The Economics of the Welfare State

The Economics of the Welfare State

FOURTH EDITION

Nicholas Barr

OXFORD

UNIVERSITY PRESS

OXFORD
UNIVERSITY PRESS

Great Clarendon Street, Oxford OX2 6DP
Oxford University Press is a department of the University of Oxford.
It furthers the University's objective of excellence in research, scholarship,
and education by publishing worldwide in

Oxford New York

Auckland Cape Town Dar es Salaam Hong Kong Karachi
Kuala Lumpur Madrid Melbourne Mexico City Nairobi
New Delhi Shanghai Taipei Toronto

With offices in

Argentina Austria Brazil Chile Czech Republic France Greece
Guatemala Hungary Italy Japan South Korea Poland Portugal
Singapore Switzerland Thailand Turkey Ukraine Vietnam

Oxford is a registered trade mark of Oxford University Press
in the UK and in certain other countries

Published in the United States
by Oxford University Press Inc., New York

A catalogue record for this book is available from the British Library

Library of Congress Cataloging in Publication Data
(Data available)

ISBN 978-0-19-926497-1

7

Typeset by Graphicraft Limited, Hong Kong
Printed in Great Britain by
Antony Rowe Ltd, Chippenham, Wiltshire

For my Mother and Father

■ PREFACE TO THE FOURTH EDITION

The world has changed since the first edition of this book was published in 1987, when the Thatcher and Reagan administrations were in their pomp in the West, and the Communist threat was still regarded as very real. Possibly as a result, discussion of the market versus the state at that time was something of a Punch and Judy debate between the two polar extremes. With the end of the cold war came a more balanced view. The considerable virtues of private markets for most commodities is appreciated in the former Communist countries—certainly those that have now joined the European Union or are on the threshold—while governments in the West are more aware that unregulated markets are not always and everywhere a complete answer. In part the ideological pendulum has swung slightly, but the change has also resulted from experience of the problems that arise if markets are not properly regulated—scandals over mis-sold pensions and the continuing problems of the US health-care system being cases in point, and from a realization that risks are, if anything, intensifying—for example, natural disasters, technological accidents, infectious diseases, and food safety. Actuarial insurance cannot readily address problems of this type or on this scale.

Like previous editions, this book is not only about Britain; it also sets out the economic theory of the welfare state, which is relevant to all industrial countries, to transition countries, and to many middle-income developing countries. As previously, though an economics book, it is written to be accessible to readers in related areas: the theory in Chapters 3–6 is summarized in an appendix at the end of each chapter; though algebra is used where necessary to pin down some important concepts precisely, the results are always explained verbally so that the equations can be skipped by those who are prepared to take their conclusions on trust; and the Glossary explains the meaning of technical terms, and disentangles differences of usage in various countries. Thus the book should be of interest also in related areas such as political economy and social policy, and to colleagues studying post-communist transition or economic development. The book is also relevant to the policy community in the OECD, and in post-communist and middle-income developing countries, including officials in Ministries of Finance, in departments of Social Security, of Health, and of Education, and in international organizations such as the International Monetary Fund, the World Bank, and the United Nations.

The book's main thrust remains unchanged. Many people (including me) believe that it is an essential part of a civilized society that the state should ensure a generous social safety net. That, however, is only part of the case for the welfare state. The economics of information yields two powerful sets of conclusions. First, the issues raised by the welfare state fit naturally into the conventional theoretical framework used by economists. Secondly, public involvement in institutions of the general sort that comprise the welfare state can be justified strongly in efficiency terms; the welfare state does things which markets either would not do at all, or would do badly. To the extent that this is so, it is no longer public involvement *per se* that is controversial but only its precise form and the choice of its distributional objectives.

The arguments in support of that view have been tightened in various ways. I have shortened the book slightly to eliminate potential middle-age flab. UK institutional description is less detailed, on the grounds that it rapidly goes out of date, that international information is readily available from the OECD and the EU, and that it is now easy to find such information electronically (for which purpose I have included a list of useful web sites on institutional arrangements in the UK and other countries). Alongside a slightly weaker focus on the UK is a broadening of the policy discussion, making the analysis more obviously applicable to all industrialized countries and, in many instances, also to middle-income developing countries. The book also includes more references to, and somewhat more discussion of, the wider Europe and some tables giving international comparative data—for example, on levels of spending on different parts of the welfare state in different countries.

Secondly, I have reshaped the book to sharpen its focus. One element is to drop the chapter on housing, which is increasingly being allocated by the market, supported by income transfers. Thus the topic is no longer central to a book about economic aspects of the welfare state, any more than is a chapter on food. Both are fundamental to individual welfare, but neither is primarily a public responsibility—the book explains why.

For exactly symmetrical reasons, I have expanded the treatment of higher education finance by giving it a separate chapter and anchoring the discussion more explicitly in the economics of information. It is an area where much has happened, with more to follow in many countries, much of it intensely relevant to the book's intellectual framework. In addition, it strengthens the book's message to have two chapters on education, one on schools and one on post-compulsory education, the first sceptical about market forces, the second supportive—both sets of arguments entirely consistent with the core theoretical analysis of the book.

A third change in focus is to reshape discussion throughout the book to bring out more explicitly three key purposes of the welfare state—insurance, life-cycle consumption smoothing, and poverty relief. The way the analysis is framed thus continually answers the book's core question 'Why do we have a welfare state?'. For the same reason, I have strengthened the discussion of consumption smoothing by incorporating the simple Fisher model in the theoretical discussion of Chapter 4.

The policy discussion, including new empirical literature, has also been updated, and new topics introduced. The chapter on pensions emphasizes that the fact that we are all living longer is not a problem but a triumph, and includes a new section on why raising the age of retirement is the only fundamental solution (and a good one) for the pensions 'crisis'. There is new analysis of what is known alternatively as 'activation policies', 'welfare to work', and 'making work pay'; and discussion of education, and of social exclusion more generally, incorporates recent findings on the critical importance of early child development.

Finally, I have taken the opportunity to add questions for further discussion at the end of most of the chapters, some of them pulling together material in the chapter, others challenging wider thinking.

The quickest way to get the book's central messages is to read Chapters 1 and 15; the next quickest is to read those chapters plus the concluding sections of Chapters 4 (economic theory), 11 (cash benefits), and 12, 13, and 14 (health, school education, and higher education, respectively). For those who want to read round the subject, three volumes are, in many ways, companions to this one. Howard Glennerster's book (2003*a*) discusses the detailed finances of the welfare state. Barr (2001*a*) digs more deeply into the core efficiency justification of state activity in social policy and Barr (2001*b*) is a three-volume series containing 100 articles on the welfare state, many of them referred to in the text or Further Reading of this book.

I have many people to thank, including everyone who helped with earlier editions. Zheng Bingwen's careful editing of the Chinese translation of the third edition revealed some minor errors that I have taken the opportunity to correct, and Riccardo Puglisi also gave useful comments on the third edition. As in earlier editions, my colleagues and friends have been generous in letting me pillage their bookshelves, their writings, their brains, and their time. Anne West gave me access to her new book before it was published. Howard Glennerster did likewise, and commented on several chapters; and the book as a whole has benefited greatly from discussions with him. Chapter 14 draws on my fifteen-year partnership on UK higher education with Iain Crawford. Jonathan Leape and Elias Mossialos gave very helpful comments and advice on one or more chapters, and Waltraud Schelkle volunteered a shedload of useful references. I am also grateful to officials at the UK Department for Work and Pensions, Department of Health, and Department for Education and Skills for help with factual matters, particularly statistical sources, and to Hilary Walford for her customary precision in copy-editing. I owe a continuing debt to my students. They ask awkward questions (all the time), see things in clearer ways (often), or provoke me into seeing things in clearer ways (sometimes). Michael Barr, who has graduated from drawing pictures on the back of printouts of draft chapters of the first edition, provided IT training and research assistance with this edition, and Stephanie Abdulin helped in preparing the text. Once more, my biggest debt is to my wife, Gill, for encouragement and help, and for her patience when work–life balance required some elasticity. None of them should be implicated in remaining errors.

Nicholas Barr
London
December 2003

■ CONTENTS

■ DETAILED CONTENTS

PART ONE **CONCEPTS**

■ LIST OF FIGURES

■ LIST OF TABLES

ABBREVIATIONS

AC	average cost
AFDC	Aid to Families with Dependent Children
ATR	average tax rate
CPAG	Child Poverty Action Group
DES	Department of Education and Science
DfEE	Department for Education and Employment
DfES	Department for Education and Skills
DHSS	Department of Health and Social Security
DoE	Department of the Environment
DoH	Department of Health
DRG	diagnosis-related group
EU	European Union
GCSE	General Certificate of Secondary Education
GP	general practitioner
GPV	gross present value
HEFCE	Higher Education Funding Council for England
HMO	health maintenance organization
LEA	Local Education Authority
LSE	London School of Economics
MC	marginal cost
MPC	marginal private cost
MPV	marginal private value
MSC	marginal social cost
MSV	marginal social value
MTR	marginal tax rates
MV	marginal value
NBER	National Bureau of Economic Research
NCIHE	National Committee of Inquiry into Higher Education
NHS	National Health Service
NIC	National Insurance Contribution
NPV	net present value
OAI	Old Age Insurance
OASI	Old Age and Survivor Insurance
OASDI	Old Age, Survivor, and Disability Insurance
OASDHI	Old Age, Survivor, Disability, and Health Insurance
OECD	Organization for Economic Cooperation and Development
PAC	Public Assistance Committee
PAYG	Pay-As-You-Go
PI	Pareto improvement

PPO	preferred provider organization
PVB	present value of benefits
PVC	present value of costs
QALY	Quality Adjusted Life Year
RI	Rawlsian improvement
SERPS	state earnings-related pension scheme
SI	socialist improvement
SLC	Student Loans Company
UGC	University Grants Committee

■ USEFUL WEB SITES

An increasing number of countries have a portal that leads to government web sites: Belgium: www.belgium.be; France: www.service-public.fr/accueil/english.html; Germany: www.bund.de/Service/english-.6118.htm; UK: www.ukonline.gov.uk; USA: www.gpoaccess.gov;

For UK official statistics, see the Office for National Statistics web site (www.statistics.gov.uk). On UK taxes and benefits, see the web sites of the Institute for Fiscal Studies (www.ifs.org.uk) and the Centre for the Analysis of Social Exclusion (http://sticerd.lse.ac.uk/case/). On UK government publications, see the web site of the British Offical Publications Current Awareness Service (www.bopcas.soton.ac.uk) (subscribers only)

For EU statistics, see the Eurostat web site (http://europa.eu.int/comm/eurostat/).

On the USA, see the US government portal (www.gpoaccess.gov) and the web sites of the National Academy of Social Insurance (www.nasi.org) and the Brookings Institution (www.brookings.org).

For a summary of systems of cash benefits worldwide, see US Social Security Administration (2002, 2003) (http://www.ssa.gov/policy/pubs/index.html).

Justice is the first virtue of all social institutions, as truth is of systems of thought. A theory however elegant and economic must be rejected or revised if it is untrue; likewise laws and institutions no matter how efficient and well-arranged must be reformed or abolished if they are unjust.

(John Rawls, 1971)

Let us remember that it [laissez-faire] is a practical rule, and not a doctrine of science; a rule in the main sound, but like most other sound rules, liable to numerous exceptions; above all, a rule which must never for a moment be allowed to stand in the way of any promising proposal of social or industrial reform.

(J.E. Cairnes, 1873)

■ PART ONE

Concepts

The chapters in Part 1 establish the concepts used throughout the book to assess the existence and institutions of the welfare state, including relevant definitions (Chapter 1), the historical backdrop (Chapter 2), political theory (Chapter 3), economic theory (Chapters 4 and 5), and problems of defining and measuring poverty and inequality (Chapter 6).

Readers with less technical background (or less time) can read the non-technical summaries at the end of Chapters 3–6.

1 Introduction

[The duties of the state are] . . . first . . . that of protecting the society from the violence and invasion of other independent societies . . . second . . . that of protecting, as far as possible, every member of the society from the injustice or oppression of every other member of it . . . third . . . that of erecting and maintaining those publick institutions and those publick works which, though they may be in the highest degree advantageous to a great society, are of such a nature, that the profit could never repay the expence to any individual or small number of individuals.

(Adam Smith, 1776)

1. The approach

1.1. The central argument

One of the wellsprings of this book was the exuberant insistence of some of my students and colleagues that economics appeared largely irrelevant to the central concerns of social policy. They had a point, and this book, like previous editions, is an attempt to remedy their grievances and to assert the importance of economics. To address the concern about relevance, discussion relates economic theory to different notions of social justice and to the historical development of the welfare state. In stressing the importance of economics, two results stand out. First, the welfare state is not a subject apart, but fits naturally into the framework of economic analysis. Secondly, the theoretical arguments support the existence of the welfare state not only for well-known equity reasons but also—and powerfully—in efficiency terms. This is an area in which economic theory is capable of strong results that can justify the general idea of the welfare state and, to a surprising extent, can do so without resort to ideology.

To keep the subject manageable, the book is explicitly about economic theory and its application to the welfare state. It is not a book about comparative systems, since the welfare state, though existing in all countries in the wider Europe and, more generally, in all advanced industrial countries, takes very different forms (Esping-Andersen et al. 2002; Neil Gilbert 2002). The book has a very brief institutional description, mainly of the UK, to motivate the theory, plus references to more detailed information and, where possible, wider European and US examples, but with no attempt at systematic coverage. A second restriction is that, though the book discusses in some detail how welfare-state services can be financed, there is less detailed discussion of how they should be delivered. Economic theory has much to say about funding; in contrast, though economic fundamentals (for example, a sensible incentive structure) are important on the delivery side, institutional organization and institutional change are things about which economic theory has less to say.

The book addresses two broad questions: what theoretical arguments justify the various parts of the welfare state in an industrial economy; and, given these arguments of principle, how sensible (or otherwise) are arrangements in the UK[1] and other countries?

The approach is best illustrated by two questions that permeate throughout.

1. What are the *aims* of policy?
2. By what *methods* are those aims best achieved?

Question 1 is broad ranging. There is general agreement that the major aims of policy in Western societies include *efficiency* in the use of resources; their distribution in accordance with *equity* or *justice*; and the preservation of *individual freedom*. These aims, however, can be defined in different ways, and may be accorded different weights. To a utilitarian,[2] the aim of policy is to maximize total welfare; to Rawls the aim is social justice, defined in a particular way; libertarians make their main aim individual freedom, and socialists their prime concern equality. The answer to question 1 is explicitly normative and largely ideological. The objectives of the welfare state are discussed in more detail in Section 2.2.

In contrast, once question 1 has been answered, question 2 should be treated not as *ideological* but as *technical*—that is, it raises a *positive* issue. Whether a given aim should be pursued by market allocation or by public provision depends on which of these methods more nearly achieves the chosen aim. Market allocation is neither 'good' nor 'bad'—it is useful in some instances—for example, private markets for food are generally effective in achieving the aim that people should not starve; in others, however (it is argued in Chapter 12 that health care is one), the market mechanism works less well, and substantial state intervention can contribute to efficiency and to justice. Similarly, public provision is neither good nor bad, but useful in some cases, less so in others. One of the questions throughout is which method is more useful in different areas of the welfare state.

The distinction between aims and methods is fundamental, and bears reinforcement. Consider two central questions that all societies face.

- How much redistribution (of income, wealth, power, etc.) should there be?
- How should economic activity be organized, through markets, or central planning, or as a mixed economy?

The first question is clearly ideological and normative; it is an aims question and so properly the subject of political debate. But, *once that question has been answered*, the second question is largely one of method (i.e. a positive issue) and better treated as technical than as political. The approach is explained in detail in Chapters 3 and 4, and summarized in the concluding section of Chapter 4.

---

[1] The United Kingdom (UK) is Great Britain and Northern Ireland (Act of Union with Ireland 1800; Government of Ireland Act 1920). Britain (or Great Britain) consists of England, with Wales and Scotland (Act of Union with Scotland 1706).

[2] Utilitarianism and other theories of society, including those of Rawls and libertarian and socialist writers, are discussed in Chapter 3.

1.2. Organization of the book

Part 1 sets the scene, starting in Chapter 2 with the historical development of the welfare state in the UK, including some comparison with other countries, particularly the USA. The three chapters that follow are the theoretical heart of the book: Chapter 3 discusses definitions of social justice and their different implications for the welfare state; Chapter 4 sets out the economic theory of state intervention and Chapter 5 the theory of insurance. Chapter 6 discusses problems of definition and measurement, particularly of poverty and inequality. For readers who are diffident about their theoretical background, each of the conceptual chapters (3, 4, 5, and 6) has a non-technical appendix summarizing the essential material; and technical terms are explained in the Glossary.

Three major threads developed in Part 1 run through the rest of the book: the social-welfare-maximization problem; alternative definitions of social justice; and measurement problems. The social-welfare-maximization problem (set out in Chapter 4) is the conventional starting point for economic theory. An important theorem states that under appropriate assumptions a competitive market equilibrium will allocate resources efficiently. It is argued that, where these conditions hold, the role of the state, if any, is limited to redistribution; conversely, where these conditions fail, there may be efficiency grounds for intervention in a variety of forms. The second major theme is social justice. The definition chosen will determine the weights assigned to different individuals, with major implications for the form and extent of intervention—for example, whether people with no income should be supported at subsistence or at a higher level. The third thread, discussed in Chapter 6, concerns problems of definition and measurement. Many variables are hard to define and, once defined, hard to measure. A crucial and recurrent difficulty is that utility[3] is not measurable. This makes it hard both to measure living standards and to compare them. Costs or benefits—of health care or education, for example—may also be hard to measure.

As far as possible, each chapter in Parts 2 and 3 has a similar layout to clarify the structure of the argument. Each chapter discusses in turn: the *aims* of policy; the *methods* by which they might be achieved—that is, the theoretical arguments about intervention for reasons of efficiency and social justice; *assessment* in the light of this theoretical discussion of the appropriateness (or otherwise) of the UK and other systems, including discussion of the empirical literature; and *reform*.

Part 2 analyses cash transfers. Chapter 7 briefly describes the finances of the welfare state. Chapter 8 looks at unemployment and sickness benefits, whose primary purpose is insurance; Chapter 9 discusses retirement pensions, whose main purpose is consumption smoothing;[4] and Chapter 10 reviews non-contributory benefits, whose main purpose is poverty relief. Each chapter starts with the theory and then assesses the practice. Chapter 11 considers a variety of reform strategies. Part 3 discusses provision in kind. Chapter 12, on health, analyses the theoretical arguments for public production and allocation, assesses the effectiveness of the UK National Health Service in comparison with systems in other countries, and discusses alternative ways in which health care might be organized. Chapters 13 and 14 cover similar ground for school education and higher education.

---

[3] See the Glossary.   [4] See the Glossary.

The conclusions of the book are summarized in Chapter 15, which picks up some of the questions asked at the end of this chapter. Readers in a hurry can get an idea of the book's approach and its main conclusions by reading Chapter 15 and the concluding sections of Chapters 4 (economic and political theory), 11 (income support), and 12, 13, and 14 (health care, school education, and higher education, respectively).

2. The welfare state and its objectives

2.1. Defining the welfare state

This section defines the welfare state in three ways: in principle, for the purposes of this book, and in practice.

THE WELFARE STATE IN PRINCIPLE. We shall see in Chapter 6 that important concepts such as poverty and equality of opportunity are hard, if not impossible, to define in principle, and even harder to measure. The concept of the welfare state similarly defies precise definition, and I make no serious attempt to offer one. Even Richard Titmuss (1958) ducked the problem—that book is called *Essays on 'The Welfare State'* (his quotes). As he later put it, 'I am no more enamoured today of the indefinable abstraction "The Welfare State" than I was some twenty years ago when . . . the term acquired an international as well as a national popularity' (Titmuss 1968: 124). Three areas of complication stand out (for fuller discussion, see Glennerster 2003*a*: ch. 1).

1. *Welfare derives from many sources in addition to state activity.* Individual welfare derives from at least four sources.

- *The labour market* is arguably the most important, first through *wage income*. Full employment is a major component of welfare broadly defined. High levels of employment and rising labour productivity over the 1950s and 1960s were at least as much an equalizing force as redistribution.[5] In addition to wage income, firms (individually or on an industry-wide basis, voluntarily or under legal compulsion) provide *occupational welfare* in the face of sickness, injury, and retirement.

- *Private provision* includes voluntary private insurance and individual saving.

- *Voluntary welfare* arises both within the family and outside, where people give time free or at a below-market price, or make voluntary charitable donations in other forms.

- *The state* intervenes by providing cash benefits and benefits in kind. It also contributes through tax concessions to the finance of occupational and private provision.

2. *Modes of delivery* are also diverse. A service may be *funded* by the state, but it does not follow that it must necessarily be publicly *produced*. The state can produce a service itself and supply it to recipients at no charge (e.g. health care under the National Health Service); or it can pay for goods produced in the private sector (e.g. free pharmaceutical

---

[5] As discussed in Chapter 2, Section 5.1, full employment was one of Beveridge's central assumptions.

drugs under the National Health Service); or it can give individuals money (either explicitly or in the form of tax relief) to make their own purchases (e.g. tax relief in some countries for private medical insurance premiums). The issue of 'privatization', as we shall see in Chapter 4, Section 6, is more complex than is often recognized in public discussion.

3. *The boundaries of the welfare state are not well defined.* Though the state's role should not be exaggerated, neither should it be understated. Some typically excluded activities such as public health and environmental policies are very similar in purpose to ones that are included.

Welfare is thus a mosaic, with diversity both in its source and in the manner of its delivery. Nevertheless the state, through various levels of government, is much the most important single agency involved in most industrialized countries. Throughout the book the term 'welfare state' is used as a shorthand for the state's activities in four broad areas: cash benefits; health care; education; and food, housing, and other welfare services.

In broad terms the modern welfare state comprises cash benefits and benefits in kind. The latter embrace a wide range of activities that can include education, medical care, and more general forms of care for the infirm, the mentally and physically handicapped, and children in need of protection. Cash benefits have two major components.

1. *Social insurance* is awarded without an income or wealth test, generally on the basis of (*a*) previous contributions and (*b*) the occurrence of a specified contingency, such as becoming unemployed or reaching a specified age.

2. *Non-contributory benefits* are of two sorts. So-called *universal benefits* are awarded on the basis of a specified contingency, without either contributions or an income test. Major examples in the UK are child benefit and the National Health Service (discussed in Chapters 10 and 12, respectively). *Social assistance* is awarded on the basis of an income test. It is generally a benefit of last resort, designed to help individuals and families who are in poverty, whether as an exceptional emergency, or because they are not covered by social insurance, or as a supplement to social insurance.

THE WELFARE STATE FOR THE PURPOSES OF THIS BOOK. The welfare state exists to enhance the welfare of people who (*a*) are weak and vulnerable, largely by providing social care, (*b*) are poor, largely through redistributive income transfers, or (*c*) are neither vulnerable nor poor, by organizing cash benefits to provide insurance and consumption smoothing, and by providing medical insurance and school education.

This book is mainly about (*b*) and (*c*), covering cash benefits, health care, and education. Two omissions are deliberate. There is little discussion of element (*a*)—for example, protection of vulnerable children, the frail elderly and people with emotional and physical disabilities. This is not because they are unimportant (absolutely not the case), but because they are topics about which economics has relatively little to say. Secondly, welfare depends also on access to food and housing. These topics do not figure prominently for different reasons: each raises economic issues that are largely settled territory: markets, it will be argued, work well for these two vitally important goods. Both sets of markets need regulation; but in both cases, the poor are best protected by income transfers, allowing them to buy food and shelter. Thus food is discussed in the following chapters mainly in terms of regulation to ensure it is safe, and housing largely in terms of income transfers

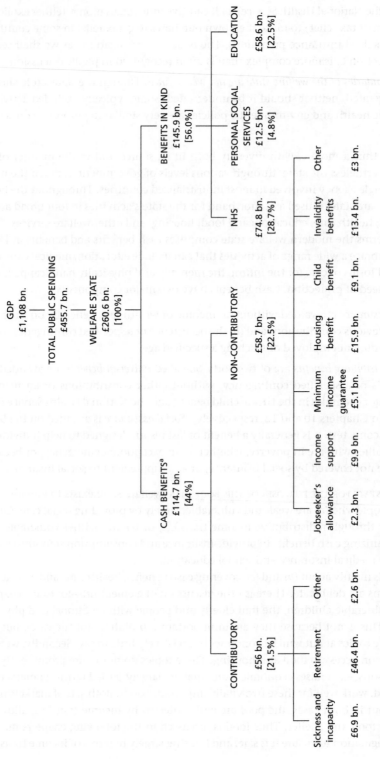

Fig. 1.1 Overview of the welfare state, UK, 2003/4 (est.) (£ bn. and %)

[a] The figure excludes about £12 billion of tax credits whose function is identical to cash benefits.
Sources: UK Treasury (2002a: table A3; 2003a: tables C3, C11), UK DWP (2002a: table 7).

to poor people to support their housing needs. Other, equally important aspects of housing—such as unsafe neighbourhoods—raise issues more usefully tackled by disciplines other than economics.

THE WELFARE STATE IN PRACTICE. The UK welfare state can be taken to comprise, at a minimum, the publicly provided benefits (representing about 23.5 per cent of gross domestic product) shown in Figure 1.1, together with the contributions that pay for them. Cash benefits follow the pattern described above. National insurance is payable to people with an adequate contributions record; benefits cover, *inter alia*, unemployment, sickness (short- and long-term), and retirement, of which the last (about 18 per cent of social spending) is much the largest. Non-contributory benefits include child benefit (a weekly cash payment to the parent or guardian of every child), and income support (i.e. social assistance for people with little or no other income). The major benefits in kind are the National Health Service (29 per cent of total social spending) and education (22.5 per cent).

As Figure 1.2 shows, the UK is by no means unusual. The data show 1998 figures for public social spending, which the OECD define to include all cash benefits, health care, and social services, but to exclude spending on education. Spending was highest in the Nordic

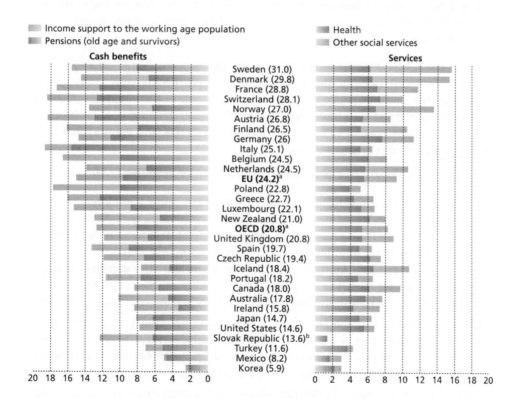

Fig. 1.2. Public social expenditure by broad social policy area, OECD 1998 (% of GDP.)

Note: Countries are ranked by decreasing order of total public social expenditure as a percentage of GDP.
[a] OECD and EU are unweighted averages.
[b] Slovak Republic: data for total are underestimated because data about health are not available yet.
Source: OECD (2003c: 55).

countries and, among the richer countries, lowest in Japan and the USA. UK spending was equal to the OECD average, somewhat below the average for the EU.

2.2. The objectives of the welfare state

The objectives of social institutions, as in any other area of economic policy, are efficiency, equity, and administrative feasibility. In this context, however, it is useful to adopt a more refined categorization.

EFFICIENCY has at least three aspects.

1. *Macro-efficiency*. The efficient fraction of GDP should be devoted to the totality of welfare-state institutions—for example, policy should avoid distortions leading to cost explosions.

2. *Micro-efficiency*. Policy should ensure the efficient division of total welfare-state resources between the different cash benefits, different types of medical treatment, and different kinds of educational activity.

3. *Incentives*. Where institutions are publicly funded, their finance and the structure of benefits should minimize adverse effects on labour supply, employment, and saving.

Objectives 1–3 are different aspects of *allocative efficiency*, sometimes—particularly in the context of health care and education—referred to as *external efficiency*. As an example, if the objective of health policy is to maximize the health of the population, external efficiency is concerned with producing the quantity, quality, and mix of health interventions (including preventive care and education about diet and lifestyle) that bring about the greatest improvement in health.

SUPPORTING LIVING STANDARDS, the second strategic aim, has at least three components.

4. *Poverty relief*. No individual or household should fall below a minimum standard of living. The aim could be to *eliminate* poverty or to *alleviate* it. As discussed in Chapter 6, there is no analytically satisfactory way of defining a poverty line, so the definition of the minimum standard is largely normative. Once the poverty line has been decided, the effectiveness of the system is measured by statistics relating to *how many* people are below the poverty line ('headcount' measures), by *how much* ('poverty-gap' measures), and for *how long* (life-cycle and intergenerational matters).

5. *Insurance*. No one should face an unexpected and unacceptably large drop in her living standard. This is a major objective of unemployment benefits and most health-related benefits. Its success is measured by the replacement ratio, which shows a person's income when on benefit in comparison with her previous income.

6. *Consumption smoothing*. Institutions should enable individuals to reallocate consumption over their lifetime. As discussed in Chapter 9, individuals can redistribute from their younger to their older selves (an actuarial private pension scheme); or such redistribution could be notional (an unfunded state pension (Samuelson 1958)). Alternatively, there could be tax-funded provision, with no pretence of individual

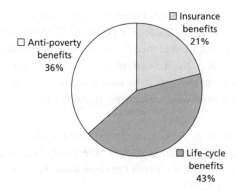

Fig. 1.3. Spending on cash benefits by type of benefit
Source: UK DWP (2002a: table 7).

contributions, to groups whose stage in the life cycle suggests that they are likely to be financially constrained (e.g. benefits for families with young children). Analogously, student loans, discussed in Chapter 14, allow people to redistribute from their middle years to their younger self.

These three objectives largely shape the rest of the book. The simple Fisher model discussed in Chapter 4, Section 3.2 and illustrated in Figure 4.5 illustrates a person's choices between consuming now (period 1) or later (period 2)—that is, his or her options for consumption smoothing. A person can consume less in period 1 and save, so as to be able to consume more in period 2; similarly, someone who wants to consume more earlier can borrow, thus consuming more in period 1.

The simple model assumes rational behaviour in a world of certainty and competitive markets. In that world, the welfare state is largely unnecessary: there is no risk, and hence no need for insurance; people provide for their old age through voluntary saving; and temporary poverty is dealt with by borrowing or saving. Thus the only role for the welfare state is to provide poverty relief for someone who is lifetime poor.

The rest of the book is largely about the effects of relaxing the certainty assumption. A central argument is that imperfect information, risk, and uncertainty give the state (or parastatal agencies) a key role, not only in providing poverty relief, but also in ensuring that people have access to insurance and consumption smoothing that the private market would provide ineffectively or not at all.

Figure 1.3 shows the broad division of cash benefits into spending on the three objectives. Just over one-third of spending on cash benefits is directly redistributive from rich to poor, the remaining two-thirds, involving insurance and consumption smoothing, being life-cycle redistribution. Though the task of poverty relief is central, it is clear that the welfare state exists also for much wider reasons.

THE REDUCTION OF INEQUALITY, in contrast, is almost entirely an equity issue.

7. *Vertical equity*. The system should redistribute towards individuals or families with lower incomes. This aim is contentious. All income-tested benefits contribute to it;

so, secondly, do non-means-tested benefits whose recipients disproportionately have lower incomes (e.g. the UK flat-rate pension). A third form of redistribution arises where the benefit formula favours lower-income individuals. 'Free' provision of a tax-funded service (e.g. health care in the UK) is also generally redistributive. The success or otherwise of benefits in reducing inequality is assessed by inspection over time of aggregate inequality measures, though with all the caveats noted in Chapter 6.

8. *Horizontal equity*. Differences in benefits should take account of age, family size, etc., and differences in medical treatment should reflect only factors that are regarded as relevant (e.g. whether or not the patient has dependent relatives), but not irrelevant factors like ethnic background.

SOCIAL INCLUSION. So far the objectives have been conventional economic ones. Some commentators also include broader goals.

9. *Dignity*. Cash benefits and health care should be delivered so as to preserve individual dignity and without unnecessary stigma. Beveridge emphasized the importance of contributions in this context: 'The popularity of compulsory social insurance today is established, and for good reason; by compulsory insurance . . . the individual can feel assured that [his] needs will be met . . . by paying . . . a contribution, he can feel that he is getting security not as a charity but as a right' (Beveridge Report 1942: para. 296).

10. *Social solidarity*. Cash benefits and health care should foster social solidarity— a frequently stated goal in mainland Europe. So far as possible, benefits should depend on criteria that are unrelated to socio-economic status. Retirement pensions are an example; so is medical care in many countries. Additionally, benefits should be high enough and health care and education good enough to allow recipients to participate fully in the life of the society in which they live—a broader aim than that of relieving income poverty.

ADMINISTRATIVE FEASIBILITY has two aspects.

11. *Intelligibility*. The system should be simple, easy to understand, and as cheap to administer as possible.

12. *Absence of abuse*. Benefits should be as little open to abuse as possible.

PROBLEMS of definition and measurement abound. Efficiency objectives 1–3 have precise analytical definitions, but measurement problems—particularly the incidence of taxes, contributions, and benefits—make it difficult to assess how far they are achieved. How do we define a poverty line in objective 4; and how large a drop in living standard is 'unacceptable' (objective 5)? The appropriate extent of vertical redistribution and a workable definition of horizontal equity (objectives 7 and 8) have occupied economists, philosophers, and political theorists almost since the dawn of time, and have plagued policy-makers at least since the British Poor Law Act of 1601. Even 'equality' is difficult to define unambiguously (Okun 1975: ch. 3; Le Grand 1982: ch. 2), especially in the context of benefits in kind like health care. Concepts such as 'dignity', 'stigma', and 'social solidarity' (objectives 9 and 10) are hard to define and raise major measurement problems.

Writers like Hayek (1976) argue in addition that the term 'social solidarity' is devoid of meaning, and that its pursuit is both pointless and dangerous. These problems are discussed in some detail in Chapters 3–6.

Even were these problems assumed away, a second set of difficulties arises, in that some objectives are inherently in conflict and others may be. The trade-off between efficiency and distributional objectives is no less intractable for its familiarity; the same is true of the trade-off between horizontal equity and administrative simplicity. Other objectives conflict almost by definition. Consumption smoothing implies that an individual with higher earnings should receive higher benefits, which sits uneasily with the requirement that benefits should redistribute towards those with lower incomes, and with the objective that benefits should contribute to social solidarity. On one interpretation of equity everyone should receive benefits proportional to their past contributions, but that, again, conflicts both with redistribution towards lower incomes and with social solidarity. The choice of objectives and of priorities between them is a fundamental normative issue.

3. A changing world: Challenges and responses

A number of longer-term trends have major implications for the design of the welfare state and recur throughout the book.

DEMOGRAPHIC CHANGE. Life expectancy has increased in all industrial countries while birth rates have declined, simultaneously increasing the number of older people and reducing the number of younger workers. As a result, from about 2005 onwards, the ratio of people over 60 to those of working age will increase sharply. If present policies continue unchanged, spending on pensions and health care in some countries is set to double. Policies to accommodate these changes are discussed in detail in Chapter 9.

GLOBALIZATION has at least two roots. First, since 1970 the international trade regime has become increasingly open. Secondly, as a result of technological change, in Quah's terms, economic activity is increasingly 'dematerialized'—that is, it is in the form of encoded binary bits (computer programs, music, videos) rather than solid, such as a Boeing 747. One of many implications of this trend, according to Quah (1996: 7; see also Quah 2003), is that 'international trade becomes not a matter of shipping wine and textiles . . . but of bouncing bits off satellites'. In these circumstances, national boundaries become increasingly porous.

For both reasons, globalization reduces the ability of a country to act independently in designing its institutions. Countries with expensive welfare states, it is argued, will increasingly be at a competitive disadvantage relative to those with more parsimonious ones. At the same time, however, demands on the welfare state are rising: there are more old people, and in many countries rising numbers of unemployed; in addition, as discussed below, there are more lone-parent families, and increasing numbers of low-paid and part-time workers.

CHANGES IN FAMILY STRUCTURE have taken several forms. First, families have become more fluid. The institutions of the immediate post-war period assumed an archetypal nuclear family: the main (frequently the only) source of income was the wages of the husband; and husband and wife stayed married, so that the husband's pension entitlement also covered his wife. Though not wholly valid even then, the assumption was true enough to form the basis of most social policy. Today, in contrast, many more marriages end in divorce; and parenthood is less closely tied to marriage. These changes have major implications for social policy, particularly so far as child support and pension arrangements for women are concerned. A second set of changes arises from the increasing number of women who have jobs outside the home.

CHANGES IN THE STRUCTURE OF JOBS. The nature of work is also changing. Post-industrial employment tends to favour professional and highly skilled occupations. The demand for unqualified workers is lower than in the past and, in consequence, their wages are low and their employment often precarious and part-time. There are worries about increasing polarization between a core of skilled workers and a peripheral workforce. Contributory social insurance is of doubtful relevance to the latter group.

RISING EXPENDITURE ON THE WELFARE STATE over past decades has been universal. Rising income leads to demands for higher insurance benefits and more extensive consumption smoothing, and to the adoption of a poverty line that rises in real terms. A second cause is technological advance: more advanced medical technology extends the range of what is possible, fuelling the drive for higher spending on health care; and technological advance is a major driver of mass tertiary education. Thirdly, population ageing will increase spending on age-related benefits, notably pensions, health care, and social care.

RESULTING CHALLENGES AND RESPONSES. Two challenges stand out. A problem—both for economic policy and for social policy—is the possibility that the strategic design of the welfare state is based, at least in part, on a past social order with stable, two-parent families, with high levels of employment, and where most jobs were full-time and relatively stable.

Secondly, the conflict between economic growth and equality has become sharper over the years. 'The harmonious coexistence of full employment and income equalization that defined the postwar epoch appears no longer possible' (Esping-Andersen 1996a: 4). There is a major debate, discussed in Chapter 15, Section 2.2, about why this is so.

Despite much public discussion of a 'crisis' of the welfare state, change has been mainly marginal. Esping-Andersen (1990, 1999, 2002 et al.) distinguishes three broad approaches to economic and social change since the first oil shock of the 1970s.

Under what Esping-Andersen calls the social-democratic approach (broadly that in the Scandinavian countries, and particularly in Sweden), policy was aimed at increasing the demand for labour through active labour-market policies and increased public-sector employment. The problem with this approach was its cost. By the mid-1990s Sweden faced major fiscal problems at a time of rising pressure on public jobs. Part of the response was a move towards wage flexibility; there was also reform to the state pension system.

The corporatist approach—that in the rest of mainland Europe—tried to reduce the supply of labour, notably through early retirement. In many ways this is the Scandinavian solution by a different route: instead of finding jobs, frequently in the public sector, for people who would otherwise be unemployed, this approach tries to open up jobs by offering early retirement, either explicitly or through the award of a disability pension.

The cost in this case is not that of public employment but of public pensions. The approach is coming under increasing fiscal pressure.

The neo-liberal approach—broadly the Anglo-Saxon model (the UK, the USA, Australia, and New Zealand)—sought to increase the demand for labour by liberalizing labour markets, not least through increased wage flexibility. This approach has two advantages: it avoids the heavy fiscal cost of the Scandinavian or mainland European arrangements; and employment growth in the Anglo-Saxon countries over the 1980s was significantly higher than in the rest of the OECD. The besetting problem of the approach is rising inequality and poverty, particularly among unskilled workers and single-parent households. As discussed in Chapter 2, Section 6, in the later 1990s reform in both the UK and the USA refined this approach by combining labour-market flexibility with policies of 'activation' based round benefit structures that gave strong labour-market incentives, together with policies aimed at improving people's labour-market skills.

This book is primarily about what economic theory tells us about how to respond to these challenges. The resulting debates are drawn together in the concluding part of the final chapter.

■ **QUESTIONS FOR FURTHER DISCUSSION**

1. What is the welfare state?

2. What are the main purposes of the welfare state?

■ **FURTHER READING**

On the welfare state generally, see Barr (2001*a,b*), the latter a collection of 100 articles about the welfare state, and, for an introduction, see Glennerster (2003*a*).

Titmuss (1958) attempts to define the welfare state; see also Esping-Anderson (1996*b*).

Esping-Andersen (1996*b*) also gives a wide-ranging overview of the challenges facing welfare states across a broad range of countries, including the former Communist countries, Latin America, and the newly industrializing countries of East Asia. For contrasting views on the debate about the welfare state, see Lindbeck (1997), Atkinson (1999*a,b*), and Neil Gilbert (2002).

2   The historical background

The principle of *laissez-faire* may be safely trusted to in some things but in many more it is wholly inapplicable; and to appeal to it on all occasions savours more of the policy of a parrot than of a statesman or a philosopher.

(J. R. McCulloch, 1848)

The poverty of the poor is the chief cause of that weakness and inefficiency which are the cause of their poverty.

(Alfred Marshall, 1885)

The UK welfare state is neither the outcome of the Second World War nor simply the creation of the first post-war Labour government. Its roots are ancient and complex. Christian charity to relieve poverty has gradually, though not wholly, been taken over by state action. And state activity has grown over the years from small scale to large; from local to central; from permissive to mandatory; and from piecemeal to complex and interrelated. From this tangle, however, four events stand out: the *Poor Law Act* 1601 and the *Poor Law Amendment Act* 1834 were the main legislative bases of poverty relief before the twentieth century; the *Liberal reforms* of 1906–14 represented a substantial departure from *laissez-faire* capitalism and so can be argued to form the basis of the welfare state; and the *post-war legislation* of 1944–8 set the foundations of the welfare state as we know it today.

It should be clear that the question 'how did the welfare state come about?' is vast, so discussion is limited in two strategic ways. No attempt is made at complete coverage; the story is confined mostly to the UK, with only a sideways glance at other countries, notably the USA. The question is also controversial; I shall sketch out the major areas of historical dispute, but make no attempt at resolving them. The chapter is organized chronologically, discussing in turn the period up to the end of the nineteenth century (Section 1); the Liberal reforms of 1906–14 (Section 2); developments in the UK between the two world wars (Section 3); inter-war poverty relief in the USA (Section 4); the Second World War and its immediate aftermath in the UK (Section 5); and developments since 1948 in the UK and the USA (Section 6). Section 7 draws the threads together by considering the forces that created the welfare state.

1. Early days

1.1. Poor relief

Early public poor relief in Britain was motivated by the fear of social disorder and chronic labour shortages in the years after the Black Death of 1348–9. As a result, the state attempted to control wages and labour mobility in the Statute of Labourers 1351 and the Poor Law Act 1388. Tudor legislation grew away from this repressive and not very effective regime:

In 1576 the concept of 'setting the poor on work' was enshrined in statute law where it was to remain for something like three and a half centuries. If the able-bodied required assistance they had to work for it, and in the 1576 Poor Relief Act [magistrates] were instructed to provide a stock of raw materials on which beggars could work in return for the relief they received. (Fraser 1984: 32)

THE 1601 POOR LAW ACT, built on the 1576 Act, adopted a twofold approach: each parish was required to assume responsibility for its poor; and different treatment was prescribed for three categories of pauper. The 'impotent poor' (the old and the sick) were to be accommodated in almshouses; the able-bodied were to be given work in a 'house of correction' (not at first a residential workhouse); and those who refused to work were to be punished in this house of correction. The idea was that paupers not able to work should be cared for and the able-bodied should be given work; neither regime was intended to be punitive.

This arrangement stood for nearly 200 years; but eventually its institutions, locally financed and adapted to a pre-industrial economy, came under pressure from population growth, increased social mobility, industrialization, and economic fluctuations. By 1795 food shortages and inflation, the results of war and bad harvests, had spread poverty from the unemployed to those in work, giving rise to various local initiatives, notably the Speenhamland system, which supplemented wages with an 'allowance' based on the price of bread. The novelty of these changes was that they extended aid to people in work. Poor relief, whether under the Poor Law or a local variant, carried less social stigma than it was later to acquire.

These arrangements soon came under attack. Bentham believed that they caused moral degeneracy among recipients. Malthus argued that poor relief would cause excessive population growth, and Ricardo that it would depress wages and thereby worsen poverty. Possibly more important than these theoretical arguments was the escalating cost of relief because of rising prices and rising unemployment as soldiers returned from the Napoleonic Wars. As a result, the costs (which were met from local revenues) rose sharply.

THE POOR LAW REPORT AND THE POOR LAW AMENDMENT ACT 1834 were consequences of this philosophical and financial climate. A Royal Commission was set up in 1832. Its report, which was *laissez-faire* in tone, was written by Nassau Senior and Edwin Chadwick, a former secretary to Bentham. The intellectual background to the report, and particularly the position of the classical economists on the Poor Law, is often misunderstood. It is true that Malthus and Ricardo, worried by population growth and shocked by the earlier effect of the Poor Law, advocated its gradual repeal. But it is not the case that Nassau Senior (who was, according to Robbins, more in the mainstream of classical thought) was against poor relief. In Senior's view, 'the great test which must be applied to any project of state action in regard to relief is the question *whether it has any tendency to increase that which it is proposed to diminish*' (Robbins 1977: 128, emphasis in original). Thus, he supported public provision for orphans, the blind, and the disabled, including provision of medical treatment and hospitals. He was not in favour of abolishing relief for the able-bodied and their dependants, but insisted on the principle of 'less eligibility'—that is, that relief should be limited to an amount and administered in a manner that left the recipient worse off than the employed.

The Poor Law Report was entirely consistent with this approach when it argued that the new system should contain three elements (often referred to as 'the Principles of 1834'): the notion of less eligibility, the workhouse test, and administrative centralization. Less eligibility was the central doctrine of 1834. It was not intended to apply to the old or sick, but only to the able-bodied whose indigence, it was argued, would be encouraged by higher benefits. The workhouse test (i.e. relief conditional upon living in the workhouse) was not a principle, but simply a means of enforcing less eligibility. As far as possible, the workhouse would provide a standard of living lower than that of the lowest worker. Additional restrictions were imposed, including the strict segregation of husbands, wives, and children. The purpose of centralization was to avoid local corruption and incompetence; to ensure uniformity; to enhance cost effectiveness; and to promote labour mobility. The difference between the 1601 Poor Law and the Principles of 1834 is important. The former was intended to give work to the able-bodied without stigma; the latter discouraged claims for relief by making its receipt unpleasant and stigmatizing.

The Poor Law Amendment Act followed quickly in the wake of the Poor Law Report. Despite controversy among historians, it is now clear that, though the intention of the Act was largely (though in important respects not fully) to implement the recommendations of the report, the effect of the Act in practice was less than appeared in principle. The Poor Law Commission (in whom the powers of central government were vested) was never able to bend local administration to its will, particularly in respect of enforcing the workhouse test. But in other respects, it is argued, the implementation of the Act was more unpleasant than was intended by its architects (Bowley 1937: pt. II, ch. 2). Many people were forced to accept the harsh conditions of the workhouse, and many others endured appalling privation to avoid it. Because of its very cruelty, however, the system became over time a force for change, and thus the 1834 Act may be seen as one of the roots of later developments.

1.2. Other early social legislation

Notwithstanding the philosophical underpinnings of the Principles of 1834, *laissez-faire* was increasingly eroded over the nineteenth century.

FACTORY LEGISLATION. The first Factory Act, passed in 1802, protected women and children by limiting hours and regulating working conditions. Althorp's Factory Act 1833 tightened the rules and, probably of greater long-run importance, appointed four inspectors to enforce its provisions. The latter implicitly acknowledged the right of the state to regulate certain social conditions.

EDUCATION. The role of the state in education started more gradually (Edwin West 1970; Fraser 1984: ch. 4). Most schools in the early nineteenth century were charitable and reflected the prevailing ethos of social deference, Christian morality, and voluntarism. The Sunday school movement had an important role in teaching reading, often with the Bible as the only text. State intervention started in 1833 with a grant to Protestant schools for school building—i.e. as financial help for voluntarism—and from 1847 a grant was paid for a limited scheme of teacher training. As government involvement grew, a Royal Commission was established, though its recommendations were largely super-seded by the Education Act 1870, which gave every child the right (at least in principle) to some form of schooling. School Boards were empowered (but not compelled) to provide elementary education, financed by a mixture of central and local revenues. The resulting system was a compromise in which the new board schools coexisted with the voluntary sector. Later developments made elementary school attendance com-pulsory between 5 and 10 (Mundella's Education Act 1880) and virtually free (the Fee Grant Act 1891).

Thus a process of gradual accretion over the nineteenth century led to a system of primary education that was compulsory and largely publicly funded. Of the many explanations of these changes one in particular is a recurring theme—the *national-efficiency* argument, justifying state involvement in education on the grounds that it made labour more productive, thus contributing to national economic performance.

PUBLIC-HEALTH ACTIVITIES were the third breach in *laissez-faire* (Finer 1952: chs. 5, 7, 8; Fraser 1984: ch. 3). In the first half of the nineteenth century, urbanization (largely the result of the Industrial Revolution) and population growth caused cities to grow rapidly, leading to a housing shortage and, connected, a sanitation problem. The poor in parti-cular were afflicted by typhus and tuberculosis; and a series of cholera epidemics, being water-borne, attacked everyone, including the middle classes with their ready access to water.

This was the problem. The solution again involves Edwin Chadwick (1842), whose *Inquiry into the Sanitary Condition of the Labouring Population of Great Britain* was remark-able for the high quality of its statistical analysis. Chadwick originally advocated sewage disposal as a public enterprise on the grounds that ill health, by causing poverty, added to the cost of the Poor Law. The report, however, included wider grounds for intervention. Its main recommendation was that sewage should be separated from other water through the use of glazed pipes. The report met considerable opposition and, as a result, legislation was delayed and initially ineffective. After several false starts, the Public Health Act 1875 established clear duties for local authorities, and remained the basis of most public-health activities until 1936.

This, then, was the situation in the 1870s. The state was slowly becoming involved in increasing areas of social and economic life; but, though the classical economists supported much of the new legislation, the prevailing doctrine was still largely *laissez-faire*.

2. The Liberal reforms

2.1. The origins of the reforms

The next major development was the period of the Liberal reforms between 1906 and 1914.[1] There has been much debate about this burst of activity so much at variance with the ideology of the nineteenth-century Liberal Party. Hay (1975) distinguishes three influences in particular: pressure from below, changing attitudes to welfare provision, and institutional influences.

PRESSURE FROM BELOW. There is a measure of agreement (see Hobsbawm 1964; Pelling 1979) that working-class political pressure was one of the origins of the reforms, though the relationship is not simple. If reform was so popular, why was it not a major election issue; and why the long lag between electoral reform in 1867 and social reform in 1906–14?

CHANGING ATTITUDES to welfare provision among the political elite arose in part out of the national-efficiency issue. The argument at its simplest was that economic growth depended on a healthy, educated workforce. In dramatic contrast with the Principles of 1834, a speaker in parliamentary debate could argue: 'The future of the Empire, the triumph of social progress and the freedom of the British race depend not so much upon the strengthening of the Army as upon fortifying the children of the State for the battle of life' (*Hansard* (Commons), 18 Apr. 1905, col. 539, quoted by Bruce 1972: 152–3). The influence of the national-efficiency arguments is debated. At a minimum they made social reform politically respectable.

A second reason for greater acceptance of intervention was a changed attitude towards poverty. Social surveys by Rowntree (1901) and Booth (1902) and the study of the health of Boer War recruits yielded much empirical information. The effects of these data on attitudes were complex: they suggested that poverty was more widespread than had been believed, and that not all poverty, even among the able-bodied, was due to moral defect. They also raised doubts about the effectiveness of private philanthropy.

A third influence was the rise of collectivism. The 'Old Liberalism', which opposed state intervention, had twofold roots in the 'natural-rights' individualist philosophy of writers like Spencer (1884) and in utilitarianism.[2] Between 1860 and 1900, however, several philosophers, though in no sense advocating collectivism, suggested that the traditional definition of individual freedom as *absence of coercion* was too narrow. It was argued (e.g. Hobson 1909: pt. II, ch. II) that 'positive freedom' should include not only economic freedom but also a measure of *economic security*. It followed that the state, in advancing individual freedom, should adopt an active role in social reform. This was the 'New Liberalism' (Freeden 1978).

Against a backdrop of these changing ideas the German example became important. Between 1883 and 1889, largely to counter socialist agitation, the German government

---

[1] This section draws on Hay (1975). See also the Further Reading.
[2] The important distinction between a natural-rights and a utilitarian defence of individual freedom is discussed in Chapter 3, which also discusses the ideas of collectivist writers.

under Bismarck had created a broad system of social insurance under which compulsory contributions gave entitlement to guaranteed benefits, thereby removing the threat of the means test and poorhouse. The scheme was investigated by Lloyd George, and had a major influence on the shape of the National Insurance Act 1911, discussed below.

INSTITUTIONAL INFLUENCES on the reforms included pressure groups such as the Friendly Societies, which represented the idea of working-class self-help. It is also argued that bureaucracies like the civil service exerted an independent influence. McDonagh (1960) describes a process whereby, as awareness of a problem grew, a body of experts would be set up to investigate. As a result of its findings, awareness of the problem increased, and so did the volume of resources devoted to combating it. Experts thus contributed not only to the *manner* in which social problems were tackled, but also to the *range* of issues regarded as the proper province of public policy.[3]

The reforms were central rather than local mainly because central government was reluctant to reform local-authority finance, and because local revenues failed to keep pace with rising expenditure. Finally, the reforms were outside the Poor Law partly because the latter was financed locally, partly to sidestep the long-established vested interests of local Poor Law institutions, and partly because of popular hostility towards the old system.

2.2. The new measures

Whatever their causes (about which historians continue to argue) and motives (discussed below), the reforms of 1906–14 were substantial by any standards and particularly so in the context of the times. The new measures concerned children, pensions, unemployment, health, and fiscal policy.

CHILDREN. The Education (Provision of Meals) Act 1906 permitted, but did not compel, local authorities to provide school meals for needy children; the Education (Administrative Provisions) Act 1907 introduced medical inspection of schoolchildren; and the Children Act 1908 made it a punishable offence for parents to neglect their children. The motives for these Acts were partly humanitarian and partly on national-efficiency grounds.

PENSIONS. The Old Age Pensions Act 1908 'introduced a new principle into social policy. Hitherto relief had been provided . . . from *local* funds and only after a test of destitution. Now . . . payments were to be made, as of right, from *national* funds . . . within strict limits of age and means, but with no test of actual destitution' (Bruce 1972: 178, emphasis in original). The Act introduced a non-contributory pension of five shillings (25 pence) per week for people over 70 whose income was below £31 per year, though it excluded previous recipients of Poor Law relief, and some people on moral grounds.[4]

---

[3] The government-failure literature, discussed in Chapter 4, Section 5, argues that these forces can go too far and create inefficient upwards pressure on the size of government.

[4] History is full of small anomalies. An additional reason for the pensions legislation, according to Pelling (1979: 11), was 'a loosening of the Treasury's purse strings (because of) the temporary lull in the naval building race, which was due to the destruction of Russian battleships in the Russo-Japanese War . . . Thus in a sense it was Admiral Togo, the victor of Tsushima, who laid the groundwork of Old Age Pensions and deserves to be remembered as the architect of the British Welfare State.'

UNEMPLOYMENT AND MINIMUM WAGES. Earlier proposals to resolve growing unemployment had met with little success (see Harris 1972). Any acceptable solution had to meet four criteria (Hay 1975: 50–1). It had to 'make the minimum alterations in the normal work-ings of the labour market to satisfy individualists, economists and industrialists'. Secondly, 'it . . . had to be largely self-financing in order to avoid unacceptable increases in direct taxation or the reintroduction of tariffs'. It had to be separate from the Poor Law to avoid the need to discriminate between the 'deserving' and 'undeserving' poor. Lastly, it had to be sufficiently attractive to head off any socialist threat. The resulting package had three elements: voluntary labour exchanges would assist the working of the labour market; there was to be a limited scheme of unemployment insurance; and a Development Fund would finance counter-cyclical public-works expenditure, mainly by local authorities.

The scheme of unemployment insurance was limited: it applied only to a narrow range of industries; only workers earning less than £160 per year were covered; and benefits were low, to discourage deliberate unemployment. A variety of other industrial legislation gave government limited powers to set minimum wages. It was recognized that unemploy-ment and sickness were interrelated, so the National Insurance Act 1911 also contained health insurance. The combined package was financed by a weekly contribution of 9d. (3.75 pence), of which 4d. (1.67 pence) was paid by the worker, the rest by the employer.

HEALTH. Whereas unemployment insurance, according to Hay, was largely the result of working-class pressure, health insurance arose more from considerations of national efficiency. Prior to 1911 there were voluntary hospitals for those who could afford to subscribe to them; for others Poor Law hospitals offered free and (for the most part) non-stigmatizing health care (Abel Smith 1964: ch. 15). The 1911 Act did little to change these arrangements. Cover was extended only to the breadwinner, who was entitled to a sickness (i.e. cash) benefit, free medical treatment and drugs from a panel doctor, and access to a sanatorium.

FISCAL POLICY. The fiscal controversies of the time concerned tariffs (not the issue here), and progressive income tax. The traditional economic argument was that taxation should be based on 'equal sacrifice' (implying a poll tax) or 'equi-proportional sacrifice' (implying a proportional tax). Both approaches ruled out redistribution through the tax system. By the turn of the century, however, there was limited support for redistribution through tax-financed public spending. Edgeworth justified progressive taxation via the 'least-aggregate-sacrifice' principle under which *marginal* rather than *total* sacrifice was to be equalized. Equal marginal sacrifice plus the assumption of diminishing marginal utility of income together imply progressive taxation.

A different line of argument (Hobson 1908) was that monopoly resulted in a suboptimal income distribution, leading to under-consumption. By thus attributing unemployment to under-consumption, which could be remedied by income redistribution, Hobson fore-shadowed Keynes some thirty years before the publication of *The General Theory*. Others, notably socialists, saw progressive taxation as an issue of social justice, a subject to which we return in Chapter 3.

BRIEF ASSESSMENT. In assessing the reforms, two hotly debated issues arise: what was their motive (discussed in Section 7.1); and were they particularly radical? It can be argued

(Marsh 1980: 17) that the virtually simultaneous introduction of old-age pensions, unemployment insurance, sickness benefits, and progressive taxation, supported by the interventionist philosophy of the New Liberalism, constituted a fundamental break with earlier economic and political doctrines.

However, a closer look at the individual programmes gives a less clear answer. The pension scheme, albeit non-contributory, was partially means-tested, and applied only to people over 70 who had never received poor relief. Its main purpose, it can be argued, was to improve national competitiveness by weeding out inefficient labour (the national-efficiency argument again). Unemployment insurance was based in part on a weekly employee contribution of 4*d*. (i.e. lump sum and therefore regressive) and applied only to a few relatively skilled workers in some industries. Sickness benefits were financed by the same contribution, with similar coverage; and the health-care benefits applied only to the breadwinner. It can be argued, therefore, that the reforms were relatively minor and had limited coverage; and that only the pension scheme was substantially redistributive from rich to poor. The New Liberalism, from this viewpoint, was not very new; it still accepted capitalism unquestioningly, and in that sense was only a reinterpretation of the Old Liberalism. As we shall see in Section 4, strikingly similar issues arise in considering the novelty (or otherwise) of the 1935 US Social Security Act.

Nor, in conclusion, were the Liberal reforms in any way unique. Germany, as we have seen, had introduced social insurance in the 1880s, motivated in part by fears of social unrest. New Zealand introduced non-contributory pensions in 1898, *inter alia* for reasons of national efficiency, in the face of increased international competition on an economy highly dependent on its exports. By 1908 Denmark, Ireland, Austria, Czechoslovakia, and Australia also had social legislation of some sort. The Liberal reforms, though one of the earlier examples of nationally organized income support, were not the first; nor did they represent a major discontinuity either with previous arrangements or with developments in other countries.

3. The First World War and the inter-war period in the UK

3.1. Housing

In contrast with the eventful years between 1906 and 1914, the period thereafter was largely a time of stagnation in social policy, with the important exception of housing. There were also major changes in unemployment insurance (Section 3.2).

THE ROOTS OF STATE INVOLVEMENT. In housing, probably more than any other part of the welfare state, past policies, notably during and after the First World War, had a crucial bearing on institutions for most of the rest of the twentieth century. Before 1914, virtually all housing was privately provided. By and large the system worked well for those who could afford it, but for the poor, particularly in large cities, it led to overcrowding and squalor (Gauldie 1974). In a strictly technical sense the housing market cleared, but policy-makers found the result unacceptable both for reasons of public health and public order, and for more charitable motives. Early legislation had little effect, mainly because it imposed no *duty* on local authorities to remedy poor housing. Though working-class housing conditions continued to cause concern in the latter part of the nineteenth century, the response was limited mainly to philanthropic efforts (see Merrett 1979).

By 1918, however, for at least three reasons, housing had become a problem requiring action. First, there was an acute housing shortage because of falling supply (due to the cessation of building during the First World War, and the deterioration of older property) and rising demand (because people were living longer and marrying earlier, and mobility among young people was increasing). Secondly, this shortage was politically too sensitive to be left to private charity and discretionary local action. In 1918 large numbers of soldiers were demobilized, and there were fears of social unrest (the Russian Revolution having occurred in the previous year). Lloyd George's promise in November 1918 'to make Britain a fit country for heroes to live in' was seen as a commitment on which it would have been politically dangerous to renege.

The third reason why housing was thought to warrant government action was because intervention had already occurred, through the imposition of rent control in 1915 as an emergency wartime measure. By 1918 many people were unable to pay the market price of housing, which had risen sharply because of the shortage; at least as important, controlled rents had already assumed an aura of 'fair' rents.

Since immediate decontrol was politically impossible, the government assumed some responsibility for people dependent on renting at the lower end of the market, through direct provision of housing at rents equivalent to controlled rents.

RESULTING ACTION. The resulting Housing and Town Planning Act 1919 (the Addison Act) contained three provisions: local authorities were invested with the *duty* of remedying housing deficiencies in their areas; house building was to meet *general* needs rather than concentrating only on slum clearance; and the operation received a central government subsidy. In contrast with nineteenth-century thought, the Act embodied three new principles—central supervision, compulsion, and subsidy. It had three long-term effects: the acceptance of housing as a legitimate area of government intervention, in the sense of public production as opposed only to regulation; the provision of accommodation at a subsidized rent, implying a view of housing as a social service; and the delivery of service by local authorities. The Act, together with rent control, laid a foundation for housing policy that lasted into the latter part of the twentieth century.

3.2. Unemployment insurance

From 1920 to 1940 unemployment never fell below one million and reached a peak of over three million, in the face of which unemployment insurance qua insurance virtually collapsed. The story in many other countries involves similar problems, similar debates, and, in broad terms, similar solutions (Kaim-Caudle 1973). The case of the USA is taken up in Section 4.

DEVELOPMENTS IN THE 1920S. The Unemployment Insurance Act 1920 extended the 1911 Act to more workers, and also paid an allowance for dependants. It was introduced hastily in the face of rising unemployment after the war, not least among demobilized soldiers. The Act was doomed to failure, since rising unemployment inevitably undermined the insurance aspect of the scheme. This led to continual juggling with contribution and benefit levels, and to a series of devices that sought to preserve the fiction of insurance while in reality paying benefits not financed by contributions, thereby violating the insurance principle. The payment of such benefits out of the insurance fund was partly because the locally financed Poor Law could not cope with mass unemployment and, equally important, because the unemployed strenuously resisted the Poor Law. The realization grew only slowly that insurance has problems even with short-term unemployment, and is totally inadequate in the face of long-term or mass unemployment (a central topic of Chapters 5 and 8).

As a result of the report of the Blanesburgh Committee, two benefits were introduced in 1927. Standard benefit was paid as an insurance benefit of indefinite duration to anyone who had made *any* contributions. Transitional benefit was payable as of right to those who did not satisfy even the minimal requirements of the insurance scheme, provided that they were 'genuinely seeking work'. Both benefits were paid from the insurance fund. Transitional benefit protected the unemployed from the Poor Law, which was reorganized in 1929, when the powers of the Guardians were transferred to Public Assistance Committees (PACs) run by local authorities.

In 1930 the Labour government changed the regulations for transitional benefit in two ways: they made the benefit a charge on general government revenues rather than the insurance fund; and they relaxed the 'genuinely seeking work' clause. As a result, the numbers receiving transitional benefit doubled within two months, at a cost of £19 million in its first year, just as the economic crisis came to a head.

THE 1931 CRISIS AND THE BENEFIT CUTS. By the late 1920s one strand of policy concerned the finance of unemployment benefits; another concentrated on the economic crisis more generally, and particularly on how to reduce unemployment. Economic radicals like Keynes, with support from the Liberal Party and from various politicians in other parties, favoured expansionary public-works expenditure. Economic conservatives followed the traditional orthodoxy, supporting expenditure cuts, a balanced budget, and lower government borrowing. In the 1931 crisis the economic conservatives dominated. The decision to preserve the gold standard by stringent fiscal and monetary policy, particularly a cut in unemployment benefit, split the Labour Cabinet and led to the formation of a National Government. In the face of expenditure cuts, unemployment and controversy mounted.

The rapid escalation of benefit payments at a time of economic crisis led to immediate action. Benefits were cut by 10 per cent from 17s. (85 pence) to 15s. 3d. (76 pence) in 1931. Standard benefit was limited to twenty-six weeks, and the administration of transitional benefit was transferred to the local PACs, though still paid from central funds.

It is a matter of controversy whether *real* benefits fell, since prices had also declined. Between 1921 and 1931 the overall price of consumer goods fell by 28 per cent, and those of food, clothing, and fuel and light by even more. Compared with 1927 (when standard and transitional benefits were introduced), the price of consumer goods fell by 8 per cent, though the price of housing increased by 2 per cent (C. H. Feinstein 1972: tables 61, 62). Possibly of greater importance as an explanation of the anger engendered by the cuts was the way they were implemented. Eligibility for benefit was tightened, though with regional variation, which was itself a further cause of anger. The interpretation of the 'genuinely seeking work' condition became more harsh. Additionally, from 1931, in sharp contrast with arrangements after 1927, the PACs administered transitional payment on the basis of the stringent Poor Law *household* means test, which, 'like the workhouse before it, was destined to leave an indelible mark on popular culture . . . long after its official demise . . . Receipt of transitional payment through the PACs in effect put the unemployed right back on to the Poor Law' (Fraser 1984: 194).

It is often not appreciated that the desperate plight of many of the unemployed in the 1930s was not typical of the country as a whole. The unemployment rate varied widely between regions, and long-term unemployment was concentrated in a limited number of decaying areas. While the unemployed suffered, living standards rose substantially for those in regular work.

THE UNEMPLOYMENT ACT 1934 separated unemployment insurance proper from measures to support the long-term unemployed. Part I of the Act extended compulsory insurance to more workers; restored benefits to their level prior to the 1931 cut; organized contributions on the basis of one-third each from worker, employer, and government; and established an independent committee to run the scheme, with responsibility only for those receiving *insurance* benefits. Part II dealt with unemployment assistance for people with no insurance, or whose cover had expired. Benefits were paid from general government funds, and run on a *national* basis by the newly established Unemployment Assistance Board. Payment was on the basis of need, in the light of family circumstances. The principle of less eligibility was finally laid to rest. Sixteen years after the end of the First World War, the UK had a system of unemployment relief that worked reasonably smoothly.

The social measures of the 1906–14 period were inadequate for the mass unemployment of the inter-war years. The Widows, Orphans and Age Contributory Pensions Act 1925 (extended by a further Act in 1929) introduced the first national scheme of contributory pensions; the 1911 health-insurance scheme was enlarged; and there was action on housing. For the most part this legislation was a product of the 1920s. In the 1930s the welfare state was in abeyance, and new measures were little more than crisis management. The main lesson for the future was that *laissez-faire* capitalism could not solve the problem of unemployment—in this area, too, state intervention was necessary. When intervention came, in the form of rearmament and war production, the unemployment problem disappeared—an unhappy way of ending an unhappy period in British social policy.

4. Inter-war poverty relief in the USA

4.1. The roots of the 'New Deal'

Government involvement in income support in the USA, at least at the federal level, began late by international standards.[5] There was no American equivalent of the Liberal reforms, nor any analogue to the broadening of the UK welfare system during and

---

[5] For additional detail, see the Further Reading.

after the First World War. Until 1935 it was accepted that, except in times of disaster, no able-bodied person need be without work. Public assistance was regarded as charity, and its receipt generally carried stigma. Until the 1930s such aid as existed came mainly from state and local government, though private schemes also had a limited role. By 1929 approximately 75 per cent of all relief derived from public funds, mostly local. *Until 1933 the federal government paid no grants and organized no programmes for relief or insurance, except for its own employees.* Emergency appropriations were made occasionally in the face of local disasters, but *no federal relief had ever been granted to the unemployed.*

Eligibility requirements and benefit levels varied widely by locality. Common among eligibility rules were taking the 'pauper's oath', disenfranchisement (in fourteen states), residency requirements, and the condition that recipients live in almshouses (US National Resources and Planning Board 1942: 26–8). In states where relief was granted to people outside almshouses, payments were low; and many localities gave benefits only in kind.

Detailed explanation of why these arrangements changed sharply in the 1930s is controversial. I shall do no more than set out the main questions. First, why did income support at a national level begin in the USA later than in almost any other industrialized country[6] and, moreover, at a level that by international standards was low?[7] The arguments are complex (see Higgins 1981: ch. 4). Most writers concentrate on one or more of three sets of factors: the influence of ideology (see Section 7.1); the cultural and political heterogeneity of the USA (Gronbjerg et al. 1978; Katznelson 1978); and the influence of pressure groups (Menscher 1967; Derthick 1979; Weaver 1982: ch. 4).

A second question is why the 1930s legislation took the shape it did. To a minor extent it was influenced by experience in other countries, notably the UK, Germany, France, Sweden, and Canada. Considerably more important was the desire to head off more radical proposals. Douglas (1925) advocated a system of family allowances for dependants. The Townsend Plan in the early 1930s called for a monthly pension of $150 for everyone over 60. Simultaneously, Huey Long was pursuing his populist campaign to 'share our wealth'. The Social Security Act 1935 was in part 'a compromise measure to blunt the political appeal of the enormously expensive and essentially unworkable Townsend Plan' (Pechman et al. 1968: 32).

Why did reform occur when it did? Well before the 1930s, pressures for change were emerging out of various long-run developments, notably technological innovation, the decline of the family farm, and decreasing household size. The crisis of the 1930s brought developments to a head. As unemployment rose after 1929, local expenditure on relief and emergency assistance by states both outstripped declining tax revenues, making federal participation inevitable. Under the Emergency Relief and Construction Act 1932, $300 million in federal funds were made available for loans to states to help in their relief efforts.[8]

---

[6] By 1930, twenty-seven countries had public schemes of poverty relief of some sort. Among industrialized countries only Norway, Japan, and Switzerland started later than the USA (Pechman et al. 1968: app. C).

[7] Why, to use Wilensky and Lebeaux's concept (1965), did the USA adopt a *residual* model of welfare? We return to this issue in Section 7.1.

[8] Repayment of these loans was eventually waived.

4.2. The Social Security Act 1935

Between 1933 and 1935 the federal government played an increasing role. The Civilian Conservation Corps, the Public Works Administration, and the Federal Civil Works Administration organized public works; the Federal Surplus Relief Corporation distributed surplus commodities to the needy; and the Federal Emergency Relief Administration supervised federal grants to states for unemployment relief. This last had the greatest impact, both at the time and through its influence on subsequent legislation. The use of federal funds gave federal government influence over the state programmes, in particular on benefit levels and administration, and these features were carried over into the permanent legislation.[9]

THE 1935 SOCIAL SECURITY ACT created what, for the USA, was a broad-ranging scheme. It established two major insurance schemes and three major forms of assistance, administered by a new Social Security Board whose powers and duties were set out in Title VII of the Act.[10]

Federal Old Age Benefits (Title II) were financed by contributions from employees and employers under Title VIII and, as originally envisaged, were to be run largely on actuarial lines (as discussed shortly, this resolve was not put into effect).

Federal assistance to states for unemployment compensation was granted under Title III, financed by taxes levied on employers under Title IX. Unlike the pension scheme, which was federal, unemployment insurance was organized by states, which had wide discretion over the precise form of their arrangements. Though the scheme (being insurance) provided no benefits for individuals currently out of work, this was much the most controversial part of the Act, many employers bitterly opposing any form of unemployment compensation. Nevertheless, by 1937 all states and territories had such a scheme.

Old Age Assistance (Title I) provided for means-tested cash payments to the elderly through federal grants to states with approved schemes. It was envisaged that costs would decline as the insurance benefits under Title II became payable. By 1940, fifty-one jurisdictions offered Old Age Assistance.[11]

Aid to the Blind (Title X) provided federal grants to approved state plans of aid to the needy blind. By 1940, forty-three states qualified for federal funds.

Aid to Dependent Children (Title IV) paid federal grants to states giving cash assistance to families with needy children 'under the age of 16 (or under the age of 18 if found by the State agency to be regularly attending school) . . . deprived of parental support or care by reason of the death, continued absence from the home, or physical incapacity of a

[9] For further details of the emergency programmes, see US Federal Emergency Relief Administration (1942), and US National Resources and Planning Board (1942: 26–7).

[10] For the wording of the Act itself, see Social Security Act, 14 Aug. 1935, ch. 531, 49 Statutes at Large 620, or, for an edited version, R. B. Stevens (1970: 167–80).

[11] The forty-eight continental states, plus Washington DC, Alaska, and Hawaii.

parent'.[12] By 1949, forty-two jurisdictions had schemes of this sort which qualified for federal funds.[13]

THE 1939 AMENDMENTS to the Social Security Act stressed its welfare objectives and broadened its scope. The strict actuarial principles of the 1935 legislation were diluted; insurance benefits became payable to dependants of aged recipients, and to widows and children of workers covered by the scheme; payments began in 1940 rather than 1942; benefits were tied to average earnings over a minimum period, thus breaking the link with lifetime contributions; and the earnings test prescribed by the 1935 Act was liberalized before the first benefits were paid.[14] The financial basis of the scheme also changed. The intention of accumulating an actuarial fund was abandoned, benefits for the elderly and their dependants being paid almost entirely out of current contributions (i.e. the scheme was organized on a Pay-As-You-Go (PAYG) rather than a funded basis, an issue discussed in Chapter 9).

BRIEF ASSESSMENT. To a greater extent than the Liberal reforms, the Social Security Act can be criticized as timid. The Act, admittedly, improved earlier arrangements: the range of benefits was broader, the age requirements for retirement more liberal, and the eligibility restrictions on residence and citizenship less stringent; and benefits were paid in cash, this being a condition of the federal contribution to state schemes.

In important respects, however, 'the . . . Act may be reasonably regarded as a conservative legislative solution to a difficult and explosive problem' (Pechman et al. 1968: 32). First, though the federal government ensured some uniformity, state programmes still varied widely in terms of benefit levels and eligibility requirements. Secondly, the insurance arrangements were severely constrained: in 1940 only about 60 per cent of workers were covered; benefits were intended originally to bear a simple relationship to contributions, ruling out any substantial redistribution (though this aspect was relaxed somewhat by the 1939 amendments); and the insurance benefits were subject to an earnings test. Thirdly, the assistance measures were categorical—that is, they granted aid only to individuals falling into one of the three categories: aged, blind, or dependent child—since it was felt that only these groups should ever require assistance.

The importance of the original Social Security Act, it can be argued, lies less in its content, which was in many ways rather conservative, than in the reform process itself: the Act gradually brought about public acceptance of income support as a permanent institution; secondly, and acutely relevant to reformers elsewhere, the use of carefully designed subsidies to states enabled the federal government to impose some uniformity on state programmes.

---

[12] Social Security Act 1935, Title IV, section 406(*a*). Phrase in parentheses added by an amendment in 1939.

[13] A further eight states (Alaska, Connecticut, Illinois, Kentucky, Mississippi, Nevada, South Dakota, and Texas) operated schemes without federal funds (US National Resources and Planning Board 1942: 83).

[14] These changes were based on recommendations in US Advisory Council on Social Security (1938), which contains valuable background information. For details of the legislative history, see Myers (1965: ch. 4) or, more briefly, Pechman et al. (1968: app. B).

5. The Second World War and its aftermath

5.1. Wartime activity

POLICY. The final climacteric in the development of the welfare state occurred in the years 1940–8. The Second World War was a total war; *everyone's* life was affected, and this, it is argued, led to important changes in attitude. The totality of the war effort forced the UK government to adopt powers (rationing and the direction of labour, for example) on a scale hitherto unknown. It also reduced social distinctions; unlike the divisive unemployment of the 1930s, food shortages and bombs affected all social classes. The pressure of common problems prompted common solutions. Attitudes were changed also by increased awareness of social problems as social classes mingled. In the armed services men who would otherwise have led separate lives were thrown together. Evacuation, too, 'was part of the process by which British society came to know itself, as the unkempt, ill-clothed, undernourished and often incontinent children of bombed cities acted as messengers carrying the evidence of the deprivation of urban working-class life into rural homes' (Fraser 1984: 210).

As well as planning for the future, some social policy was a direct result of the war, including action on school meals, the transformation of the Unemployment Assistance Board, and dramatic changes in the organization of health care. As a result of wartime food shortages, school meals and school milk, previously a form of charity, became a normal feature of school life. The needs of wartime diversified the activities of the Unemployment Assistance Board (renamed the Assistance Board). In particular, wartime inflation adversely affected pensioners, and legislation in 1940 allowed the Board to pay supplementary pensions on the basis of need. By 1941 it dealt with ten pensioners to every one unemployed person. It also helped others who fell outside the traditional categories—victims of bombing, evacuees, dependants of prisoners of war, etc. As a direct result of the war, the Assistance Board became a generalized relief agency and so foreshadowed the National Assistance Board of 1948.

From 1939 there were two sorts of hospital patient. Some received emergency treatment, which was free, and financed and organized nationally. Others took their turn, as previously, in a voluntary or municipal hospital, for which payment was generally through membership of a contributory scheme or through a means test (Abel Smith 1964: ch. 26). Initially only military personnel fell into the emergency category, but wartime exigencies extended the services to an ever-widening group of people. This served as an example of large-scale, state-financed health care and also exposed the deficiencies of the old system.

PLANNING FOR THE POST-WAR PERIOD. The Beveridge Report (1942) has pride of place on the planning front. It was based on three assumptions: that a scheme of family allowances would be set up; that there would be a comprehensive health-care service; and that the state would maintain full employment. The report envisaged a scheme of social insurance that would be 'all-embracing in scope of persons and of needs. . . . Every person . . . will pay a single security contribution by a stamp on a single insurance document each week. . . . Unemployment benefit, disability benefit [and] retirement pensions after a transitional period . . . will be at the same rate irrespective of previous earnings' (ibid. 9–10). Benefits were to be paid also for maternity, and to widows and orphans. Coverage was to be compulsory and (in contrast with the 1935 US Social Security Act) universal in respect of individuals and risk. Flat-rate contributions would give entitlement to flat-rate, subsistence benefits; there would be no means test; and the scheme was to be administered nationally.

The 1944 White Paper, *Social Insurance* (UK Government 1944), accepted most of these recommendations, and became the basis of the National Insurance Act 1946. In the same year two other major White Papers were published. *A National Health Service* (UK DoH 1944) envisaged 'a comprehensive service covering every branch of medical and allied activity' providing free treatment on a universal basis, financed out of general taxation. *Employment Policy* (UK Department of Labour 1944) was very much a Keynesian document. It committed the government to 'the maintenance of a high and stable level of employment', brought about, where necessary, by counter-cyclical deficit spending. The economic radicals of 1931 had finally come into their own.

The major piece of social legislation during the war was the Education Act 1944, based on Butler's 1943 White Paper (UK Board of Education 1943), which set the foundation for post-war education. It created a comprehensive national system of primary, secondary, and further education. Primary and secondary education were to be free up to school-leaving age, which was to be raised to 15 in 1945 and to 16 as soon as possible thereafter.

ASSESSING BEVERIDGE. The original Beveridge proposals have four central characteristics (see Glennerster 2000: ch. 2 or, for fuller discussion, Harris 1997).

- *Strategic*. The true novelty of the proposals was their replacement of the old, haphazard system by a coherent *strategy* embracing social insurance, family allowances, national assistance paid out of central revenues, the National Health Service, and (possibly crucially) a presumption of high employment. Thus the Report was not a ragbag of recommendations, but a strategic whole.

- *Universal*. Coverage was mandatory for everyone with an employment record. The motivation was not a predilection for collective provision, but Beveridge's insistence that this was the only way to avoid the gaps experienced during the Great Depression.

- *Actuarial*. The proposals were modelled as closely as possible on private, actuarial insurance: flat-rate benefits were based on flat-rate contributions related to the average risk, and the original proposal was that the state pension scheme should be funded.

- *Parsimonious*. Beveridge argued that the main insurance benefits should be at or above the poverty line, so that recipients would not need to apply for means-tested benefits. For incentive and fiscal reasons, however, he advocated a parsimoniously defined poverty line, with a stringent test to ensure that unemployment was genuine.

The central emphasis on poverty relief contrasts sharply with the Bismarck approach (earnings-related contributions giving entitlement to earnings-related benefits), with its explicit emphasis on consumption smoothing.

5.2. Policies 1946–1948

The 1945 Labour government was armed with a large parliamentary majority and a stack of White Papers, many of them approved by the Conservatives during the wartime coalition. Under the Family Allowance Act 1945 a payment of 5 shillings (25 pence) was made for the second child and subsequent children in each family. The benefit was universal and paid from general taxation.

The National Health Service Act 1946, based on the 1944 White Paper, established a national system of comprehensive health care available universally at no charge. The system was financed from general taxation, except for a small proportion from national-insurance contributions. The detailed arrangements (Abel Smith 1964: chs. 27–9; Glennerster 2000: ch. 3) involved considerable discussion with the medical profession.

The National Insurance Act 1946 was based on the 1944 White Paper, which in turn followed closely the recommendations of the Beveridge Report. All insured persons were required to buy a weekly stamp (to which the employer also contributed), whose cost varied by age, sex, and marital and employment status. An employed person was eligible for flat-rate benefit under seven heads, including unemployment, maternity, sickness, widowhood, retirement, and a death grant to cover funeral costs. Beveridge had envisaged that it would take twenty years to build up entitlement to a full retirement pension, but in the event the Labour government implemented full pensions from October 1946.

The National Insurance (Industrial Injuries) Act 1946 entitled those injured at work to various benefits financed by an identifiable component of the national-insurance contribution. Because the scheme was compulsory, it was possible to pool risks across industries with higher and lower accident rates (see Chapter 5, Section 4.1).

The National Assistance Act 1948 established a safety net for those whose needs were not covered (or not fully covered) by insurance. The Act, like the other major Acts, was universal in approach. The old Assistance Board became the National Assistance Board, administering means-tested benefits to those not in full-time work whose income was below subsistence. In doing so it assumed the residual functions of the local PACs left over from the Poor Law, which were explicitly repealed by the Act.

The legislation of 1944–8 was, on the whole, successful. If the welfare state has any official birthday, it is 5 July 1948, when the provisions of the National Insurance, Industrial Injuries, National Assistance, and National Health Service Acts came simultaneously into effect, family allowances and higher pensions having been implemented in 1946. With unemployment below 250,000, the insurance fund made a surplus of £95 million in its first year, but the National Health Service cost more than anticipated.

There is considerable debate about the importance, or lack of it, of the Second World War in bringing about this legislation. Some writers (Titmuss 1958: ch. 4; Marshall 1975) regard the war as a sine qua non for subsequent events, others (Glennerster 2000: ch. 1) as merely one of a long chain of formative influences.

6. Post-war developments in the UK and USA

This section reviews post-war developments in the UK and USA, concentrating mainly on cash benefits. Discussion of health care and education is deferred to the relevant chapters. For fuller assessment, see Glennerster (2000), and for trends in the advanced industrial countries, (Neil Gilbert 2002: ch. 1).

6.1. The UK

At risk of oversimplifying, the post-war story can be divided into three phases: the first period (the post-war consensus) saw consolidation and extension; the second (the watershed of the 1976 economic crisis and the subsequent period of 'Thatcherism') comprised a series of attempts to restrict the growth of social spending; the third (post-1997—New Labour) tried to address both sets of concerns.

CONSOLIDATION AND EXTENSION: THE POST-WAR CONSENSUS (see Glennerster 2000: chs. 4–7). The contributions regime was the first to show stress. An implication of a self-balancing fund is that total contributions must match total benefits. Since contributions (being flat-rate) could not exceed the reach of a low-paid worker, benefits, too, had to be low. In a fundamental reform, the 1975 Social Security Act replaced the weekly stamp with an earnings-related contribution for all employed persons. One effect of the changes was to enable the insurance system to redistribute from rich to poor (see Chapters 8 and 9).

National-insurance benefits remained broadly unchanged for twenty years. In the later 1960s and early 1970s there was much political wrangling over a series of proposed pension reforms. The Social Security Pensions Act 1975—one of the most important pieces of social legislation since 1948—was in some ways a blend of these proposals (see UK DHSS 1974). It introduced wide-ranging earnings-related pensions and, for the first time, gave a statutory basis for the indexation of benefits, which were intended to rise in line with average earnings.

The system of family support advocated by Beveridge remained largely intact until the late 1970s. It had two strands: a taxable family allowance for the second child and subsequent children in any family; and an income-tax allowance for all children. The resulting system was complex and did not give the greatest benefit to the poorest families (such inter-relations between the tax and benefit systems will be a recurring theme). To avoid these difficulties the Child Benefit Act 1975 (a remarkable year for social legislation) abolished family allowances and child tax allowances, replacing them with child benefit, a weekly, tax-free cash payment in respect of *all* children in the family, with an additional payment for single parents (see Chapter 10).

Assistance benefits are also discussed in Chapter 10. The National Assistance Board was abolished in 1966, and a Supplementary Benefits Commission with wide discretionary powers established. Contrary to Beveridge's expectations, there was a large increase over the years in the number of recipients.

The 1960s saw the 'rediscovery' of poverty (Abel Smith and Townsend 1965), including poverty among working families, who were normally not eligible for supplementary benefit. One response was the introduction in 1971 of family income supplement, a cash benefit for working families with children. The scheme's success was limited by problems with take-up (i.e. potentially eligible families not applying), and (again) anomalous inter-actions between the tax and benefit structures. At certain income levels, for instance, a family was eligible for family income supplement, but also liable to income tax.

More generally, the years after 1960 saw a proliferation of assistance benefits. Some paralleled the insurance scheme (e.g. pensions for people too old to have an adequate post-1948 contributions record); others were means-tested; and the relation between dif-ferent benefits, and between benefits generally and the tax system, became complex and muddled, raising problems of the 'poverty trap' discussed in Chapter 10, Section 3. By the early 1970s there were over fifty benefits outside national insurance (UK Select Committee on Tax Credit 1973: 47–8).

A snapshot of the welfare state in the mid-1970s shows a system with earnings-related contributions, with the major benefits at least partially earnings related and indexed to average wages, and with a growing array of assistance benefits. The welfare state, it must have seemed to its proponents, was coming into full flower. The seeds of retrenchment, however, had already been sown. The effects of the first oil shock in late 1973 included rapidly accelerating inflation. The economic situation deteriorated rapidly, forcing the government sharply to tighten its macroeconomic policy. In the wake of the economic crisis of 1976, the later 1970s were times of tight spending limits. The first Thatcher government took office in 1979.

ATTEMPTED RETRENCHMENT ('THATCHERISM') (see Glennerster 2000: chs. 8–9). By the late 1980s the picture was different (see Martin Evans 1998). Unemployment benefit became less generous through a series of cumulative changes (Atkinson 1995a: ch. 9, app.); indexa-tion became less generous by tying the major benefits to changes in prices rather than earnings; and a series of measures tipped the balance increasingly towards means-tested benefits (Martin Evans 1998: tables 7.3, 7.15).

A 'fundamental review' of income transfers (UK DHSS 1985a,b) set out with radical intentions, including privatizing all pensions except the basic pension. In the event (UK DHSS 1985c), the main changes were to reduce the state pension for individuals retiring after the turn of the century (see Chapter 9, Section 5) and to allow individuals to opt out of the state earnings-related scheme and occupational schemes and instead to have a personal pension. The review also introduced changes to income-tested benefits, mainly through measures to alleviate the poverty trap (Chapter 10, Section 3).

The real income of the population as a whole increased by 36 per cent between 1979 and 1990. However, inequality increased to such an extent that the poorest 10 per cent of the population were 13 per cent absolutely worse off in 1993/4 than they had been in 1979, while the real income of the richest decile rose by 60 per cent (Hills with Gardiner 1997: 37). Though poverty can be measured in different ways (Chapter 6, Section 2), poverty increased unambiguously (Chapter 6, Section 2.3, and Chapter 10, Section 3.5).

It is widely believed that attempts at retrenchment (a) were driven by ideology and (b) reduced the size and scope of the welfare state. The evidence (Glennerster and Hills 1998; Glennerster 2000: ch. 1) does not support that view. Though ideology was doubtless part of the story, external factors—successive oil shocks, increasing global pressures (Chapter 1, Section 3), and ageing populations (Chapter 9)—were more potent driving forces. Furthermore, contrary to their stated aim, successive Thatcher administrations did not reduce the share of national income devoted to welfare-state spending.

1997 ONWARDS (NEW LABOUR). The concerns of the 1960s and 1970s were coverage and adequacy; those of the 1980s were efficiency, labour-market incentives, and fiscal constraint; New Labour sought to pursue both agendas simultaneously (see Glennerster 2000: ch. 10).

One element in the New Labour approach had much in common with previous Conservative governments. Competitive markets rather than central planning were regarded as the way to pursue growth in a modern economy (this was the decade in which Communism in Central and Eastern Europe and the former Soviet Union collapsed). High tax rates were to be avoided because of their adverse incentives. The best way to reduce unemployment was through low rates of inflation, rather than counter-cyclical deficit spending.

On the other hand, New Labour, like old Labour, was committed to the objectives of reducing poverty and addressing social exclusion (a broader concept than poverty); it also pursued (albeit quietly) policies that were significantly redistributive.

Where New Labour differed—in degree if not in kind—from its predecessors was in its strategy for achieving those objectives, based primarily on 'activation'. One plank was that benefit design and access to advice should encourage people to work, based on the idea that 'work was the best form of welfare. It gave dignity and independence while benefits could never do so' (Glennerster 2000: 206). A second plank was to equip people for work: thus inequality should be attacked via its causes, by improving people's job skills.

The detailed story is taken up in the relevant chapters.

6.2. The USA

The US story, too, is one of expansion followed by retrenchment.

EXPANSION. Developments in the USA in the 1940s lay outside the social-security system. The Full Employment Act 1946—a considerable departure from previous policies—imposed on federal government the implicitly Keynesian responsibility for maintaining full employment.

In the years after 1950 the insurance scheme was steadily broadened to the point where, together with related programmes, virtually all workers and their families were covered. The extension is summarized by the changing name of the scheme: the 1935 Act concentrated on Old Age Insurance (OAI); survivor benefits were added in 1939 (OASI); disablement benefits in 1956 (OASDI); and various health benefits for the elderly and the poor in 1965 (OASDHI) (for legislative details, see R. B. Stevens 1970: 758–75).

The benefit regime established by the 1935 Act was also liberalized: there were proportionately larger increases for lower-income workers (increasing the scheme's redistributive impact); benefits for survivors and dependants were raised relative to those for the insured person (increasing the support given to families); and the rules about the age of retirement were relaxed.

There was less change in assistance benefits. Aid to the Permanently and Totally Disabled was established in 1950; and Aid to Dependent Children (renamed Aid to Families with Dependent Children) was liberalized in the 1960s. Of particular note, states were given the option of paying benefit not only where the father was absent or disabled, but also where he was unemployed.

Health care for recipients of assistance ('Medicaid') was introduced in 1965, at the same time as its inclusion for the elderly under the main insurance scheme ('Medicare'), with major implications for expenditure on health care (see Chapter 12, Section 4.1).

The 1960s saw a 'welfare explosion'—a dramatic expansion in the size and cost of Aid to Families with Dependent Children. The increase was particularly great in the states with the largest cities, especially in New York and California. 'Governor Reagan complained last night that California's "permissive" welfare system is encouraging teenaged girls to become pregnant and subsidizing hippie communes at poor folks' expense. "The Age of Aquarius smells a little fishy," he told a sympathetic audience of conservative Republicans' (*San Francisco Chronicle*, 14 Sept. 1970, p. 37). The phenomenon evoked considerable concern, particularly because it coincided with a period of low unemployment and sustained economic growth (see David Gordon 1969; Barr and Hall 1981).

Poverty became a major political issue in the 1960s for the first time in thirty years (see US President's Commission on Income Maintenance Programs 1969). With hindsight, however, the response was long on words but muted in action. There were a number of experiments with negative income tax (see the Further Reading to Chapter 11), but changes *ex post* were small.

THE GROWTH SLOWDOWN. Two overarching facts explain much of US social policy since 1973: growth slowed down, and inequality increased sharply, as discussed in more detail in Chapter 6, Sections 2.3, 4.3. In principle, more—and more redistributive—transfers might have been able to protect the poor. In practice, the USA provides income transfers to working-age people only parsimoniously (Burtless 1987 describes how eligibility requirements for unemployment benefit tightened; for fuller assessment, see Blank 1997: ch. 3). Americans of working age are thus very dependent on earnings; and, since there is no equivalent of family allowance, American children are very dependent on their parents' earnings. The combined effects of stagnating growth, rising inequality, and parsimonious transfers thus led inexorably to an increase in poverty. The poverty rate fell from 22 per cent of the population in 1950 to 11 per cent in 1973; over the following two decades, notwithstanding a 27 per cent increase in real per capita income, it increased to 14.5 per cent (Gottschalk 1997). The composition of the total changed sharply, with less poverty among the elderly (reflecting expanding social-security and private pensions) and more among children (reflecting rising numbers of single-parent families). Welfare reform in 1996, shifting much of the responsibility for poverty relief to states, did nothing to reverse the trend (see Blank 1997, 2000).

In 1965, Wilensky and Lebeaux (1965: pp. xvi–xvii) argued that the 'United States is more reluctant than any rich democratic country to make a welfare effort appropriate to its affluence. Our support of national welfare programs is halting; our administration of services for the less privileged is mean. We move toward the welfare state but we do it with ill grace, carping and complaining all the way.' Forty years later, little had changed:

'Government transfer programs had little effect in ameliorating the trend towards inequality. If anything, these programs become less effective in redistributing incomes to low-income families after 1979' (Burtless 1996: 289).

6.3. Comparative issues

Four strategic issues are the subject of much of the rest of the book: the role of employment; the importance of social insurance; the relation between the benefit and tax systems; and the continued and substantial reliance on means-tested benefits.

A high level of employment was initially seen in both countries as the primary method of income support. The UK government committed itself to such policies in its wartime White Paper (UK Department of Labour 1944). The US analogue was the Full Employment Act 1946. The retreat from these commitments and the increased emphasis on labour-market flexibility in both countries in the 1980s is discussed in Chapter 1, Section 3.

Social insurance was the major line of defence. The coverage of the UK 1946 National Insurance Act was broader in three important ways than the US Social Security Act as amended in 1939: it dealt with contingencies such as sickness and maternity, which were not covered by US legislation; its coverage of individuals was virtually universal; and it was a *national* scheme (so, too, were assistance payments). In contrast, the US system (apart from federal retirement and disability insurance and, later, health insurance for the elderly) was organized by states.

The original intention of both Acts was to emulate actuarial insurance, particularly the intention to pay pensions from an accumulated fund. But political pressures and favourable demographic and economic trends resulted instead in pensions paid largely out of current contributions, starting in 1940 (USA) and 1946 (UK); and over the years political pressure led to further erosion of actuarial principles, as the coverage of both schemes was broadened and the relation between contributions and benefits relaxed. The overall result, in a UK context, was considerable erosion of the Beveridge strategy. The extent to which such benefits are (or should be, or can be) true insurance is one of the main topics of Chapters 5, 8, and 9.

Tax expenditures (see Chapter 7, Section 1.1) buttressed social insurance in both countries. Parallel to public pensions, for example, was tax relief for private schemes. Both methods provide income support for the elderly, though often with very different distributional consequences. Income tax is relevant also because of the increasing overlap between taxpayers and benefit recipients. Some social-insurance benefits are taxable, an issue of acute relevance when (in sharp contrast with the 1940s) most earners are above the income tax threshold and where husband and wife pay income tax as separate individuals. The overlap is crucial also in connection with income-tested benefits, as we shall see in Chapters 10 and 11.

Reliance on means-tested benefits continued in both countries (and in many others) on a substantial scale, despite wide-ranging social insurance and tax expenditures, and notwithstanding Beveridge's expectation that the assistance measures would become residual. This was partly because in the UK most of the insurance benefits were below the subsistence level established by national assistance (violating what Beveridge regarded as an essential ingredient of his proposals), and partly because of problems with take-up.

As a result, means-tested assistance continued in cash (income support, Aid to Families with Dependent Children) and kind (free medical prescriptions in the UK, 'medicaid' in the USA).

The persistence of these benefits, and the large numbers of people involved, demonstrate that insurance and related measures were only partially successful in abolishing 'want'.[15] Studies in both countries (US Panel on Poverty and Public Assistance 1995; Hills with Gardiner 1997) showed continuing and widespread poverty, partly due to factors outside the direct scope of income support (e.g. racial discrimination). But poverty was also found among the elderly and the unemployed, to whom social insurance was directly relevant.

Finally, as we have seen, there were two substantial differences. There remained a complete absence in the USA of any analogue of child benefit, notwithstanding the many countries that had such arrangements (France introduced the first scheme before the First World War).[16] Nor, despite attempts at major reform in the early 1990s, was there anything remotely resembling the UK National Health Service. This remained true in 2004.

7. Concluding issues: From the past to the present

7.1. Interpreting the forces creating the welfare state

Given the variety of influences on the welfare state, it is not surprising that there is controversy over their relative importance (for a summary, see Neil Gilbert 2002: ch. 1). The key issue is whether the dominant factor was ideology or the nature of the industrial process. The ideological debate concentrates on the motives underlying social legislation. A *liberal* (as defined in Chapter 3, Section 1) interpretation of history attributes the development of the welfare state to the quest for social justice, and sees the events described earlier as progress along a road towards the good society. Fraser (1984: 157) writes of Lloyd George's 1909 'People's Budget' that '[here] was the essence of the novel approach: financial policy geared to the social needs of the people; the budget as a tool of social policy'.

In contrast, Marxists did not see the welfare state as arising out of a concatenation of disparate events, and certainly not as part of a quest for social justice. They argue that the primary purpose of social legislation was to protect and preserve the capitalist system: the welfare state helps to meet the needs of the capitalist industrial system for a healthy, educated workforce; and it is the 'ransom' paid by the ruling elite to contain social unrest. To a Marxist, the Liberal reforms were very limited and intended mainly to preserve the existing economic system. Unemployment, sickness, and health benefits under the 1911

---

[15] This is not to imply that income testing is *necessarily* a sign of a failing system of income support. The Australian system uses means testing, but more to exclude the rich than to try to include only the poor. For a summary of social-security institutions worldwide, see US Social Security Administration (2002, 2003).

[16] For a review and international comparison of family allowances, see Bradshaw and Finch (2002).

National Insurance Act applied only to limited classes of worker; and some historians argue that one of the main motives of the 1908 Pension Act (the only substantially redistributive measure) was to weed out of the workforce older men and women whose presence was reducing Britain's industrial efficiency in the face of international competition. These different views of the welfare state are discussed in more detail in Chapter 3, Section 5.3.

In more modern guise, Esping-Andersen (1990) seeks to connect socio-political forces with different welfare-state regimes. As discussed in Chapter 1, he distinguishes three types of welfare state: social democratic (the Nordic countries), corporatist (mainly Western Europe) and neo-liberal (the Anglo Saxon world). Later work (Esping-Andersen 1999; Esping-Andersen et al. 2002: chs. 2 and 3) extended the framework to incorporate the family. Other writers (see Castles 1996) suggest a fourth type of welfare state, significantly needs-based, in Australia and New Zealand. There are two strategic counter-arguments: first, 'efforts to distinguish distinct regimes tend to slice the conceptual patterns of welfare thinner and thinner, advancing towards the ultimate conclusion that each country's system evolves out of its unique heritage' (Neil Gilbert 2002: 20).

A second set of counter-arguments questions the underlying premiss that ideology matters. Theories of convergence (see Neil Gilbert 2002: ch. 1 and the Further Reading) derive from two propositions: that all countries, whatever their socio-political history, have developed similar industrial structures, and that a welfare state is an inevitable concomitant of that structure. The theory therefore bases its argument on technological determinism. At its strongest, it asserts that the dominant force in the development of the welfare state is industrialism—and, more recently, global pressures—and, by implication, that ideology is largely irrelevant.

The issue, therefore, is whether 'welfare states converge under the pressure of broad impersonal structural forces or diverge in response to human interventions shaped by sociopolitical factors in different countries' (Neil Gilbert 2002: 22). I make no attempt to judge the two approaches. The world, however, is a complicated place, and I have a profound suspicion of almost any unicausal explanation of anything. Most industrial countries face similar problems of unemployment and pockets of poverty, so it is not surprising that many have adopted broadly similar solutions; the logic of industrialism clearly has some validity. Similarly, the technical problems with private markets discussed in Chapters 4 and 5 afflict all industrialized countries.

But ideology also plays a part, if only in determining whether a country adopts a *residual* or an *institutional* model of welfare. The former accords welfare a role only when market or family structures break down; the latter regards it as an integral part of modern industrial society (Wilensky and Lebeaux 1965: 138–9). Thus a 'capitalist' country like the USA has (and has always had) a system of income support and social services that is small relative to its population and national income (though it has a wide-ranging system of publicly provided education). A 'socialist' country like Sweden has a highly articulated welfare state; Denmark and New Zealand (which were not highly industrialized) were among the first countries with a public system of old-age pensions; and Saskatchewan was the first Canadian province to have publicly organized health insurance.

It is clear, in conclusion, that the forces that created the UK (or any other) welfare state are diverse and complex. The question 'how did it come about?' has no easy answer.

7.2. What was created?

The nature of what was created, as we have just seen, is a matter of controversy. Is the welfare state a step towards the good society (discussed in Chapter 3, Section 3), an expensive and demeaning road towards totalitarianism (Chapter 3, Section 2), or a cynical device to prop up the capitalist system (Chapter 3, Sections 4.2, 5.3)? Setting these issues to one side, the successes of the post-1948 arrangements are twofold and clear. There is, first, a comprehensive system of income support, with insurance arrangements underpinned by a broad safety net in the form of income support (i.e. means-tested social assistance), which is organized nationally and for which *everyone* is potentially eligible. Many other countries have considerably less comprehensive systems. The second major success was the National Health Service, which 'brought to all the most obvious and immediate benefits. To many it *is* the Welfare State, and every survey . . . has shown how much it is . . . valued and taken for granted as part and parcel of British life' (Bruce 1972: 330).

The failures are also clear. It is striking how many current problems have their roots or their parallels in the past. The inter-war difficulties with unemployment insurance raised questions about the extent to which unemployment is an insurable risk (Chapters 5 and 8); the introduction of state pensions in 1908 was motivated in part by demographic problems (Chapter 9); the British antipathy to means testing (Chapters 10 and 11) is strongly influenced by the folk memory of the stringent household means test between the wars; the post-war distributional complexities arising out of the interaction between family allowances and child tax allowances will emerge in many guises; and the exploding costs of medical care in the USA (Chapter 12, Section 4.1) stem in part (though not wholly) from the design of 'Medicare' and 'Medicaid', introduced in 1965.

Over and above these problems is the fact, despite the relative success of the cash benefit system, that poverty, far from being eliminated, has risen since the early 1980s. In part this is because the poverty line has moved up as living standards and expectations have risen; but for many the issue is one not just of *relative* poverty, but of uncertainty and harsh discomfort. In addition, inequality has increased in many countries. For some, the most important problem of all has been the pressure to retrench. The 'welfare consensus' on both sides of the Atlantic weakened during the 1980s for both ideological and economic reasons. Around the turn of the century, UK governments sought to address social exclusion, in part by encouraging people back into the labour market. Not least because of fiscal constraints, however, the high summer of 1948 has passed, to be replaced by what Neil Gilbert (2002: 193) calls 'the silent surrender of public responsibility.' To some commentators at least, the Principles of 1834 (Section 1.1) come to mind, completing a historical circle.

■ **QUESTIONS FOR FURTHER DISCUSSION**

1. What were the main historical forces creating the welfare state?

2. 'The British welfare state was a result of the Second World War.' Discuss.

■ FURTHER READING

Good general texts on the historical development of the UK welfare state are Bruce (1972), Marshall (1975), Thane (1982), and Fraser (1984). For the period since 1945, see Timmins (1996) and Glennerster (2000), and for a detailed account since the mid-1970s, Glennerster and Hills (1998).

Contemporary discussion of the 'New Liberalism' can be found in Hobson (1909); for more recent analysis of economic and political thought at the time, see Robbins (1977) and Freeden (1978). For a brief introduction to early poor relief, see Rose (1972); on the principle of *laissez-faire*, Taylor (1972); and on the Liberal reforms, Bentley Gilbert (1973) (compendious) or Hay (1975) (brief). The early debates on unemployment are detailed in Harris (1972) and a history of health care prior to 1948 is given in Abel Smith (1964).

The origins of the modern welfare state are discussed by Glennerster (2000: ch. 1), and more fully by Harris (1997) (a magisterial biography of Beveridge) and Titmuss (1958) (who stresses the influence of the Second World War). The proposals contained in the Beveridge Report (1942) are still well worth reading, as are those for the National Health Service in UK DoH (1944). Detailed historical statistics for the UK from 1855 to 1965 can be found in C. H. Feinstein (1972).

For contemporary accounts of US developments in the 1930s, see Douglas (1939), US Federal Emergency Relief Administration (1942), and US National Resources and Planning Board (1942). For retrospective analysis, see Witte (1962), Schottland (1963), or Altmeyer (1966); and, for later debates, Tobin (1968) and US President's Commission on Income Maintenance Programs (1969) (a remarkable document). Details of US legislation are given in R. B. Stevens (1970). On more recent developments, see Blank (1994, 1997), Karoly and Burtless (1995), and US Panel on Poverty and Public Assistance (1995).

For differing interpretations of the origins of the welfare state, see Neil Gilbert (2002: ch. 1) for a summary, Wilensky and Lebeaux (1965), Rimlinger (1971), Higgins (1981: ch. 4), and Mishra (1981: ch. 3).

UK policy in recent years is evaluated by Glennerster (2000, ch. 10), Brewer et al. (2002), and Hills (2002); on the USA, see Blank (2000), and for a broader international assessment, Neil Gilbert (2002).

For the modern institutions, see Child Poverty Action Group (2003) (the 2003 version of an annual publication) or the Department for Work and Pensions web site (http://www.dwp.gov.uk). For a compendious summary of institutions internationally, see US Social Security Administration (2002, 2003).

3 Political theory: Social justice and the state

The fundamental issue [of the welfare state] is not economic. It is moral . . . The issue is the responsibility of people to manage their own affairs . . . Is it not the case that while adults manage incomes children receive pocket money? The operation of the welfare state tends to reduce the status of adults to that of children.

(Peter Bauer, 1983)

[The] major evil [of paternalistic programs] is their effect on the fabric of our society. They weaken the family; reduce the incentive to work, save and innovate; reduce the accumulation of capital; and limit our freedom. These are the fundamental standards by which they should be judged.

(Milton Friedman, 1980)

Traditional socialism was largely concerned with the evils of traditional capitalism, and with the need for its overthrow. But today traditional capitalism has been reformed and modified almost out of existence, and it is with a quite different form of society that socialists must now concern themselves.

(Anthony Crosland, 1956)

1. Theories of society

A society is a cooperative venture for the mutual advantage of its members. It generally contains both an identity of interests and conflicts of interest between individuals and groups. The institutions of any society (its constitution, laws, and social processes) profoundly influence a person's life chances. The purpose of a theory of society is to offer principles that enable us to choose between different social arrangements. In analysing the welfare state it is helpful to distinguish three broad types of theory: libertarian; liberal; and collectivist.[1]

LIBERTARIANS (discussed in Section 2) are in many ways the descendants of the 'Old Liberalism' of the nineteenth century (Chapter 2, Sections 1.1, 2.1), although, as we shall see, there are important differences between 'natural-rights' and 'empirical' libertarians. The former (e.g. Nozick) argue that state intervention is *morally wrong* except in strictly limited circumstances. The latter, including writers such as Hayek and Friedman and

---

[1] Readers with limited political theory can find the gist of the argument in the Appendix at the end of the chapter.

practitioners such as Margaret Thatcher, are the modern inheritors of the classical liberal tradition;[2] they argue against state intervention not on moral grounds, but because it *will reduce total welfare*. Both groups analyse society in terms of its individual members (as opposed to the group or social class), give heavy weight to individual freedom, and strongly support private property and the market mechanism. As a result, the state's role *vis-à-vis* taxation and redistribution is severely circumscribed.

LIBERAL theories (Section 3) are the modern inheritors of the 'New Liberalism' (Chapter 2, Section 2.1). They find their philosophy in utilitarianism (Section 3.1) and in writers like Rawls (Section 3.2); their policy advocates in Beveridge, Keynes, and Galbraith; and their practitioners in politicians such as Harold Macmillan and John Kennedy. The theory has three crucial features. First, societies are analysed in terms of their individual members. Secondly, 'private property in the means of production, distribution and exchange [is] a contingent matter rather than an essential part of the doctrine' (Barry 1973: 166)—that is, the treatment of private property is explicitly regarded not as an end in itself, but as a means towards the achievement of policy goals. Finally, liberal theories contain 'a principle of distribution which could, suitably interpreted and with certain factual assumptions, have egalitarian implications' (ibid.)—that is, in certain circumstances income redistribution is an appropriate function of the state. This book, as Chapter 4 will amplify, is firmly in the liberal tradition.

COLLECTIVIST theories, too, are varied. *Marxist* theory (Section 4.2) draws its philosophy from Marx and its policies from writers such as Harold Laski, Lytton Strachey, and Ralph Miliband. The theory sees industrial society as consisting of social classes, defined narrowly in terms of their relation to the means of production. Private property has only a limited role, and the allocation and distribution of resources in accordance with in-dividual need is a primary concern of the state. *Democratic socialists* (Section 4.1) present an intermediate case. They derive their philosophy from writers like Tawney, and find their policy advocates in, for example, Antony Crosland and Richard Titmuss, and their practitioners in politicians such as Clement Attlee and Harold Wilson. Though sharing to some extent the egalitarian aims of Marxists, their analysis has much in common with liberal thinking.

In practice the theories blur into each other like the colours of the rainbow. Should Tony Blair be thought of as a democratic socialist or as a liberal coming from a socialist back-ground? But it is useful for exposition to discuss them as separate entities, especially when contrasting their implications for policy (Section 5). Nevertheless, their differences and similarities are complex, and involve subtleties well beyond the scope of one brief chapter. The purpose here is limited to outlining the ideological debate. Knowledgeable readers will, I hope, be forgiving.

---

[2] There is a confusing ambiguity in the use of the word 'liberal'. In the nineteenth century it was used to describe *laissez-faire* thinkers such as Bentham and Nassau Senior (Chapter 2, Section 1.1); and today a writer like Friedman, in calling himself a liberal, is using the term in the same way. I shall, throughout, refer to such writers as libertarians.

2. Libertarian views

It is necessary to return briefly to nineteenth-century debates (Chapter 2, Sections 1.1, 2.1). The ideology of *laissez-faire* derived from two very different philosophical roots. When modern writers such as Hayek and Friedman advocate free markets and private property, they follow Hume (1770), Adam Smith (1776), Bentham (1789), and Mill (1863) in doing so on a *utilitarian* or *empirical* basis, out of a belief that such institutions maximize total welfare. Nozick, in contrast, follows Spencer (1884) by defending private property on *moral* grounds, as a *natural right* (see Robbins 1978: 46 ff.). Though not watertight, the distinction between the two views (exemplified by the first two quotes at the head of the chapter) is crucial to debates about policy (Section 5), and so merits closer attention.

NATURAL-RIGHTS LIBERTARIANS. To Nozick (1974) everyone has the right to distribute the rewards of his own labour. He calls this *justice in holdings*, which has three elements. A person is entitled to a holding if he has acquired it (*a*) through earnings (so-called justice in acquisition), or (*b*) through the inheritance of wealth that was itself justly acquired (justice in transfer). Holdings that fall under neither principle cannot be justified, hence (*c*) government may redistribute holdings acquired illegally (the principle of rectification).

These propositions support the libertarian predilection for a 'nightwatchman' state with strictly circumscribed powers: the state can provide one and only one public good—the defence of our person and property, including enforcement of contracts; but apart from correcting past wrongs it has no distributional role. Nozick regards taxation as theft (since it extracts from people money (legitimately acquired) that they would otherwise have allocated in other ways), and also as slavery, in that people are forced to spend part of their time working for government.

EMPIRICAL LIBERTARIANS. Hayek's theory has three strands: the primacy of individual freedom; the value of the market mechanism; and the assertion that the pursuit of social justice is not only fruitless (because there is no such thing) but actively harmful. Freedom to Hayek (1960: ch. 1) and other libertarians is defined narrowly as the absence of coercion or restraint; it includes political liberty, free speech, and economic freedom. The central argument of Hayek (1944) is that the pursuit of equality will reduce or destroy liberty.

To Hayek the market is beneficial because it protects individual freedom and creates economic benefits. '[It is] a procedure which has greatly improved the chances of all to have their wants satisfied, but at the price of all individuals . . . incurring the risk of unmerited failure . . . It is the only procedure yet discovered in which information widely dispersed among millions of men can be effectively utilised for the benefit of all' (1976: 70–1). These advantages arise only if prices and wages are allowed to act as signals that tell individuals where to direct their efforts. A person's reward is that which induces him to act in the common good; it will often bear no relation to either his individual merit or his need.

Hayek's view of social justice contrasts sharply with that of Rawls. According to Hayek, a given circumstance (e.g. winning the lottery or dying young) can be regarded as good or bad, but is just or unjust 'only in so far as we hold someone responsible for . . . allowing it to come about' (ibid. 31). Thus something is just or unjust *only if it has been caused by the action or inaction of an individual or individuals*. The market, in contrast (ibid. 64–5), is an impersonal force like 'Nature', akin to an economic game with winners and losers, whose outcome can be good or bad, but never just or unjust. To Hayek, therefore, the whole notion of social justice is 'a quasi-religious superstition of the kind which we should respectfully leave in peace so long as it merely makes those happy who hold it' (ibid. 66). However, 'the striving for [social justice] will . . . lead to the destruction of . . . personal freedom' (ibid. 67). The reason is that

the more dependent the position of individuals . . . is seen to become on the actions of govern-ment, the more they will insist that the governments aim at some recognisable scheme of dis-tributive justice; and the more governments try to realise some preconceived pattern of desirable distribution, the more they must subject the position of the different individuals . . . to their con-trol. *So long as the belief in 'social justice' governs political action, this process must progressively approach nearer and nearer to a totalitarian system.* (ibid. 68, emphasis added)

For Friedman, too, the primary value is individual freedom. Hence,

the scope of government must be limited. Its major function must be to protect our freedom both from the enemies outside our gates and from our fellow-citizens: to preserve law and order, to enforce private contracts, to foster competitive markets. Beyond this major function, government may enable us at times to accomplish jointly what we would find it more difficult . . . to accom-plish severally. However, any such use of government is fraught with danger. We should not and cannot avoid using government this way. But there should be a clear and large balance of advantages before we do. (1962: 2–3)

To Friedman and Hayek the state has no distributional role, other than for certain public goods and for strictly limited measures to alleviate destitution.

This line of thinking re-emerged in the 1970s and 1980s in the arguments of the New Right (see George and Wilding 1994: ch. 2). British adherents of this approach see Keynes and Beveridge as unhelpful influences. In the USA, writers like Murray (1984) argue that social benefits exacerbated poverty and should largely be abolished. The New Right puts great faith in individuals and little faith in government. The market, according to its view, is the best coordinator of vast amounts of decentralized information and is thus efficient. It benefits consumers because competitive pressures maximize choice, minimize costs, and reduce the power of providers. It does not depend on the goodwill of service providers and hence, it is argued, accords better with the realities of human nature. Accordingly, the New Right advocates a larger role for markets and a severely circumscribed role for the state.

3. Liberal theories of society

Liberal theories start from three premises very different from the New Right (see George and Wilding 1994: ch. 3): capitalism is regarded as more efficient than any other system; but it has major costs in terms of poverty and inequality; and government can ameliorate those costs. Thus a combination of capitalism and government action jointly maximizes

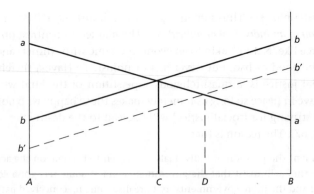

Fig. 3.1. The optimal distribution of income under utilitarianism

efficiency and equity. This approach derives from two strands of thinking: utilitarian analysis and the writing of the philosopher John Rawls.

3.1. Utilitarianism

The utilitarian arguments that form the basis of much of this book derive from the 'New Liberalism' of the early twentieth century (Chapter 2, Section 2.1), which was itself firmly rooted in the nineteenth-century classical tradition. Thus modern utilitarians have common intellectual roots with empirical libertarians.

THE THEORY. The utilitarian aim is to distribute goods so as to maximize the total utility[3] of the members of society. 'Goods' are interpreted broadly to include goods and services, rights, freedoms, and political power. Maximizing total welfare has two aspects: goods must be produced and allocated *efficiently* (discussed in Chapter 4); and they must be distributed in accordance with *equity* (though not necessarily equally). The equitable distribution is shown in Figure 3.1. Total income to be distributed is *AB*. Individual A's marginal utility (read from left to right) is shown by the line *aa*, and is assumed to diminish as his income rises. Individual B's marginal utility, which declines from right to left, is shown by the line *bb*. Total utility is maximized when income is shared equally; A's income is *AC*, and B's is *BC*.

Utilitarianism can therefore justify redistributive activity by the state in pursuit of an egalitarian outcome, but this result depends crucially on two conditions. First, A and B must have identical marginal utility of income functions.[4] If B's marginal utility is shown by *b'b'*, then the distribution that maximizes total welfare is unequal, since A now has an income of *AD*. Secondly, utilitarianism can fully specify the optimal distribution only where the utility of A and B can be measured cardinally (see the Glossary).

---

[3] Synonymously, to maximize total happiness, total welfare, or total well-being.
[4] Strictly, several other technical conditions are necessary—e.g. that the underlying social-welfare function is symmetric and concave (see Chapter 6, Section 1.2).

CRITICISMS include questions such as: is utility capable of precise definition; does interpersonal comparison of utility have any meaning; and whose utility counts (e.g. future generations, animals, etc.)? These issues are set to one side to focus on two fundamental criticisms.

An unjust outcome. Utilitarianism can sanction injustice by justifying harm to the least well-off if this maximizes total utility. 'The trouble with [utilitarianism] is that maximising the sum of individual utilities is supremely unconcerned with the interpersonal distribution of that sum' (Sen 1973: 16). Formally, suppose that individual B in Figure 3.1 derives less pleasure from life than A because he has major health problems. His marginal utility is shown by the line *b'b'*, and the optimal distribution of goods by point *D*. Thus B should receive *less* income than A because of his health problems. This outcome is criticized as being unjust.

The impossibility of a Paretian liberal. Consider two desirable objectives: individual freedom (which includes the idea that an individual is the best judge of her own welfare), and maximizing total welfare. Sen (1970, 1982) (see also Brittan 1995: ch. 3) argues that it is not always possible to achieve both objectives simultaneously—that is, individual freedom may not be compatible with simple utilitarianism. The argument goes as follows.

Suppose that my action imposes a cost on other people, not in economic terms (e.g. polluting their garden with smoke) but because *they* have views about *my* actions. They might think it wrong that I have long hair. More generally, they might think it wrong that a wealthy person has a yacht in Monte Carlo, or that people live together before marriage. Thus the action of one person can affect the welfare of another for aesthetic or moral reasons.

What does this imply for public policy? If policy-makers take such interdependencies into account, 'people will be penalized for carrying out private personal acts which affect others only because thinking makes it so' (Brittan 1995: 74). Accepting such preferences can make utilitarianism an illiberal doctrine, because they 'are a disguised form of coercion which arise from a desire to regulate the way other people spend their lives . . .' (ibid.).

To avoid this difficulty, policy-makers may choose to ignore the preferences of some people (e.g. those who wish to impose mandatory haircuts). In that case, however, policy is no longer decided *only* on a utilitarian basis; it will incorporate judgements about which forms of interdependence are allowable and which not. The heated debates about appropriate public policy (if any) about personal appearance, soft drugs, and sexual behaviour illustrate the point.

3.2. Rawls on social justice

Rawls in some ways is Nozick's liberal counterpart. Nozick is a natural-rights defender of liberty. For Rawls the natural right, and hence the primary aim of institutions, is *social justice*: thus 'each person possesses an inviolability founded on justice that even the welfare of society as a whole cannot override' (1972: 2). Justice, to Rawls, has a twofold purpose: it is desirable for its own sake on moral grounds; also, and importantly, institutions will survive only if they are perceived to be just. Rawls argues that there exists a definition of justice that both is *general* (i.e. not specific to any particular culture) and can be derived by a process that everyone can agree is fair. The resulting principles deal with the distribution of goods, interpreted broadly to include also liberty and opportunity.

THE ORIGINAL POSITION is Rawls's starting point. He invites us to contemplate a group of rational individuals, each concerned only with his own self-interest, coming together to negotiate principles to determine the distribution of goods. They are free agents in the negotiation, but they must abide by the resulting principles. Rawls thus uses the convention of a *social contract*.

In this situation no discussion between interested parties will yield principles of justice that command universal acceptance. Rawls therefore abstracts the negotiators from their own society by placing them behind a *veil of ignorance*. They are assumed to be well informed about the general facts of the world—psychology, economics, sociology —but each is *deprived of all knowledge about himself*—that is, of his characteristics or endowments, his position in society, and the country or historical period into which he is born. The negotiators seek to advance their own interests, but are unable to distinguish them from anyone else's.

The role of the veil of ignorance is best illustrated by example. To distance ourselves from personal interests we (i.e. citizens through our elected representatives) may decide that aircraft hijackers' demands should never be met, even if innocent lives are lost. We do this in order to save even more lives in the long run; and we establish this doctrine in advance of the event (i.e. behind the veil of ignorance) because if it were our personal loved ones who were kidnapped we would be likely to do anything to save them, irrespective of the possible consequences for others in the future.

The negotiators can consider any principle of justice—for example, the just action is that which is in the interests of the stronger, or that which ennobles the species or that which maximizes total utility. According to Rawls, the rational negotiator will reject these because under each he might systematically be underprivileged. The only rational choice is to select principles in terms of what Rawls calls the 'maximin rule', which maximizes the position of the least well-off individual or group. The negotiators do this because 'for all they know they may turn out to be the least privileged inhabitants of a country like [pre-reform] South Africa' (McCreadie 1976: 117).

The original position, together with the veil of ignorance, plays two distinct roles. It is an analytical device, which 'reduc[es] a relatively complex problem, the social choice of the principles of justice, to a more manageable problem, the rational individual choice of principles' (Daniels 1975: p. xix). Secondly, Rawls sees the procedure as a *moral justification* of the resulting principles—they will be seen to be fair, he argues, because they are selected in a manner that is both rational and fair; hence his term 'justice as fairness'.

THE PRINCIPLES OF JUSTICE that follow are those that Rawls claims would be chosen rationally and unanimously by the negotiators. Because of the veil of ignorance, they will choose to maximize liberty for everyone. Hence:

The first principle (the 'liberty principle'). 'Each person is to have an equal right to the most extensive basic liberty compatible with a similar liberty for others' (Rawls 1972: 60).

The negotiators then turn to the distribution of goods other than liberty. Each will reject any principle of distribution that could leave him disadvantaged or exploited.

The negotiators may consider a principle that mandates a thoroughly equal distribution of goods . . . But they will soon come to realise that they stand to benefit by the introduction of certain inequalities . . . For example, giving a rural [doctor] an airplane would make him relatively advantaged, but even—and perhaps especially—the least advantaged among the rural populace stand to benefit as a result, and thus should sanction such inequality.   (Gorovitz 1975: 281)

Hence:

The second principle (the 'difference principle'). 'Social and economic inequalities are to be arranged so that they are both (*a*) to the greatest benefit of the least advantaged and (*b*) attached to offices and positions open to all under conditions of fair equality of opportunity' (Rawls 1972: 83).

Possible conflict between the two principles is ruled out by a *priority principle*, which gives the first principle absolute priority over the second. A reduction in the liberty of the least well off cannot be justified even if it is to their economic advantage. Subject to these priorities the two principles can be regarded as a special case of a simpler, more general conception of justice, in which 'all social primary goods—liberty and opportunity, income and wealth . . . are to be distributed equally unless an unequal distribution of any or all of these goods is to the advantage of the least favoured' (ibid. 303). At its simplest, the distribution of goods between individuals A and B in Figure 3.1 should be that shown by point *C* unless any other distribution benefits the less advantaged of the two.[5] If goods are not so distributed, any policy that improves the position of the less well off is an improvement according to Rawls.[6]

RAWLS AND UTILITARIANISM. Rawls is an explicit opponent of utilitarianism. He regards it as illogical (inasmuch as it would be rejected by rational negotiators in the original position) and unjust (in that it can sanction injustice in the interests of maximizing total welfare). The two theories can have very different implications. Suppose a given policy change makes at least one person better off without making anyone else worse off. This is an increase in Pareto efficiency,[7] and hence desirable to utilitarians even if the individual thus benefited were rich. Rawls's difference principle, in contrast, would oppose the policy unless it were also (though not necessarily only) to the advantage of the least well off. Thus an efficient answer in Paretian terms will not always be a just answer in a Rawlsian sense (though, as argued in Chapter 4, Section 2.2, it may be possible to find a distribution that is both efficient and just).

CRITICISMS OF RAWLS'S THEORY. It has been argued that the negotiators would be unable to make any decisions behind the veil of ignorance. According to Nisbet (1974: 112),

[the negotiators] don't know much of anything—anything, that is, that we are justified by contemporary psychology in deeming requisite to thought and knowledge of any kind whatever. Nevertheless, Professor Rawls is shortly going to put his happy primitives through feats of

---

[5] Under the lexical extension of the difference principle, any policy should benefit the worst off; if he is indifferent, it should benefit the next worse off, and so on. Rawls thus admits a policy that benefits *only* the best off, provided that everyone else is indifferent to it.

[6] A utilitarian social-welfare function (see Chapter 4, Section 1) does not constrain the way individuals are weighted; a Rawlsian social-welfare function gives infinite weight to the least-advantaged individual or group.

[7] See Chapter 4, Section 2.1, and the Appendix to Chapter 4, paras. 2–4.

cerebration that even the gods might envy. Out of the minds of his homunculi, these epistemological zombies who don't know their names, families, races, generation or societies of origin, are going to come principles of justice and society so vast in implication as to throw all present human societies into a philosopher's limbo.

Miller (1976) (discussed shortly) similarly argues that removing *all* cultural knowledge will immobilize the negotiators; but failure to do so, though permitting them to make a decision, will result in a culture-bound definition of justice.

The first principle is criticized[8] because Rawls's list of liberties may be too narrow, because the principle of toleration (e.g. of diversity of goals) inherent in Rawls's definition of liberty may reflect class bias, and because some issues are left unresolved—for example, what liberty should be accorded racists? Additionally, Barry (1973: 6) and Hart in Daniels (1975: p. xxx) dispute the priority given to liberty. Poor people might well be willing to trade some liberty for greater social or economic advantage. The second principle is criticized for its crucial dependence on maximin, which, it is argued (Arrow 1973; Letwin 1983: 22–9), is the optimal outcome only under very restrictive assumptions.

MILLER'S ANALYSIS OF SOCIAL JUSTICE. A final criticism of Rawls is that he developed not a general theory of justice but a liberal theory. Miller (1976) argues that a completely general theory of justice is logically impossible, and that in this respect Rawls was bound to fail. According to Miller, social justice has three distinct elements:

- *rights*—e.g. political liberty, equality before the law;
- *deserts*—i.e. the recognition of each person's actions and qualities;
- *needs*—i.e. the prerequisites for fulfilling individual plans of life.

The 'deserts' aspect implies that someone who works longer hours should receive more pay, and the 'needs' aspect that an individual incapable of work should not be allowed to starve. Though admitting the difficulty of precise theoretical definition, Miller argues that each element is a logically distinct principle embodying a particular type of moral claim.

It is easy to see that rights and deserts can be reconciled (e.g. a person should have the right to keep all her income if she has earned it legally); similarly, rights and needs can be compatible (e.g. a person should be entitled to health care if she is ill). But conflict can arise between desert and need: if I am rich and healthy and you are poor and ill, then either I am taxed (and do not receive my deserts) to pay for your medical treatment, or you receive no treatment (hence your need is not met) so as to protect my deserts.

The core of Miller's argument is that the definition of social justice depends crucially on the type of society being discussed. In a pure market economy, justice will be defined in terms of rights and deserts. A collectivist defines justice as distribution according to need.

Miller thus argues that the different principles of justice are connected to wider views of society. He criticizes utilitarians and Rawls because they take no explicit account of the conflicting claims of rights, deserts, and needs, but blur them into a single, indistinct

---

[8] See Daniels (1975: pp. xxviii–xxix) and the chapters therein by Hart, Scanlon, Daniels, and Fisk.

whole. Miller also criticizes the view implicit in Rawls that there is a single conception of justice upon which everyone's definition will converge, arguing instead that justice comprises conflicting principles, the relative weights attached to which may vary sharply between different societies. 'The whole enterprise of constructing a theory of justice on the basis of choice hypothetically made by individuals abstracted from society is mistaken, because these abstract ciphers lack the prerequisites for developing conceptions of justice' (Miller 1976: 341). Or, if they do manage to make choices, it must be in terms of culturally acquired attitudes. In short, the negotiators in the original position will be immobilized unless they have some knowledge of the nature of the society for which they are choosing rules of justice. Finally, 'Rawls's individuals are given the attitudes and beliefs of men in modern market societies, and it is therefore not surprising that the conception of justice they . . . adopt should approximate to the conception . . . dominant in those societies' (ibid. 342). Hence, he argues, Rawls fails to develop a *general* theory of social justice; such generality is not possible.

4. Collectivist views

4.1. Democratic socialism

Collectivist writers agree on the importance of equality. They regard resources as available for collective use, and consequently favour government action; but historically they have disagreed about whether socialist goals could be achieved within a market order. Some writers advocate a mixed economy that blends private enterprise and state intervention; Marxists (discussed in Section 4.2) argue that this is not possible; that capitalism is inherently unjust; and that socialism is possible only where the state controls the allocation and distribution of most resources.

SOCIALIST AIMS vary widely, but three—equality, freedom, and fraternity—are central. Equality is a variant of vertical equity discussed in Chapter 1, Section 2.2, and fraternity of the social solidarity aim. It is recognized that these aims can clash; and different writers accord them different weight; but together they make up the socialist definition of justice. In Miller's terms, the dominant themes are rights and needs, with deserts assigned a smaller role.

There is a measure of agreement (Tawney 1953, 1964; Crosland 1956) that the crucial element of justice is equality, which to socialists is an active concept. Equality of opportunity on its own may be insufficient (Tawney 1964; Laski 1967: ch. 4; Hattersley 1987), since substantial inequality of outcome may persist. Positive equalizing measures are needed, though not necessarily complete equality of outcome (see Daniel 1997).

Such emphasis on equality bears closely on Miller's concept of need. Weale points out that 'in some political arguments . . . the assumption is made that to distribute according to need is to satisfy the claims of equality' (1978: 67), but suggests (ch. 5) that the relationship is rather more complicated. For present purposes we need note only that equality and meeting need are closely related concepts, though not logically equivalent.

The socialist concept of freedom is broad. It embraces freedom of choice (which is possible only if there is no poverty and no substantial inequality of wealth and power), and extends from legal and political relations to economic security. Thus individuals should have some power in relation to their conditions of work, including stability of employment, and should not be subject to the arbitrary power of others. In sharp contrast with libertarian views, socialists regard government action as an essential and active component of freedom.

The third major value is fraternity. To a socialist this means cooperation and altruism rather than competition and self-interest. Altruism (e.g. Titmuss 1970) is a recurring theme.

SOCIALIST CRITICISM OF THE FREE MARKET starts with the motive given to individuals to pursue personal advantage rather than the general good, and denies the libertarian assertion that the former brings about the latter. Secondly, the market is regarded as undemocratic, inasmuch as some decisions with widespread effects are taken by a small elite, and others are left to the arbitrary distributional effects of market forces. Thirdly, the market is unjust because it distributes rewards that are unrelated to individual need or merit, and because the costs of economic change are distributed arbitrarily. Fourthly, the free market is not self-regulating; in particular, left to itself, it is unable to maintain full employment. Lastly, the market has not been able to abolish poverty, let alone inequality. In sum,

> production is carried on wastefully and without adequate plan. The commodities and services necessary to the life of the community are never so distributed as to relate to need or to produce a result which maximises their social utility. We build picture palaces when we need houses. We spend on battleships what is wanted for schools. . . . We have, in fact, both the wrong commodities produced, and those produced distributed without regard to social urgency. (Laski 1967: 175)[9]

Socialists have generally agreed broadly over aims but have argued about the best way to achieve them. Though the distinction is not watertight, it is useful to contrast the 'fundamentalists' (largely Marxists), who reject capitalism, with what—at least since the collapse of Communism in Central and Eastern Europe and the former Soviet Union— has become the mainstream, which holds that the ills of society can be corrected within a broadly capitalist framework.

DEMOCRATIC SOCIALISM. Mainstream writers see two great changes in the capitalist system: first, government today has a large role in economic life as well as in other areas; secondly, the classic entrepreneur has largely disappeared, the ownership of modern corporations being both diffuse and largely separate from the people who manage them. It is argued in consequence (see the quote by Crosland at the head of the chapter) that capitalism has been 'tamed', and that the resulting mixed economy, with an active role for government in the distribution of goods, income, and power, is compatible with socialist objectives.

Latterly democratic socialism appears to have moved closer to liberalism, with more worry about the trade-off between efficiency and distributional objectives, and hence less crisp adherence to older definitions of equality. Daniel (1997) puts it bluntly.

---

[9] Once you have read this paragraph, it is instructive to reread the diametrically opposite quote from Hayek (1976: 70–1) in Section 2, on the virtues of the market. Laski and Hayek were on excellent personal terms.

The current academic and political climate has come a long way from the ambitions of George Bernard Shaw, and even those set out in Labour's 1974 Manifesto which called for 'a fundamental and irreversible shift in the balance of power and wealth . . . far greater economic equality—in income, wealth and living standards . . . and an increase in social equality . . . [through] full employment, housing, education and social benefit.

It is an illustration of how attitudes to equality have changed that this declaration seems absurdly extreme.   (pp. 23–4)

There is not enough political will to see through an aggressive direct attack on money inequalities . . . It seems clear that the focus will be on redistributing opportunities, not income—an emphasis on preventive medicine, through boosting skills, not invasive surgery, through higher taxes.   (p. 25)

4.2. Marxists

This is not a Marxist book and I am no Marxist writer, so this section seeks only to sketch out as much Marxist thought as is necessary to contrast it with other theories (see George and Wilding 1994: ch. 5, and the Further Reading). In discussing the Marxist view of capitalism, we need to consider three things: the contrast between the Marxist approach and that of conventional economic analysis; its analysis of the exploitation of labour; and its view of the role of government in supporting capitalism.

THE MARXIST APPROACH differs substantially from that of the classical political economists such as Adam Smith (1776) and Ricardo (1817), for whom the production of commodities was largely independent of the society in question. This approach has continued to dominate economic thinking. It is argued that conventional economic theory is applicable to the USA, to the UK, to Sweden, and to the former Communist countries; and such economic analysis is seen as almost entirely separate from political and social arrangements. Thus to Sweezy (1942: 5), 'economic theorising is primarily a process of constructing and interrelating concepts from which all specifically social content has been drained off'. A key part of Marx's thought, in contrast, is that the economic, political, and social structure of a society is determined largely by its dominant mode of production. It is argued that the capitalist *mode of production* will result not only in a particular form of economic organization, but also (and inevitably) in a particular and inequitable structure of social class and political power.

THE EXPLOITATION OF LABOUR UNDER CAPITALISM is central to Marxist thought. Conventional economic theory sees individuals as selling their labour services (more or less) freely in a (more or less) competitive market; the wage is established when the demand for labour equals its supply, which, under competitive conditions, results in a wage rate equal to the marginal product of labour. Capital, similarly, receives its marginal product, which, under competitive conditions and in the long run, is equal to the 'normal' rate of profit plus any premium for risk. Under certain conditions[10] these payments to factors exhaust the product leaving no surplus; thus, it is argued, there is no exploitation. In a Marxist

[10] Euler's theorem states that paying all factors their marginal product will lead to product exhaustion under constant returns to scale. This can occur either where the production function exhibits constant returns to scale at all levels of output or at the point of minimum long-run average cost.

analysis of the labour market this *apparently* free exchange of labour services (called *labour power*) for the wage is seen as a key feature of the capitalist mode of production. But for most people the sale of their labour is their only means of subsistence, since other methods (e.g. the cultivation of common land) are largely blocked. Thus, 'in the capitalist mode of production the worker is *forced* to sell his/her labour power because he/she has no substantial savings or independent access to the means of production . . . Hence the relations of production are *enforced* through the institution of the labour market' (Ginsburg 1979: 21, emphasis added). Because of this compulsion, the capitalist can extract *surplus value* from the labour he employs.

Marx's argument is complex, but in essence exploitation arose because the capitalist was obliged to pay only a weekly wage sufficient to support the worker and his family at around subsistence, but could then extract as much output as possible by imposing long working hours. The surplus value is the difference between the value of a worker's output and his wage and is, according to Marx, much greater than that necessary to yield a 'normal' rate of profit. Individuals whose only source of income is the sale of their labour thus have less power than the (fewer) people who own wealth or have independent access to the means of production. Marx argued that this inequality of power is inevitable in a capitalist society, and consequently the more powerful few are able to exploit labour by extracting its surplus value, hence enjoying a disproportionate share of output.

Because of its exploitative nature, Marx's attitude to capitalism 'was one of total rejection rather than reform and much of his intellectual effort went into proving that the capitalist system was both unworkable and inhuman' (Mishra 1981: 69). The heart of the argument is that the capitalist mode of production causes conflict between one class (the large, poor, exploited working class) and another (the small ruling class, which derives power from wealth and/or political influence); that conflict, according to Marx, is inherent and inevitable.

THE ROLE OF GOVERNMENT IN A CAPITALIST SOCIETY. Given this position, it is necessary to ask why capitalism has survived despite the numerical superiority of the working class. The first reason, according to Marxists, relates to *economic* power, which is concentrated in a small number of hands. The second is the distribution of *political* power. The ruling class dominates government decisions, Marxists argue, both because of its economic power and because members of the economic elite share a common education and social class with the political elite. Accordingly, government in a capitalist society always favours the ruling elite (Miliband 1969: chs. 4–6). Thirdly, there is the power of the ruling class over *ideas* (Miliband 1969: ch. 8). From this prop to capitalism derives the Marxist emphasis on 'consciousness raising'.

All three factors constitute the Marxist explanation of the survival of capitalism despite class conflict. But there is disagreement about whether the resulting structure supports *only* the ruling class, or whether the state, in supporting the capitalist *system*, also benefits workers. Gough (1979: 13–14), criticizing some Marxist writers for ignoring the effects of class conflict, argues that, to protect the capitalist system in the face of working-class pressure, the welfare state has been extended, with gains for the ruling elite, but also for workers.

THE MARXIST STATE. The next step is to outline the Marxist definition of a just society and the role of government in achieving it. Marxists broadly share the socialist triad of liberty, equality, and fraternity. Liberty is a more active concept than the absence of coercion. It cannot exist where economic or political power is distributed unequally, nor where the actions of the state are biased (Laski 1967: ch. 4; Miliband 1969: ch. 7); freedom, moreover, includes substantial equality and economic security. Thus to Marxists freedom and equality are two intermingled aspects of social justice, in sharp contrast with the liberal view, in which potential conflict between freedom and equality creates the central problem of political economy.

Equality to a Marxist does not necessarily imply complete equalization. According to Laski (1967: 157), 'the urgent claims of all must be met before we can meet the particular needs of some'. Once this basic condition has been met, differences in rewards should depend on effort or ability. It can, therefore, be argued that the Marxist aim is not equality but meeting need, which, as we have seen (Weale 1978), is a related but logically distinct objective. In Miller's terms, the Marxist definition of justice is based largely on needs, with rights somewhat secondary and with a small place for deserts.

Finally, we turn to the methods advocated by Marxists for the achievement of these aims. It is clear that their view of society, particularly the emphasis on economic equality and analysis of class conflict, implies a highly active role for government. They stress the importance of nationalizing the means of production, both because profits though produced socially generally accrue to a few large shareholders, and because private ownership of productive resources is incompatible with the Marxist definition of freedom. Though not a panacea, nationalization is regarded as essential to the achievement of Marxist aims, including industrial democracy, which is seen as a necessary concomitant of political democracy. An additional purpose is to ensure that industry is run for social rather than private benefit.

A Marxist society, therefore, would combine public ownership and government planning with wide-scale participation by workers in decisions affecting their lives. Libertarians argue that there is too much planning in the welfare state, Marxists that there is not enough—planning, they argue, far from reducing individual freedom, enhances it. It is logical that each side should reach the conclusion it does—planning reduces freedom defined by libertarians as the absence of coercion, but (if successful) enhances freedom defined by socialists to include some guarantee of economic security.

5. Implications for the role of the state

5.1. Theoretical issues

This section compares the theories, and discusses their implications for policy generally (Section 5.2) and the welfare state in particular (Section 5.3).

CRITICISMS OF LIBERALISM BY LIBERTARIANS centre largely on the definition of individual freedom. The liberal concept includes economic security, so that social justice embraces needs as well as rights and deserts. Libertarians criticize the inclusion of needs, at any rate above subsistence, because the resulting institutions (e.g. taxation) reduce efficiency, abridge natural rights (Nozick), and are part of a slippery slope towards totalitarianism

(Hayek). There are several counter-arguments. The first concerns Hayek's argument that it is not possible to define social justice. As we shall see in Chapter 6, many concepts, including poverty and inequality, are hard, if not impossible, to define; but this does not imply that no such phenomenon exists. Defenders of Rawls would argue, in addition, that the priority of the liberty principle is explicit protection against the Hayekian slippery slope; and also that redistribution does not violate individual rights where it was agreed behind the veil of ignorance, as part of the social contract.

CRITICISMS OF LIBERALISM BY COLLECTIVISTS arise, first, because of the greater collectivist emphasis on needs. Additionally, collectivists adopt a broader definition of freedom. As a case in point, Daniels (1975) criticizes Rawls's liberty principle, because it underestimates the effect of economic inequality on political liberties; as a result, the two principles may be incompatible. Marxists also criticize liberal theories because they leave out class conflict.

CRITICISMS OF LIBERTARIANISM. There is no opposition by liberals to markets *per se*. But they attack the libertarian emphasis on free markets, which can distribute resources unjustly by failing to meet individual need. More specifically, Hayek (1976: 64–5) has a view of markets as a game with winners and losers; but it can be argued that it is a game without rules, like a boxing competition where participants are not divided into different classes by weight. To liberals this violates the assumption of equal power on which, *inter alia*, the advantages of a market system depend (see Chapter 4, Section 3.2). Collectivists criticize the libertarian definition of freedom as too narrow, and regard equality and economic security as inseparable aspects of freedom (contrast Hayek 1944: ch. 9, and Laski 1967: 520). Marxists reject the market system entirely.

CRITICISMS OF COLLECTIVISM. Natural-rights libertarians, in consequence, entirely reject collectivist views, since attempts to redistribute resources equally or in accordance with need are seen as violations of individual freedom. Empirical libertarians and liberals criticize collectivism not because it includes meeting need as an objective, but because it gives it pride of place.

A different line of criticism is that collectivism (particularly when combined with central planning and state ownership) is inefficient—as shown by the growth slowdown after 1960 in the countries of Central and Eastern Europe and the former Soviet Union (see Estrin 1994; World Bank 1996: ch. 1). The major purpose of the late 1980s revolution throughout the region was to replace central planning by a market system, with the objectives of improved efficiency and increased individual freedom. It is important, however, not to misinterpret these events. It can be argued that collectivism defined, as by Marxists, in terms of its *methods* (e.g. state ownership and control), has been discredited. Democratic socialism, however, is defined in terms of its *aims*—for example, the pursuit of more or less egalitarian goals. This form of socialism, which blurs into a liberal analysis, remains firmly on the agenda.

5.2. Policy implications

PRIVATE PROPERTY is inviolate only to natural-rights libertarians like Nozick (1974: ch. 7), for whom justice in holdings implies total freedom for the individual to allocate as she chooses those resources that she has justly acquired. To Marxists, resources are available collectively to be distributed according to need; hence their emphasis on public ownership, and the view that 'property is theft' (see Laski 1967: chs. 5 and 9).

To liberals, private property and public ownership are a pragmatic matter, with government free to adopt whichever mix of the two is most helpful in achieving policy aims. Rawls maintains that his two principles are compatible with either private or public ownership, or with a mixed economy. Empirical libertarians accord private property a major but not overriding role; and democratic socialists allow it a more important role than formerly.

TAXATION to Nozick means that an individual will work (say) three days a week for himself, and two days compulsorily for the government; to Nozick, therefore, it is taxation, not private property, which is a form of theft. It is, however, mistaken to attribute this view to all libertarians. The necessity of taxation was always acknowledged by the classical liberals (Robbins 1978: ch. 2), albeit with some reluctance because of the consequent interference with liberty. The modern inheritors of this position such as Hayek and Friedman and the New Right concede the necessity of some taxation for the provision of public goods (narrowly defined) and for poverty relief (generally at subsistence).

To collectivist writers (Tawney 1964: 135–6) taxation for any social purpose is entirely legitimate. Liberals, also, regard taxation as an appropriate means towards policy objectives, though they are concerned about its disincentive effects, particularly on labour supply and capital formation, and more generally with selecting an optimal trade-off between efficiency and social justice (Atkinson and Stiglitz 1980: lectures 12–14).

REDISTRIBUTION. Distributive justice is not a problem for everyone. To Marxists, resources are available for collective allocation on the basis of need, which is given clear priority. Natural-rights libertarians like Nozick concentrate entirely on rights and deserts. Resources are produced by *individuals*, who thereby acquire the right to allocate them; the question of *societal* allocation does not arise. Distributive justice is therefore removed from the agenda.

Other groups have difficulties with distribution precisely because they are concerned with both desert and need. Empirical libertarians may oppose progressive taxation, but do not entirely rule out redistribution, accepting public action to relieve destitution. Utilitarians favour redistributive activity which increases total welfare, but are concerned about the trade-off with efficiency. Rawls, too, is not a complete egalitarian, since privilege is acceptable if it improves the position of the least well off. For general discussion, see Brittan (1995: ch. 12).

PUBLIC PRODUCTION raises similar arguments. Libertarians countenance provision by the state of at most limited public goods such as law and order, and even those only if no method of private supply can be found (Hayek 1960: 223; Friedman 1962: ch. 2). Completely opposite, the Marxist state supplies all basic goods and services, and distributes them in accordance with individual need. To liberals the issue of public versus market production and allocation is a pragmatic question of which method is more effective—the subject of most of this book.

5.3. Attitudes towards the welfare state

The welfare state is a complicated set of institutions, so it is not surprising that attitudes towards it are complicated (for detailed discussion, see George and Wilding 1994).

NATURAL-RIGHTS LIBERTARIANS like Nozick regard a welfare state of any sort as an anathema, seeing its pursuit of the spurious (or immoral) goal of equality as an unacceptable violation of individual liberty.

EMPIRICAL LIBERTARIANS such as Hayek and Friedman require careful discussion. The distinction between an institutional welfare state, which pursues substantially redistributive goals, and a residual welfare state was discussed in Chapter 2, Section 7.1. The former is strongly opposed by all libertarians. It is seen as a coercive agency that stifles freedom and individualism and courts the risk of totalitarianism through the amalgamation of economic and political power under central planning, in contrast with their separation in a market system. It also creates inefficiency because at a zero or subsidized price demand is excessive, because government monopoly is insulated from competition, and because of the distortionary effects of the taxation necessary to finance it.

A residual welfare state has much more limited aims. It is recognized that a free society based on private property and competitive markets is likely to distribute income unequally. Limited state activity may therefore be appropriate to relieve destitution and to provide certain public goods. Empirical libertarians consider this rather austere welfare state as essential to their idea of a civilized society. It is therefore not inconsistent when they attack existing social arrangements in the strongest terms (for example, the quote from Friedman at the head of this chapter), but support more limited welfare institutions (see Friedman 1962: chs. 6, 12; George and Wilding 1994: ch. 2).

LIBERALS AND DEMOCRATIC SOCIALISTS tend unambiguously to support the welfare state (George and Wilding 1994: chs. 3, 4). To Beveridge (1944: 254) it was necessary 'to use the powers of the State, sofar as may be necessary without any limit whatsoever, in order to avoid the five giant evils'.[11] Writers like Gilmour (1992) argue that the welfare state is not just an outcome of working-class pressure nor a creation of the post-war Labour government but an all-party creation deeply rooted in British history.

For most socialist writers, however, the welfare state is not a complete solution to society's ills, but only a step along the way.

For [Democratic Socialists], the welfare state is a significant staging post in the transition from laissez-faire capitalism to socialism . . . They have always understood and accepted that this transition . . . would be both gradual and slow for they have consistently rejected any other form of transition but the parliamentary process. . . . Social policy plays a very special role in this transition . . . (George and Wilding 1994: 74)

It is not surprising that liberals and socialists share some common ground. Robson (1976: 17), citing Hobhouse, writes:

---

[11] Want, disease, ignorance, squalor, and idleness.

The liberal . . . stands for emancipation, and is the inheritor of a long tradition of those who have fought for liberty, who have struggled against government and its laws or against society because they crushed human development . . . The socialist stands for solidarity of society, for mutual responsibility and the duty of the strong to aid the weak . . . On this analysis the ideals of the liberal and socialist were seen as complementary rather than conflicting.

MARXISTS disagree among themselves (George and Wilding 1994: ch. 5). Is the welfare state *only* an instrument of capitalist oppression, or does it *also* represent a progressive outcome of working-class pressure? Under the first view, the welfare state is at best irrelevant, a 'ransom' paid by the dominant class, and an institution dealing with symptoms rather than causes of economic and social problems; at worst, the welfare state is actively malign, in that it has sustained the capitalist system. 'Social control . . . has to do with the maintenance of order and the reduction of social conflict and tension. From the viewpoint of the ruling classes this often means reducing the workers' hostility towards the capitalist regime . . .' (Mishra 1981: 82). This, according to some Marxists, is the major purpose of the welfare state.

Other writers see the welfare state as serving the interests of the capitalist class *and* those of workers. A central insight (Gintis and Bowles 1982) is the contradictory position of the welfare state in a market economy; the former is based on rights (e.g. of citizenship) and needs, the latter recognizes claims based on deserts (e.g. through the ownership of property). Thus Gough (1979) sees the state not as a neutral umpire, nor as acting *merely* in the interests of the capitalist class (as opposed to the capitalist *system*), but as responding to pressure: from the working class to meet needs and extend rights; and from capital to foster capital accumulation.

The welfare state thus has contradictory functions. 'It simultaneously embodies tendencies to enhance social welfare, to develop the powers of individuals, to exert social control over the blind play of market forces; and tendencies to repress and control people, to adapt them to the requirements of the capitalist economy' (Gough 1979: 12).

As a result it is not surprising that some Marxists have ambivalent attitudes. Is the welfare state an 'agency of repression, or a system for enlarging human needs and mitigating the rigours of the free-market economy? An aid to capitalist accumulation and profits or a "social wage" to be defended and enlarged like the money in your pay packet? Capitalist fraud or working-class victory?' (ibid. 11).

Whether the welfare state contributes to justice is clearly a matter of perspective, and hence susceptible of no definitive answer. Miller (1976: 343–4) admits that 'readers with a yearning for Rawlsian "moral geometry" may . . . find this [conclusion] disappointing. Can there be no . . . arguments of universal validity that hold good across social and historical barriers? This is indeed a pleasant prospect, but since there seems little hope of it being realised, I conclude that we shall have to make do with more modest results.'

It is, nevertheless, instructive to conclude with a few words on who can usefully talk with whom, and about what. It is not possible to enter debate with natural-rights defenders of free markets and the nightwatchman state, save by disputing their values, nor with Marxists, to whom the evils of the market system are axiomatic. But dialogue *is* possible between empirical libertarians, liberals, and democratic socialists. Writers such as Hayek and Friedman share common roots in nineteenth-century classical liberalism with the largely utilitarian arguments of this book. Their position rests less on an ethical than on a theoretical and empirical view about the institutions likely to maximize total utility. The distinction is vital. The issues dividing a liberal defence of the welfare state from the views of empirical libertarians are not moral but largely factual. The main thrust of the argument is that technical problems with markets as both a theoretical and an empirical matter are more pervasive than Hayek and Friedman allow. These are the grounds of the debate; the theoretical heart of the argument is the subject of Chapter 4.

■ QUESTIONS FOR FURTHER DISCUSSION

1. 'Property is theft' (Karl Marx). 'Taxation is theft' (Robert Nozick). Who is right?

2. What sort of welfare state would writers such as Hayek and Friedman advocate? Does any country have a welfare state like that?

■ FURTHER READING

For more detailed discussion of the ideas in this chapter and their application to the welfare state, see George and Wilding (1994).

Libertarian ideas are set out by Nozick (1974) (a natural-rights defence), Hayek (1944, 1960, 1976), Friedman (1962), and Friedman and Friedman (1980). For an appreciation of Hayek, see Brittan (1995: ch. 6). The intellectual roots of these ideas are discussed by Robbins (1978).

The liberal approach is analysed by Barry (1973) and Miller (1976). On utilitarianism, see, for instance, Sen (1973). On the impossibility of a Paretian liberal, see Sen (1982), Sen and Williams (1982), and for a summary of the main arguments, Brittan (1995: ch. 3). For an introduction to Rawls (1972), see Gorovitz (1975) (one of the best teaching articles I have read). For more detailed commentary, see the contributions in Daniels (1975), and Sen (1992: ch. 5); for liberal critiques, Barry (1973) and Miller (1976); and for cogent libertarian criticism, Nisbet (1974). McCreadie (1976) offers an interesting application to the UK National Health Service.

A simple introduction to socialist thought (and also to the other theories of society) is by George and Wilding (1994), and discussion in greater depth by Crosland (1956), Tawney (1964) (a defence of equality), Laski (1967), and Miliband (1969).

The classic exposition of Marxist economic theory is Sweezy (1942). See also Mandel (1976), J. Harrison (1978), and Desai (1979). Marxist attitudes to the welfare state are discussed by Ginsburg (1979), Gough (1979), and Mishra (1981).

On arguments about equality, see the essays in Franklin (1997) (a defence of equality) and Letwin (1983) (a libertarian critique of egalitarianism).

Gender aspects of the welfare state are discussed by George and Wilding (1994: ch. 7), Sainsbury (1994), and Anne Phillips (1997).

Appendix: Non-technical summary of Chapter 3

1. Chapter 3 discusses different theories of society—libertarianism, utilitarianism, Rawlsian arguments, and socialism. In practice the theories blur into each other like the colours of the rainbow, but it is useful for exposition to talk about them as separate entities.

Libertarian theories

2. To libertarians (Section 2), as their name implies, the primary aim of institutions is individual liberty, and the best method of achieving its economic dimension is through the operation of private markets. *Natural-rights libertarians* like Nozick (1974) defend a minimal (or 'nightwatchman') state on ethical grounds; *empirical libertarians* such as Hayek and Friedman out of a belief that such a regime will maximize total welfare. For natural-rights libertarians the state has no legitimate distributional role; to empirical libertarians its distributional activities are strictly circumscribed.

3. Hayek argues in addition that the pursuit of social justice is not only fruitless because there is no such thing, but also dangerous because it will destroy the market order, which is both efficient and the only guarantee of personal freedom. According to Hayek (1976), a given circumstance is just or unjust only if it has been caused by the action/inaction of a *named* individual or individuals. The outcome of impersonal forces ('Nature') can be good or bad, but never just or unjust. The market is seen as an impersonal force, akin to an economic game with winners and losers, and so the market-determined distribution of goods can be neither just nor unjust. The notion of social justice therefore has no meaning. Its quest, however, is dangerous according to Hayek, because, once governments start to interfere with the market-determined distribution, a process is set in motion that progressively approaches totalitarianism.

Liberal theories

4. Liberal theories (Section 3)—e.g. utilitarianism and Rawlsian thinking—contrast with libertarian views first by allowing the state a greater distributional role, and secondly through a weaker presumption that the free market is necessarily the best means of production and distribution. The treatment of property rights is not an end in itself, as with libertarians, but a means towards the achievement of stated policy aims. In certain circumstances this can justify a mixed economy.

5. The utilitarian aim is to distribute goods so as to maximize the total utility of society's members (Section 3.1). Where individuals have identical marginal utility of income functions, this occurs when income is shared equally (Figure 3.1). Utilitarianism thus enables statements to be about the optimal distribution of goods (which in certain circumstances can be egalitarian), and so legitimates a redistributive role of the state.

6. This approach is criticized by Rawls and others because it can justify harm to the least well-off individual or group, if this raises total utility.

7. Rawls, in contrast, makes justice the primary aim of policy (Section 3.2) (for a very clear introduction, see Gorovitz 1975). Rawls defines social justice in terms of two principles, the first dealing with the distribution of liberty, the second with that of other goods. Taken together they imply that all goods (interpreted broadly to include liberty and opportunity) should be distributed equally unless an unequal distribution is to the advantage of the least well-off individual or group. No policy should be undertaken, according to Rawls, unless it benefits also (though not necessarily only) the least well off. Again, there is a legitimate, and generally egalitarian, redistributive role for the state.

8. The theories of utilitarians and Rawls can have different policy implications. Suppose a given policy change makes at least one person better off without making anyone worse off. This is a Pareto improvement (see Chapter 4, Section 2.1); hence utilitarians would regard the policy as desirable, even if the individual who benefited was rich. Rawls's principles of justice would oppose the policy unless it was also to the advantage of the least well off. Thus an efficient answer in a Paretian sense is not always just in a Rawlsian sense (see Chapter 4, Section 2.2).

Socialist theories

9. The main socialist aims are equality, freedom, and fraternity. These values can conflict, and different writers accord them different weights. But there is general agreement about the importance of equality, which is closely related (though not logically equivalent) to the further socialist aim of meeting need.

10. Despite agreement about their aims and in their diagnosis of the failings of the free market, socialists are divided over how best to achieve them, most fundamentally over the role, if any, of the market system.

11. Democratic socialists (Section 4.1) argue that institutional changes, not least the enlarged role of government in economic life, have greatly reduced the evils of capitalism and made it possible to harness the market system to socialist goals. Adherents of this view accept a role for private property and the market mechanism, though modified in both cases by state intervention—i.e. like liberals they feel that their aims are likely to be best achieved by some sort of mixed economy.

12. Other socialists, e.g. Marxists (Section 4.2), argue that private ownership and the market system are inherently in conflict with socialist aims. In particular they regard the market as exploitative and therefore incompatible with equality. Marxists therefore reject capitalism outright, whether or not it makes up part of a mixed economy, and give the state a primary role in production and allocation, as well as in distribution and redistribution.

Attitudes towards the welfare state

13. The appropriate role of the state depends crucially on the underlying theory of society (Sections 5.1 and 5.2), as also do attitudes towards the welfare state (Section 5.3).

14. Natural-rights libertarians reject all but minimal intervention and are unambiguously hostile to the welfare state, which they regard as a coercive agency that stifles freedom and individualism, and encourages waste and inefficiency in pursuit of the spurious and dangerous goal of social justice.

15. Empirical libertarians have a broadly similar attitude towards a large-scale welfare state with substantial redistributive goals. They do, however, recognize that a free society based on private property and competitive markets will distribute income unequally, and are therefore prepared to support an austere welfare state whose primary aim is the relief of destitution.

16. The main support for the welfare state comes from liberals and democratic socialists, in the latter case unreservedly, because it is seen as an equalizing force. For liberals its existence is a contingent issue: they support the institutions of the welfare state where (and only where) they contribute more than alternative arrangements to the achievement of society's aims. In such cases their support is unreserved.

17. Marxists are generally hostile to the welfare state, though with some controversy. 'Hardline' commentators regard it as an actively malign agency that serves *only* (or mainly) as an instrument

of social control, to protect the continued existence of the capitalist system. Other writers argue that, though the welfare state is indeed a 'ransom' paid by the dominant class, it *also* represents a genuine improvement in working-class conditions.

18. Finally, who can talk with whom, and about what? No debate is possible between liberals and natural-rights libertarians, on the one hand, or between liberals and Marxists, on the other. Debate *is*, however, possible between liberals and libertarians such as Hayek and Friedman, who argue less from a moral position than from an empirical view about the institutions likely to maximize total utility. The main thrust of this book is that technical problems with markets, as both a theoretical and an empirical matter, are much more pervasive than Hayek and Friedman allow. In other words, the issues that separate a liberal defence of the welfare state from the views of empirical libertarians are at least as much factual as ideological.

4 Economic theory 1: State intervention

Every individual . . . generally . . . neither intends to promote the public interest, nor knows by how much he is promoting it. By preferring the support of domestic to that of foreign industry he intends only his own security; and by directing that industry in such a manner as its produce may be of the greatest value, he intends only his own gain, and he is in this, as in many other cases, led by an invisible hand to promote an end which was no part of his intention.

(Adam Smith, 1776)

[The] market needs a place, and the market needs to be kept in its place. It must be given enough scope to accomplish the many things it does well. It limits the power of bureaucracy . . . responds reliably to the signals transmitted by consumers and producers . . . Most important, the prizes in the market place provide the incentives for work effort and productive contribution . . . For such reasons I cheered the market; but I could not give it more than two cheers. The tyranny of the dollar yardstick restrained my enthusiasm.

(Arthur Okun, 1975)

I see the critical failing in the standard neoclassical model to be in its assumptions concerning information . . . however, while it is the informational assumptions underlying the standard theory which are perhaps its Achilles heel, its failures go well beyond that: The assumptions concerning completeness of markets, competitiveness of markets, and the absence of innovation are three that I stress.

(Joseph E. Stiglitz, 1994)

1. The formal structure of the problem

We now change gear and move from the world of political philosophy to economic theory.[1] The main aim is to develop a framework that (*a*) explains and (*b*) justifies (or fails to justify) the fact that the state produces and/or allocates some goods such as health care and education, but leaves others like food to the private market. The main issues concern economic efficiency and social justice. Section 1 sets out the formal structure of the problem. Section 2 shows that the efficiency aim is common to all theories of society, but that redistributive goals depend crucially on which definition of social justice is chosen.

---

[1] Non-technical readers can find the gist of the argument in the Appendix at the end of the chapter.

The next step (Section 3) is to consider the conditions under which the market will allocate efficiently, and appropriate forms of intervention where those conditions fail. The pursuit of social justice (Section 4) raises such questions as: why does redistribution occur; should it be voluntary; should it be in cash or in kind; and what role (if any) should the state adopt to bring about equality of access, opportunity, or outcome? One set of counter-arguments to government intervention comes from the 'government-failure' analysis, summarized in Section 5. As a precursor to policy discussion in later chapters, Section 6 sets out the logic of privatization. Section 7 pulls together the major threads running through Chapters 3 and 4 by discussing the appropriate boundary between the market and the state, summarizing the main theoretical argument of the book, and establishing the areas of debate with its opponents, particularly libertarian writers such as Hayek and Friedman.

The conventional starting point for economic theory is the social-welfare-maximization problem. The aim of policy is to maximize social welfare subject to the three basic constraints of tastes, technology, and resources, i.e.

Maximize:
$$W = W(U^A, U^B) \tag{4.1}$$

Subject to:
$$\left. \begin{array}{l} U^A = U^A(X^A, Y^A) \\[6pt] U^B = U^B(X^B, Y^B) \end{array} \right\} \text{Tastes} \qquad \begin{array}{l} (4.2) \\[6pt] (4.3) \end{array}$$

$$\left. \begin{array}{l} X = X(K^X, L^X) \\[6pt] Y = Y(K^Y, L^Y) \end{array} \right\} \text{Technology} \qquad \begin{array}{l} (4.4) \\[6pt] (4.5) \end{array}$$

$$\left. \begin{array}{l} K^X + K^Y = \bar{K} \\[6pt] L^X + L^Y = \bar{L} \end{array} \right\} \text{Resources} \qquad \begin{array}{l} (4.6) \\[6pt] (4.7) \end{array}$$

The aim in equation (4.1) is to maximize social welfare, W, as a function of the utilities of individuals A and B, U^A and U^B; thus the problem is a joint maximization of efficiency and social justice. The utilities of individuals A and B are constrained by their consumption of goods X and Y (equations (4.2) and (4.3)); consumption is constrained by equations (4.4) and (4.5), which show the production functions for X and Y in terms of the inputs of capital, K, and labour, L; the inputs used to produce X and Y are constrained by the total availability of capital and labour, $\bar{K}$ and $\bar{L}$ (equations (4.6) and (4.7)).

The problem as formulated relates to a *first-best economy*. This implies one of two situations: either there is no impediment to efficiency, and also an optimal distribution of endowments; or government can counter inefficiency or maldistribution with first-best policies (e.g. through lump-sum taxation). An important theorem discussed in Section 3 establishes the (first-best) assumptions under which a competitive market will allocate resources efficiently. Where these conditions hold, the state has no role except possibly a distributional one.

The conditions, however, are stringent, as is the assumption that lump-sum taxation is feasible. A *second-best economy* faces additional constraints: imperfect information is a recurring theme, e.g. if U^A is not well defined with respect to X^A. As a result, unrestricted markets may be inefficient or inequitable, and intervention may improve matters. Externalities are another problem. If U^A depends on X^B we have a consumption externality that

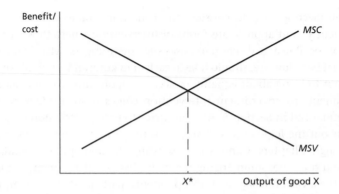

Fig. 4.1. Pareto optimal output: The simple case

constitutes a constraint additional to those in equations (4.2) to (4.7). This may justify intervention in various forms. We return to these issues in Sections 3 and 4.[2]

2. Why economic efficiency is one of the aims of policy

2.1. The concept of economic efficiency

The concept of efficiency is fundamental, so a brief introduction is included here, rather than relegated to the Appendix.[3] Technical readers should proceed directly to Section 2.2.

Economic efficiency[4] is about making the best use of limited resources given people's tastes. It involves the choice of an *output bundle*

$$X^* = (X_1, X_2, \ldots, X_N) \tag{4.8}$$

(where X_i is the output of the ith good) with the property that any deviations from these quantities will make at least one person worse off. The intuition is shown in a partial equilibrium framework in Figure 4.1: the optimal quantity of any good, *ceteris paribus*, is that at which the value placed by society on the marginal unit equals its marginal social cost.[5]

For a general equilibrium, three conditions must hold simultaneously.[6]

1. *Productive efficiency* means that activity should be organized to obtain the maximum output from given inputs. This is what engineers mean when they talk about efficiency. It is about building a hospital to a specified standard with as few workers as possible

---

[2] For a survey of the literature on first- and second-best analysis within the social-welfare-maximization framework, see Atkinson and Stiglitz (1980: lectures 11–14).

[3] Non-technical readers should consult the relevant chapters (see the following footnotes) in Le Grand et al. (1992), Baumol and Blinder (2000: ch. 4), Stiglitz and Walsh (2002: chs. 2, 10), Varian (2002: ch. 1), or Begg et al. (2003, ch. 15).

[4] Referred to synonymously as Pareto efficiency, Pareto optimality, allocative efficiency, or external efficiency.

[5] See Le Grand et al. (1992: ch. 1), Stiglitz and Walsh (2002: ch. 10), or Begg et al. (2003, ch. 15).

[6] See Stiglitz (2000: ch. 3) or Varian (2002: ch. 1).

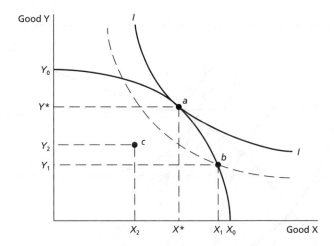

Fig. 4.2. A simple general equilibrium representation of Pareto optimal output

standing around waiting for something to do. It is also about the choice of technique, taking the prices of inputs into account. The transformation curve Y_0X_0 in Figure 4.2 shows the maximum quantities of the two goods that can be produced with available resources. Productive efficiency means that production is at a point on—rather than inside—the transformation curve. Thus all points on the transformation curve conform with productive efficiency.

This, however, is not enough for allocative efficiency, which requires two additional conditions to hold.

2. *Efficiency in product mix* means that the optimal combination of goods should be produced, given existing production technology and consumer tastes. The fact that it is possible to build a hospital cheaply is not *per se* justification for building it. The resources involved could perhaps give the local population greater satisfaction if used to build a school; or the land could be used as a park, and the money saved by not building a hospital used to reduce taxes.

Formally, production is not at *any* point on the transformation curve in Figure 4.2, but at the specific point *a*, at which the ratio of marginal production costs (i.e. the slope of the transformation curve) is equal to the ratio of marginal rates of substitution in consumption (i.e. the slope of the 'social' indifference curve, *I–I*).

3. *Efficiency in consumption* means that consumers should allocate their income in a way that maximizes their utility, given their incomes and the prices of the goods they buy—in formal terms, the marginal rate of substitution must be equal for all individuals.

The meaning of the third condition is analysed further in the Edgeworth box in Figure 4.3. The size of the box shows the total output to be divided between individuals A and B, O_AX^* of good X and O_AY^* of good Y, where the quantities X^* and Y^* are those in Figure 4.2 (hence fulfilling efficiency in production and in product mix). The output allocated to A is measured from the origin O_A, and that to B from O_B; at point g the two individuals share output equally. The contract curve, represented by the line O_AO_B, shows those combinations of X and Y at which the marginal rate of substitution between the

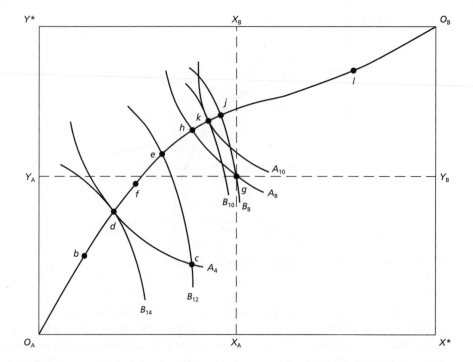

Fig. 4.3. The Edgeworth box (distribution)

two goods is the same for both individuals. Any movement away from the contract curve makes at least one person worse off. Hence any point on the contract curve constitutes an efficient allocation.

Thus in Figure 4.2, point c is neither productively nor allocatively efficient. Point b, like all other points on the transformation curve, conforms with productive efficiency. Only point a conforms with both productive and allocative efficiency. Thus allocative efficiency conforms simultaneously with all these requirements. It will depend on external conditions (more resources are devoted to hotels on the Mediterranean than in Murmansk); it will depend on tastes (the French spend more on food than the English; the English spend more on gardens than the Germans; Hungarians consume more paprika than anyone else); it will depend on the age of the population (more resources are spent on schools in a country with many children); it will depend on income levels (private ownership of cars and personal computers is more widespread in better-off countries). The argument in favour of markets, discussed in detail in Section 3, is that they can achieve this efficient result with minimal intervention.

The concept of a *Pareto improvement* is important for the analysis that follows. Suppose the initial allocation is shown by point c in Figure 4.3; then individual A on indifference curve A_4 is 'poor' and B on indifference curve B_{12} 'rich'. If trade moves the allocation to point d, then B is better off (he has moved to the higher indifference curve B_{14}) and A is no worse off; this is a Pareto improvement. Similarly, a move to the allocation shown by e makes A better off without harming B; and a move to an intermediate allocation like f

benefits both parties. Thus any move from the distribution shown by *c* to any distribution on the contract curve between *d* and *e*, including points *d* and *e* themselves, increases efficiency and constitutes a Pareto improvement.[7] The next question is which of these allocations is socially optimal.

2.2. The relevance of efficiency to different theories of society

The relationship between efficiency and social welfare is shown in Figure 4.3.[8] We have seen that a move from point *c* to a point like *e* is a Pareto improvement. The next step is to show that this is not just a utilitarian result. In each case two questions are considered: (*a*) given an initial suboptimal allocation, what constitutes a welfare improvement; and (*b*) what is the optimal distribution of goods—that is, what allocation is both efficient and socially just? Two results are established: economic efficiency, in the sense of a movement to an appropriate subset of the contract curve, is an important aim under *all* the definitions of social justice discussed in Chapter 3; and in a first-best economy no distribution can be socially just unless it is also efficient.

These, however, can be murky waters. Pareto efficiency incorporates two value judgements: social welfare is increased if one person is made better off and nobody worse off; and individuals are the best judge of their own welfare. As discussed in Chapter 3, Section 3.1, these assumptions can be problematic. Thus 'Pareto-type definitions . . . are not uncontested . . . for they incorporate values that are less innocuous than might be at first apparent' (Le Grand 1996: 152; see also Le Grand 1991*a*: ch. 3). This section abstracts from these problems.

THE FIXED-FACTOR CASE assumes an Edgeworth box of given size, and also that the conditions for efficiency in production and in product mix hold. This is equivalent to discussing a first-best solution.

Libertarianism.[9] Welfare is increased by any Pareto improvement, which to writers like Nozick is the only source of welfare gain. Thus a movement from *c* in Figure 4.3 to any point on the contract curve between points *d* and *e* (including the end points) increases welfare.

Natural-rights libertarians have little to say about the optimal distribution of goods. If the initial distribution is at *c*, then any point on the contract curve between *d* and *e* is optimal, provided that *c* accords with Nozick's idea of justice in holdings, and that the movement from *c* to the contract curve is the result of voluntary trading in a competitive market system. More generally, depending on the initial distribution, *any* point on the contract curve can be an optimum. Empirical libertarians such as Hayek and Friedman support this conclusion, save that they accept redistributive activity up to (but not beyond) a guarantee of subsistence—that is, they would have nothing to say about movements along the contract curve between points *b* and *l*, if these show subsistence for individuals A and B, respectively.

---

[7] For an amusing and informative example taken from a prisoner-of-war camp, see Radford (1945).

[8] The issue can be approached also via a utility-possibility frontier, which can be derived as a simple transformation of the contract curve in Figure 4.3; see Atkinson and Stiglitz (1980: lecture 11.2).

[9] The libertarian theory of society is discussed in Chapter 3, Section 2. Utilitarianism, Rawls, and socialism are discussed in Chapter 3, Sections 3.1, 3.2, and 4, respectively, and in the Appendix to Chapter 3.

Utilitarians aim to maximize total utility. Again, any Pareto improvement, such as a move from c to the contract curve between (and including) points d and e, increases welfare.

Is any point on the contract curve superior to any other—that is, do movements *along* the contract curve raise welfare? The utilitarian answer, which is often misunderstood, depends on whether utility is ordinally or cardinally measurable (see the Glossary). When utility is cardinally measurable and A and B have identical marginal utility of income functions (as in Figure 3.1), welfare is maximized by starting from an equal distribution of goods, shown by point g in Figure 4.3. From this egalitarian endowment, Pareto improvement is possible; under the stated assumptions total utility will be highest at point k. Individuals A and B are on indifference curves A_{10} and B_{10}, respectively; each enjoys ten units of utility (because utility is cardinally measurable); and (because marginal utility of income declines) total utility is lower at all other points on the contract curve. In these circumstances a move *along* the contract curve from a point like e towards k constitutes a utilitarian welfare improvement.

This egalitarian outcome, however, depends on A and B having identical marginal utility of income functions. If A is a gloomy guy and B a cheerful chappie, social welfare is maximized at a point like d, and with roles reversed at a point like l. The same logic applies when utility is measurable only ordinally, but here, though we know that there exists a single optimum distribution at a point like k (or d or l), we cannot say which point because we cannot compare the utility of the two individuals. The latter conclusion is fundamentally different from the libertarian argument that there is no ethical difference between points like d, k, and l.

Rawls's aim is to distribute resources in accordance with social justice. Starting again from point c, a movement to e is a Rawlsian improvement (RI) because it benefits the less advantaged individual A. But a movement from c to d, though a Pareto improvement (PI), is *not* RI because it violates Rawls's principle that matters are to be arranged to the benefit of the least advantaged. A movement from c to a point between d and e is RI (and PI), because it benefits A at least to some extent. In addition, a movement from c to points between (and including) e and k, though it is not PI (since individual B is made worse off), is RI because it benefits the less-advantaged A. Hence a movement from c to the contract curve between d and e, *including* points d and e, is PI; RI excludes point d[10] and includes points between e and k. The conclusion is that, if we are off the contract curve at a point like c, there will always be a subset of the contract curve that is RI. Thus, in a first-best economy *all Rawlsian socially just distributions lie on the contract curve.*

According to Rawls, goods should be distributed equally, unless any other distribution benefits the least well off. Hence the just distribution is generally point g, and the optimum outcome point k—that is, a single, known, and (generally) egalitarian point. Any movement along the contract curve towards k is an unambiguous improvement.

Socialism. Under one interpretation resources should be shared equally. A movement from c to e raises the welfare of (poor) individual A, thereby reducing relative inequality. Such a move is a socialist improvement (SI). But a movement from c to d helps only (rich) individual B. If output is fixed (i.e. ruling out the case where B uses the extra resources to

---

[10] Unless the lexical extension to the difference principle applies (see Chapter 3, note 5).

bring about economic growth to the advantage of A), this increases relative inequality and is therefore not SI. A movement from c to an intermediate point like f is arguable. I shall define (though others may disagree) SI to refer to any movement that increases individual A's *relative share* of output, thereby reducing inequality. Suppose f is the point on the contract curve at which A's relative share is the same as at c. We can then interpret as SI a movement from c to any point on the contract curve between (and including) e and k, and arguably also to any point between e and f (excluding point f itself). *SI is thus a subset of RI*, and all first-best solutions that are just in a socialist sense lie on the contract curve; and, like Rawls, socialists will favour any movement along the contract curve towards k.

RELAXING THE FIXED-FACTOR-SUPPLY ASSUMPTION complicates matters because of the need, in the absence of lump-sum taxation, to analyse policies in a second-best economy. It is a standard proposition (Atkinson and Stiglitz 1980: 343) that lump-sum transfers, being based on characteristics exogenous to the taxpayer, can bring about any desired distribution of income without efficiency loss. Taxes related to income, including any indirect tax whose payment rises with income, are not lump sum, and generally cause inefficiency, *inter alia* through their effect on individual labour supply. But attempts to achieve social justice (such as a movement from e to k in Figure 4.3) involve redistribution; hence taxation must inevitably be income related. As a result, any practicable system of taxation may cause inefficiency in production and/or product mix. Thus there may be a trade-off between efficiency and equity.

This trade-off is analysed in the optimal taxation literature[11] within the social-welfare-maximization framework in Section 1. The distribution that jointly optimizes efficiency and social justice depends on two sets of factors: the efficiency costs of redistribution (mainly a technical matter depending, *inter alia*, on the compensated elasticity of factor supply); and the relative weights attached to efficiency and equity (an ideological matter).

When account is taken of the efficiency impact of redistribution, it may not be possible, for instance, to move from point c to point e. The only feasible possibilities might be:

- a movement to a point like b, which is efficient and leaves total production unaffected, but which, in most theories of society, is less just than the distribution shown by c; or

- a movement to a distribution less unequal than b. In this case redistributive taxation will cause efficiency losses, generally by reducing output (i.e. attempts to move from c towards e will shrink the size of the box in Figure 4.3).

In the face of this trade-off there will be different views about the desirability of an increase in efficiency, which will not be seen as a welfare gain if its equity cost is 'too' high. To some libertarians equity has a zero weight; a movement from c to b will therefore increase both efficiency and welfare. To utilitarians the weight given to social justice is an open question. A given efficiency gain may or may not increase welfare; and the

---

[11] See Cullis and Jones (1998: chs. 15, 16), Stiglitz (2000: ch. 20), Rosen (2002: ch. 14) or, more formally, Atkinson and Stiglitz (1980: lectures 11, 12).

utilitarian optimum will not necessarily be efficient (i.e. utilitarians will tolerate some efficiency loss in the interests of greater justice). Rawlsians and socialists give social justice more weight, and will therefore tend to accept a higher efficiency loss to achieve a just distribution. Note, however, that no theory of society gives social justice complete priority. Even a Marxist would resist the pursuit of distributional objectives if the resulting efficiency costs reduced output to zero.

CONCLUSIONS focus particularly on the relationship between efficiency and social welfare. The overall conclusion is that the analysis of this chapter is general in its application.

Conclusion 1. The meaning of efficiency: an increase in efficiency (e.g. a movement from point *c* to a point on the contract curve) has the same meaning in all theories of society. Though the underlying concept, Pareto efficiency, is not value free, its implicit value judgements apply widely. Thus an interest in efficiency is not restricted to utilitarians.

Conclusion 2. Welfare improvements: welfare is increased under all the theories of society by a movement from a point like *c* to an appropriate subset of the contract curve. Additionally, a movement from *c* to a point between *e* and *f* (excluding *f*) is SI *and* RI *and* PI. *Efficiency gains of this sort raise social welfare under all the theories of society discussed in Chapter 3.* Where such a movement is feasible, this conclusion is valid whether factor supply is fixed or variable.

Conclusion 3. The optimal distribution in a first-best economy: for any of the theories of society discussed earlier *all first-best socially just distributions are also Pareto efficient.* Efficiency in this case is a necessary condition for social justice.

Conclusion 4. The optimal distribution in a second-best economy: in this case an increase in efficiency may be possible only at the expense of social justice. Whether such an efficiency gain raises social welfare depends on the relative weights accorded efficiency and equity, weights that will vary with different theories of society. Thus, the second-best optimum distribution may be a point that is not Pareto efficient.

3. Intervention for reasons of efficiency

3.1. Types of intervention

Discussion so far has concerned the *objectives* of policy. The next step is to consider *methods*. This section discusses the circumstances in which market allocation is efficient and, if it is not, which types of intervention might be justified. The analysis here (and for most of the book) looks mainly at static efficiency, though in later chapters issues of economic growth (i.e. dynamic efficiency) are discussed where relevant.

The state can intervene in four ways: regulation, finance, and public production interfere indirectly in the market mechanism; income transfers may have indirect effects.

REGULATION. The state interferes with the free market through many regulations. Some (e.g. relating to shop-opening hours) have more to do with social values than economics. But many are directly relevant to the efficient or equitable operation of markets, especially where knowledge is imperfect. Regulation of *quality* is concerned mainly with the supply side—for example, hygiene laws relating to the production and sale of food and pharmaceutical drugs; laws forbidding unqualified people to practise medicine; and consumer protection legislation generally. Regulation of *quantity* more often affects individual demand—the requirement to attend school, mandatory automobile insurance, and compulsory social-insurance contributions. Examples of *price* regulation include minimum wages and rent control.

FINANCE involves subsidies (or taxes) applied to the *prices* of specific commodities or affecting the *incomes* of individuals. Price subsidies affect economic activity by changing the slope of the budget constraint facing individuals and firms. They can be partial (e.g. for public transport or local-authority housing) or total (e.g. free pharmaceutical drugs for the elderly). Similarly, prices can be affected by a variety of taxes (e.g. on pollution or congestion). Income subsidies raise different issues that are discussed shortly.

PRODUCTION. Though regulation and finance modify market outcomes, they leave the basic mechanism intact. Alternatively, the state can take over the supply side by producing goods and services itself; in such cases the state owns the capital inputs (e.g. school buildings and equipment) and employs the necessary labour (e.g. teachers). Other (more or less pure) examples are national defence and (in some countries) most health care. It is important to be clear that finance and production are entirely separate forms of intervention, both conceptually and in practice, a distinction of considerable relevance to privatization (Section 6).

INCOME TRANSFERS can be tied to specific types of expenditure (e.g. education vouchers or housing benefit) or untied (e.g. social-security benefits). First-best transfers take the form of a lump sum, and therefore affect economic activity by changing the incomes of individuals, with no extra-market effect on product or factor prices. As we saw in Section 2.2, however, redistributive transfers in practice are not of this sort, and so cannot be regarded in efficiency terms as wholly neutral.

3.2. The assumptions under which markets are efficient

This section is in some ways the theoretical heart of the book. The *invisible hand theorem* asserts that the market clearing set of outputs, X_M, will be the efficient output bundle X^* in equation (4.8) if and only if a number of assumptions hold. These (henceforth collectively called the *standard assumptions*) concern perfect competition, complete markets, the absence of market failures, and, crucially, perfect information. Where the assumptions hold, there is no justification for intervention on efficiency grounds, but, if one or more fails, the resulting market equilibrium may be inefficient, and state intervention in one of the forms described above may be appropriate

Perfect competition

Perfect competition must hold in product and factor markets, and also (and importantly) in capital markets. The assumption has two essential features: economic agents must be price-takers; and they must have equal power.

PRICE-TAKING implies a large number of individuals and firms, with no entry barriers in any market. The assumption can fail—for example, in the presence of monopoly, monopsony, or oligopoly—and appropriate intervention can increase efficiency. It is a standard proposition that a monopolist can be given an incentive to produce the efficient output either through the imposition of a maximum price (i.e. *regulation*) or via an appropriate *price subsidy* (with or without the addition of a lump-sum tax). Where imperfect competition takes the form of oligopoly, other forms of regulation may be appropriate—for example, anti-trust legislation.

EQUAL POWER is not violated if some individuals have higher incomes than others and so have more 'dollar votes'. In all other respects agents must have equal power—there can be no discrimination. The assumption is frequently breached, and hard to correct. In some areas (e.g. safety legislation in factories) the state intervenes to protect workers through *regulation*. Others, such as having friends in high places, have no easy solution; nor does discrimination in terms of gender or ethnicity. Legislation (i.e. regulation) in these areas has met with only partial success.[12]

Complete markets

Complete markets would provide all goods and services for which individuals are prepared to pay a price that covers their production costs. This is not always the case. The market will generally fail to supply public goods (discussed shortly). Missing markets arise, secondly, because certain risks are uninsurable (Chapter 5). Thirdly, capital markets may in some circumstances fail to provide loans (student loans are discussed in Chapter 13). Fourthly, there may be no futures market—that is, it may not be possible to make a contract now to buy or sell a commodity on given terms at some time in the future. Finally, a commodity may not be supplied because a complementary market is absent. This is a particular problem if large-scale activities need to be coordinated—for example, in the case of urban renewal projects. Where there are missing markets, state intervention (often, though not always, in the form of public production) will generally be necessary if the commodity is to be supplied.

No market failures

This assumption can be violated in three major ways: public goods, external effects, and increasing returns to scale, discussed in more detail in the Appendix.

PURE PUBLIC GOODS exhibit three technical characteristics, non-rivalness in consumption, non-excludability, and non-rejectability, which together imply that the market is likely to produce inefficiently, if at all. Once a public good is produced, non-excludability makes it impossible to prevent people from using it, hence it is not possible to levy charges (this is the *free-rider* problem); in such cases the market may fail entirely. Non-rivalness implies that the marginal cost of an extra user (though *not* of an extra unit of output) is zero. The efficient price should therefore be based on individual marginal valuations of the good—

---

[12] Work by the World Bank (Stern 2002) emphasizes a development strategy with two elements: ensuring a favourable investment climate, and empowering individuals. The latter has strong links to ensuring that people have equal power.

that is, on perfect price discrimination; where this is not possible, the market is likely to be inefficient. If a public good is to be provided at all, the appropriate form of intervention is generally *public production*.[13]

EXTERNAL EFFECTS are a closely related phenomenon. They arise when an act of agent A imposes costs or confers benefits on agent B for which no compensation from A to B, or payment from B to A, takes place. Formally, a technological externality arises when A's utility function or production function is interrelated with B's. It is a standard proposition[14] that, in the presence of an external cost, the market clearing output will generally exceed the efficient output, and vice versa for an external benefit. The market itself can sometimes solve the problem, (*a*) through merger of the relevant parties (Meade 1952) or (*b*) where property rights are well defined, through negotiation between the parties concerned (Coase 1960). The latter, however, is not always possible—for instance, where property rights are not enforceable (air pollution) or where transactions costs are high because large numbers of people are involved (traffic congestion). In such cases, intervention may be warranted through either (*c*) *regulation* or (*d*) an appropriate Pigovian *tax or subsidy*. The choice of method depends on a complex of factors. Taxation/subsidy is the usual solution if the intention is marginally to change levels of consumption or production. But regulation may be useful where the aim is to enforce at least a minimum level of some activity (compulsory automobile insurance), or to restrict it below some maximum (mandatory pollution controls) or where measurement problems prevent assessment of the appropriate tax/subsidy.[15]

INCREASING RETURNS TO SCALE at all levels of output imply that average cost will exceed marginal cost, as in Figure 4.4. The consequent long-run losses will drive competitive firms from the industry, which will either become monopolized or (if even a monopolist makes losses) will cease to exist at all. Intervention can take one of two forms. The industry could remain private, buttressed by an appropriate lump-sum subsidy $(AC_0–P_0)X_0$ in Figure 4.4;[16] or it could be nationalized and similarly subsidized. The appropriate intervention, therefore, is *subsidy* or *public production* or both.

Perfect information

The analysis of imperfect competition and market failures has two noteworthy features: for the most part it has a long pedigree in the economic literature; and it justifies regulation and subsidy but (with the exception of public goods) gives no efficiency argument for public production. Two conclusions follow (for fuller discussion, see Barr 1992: section III (A)): when applied to the welfare state, these traditional arguments give little justification,

---

[13] See, in ascending order of difficulty, Baumol and Blinder (2000: ch. 14), Begg et al. (2003: ch. 16), Stiglitz (2000: ch. 6), Rosen (2002: ch. 4), or Varian (2002: ch. 35). The classic exposition of the theory of public goods is Samuelson (1954).

[14] On the welfare effects of externalities, see, in ascending order of difficulty, Le Grand et al. (1992: ch. 2), Baumol and Blinder (2000: ch. 14), Begg et al. (2003: ch. 15), Stiglitz (2000: ch. 4), or Varian (2002: ch. 33).

[15] For discussion in the context of environmental issues, see Stephen Smith (1992), the various contributions in the special issue 'Public Finance and the Environment', *International Tax and Public Finance*, 2/2 (Aug. 1995), and Stiglitz (2000: ch. 9).

[16] Though the taxation to finance the subsidy would itself be distortionary unless levied on a lump-sum basis.

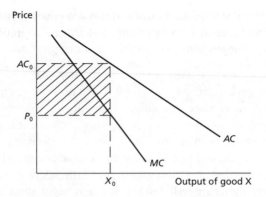

Fig. 4.4. The loss resulting from marginal cost pricing under increasing returns to scale

at least in utilitarian terms, for large-scale, publicly organized welfare-state services; and, to the extent that they support such institutions at all, they justify only a *residual* welfare state.[17]

A more recent body of theory, for which the Nobel Prize was awarded in 2000, focuses on the extent to which economic agents are well informed. Simple theory assumes that consumers know what goods are available and their nature. The assumption can fail because agents may have imperfect knowledge of the *quality* of goods or their *prices*. The literature thus has two strands. The first analyses the effects of imperfect information about quality: consumers might be badly informed (e.g. about the quality of an automobile), so might producers (e.g. about the riskiness of an applicant for insurance or a loan). The resulting literature investigates such topics as 'lemons' and signalling. The second strand, imperfect information about prices, embraces search theory and reservation wages.[18]

As emerges in much of the rest of the book, this literature, particularly the first strand, provides the analytical key to the economic explanation of the welfare state.[19] Complete information requires at least three types of knowledge: about the quality of the product, about prices, and about the future.

QUALITY. The assumption that economic agents have perfect knowledge about the nature of the product (including factor inputs) implies that individuals have well-defined indifference maps, and firms, similarly, well-defined isoquants. This is plausible for some goods (e.g. food), but less so for others. New (1999) distinguishes two distinct problems: an information problem can be solved by providing the relevant information; with an information-*processing* problem, in contrast, the information is so complex that agents cannot make rational choices even if the information is provided. The latter can occur

---

[17] Chapter 2, Section 7.1, explains the distinction between a residual and an institutional welfare state.

[18] See Hirschleifer and Riley (1992), Riley (2001), and the Nobel Symposium in the *American Economic Review*, June 2002 (Akerlof 2002; Spence 2002; and Stiglitz 2002) and the references therein. See also the Further Reading at the end of Chapter 5.

[19] It has also led to major advances in other areas, as suggested in the quote by Stiglitz at the head of the chapter. See the references in the previous note.

(*a*) where the time horizon is long (this can be regarded as in some sense a failure of information), (*b*) where the good or service has a very small probability of harming the individual (the failure in this case is an inability to process small probabilities), or (*c*) where the information is inherently complex.

Where there is a straightforward information failure, the market itself may provide the necessary information. When I buy a house, I do not know whether it is structurally sound, but I can hire the services of a surveyor. More generally, information is available from a large number of consumer publications. In such cases intervention is unnecessary.

Other information failures may justify regulation. Consumers usually have sufficient knowledge about the characteristics of food to choose a reasonably balanced diet, but may be imperfectly informed about the conditions in which the food was prepared. The state therefore intervenes with hygiene laws (i.e. *regulation*), whose effect is to improve consumer information, thereby increasing efficiency.

In contrast, where the issue is an information-processing problem, market outcomes may be less efficient than some sort of administrative solution. Markets are generally more efficient:

(*a*) the better is consumer information,

(*b*) the more cheaply and effectively it can be improved (e.g. computer magazines),

(*c*) the easier it is for consumers to understand available information (i.e. an information problem rather than an information-processing problem),

(*d*) the lower are the costs of choosing badly, and

(*e*) the more diverse are consumer tastes.

Commodities that conform well with these criteria are food and such consumer durables as personal computers and automobiles. As discussed later, health care conforms less well: consumer information is often poor; people generally require individual information, so that the process will not be cheap (violating (*b*)); much of the information is highly technical (violating (*c*)); and the costs of mistaken choice can be high (violating (*d*)). In these circumstances, there may be a justification for *public production and allocation*.

PRICE. Rational choice requires also that agents are perfectly informed about prices—that is, that they face a well-defined budget constraint. This is plausible for commodities like clothes, less so for things like car repairs. Where the assumption fails, the market, again, may supply the necessary information—for example, a house or a piece of jewellery can be professionally valued. In such cases the services of the valuer improve knowledge about prices, and so increase efficiency. Where the market does not resolve the problem, state intervention via *regulation* may be necessary—for instance, a requirement to issue price lists.

It should be noted that rational choice depends on both indifference/isoquant map and budget constraint; hence perfect information is needed about the nature of the product *and* about prices—neither on its own is sufficient. The two together have a critical efficiency role: it is conventionally argued, not least by writers such as Hayek and Friedman, that the advantages of competition are the maximization of consumer choice and the minimization

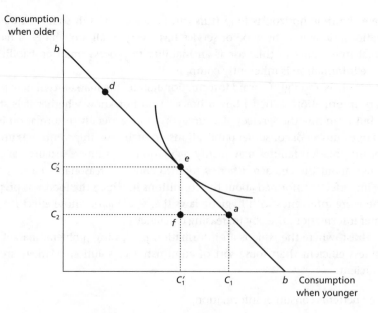

Fig. 4.5. Rational choice in the Fisher model

of cost. Without perfect information, however, agents are unable to exercise their consumer sovereignty rationally; nor can they tell whether competitive cost reductions are associated with an unacceptable reduction in quality. An important conclusion follows—that *the efficiency advantages of perfect competition are contingent on perfect information.*

THE FUTURE. Intertemporal utility maximization requires perfect information also about the future. The simple Fisher model in Figure 4.5 shows the options available to an individual over time. The horizontal axis shows a person's potential consumption in period 1 (her younger years), the vertical axis that in period 2 (her older years). Suppose she has an initial endowment shown by point *a*: she can consume C_1 units in period 1 and C_2 units in period 2. However, she can increase her options by trading with other individuals—that is, by saving or borrowing. For example, she could save $C_1–C_1'$ units of consumption in period 1 in exchange for $C_2'–C_2$ units in period 2, thus moving to point e.[20]

Thus a person whose initial endowment is C_1 in period 1 and C_2 in period 2 faces a lifetime budget constraint $b–b$. The consumption pattern that maximizes lifetime utility is shown by point e, which the person attains by saving $C_1–C_1'$ when younger, making possible consumption of C_2' when older—that is, she redistributes from her younger to

[20] If the interest rate is zero, she can save (say) 1 unit in period 1 and consume an extra unit in period 2. If her initial endowment shown by *a* comprises 7 units in period 1 and 3 units in period 2, she could, by borrowing 3 units, consume 10 units in period 1 and 0 in period 2 or, by saving 7 units, could consume 0 in period 1 and 10 units in period 2, or anywhere in between. Thus her consumption opportunities are shown by a budget constraint with a slope of –1. If the interest rate is 10%, the budget constraint becomes steeper. For each unit she saves in period 1, she receives 1.1 units in period 2. By saving she can therefore move from *a* to *e*. Thus the budget constraint $b–b$ goes through the initial endowment point, *a*, and its slope is determined by the interest rate.

her older self. Similarly, with an initial endowment of d on the same budget constraint, the person could move to e by borrowing in period 1.

The simple model assumes a well-behaved utility function, rational behaviour, certainty, and competitive markets. The assumption of certainty is fundamental. First, it implies perfect information: consumers are well informed about the quality of the goods and services they buy; thus people are assumed to be able to make well-informed choices between different pension schemes, different medical treatments, and different educational activities. Secondly, the assumption rules out stochastic outcomes such as risk (where the probability distribution of outcomes is known) and uncertainty (where it is not). The absence of risk means that there is no need for insurance; it also means, for example, that lenders do not have to form a view about the riskiness of applicants for student loans. The absence of uncertainty rules out common shocks such as inflation.

In a world of certainty, the welfare state has only a small role.

- Insurance is unnecessary, since there is no risk.

- People provide for their old age through voluntary saving, and finance their education by borrowing in perfect capital markets. Thus consumption smoothing takes place through voluntary action using private institutions.

- Transient (i.e. temporary) poverty is also dealt with by borrowing or saving. If the poverty line in period 2 is shown by C_2' in Figure 4.5, someone with an initial endowment of a is poor in period 2, but can deal with the problem by saving in period 1, thus moving from a to e. Dealing with poverty for someone who is not lifetime poor is more akin to consumption smoothing than to traditional poverty relief.

- The only reason for a welfare state in such a world is to provide poverty relief for a person who is lifetime poor—for example, someone with an initial endowment of f in Figure 4.5, whose income is not enough to keep him or her above the poverty line in both periods.

Much of the rest of the book is concerned with relaxing the certainty assumption. Discussion includes (a) imperfect information in product markets, insurance markets, and capital markets, (b) risk and uncertainty, particularly in a context of imperfectly informed insurers, and (c) external shocks—for example, demographic change.

Item (a) is discussed in this chapter. Item (b), risk and uncertainty, creates a need for insurance: I know that I will need food this week and again next week, and shop accordingly; but I do not know how much furniture I will consume over the next ten years because I do not know whether my house will burn down. In such cases, the market solution is actuarial insurance, which gives me certainty, since any losses I suffer will be made good by the insurer. As discussed in Chapter 5, however, technical problems (due largely to information failures in insurance markets) can make private insurance inefficient or impossible. In this case *public funding* might be appropriate. Chapters 8 and 12 discuss insurance against unemployment, ill health, and other contingencies. Finally, (a), (b), and (c) together have major implications for consumption smoothing from middle years to later years to finance retirement pensions (Chapter 9) and to younger years to finance investment in human capital (Chapter 14).

3.3. Policy implications

LESSONS FROM ECONOMIC THEORY. It is important to be clear about what has been said, and what not said, about the size of the public sector. As a theoretical proposition, the market allocates efficiently when *all* the necessary assumptions hold. In such cases intervention on efficiency grounds is neither necessary nor desirable. Where one or more of the assumptions fails, it is necessary in each case to ask three questions.

- Can the market solve the problem itself?
- If not, which type of intervention—regulation, finance, or public production—or mix of interventions might improve efficiency?
- Would intervention be cost effective?

As a practical matter, the necessary conditions rarely apply fully; it is generally sufficient that they are broadly true. Competition may operate with a relatively small number of suppliers, and minor forms of consumer ignorance can often be ignored. Nevertheless, the market's efficiency advantages are tempered by the possibility of market failure and, completely separately, by the fact that market outcomes can be inequitable.

A second lesson is that a prima-facie case for intervention—because one or more assumptions fails significantly—translates into a case for action only if intervention can improve on an imperfect market outcome. Intervention, in short, must be cost effective. This is more likely (*a*) the larger the market failure and (*b*) the more effective and non-corrupt is government. Government failure is discussed in Section 5.

Thirdly, the size of the public sector depends also on demand. If there are only two goods, food (produced privately) and education (produced publicly), the optimal size of the public sector will depend on preferences over food and education, and will vary over time and across countries. Thus the size of the public sector has a political-economy as well as a narrowly economic dimension.

MARKET SUCCESS. Food, by and large, conforms with the standard assumptions. People generally have sufficient information to buy a balanced diet; food prices are known, not least because food is bought frequently; and most people know roughly how much they will need over a given period. Food production and (especially) distribution are competitive; and there are no major market failures. That does not mean that food conforms perfectly. One violation is ignorance about the conditions under which food is produced and about its ingredients. The state therefore intervenes with hygiene regulations; it may also require packaging to display ingredients and a 'sell-by' date. A second potential violation, notwithstanding the availability of information, is that obesity is a growing problem, again suggesting that regulation (e.g. about accurate labelling of the fat, sugar, and salt content of food) might be beneficial. Since such regulation can readily be understood, it enhances consumer information. Even where there are reservations about the effectiveness of regulation, consumer choice and market allocation are more efficient than any alternative, not least because of the enormous diversity of consumer tastes. It is not surprising that there are no serious advocates of a national food service.

Clothing, too, mostly conforms with the assumptions. It can, however, be argued that people are less well informed about the quality of clothing than about food. Yet there is less regulation about the quality of clothing, not least because the costs of mistaken choice are generally much lower than with food. The exceptions—for example, safety clothing and crash helmets—for precisely that reason *are* regulated. Except for these latter cases, it can be argued that, even where an assumption fails, intervention is not cost effective.

Consumer goods such as televisions, washing machines, kitchen appliances, and personal computers fit into the same pattern. The market supplies much information through consumer magazines, newspaper articles, and consumer programmes on radio and television; and aggrieved individuals can seek legal redress. Minor consumer ignorance is ignored where the costs of mistaken choice are small. Where the potential costs of poor quality are larger (e.g. electrical appliances that might catch fire), the appropriate form of intervention is regulation.

Cars raise two sets of issues. On the production side the arguments are similar to those for smaller consumer goods, a key feature being the extent of consumer information about quality. In particular, consumers cannot easily check that a car's brakes and steering are safe and its tyres well designed. Given the high costs of mistaken choice, regulation of such safety features is stringent and continually evolving. So far as the use of cars is concerned, regulation mainly addresses the external costs my driving imposes on others if I drive unsafely (e.g. drink-drive laws), or operate a car in unsafe mechanical condition (worn tyres).

MARKET FAILURE. Since much of the rest of the book discusses areas where—to a greater or lesser extent—markets fail, this section takes only one illustration, health care (discussed in Chapter 12). Since much medical treatment is complex and technical, health care raises not only information problems but also information-processing problems.[21] In addition, knowledge of prices is scant. Nobody knows how much health care he will need and, as shown in Chapters 5 and 12, there are major technical (again, largely information) problems with private medical insurance. It is also argued that health care is not competitive. Finally, some medical care can generate externalities. What type of intervention is then appropriate? Information failures and the lack of competition justify regulation; the externality, coupled with major insurance problems, may justify public funding; and information-processing problems create a strong (though not overriding) argument for public production and allocation.

These arguments, though applied in this book to the components of the welfare state, are general, and it is instructive to apply them to past or present public enterprises well outside the welfare state, such as railways, electricity, telephones, steel, coal and airlines, and to reform in the European former Communist countries.

4. Intervention for reasons of social justice

Different definitions of social justice (or equity) were discussed in Chapter 3. The main questions asked here are: why does redistribution occur; should it be in cash or kind; and is there enough redistribution?

---

[21] The important distinction between an information problem and an information-processing problem is explained in Section 3.2.

4.1. Why does redistribution occur?

COERCED REDISTRIBUTION. According to writers such as Downs (1957) and Tullock (1970),[22] the 'poor', acting as individuals or as part of a coalition, use their voting power to enforce redistribution from the 'rich'. Downs assumes that politicians seek office for reasons of income, status, and power, and therefore choose policies that maximize the votes they receive at the next election; and that citizens vote for the party whose programme promises them the highest expected utility. Since the income distribution in most countries contains relatively few people with high incomes and many with lower incomes, governments maximize votes by redistributing from the rich, thereby gaining the (many more) votes of those with lower incomes.

The logic of the argument is that the system will redistribute towards equality. That equality is not reached is attributed to three countervailing pressures: fear of the efficiency losses of high taxation; the fact that the rich generally have more power; and the fact that the poor might want some inequality to remain, in the hope that they might some day themselves become rich.

Tullock discusses how different income groups might form voting coalitions, noting in particular that any coalition of at least 51 per cent of the electorate must contain not only the very poor but also many in the middle-income group. His theory therefore offers an explanation of the commonly observed phenomenon that public expenditure on the poor is often lower than on the middle-income group (which tends, for example, to make more intensive use of the educational system). There is a direct relationship between these arguments and the government-failure analysis discussed in Section 5.

VOLUNTARY REDISTRIBUTION. According to Downs (1957) and Tullock (1970), redistribution is motivated by selfishness and enforced by political coercion. Hochman and Rodgers (1969), in contrast, recognize the possibility of altruistic motives. Their theory seeks to explain both voluntary giving, and the fact that people with high incomes may vote for political parties which propose to tax them more heavily to finance redistributive policies. At the heart of this approach lies the notion that individual welfares are interdependent.

The simplest explanation of *voluntary* redistribution is based on a particular type of externality. Assume a two-person world with representative 'rich' and 'poor' individuals, R and P. If R is concerned with P's utility as well as his own, both may gain by a gift from R to P. Where redistribution makes some people better off without making anyone worse off, transfers from rich to poor may be justified on quasi-efficiency grounds.[23]

Formal analysis. In the simplest case R and P each has a utility function that is dependent only on his own income. Thus

$$U^R = f(Y^R) \qquad\qquad (4.9)$$

and

$$U^P = f(Y^P), \qquad\qquad (4.10)$$

---

[22] See also Buchanan and Tullock (1962), and, for a non-technical introduction, Tullock (1976).

[23] For a fuller exposition, see Hochman and Rodgers (1969). A similar approach treats the size distribution of income as a public good; see Thurow (1971).

where U^R and U^P are the utilities of the rich and the poor man, respectively, and Y^R and Y^P their incomes. But now suppose that R's utility depends not only on his own income, but also on P's. Then,

$$U^R = f(Y^R, Y^P), f_1 > 0, f_2 \geq 0 \tag{4.11}$$

where f_1 and f_2 are the partial derivatives of U^R with respect to Y^R and Y^P, respectively. There is an externality since *ceteris paribus* R's utility rises with P's income.[24] In this situation redistribution from rich to poor can be rational: it will raise P's utility (because his income goes up) and also R's utility (because of the increase in P's income), so long as

$$\frac{\partial U^R}{\partial Y^P} - \frac{\partial U^R}{\partial Y^R} \geq 0, \tag{4.12}$$

where the first term shows the increase in R's utility as a result of the increase in P's income, and the second the reduction in R's utility because of the reduction in his own income. Voluntary redistribution from R to P will be rational so long as the first term exceeds the second.

Criticisms of voluntarism. This approach leaves no distributional role for the state through compulsory taxation unless voluntarism can be shown to be suboptimal. Two such arguments have been proposed. The first concerns the problem of free-riders, which can arise when the model is extended from the two-person case to the *n*-person. Suppose that it is not the income of specific *individual* poor people that affects the utility of the rich, but the *overall* distribution, which then displays all the characteristics of a public good.

Each individual in society faces the same income distribution. No one can be deprived of the benefits flowing from any particular income distribution. My consumption of whatever benefits occur is not rival with your consumption. In short, the income distribution meets all the tests of a pure public good. Exclusion is impossible; consumption is non-rival; each individual must consume the same quantity. The same problems also occur. *Each individual has a vested interest in disguising his preferences concerning his desired income to avoid paying his optimal share of the necessary transfer payments.* (Thurow 1971: 328–9, emphasis added)

Hence, 'It can be argued that private charity is insufficient because the benefits from it accrue to people other than those who make the gifts . . . [We] might . . . be willing to contribute to the relief of poverty, *provided* everyone else did' (Friedman 1962: 191, emphasis in original).

Formally, suppose that the *i*th rich person in an *n*-person world makes voluntary gifts of g_i. His or her utility is then

$$U_i^R = f(Y_i^R, G), \tag{4.13}$$

where $G = \sum_j g_j$—that is, G is the total sum of voluntary transfers to the poor. G is non-rival and non-excludable: other people's donations are a perfect substitute for one's own

---

[24] In formal terms we are relaxing the assumption that the social-welfare function is additive—see Chapter 6, Section 1.2.

donations. Thus it may be rational for rich people to vote for redistributive taxation, which avoids free-riding. I shall refer to this as 'voluntary compulsion'. Since it is, up to a point, imposed by the rich upon themselves, this is very different from the 'coercion via the ballot box' of Downs and Tullock.

On the other hand, suppose that the externality takes a different form, in which it is not only the *income of the poor* that matters to the rich, but also the *act of giving*—what is known as the 'warm-glow' model. In that case, a rich person is concerned not only with total giving to the poor, G, but also with his or her own giving, g_i. Thus equation (4.13) becomes

$$U_i^R = f(Y_i^R, G, g_i) \tag{4.14}$$

and giving is partly a public good and partly a private good. For the latter reason, free-riding becomes less of a problem.[25]

A second and completely separate criticism of voluntarism is that, if redistribution were *only* that which the rich volunteered, it might be suboptimal even in the absence of free-riders. Suppose the initial situation is shown by point d in Figure 4.3, and the social welfare maximizing distribution by point k (as for Rawls or a socialist). The rich might be prepared through voluntarism to move the distribution from d to f, or through compulsory taxation to e. But if the income externality is 'exhausted' at e then a movement to k, though possibly raising *total* utility, would reduce the utility of the rich. In such a case voluntary transfers would be insufficient to bring about the egalitarian distribution advocated, for example, by Rawls.

It follows, in conclusion, that voluntary redistribution *alone* will be suboptimal unless one believes *both* that free-riding is not a problem *and* that the optimal amount of redistribution is that which the rich wish to volunteer.

4.2. Redistribution in cash or kind?

What, if any, are the arguments for redistribution in kind (i.e. transferring commodities directly to the poor at zero or non-market prices)?

ECONOMIC ARGUMENTS. The efficiency case for overriding consumer sovereignty has two legs.

- Where consumer information is poor *and* an agent's decisions likely to be better, the consumption decision might be more efficient if made on the individual's behalf by an agent. This is the efficiency case for 'merit goods', discussed below, where individual preferences are overridden—for example, parents are obliged to ensure that their children receive education till age 16.

- Even where it might be *desirable* to override preferences, it is *possible* only where the individual cannot subvert the agent's choices. This requires that (*a*) the commodity

---

[25] For precisely this reason, many charitable organizations now attempt to reduce free-riding by assigning a specific, named family to the giver. Attempts have been made to defend voluntarism against the free-rider argument. See Sugden (1983b), Andreoni (1989, 1990), Andreoni and Payne (2003), and, for a survey, Jones and Posnett (1993).

is not easily tradeable (otherwise the individual could sell the good and use the money to finance a different consumption mix), (*b*) the commodity is not easily fungible in family income (otherwise, if given free food, I could buy whisky with the money I would otherwise have spent on food), and (*c*) it not easy to reject the good.

There are two further reasons why policy-makers might wish to override consumer preferences. Individuals may have unequal power, leading to horizontal inequity. In some societies a daughter's income is transferred to her husband's family whereas a son's stays in his parents' household. Parents may therefore give daughters less education or feed them less well. In such circumstances, the freedom of parents might partly be overridden —for instance, through school-feeding programmes. Secondly, consumer sovereignty might be set aside in cases of supply-side disruption (food rations in wartime). The problem is less that market allocation is inefficient than that it is more inequitable than policy-makers regard as tolerable.

This suggests that, in strict economic terms, the use of in-kind transfers for distributional purposes is limited unless they are also justified on *efficiency* grounds.

POLITICAL ECONOMY ARGUMENTS. The counter-argument suggests that it may sometimes be politically easier to redistribute in kind.

Formal analysis. In equation (4.11), the utility of the rich person depends both on his own income, and that of the poor man. But suppose the externality is caused not by P's *income* but by his *consumption*. Then

$$U^R = f(Y^R, C^P) \tag{4.15}$$

where C^P is P's consumption. However, not all increases in C^P will raise the utility of the rich—consumption of alcohol by the poor might not do so. It is necessary to disaggregate so that

$$C^P = G^P + B^P, \tag{4.16}$$

where G^P is 'good' consumption by the poor (children's clothing, basic food), and B^P is 'bad' consumption (whisky, welfare Cadillacs), where 'good' and 'bad' are defined by the rich.

From equations (4.15) and (4.16) we have

$$U^R = f(Y^R, G^P, B^P) \; f_1 > 0, \; f_2 \geq 0, \; f_3 \leq 0, \tag{4.17}$$

where f_1, f_2, and f_3 are the partial derivatives of U^R with respect to Y^R, G^P, and B^P, respectively. R's utility increases with his own income, and with 'good' consumption by P, but decreases with P's 'bad' consumption. In this situation, transfers of 'good' consumption take place as long as

$$\frac{\partial U^R}{\partial G^P} - \frac{\partial U^R}{\partial Y^R} \geq 0, \tag{4.18}$$

where the first term shows the increase in R's utility resulting from the increase in P's 'good' consumption, and the second the decrease in R's utility because of the decrease in his own income.

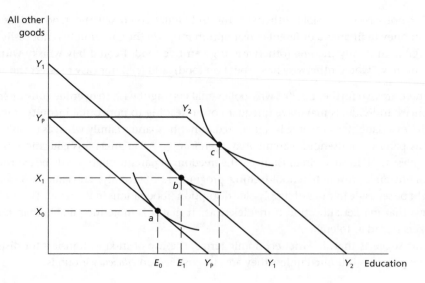

Fig. 4.6. Redistribution in cash and kind

Merit goods. School education is compulsory, irrespective of the wishes of parents or children. As discussed above, if the standard assumptions hold, there is no efficiency justification for merit goods. Figure 4.6 shows how their existence can be explained in political economy terms by a consumption externality. Suppose individual P initially faces the budget constraint $Y_P Y_P$ and maximizes utility by choosing point *a*. Now compare a cash transfer with a compulsory in-kind transfer. Suppose that the cash transfer shifts P's budget constraint out to $Y_1 Y_1$ so that he maximizes utility at point *b*. Alternatively, a compulsory transfer of $Y_2 - Y_P$ units of education shifts P's budget constraint to $Y_2 Y_2$, and utility is maximized at *c*. Given the choice, a rational poor person will favour the in-kind transfer, since *c* is on a higher indifference curve than *b*.

Now consider matters from the viewpoint of individual R. It is clear that the in-kind transfer is more costly (i.e. measuring along the horizontal axis, the in-kind transfer consists of $Y_2 - Y_P$ units of education, whereas the cash transfer buys only $Y_1 - Y_P$ units). However, though R gives up more *income* to finance the in-kind transfer, he might give up less *utility*. In the presence of a consumption externality, an income transfer can reduce the utility of the rich both *per se* and because it might be used by the poor to finance 'bad' consumption. Transfers in kind, though costing more in financial terms, have the advantage, from R's point of view, that they are entirely 'good' consumption. If f_2 in equation (4.17) is large and positive, and f_3 large and negative, then R too might prefer the in-kind transfer.

In this case social welfare might be higher with in-kind transfers, despite the absence of any efficiency reasons for public production or allocation, simply because both rich and poor prefer it that way.

4.3. Horizontal equity

Discussion thus far has concentrated on *vertical equity*—that is, the redistribution of income or consumption from rich to poor. Social justice also involves *horizontal equity*, which concerns goals like minimum standards for certain goods and services, or equal access to them, and equality of opportunity.[26]

MINIMUM STANDARDS are a form of regulation, and may therefore be justified by the failure of one or more of the standard assumptions. This can occur in three ways. Where agents face an information problem, they may be unable to make efficient choices, hence the case for minimum standards of food hygiene, schools, and hospitals. Secondly, if agents have unequal power, they might not be able to enforce their decisions; this justifies regulations about safety standards at work. Finally, there may be externalities. If my house has inadequate sewage disposal, the resulting public-health hazard is an argument for appropriate building codes.[27]

If the standard assumptions hold, however, consumers are able to make rational choices, and to enforce them, provided that they have sufficient income to do so. In such cases, concern with the quality of consumption should manifest itself in income transfers rather than minimum standards, except, possibly, in the presence of consumption externalities. The latter, however, is a dangerous argument, since minimum standards imposed on the poor 'for their own good' (i.e. 'good' consumption) may end up harming the poor if pitched at a higher level than is justified in efficiency terms.

EQUAL ACCESS. Where the standard assumptions hold, the only cause of unequal access is shortage of income. But action to ensure equal access may be justified in particular by imperfect information or unequal power.[28] A case in point is 'know-how', inequality of which is a major cause of inequality generally. Know-how includes understanding the value of education, knowing your legal rights, and your social and professional contacts. In the face of such inequality the state can intervene through regulation (e.g. legislation against discrimination), through subsidy (e.g. legal aid for people with low incomes), or through public production (e.g. the provision of compulsory, free education, which is supposed to be of an equal standard for all).

EQUALITY OF OPPORTUNITY is closely related to equal access. We return to the issue in Chapter 6, Section 3.1.

4.4. Is there enough redistribution?

We saw in Section 2.2 that social justice is concerned with movements along the contract curve towards the optimal distribution. What is that distribution; and have we achieved it?

---

[26] For the place of horizontal equity in the social-welfare-maximization framework of Section 1, see King (1983).

[27] In the light of these theoretical arguments, it is noteworthy that much early social legislation in Britain was concerned with factory conditions and public health—see Chapter 2, Section 1.2.

[28] For a powerful theoretical analysis of how the failure of the equal-power assumption leads to discrimination against women, see Apps (1981) and Apps and Rees (1996).

Libertarians[29] see the optimal distribution as the result of competitive market forces on legally acquired endowments. They support the relief of destitution through voluntary charity, which writers like Nozick regard as the only legitimate method, all redistributive taxation being coercive. It follows from earlier discussion that, if the free-rider problem is non-trivial, voluntary giving will be suboptimal even in libertarian terms. Empirical libertarians such as Hayek and Friedman allow taxation to bring incomes up to subsistence if voluntary giving fails to do so, not least because of the free-rider problem, which Friedman explicitly accepts (see the quote in Section 4.1). However, as discussed in the next section, most libertarians argue that benefits are too high, and therefore that we have *too much* redistribution (see Brittan 1995: ch. 12).

Utilitarians are unsure which distribution maximizes social welfare because of the impossibility of measuring utility cardinally. They are therefore unclear whether there has been too much redistribution or not enough.

Rawls argues unequivocally that goods should be distributed equally unless any other distribution is to the advantage of the least well off. This is not the actual situation, and therefore there has been too little redistribution. Rawls disagrees with the Downs–Tullock argument that democratic politics have resulted in excessive redistribution, arguing that voting and other political activity in practice takes place outside the veil of ignorance. Negotiation is therefore hindered by special pleading, particularly because the rich generally have greater power. The resulting distribution is nowhere near the Rawlsian optimum. Socialists, too, are clear that their goal of equality has not been reached.

5. Public choice and government failure

THE ARGUMENT. Mueller (2003) surveys the public-choice literature, of which this section is a very brief account (see also the Further Reading). There are four explanations of the extent of and growth in government activity. The role of government (*a*) in dealing with market failures and (*b*) as redistributor of income and wealth has been the major focus of this chapter and the previous one. The literature analyses in addition (*c*) the response of government to the electorate in the form of coalitions of voters or through pressure groups, and (*d*) the role of bureaucrats. The government-failure arguments point to the latter two as important distorting influences. The essence of the argument is that government actions are based on self-interest rather than on maximizing social welfare.

The influence of the electorate operates in various ways. The coercion-via-the-ballot-box arguments were discussed in Section 4. Writers such as Buchanan and Tullock (1962) and Tullock (1970, 1971) argue that most transfers from the rich are captured by the middle class through their electoral power as median voters or acting as interest groups. Other arguments stress the broader role of interest groups on redistributive transfers (e.g. the poverty lobby). Interest groups use their lobbying power to bring about redistribution also through regulation. It is argued that regulators are frequently captured by those whom

---

[29] See note 9.

they are supposed to regulate. According to this view, regulation (e.g. of the medical profession) is an entry barrier that allows the extraction of monopoly rent.

Distortions can arise also within government. Public agencies may be run partly for the benefit of the bureaucrats who run them (Niskanen 1971). Such 'organizational slack', it is argued, occurs because politicians cannot fully monitor the actions of utility-maximizing officials.

For one or more of these reasons, it is argued, the size of the public sector may be inefficiently large; or its composition may be distorted to meet the needs of the bureaucracy, powerful interest groups, voters in marginal constituencies, etc.

ASSESSMENT. These insights, however, should not be overstated. Even within a strict utilitarian framework, as discussed in Section 4, writers such as Friedman (1962) and Hochman and Rodgers (1969) explain tax-financed redistribution in ways that do not rely on electoral coercion. Interest groups may enhance efficiency (Becker 1983, 1985). Regulation *may* result in monopoly rents (e.g. doctors in some countries) but, as discussed in Section 3.2, it also serves to protect imperfectly informed consumers (e.g. regulation of medical training).

The power of bureaucrats can be overstated and their motivation misunderstood (Dunleavy 1985). Organizational slack should not be exaggerated: it is reduced by competition between agencies; it can be exploited only where the true benefits and costs of the agency are hard to measure; increases or enlarged departments can be monitored; voters may be able to vote with their feet against high local taxation (Tiebout 1956); and bureaucratic utility maximization can just as easily lead to *less* government (Treasury officials under Margaret Thatcher won favour by cutting expenditure). In addition, organizational slack may be more pronounced where the state regulates private activity than with public production: as discussed in Chapter 12, Section 4.1, countries where private, fee-for-service medical care is publicly funded find it more difficult to contain costs than those with public production.

Nor do the government-failure arguments necessarily apply equally everywhere. Tullock's claim (1971) that benefits go disproportionately to the middle class may be more true of the USA than elsewhere. In Germany and Sweden, for instance, the lowest-income quintile in the mid-1980s received net transfers of about 10 per cent of GDP.

The borderline between the market and the state is discussed further in Section 7.1.

6. From theory towards policy: The issue of privatization

THE CONCEPT OF PRIVATIZATION is by no means simple. A good can be *financed* publicly or privately, and it can be *produced* in either sector; thus there are four cases. Food is generally financed and produced in the private sector (Box 1 of Figure 4.7); at the other extreme, most school education is produced publicly and paid out of tax revenues (Box 4). Two intermediate cases are frequently overlooked. Public transport is produced in the public sector but financed by charges on the private sector (Box 2). Other goods are produced privately but sold to the public sector, including many inputs to the National Health Service—for example, drugs, blankets. Those who favour privatization often mean

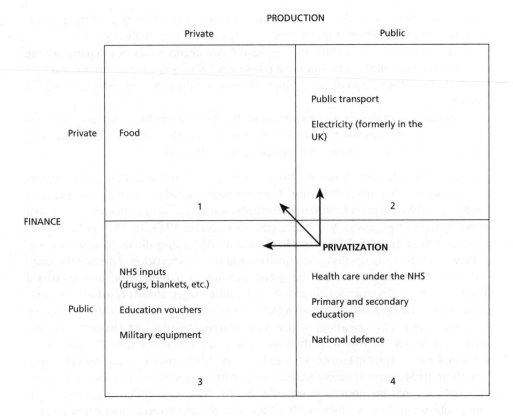

Fig. 4.7. An overview of public and private provision

Note: The examples in boxes 1–4 are only approximate.

a movement from Box 4 to Box 1. But it can be any movement up and/or to the left in Figure 4.7.

This analysis, unfortunately, is too oversimplified to be of much use. Markets in reality are virtually never purely private: food is subject to regulation about quality, and its price is distorted *inter alia* by agricultural subsidies; and it may be purchased out of transfer income (social-security benefits), or provided without charge (free school meals). Nor are there many pure cases of free public provision—for example, charges are levied under the National Health Service for prescriptions and dentistry.

To clarify the situation, even keeping matters as simple as possible, it is necessary to distinguish not only (*a*) in which sector *production* takes place and (*b*) which sector *finances* it, but also the influence of *regulation*, in particular of (*c*) the total quantity produced of any good and (*d*) how much each individual consumer receives. These are illustrated in Table 4.1, though the analysis is still far from exhaustive. The first part shows different examples of private production. Row 1 (which corresponds to Box 1 in Figure 4.7) shows the pure private case—for example, food purchased out of non-transfer income. Production is private, and total supply determined by producers; individuals decide how

Table 4.1 Public and private provision: A more complete view

Type of allocation	Production (1)	Regulation: Decision about total production (2)	Regulation: Decision about individual consumption (3)	Finance (4)	Examples
1. Pure private (= Box 1 in Figure 4.7)	PRIVATE		PRIVATE	PRIVATE	Food purchased out of non-transfer income
2. Private market plus state finance (income subsidy)	Private		Private	Public	All consumption of privately produced goods purchased out of transfer income; food stamps, Medicare, and Medicaid (USA)
3. Private market plus regulation					
(a) regulation of individual consumption	Private		Public	Private	Mandatory automobile insurance
(b) regulation of total supply	Private	Public	Private	Private	Health care (Canada, approx.)
4. Private production, state regulation and finance (= Box 3 in Figure 4.7)					
(a) supply wholly private	Private	Private	Public	Public	Education vouchers
(b) total supply determined by state	Private	Public	Public	Public	Inputs for NHS and national defence
5. Public production, private allocation and finance (= Box 2 in Figure 4.7)					
(a) total supply determined by private demand	Public	Private	Private	Private	Public transport
(b) supply wholly public	Public		Private	Private	NHS pay beds
6. Public apart from private finance	Public		Public	Private	National insurance (UK), health-care insurance (Canada, approx.)
7. Public apart from private consumption decision	Public		Private	Public	Post-compulsory education
8. Pure public (= Box 4 in Figure 4.7)	PUBLIC		PUBLIC	PUBLIC	NHS, national defence

Note: The examples are only approximate.

much to consume, and pay for it themselves. Row 2 is identical except that individual consumption is financed by the state. The simplest case is food purchased out of transfer income; other examples are food stamps, Medicare, and Medicaid in the USA. Row 3 illustrates a private market subject to regulation. In row 3(*a*) the individual-consumption decision is made by the state (mandatory automobile insurance); in row 3(*b*) the state puts a ceiling on total production, though allocation to individuals remains private (very roughly the case of health care in Canada). Row 4 illustrates private production modified by both regulation and finance (i.e. roughly Box 3 in Figure 4.7). In row 4(*a*) production decisions are wholly private (e.g. education vouchers). Row 4(*b*) shows the case where allocation and finance are wholly public, but production itself takes place in the private sector (National Health Service inputs such as blankets and X-ray machines, certain types of military equipment).

The second half of the table looks at public production. In row 5(*a*) output is produced in the public sector but allocated and financed privately (public transport); in row 5(*b*) supply is determined publicly, but demand decisions and finance are private (pay beds in Health Service hospitals). These cases approximate Box 2 in Figure 4.7. Row 6 covers public production and allocation with private finance—for example, social insurance. Row 7 illustrates public production and finance, though the individual consumption decision is private—for example, secondary education after minimum school-leaving age. Pure public production is shown in row 8 (i.e. Box 4 in Figure 4.7); examples include (as approximations) compulsory school education, the National Health Service, and national defence.

We can now see what privatization means. Libertarians favour private production under column (1), producer and consumer sovereignty under columns (2) and (3), and private finance under column (4). They would therefore choose row 1 or, failing that, the private market underwritten by income transfers, shown in row 2. Privatization can therefore be seen as an upward movement in the table from a lower line to a higher.

THE ISSUES. How, then, should proposals for privatization be analysed? Section 3 argued that, where the standard assumptions all hold, there are no efficiency grounds for intervention, and distributional objectives are generally best approached through income transfers.

The issues raised by the privatization debate (see the Further Reading) fall naturally into this framework. It is necessary to consider the extent to which any activity conforms with the standard assumptions. And in this context information problems assume considerable importance. Because of technological change over the century, the optimal scale of many types of industry is large; and in any large organization information (i.e. management) problems are likely to arise whether the industry is public or private. It is, therefore, not surprising that 'the fundamental problems concerned with the control of public utilities are very similar, irrespective of whether they are in the public or private sectors' (Webb 1984: 99).

Whatever the answers about privatization, the technical element of analysis should not be obscured by ideology, an observation that leads naturally to the final part of the chapter.

7. Conclusion: Economic and political theory

7.1. Drawing the borderlines between government and markets

This section brings together the analysis of Chapters 3 and 4. The efficiency arguments for intervention were set out in Section 3, and the government-failure counter-arguments in Section 5. The important contribution of the public-choice literature is that analysis of government should treat its activities as endogenous. It does not, however, follow that the social-welfare outcome of the political marketplace is necessarily inferior to that of conventional markets. Markets can be efficient or inefficient; so can governments. Thus market failure is a counterpoint to government failure.

Inman's survey (1987) concluded:

Markets fail. They fail for the fundamental reason that the institution of market trading cannot enforce cooperative behavior on self-seeking, utility-maximizing agents, and cooperative behavior between agents is often required for beneficial trading. In each instance of market failure . . . agents were asked to reveal information about their benefits or costs from trades with no guarantee that that information would not be used against them. Without that guarantee, information is concealed, trades collapse, and the market institution fails.   (p. 672)

While democratic processes do not generally guarantee an efficient allocation of social resources, *we cannot go the next step and conclude that collectively-decided allocations . . . are inferior to individually-decided market allocations.*   (p. 727, emphasis added)

neither the institution of markets, or voluntary trading, nor the institution of government, or collectively decided and enforced trading, stands as *the* unarguably preferred means for allocating societal resources. Each institution has its strengths and its weaknesses.   (p. 753, emphasis in original)

Libertarians properly criticize a naïve predisposition towards state intervention at the slightest sign of problems in private markets; but to argue that public-sector inefficiency *automatically* implies that private markets increase social welfare is to make the same mistake. Decisions about the borderline between market and state involve judgement, so that different interpretations are possible. Le Grand (1987*b*), with echoes of Tullock (1971) (though from a very different perspective), argues that the UK welfare state has been 'captured' by the middle class, and goes on to suggest that this is a matter for ambivalence. It is 'bad' because the welfare state's major benefits should go to the poor; but it is 'good' because it keeps the articulate middle class as consumers of the welfare state, creating pressure to maintain standards. The arguments above suggest that we should not be ambivalent: as subsequent chapters explain, many parts of the welfare state are a response to pervasive technical problems in private markets, and therefore serve not only the distributional and other objectives listed in Chapter 1, Section 2.2 (poverty relief, vertical and horizontal equity, dignity and social solidarity), but also efficiency objectives such as consumption smoothing and insurance. As such, the welfare state exists quite properly both for lower-income groups *and* for the middle class. In the Wilensky and Lebeaux (1965) sense discussed in Chapter 2, Section 7.1, there is an *efficiency* case for an institutional welfare state.

7.2. Achieving policy aims: A liberal view

The vital distinction between the *objectives* of policy and the *methods* available to achieve them should by now be clear. Objectives include social justice and economic efficiency: the definition of social justice will vary with different theories of society (Chapter 3); economic efficiency has broadly the same meaning in all theories of society (Section 2). Methods embrace income transfers and direct intervention in the market through regulation, finance, and public production. The resulting form of economic organization, at one extreme, is the free market (with or without redistribution) and, at the other, central planning and public production of all basic goods and services (with or without charges). In between are different types of mixed economy involving both private markets (with or without intervention in the form of regulation and finance) and public production.

The central argument of this book is that the proper place of ideology is in the choice of objectives, particularly in the definition of social justice and in its trade-off with economic efficiency; but, *once objectives have been agreed*, the choice of method should be regarded as a *technical* issue much more than an ideological one. Whether a particular good or service is provided publicly or privately should depend on which method more nearly achieves the chosen objectives. Market versus state provision is thus a contingent matter rather than an item of dogma, and in that sense this book is firmly in the liberal tradition.[30]

How, then, should we choose between different methods? The analysis of Section 3 suggests:

Proposition 1: efficiency. Where one or more of the standard assumptions fails, state intervention in the form of regulation, finance, or public production may increase economic efficiency. If none of the assumptions fails, efficiency is generally best achieved without intervention.

Proposition 2: social justice. Setting political-economy arguments (Section 4.2) to one side:

(a) Only efficiency arguments can justify intervention other than cash redistribution. If no efficiency justification exists, social justice is likely to be served best by *income* transfers.

(b) But if analysis suggests that efficiency will be furthered by public production and allocation of any good or service, then social justice can be enhanced by *in-kind* transfers, e.g. redistribution in the form of free education or health care.

There are three possible exceptions to Proposition 2. The first is political-economy arguments, which may support transfers in kind even where there are no efficiency grounds for public production or allocation. The second concerns the role of giving. There is no technical argument against having a market for babies. But most societies rule this out on ethical grounds. It is argued, for instance, that health care might more appropriately be regarded as a gift than a purchase, and Titmuss (1970) makes a cogent argument for blood to be treated in this way.

---

[30] For a classic defence of the mixed economy on broadly similar grounds, see Okun (1975).

The optimal taxation literature (see the Further Reading) offers the third exception. The taxation necessary to finance income transfers may reduce labour supply; if so, a given distributional objective *may* be possible at lower efficiency cost by subsidizing the *prices* of goods consumed by the poor. The result requires (*a*) that such goods are consumed only (or mainly) by the poor, and (*b*) that their consumption is not strongly complementary to leisure.

From a purely theoretical viewpoint, this suggests that the two propositions can be criticized for their 'piecemeal' approach—that is, for discussing conformity with the standard assumptions in a given area while implicitly assuming that they hold in all other areas. This ignores second-best considerations (Lipsey and Lancaster 1956). Several defences are possible. First, in a limited number of cases the approach is *theoretically* valid (Davis and Whinston 1965). Secondly, the measurement problems involved in applying the optimal taxation approach to policy are intractable. Thirdly, none of the areas covered by the welfare state conforms closely with the two conditions at the end of the previous paragraph.

Finally, I want to nail a wholly fallacious line of argument. In one form it runs, 'we must have a National Health Service because otherwise the poor could not afford adequate health care'—an argument that does the cause of its proponents little service. The fallacy is that, if inability to pay were the *only* difficulty, there would not be a *market-allocation problem* but an *income-distribution problem*, which could be solved by income transfers, as currently with food. The justification for the National Health Service, as argued in Chapter 12, lies not in Proposition 2(*a*) (which applies to food) but in Proposition 2(*b*).

Even more woolly is the assertion that 'we must have a National Health Service because everybody has a right to health care'. The fallacy lies in the word 'because'. It can equally be argued that everybody has a right to good nutrition, yet there are few advocates of a national food service. The statement confuses objectives with methods. There is wide acceptance of the value judgement that people have a right to adequate nutrition and health care. These are *objectives*; but the existence of these rights does not, *per se*, have any implications for the best method of achieving them. As we shall see, there are good reasons why the UK has a National Health Service but not a national food service—entitlement to food and health care, however, is not one of them.

7.3. The debate with libertarians

Propositions 1 and 2 would meet with general agreement from liberals and democratic socialists. Marxists would reject them for the reasons discussed in Chapter 3, Section 5. They accept the idea of social justice, but argue that too little has been done to achieve it. The efficiency arguments embodied in Proposition 1 are in large measure rejected because the market system, though possibly in some respects efficient, is the fundamental *cause* of the failure to achieve social justice.

The debate with empirical libertarians such as Hayek and Friedman is in many ways the most instructive. The less interesting part of the argument is ideological. Libertarians reject almost in their entirety the social-justice arguments of Section 4, and in consequence reject Proposition 2. Hayek argues (Chapter 3, Section 2) that there is no such thing as social justice, and that its quest risks eventual totalitarianism. Libertarians argue—largely for the government-failure reasons set out in Section 5—that there is too much redistribution, and that redistribution in kind is even more dangerous than transfers in cash. Taken as an ideological view, little counter-argument is possible, save to assert a different set of values.

The debate over efficiency is much more important. As we saw in Chapter 3, Section 2, empirical libertarians are the direct descendants of Classical liberalism (compare the views in Friedman (1962: ch. 2) on the role of the state with those of Adam Smith quoted at the head of Chapter 1). Writers such as Hayek and Friedman therefore admit a limited role for the state in the presence of market failures, and both accept a very restricted welfare state. Beyond this, however, both would resist the efficiency arguments of Section 3. State intervention, it is argued, is often the *cause* of imperfect information rather than its result (e.g. if there were a competitive market for health care, people would acquire better information, in part because market institutions would arise to supply it). They support intervention to break monopolies or near-monopolies in product and (particularly) factor markets, and argue that domestic monopolies of tradeable goods need not be a problem if there are no barriers to trade. As a result they argue that state intervention is excessive.

In sum, libertarians such as Hayek and Friedman accept the analytical framework of Section 3, but interpret facts differently. To that extent the debate is empirical. But it is also (and importantly) theoretical. What is not in dispute is the aim of maximizing social welfare, nor the existence of imperfections in the form of monopolies, externalities, public goods, and increasing returns to scale. The critical difference, as suggested in Section 3, is that the analysis of Hayek and Friedman takes little account of information problems. These afflict consumers of increasingly complex products, and managers of increasingly large-scale enterprises, and they include technical—again largely information—problems in insurance markets (Chapter 5). The existence of information problems, more than any other theoretical consideration, suggests that a properly designed welfare state is much more than an instrument of social justice. It also has a major efficiency role.

■ QUESTIONS FOR FURTHER DISCUSSION

1. 'The best form of government intervention is no intervention at all.' Discuss.

2. Why not leave redistribution to private charity?

3. Should government intervene for all market failures?

4. [More difficult] 'If all information problems could be solved, there would be no need for a welfare state.' Discuss.

FURTHER READING

The most comprehensive treatment of the subject matter of this chapter is Atkinson and Stiglitz (1980: lectures 11–18), Stiglitz (1989, 1993), and Salanié (2000), or, at a less technical level, Stiglitz (2000: chs. 3, 4) or Rosen (2002: chs. 4–7). For a gentler introduction to the economic theory of markets and welfare economics, see Le Grand et al. (1992: chs. 1, 2), Stiglitz and Walsh (2002: chs. 2, 4, 10, 14–16); and Begg et al. (2003: chs. 15, 16), also Baumol and Blinder (2000) (elementary) or Varian (2002) (intermediate). Barr (1994a) covers similar theoretical ground at a non-technical level with particular reference to the former Communist countries of Central and Eastern Europe and the former Soviet Union. For a lucid, non-technical discussion of efficiency, equity, and their trade-off, see Okun (1975) (a classic, strongly recommended defence of the mixed economy) and Le Grand (1991a: ch. 3) and, for wide-ranging discussion, Brittan (1995) and Kay (2003). References to the literature on information problems are given in the Further Reading at the end of Chapter 5.

For a simple introduction to the theory of externalities, see Le Grand et al. (1992: ch. 2) and, for fuller discussion of market failures, Stiglitz (2000: chs. 4, 6) or Rosen (2002: chs. 4, 5). A complete technical account of the optimal taxation literature and the trade-off between efficiency and equity is given by Atkinson and Stiglitz (1980: lectures 11–18); for less technical discussion, see Stiglitz (2000: ch. 20) or Rosen (2002: ch. 14).

Different definitions of equity are discussed in Chapter 3; for an excellent brief summary, see also Le Grand (1984). A non-technical introduction to the theory of coerced redistribution through the ballot box is given by Tullock (1976), and in more complete form by Downs (1957) and Tullock (1970). The theory of voluntary (Pareto optimal) redistribution is developed by Hochman and Rodgers (1969); see also Thurow (1971). For general discussion of the economics of charity, see Sugden (1983b) (a simple introduction), and for a more complete treatment Sugden (1982, 1984) and the discussion in Collard (1983) and Sugden (1983a). The literature on the economics of charity is surveyed by Jones and Posnett (1993) and the references therein.

The large literature on public choice is surveyed by Mueller (2003); for a shorter summary, see Stiglitz (2000: ch. 7).

For argument about privatization in the context of the welfare state, and public enterprise generally, see the contributions in Le Grand and Robinson (1984). For more general discussion, see Vickers and Yarrow (1988), Boardman and Vining (1989), Galal et al. (1994), Megginson et al. (1994), and Stiglitz (2000: chs. 8, 12, 14, 16). On privatization in the former Communist countries, see Megginson and Netter (2001) and Estrin (2002).

Appendix: Non-technical summary of Chapter 4

1. Chapter 4 sets out the economic theory of state intervention, with particular emphasis on why intervention might foster efficiency and/or social justice (also referred to as equity).

The efficiency objective

2. *The meaning of economic efficiency.* Efficiency is concerned with making the best use of limited resources given people's tastes and available technology. A key underlying concept is that of *resource scarcity*—that is, if resources (labour, capital, raw materials, land) are used for one purpose they cannot be used for another (this is what economists mean by *opportunity cost*). Since those resources are limited, it follows that output is limited. Thus it is not possible to satisfy everyone's demands completely: policy should seek to satisfy people as much as possible—that is, should seek to use limited resources as effectively as possible. This is precisely what economic efficiency is about. As discussed in Section 2.1, the efficient (or Pareto optimal) output of any good is the quantity that maximizes the excess of benefits over costs. This is the output X^* in Figure 4.1 at which the value placed by society on the marginal unit of output equals its marginal social cost (see Le Grand et al. 1992: 9–14).

3. *A Pareto improvement* (i.e. an increase in efficiency) takes place if any change in production or distribution makes one person better off without making anyone else worse off.

4. *Efficiency and ideology.* Section 2.2 shows that an increase in efficiency can raise welfare under any of the theories of society discussed in Chapter 3. The aim of efficiency is therefore common to all these ideologies, though the weight attached to it will vary when its achievement conflicts with distributional goals.

Intervention for reasons of efficiency

5. The state can intervene in four ways (Section 3.1).

- *Regulation* mainly concerns the quality of supply (e.g. hygiene laws relating to food, minimum building standards) and the quantity of individual demand (e.g. the legal requirement to attend school, compulsory membership of national insurance).

- *Finance* can involve subsidies (or taxes) that change the price of specific commodities. Subsidies can be partial (e.g. local-authority housing) or total (e.g. free drugs under the National Health Service).

- *Public production* covers defence, education, and in some countries health care.

These three types of intervention all involve direct interference in the market mechanism.

- *Income transfers* do not do so directly, but enable recipients to buy goods of their choice at market prices—for example, elderly people receive a retirement pension with which they buy food.

6. *The invisible-hand theorem* asserts that markets are efficient if and only if a number of assumptions hold (Section 3.2). These conditions (collectively called the standard assumptions) are discussed in paragraphs 7–16 below, which, together with paragraphs 22–6, summarize the theoretical heart of the book. The conditions relate to perfect information, perfect competition, and the absence of market failures.

7. *Perfect information* implies, first, that consumers and firms are well informed about the nature of the product, and also about prices. This is plausible for some goods (e.g. food and clothing), less so for others (e.g. health care). Where the assumption fails, several solutions are possible: the market itself may develop institutions to supply information (e.g. professional valuers, consumer magazines); or the state may respond with regulations (e.g. hygiene laws in the case of food); where information problems are serious, the market might be so inefficient that public production might be a better answer.

8. Individuals need perfect information also about the future, so as to make rational choices over time. This is broadly true of food (since I know that I will need to eat tomorrow, next week, next month); it is not true with motor cars, because I do not know whether my car will be involved in an accident. The market can frequently cope with this sort of uncertainty through the mechanism of insurance (the main topic of Chapter 5). But private insurance can be inefficient or impossible, largely because of information problems in insurance markets. Thus some risks (e.g. unemployment) are not insurable. In such cases public funding may increase efficiency.

9. *Perfect competition* must apply in all input and output markets and also to capital markets (i.e. access to borrowing). Two conditions must hold: individuals must be price-takers; and they must have equal power.

10. Price taking implies free entry and exit into/from an industry with a large number of consumers and firms, none of whom individually is able to influence market prices. Where the assumption fails (e.g. in the case of a monopoly), intervention generally involves regulation (e.g. a price ceiling) or an appropriate mix of taxation and subsidy.

11. Equal power is violated by any difference (apart from differences in individual incomes) in the ability of individuals to choose their consumption. The assumption rules out all forms of discrimination; where it fails, solutions (where they exist) generally involve regulation.

12. *Market failures* arise in three forms: public goods, external effects, and increasing returns to scale.

13. *Public goods* in their pure form exhibit three technical characteristics: non-rivalness in consumption; non-excludability; and non-rejectability. Private (i.e. 'normal') goods are rival in consumption in the sense that if I buy a cheese sandwich there will be one sandwich less available for everyone else; excludability means that I can be prevented from consuming the sandwich until I have paid for it; and rejectability implies that I do not have to eat it unless I wish to. Not all goods display these characteristics, the classic example being national defence. If the Royal Air Force is circling over the UK, the arrival of an additional person does not reduce the amount of defence available to everyone else (non-rivalness in consumption); nor is it possible to exclude a new arrival by saying that the bombs will be allowed to fall on him until he has paid his taxes (non-excludability); nor is the individual able to reject the defence on the grounds of pacifist beliefs (non-rejectability). Similar considerations apply wholly or in part to roads, public parks, and television broadcast signals.

14. In discussing public goods, an important distinction should be noted. For a private good the marginal cost associated with an *extra unit of output* and the marginal cost of an *extra user* are one and the same thing—if it costs £1 to produce an extra cheese sandwich, it also costs £1 to provide for an extra cheese-sandwich-consumer. But this identity does not hold for public goods—the marginal cost, for example, of an extra hour's broadcasting is positive and generally large, whereas the marginal cost of an extra viewer is zero. This has important implications. If a public good is provided at all, non-excludability makes it impossible to charge for it (this is the *free-rider* problem); in such cases the market will generally fail entirely. Non-rivalness implies that the marginal cost of an extra user (though *not* of an extra unit of output) is zero, and therefore the efficient price should

be based not on costs, but on the value placed by each individual on an extra unit of consumption. Since the latter is impractical, the market is likely to produce an inefficient level of output. Thus the market is either inefficient or fails altogether; if the good is to be provided at all, it will generally have to be publicly produced.

15. *External effects* arise when an act of individual A imposes costs or confers benefits on individual B, for which no compensation from A to B or payment from B to A takes place, or, more formally, when A's utility or production function is interrelated with B's. The effect of externalities is to create a divergence between private and social costs and benefits. As a result, the market output in the presence of an external cost will generally exceed the efficient output, X^* in Figure 4.1, and vice versa for an external benefit. On occasion the market can resolve this inefficiency itself. Coase (1960) shows that, where the law assigns unambiguous and enforceable property rights, the externality problem may be solved by negotiation between the parties concerned. But this is not always possible—for instance, where property rights are not enforceable (air pollution) or where large numbers of people are involved (traffic congestion). In this case intervention may be justified either through regulation (e.g. mandatory filtering equipment) or via an appropriate tax (sometimes referred to as a Pigovian tax) on the activity generating the external cost (e.g. a congestion charge) (see Le Grand et al. 1992: ch. 2; Stiglitz 2000: ch. 4).

16. *Increasing returns to scale* arise when doubling all inputs leads to more than twice the output. If a production function exhibits increasing returns to scale at all levels of output, average cost will always exceed marginal cost, as in Figure 4.4. It follows that, at an output of X_0, the marginal cost price P_0 is less than average cost, AC_0. Hence competitive pricing results in an inherent loss, shown by the shaded area. If firms in a competitive industry make long-run losses, they will leave the industry, which will become monopolized or, if even a monopolist is unable to make a profit, will cease to exist. The result, therefore, is a suboptimal output or a failure by the market to produce at all. Two solutions are possible: paying firms a lump-sum subsidy equal to the loss associated with competitive pricing; or nationalizing the industry and paying an identical subsidy. The appropriate intervention is therefore subsidy or public production, or both.

17. The market will allocate efficiently only when *all* the assumptions in paragraphs 7–16 hold, in which case no intervention on efficiency grounds is necessary. Where one or more of the assumptions fails, it is necessary in each case to consider which type of intervention (regulation, finance, or public production) is most likely to improve efficiency.

Intervention for reasons of social justice

18. Section 4.1 sets out two broad explanations of why redistribution occurs. To libertarians it is enforced on the rich by the voting power of the poor. Utilitarians argue that the rich may *choose* out of altruistic motives to vote for political parties that propose to tax them more heavily to finance redistributive policies.

19. In certain circumstances there may be political-economy arguments for direct in-kind transfers —for instance, of education. The formal analysis (based on the idea of a consumption externality) is shown by the voting model in Section 4.2. Suppose the utility[31] of rich individual, R, rises with his own consumption, and also with the consumption of poor man, P. In particular, suppose that R's utility rises with 'good' consumption by P (e.g. education), but falls with P's 'bad' consumption (e.g. whisky), where 'good' and 'bad' are defined by R. In this circumstance it might be rational for R to offer P an education costing (say) £1,000, but to offer a cash transfer of only £200 (since P

---

[31] See the Glossary.

might spend the latter in part on 'bad' consumption). Faced with these offers, P might prefer the in-kind transfer to the lower cash sum (see Figure 4.6)—that is, both rich and poor might vote for compulsory in-kind transfers.

Privatization

20. The term 'privatization' is more complicated than many of its users realize (Section 6). As a first approximation, commodities like food are *produced* and *financed* privately whereas, at the opposite extreme, most school education is produced in the public sector and paid for out of tax revenues. But intermediate cases are possible (Figure 4.7). Some goods are publicly produced, but are financed by user charges (e.g. public transport); others are paid from tax revenues but produced in the private sector (e.g. pharmaceutical drugs under the National Health Service).

21. Matters become considerably more complicated when regulation is included. It is then necessary to distinguish not only the sector in which (*a*) production and (*b*) finance take place, but also who decides (*c*) how much in total of any good will be produced and (*d*) how much each individual consumer will receive. Some of these cases are set out in Table 4.1.

Achieving the aims of policy

22. Section 7 draws together the main arguments of Chapters 3 and 4 by repeating the distinction between the *objectives* of policy and the *methods* available to achieve them. Objectives embrace social justice and economic efficiency; methods include income transfers and direct interference in the market through regulation, subsidy, or public production.

23. The central argument of this book is that the proper place of ideology is in the choice of objectives, particularly the definition of social justice and its trade-off with economic efficiency; but, once these aims have been agreed, the choice of method should be regarded as mainly a *technical* issue, not an ideological one. Whether a good like health care is produced publicly or privately should be decided on the basis of which method more closely achieves agreed objectives. A rationale for choosing between the different methods is given in Section 7.2 in the form of two propositions.

24. *Proposition 1: efficiency.* Where one or more of the standard assumptions fails, state intervention in the form of regulation, finance, or public production may increase economic efficiency. If none of the assumptions fails, the efficiency aim is generally achieved best by the market with no intervention.

25. *Proposition 2: social justice.* Subject to minor qualifications it is possible to argue:

(*a*) Only efficiency arguments can justify intervention other than cash redistribution. If no such efficiency justification exists, the interests of social justice are best served by *income* transfers.

(*b*) But if there exist arguments that suggest that efficiency will be furthered by public production and allocation of any good or service, then social justice can be enhanced by *in-kind* transfers (e.g. redistribution in the form of free education or health care).

26. The two propositions make the issue of market versus public production and allocation a contingent matter, placing this book firmly in the liberal tradition (as defined in Chapter 3, Section 1). The debate between this book and libertarian writers such as Hayek and Friedman is set out in Section 7.3.

5 Economic theory 2: Insurance

Insurance, *n*. An ingenious modern game of chance in which the player is permitted to enjoy the comfortable conviction that he is beating the man who keeps the table.

(Ambrose Bierce, 1842–1914)

1. Introduction

The term 'insurance'[1] is used by different people to mean different things:

- as a device that offers individuals *protection against risk*, or
- as an *actuarial mechanism* (equation 5.12), normally organized in the private sector.

The first defines insurance in terms of its objective, the second in terms of a method by which that objective might be pursued. Even where institutions are not insurance in the second sense, they might still be insurance in that they offer protection against risk.

It is possible to insure against many common mishaps such as burglary, death, or car accidents, and for holiday deposits lost through illness. It is even possible to buy life insurance for one's dog or cat. On the face of it this is curious, since insurance companies usually make a profit: thus a representative individual receives less in benefit in the long run than he pays in contributions.

This gives rise to two questions: why do people insure voluntarily; and under what conditions will the private market provide insurance? These questions concerning, respectively, the demand and supply sides of the insurance market are discussed in Sections 2 and 3. Section 4 considers the circumstances in which a market equilibrium will exist, and will be efficient. Many of the problems discussed are examples of a more general class of information problem (see the Further Reading). The parallels will be noted as we proceed.

---

[1] Non-technical readers can find the gist of the argument in the Appendix at the end of the chapter.

2. The demand for insurance

2.1. Individual demand

Why might a rational individual choose to insure when the expected pay-out is less than his premium payments? The answer, if he is risk averse, is that uncertainty *per se* causes disutility; hence certainty is a commodity yielding positive marginal utility, for which he will pay a positive price. The formal argument starts with the definition of a risk-averse individual as someone with diminishing marginal utility of income, shown in Figure 5.1.[2] Suppose there is a 'bad' outcome, y_1, yielding utility $U(y_1)$, and a 'good' outcome, y_2, yielding utility $U(y_2)$, occurring with probabilities p_1 and p_2, respectively. The individual's expected income and expected utility are:

$$\text{expected income: } E(y) = \bar{y} = p_1 y_1 + p_2 y_2, \tag{5.1}$$

$$\text{expected utility: } E(U) = \bar{U} = p_1 U(y_1) + p_2 U(y_2). \tag{5.2}$$

If $p_1 = p_2 = 0.5$, expected income, $\bar{y}$, is midway between y_1 and y_2 (if $y_1 = £100$ and $y_2 = £1,000$, then $\bar{y} = £550$); and expected utility, $\bar{U}$, is midway between $U(y_1)$ and $U(y_2)$.

It is important to realize that a risk-averse individual can obtain the utility $\bar{U}$ in two entirely different ways.

- It could be obtained as the *expected* utility from an uncertain income of y_1 or y_2. Note that the individual never receives $\bar{y}$; each year she receives *either* y_1 or y_2 with corresponding utilities $U(y_1)$ and $U(y_2)$; the expected (or average) outcome is $\bar{y}$.

- Alternatively, she could obtain $\bar{U}$ from a *certain* income y^*, as shown directly by the utility function in Figure 5.1. When a person insures, what she is buying is *certainty*.

A rational individual will be indifferent between (*a*) an expected income $\bar{y}$ arising from uncertain outcomes y_1 and y_2 and (*b*) a lower income y^*, with certainty. The value of certainty is thus

$$V = \bar{y} - y^* \tag{5.3}$$

and a rational individual will pay a net price, ϕ, so long as:

$$\phi < V. \tag{5.4}$$

The net price of insurance, ϕ, should be carefully distinguished from the gross premium. The difference is shown in Table 5.1, where the insurance company charges an annual premium of £550, and compensates for up to £900 of lost income. In a 'good' year the individual has an income of £1,000, and pays a gross premium of £550, leaving a net income of £450. In a 'bad' year her income is £100; she pays a premium of £550 but receives compensation of £900. Thus the effect of insurance is to guarantee a net income of £450.

---

[2] For an introduction, see Varian (2002: ch. 12), Begg et al. (2003: ch. 13), and the Further Reading.

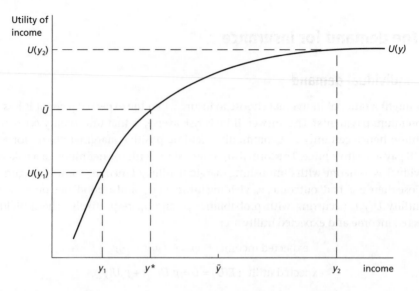

Fig. 5.1. The demand for insurance by a rational risk-averse individual

Table 5.1. Gross and net insurance premiums, and net income in good and bad years (£)

Income, insurance premium, and benefit	Good year	Bad year
1. Income	1,000	100
2. Insurance premium	550	550
3. Insurance benefit	—	900
4. Net Income ((1) − (2) + (3))	450	450
5. Net Premium ((2) − (4))	100	100

The net premium, ϕ, is the difference between the gross premium and the average payout. The latter is the individual's expected loss

$$E(L) = pL, \tag{5.5}$$

defined as the size of the loss, L, times the probability, p, that it will occur. Thus the net price of insurance is

$$\phi = \pi - pL, \tag{5.6}$$

where π is the gross premium. In the example, the individual's expected loss is £450; so £450 of the gross premium can be regarded as a form of saving to cover her own losses in the long run. The *net* price of insurance is £100, which the individual will pay so long as it does not exceed the value to her of certainty, V, in equation (5.3). We return to the calculation of insurance premiums in Section 3.1.

2.2. The nature of the product: Insurance as a mechanism for pooling risk

The twin intellectual bases of insurance are the law of large numbers and gains from trade. Under the former, *individuals* may face uncertainty, but groups can face approximate certainty—for example, I do not know whether I will die this year, but the death rate for men aged 50 to 65 is known and stable. It is the relative certainty about the *aggregate* probability resulting from the law of large numbers that opens up to individuals the possibility of exploiting gains from trade by agreeing to pool risks.

Suppose each individual's income is a random variable y with mean, μ, and variance, $\text{var}(y)$; there are N such individuals with incomes $y_1, y_2, \ldots y_N$, respectively. We assume:

- all individuals face the same probability distribution of outcomes,

- y, μ, and $\text{var}(y)$ for each individual are independent of those for every other individual.

In the absence of insurance, the variance (i.e. risk) facing the ith individual is $\text{var}(y_i)$. Now suppose all N individuals put their income into a pool agreeing that each will receive

$$\bar{y} = \frac{1}{N}(y_1 + y_2 + \ldots + y_N). \tag{5.7}$$

This pooling is a form of insurance. The variance for society is

$$\text{var}(y_1 + y_2 + \ldots + y_N) = N\,\text{var}(y),$$

since all incomes are independent and have the same variance. But the variance for the *individual* is smaller. He receives the average income, $\bar{y}$ in equation (5.7), and

$$\text{var}(\bar{y}) = \text{var}\left(\frac{y_1}{N} + \frac{y_2}{N} + \ldots + \frac{y_N}{N}\right)$$

$$= N\,\text{var}\left(\frac{y}{N}\right)$$

$$= \frac{\text{var}(y)}{N} \to 0, \text{ as } N \to \infty. \tag{5.8}$$

What equation (5.8) shows is that, if N identically distributed and independent incomes are pooled, the variance of average income (and hence the risk to the individual) tends to zero as N tends to infinity. By 'trading' (i.e. pooling), individuals can acquire certainty.

2.3. An example: Annuities

Annuities (i.e. an annual income stream) are another form of pooling. An individual could buy a pension of £y per year for a lump sum A, where A is the present value of the pension stream for the rest of her life, n years, and r is the rate of interest.[3] Thus

---

[3] See Cullis and Jones (1998: ch. 6) or Stiglitz (2000: ch. 11).

$$A = y + \frac{y}{1+r} + \frac{y}{(1+r)^2} + \ldots + \frac{y}{(1+r)^{n-1}}. \tag{5.9}$$

More generally, the capital cost of a given income stream is

$$A = f(y,n,r). \tag{5.10}$$

Consider someone with £50,000 accumulated in pension contributions over his working life. He could finance his retirement by consuming this lump sum at a rate of, say, £5,000 per year; but that way he risks outliving his savings. He can avoid this uncertainty by exchanging £50,000 plus an uncertain lifespan for a pension of £y, with certainty and for life. He is, in effect, making a bet with the insurance company: if he hands over the lump sum and immediately drops dead, he loses, but if he lives to 98, he wins. This arrangement is exactly analogous to income pooling. All retired persons put their lump sums into a pool and draw the average income; those who live longer draw more than those who die younger, but the fund can pay for the long-lived because it is based on average life expectancy.

How large is the annuity? Equation (5.10) can be rewritten as

$$y = g(A,n,r), \tag{5.11}$$

which shows that the annual payment, £y, for a given lump sum, A, depends on the insurance company's view of n (the applicant's life expectancy) and r (its expected interest rate).

LIFE EXPECTANCY. The insurance company will pay a lower annual income the longer it expects to pay benefit. In principle, this depends on four broad factors.

Age. The younger a person, the longer, on average, he has to live and the smaller the annuity in respect of a given lump sum.

Gender. On average, women live longer than men. Other things being equal, a woman will therefore receive a smaller annuity than a man. In practice, many pension schemes pool across men and women, not least for the equity reasons discussed in Chapter 9, Section 4.2.

Health. With annuities, it is the long-lived who are 'bad' risks. But it is easier to detect health problems than to prove their absence, hence companies usually pool across health for annuities. There is no such pooling for life insurance, where it is the short-lived, often with detectable health problems, who are bad risks.

Marital status. Where an annuity is payable also to a surviving spouse, the age difference between husband and wife is relevant. If I retire at 65, and my wife is considerably younger, she is likely to outlive me by many years, in which case the payout period, n, is longer, and the annuity correspondingly smaller. However, where a scheme is compulsory, insurers usually pool across men aged 65 irrespective of the age of their wives. This is feasible because for the *group* the average age difference is predictable.[4]

THE RATE OF INTEREST. If changes in the price level are not to affect the real value of an annuity, it is necessary to base calculations on the real rate of interest (i.e. the excess of

---

[4] The fact that such schemes are compulsory is important, an aspect discussed in more detail in Sections 3.2 and 4.2.

the nominal interest rate over the rate of inflation). Suppose an individual has accumulated a lump sum of £50,000, and the insurance company expects him to live for 12 years ($n = 12$) and anticipates a real rate of interest of 3 per cent ($r = 0.03$). The actuarial value of an annuity is obtained by substituting these values into equation (5.11) to obtain a value for y. The subject of annuities in the context of pension finance is a major topic in Chapter 9.

3. The supply side

3.1. The supply of insurance

This part of the chapter discusses the price at which the private market will supply insurance, and then turns to a number of technical problems.[5]

THE ACTUARIAL PREMIUM. Suppose that I insure the contents of my house for £1,000, when the probability of being burgled is 1 per cent. From equation (5.5) my expected loss is the insured loss, L, multiplied by the probability, p_i, that I will experience the loss. The insurance company knows that on average it will have to pay out £10 per year (i.e. 1 per cent of £1,000). The actuarial premium for the ith individual, π_i, is then defined as

$$\pi_i = (1 + \alpha)p_i L, \tag{5.12}$$

where $p_i L$ is the individual's expected loss, and α is the loading that the insurance company adds to cover administrative costs (e.g. sending an expert to assess the damage) and normal profit. π is the price at which insurance will be supplied in a competitive market.

The actuarial premium in equation (5.12) rests on a number of conditions on the probability, p_i. Some are strictly technical, others bring us directly back to the issue of perfect information. Problems of either sort can make insurance inefficient or impossible, interfering with a person's ability to choose an optimal time path of consumption (see the discussion of the Fisher model in Chapter 4, Section 3.2).

INDEPENDENT PROBABILITIES. Actuarial insurance requires, first, that the probability of the insured event for any individual is independent of that for anyone else. This condition is necessary because insurance depends on the existence in a given period of a predictable number of winners and losers. If, in the extreme, individual probabilities are completely linked, then, if one person suffers a loss, so does everyone else. Thus actuarial insurance can cope with *individual* risk (sometimes also called idiosyncratic risk) but not with *common* or *systemic* shocks. An important problem under this head (discussed in Chapter 9, Section 3) is inflation, which, if it affects any one member of an actuarial pension scheme, will affect all.

PROBABILITY LESS THAN ONE. The relevant probability must be less than one. If not, equation (5.12) simplifies to

$$\pi = (1 + \alpha)L > L \tag{5.13}$$

---

[5] See, in ascending order of difficulty, Burchardt and Hills (1997: ch. 1), Begg et al. (2003: ch. 13), Culyer (1993), and Rees (1989).

and the actuarial premium exceeds the insured loss. I might, for example, have to pay a premium of £1,500 to insure against potential burglary losses of £1,000. Actuarial insurance will not be offered because there will be no demand for it. In economic terms there is no possibility of spreading risk, and hence no gains from trade.

This problem can arise for the chronically ill, where the probability of ill health is equal to one unless insurance is taken out before the condition is diagnosed. Medical insurance usually excludes cover for pre-existing conditions precisely because the probability of needing treatment is too high to insure. Advances in genetic testing will create major problems: the better the information about a person's future health, the greater the extent of pre-existing, and hence uninsurable, conditions (see Chapter 12, Section 3.1, and Barr 2001a: ch. 5).

We have seen (Chapter 4, Section 3.2) that market efficiency requires perfect information on the part of consumers and firms. Firms may face problems in a number of ways: employers may not be well informed about the quality of labour, nor lending institutions about the degree of riskiness of prospective borrowers. A particular class of information problem concerns insurers.

KNOWN PROBABILITIES. The relevant probability must be known or estimable. Insurance addresses *risk*, but cannot cope with *certainty* (the previous condition) nor with *uncertainty*, the issue here.[6] If the insurer does not know the probability, he cannot calculate a premium from equation (5.12), making actuarial insurance impossible. The problem can arise in a number of ways. The insured event may be rare, so that, with few observations, any estimate of the probability will have a large variance. Secondly, the problem might be unknown because of the complexity of the problem—for example, estimating future rates of inflation, or the risk of exposure to variant-CJD. Thirdly, the problem can arise where insurance involves long-term contracts. In the long run a known risk can become unknown (i.e. a risk can turn into uncertainty). Thus private insurers are generally unable to offer contracts which index pensions against future inflation, *inter alia* because it is not possible to estimate the probability distribution of different levels of future price change (Chapter 9, Section 3.1). Similar problems arise for insurance for long-term care (Chapter 8, Section 2.3).

Further problems are caused by asymmetric information, where the insurer has less information than the customer. Specifically there should be no *adverse selection*, and no *moral hazard*. The former arises where the purchaser can conceal from the insurer that he is a high risk—for example, it may be possible for people to conceal potential ill health from medical insurers. Adverse selection thus arises where there is *hidden knowledge*. Moral hazard arises where there is *hidden action*—that is, situations where (slightly to oversimplify) the customer can costlessly manipulate the probability of the insured event. Pregnancy, for example, can be the result of deliberate choice. Thus the probability cannot be regarded as exogenous, and individual medical cover will generally exclude the costs of a normal pregnancy.[7]

---

[6] See the Glossary for the important distinction between risk and uncertainty.
[7] But many policies will cover the extra costs of complications because the probability of *complications* is exogenous.

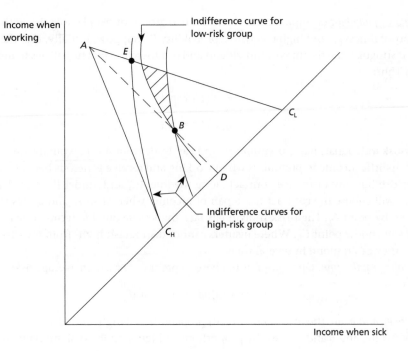

Fig. 5.2. Effects of adverse selection on a competitive equilibrium

3.2. Asymmetric information

Adverse selection and moral hazard are central to efficiency arguments about the welfare state, and so merit further discussion.[8]

ADVERSE SELECTION is a manifestation in insurance markets of the more general concept of 'lemons' (Akerlof 1970). The purchaser of insurance may know better than the supplier that he is a 'lemon' (i.e. a poor risk), and may conceal the fact in order to choose a policy that would be unattainable if the insurer were perfectly informed.

Akerlof's competitive analysis was extended by Rothschild and Stiglitz (1976) to cover strategic behaviour by firms.[9] Point *A* in Figure 5.2 shows the income of an uninsured individual when working and when unable to work because of illness. Under simplifying assumptions (e.g. no administrative costs), a rational, risk-averse individual will insure fully, so that income (net of the insurance premium) will be the same when ill as when working, i.e. at a point on the 45-degree line.

---

[8] The literature starts from Arrow (1963), followed by Akerlof (1970), Pauly (1974), Rothschild and Stiglitz (1976), and Stiglitz (1983).

[9] For further discussion see, in ascending order of difficulty, Atkinson (1989: ch. 7), repr. in Barr and Whynes (1993: ch. 2), Culyer (1993), and Rees (1989).

Known probabilities. Suppose that there are two groups of people, low risk with a probability of illness p_L, and high risk with a probability P_H. Suppose, initially, that the insurer can distinguish the riskiness of individuals and can therefore match policies to individual risk. Thus:

$$\pi_L = (1 + \alpha)p_L L, \tag{5.14}$$

$$\pi_H = (1 + \alpha)p_H L. \tag{5.15}$$

Low-risk individuals pay a premium π_L and can trade from A on favourable terms. They give up little income in premiums when working and receive generous benefits when ill. They can buy any insurance contract along the line AC_L and, under the stated assumptions, will choose the contract (i.e. a pair of incomes when at work and ill, respectively) shown by point C_L. High-risk individuals face the less-favourable terms shown by AC_H, and will choose point C_H. Where insurers cannot distinguish high- from low-risk applicants, they can respond in several ways.

Pooling equilibrium. One option is to charge a premium based on average risk:

$$\bar{\pi} = (1 + \alpha)[\theta p_H + (1 - \theta)p_L]L, \tag{5.16}$$

where p_H and p_L are the (now unobserved) probabilities of high- and low-risk individuals, respectively, and θ and $(1 - \theta)$ the proportions of high- and low-risk individuals buying insurance. The locus of potential insurance contracts is illustrated by the line AD in Figure 5.2.

If low risks buy less cover and high risks more at an average premium, π, the resulting policies are less efficient than would exist with individually tailored policies, π_L and π_H Consider the contract shown by B. Any contract in the shaded area above B would (*a*) be preferred by the low-risk group, and (*b*) still be profitable. However, the pooling equilibrium (i.e. a common premium for all applicants) at B is not stable—if any company offered such a contract, another company could bid away the low-risk group by offering a policy in the shaded area above B. This instability applies to any other contract along AD.

Separating equilibrium. Suppose instead that the insurer tried to offer separate policies to the two groups. It cannot verify the riskiness of each individual. It might, however, appeal to *self-selection* by offering policies that embody incentive structures such that customers' market behaviour reveals their true probability (see Ravallion and Datt 1995 for analysis of such self-selection in different contexts). Thus the policy offered to the low-risk group along AD must lie to the left of point E (anywhere to the right would attract high-risk applicants). As Figure 5.2 is drawn, however, low-risk individuals prefer the pooling contract shown by B to any contract between A and E. The problem in this case is that no separating equilibrium exists. Even if it did, it would still be inefficient because low-risk individuals cannot buy complete cover.

Outcomes of adverse selection. Attempts by insurers to recruit good risks and avoid bad risks is known as *cream skimming*. Paradoxically, however, though insurers fear that mainly bad risks will buy cover, the outcome is gaps in coverage for *low risks*. In the face of adverse selection, the market either is inefficient or fails entirely. A partial solution is to restrict the range of choice the insured is allowed—for instance, making membership compulsory to prevent low risks opting out of a pooling equilibrium (i.e. seeking to move into the shaded area above point *B*). If preferences are sufficiently similar, the welfare loss from compulsion may be small.

MORAL HAZARD. At its strongest, the condition that there should be no moral hazard requires that both the probability, p, and the insured loss, L, should be exogenous to the individual. Slightly less stringently, moral hazard can be avoided so long as individuals can influence p or L only at a cost to themselves greater than the expected gain from so doing. Where the assumption fails, customers can affect the insurer's liability without its knowledge.

Pauly (1974) considers the case of individual expenditure on a preventive activity, z, which can reduce the probability of the insured event. From a social point of view, the efficient level of z is where its marginal cost is equal to the marginal reduction in insured losses. But if losses are fully insured and the insurance company cannot monitor individual preventive activity, the private incentive is to spend little or nothing on it—people, in short, will behave differently if they are insured. At its simplest, my extra spending on z reduces my premium by only an infinitely small amount: the main beneficiaries are other insured people who now pay slightly lower premiums. As a result of this type of externality, Pauly argues, individuals face private incentives to under-invest in preventive activities.

Pauly's analysis is sensitive to one strong assumption—namely, that all losses, *including* non-material losses, are insurable. If that assumption is relaxed, there are several possible outcomes, of which Pauly's is only one. To show the effects of uninsurable psychic losses, it is useful to distinguish four cases.[10]

Case 1: Endogenous p_i, but only at substantial psychic cost. An example is suicide. Here the problem of moral hazard is more apparent than real. It is possible to influence the probability of dying, but generally only at a high utility cost to the person concerned. People do not commit suicide *only* to make their legatees rich. (It is true that someone intending to commit suicide for other reasons might do so; but that is a problem of adverse selection, to deal with which most policies exclude cover during the first year of the policy.) Because individuals cannot insure against the psychic cost to themselves of death, insurance is incomplete. Moral hazard in such cases does not cause a problem.

Case 2: Endogenous p_i, with no substantial psychic cost. People might drive less carefully if they are insured, or buy fewer fire extinguishers, since insurance reduces the cost to the insured individual of those unwelcome events. In this case, the Pauly result holds: moral hazard does not make insurance impossible but causes inefficiency, since people take less care than if they had to bear the full loss themselves.

Case 3: Endogenous p_i, with substantial psychic gains. This is the case of voluntary pregnancy or elective health care (e.g. a hair transplant). Here the insured event is not an undesired outcome but a deliberate act of consumer *choice*. Individuals can control at small cost the probability, p_i, in equation (5.12), and the insurance company can calculate neither the expected loss nor the actuarial premium. This is a far cry from an insurable

---

[10] For fuller discussion of moral hazard, see Stiglitz (1983), Rees (1989), or Culyer (1993).

risk. Such activities are generally uninsurable for individuals,[11] though the problem can sometimes be sidestepped where insurance is compulsory. If, for example, all workers in the steel industry are compelled to join a particular scheme, the insurer can impose a pooling solution based on the average expected number of births. In contrast, if insurance were voluntary, a disproportionate number of intending parents might join, raising issues of adverse selection as well as moral hazard.

Case 4: Endogenous L at zero or low cost (the so-called *third-party-payment problem*). Here it is not the probability, p_i, that is endogenous but the size of the insured loss. To see intuitively what is going on, contrast behaviour in a conventional restaurant with that in an 'all-you-can-eat-for-£9.95' restaurant. In the case of medical care, for instance, if the insurer pays all medical costs, neither patient nor doctor is constrained by the patient's ability to pay. The marginal private cost of health care is zero for both doctor and patient, even though social cost is positive. The results of this form of moral hazard are twofold: because of the divergence between private and social costs, consumption of health care (and consequently the insurance payout) is inefficiently large (Chapter 12, Section 3.1); and there is an upward bias in insurance premiums.

Similarly, suppose automobile insurance pays for all car repairs. I then have an incentive both to drive recklessly (p endogenous) and to have my car repaired lavishly (L endogenous). The result of this type of moral hazard, once more, is inefficiency in the form of over-consumption.

Thus moral hazard creates incentives to over-consumption on the demand side (cases 2 and 3) or supply side (case 4). The problem is fundamental: the more complete the cover and the lower the psychic loss from the insured event, the less individuals have to bear the consequences of their actions and the less, therefore, the incentive to behave as they would if they had to bear their losses themselves. A number of devices try to reduce the problem, either through regulation or through incentives.

- *Inspection* (a form of regulation) is frequently used for damage claims (e.g. for house contents or automobile repairs). The insurer inspects the damage and pays benefit only in respect of what it regards as the true insured loss.

Incentive mechanisms share the cost between the individual and the insurer.

- Frequent claimants (e.g. accident-prone car drivers) pay *higher premiums*.
- *Deductibles* make the insured person pay the first £X of any claim.
- With *coinsurance* the insured person pays x per cent of any claim.

None of these, however, faces the individual with the full marginal cost of making good the loss.

In analytical terms, adverse selection and moral hazard both derive from information failure. Neither would arise if the insurer could 'get inside the head' of insured persons (i.e. could read their thoughts), hence ruling out both hidden knowledge and hidden action.

---

[11] Insurance policies generally have exclusions for such procedures as adult bat ears, breast augmentation, cosmetic rhinoplasty, tattoo removal, and the removal of warts.

4. The insurance market as a whole: Private and social insurance

4.1. The existence and efficiency of private insurance markets

THE EXISTENCE OF PRIVATE INSURANCE MARKETS requires three conditions to hold.

1. There must be positive demand. From equation (5.3) this requires that

$$V = \bar{y} - y^* > 0.$$

This condition holds if some individuals are risk averse.

2. It must be technically possible to supply insurance—that is, none of the problems discussed previously must make actuarial insurance impossible.

3. It must be possible for insurance to be supplied at a price that the individual is prepared to pay—that is, the demand price must exceed or equal the net supply price. From equation (5.4) this requires

$$V = \bar{y} - y^* \geq \phi.$$

Equation (5.6) defines the net premium as the gross premium, π, minus the expected benefit, pL:

$$\phi = \pi - pL.$$

Hence, from equation (5.12),

$$\phi = \alpha pL.$$

Thus, a market for insurance exists only if

$$\bar{y} - y^* \geq \alpha pL. \tag{5.17}$$

Insurance can be supplied at an acceptable price only where the individual's risk aversion (represented by the difference between $\bar{y}$ and y^*) is sufficient to cover the insurer's mark-up, αpL.

SHOULD INSURANCE BE COMPETITIVE? The three conditions hold for the examples of actuarial insurance in Section 1. Consider the case of a head teacher who wants to insure against the loss to the school if it rains on the day of a fund-raising event. Since she wants to insure, it follows that she is risk averse, hence the demand condition holds. Nor are there technical problems on the supply side; the probability of rain on a given day is known and less than one; there is no adverse selection (since she cannot hide rainfall statistics from the insurer) and no moral hazard (since she cannot influence the weather). Finally, administrative costs are low, since it is easy to establish whether or not the weather was bad, and so insurance can be provided at a low net price. Thus actuarial insurance is technically possible.

Is competitive insurance desirable? It was argued in Chapter 4 that an unrestricted market allocates resources efficiently provided that the standard assumptions hold.

These conditions apply equally to insurance. Perfect information is relevant to people who buy insurance, and to the companies that supply it. Where both sides of the market are well informed, competition provides consumers with their desired type and mix of policies and ensures that suppliers make no long-run excess profits. In such cases—for example, automobile insurance and burglary insurance—competition is both possible and desirable.

The strength of this argument is not diminished by the fact that the necessary conditions do not always hold, creating areas where the case for competitive actuarial insurance is weaker or non-existent. Three types of problem stand out.

1. *Imperfectly informed consumers.* With long-term contracts, buyers face information problems: they may not know what cover they will need many years hence (e.g. long-term care insurance); and with technically complex contracts (e.g. pensions) they may not understand the issues fully. In some cases the market may supply the necessary information, for example, through insurance brokers. Where information problems are serious, however,[12] the benefits from competition are diminished and may largely disappear. Competitive insurance is likely to be inefficient; it may also create inequities (for example, missold pensions policies). These issues are taken up in later chapters (see also Burchardt and Hills 1997).

2. *Imperfectly informed insurers.* The resulting problems were discussed in Section 3. Competitive pressures can create problems in the form of cream skimming, gaps in coverage, and third-party incentives to inefficiently high spending.

3. *Administrative costs.*[13] From equation (5.12), the higher the administrative loading, α, the less likely that people will buy insurance. As equation (5.17) shows, the effect of α is to drive a wedge between people's risk aversion, $\bar{y} - y^*$, and the net return, pL, they derive from insurance. As a result, risk-averse individuals, whose welfare could be increased by insuring, do not buy insurance.

This outcome is not necessarily inefficient: an individual's risk aversion may be slight, and *some* administrative costs are unavoidable. The administrative costs associated with individual policies include marketing costs, processing costs, reimbursement costs, and forgone economies of scale that a larger company might enjoy. These costs are efficient (and hence competition desirable) if they generate significant welfare gains by enabling insurers to offer policies that match individual preferences more accurately. They are inefficient, however, if (*a*) their costs outweigh the welfare gains from individually tailored policies or (*b*) some other form of organization would be cheaper. With badly informed consumers, for example, the welfare gains from improved individual choice might be low; thus social insurance, which has no marketing costs, low costs of processing and reimbursement (because of standardization), and economies of scale, may be more efficient.

In the face of any of these problems, actuarial insurance may be (*a*) inefficient or (*b*) not supplied at all. The central point of later discussion is that difficulties often arise because two sets of needs—those of actuarial insurance and those of social policy—

---

[12] i.e. where there is an information-processing problem; see Chapter 4, section 3.2.
[13] For fuller discussion, see Culyer (1993: 156–7).

do not match. The solution is not to berate insurers for failing to meet social-policy objectives, still less to ignore social-policy needs because actuarial insurance cannot meet them. What is needed is a bridge between the two sets of objectives. Such a bridge may involve regulating or subsidizing private insurance or it may involve public funding through social insurance or taxation. These issues arise repeatedly, particularly for unemployment insurance (Chapter 8, Section 2.2), the protection of pensions against inflation (Chapter 9, Section 3.1), and medical insurance (Chapter 12, Section 3.1).

PREMIUM DIFFERENTIALS. Earlier discussion of adverse selection poses the question of whether efficiency requires that differences in individual probabilities should *always* result in different premiums. Where the decision to insure is voluntary, efficiency requires that insurers should seek to discover who is high and who is low risk, and charge premiums accordingly, as in equations (5.14) and (5.15).

In contrast, where insurance is compulsory, it might be possible to pool high and low risks and charge everyone the average premium (equation (5.16)), since low-risk people cannot choose not to insure. Thus, for example, the 1946 National Insurance Act (Chapter 2, Section 5) applied pooling explicitly both to individuals and to risks. All employed men of working age paid the same lump-sum contribution to buy entitlement, *inter alia*, to the same unemployment benefit, even though some groups (e.g. doctors) were less likely to be unemployed than others (e.g. construction workers). All individuals paid an average premium (equation (5.16)); and, because contributions were compulsory, it was not possible for overcharged low-risk individuals to opt out. Analytically, the low-risk group paid an actuarial premium (equation (5.14)) plus an unavoidable lump-sum tax, and the high-risk group paid an actuarial premium shown by equation (5.15) and received a lump-sum transfer. Thus a system that charges a compulsory average premium irrespective of risk can alleviate problems of adverse selection.[14] Another example (Chapter 9, Section 4.2) is the pooling of men and women in pension schemes, despite the fact that on average women live longer. In contrast, automobile insurance is also compulsory, but there is no pooling across groups—people with worse accident records generally pay higher premiums.

Thus if insurance is compulsory, charging all categories of risk the same premium causes little inefficiency in *insurance* markets, though it might cause secondary inefficiency in related activities.

FALLACIOUS EQUITY ARGUMENTS appear in a number of guises. The first is that insurance is inequitable because it redistributes from those who do not make claims to those who do. This assertion merits little discussion. The whole point of insurance is that people do not know whether they will need to claim (i.e. whether the 'good' or the 'bad' outcome will occur). A rational risk-averse individual increases her utility by choosing a lower income with certainty (y^* in Figure 5.1), in preference to a higher expected income, $\bar{y}$. Insurance can bring about this increase in utility precisely because the individual is a net contributor in a 'good' year and a net beneficiary in a 'bad' year.

---

[14] It might, however, cause inefficiency in other ways: standard policies do not allow for differences in preferences; and a common structure of premiums for employers might lead to inefficient expansion of risky industries.

A second fallacious argument is that 'private insurance is inequitable because the poor cannot afford adequate cover'. This proposition can be attacked in a number of ways. First, if the *only* difficulty is that the poor cannot afford cover, the problem is one not of market allocation but of income distribution, and can be solved by cash redistribution. Secondly, who decides what level of cover is 'adequate'? Public provision on these grounds can be justified only where there are efficiency problems with private insurance, or if the poor have imperfect information. The arguments developed earlier, in particular the two propositions in Chapter 4, Section 7.2, apply equally to insurance.

4.2. Social insurance

SOCIAL INSURANCE AS A RESPONSE TO INFORMATION FAILURE. Arrow argues that, where markets fail, other institutions may arise to mitigate the resulting problems, sometimes through public production and sometimes through private institutions using non-competitive allocation mechanisms: 'the failure of the market to insure against uncertainties has created many social institutions in which the usual assumptions of the market are to some extent contradicted' (Arrow 1963: 967). In other words, as discussed in the first paragraph of this chapter, institutions (public or private) may arise that are insurance in the sense of protecting against risk, even if they are not insurance in a narrow actuarial sense.

The Arrow arguments and their subsequent elaboration contrast strongly with those of Hayek (1945). Both writers started from the assumption of asymmetric information. To Hayek the fact that different people know different things is an argument *in favour* of markets. He argued (analogous to the existence of skill differences) that the market makes beneficial use of such differences by allowing gains from trade to be exploited. Arrow showed that the market is an inefficient device for mediating certain important classes of differences in knowledge between people. Nor is the Arrow view idiosyncratic. The Rothschild and Stiglitz (1976) and similar arguments were discussed in Section 3.2. Lucas (1987: 62), in discussing unemployment, reached an identical conclusion:

Since . . . with private information, competitively determined arrangements will fall short of complete pooling, this class of models also raises the issue of *social insurance*: pooling arrangements that are not actuarially sound, and hence require support from compulsory taxation. The main elements of Kenneth Arrow's analysis of medical insurance are readily transferable to this employment context.   (emphasis in original)

Social insurance thus derives from two sources. The need for insurance arises because in industrialized countries employment is largely a binary phenomenon (i.e. a person is either employed or unemployed) and retirement, similarly, is a discrete event. Thus the risks against which social insurance offers protection are to some extent a social construct.[15] Secondly, on the supply side, information failures provide both a theoretical *justification of* and an *explanation for*, a welfare state that is much more than a safety net. A central argument in later chapters is that actuarial insurance cannot cover contingencies such as unemployment, inflation, and important medical risks. Social insurance is one response.

---

[15] Atkinson (1995*a*: ch. 11) stresses the importance of labour-market institutions. On retirement, see Hannah (1986).

THE NATURE OF THE BEAST. An important characteristic of most social insurance is that membership is compulsory, thus preventing low risks from opting out. Compulsion makes possible the three generic forms of organization described in Chapter 1, Section 2.1, all of which are insurance in the sense of offering protection, but which diverge increasingly from insurance in conventional actuarial terms.

- *Social insurance* (i.e. benefits based on a contributions record and the occurrence of a specified contingency) takes two broad forms. Quasi-actuarial contributions are related to the average risk (e.g. the flat-rate weekly contribution of the UK scheme between 1948 and 1975); this is a pure pooling equilibrium. Income-related contributions break the link with individual risk; the contribution in this case looks like a hypothecated tax.
- *'Universal' benefits* abandon the attempt to mimic private insurance. Tax-financed benefits are awarded on the basis of specified contingencies without a contributions or income test (a flat-rate citizen's pension in some countries, health care in some countries including the UK).
- *Social assistance* is awarded on the basis of specified contingencies and an income test.

Administration can be by the state at central level (the UK) or at a lower level (as for most programmes in the USA, and for health care in Australia, Canada, and Sweden). Alternatively, administration can be hived off to private-sector institutions such as friendly societies or trades unions (as with unemployment compensation in Sweden and medical care in Germany); in such cases the private sector is acting, in effect, as an agent of the state.

The social-insurance arrangements just described are based on private institutions: benefits are conditioned on an implicit or explicit contributions record and on the occurrence of a specified event, frequently related to employment status, in that one of their major purposes is to replace lost earnings.

Social insurance, however, differs from private insurance in two important respects. First, because membership is generally compulsory, it is *possible* (though not essential) to break the link between premium and individual risk; a pooling solution is therefore an option. Secondly, the contract is usually less specific than private insurance, with two advantages: protection can be given against risks that the private market cannot insure (Chapter 8 argues that unemployment is one); and the risks can change over time. Atkinson (1995a: 210) points out that 'the set of contingencies over which people formed probabilities years ago may have excluded the breakdown of the extended family, or the development of modern medicine, simply because they were inconceivable'.

Thus social insurance, in sharp contrast with actuarial insurance, can cover not only *risk* but also *uncertainty*. Social insurance, in various guises, will appear repeatedly in later chapters.

■ QUESTIONS FOR FURTHER DISCUSSION

1. Why does a middle-aged person driving a three-year-old small car pay a lower premium for automobile insurance than a student driving a Ferrari?

2. 'Annuities are a form of insurance. Women on average live longer than men and therefore, from the point of view of annuities, are a worse risk than men. For a given contribution, women should therefore receive a lower monthly annuity benefit than a man.' Are the statements logical? Is the conclusion correct?

3. How does social insurance differ from actuarial insurance?

■ FURTHER READING

Burchardt and Hills (1997: ch. 1) give an excellent, non-technical introduction to the economics of insurance. See also, in ascending order of formality, Begg et al. (2003: ch. 13), Varian (2002: ch. 12), and Rees (1989). For discussion in the context of cash benefits and medical insurance, see Stiglitz (2000: chs. 12, 14) and Rosen (2002: chs. 9, 10); on medical insurance, see also Culyer (1993). Barr (2001a: ch. 5) discusses the implications of genetic testing for insurance.

On information problems more generally, see Varian (2002: ch. 36) for an overview. The classic articles are by Arrow (1963) (who discusses medical insurance), on adverse selection by Akerlof (1970) and Rothschild and Stiglitz (1976), on moral hazard by Pauly (1974) and Stiglitz (1983), and on signalling by Spence (1973). For surveys, see Hirschleifer and Riley (1992), Riley (2001), and the Nobel Symposium in the *American Economic Review*, June 2002 (Akerlof 2002; Spence 2002; and Stiglitz 2002).

Appendix: Non-technical summary of Chapter 5

1. Chapter 5 discusses the demand and supply of insurance, and some problems that can arise on the supply side of a private insurance market.

2. The term 'insurance' is used by different people to mean different things. Two meanings above all should be distinguished. Insurance can be defined (*a*) as a device that offers individuals *protection against risk*, and/or (*b*) as an *actuarial mechanism* (as defined in equation (5.12) below) that the private sector can organize. The first defines insurance in terms of its purpose, the second in terms of a method by which that purpose might be pursued. Even where institutions are not insurance in the sense of (*b*), they might still be regarded as insurance in that they offer protection against risk.

The demand and supply of insurance

3. Uncertainty reduces the utility of an individual who is risk averse; hence certainty has a positive value, and a risk-averse individual will be prepared to pay a positive price for it. When I take out insurance, the commodity I am buying is *certainty* (e.g. that if my car is stolen it will be replaced). The formal argument is presented in Section 2.1.

4. The supply of insurance is discussed in Section 3.1. Suppose that the probability, p, of being burgled is 1 per cent; and that, if I am burgled, my loss, L, will be £1,000. On average, therefore, I can expect a loss of £1,000 once every 100 years. In annual terms my expected loss is $p \times L = 1\% \times £1,000 = £10$—that is, the insurance company knows that on average it will have to pay me £10 per year. Formally, an *actuarial premium*, π, is defined as

$$\pi = (1 + \alpha)pL, \tag{5.12}$$

where pL is the expected loss of the individual buying insurance, and $(1 + \alpha)$ is the insurance company's mark-up of α per cent to cover its administrative costs and normal profit. π is the price at which insurance will be supplied in a competitive market.

Technical problems on the supply side

5. Private insurance will be inefficient or non-existent unless the probability, p, in equation (5.12) meets five conditions (Sections 3.1 and 3.2). First, the probability of a given individual being burgled must be *independent* of the probability of anyone else being burgled. What this means (roughly speaking) is that insurance depends for its financial viability on the existence in any year of a predictable number of winners and losers.

6. Secondly, p must be *less than one*. If $p = 1$, it is certain that my car will be stolen; hence there is no possibility of spreading risks, and the insurance premium will equal or exceed the cost of a new car. This problem can arise for the chronically or congenitally ill, for whom the probability of ill health equals one unless insurance is taken out *before* the condition is diagnosed.

7. A third condition is that p must be *known or estimable*. If it is not, insurance companies will be unable to calculate an actuarial premium, and actuarial insurance will be impossible. This problem can arise for policies with a long-time horizon, where risk (which is insurable) turns in the long run into uncertainty (which is not). The private market, for example, is generally unable to supply insurance against future inflation because the probability of different levels of future price increases cannot be estimated.

8. Fourthly, there must be *no adverse selection*, which arises when a purchaser is able to conceal from the insurance company the fact that he is a poor risk. If the insurance company cannot distinguish high- and low-risk customers, it will have to charge everyone the same premium, based on the average risk. As a result, low-risk individuals will face an inefficiently high premium and may choose not to insure even though, at an actuarial premium, it would be efficient for them to do so. This problem arises particularly in the case of medical insurance for the elderly.

9. Finally, there must be *no moral hazard*. The problem can arise in two ways: first, where the customer is able costlessly to manipulate the probability p in equation (5.12) that the insured event will occur; and, secondly, where the customer can manipulate the size of the loss, L. The latter difficulty is conventionally called the *third-party-payment problem*.

10. There are numerous ways in which consumers can manipulate the relevant probability. The chances of developing appendicitis are beyond individual control, and so medical insurance for this sort of complaint is generally possible. In contrast, the probability of becoming pregnant, and visits to one's family doctor, can both be influenced by individual actions and are therefore generally not well covered by actuarial insurance. Where the problem is serious, the supplier is unable to calculate the actuarial premium, and private insurance may be impossible.

11. The third-party-payment problem does not make insurance impossible, but causes over-consumption. The problem is particularly relevant to health care. If an individual's insurance pays all medical costs, then health care is 'free' to the patient. Similarly, on the supply side, the doctor knows that the insurance company will pay her charges; she is therefore not constrained by the patient's ability to pay. As a result, both doctor and patient can act as though the cost of health care were zero. This is inefficient: it causes over-consumption and creates upward pressure on insurance premiums.

12. The problems discussed in paragraphs 5–11 can cause inefficiency, and may make private insurance impossible. Both difficulties are acutely relevant to unemployment insurance (Chapter 8, Section 2.2), to the protection of pensions against inflation (Chapter 9, Section 3.1), and to medical insurance (Chapter 12, Section 3.1).

6 Problems of definition and measurement

To criticise inequality and to desire equality is not . . . to cherish the romantic illusion that men are equal in character and intelligence. It is to hold that, while their natural endowments differ profoundly, it is the mark of a civilised society to aim at eliminating such inequalities as have their source, not in individual differences, but in its own organisation.

(R. H. Tawney, 1964)

Common prosperity cannot and never will mean absolute egalitarianism or that all members of society become better off simultaneously at the same speed . . . Such thinking would lead to common poverty.

(People's Republic of China, Central Committee's Decision on Reform of the Economic System, 1984)

1. Measuring welfare

Measurement problems are a recurring theme.[1] They are illustrated here in the context of poverty (Section 2) and inequality (Sections 3 and 4). Two sets of issues are discussed: how do we define poverty and inequality; and how do we measure them in principle and in practice? It is helpful to start by considering the definition and measurement of welfare for individuals and for society as a whole.

1.1. Individual welfare

Defining individual income

WEALTH AND INCOME. The theoretical concept of income is complex and the literature vast (see the Further Reading). For present purposes it is possible to simplify matters by considering income as the flow deriving from a stock of wealth. Individual wealth can arise, broadly, in three forms. *Physical wealth* consists of consumer durables such as houses, machines (e.g. cars, television sets), Picassos, and Persian rugs. *Financial wealth* includes shares, government bonds, and bank accounts.[2] *Human capital* is wealth embodied

---

[1] Non-technical readers may omit Sections 1.2, 4.1, and 4.2. The gist of the argument is in the Appendix at the end of the chapter.

[2] It is legitimate to include both physical and financial wealth for *individuals*. But, for society as a whole, care is needed to avoid double counting, which would arise if, for example, Ford factories and Ford shares were both included in the definition of wealth.

in individuals as a result of skill and training, and has two quite separate sources: it is the result of past investment in education and training (which is what most people mean when they talk about human capital); it also arises from 'natural talent'. The latter requires explanation. Obvious examples are Shakespeare and Mozart, whom most of us could not emulate, however much training we had. The concept, however, is much broader, including, for example, the ability to walk, dress, wash oneself, etc., which forms of human capital may be denied to individuals with serious health problems.

Each type of wealth yields a flow of income. Physical wealth produces non-money income in the form of a flow of services (e.g. housing, or televisual services), but can also yield money income (e.g. a house to a landlord, or an automobile to a taxi driver). Financial wealth yields money income (e.g. the annual flow of interest from a £1,000 bank account). Human capital produces income in several forms. Suppose an individual divides his time between 'work' and 'leisure'.[3] When working, his human capital yields wages and non-money income like job satisfaction (which can be positive or negative); when not working, he receives non-money income through the enjoyment of leisure (again positive or negative), and also in the form of own production (household chores, gardening, etc.).

FULL INCOME, Y_F, consists of the flow of services from *all* individual wealth—that is, money income, Y_M, plus all forms of non-money income, Y_N:

$$Y_F = Y_M + Y_N, \tag{6.1}$$

where money income comprises wage and non-wage money income (e.g. dividends and interest),[4] and non-money income includes job satisfaction, the flow of services from physical wealth, the value of own production, and, importantly, the enjoyment of leisure. For given prices, full income thus defined is a measure of an individual's *opportunity set*.

The word 'opportunity' is crucial. The opportunity set measures the individual's *potential* consumption, including leisure. In Figure 6.1 the lines *eA* and *eB* show the earning opportunities of individuals A and B, respectively. A and B are both poor as conventionally measured, since their income, shown by points *a* and *b*, is below the poverty line *cd*. However, A's full income, including the value of leisure, shown by *OA* is well above the poverty line; B's full income, *OB*, is not. A is 'poor' because *by choice* he works for only four hours per day; B is poor *despite* working twenty-two hours per day.[5] By defining full income as the return to *all* forms of individual wealth it is possible to construct a measure of consumption opportunities that makes theoretical sense.

Full income is not, however, a complete measure of individual well-being. Even in its own terms, it omits important factors. Uncertainty can be a major source of welfare loss. Insurance can help but, as discussed in Chapter 5, may be incomplete, not least because it is possible to insure against risk but not against uncertainty. Secondly, individual

---

[3] The distinction between work and leisure is in many respects suspect (see e.g. Apps and Rees 1996). But it does no harm to retain the distinction for present purposes, and makes the exposition clearer.

[4] This definition leaves unanswered the difficult question of whether, and to what extent, capital gains should be included in income. See Prest and Barr (1985: ch. 13, sect. 4).

[5] See Atkinson and Stiglitz (1980: 260–1) on the importance of including leisure, and Le Grand (1984) on the central importance of choice in assessing individual welfare.

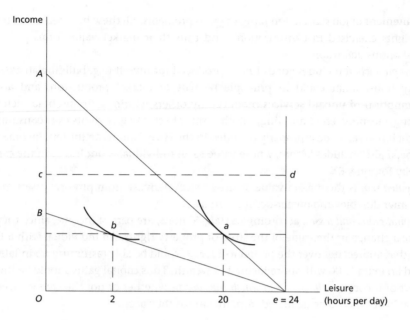

Fig. 6.1. Poor by choice or constraint?

welfare depends not only on potential consumption but on factors such as health (Sen 1985, 1995a; Dasgupta 1993: ch. 4). Sen (1985; 1992: ch. 3) extends the argument to define well-being in terms of people's 'capabilities', which includes important dimensions of choice and freedom. 'Just as the . . . "budget set" in commodity space represents a person's freedom to buy commodity bundles, the "capability set" . . . reflects the person's freedom to choose from possible livings' (Sen 1992: 40). While we note these criticisms, they are set to one side in the discussion that follows, since even the more limited concept of a consumption opportunity set cannot easily be put into practice.

THE HAIG–SIMONS DEFINITION. How might full income be translated into practice? The classic definition of individual income is by Simons (1938: 50), also called the Haig–Simons definition: 'Personal income may be defined as the algebraic sum of (1) the market value of rights exercised in consumption and (2) the change in the value of the store of property rights between the beginning and the end of the period.' More simply, 'income in a given period is the amount a person could have spent while maintaining his wealth intact' (Atkinson 1983: 39). The word 'could' is important. My income is increased if my *potential* to consume is raised, whether or not I actually choose to consume more.

The Haig–Simons definition has twofold importance: it indicates how income might be measured in practice; and it is comprehensive (and therefore theoretically sound) because it includes the following types of income that are omitted from conventional definitions.

Non-pecuniary benefits from work. Where fringe benefits are marketable (e.g. a chauffeur-driven car), they can be valued fairly easily. But problems arise where benefits are non-marketable and/or a mixture of 'work' and 'leisure'. Is a business trip abroad work, or leisure in disguise, or a mixture? And how should 'enjoyment' of the trip be valued? The measurement of job satisfaction raises obvious problems. All these non-pecuniary benefits are 'rights exercised in consumption', and thus their market value forms part of the Haig–Simons definition.

Own production includes goods I have produced for myself (e.g. building an extension to my house) that could in principle be part of market production, and also the consumption of unpaid services produced by others within the household sector (e.g. cooking, cleaning, child minding).[6] Both forms of activity give rights over consumption, and their market value is properly included in the Haig–Simons definition. Income under this head also includes leisure, whose value to an individual is not less than the earnings thereby forgone, £X.

Imputed rent is the market value of the services deriving from physical assets, notably consumer durables and owner-occupied houses.

Capital gains and losses, according to Haig–Simons, are part of income, since they constitute a change in the value of the store of property rights. An individual with a £1,000 asset that appreciates over the period to £1,100 would be able (assuming no inflation) to spend an extra £100 without reducing her wealth. Thus capital gains should be included as part of income *in the period in which they accrue* whether or not they are realized; and capital losses should be deducted from income as they accrue.

Measuring individual income

The next step is to consider how a theoretically sound definition of income might in practice be measured. This raises three sets of problems.

WHAT DO WE INCLUDE IN INCOME? A workable version of Haig–Simons is the sum of wage income, non-wage money income, fringe benefits, imputed rent, and realized capital gains. But this measure deviates from full income as defined in equation (6.1) through the omission of job satisfaction, extra-market production, and forgone income taken as leisure, and also because capital gains are not measured as they accrue. Further problems arise in attributing to individuals the benefits of publicly provided goods and services (e.g. education, roads).

Because non-money income is largely unmeasurable, we must focus on money income. This would not matter if money income were a good proxy for full income, but in practice money income as a proportion of total income varies widely and unsystematically. Non-observability of full income prevents a complete characterization of the individual opportunity set, forcing us to use the unreliable yardstick of money income. Full income is useful less as a guide to policy than as an explanation of why conventional definitions of poverty and inequality, based on money income, are severely limited as measures of welfare.

THE INCOME UNIT. What is the relation between household income and individual welfare? Part of the story—the comparison of households of different sizes—is discussed in Section 3.3. The other part concerns relations within a household. Consider a man, a woman, and two children, whose only source of income is £25,000, earned by the man. Regarded as a

---

[6] In formal terms these two sorts of activity correspond to production for own consumption and production for trade within the household sector (see Apps and Rees 1996).

family, four people share an income of £25,000; no one is poor; nor is there necessarily substantial inequality. But, if the man is regarded as a separate unit, the woman and child have no income; they are counted as poor; and there is substantial measured inequality. Thus the narrower the definition of the income unit, the greater are measured poverty and inequality.

The heart of the problem is the difficulty of measuring how income is shared. Since this is unobservable, policy is often based on the observable but not strictly relevant fact that two people are married, and thereby infers (rightly or wrongly) that income is shared. This is a strong assumption and one that is clearly unsatisfactory. The large literature on richer (Okin 1989; Sainsbury 1994; Sutherland 1997) and poorer countries (Dasgupta 1993: ch. 11) confirms widespread gender inequality. Any measure of income, however complete, will fail to capture important aspects of the distribution of welfare within households.

OVER WHAT TIME PERIOD IS INCOME MEASURED? Problems arise because income rarely flows continuously. Consider someone who earns £500 per week in commission but receives no wage; during the year he works fifty weeks, earning £25,000, and in the remaining two weeks, because of illness, earns nothing. Measuring income over a year he is not poor, but on a weekly basis he is poor for two weeks. For some purposes (e.g. setting the level of student support) it might be appropriate to use long-run income. On the other hand, if a student with no family support or job applied for social assistance during the summer vacation, it would not be helpful to refuse benefit because he had a high expected life-time income. In cases of immediate need, the relevant definition of income is usually short run.

1.2. Social welfare

Similar arguments apply at an aggregate level. A comprehensive measure of national income would include both money and non-money income.

We cannot measure . . . national achievement by the gross national product. For the gross national product includes air pollution and advertising for cigarettes, and ambulances to clear our highways of carnage . . . It swells with equipment for the police to put down riots in our cities; and though it is not diminished by the damage these riots do, still it goes up as slums are rebuilt on their ashes . . . And if the gross national product includes all this, there is much that it does not comprehend. It does not allow for the health of our families, the quality of their education or the joy of their play . . . It allows neither for the justice in our courts, nor for the justice of our dealings with each other . . . It measures everything, in short, except that which makes life worthwhile. (Robert Kennedy in 1967, reported by Newfield 1978: 59–60)

More formally, the *social-welfare function* in equation (4.1) is the explicit relation between aggregate welfare and the welfare of the individuals who make up society. If U^i, the utility of the ith individual, depends on his income, y^i, social welfare, W, can be expressed as

$$W = W(U^1(y^1), U^2(y^2), \ldots, U^n(y^n)),\tag{6.2}$$

or, more simply, as

$$W = W(y^1, y^2, \ldots, y^n).\tag{6.3}$$

Thus $y^1, \ldots, y^n$ measure the welfare of each of the n individual members of society; these are aggregated into a measure of social welfare through the function W. Social-welfare functions are categorized in terms of their formal properties (see Cowell 1995: 35–41), an explanation of which is a necessary prelude to the discussion of aggregate inequality in Section 4.

PROPERTY 1: NON-DECREASING. Let social welfare in state A be

$$W_A = W(y^1, y^2, \ldots, y^{iA}, \ldots, y^N)$$

and, in state B,

$$W_B = W(y^1, y^2, \ldots, y^{iB}, \ldots, y^N).$$

In other words, the distribution in states A and B differs only because the ith individual has a higher income in state B than in state A. Then a social-welfare function is non-decreasing if and only if

$$W_B \geq W_A \text{ if } y^{iB} \geq y^{iA}. \tag{6.4}$$

Non-decreasing implies that, if any individual's income rises, social welfare cannot decrease.

PROPERTY 2: SYMMETRIC. A social-welfare function is symmetric if

$$W(y^1, y^2, \ldots, y^n) = W(y^2, y^1, \ldots, y^n) = \ldots = W(y^n, \ldots, y^2, y^1). \tag{6.5}$$

Social welfare depends on the distribution of income, but not on who gets which income—that is, social welfare is unchanged if two people 'swap' incomes. This is equivalent to assuming that all individuals have identical utility functions.

PROPERTY 3: ADDITIVE. A social-welfare function is additive if

$$W(y^1, y^2, \ldots, y^n) = \sum_{i=1}^{n} U^i(y^i) = U^1(y^1) + U^2(y^2) + \ldots + U^n(y^n). \tag{6.6}$$

This is the utilitarian social-welfare function, under which social welfare is the sum of the utilities experienced individually by members of society. Additivity implies that a person's utility depends only on his own income, independent of anyone else's income—a strong assumption that rules out the possibility of welfare interdependence discussed in Chapter 4, Section 4.1, and also rests uneasily with the relative definition of poverty discussed shortly.

These three properties taken together have important implications. If a social-welfare function is non-decreasing, symmetric, and additive, it has the general form

$$W = U(y^1) + U(y^2) + \ldots + U(y^n), \tag{6.7}$$

where: (a) (in contrast with equation (6.6)) U is the same for each individual (a consequence of symmetry); and (b) $U(y^i)$ increases with y^i (because the social-welfare function is non-decreasing).

Equation (6.7) makes it possible to use $U(y^i)$ as an index of social welfare. If there is an increase in the income of the ith individual, the increase in social welfare will be

$$U'(y^i) = \frac{dU(y^i)}{dy^i} \geq 0. \tag{6.8}$$

The welfare index $U(y^i)$ is *not* an ordinary utility function. It shows the social marginal valuation or *welfare weight* of changes in the *i*th person's income. To show why $U'(y^i)$ is the welfare weight, consider tax/transfers leading to a series of (small) changes in individual incomes, $\Delta y^1, \Delta y^2, \ldots, \Delta y^n$. The resulting change in social welfare is the total differential ΔW; and, if the social-welfare function takes the simple form of equation (6.7), then

$$\Delta W = U'(y^1)\Delta y^1 + U'(y^2)\Delta y^2 + \ldots + U'(y^n)\Delta y^n \tag{6.9}$$

and the terms $U'(y^i)$ act as weights when summing the effects of the scheme on social welfare. The next step is to discuss what value the weights might take. This brings us to:

PROPERTY 4: CONCAVE. A social-welfare function is concave if the welfare weight always decreases as y^i increases—that is, concavity implies diminishing social marginal utility of income. A £1 increase in income raises social welfare more if it goes to a poor person than to a rich person; thus a small redistribution from rich to poor raises social welfare. For some purposes it is useful to know how concave a social-welfare function is—that is, how rapidly the welfare weight falls as an individual's income rises. Thus:

PROPERTY 5: CONSTANT RELATIVE INEQUALITY AVERSION. A social-welfare function has constant relative inequality aversion (or constant elasticity) if the utility index $U(y^i)$ has the form

$$U(y^i) = \frac{1}{1-\varepsilon} y^{i(1-\varepsilon)}, \tag{6.10}$$

where ε is a non-negative *inequality aversion parameter*. The welfare index in equation (6.10) has the property that a 1 per cent increase in someone's income reduces her welfare weight by ε per cent whatever her income (i.e. by 1 per cent from £100 to £101 or from £10,000 to £10,100). The larger is ε, the more rapid the decline in the welfare weight as income rises; hence the name 'inequality aversion parameter'. We return to these issues in Section 4.2.

2. Poverty

Attempts to define a value-free poverty line (Section 2.1) face a series of largely intractable problems. The first concerns the choice of *indicator of welfare*, specifically (*a*) *which* indicator of consumption opportunities, and (*b*) *whose* income, i.e. the issue of the income unit. A second set of issues concerns which *concept of poverty* should be used. A third issue is how poverty should be *measured* (Section 2.3).

2.1. Defining poverty

WHICH INDICATOR OF WELFARE? Individual consumption opportunities should be measured in terms of full (i.e. money plus non-money) income. Because this is not possible, it is necessary to turn to more measurable indicators. Three measures are common: actual consumption of a specific bundle of goods, total expenditure, and total money income.

Each has its difficulties, of which the following is the barest of summaries.[7] The first approach requires a definition of the appropriate consumption bundle, and, when that difficult task has been accomplished, leads to a multidimensional (and hence complex) definition of poverty. Expenditure is difficult to measure and needs adjustment for inefficient spending.

Money income is a flawed measure of individual welfare (see the Further Reading). Three problems were discussed in Section 1.1: the unsystematic relation between money income and full income; the definition of the income unit; and the time period over which income is measured. None has an unambiguous answer, so any definition of poverty in terms of money income is somewhat arbitrary, a point reinforced in Section 3.2.

All three measures—consumption, expenditure, and income—face an additional and major problem. They look only at *ex post* magnitudes, ignoring the issue of choice illustrated by Figure 6.1. I may eat no meat and have low expenditure and income, and so be poor according to all three measures. But if by choice I am a vegetarian ascetic, then my *potential* living standard may exceed the poverty line. For these and other reasons, and notwithstanding a large body of work on measuring individual welfare, Ravallion (1996: 1331) concludes that 'even the best . . . measures found in practice are incomplete on their own'.

WHOSE INCOME? This is the issue of the income unit. There are two core issues: income sharing within households (Section 1.1), and the treatment of households of different size (Section 3.3). Again, there is no wholly satisfactory solution.

WHICH CONCEPT OF POVERTY? Even if these problems had been solved, major problems remain. In particular, should poverty be regarded as an absolute or a relative concept? With an *absolute* definition, a person is poor if her money income is too low to keep her alive and healthy. Early studies (see the Further Reading) attempted to define poverty 'objectively' by reference to basic nutritional requirements. There are serious objections to this approach. People have different nutritional requirements, so that no universally applicable standard is possible; nor is it reasonable to expect people to fill these requirements at minimum cost. Philosophically, the idea of an absolute poverty line stems from times when it was natural to think in subsistence terms; but this can be argued to be out of place, at least in richer countries, when people live well above subsistence, and where the concept of deprivation is applied to emotional and cultural standards as well as to physical ones.

Under a *relative* definition, with deceptive simplicity, a person is poor if he feels poor. The definition of poverty will vary by time and place according to prevailing living standards; and whether or not a person feels poor will depend in part on what he sees around him. It is argued, for example, that the collapse of the Berlin Wall was hastened because people in East Berlin could see much higher Western living standards on West Berlin television.

An absolute poverty line will remain fixed at subsistence; with a relative definition it will rise with living standards generally. In the latter case it is argued that a person is poor if

---

[7] For fuller discussion, see Atkinson (1989: ch. 1), Sen (1985, 1987), Chaudhuri and Ravallion (1994), Ravallion (1996), Jäntti and Danziger (2000), and various of the articles in Cowell (2003).

he cannot participate in the sorts of activities pursued by the generality of the population (this is known as a participation poverty standard). Thus a person without access to television is culturally deprived, and, at least in richer countries, a child is deprived if she does not have access to a computer. A relative poverty line has to increase to include such items.

A different argument for real increases in the poverty line is that, as income rises, the demand for inferior goods falls, and they tend to disappear from the market. 'The paradox of affluence is that [it] actually creates, as a by-product, a new poverty . . . [M]ore people have cars, so that buses carry fewer passengers at higher fares, and services are cut . . . The more people who have central heating, the harder and dearer it becomes, as the number of coal merchants dwindles, for the others to buy coal' (*Sunday Times*, 19 Sept. 1982). In such cases it is necessary to raise the poverty line so that people can buy the next cheapest substitute.

Formally, an absolute definition of poverty is more appropriate the more the utility of rich and poor depends only on their own incomes, and a relative definition is more appropriate the greater are income externalities. Suppose the relevant utility functions are

$$U^R = f(Y^R), \tag{6.11}$$

$$U^P = f(Y^P), \tag{6.12}$$

where U^R and U^P are the utilities of a representative rich and poor person, respectively, and Y^R and Y^P their incomes. This is the case implied by an additive social-welfare function (equation (6.6)), and an absolute definition of poverty might be appropriate. But if the utility functions are

$$U^R = f(Y^R, Y^P) \, f_1 > 0, f_2 > 0, \tag{6.13}$$

$$U^P = f(Y^R, Y^P) \, f_1 < 0, f_2 > 0 \tag{6.14}$$

(where f_1 and f_2 are the partial derivatives of utility with respect to Y^R and Y^P, respectively), we have an income externality of the type discussed in Chapter 4, Section 4.1, and both rich and poor might prefer a poverty line that rose over time.

SOCIAL EXCLUSION. Policy in Europe has increasingly focused on a broader concept of deprivation—social exclusion. The term is less used in the USA, where commentators tend to talk about 'marginalization' and the 'underclass'. If poverty is hard to define, social exclusion is even more so (Burchardt et al. 2002*a*). The expression was used in France in the 1970s to refer to people who fell through the social-insurance safety net. In today's usage the term has increasingly been used to describe multiple sources of deprivation, including income poverty but also such factors as health problems, low educational attainment, and social isolation and disaffection. The approach leads inexorably to multidimensional measures of deprivation, as discussed by Burchardt et al. (2002*b*).[8]

---

[8] A headcount measure of income poverty, for all its imperfections, allows comparison in terms of a single number. If deprivation is multidimensional, this becomes more difficult (*a*) because it is hard to quantify each element of deprivation and (*b*) because, even were this possible, a vector of characteristics can be boiled down to a single number only by using a vector of weights for the various characteristics. Such weights inescapably introduce value judgements into the enterprise. For fuller discussion in terms of multidimensional approaches to inequality, see Barr (1999), and Sen (1999).

The conclusion is that there is no unambiguous definition of income poverty, let alone of social exclusion, a topic to which we return in Section 5.

2.2. Poverty and inequality

Absolute poverty and inequality are separate concepts that should not be confused. Absolute poverty refers to a standard of living below some benchmark. The unbroken income distribution in Figure 6.2 shows a substantial number of poor people (i.e. the area *A*), a large number of middle incomes, and few high incomes. Inequality is concerned not with the absolute living standard of the poor, but with the *differences* between income groups; the dotted distribution shows more inequality (but less absolute poverty) than the unbroken one. Various measures of this dispersion are discussed in Section 4.

The difference between poverty and inequality is illustrated more fully in Table 6.1, which shows the average income in two societies of the poor (the lowest two-thirds of incomes), the rich (the top third), and the average income of rich and poor together. In society 1 the poor have an average income of £6,000, which is one-third of the average income of the rich, £18,000. In society 2 (which is identical in all respects except income)

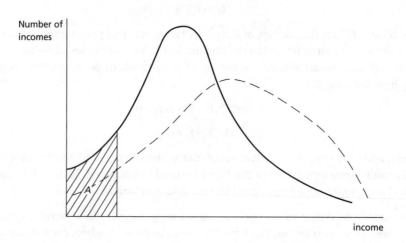

Fig. 6.2. Poverty and inequality

Table 6.1. Poverty and inequality in two different societies

Average income	Society 1	Society 2
Average income of the poor ($\frac{2}{3}$ of population)	£6,000 ($\frac{1}{3}$ income of rich)	£9,000 ($\frac{1}{4}$ income of rich)
Average income of the rich ($\frac{1}{3}$ of population)	£18,000	£36,000
Average income of rich and poor together	£10,000	£18,000

the average income of the poor, £9,000, is one-quarter of the average income of the rich, £36,000. In society 2 the poor have a higher standard of living than in society 1 (i.e. there is less absolute poverty), but are further behind both the average income and the standard of living of the rich (i.e. there is more inequality).

It is instructive to ask which society the poor would choose. Suppose a representative poor person has the utility function shown by equation (6.12); his utility depends on his own income, and his rational choice is society 2. In contrast, with equation (6.14), his utility increases with his own income but decreases as that of the representative rich person rises. If the externality (shown by f_1) is sufficiently strong, it will be rational for a poor person to choose society 1, in which the difference between rich and poor is smaller.

The distinction between poverty and inequality is important because it might not be possible to reduce both. A supply-side argument is that poverty can be alleviated by reducing the taxation of the rich, thereby encouraging economic growth and making possible further redistribution from rich to poor (i.e. reducing the top rates of tax might change society 1 into society 2). The relevance of this argument (whose truth is an empirical question) is its implicit assumption that the real enemy is absolute poverty rather than inequality—that is, it assumes an individual utility function of the form of equation (6.12). In consequence, policy design is concerned with poverty relief (objective 4 in Chapter 1, Section 2.2), but not with inequality reduction (objective 7).

Alternatively, policy that aims to 'squeeze the rich until the pips squeak' implicitly assumes that inequality rather than poverty is the main enemy—that is, that the utility of the poor is shown by equation (6.14). But, if the argument of the previous paragraph is true, then any attack on inequality might aggravate absolute poverty through the effect of higher taxation in reducing economic growth and hence the size of the tax base (i.e. attacking inequality might convert society 2 into society 1). The policy conclusion is not that attacks on inequality *will* increase absolute poverty, but that they might, making it important to be clear about the relative weights given to the different objectives of poverty relief and inequality reduction.

2.3. Measuring poverty

EMPIRICAL DEFINITIONS OF THE POVERTY LINE. Policy-makers cannot refuse to establish a poverty line just because there are conceptual problems;[9] and it is possible to infer roughly what the state thinks by looking at what it does. First, is poverty regarded as absolute or relative? With an absolute definition, the major benefits would have about the same real value today as in 1948, when the Beveridge arrangements came into effect. In fact, until the mid-1980s, benefits kept pace with changes in pre-tax average earnings.[10] Thus poverty is regarded as a relative concept, and this remains true, notwithstanding a

---

[9] On the state of play on methodology, see Atkinson (1995*a*: ch. 3), Ravallion (1996), Jäntti and Danziger (2000), Burtless and Smeeding (2001), and Glennerster (2002*a*).

[10] Since the real burden of taxation rose substantially over the post-war period, this implies that the real level of benefits *rose* relative to *post-tax* average earnings.

decline in the relative value of the major benefits since 1986.[11] The European Commission uses an explicit relative poverty line of 60 per cent of national average income (Atkinson et al. 2002; Dennis and Guio 2003).

Turning to the other issues posed earlier, the definition of the income unit for benefit purposes is fairly broad. In many countries, couples pay income tax on an individual basis; in contrast, the incomes of individuals living together are usually aggregated for benefit purposes, irrespective of marital status. In comparing families of different sizes, the UK poverty line for much of the post-war period was about 20 per cent of pre-tax average earnings for a single person, around 30 per cent for a married couple, and 40–5 per cent for a family of four. Thus the implied adult equivalents (see Section 3.3) for a single individual, a couple, and a family of four are 100, 150, and about 200, respectively. Finally, the time period over which income is measured for awarding cash benefits is frequently short. For some benefits it is necessary to show only that one has no current income; for others evidence of income in recent weeks is required.

These are the state's answers to the various definitional questions (see Barr 1981 for the earlier period; Evans 1998 for more recent trends). They are valid to the extent that over the years they have acquired the force of social convention; but they should not be regarded as having any particular intellectual merit.

HOW MUCH POVERTY? Since it is not possible to define poverty even for an individual, it is not surprising that there are no unambiguous answers about the extent of poverty overall. Aggregate poverty measures grapple with three dimensions of the problem: *how many* people are poor (the headcount measure); by *how much* do they fall below the poverty line (the poverty-gap measure); and *how long* are they poor—that is, is poverty transient or persistent?

The poverty headcount. Given a poverty line of £X per week, how many people are poor? Even this straightforward question has no simple answer. Counting the number of recipients of social assistance gives an underestimate, since not everyone who is eligible for benefit receives it.[12] Thus the number of poor people in the UK is larger than the number receiving income support, but without additional information we do not know how much greater. As a result, estimates have to be constructed from sample surveys.

The headcount, even were an accurate figure to be obtained, has major failings. It does not show how far people fall below the poverty line, and thus gives only a partial picture. Worse, a transfer of £100 from someone well below the poverty line to someone only £50 below *reduces* poverty as measured by the headcount.

The poverty gap attempts to remedy these deficiencies. It considers the total shortfall from the poverty line, divided by (*a*) the poverty line or (*b*) total income. Index (*a*) gives a measure of the average depth of poverty, (*b*) the relative cost of relieving it. Both approaches have been criticized (see Atkinson 1996), not least because a transfer from a poor person to a poorer person does not increase measured poverty.

---

[11] The retirement pension for a single person rose in real terms from £28.84 in 1948 to £75.50 in 2002 (April 2002 prices); it remained mostly between 22% and 24% of average earnings from 1948 till 1986, thereafter declining to about 16% in 2002 (UK DWP 2002c: table 5.1).

[12] The issue of these so-called take-up rates is discussed in Chapter 10, Section 3.

To address this problem, Foster (1984) proposed a poverty gap that gives greater weight to larger shortfalls. He suggested a measure

$$P_A = (1 - Y/P)^A, \tag{6.15}$$

where Y = family income and P = the poverty line. The value $A = 0$ gives the headcount; $A = 1$ gives an unweighted poverty gap; $A = 2$ gives a higher weight to greater shortfalls.

The duration of poverty. If most people dip into poverty only briefly, the problem is smaller than if poverty is long-term. Yet current household circumstances are uninformative about longer-term prospects. A static analysis (i.e. a snapshot at a single instant) gives no information about the (usually very different) characteristics of the persistently poor and the transient poor, and hence gives no guide to the (usually very different) policy measures. There is now a growing literature (see the Further Reading) on income dynamics, which seeks to disentangle persistent from transient poverty.

EMPIRICAL EVIDENCE. The fact that a definitive measure of poverty is not possible does not mean that empirical work is not useful, merely that care is needed in interpreting results.

Country studies. After 1980, poverty headcounts rose sharply in the UK. Based on a poverty line of 50 per cent of average income, poverty increased from 4.4 million people in 1979 to 10.4 million ten years later, the latter figure embracing 19 per cent of the population and 22 per cent of children (Atkinson 1995a: 292). Hills (with Gardiner (1997: 37)) finds that the poorest decile lost not only in relative terms but absolutely. Much of this poverty is persistent. Over the twenty years from the mid-1970s, the number of families with children in the bottom quintile of income recipients increased (Evans 1998). In 1997, the UK government established official poverty measures, with the aim of eradicating child poverty within twenty years (see the Further Reading). Piachaud and Sutherland (2002; see also Sutherland and Piachaud 2001) find that poverty rates declined slightly between 1997 and 2001, with further slight declines in prospect, the largest proportionate decline being in child poverty.

Poverty rose also in the USA. The facts are straightforward: after 1973, growth slowed while inequality increased. Burtless and Smeeding (2001) conclude that the incidence of poverty is higher in the USA than in other rich countries for two reasons: low wages and limited cash benefits. As in the UK, poverty fell among the elderly and rose for children (see the Further Reading). In both countries, poverty increased partly because of the response by government to economic and demographic forces (see Chapter 1, Section 3.1). We return to the topic in Chapter 10, Section 3.5.

Comparative studies face two sets of problems: for studies of absolute poverty, incomes in different countries need to be translated into a common currency (see OECD 2000); and for all comparisons of poverty, whether absolute or relative, there need to be data that are adequate in terms of detail and quality. The latter problem has been largely addressed by the availability of microdata (i.e. data on individuals), *inter alia* from the Luxembourg Income Study (LIS), which covers twenty-five countries (see Luxembourg Income Study 2000), and the European Community Household Panel (ECHP). Microdata have the two overriding advantages of comparability and completeness: it is possible to choose income units, income definitions, and equivalence scales, facilitating systematic comparison; and the data take in income from all sources, including private pensions and savings. The disadvantage is that such data are available only with a lag.

Burtless and Smeeding (2001: table 1) find that absolute poverty by headcount in the richest countries in the mid-1990s was much the lowest in the Nordic countries, followed by the mainland West European countries. It was highest in Australia, and was also high in the USA and the UK. As discussed below, the pattern of inequality was very similar. These results broadly accord with the findings of Dennis and Guio (2003) on poverty in the EU.

The former Communist countries. Analysis of transition faces additional complexities (see Atkinson and Micklewright 1992). Prior to reform, prices were often not market prices (e.g. subsidized food) and much income was received in kind (e.g. free holidays). On any measure, however, poverty increased substantially: a World Bank study (2000: 1) reports that in Central and Eastern Europe and the former Soviet Union as a whole the poverty headcount rose from about 4 per cent of the population in 1990 to 25 per cent in 1998.

Modelling poverty. The approaches discussed so far are broadly descriptive. Targeting, however, can be helped by more detailed knowledge of the characteristics of the poor —for example, are they disproportionately old, or living in certain areas. One way to construct the necessary poverty profiles is to run a regression of the poverty measure (e.g. whether the person is in receipt of social assistance) against household characteristics. This approach can be useful in identifying characteristics on which to condition benefits, a major topic in Chapter 10, and also to simulate possible changes in anti-poverty policy. For fuller discussion, see Ravallion (1996) and for recent work Hills et al. (2002).

3. Inequality 1: Individuals and families

This section discusses equality (as with poverty, no wholly satisfactory definition is possible), and then turns to inequality between individuals (Section 3.2) and families (Section 3.3).

3.1. Defining equality and inequality

DIFFERENT DEFINITIONS OF EQUALITY. The first question is: equality of what? In principle the answer is easy—individuals are equal if they face identical opportunity sets—that is, face the same full income in Figure 6.1. But full income cannot be measured, so matters in practice are more complex. Le Grand (1982: 14–15; 1991a: ch. 5) distinguishes five possible definitions. The simplest, *equality of final income*, implies that individuals are equal if they have the same level of money income plus income in kind. But complications arise in measuring income in kind. Should there be *equality of public expenditure* (i.e. spending on, say, health care is the same for everybody); or *equality of use* (e.g. everyone is allocated the same quantity of health care); or *equality of cost* (e.g. everyone faces the same cost of using the National Health Service, which implies that people visiting their doctor should be compensated for any lost earnings); or *equality of outcome* (e.g. health care is allocated so that, as far as possible, everyone enjoys equally good health)? All have valid claims as definitions of equality; all are different.

Similar problems arise when we try to define 'equality of opportunity'. An individual's income depends on three sets of factors: his *endowments* (e.g. of human capital or inherited wealth); his *tastes* with respect to work and leisure, consumption and saving, risk, etc.; and his *luck*, since outcomes have a stochastic element. Thus two individuals with identical tastes and opportunity sets may experience very different outcomes—'some people work for a firm that goes bankrupt; some people invest early in Rank Xerox' (Atkinson and Stiglitz 1980: 267).

EQUALITY OF OPPORTUNITY is best approached in several steps.

First step: equality of opportunity exists if

$$Y_F = K \text{ for all } i \quad i = 1, 2, \ldots, N, \tag{6.16}$$

where Y_F is full income as defined in equation (6.1), and includes a time dimension. Equation (6.16) states that full income should be the same for all N individuals in society. The obvious problem is that no account is taken of the stochastic element in individual income. Equality of opportunity implies that people should have an equal *chance*—that is, it is an expected value not an absolute value that should be equal. Hence:

Second step: equal opportunity can be said to exist if

$$E(Y_F) = K \text{ for all } i. \tag{6.17}$$

Here equality of opportunity requires only that expected income should be the same for all individuals. This is an adequate definition of equality of opportunity in terms of *full* income, which captures all aspects of the individual opportunity set. In practice, however, measurement problems force us to use money income, which varies not only with the individual opportunity set, but also with individual choices (see Figure 6.1); and differences in income resulting from different choices need not imply inequality. Hence, if Y is money income:

Third step: equal opportunity exists if

$$E(Y|C_i) = K_i \text{ for all } D_i. \tag{6.18}$$

Equation (6.18) requires explanation. As discussed in Section 3.2, some characteristics may affect money income without causing inequality; these include age and any differences in individual choice that are the result of differences in tastes, and so are referred to as C (choice) characteristics. But, if money income varies systematically with other characteristics (social class, gender, ethnic background, parental money income), we regard society as unequal. These are the D (discrimination) characteristics. Equation (6.18) states that equality of opportunity exists if the expected value of money income is the same for all individuals with given C characteristics, but must be invariant to their D characteristics.

At first glance equation (6.18) seems to offer a workable definition of equality of opportunity. But it contains two strategic difficulties. First, using money income as an indicator of welfare raises problems even if we control for age and tastes. Equality of opportunity must apply both to cash income and to income in kind; yet, as discussed earlier, equality of access when discussing distribution in kind can be ambiguous. In addition (Section 1.1), any measure of welfare based on material well-being is incomplete;

some non-material aspects can be analysed in economic terms as violations of the perfect-information and equal-power assumptions (Chapter 4, Section 3.2), but they stand in their own right as independent sources of inequality.

Secondly, even if full income were measurable, there remains the problem of distinguishing a C from a D characteristic. There is broad agreement that social class, gender, and ethnic background are D characteristics; and it might be argued that laziness and a long-time horizon are C characteristics. But what about 'natural ability'? If ability is entirely exogenous (i.e. 'innate'), differences in ability can be regarded as luck—that is, the stochastic element of Y. Society might take no action where people do well (e.g. the state does not confiscate the high incomes of gifted musicians or athletes), but may compensate people who do badly (e.g. someone born with a long-term health problem). A completely different case arises if ability is at least partly endogenous—for example, induced by differences in the quality of education. Ability is then in part a D characteristic, and positive discrimination might be justified.

Thus people can be unequal for two very different reasons. If incomes differ because of discrimination, 'society' is unfair, and appropriate action might involve changing the structure of society (see the quote by Tawney at the head of the chapter). In contrast, inequality can arise because of random differences in luck (i.e. 'life' can be unfair), captured by the stochastic element in equation (6.18). Bad luck may require remedial action, but does not imply that society is unfair.

The last word should go to Okun (1975: 76, repr. in Atkinson 1980), who summarizes the problem with customary eloquence.

The concept of equality of opportunity is far more elusive than that of equality of income . . . [It] is rooted in the notion of a fair race where people are even at the starting line. But . . . it is hard to find the starting line. Differences in natural abilities are generally accepted as relevant characteristics that are being tested in the race rather than as unfair headstarts and handicaps. At the other extreme, success that depends on whom you know rather than what you know is a clear case of inequality of opportunity. And it seems particularly unfair when the real issue is whom your father knows.

The inheritance of natural abilities is on one side of the line of unequal opportunity, and the advantages of a family position are clearly on the other. But much of the territory is unsettled.

3.2. Measuring inequality between individuals

Inequality between individuals is best approached by considering A and B, with money incomes of £20,000 and £10,000, respectively, and asking why they might in fact be equal. There are three reasons why differences in money income might have no bearing on an individual's opportunity set, and so be irrelevant to issues of equality.

DIFFERENT CHOICES can cause differences in money incomes in two ways. A and B may have *different tastes about money income* (i.e. different indifference maps in Figure 6.1). Suppose A likes champagne and foreign travel, and B likes walking across the hills with his dog. A (with money-intensive preferences) might choose to work longer hours; and B might work fewer hours (i.e. enjoy more leisure) and/or choose work with more job satisfaction (i.e. higher non-money income). Both A and B are maximizing their utility: there is no case for regarding them as unequal simply because one has higher money income. Secondly, there can be *differences in acquired skills* (hence different budget constraints in Figure 6.1): suppose A has chosen to forgo income early in life in order to acquire skills, while B has not. A's higher income is a return on her investment in human capital. Again there is no reason to suppose that there is any inequality provided (and the proviso is crucial) that A and B had the *same opportunity*, including access to information, to acquire skills.

AGE. Suppose A earns twice as much as B because she is 40 years old and highly skilled, whereas B is 20 years old and an apprentice. Suppose, further, that when B is 40 he will earn as much as A does now. In this case, the difference in money income is a life-cycle effect, and no long-term issue of inequality arises.[13]

THE TIME DIMENSION. If A and B have fluctuating incomes, A might earn £20,000 and B £10,000 this year, with the positions reversed next year. Taking the two years together, there is no inequality. More generally, inequality is greater if a rich person systematically has rich descendants and a poor person poor ones, an issue directly related to the earlier distinction between persistent and transient poverty.

It is possible also to ask the question in reverse. Suppose A and B each has money income of £15,000. That does not necessarily mean that they are equal. They might face different price levels. More importantly, A might have a larger family than B and so, it might be argued, has a lower standard of living. This raises issues of how to compare families of different sizes.

The conclusion is that money income is a misleading indicator of inequality. *This does not mean that there is no inequality—just that money income is bad at measuring it.*

3.3. Measuring inequality between families

If it is not possible to compare the living standards of two individuals, we are likely to make even less headway with families of different sizes. Families with the same standard of living have 'equivalent' incomes, from which can be derived equivalence scales. Suppose a couple with an income of £15,000 have a child; what increase in money income is necessary to leave them as well off as before? The issue is important. Buhmann et al. (1988) found that different equivalence scales had a significant impact on measured inequality.

The logic of the problem is illustrated by the following arguments.

- The *consumption argument* states that, if a couple have a child, per capita income in the household falls, and the couple need a higher money income to maintain their standard of living. If there are no economies of scale in household formation, a

---

[13] The need to control for age is particularly important in analysing the distribution of wealth. Consider a society where everyone has identical earnings, of which 10% is saved to finance retirement. The resulting wealth distribution is highly unequal: young people have no wealth (because they have not yet started to save); people aged 98 have very little wealth (because they have spent all their savings); and people aged 64 have substantial wealth (because they have been saving all their working lives and have yet to start dissaving).

three-person family has an adult equivalent of 3; if there are economies of scale (e.g. it costs no more to heat a house containing three people than two), it will be (say) 2. In either case, larger families require a higher income. The question is—how much higher?

- The *utility argument*, along revealed preference lines, asserts that a couple will have a child by choice only if it raises their utility. In the extreme, where two people with perfect information have a child by choice, their utility is increased, and they can maintain a given standard of living with *less* money income. More generally, the utility associated with a child reduces the additional income necessary to maintain a given living standard. This approach might be useful for better-off families,[14] but the consumption argument might be more appropriate for a low-income family.

If one person needs one unit of income, a two-person family will need (say) 1.75 units to achieve the same standard of living, and a three-person family (say) 2.25 units. More recent studies[15] encapsulate the equivalence scale in a single parameter. Economic well-being, or 'adjusted' income, W, is related to gross disposable family income, D, and family size, S, where:

$$W = D/S^E. \tag{6.19}$$

The equivalence elasticity, E, varies between 0 and 1. A value of zero implies no adjustment for family size (closer to the utility argument above), a value of one implies per capita income (a family of three people will need three times the income to maintain a given standard of living).

Atkinson et al. (1995) distinguish four approaches to setting a value on E, illustrating—yet again—that there is no unambiguously 'correct' answer.

- *Statistical scales* are developed to count people at or below a given standard of living—for example, the scales used by the European Commission or the US Bureau of Labor Statistics to count the low-income population. Atkinson, Rainwater, and Smeeding (1995) report a median value for such scales of $E = 0.72$—i.e. close to per capita.

- *Programme scales* are used for defining social assistance and similar benefits for families of different sizes. Here the median value of E is 0.59, implying some economies of scale in household formation.

- *Consumption scales* are based on observed spending patterns. For example, if food spending rises proportionately with family size but housing expenditure does not, then an increase in family size in effect raises the price of an improved diet relative to improved housing; *ceteris paribus* there will, therefore, be substitution towards housing. An implication is that families need not be fully compensated for increases in food costs. The median value of E in this case is 0.57, very close to that of the programme scales.

---

[14] Some couples are prepared to pay large amounts to adoption agencies or for medical treatment to cure infertility.

[15] See Buhmann et al. (1988), Coulter et al. (1992), Atkinson (1995a: chs. 2, 4), and Atkinson et al. (1995: ch. 2). For adjustment to accommodate the extra costs of disability, see Zaidi and Burchardt (2003).

- *Subjective scales* attempt to measure the utility associated with different income levels—i.e. the utility approach discussed above. Predictably, the median value of *E*, 0.25, is lower than for scales that do not attempt to capture the utility associated with a child.

4. Inequality 2: Aggregate measures

4.1. The descriptive approach

This section discusses the measurement of inequality in society as a whole,[16] starting with simple representations of the income distribution, and proceeding to more complex measures and a brief review of empirical studies. The aim is to construct a scalar representation of income differences within a given population. Ideally it would take on values between zero (if everyone had the same income) and one (if one person had all the income), making it possible to answer questions like: how much inequality is there in the UK today; how much more than ten years ago; is it more than the EU average? Any such measure rests on two ingredients.

- What is the unit defined to be equal or unequal—for example, the individual, family, or household? Here we talk only of 'individuals', abstracting from issues of household size and definition.

- Inequality of what—for example, income, wealth, power? The literature generally looks at 'income', which usually means money income.

An inequality measure combines knowledge of the 'incomes' of 'individuals', though we shall see that its usefulness is qualified by both conceptual difficulties and measurement problems.

THE FREQUENCY DISTRIBUTION AND ASSOCIATED MEASURES. The simplest starting point is the *frequency distribution*, which shows the number of income recipients at each level of income. It can be represented as a continuous function, as in Figure 6.2, or as a histogram. The frequency distribution has the advantage of being simple and easy to interpret, especially in the middle-income ranges. But it is weak at the tails; the left-hand tail should include negative incomes (e.g. business losses), and the right-hand tail has been severely truncated.

A dramatic way of representing the income distribution is *Pen's parade*,[17] in which each person marches past the onlooker. The parade takes an hour and each person's height corresponds to his pre-tax income (a person with average income having average height). This representation is vivid; it shows up the tails well; and we can see the distribution, and also who is where in it. It does not, however, lend itself readily to quantification.

[16] See Cowell (1995: chs. 1, 2; 2000) or, for broader discussion, Sen (1992).
[17] See Pen (1971, repr. in Atkinson 1980: 47–55), for an entertaining and non-technical description of the income distribution.

There are several measures of inequality based on the frequency distribution, of which this section discusses only the most important. A natural way of trying to capture aggregate inequality is by a summary measure of dispersion like the *variance*

$$V = \frac{1}{n} \sum_{i=1}^{n} (y_i - \mu)^2, \tag{6.20}$$

where y_i is the money income of the ith individual, μ is average income, and there are n income recipients. The advantage of the variance is twofold: it considers the whole distribution, and measured inequality is reduced by any redistribution that brings an individual's income closer to the mean. Its main disadvantage is its sensitivity to the absolute level of income; if all incomes double (or are expressed in dollars at an exchange rate of $2 = £1$), inequality does not change but V quadruples.

This problem is avoided by the *coefficient of variation* defined as

$$C = \frac{V^{0.5}}{\mu}, \tag{6.21}$$

which is the variance normalized on average income. The advantage of C is its independence of scale. But it has a number of difficulties, not least that it is neutral to the income level at which transfers take place—that is, transferring £100 from an individual with an income of £1,000 to one with an income of £500 has the same effect on C as a £100 transfer from a person with an income of £1 million to one with £999,500.

If we want to give greater weight to transfers to lower incomes, one procedure is to take some transformation such as the logarithm that staggers income levels. The *variance of the logarithm of income* has the added advantage of scale independence.[18] For this reason the variance of the logarithm of income

$$H = \frac{1}{n} \sum_{i=1}^{n} (\log y_i - \log \mu)^2 = \frac{1}{n} \sum_{i=1}^{n} \log\left(\frac{y_i}{\mu}\right)^2 \tag{6.22}$$

has been used as an inequality measure. H has the advantages that it is invariant to the absolute level of income, is sensitive to income transfers at all income levels, but gives greater weight to transfers to lower incomes. There are also disadvantages. The measure (in common with V and C) considers only differences of income from the mean; and it squares those differences. Both procedures are somewhat arbitrary. In addition, H may not be concave at higher income levels—that is, H can rise in the face of some transfers from rich to poor.[19]

THE LORENZ CURVE was devised explicitly as a representation of inequality. Though the approach is old (Lorenz 1905), it is a powerful device, intimately connected with an important theorem by Atkinson discussed in Section 4.2. In Figure 6.3 the horizontal axis shows the percentage of individuals or households, the vertical axis the percentage of total income. The Lorenz curve is shown by the line OaB. Each point shows the share of

---

[18] If income, say, doubles, this simply adds a constant to all logarithms of income, which cancel when calculating deviations from the mean.

[19] Concavity and other properties of social-welfare functions are discussed in Section 1.2.

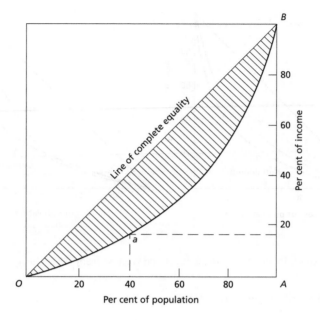

Fig. 6.3. The Lorenz curve

total income received by the lowest *x* per cent of individuals; thus point *a* shows that the bottom 40 per cent of individuals receive 17 per cent of income.

The Lorenz curve will coincide with the diagonal *OB* if income is distributed completely equally (because only then will the lowest 50 per cent of individuals receive 50 per cent of total income, and so on); and, the greater the degree of inequality, the further the curve will lie from the diagonal. If the Lorenz curve for the UK lies entirely inside that for the Netherlands (as in the historical example in Figure 6.4*a*), we can say that income inequality is lower in the UK; but where the curves cross (as in the historical comparison between the UK and West Germany in Figure 6.4*b*), an ambiguity arises. Lorenz curves thus give only a partial ordering of outcomes.[20]

The Gini coefficient (Gini 1921) is based on the Lorenz curve; diagrammatically it is the ratio of the shaded area in Figure 6.3 to the triangle *OAB*. If incomes are distributed completely equally, it will be zero; and, if one person has all the income, it will be unity. Formally, the Gini coefficient is defined as half of the arithmetic average of the absolute differences between *all* pairs of incomes, the total then being normalized on mean income:

$$G = \frac{1}{2n^2\mu}\sum_{i=1}^{n}\sum_{j=1}^{n}\left|y^i - y^j\right|. \tag{6.23}$$

---

[20] Shorrocks (1983) attempts at least partly to resolve the ambiguity. He constructs a 'generalized Lorenz curve' by scaling up the conventional Lorenz curve by the mean of the income distribution. While the measure is often successful at resolving ambiguity, it does so only because of strong assumptions about the weight given to absolute living standards. Weakening those assumptions reduces the ambiguity-resolving power of the construct.

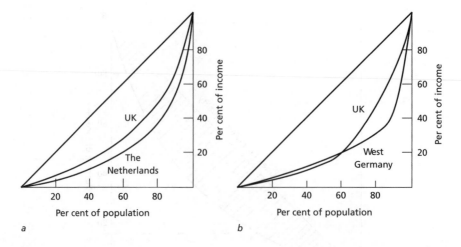

Fig. 6.4. Lorenz curves for the UK, the Netherlands, and West Germany, 1962–1964

This can also be written (Sen 1973: 31) as

$$G = 1 + \frac{1}{n} - \frac{2}{n^2 \mu}(y^1 + 2y^2 + \ldots + ny^n) \tag{6.24}$$

for $y^1 \geq y^2 \geq \ldots \geq y^n$.

The Gini coefficient has several advantages. It is independent of the absolute level of income, avoids the arbitrary squaring procedure of V, C, and H, and compares each income not with the mean but with every other income, as equation (6.23) makes clear. Its disadvantages are twofold. It gives ambiguous results when Lorenz curves cross. The second disadvantage is more subtle, and we return to it later. Formulation (6.24) shows that the Gini coefficient is a weighted sum of people's incomes, with the weights determined solely by the person's *rank order* in the distribution. Thus y^1 (the highest income) enters the term in parentheses with a relative weight of 1, y^2 (the second highest income) with a relative weight of 2, and so on. This is an entirely arbitrary social-welfare function.

GENERAL CRITIQUE OF THE DESCRIPTIVE MEASURES. To set the scene for subsequent discussion, it is helpful to bring out four sets of criticisms, which apply to all the descriptive measures.[21]

1. They lack generality. V, C, and H all incorporate the arbitrary procedures of squaring differences from the mean.

2. They all incorporate an *implicit* and *arbitrary* social-welfare function with built-in welfare weights. With V and C a given transfer from a relatively higher to a relatively lower income always has the same effect; the implied social-welfare function values all reductions in inequality equally, even if redistribution is from a millionaire to a

[21] For trenchant criticism of virtually all summary measures, see Wiles (1974: esp. pp. 7–12). He advocates the ratio of the average income of someone in the top 5% of incomes to the corresponding average for the lowest 5% as the least bad summary statistic. As discussed in Section 4.3, Gottschalk and Smeeding (2000) use this approach to measure 'social distance.'

semi-millionaire. For H the implied social-welfare function embodies weights derived from the logarithm function, which again might not be one's chosen weights. The social-welfare function underlying the Gini coefficient, as equation (6.24) shows, embraces weights based on rank order.

3. The descriptive measures give only a partial ordering of outcomes. This is obviously true of intersecting Lorenz curves and hence of the Gini coefficient. The same problem arises with the other measures.

4. In addition to these conceptual difficulties, all the measurement problems discussed earlier in the context of poverty apply equally to measures of inequality.

4.2. Inequality measures based on a social-welfare function

Normative measures start explicitly from a social-welfare function. This section discusses an important theorem by Atkinson, its implications, and the Atkinson inequality measure.[22]

THE ATKINSON THEOREM on Lorenz ranking is remarkable for its generality. Assume:

1. States A and B have income distributions given by $(y^{1A}, y^{2A}, \ldots, y^{nA})$ and $(y^{1B}, y^{2B}, \ldots, y^{nB})$, respectively.

2. Total income is the same in states A and B.

3. W is a social-welfare function that is non-decreasing, symmetric, additive, and concave (see Section 1.2).

Then: the Lorenz curve for B lies wholly inside the Lorenz curve for A *if and only if* $W_B > W_A$ for *every* social-welfare function with the four properties listed in assumption 3. To amplify, the theorem tells us:

1. If the Lorenz curve for B lies wholly inside that for A, then: (*a*) welfare in state B is higher than in state A; we can say this *without knowing what the social-welfare function is*; (*b*) the income distribution is unambiguously more equal in state B; (*c*) the Gini coefficient compares distributions unambiguously; and (*d*) conventional summary measures (e.g. V, C, and H) all show that inequality is lower in state B.

2. Conversely, if social welfare is higher in state B, then we know that Lorenz curve B must lie strictly inside Lorenz curve A.

3. As a corollary, if Lorenz curves cross: (*a*) we cannot say whether inequality is greater in state A or B; (*b*) the Gini coefficient gives an ambiguous comparison; and (*c*) different inequality measures give different results.

These conclusions link the (descriptive) Lorenz curve to the explicitly normative world of the social-welfare function. But the result is still not sufficient, both because not all Lorenz curves are non-intersecting, and because we still want a *numerical* measure of inequality. Atkinson (1970) approached the issue by considering the Lorenz curves in Figure 6.4. The theorem enables us to say unambiguously that the distribution of income

---

[22] See Cowell (1995: ch. 3), which also discusses other approaches, by Dalton (1920) and Theil (1967). For a simple introduction, see Atkinson (1983: 54–9). See also the Further Reading.

was less unequal in the UK than in the Netherlands. Figure 6.4*b* shows that the share of lower incomes was higher in West Germany than in the UK, but at higher incomes there was less inequality in the UK. By inspection, the area between the Lorenz curve and the diagonal was greater for West Germany than the UK, so that the Gini coefficient shows that the UK is *less* unequal than West Germany. But a measure that gives greater weight to lower incomes would show that the UK is *more* unequal.

Atkinson draws two major conclusions.

1. Where Lorenz curves cross, it is necessary to compare one income group with another. *Thus the degree of inequality cannot in general be compared without introducing values about the distribution* in the form of welfare weights for different income levels. This should be done *explicitly* via a social-welfare function, in contrast with descriptive measures, which all embody implicit but unstated weights.

2. Only where Lorenz curves do not intersect is it possible (subject to assumption 3 of the theorem) to avoid the necessity of explicit welfare weights; in this case all the descriptive measures will agree.

THE ATKINSON INEQUALITY MEASURE considers distributional values explicitly. It is based on a social-welfare function with the five properties discussed in Section 1.2—that is, non-decreasing, symmetric, additive, concave, and with constant relative inequality aversion, ε, as in equation (6.10), as an explicit representation of distributional values. The Atkinson measure is given by

$$A = 1 - \left[\sum_{i=1}^{N} \left(\frac{y^i}{\mu} \right)^{1-\varepsilon} f(y^i) \right]^{1/(1-\varepsilon)} \qquad \varepsilon \neq 1, \tag{6.25}$$

where y^i is the income of individuals in the *i*th income range (*N* ranges altogether), $f(y^i)$ is the proportion of the population with incomes in the *i*th range, and μ is mean income. *A* will be zero *either* if $y^i = \mu$ for all *i* (i.e. if income is equally distributed), *or* if $\varepsilon = 0$ (i.e. if policy is concerned only with the absolute level of income, not its distribution). The greater the deviation of y^i from μ and/or the higher the value of ε, the greater the value of *A*.

There is a natural connection between ε and the theories of society discussed in Chapter 3. If $\varepsilon = 0$, society is indifferent to inequality (the Libertarian position), and *A* is zero. If $\varepsilon = \infty$, society is concerned only with the position of the lowest individual or income group, as advocated by Rawls. Socialists, too, would choose a high value. Utilitarians set no *a priori* limits, but choose the value that maximizes total welfare. In general the place of ε between the two extremes determines the importance of redistribution from richer to poorer: as equation (6.25) shows, the deviation of y^i from μ is weighted by the exponent $(1 - \varepsilon)$, rather than the arbitrary squaring formula of *V*, *C*, and *H*.

The meaning of ε is shown by Atkinson's 'mental experiment', subsequently elaborated as Okun's 'leaky bucket'. Consider taking £100 from a rich man and giving a proportion £*x* to a poor man, the rest leaking away in efficiency losses (disincentives, administration). How far can *x* fall (i.e. how leaky can the bucket be) before we no longer regard the redistribution as desirable? The answer determines ε.[23] The higher is ε, the lower *x* can be

---

[23] ε is determined from the formula $1/x = 2\varepsilon$; see Atkinson (1983: 58).

(i.e. the more egalitarian the view, the more 'leakiness' is tolerable): if $\varepsilon = 1$, it is fair to take £100 from a rich person and give £50 to a poor person; if $\varepsilon = 2$, it is sufficient if the poor man receives £25.

The Atkinson measure can be interpreted both as an inequality measure *and* as an index of the potential welfare gains from redistribution. Consider the proportion of present total income necessary to achieve the same level of welfare if it were equally distributed. If $A = 0.3$, we can say that, if income were equally distributed, we should need only $(100 - 30)\% = 70\%$ of present national income to achieve the same level of social welfare. Alternatively, the gain from redistributing to equality is equivalent to raising national income by 30 per cent. The welfare gain is higher (*a*) the greater the value of ε, and (*b*) the more unequal the pre-existing distribution.

The Atkinson measure thus has powerful advantages. Conventional measures like the Gini coefficient obscure the fact that a complete ranking of states is possible only where the form of the social-welfare function is specified, and the social-welfare functions implicit in conventional measures are often arbitrary, if not unacceptable. The Atkinson measure avoids both difficulties—a complete ranking of states is possible, though precise knowledge of the social-welfare function is unnecessary.

The main criticism of the measure is not operational but philosophical—namely, its basis on an additive, individualistic social-welfare function—that is, on the assumption that social welfare is a (more or less) simple sum of individual utilities. This is restrictive: it rules out the sort of welfare interdependence discussed in Chapter 4, Section 4.1; and it ignores non-material sources of well-being.

4.3. Inequality: Some empirical results

PROBLEMS WITH EMPIRICAL WORK on the distribution of income are ubiquitous.

1. Virtually all studies are based on the current money income of households or tax units. This procedure raises serious difficulties for all inequality measures:

   - It generally omits a significant fraction of non-money income (Section 1.1) and is thus inherently a poor measure of individual opportunity sets. Additionally, cross-country comparisons may omit certain dimensions of inequality, e.g. differences in political freedom.

   - It fails to exclude differences in money income that have no bearing on inequality, e.g. life-cycle factors and individual choice (Section 3.2).

   - Adjustments for differences in the size and composition of different households face the problems described in Section 3.3.

2. Summary measures of inequality raise the following conceptual problems:

   - Conventional measures face the criticisms set out at the end of Section 4.1.

   - The Atkinson measure is based on the assumption of additivity.

   - Trends over time need to be interpreted in the light of structural change. For example, an increase in the size of a poor group—e.g. students or old people—will appear to increase inequality even though the position of each student or pensioner is unchanged.

3. Data problems:

- Information on income by type or level of income, or type of recipient, might be scant.
- The definition of income might change over time, or be incompatible with those of other countries.
- Estimation is generally based on income classes, and so neglects dispersion within each class; the use of more disaggregated data generally increases measured inequality.

EMPIRICAL EVIDENCE. The absence of any definitive measure of inequality does not mean (nor should it) that empirical work is useless, merely that it should be interpreted with all the earlier caveats in mind.

Country studies. The downward trend in inequality over the twentieth century was reversed in the years after 1980. Indeed, the UK and USA stand out for the sharpness of the increase in inequality over the 1980s. Hills (1996a) found that the Gini coefficent in the UK rose by 10 percentage points between 1977 and 1990. To illustrate the US story, in 1973 an American at the ninety-fifth percentile received slightly less than twelve times as much as an American at the fifth percentile. By 1993 the equivalent figure was over twenty-five (Burtless 1996: 272; see also the Further Reading).

Comparative studies. Much cross-country analysis uses data from the Luxembourg Income Study discussed in Section 2.3 (see Atkinson et al. 1995: table 4.8; Gottschalk and Smeeding 2000). The latter study uses various measures, including the Lorenz curve and the decile ratio—that is, the ratio of the incomes of the rich (people at the ninetieth per-centile) to those of the poor (those at the tenth percentile). The Lorenz curve shows the entire distribution; the decile ratio is a measure of 'social distance'. Both measures show a common pattern: in the mid-1990s, the Nordic countries had the least inequality, followed successively by the countries in mainland Western Europe and the Commonwealth coun-tries; the UK and the USA had the greatest inequality. The decile ratio was highest in the USA (6.44) and UK (4.56) and lowest in the Nordic countries (the Swedish ratio was 2.78).

Inequality—both facts and causation—are controversial and incompletely understood. The elements in the story include:

- labour market trends, including increased earnings inequality, polarization into households that are 'work-rich' (two or more workers) and 'work-poor' (no full-time workers), reduced job stability and increasing self-employment;
- social trends, including the changing role of women's earnings in family income;
- demographic trends, in particular the increase in the number of lone-parent families;
- changes in the benefit regime;
- changes in the distribution of wealth.

These elements are discussed in the various contributions to Hills (1996b). Danziger and Gottschalk (1995) (see also Gottschalk 1997) argue that the greater part of the increase in inequality in the USA is due to the increased earnings inequality of family heads. Fischer et al. (1996), contradicting earlier work by Murray, argue that increased inequality in the USA is largely the result of badly designed and parsimonious public policy. Atkinson (2003) discusses the major controversies surrounding both the facts (for example, whether inequality is increasing significantly or not), and causation.

The former Communist countries. As discussed earlier, there are even greater problems where measurement involves a benchmark period with non-market prices (see Atkinson and Micklewright 1992). Nevertheless, it is clear that reform has increased inequality (see World Bank 2002 for an overview, and for detail Milanovic 1998, 1999). Part of the increase —reflecting the introduction of market-determined wages and similar growth-promoting changes—was both necessary and desirable. In the late-1990s, countries such as the Czech Republic and Hungary had Gini coefficients approaching (though still below) the OECD average. In contrast, Russia had a Gini coefficient approaching 50 per cent, well above that in any OECD country, and almost certainly more than is necessary to promote efficiency. We return in the concluding section to the links between inequality and growth.

The distribution of wealth should be mentioned, if only to stress its importance. Some empirical studies are listed in the Further Reading. If anything the problems are even worse than with income. Some problems are conceptual (e.g. what should be included in personal wealth). Others are measurement problems (e.g. the valuation of estates at death). Many are problems of both concept and measurement (e.g. whether accrued pension rights should be included as part of personal wealth and, if so, how they should be valued).

5. Conclusion

DESCRIBING OUTCOMES. The main conclusion is that there is no scientifically 'correct' measure of poverty or inequality.

The following lead to more people being counted as poor—that is, to higher measured poverty:

- a higher poverty line;
- a narrower definition of income (e.g. excluding home-grown produce);
- a narrower definition of the income unit (i.e. excluding the income of the extended family);
- a larger adjustment for household size; smaller economies of scale in household formation imply a value of E (equation (6.19)) closer to one, leading to per capita adjustment or close to it, thus giving a higher weight to children;
- a shorter time period over which income is measured.

Measured inequality, similarly, will be higher with a narrower definition of the income unit, with a shorter period over which income is measured, and when based on a more continuous income distribution (the wider the bars of a histogram, the more inequality *within* groups is omitted).[24]

---

[24] The relation between measured inequality and adjustment for household size is more complex; see Coulter et al. (1992).

All these problems are compounded when comparing across countries (see Atkinson 1995a: ch. 4). Country A can have less measured poverty or inequality than country B (*a*) because of differences in the distribution of pre-transfer incomes or (*b*) because of more generous transfers, or (*c*) because poverty and inequality are measured differently (i.e. the difference could be a statistical artefact).

Since well-informed commentators can (and do) make different assumptions about the elements of (*c*), it is not surprising that estimates vary widely. These are not just technical issues. A higher weight for children will find more poor children and fewer poor old people than with a poverty line in which children receive a lower weight. Similarly, a broader definition of the income unit assumes that older people share the resources of younger family members and thus finds fewer poor old people. In short, measuring poverty and inequality involves inescapable value judgements.

EVALUATING OUTCOMES. Why does any of this matter? Measuring poverty is important because poverty is costly. It is costly in equity terms for most of the theories of society discussed in Chapter 3. It is also costly in efficiency terms: poverty is associated with ill health; and ill health is associated with poor learning outcomes (this is the national efficiency argument in Chapter 2, Section 2); poverty is also associated with crime, imposing external costs on society more broadly (Chapter 8, Section 2.1).

Measuring inequality is also important. In contrast with poverty, it is possible to have *too little* inequality. Incentives are important for static and dynamic efficiency; a flat income distribution generally requires both a fairly flat wage distribution and job security. The growth slowdown in the Communist countries of Central and Eastern Europe and the former Soviet Union show the resulting devastating efficiency costs. *Too much* inequality, however, can also be costly. As with poverty, this is partly for equity reasons. But there is also growing evidence (Aghion et al. 1999; Lundberg and Squire 2003) that, at least in developing countries with very high rates of inequality, a reduction in inequality is associated with increased growth rates.

▪ QUESTIONS FOR FURTHER DISCUSSION

1. What problems arise in trying to estimate how many poor people there are in a country.

2. Suppose a person's income is twice as high as her neighbour's. Why might such an income difference *not* reflect inequality?

3. [More difficult] Explain why definitions of poverty and inequality inescapably involve value judgements.

▪ FURTHER READING

For an overview of the problems of defining and measuring income, poverty and inequality, see Atkinson (1983) (compendious and non-technical); for wide-ranging collections, Atkinson (1980, 1989, 1995a); and for surveys, the various chapters in Atkinson and Bourguignon (2000). Cowell (2003) contains seventy-one articles on poverty and inequality published between 1896 and 2000.

For official discussion, see UK DWP (2002*b*) and Eurostat (2001), and, on social exclusion, Hills et al. (2002) and Atkinson et al. (2002).

The classic works on defining and measuring income are Fisher (1930: 3–35), Simons (1938: 41–58), Hicks (1946: 171–81), and Kaldor (1955: 54–78).

The classic historical studies of poverty are by Rowntree (1901) and Booth (1902); for follow-up studies, see Rowntree (1941) and Rowntree and Lavers (1951), and, for reworking and updating, Atkinson et al. (1983). On the definition and measurement of poverty, see Sen (1985, 1987, 1999), Piachaud (1987, 1993), Atkinson (1989: chs. 1, 2), Jäntti and Danziger (2000), and Burtless and Smeeding (2001). On measuring poverty in Europe, see Atkinson (2000), Gordon and Townsend (2000), Atkinson et al. (2002), and Dennis and Guio (2003). For a historical perspective of US poverty studies, see Glennerster (2002*a*).

On poverty in the UK, see Atkinson (1989: ch. 3), Hills with Gardiner (1997), Martin Evans (1998), and Sutherland et al. (2003). Poverty among women and poverty and ethnicity are discussed by Oppenheim and Harker (1996: chs. 5, 6), and child poverty by Sutherland and Piachaud (2001) and Piachaud and Sutherland (2002). On the USA, see US Panel on Poverty and Public Assistance (1995), Gottschalk (1997), Jorgenson (1998), Levy (1998), Triest (1998), and Blank (2000).

For comparative studies, see Atkinson (1995*a*: ch. 4; 1998), Jäntti and Danziger (2000), and Burtless and Smeeding (2001), and, on child poverty, UNICEF (2000), Vleminckx and Smeeding (2000), and Immervoll et al. (2000). Dennis and Guio (2003) discuss poverty in the EU. On poverty in the former Communist countries, see Milanovic (1998, 1999) and World Bank (2000, 2002).

On poverty dynamics, see Chaudhuri and Ravallion (1994), Ravallion et al. (1995), Jarvis and Jenkins (1997, 1998), Gardiner and Hills (1999), and Hobcraft (2002); also Burgess and Propper (2002), which includes some discussion of poverty dynamics in OECD countries.

The meaning of 'equality' is discussed by Okun (1975: ch. 3) and Le Grand (1982, 1984; 1991*a*: ch. 5). For a simple introduction to the literature on adult equivalents, see Atkinson (1983: ch. 3) and, for fuller discussion, Buhmann et al. (1988), Coulter et al. (1992), and Atkinson et al. (1995).

Aggregate inequality is illuminated in Pen (1971, repr. in Atkinson 1980), and discussed more generally by Atkinson (1983); see also Sen (1992). Cowell (1995) discusses aggregate inequality measures, and includes a useful introduction to social-welfare functions; for more advanced discussion, see Champernowne and Cowell (1998) and Cowell (2000). The classic article on the Atkinson inequality measure is Atkinson (1970), repr. with a non-mathematical summary in Atkinson (1980: 23–43) (for a simple introduction, see Atkinson 1983: 54–9). For the 'leaky-bucket' experiment, see Okun (1975: 91–100) (another piece of vintage Okun to which the reader is warmly recommended); and, for a witty and highly critical review of most inequality measures, Wiles (1974).

Inequality in the UK is discussed in UK Royal Commission on the Distribution of Income and Wealth (1979: ch. 2; repr. in part in Atkinson 1980: 71–8). On increases in inequality over the 1980s, see Atkinson (1995*a*: chs. 1, 2; 1996) and Goodman et al. (1997). Trends in the USA are discussed by Danziger and Gottschalk (1995) and Gottschalk (1997). Piketty and Saez (2003) analyse long-term trends in inequality at the top end of the distribution.

On inequality trends in the OECD, see Atkinson et al. (1995), Gottschalk and Smeeding (2000), and Atkinson and Brandolini (2001). On the former Communist countries, see Atkinson and Micklewright (1992), Milanovic (1998, 1999) and World Bank (2000, 2002), and, for a study of Russia, Brainerd (1998). For an ambitious study of inequality worldwide, see Milanovic (2002) and Milanovic and Yitzhaki (2002). On debates over the causes of widening inequality, see Fischer et al. (1996), Hills (1996*b*), and Atkinson (1999*a*, 2003).

On the distribution of wealth, see UK Royal Commission on the Distribution of Income and Wealth (1979) and, for more recent analysis, Banks and Tanner (1996) and Hamnett and Seavers (1996); on trends in the wealth distribution in the USA, see Wolff (1998).

Appendix: Non-technical summary of Chapter 6

1. Chapter 6 discusses problems that arise in defining and measuring the key concepts of income, poverty, and inequality.

Income

2. The only theoretically sound definition of individual income (Section 1.1) is *full income*, Y_F, which consists of money income, Y_M, plus all non-money income, Y_N (e.g. job satisfaction, the value of own production, and the enjoyment of leisure), i.e.

$$Y_F = Y_M + Y_N. \tag{6.1}$$

The inclusion of non-money income, including the enjoyment of leisure, is crucial. Full income defined this way is a broad measure of an individual's *potential* consumption—i.e. of her power to consume goods (including leisure).

3. The measurement of income (Section 1.1) is bedevilled by several sets of problems. First, money income is used as a proxy for full income because it is not possible to measure most non-money income. The fact that there is no systematic relation between Y_M and Y_N makes money income an unreliable yardstick of consumption opportunities, and therein lies the origin of many of the problems of defining and measuring poverty and inequality. A second difficulty concerns the definition of the unit whose income we are measuring—e.g. whom does the income unit include, and how should the incomes of families of different sizes be treated? Finally, over what time period should income be measured? The conclusion is that a theoretically sound definition of income faces intractable measurement problems.

Poverty

4. In principle poverty should be defined in terms of full income. Its measurement therefore faces all the problems described in paragraph 3. But, even if these were solved, it would still be necessary to decide whether poverty, however measured, should be defined in absolute or relative terms (Section 2.1). *Absolute poverty* means that a person's money income is too low to keep him alive and healthy. Early studies hoped in this way to measure poverty 'objectively', an approach that is increasingly out of favour, at least in developed economies. *Relative poverty* implies that a person is poor if her standard of living deviates substantially from the average of the society in which she lives—i.e. if she cannot participate in 'normal' life.

5. Poverty (in an absolute sense) and inequality are two entirely separate concepts (Section 2.2). Absolute poverty relates to a standard of living below some benchmark, inequality to the *difference* between the incomes of poor and non-poor. The distinction is important, because policies aimed at one might aggravate the other. It is, therefore, necessary to be clear whether poverty relief or inequality reduction is the major objective.

Inequality

6. Equality of opportunity (Section 3.1) would be hard to define even if full income could be measured. The main problem is to decide which causes of income differences matter. Systematic differences due to gender, ethnicity or social class are generally regarded as examples of inequality. But ambiguity can arise when differences are due to 'natural ability', depending on whether or not

it is influenced by differences in the quality of education. Equality of opportunity is not, however, violated by random differences in income (i.e. luck).

7. These problems are compounded because in practice it is necessary to use money income as a proxy for individual welfare. Differences in money income can overstate inequality between individuals A and B for at least three reasons (Section 3.2): they may have different tastes and hence have made different choices (e.g. about leisure); they may be at different stages in their life cycle (e.g. A fully trained, B an apprentice); and the difference in their incomes may be the result of random fluctuations. Other factors can understate inequality. None of this implies that there is no inequality in society—just that money income is bad at measuring it.

8. Further problems arise when comparing the incomes of families of different sizes (Section 3.3). One argument is that, if a couple has a child, per capita household income will fall; it follows that larger households need more money than smaller households to maintain an 'equivalent' stand-ard of living. Alternatively, if a couple has a child by choice, it can be argued that, though per capita money income falls, the couple's *utility* rises because otherwise they would not have had the child. In the latter case a larger household does not necessarily need a higher money income to maintain a given living standard. Again, the problem arises because it is not possible to measure full income; and again there is no wholly satisfactory solution.

9. Section 4 discusses measures of the overall degree of inequality in society. These measures, to the extent that they are valid, enable us to answer questions like: is the UK today more unequal than ten years ago; is it more unequal than the USA or the EU average?

10. A widely used measure is the *Lorenz curve* (Section 4.1). In Figure 6.3 the horizontal axis shows the percentage of individuals/households, the vertical axis the cumulative percentage of total income. The Lorenz curve is shown by the line *OaB*. Each point on the curve shows the share of total income received by the *lowest x* per cent of individuals. Thus point *a* shows that the bottom 40 per cent of individuals receive 17 per cent of income. If income is distributed completely equally, the Lorenz curve will coincide with the diagonal (i.e. the lowest 50 per cent of individuals receive 50 per cent of income, and so on). Thus the greater the degree of inequality, the further the Lorenz curve will be from the diagonal, and vice versa.

11. The *Gini coefficient* is an inequality measure based on the Lorenz curve; diagrammatically it is the ratio of the shaded area in Figure 6.3 to the triangle *OAB*. It follows that the Gini coefficient will vary between zero (if income is distributed completely equally) and one (if one person has all the income).

12. The use of the Gini coefficient as a measure of inequality is subject to criticisms (Section 4.3). First, it is based on the current money income of individuals or households: this omits all non-money income (paragraphs 2 and 3); it fails to exclude differences in money income that have no bearing on inequality, e.g. life-cycle factors and individual choice (paragraph 7); and it faces difficulties over differences in household size (paragraph 8). Secondly, the data on money income are not always accurate, complete, or consistent over time or across countries. Finally, the Gini coefficient raises a number of conceptual problems. These are discussed in Section 4.2 together with the Atkinson inequality measure, which treats inequality in a more sophisticated way, and hence avoids some of the problems of the Gini coefficient. A key conclusion is that, if the Lorenz curve for (say) Sweden lies wholly inside that for the USA, then we can (*a*) say unambiguously that inequality is less in Sweden, and (*b*) the Gini coefficient for Sweden will unambiguously be lower than that for the USA.

13. The main message of paragraph 12 for non-technical readers is that the Gini coefficient, though widely used and useful in some circumstances, is in no way definitive as a measure of over-all inequality.

PART TWO

Cash Benefits

The simple Fisher model discussed in Chapter 4, Section 3.2, shows an individual's consumption choices over time. In a world of certainty, the welfare state is necessary only to assist the lifetime poor; insurance is unnecessary, since there is no risk, and consumption smoothing (i.e. redistribution to oneself over the life cycle) takes place through saving or borrowing. A central conclusion of Chapter 5 is that relaxing the assumption of certainty introduces risk (which is insurable), uncertainty (which is not), and imperfect information, not least on the part of insurers, which creates further problems for actuarial insurance.

The welfare state thus has a central role in three of the purposes of cash benefits discussed in Chapter 1, Section 2.2:

- Insurance improves people's welfare by offering protection against contingencies that might happen or might not, notably unemployment and ill health. Chapter 8 discusses those cash benefits whose primary purpose is to offer insurance (though they also have other aspects).

- Consumption smoothing improves welfare by allowing people to redistribute to themselves over their life cycle. A central (though not the only) purpose of pensions (Chapter 9) is to allow people to redistribute from their younger to their older selves.

- Poverty relief (Chapter 10) includes benefits based on an income test, others based on indicators of poverty—for example, the presence of children in the family—and others on a mixture of income test and other conditions, such as various 'welfare-to-work' schemes.

Chapter 7 briefly describes how these various cash benefits are financed.

It is possible to categorize cash benefits in other ways. Classification by client group—for example, benefits for children, for people of working age, and for the elderly—might be a useful categorization for designing social policy. Classification by administrative method—for example, contributory or non-contributory, administered by the social-security department or by the tax authorities, or paid out of the social-security fund or from general tax revenues—might be useful for civil-service activity.

The classification adopted here—the division of benefits designed to provide insurance, or consumption smoothing, or poverty relief—is illustrated in Figure 1.3, which shows that nearly two-thirds of welfare state spending relates to the first two. This classification is the most useful for understanding the economics of the welfare state, and in particular for answering the questions this book explores: why does the welfare state exist; and why is the state so heavily involved?

The chapters in Part 2 have a broadly common structure. Section 1 establishes objectives and very briefly summarizes UK institutions. Successive sections then set out the theoretical arguments about state intervention; assess UK institutions, with some limited discussion of other countries; and discuss reform strategies in the UK and elsewhere.

7

Financing the welfare state

Taxes, after all, are the dues that we pay for the privileges of membership in an organised society.

(Franklin D. Roosevelt, 1936)

Thrift should be the guiding principle in our government expenditure.

(Mao Tse-tung, 1893–1976)

1. The structure of the UK government accounts

1.1. Conceptual issues

This chapter discusses the finances of the welfare state, and is somewhat more institutional than the rest of the book. The subject is vast, and the account here no more than a very brief summary of the ground covered in detail by Glennerster (2003*a*). National insurance and other cash benefits are discussed in Section 2, and the rest of the welfare state, mainly the National Health Service and education, in Section 3. Section 4 considers a number of important methodological issues. This section describes the structure of UK government accounts. As a backdrop it is necessary to bring out a number of conceptual points.

BOUNDARY PROBLEMS. Chapter 6 discussed difficulties in defining a poverty line—that is, the boundary between poor and non-poor people. Analogous boundary problems arise with public spending (Prest and Barr 1985: ch. 8) and are the subject of continuing review by the UK Office for National Statistics and by Eurostat.

One boundary—that between the public and private sector—is important in deciding whether a project is classified as publicly or privately financed. The issue arises when private finance of a National Health Service hospital is being considered and also, as discussed in Chapter 14, in the design of student loans. A second boundary is between different levels of government activity. The most obvious distinction is between central and local government. For instance, total spending by central and local government is *not* the simple sum of their respective expenditures. Part of central spending is a grant to local authorities, which then forms part of local spending. In producing overall public-sector accounts care is needed to avoid double counting.

TYPES OF GOVERNMENT EXPENDITURE. It is important to distinguish:

- absorption of goods and services, which (taking education as an example) includes

    (*a*) current spending (i.e. public consumption in the form of teachers' salaries), and

    (*b*) capital spending (i.e. public investment, such as new school buildings);

- transfer payments, which include (*c*) current grants to the personal sector (e.g. student scholarships), and (*d*) capital grants to the private sector (e.g. contributions to the cost of university building).[1]

Chapter 4, Section 3.1, sets out the four types of intervention—regulation, finance, public production, and income transfers. Government absorption of goods and services corresponds with public production. Transfer payments take two different forms. The first is explicit transfers, as discussed above, including all state cash benefits. Secondly there are:

TAX EXPENDITURES—that is, implicit public expenditure in the form of tax relief. Cash assistance to help tenants to pay their rent is an explicit transfer, mortgage-interest tax relief for owner-occupiers an implicit transfer. Both assist with housing costs, but only the former appears in conventional figures on public spending. Tax expenditures can take two forms. Tax allowances can subsidize particular activities—for example, private pensions (Chapter 9). Suppose a person's income tax liability is £2,000, but her pension contributions attract a deduction of £250; thus her tax bill is £1,750. The tax allowance does not appear as public spending, but results in tax revenues being £250 lower than would otherwise be the case.

Tax credits differ from tax allowances in one important respect—a person's tax bill can fall below zero. If a person's tax liability is £2,000 but she receives a tax credit of £3,000, her tax liability is minus £1,000, and she receives a £1,000 cash transfer. Tax credits can thus be a direct substitute for conventional cash benefits. As an illustration, in 2003–4, the Working Tax Credit offered a person in work a weekly cash payment of £29.20 (higher for a disabled person or lone parent, etc.) included in his or her pay packet, and clawed back at a rate of 37 pence per pound of earnings above a threshold. As discussed in Chapter 10, this policy direction was favoured by UK governments in the early 2000s because it was seen as simultaneously relieving poverty and strengthening incentives to join the workforce.

Should tax credits be treated as tax forgone, like tax allowances, hence reducing government revenues, or should they be included in public spending alongside other cash transfers? The issue is politically sensitive, since governments like to claim that they are keeping taxation down. The UK Office for National Statistics, bearing in mind international statistical guidelines, decided that 'Working Tax Credits and Child Tax Credits would be classified . . . as negative taxation to the extent that credits are less than or equal to the tax liability of the household, and as public expenditure where credits exceed that liability' (UK Treasury 2002*b*: 216). Thus tax credits paid to families who pay no income tax count as public spending; where the family pays income tax, they count as reduced taxation.

---

[1] These are transfer payments from the viewpoint of government, because universities are regarded as part of the private sector.

1.2. Government revenue and expenditure

THE REVENUE PROPOSALS of government are set out each year in the Budget, and more formally in the *Financial Statement and Budget Report* and the Finance Bill. It is a long-standing principle of UK public finance that, in general, all central government revenues, whatever their source, are paid into the *Consolidated Fund*, from which all central government expenditure is made. The only major exception is the *National Insurance Fund*, discussed in Section 2.2.

Table 7.1 gives an overview of the income and expenditure of government. The three main blocks of revenue relate to taxation, social-security contributions, and government borrowing. Total revenue of all levels of government in 2003/4 was £456 billion, mainly from current taxation.[2] Taxes on income, administered by the Inland Revenue, raised £161 billion, 75 per cent from income tax, the largest single revenue source. Taxes on expenditure, mostly administered by Customs and Excise, raised £113 billion. Other sources of revenue include business rates (i.e. property tax levied on businesses) of £19 billion and Council Tax (the only significant local tax) of £19 billion. Social-security contributions, discussed in Section 2, were £75 billion, and net public-sector borrowing £27 billion.

THE SPENDING PROPOSALS of government are set out each year in a series of departmental reports (see the Further Reading). Total spending by all levels of government in 2003/4 was £456 billion (Table 7.1). To control public spending, this figure is divided into two elements: departmental expenditure limits (£261 billion) are planned on a three-yearly basis; annually managed expenditure (£192 billion) relates to demand-led spending, notably some cash benefits and interest on the national debt. In economic terms, £232 billion is current spending on goods and services, to which is added £20 billion net investment spending; transfer payments comprise £160 billion on general transfers plus £22 billion in interest and dividend payments.

The expenditure side of Table 7.1 also shows some of the most important elements of spending by function. Total spending on cash benefits[3] in the UK was £117 billion,[4] on the National Health Service £75 billion, and on education £59 billion.[5]

One point to emerge immediately is the sheer size of the welfare state, however defined (and it consists at a minimum of cash benefits, health, and education). In 1920 the welfare state absorbed about 6 per cent of GDP, only marginally greater than debt-interest payments and about 1.75 times defence spending. In 2003/4, the welfare state absorbed close to 24% of GDP and over eight times defence spending. Table 1.2 (which omits spending on education) suggests that the resulting spending is broadly in line with the OECD average but significantly below the average for the EU.

---

[2] All figures in Section 1.2 are rounded to the nearest £ billion.

[3] As explained in the Glossary, there is an ambiguity in the use of the term 'social security'. In the USA it generally refers to retirement benefits; in the UK it refers to *all* contributory and non-contributory cash benefits, and in mainland Europe to all cash benefits and health care. The term will be avoided where possible. Where its use is inevitable, it will be used in the UK sense.

[4] The figure refers to direct cash benefits, but omits tax credits, which make up an additional £12 billion.

[5] Disaggregated figures are given in Tables 7.3 (cash benefits), 12.1 (health), and 13.1 (education).

Table 7.1. Income and expenditure of central and local government, UK, 2003/4 (est.) (£bn.)

Revenue		Expenditure	
Current receipts	424.1	Departmental expenditure limits	263.8
Net borrowing	27.1	Annually managed expenditure	191.9
Other	4.5		
General government receipts and borrowing	455.7	General government expenditure	455.7
Of which		*Of which, by economic category*	
Revenue from taxation		Current expenditure on goods and services	232.0
Inland revenue		Net investment spending	20.1
Income tax	122.1	Net social benefits and other transfers	159.7
Corporation tax	30.8	Interest and dividend payments	22.2
Other	8.4	Other	21.7
	161.3		
Customs and Excise		*Of which, by function*[a]	
VAT	66.6	Cash benefits (UK)[b]	116.7
Fuel duties	23.0	National Health Service (UK)	74.8
Taxes on alcohol & tobacco	15.4	Personal social services (England)	12.5
Other	8.1		
	113.1	Education (UK)	58.6
		Housing (England)	5.5
Other taxes		Criminal justice (England and Wales)	16.4
Business rates	18.6	Defence (UK)	30.9
Council tax	18.6	Gross debt interest	23.0
Other	16.7		
	53.9		
Social-security contributions	74.5		
Net borrowing	27.1		
Other[c]	25.8		

[a] Not exhaustive.
[b] Spending on all contributory and non-contributory cash benefits. The figure excludes about £12 billion of tax credits whose function is identical to cash benefits.
[c] Includes gross operating surplus, rent, and other current transfers, and interest and dividend receipts.
Sources: UK Treasury (2002a): tables A.2, A.3; UK Treasury (2003a): tables C8, C11, C23.

Table 7.2. National-insurance contribution rates, 2003/4

	Contribution rate	
Employed persons	Employee contribution rate[a,b]	Employer contribution rate[c]
Weekly earnings		
Below £77 (lower earnings limit)	0%	0%
£77–£89 (primary and secondary thresholds)	0%	0%
£89–£595 (upper earnings limit)	11%	12.80%
Above £595	1%	12.80%
Self-employed persons	Class 2	Class 4
Annual profits		
Below £4,095	0	
£4,095 and above	£2 per week	
£4,615–£30,940		8%
Above £30,940		1%
Non-employed persons		
Voluntary contribution	£6.95 per week	

[a] Employees receive a contracted-out rebate of 1.6% between the lower and upper earnings limits.
[b] Men aged 65 or over and women aged 60 or over do not pay employees' contributions. However, employers' contributions are payable.
[c] Employers receive a contracted-out rebate between the lower and upper earnings limits of 3.5% for qualifying final-salary (i.e. defined benefit) schemes, and 1% for qualifying money purchase (i.e. defined-contribution) schemes.

2. Cash benefits

2.1. Individual national-insurance contributions

There are three types of contributor for national-insurance purposes: employed persons, the self-employed, and the non-employed, summarized in Table 7.2.

EMPLOYED PERSONS. Class 1 contributions are paid by employees and the employers. The simple system introduced in 1948 (Chapter 2, Section 6) has become more complex over the years. Workers pay a contribution of 11 per cent of earnings between the single person's income tax threshold (£89 per week in 2003/4), and an upper earnings limit (£595 per week in 2003/4), plus 1 per cent of earnings above the upper earnings limit. Individuals contracted out of the state earnings-related pension scheme (Chapter 9, Section 1) pay contributions at reduced rates, depending on the type of pension scheme. Some people's right to benefit is protected even if they pay no contributions, including low earners[6] and people who are unemployed, ill, or caring for a disabled person.

[6] i.e. someone with earnings between the lower earnings limit (£77 per week in 2003/4) and the secondary threshold.

Unlike income tax and the other types of national-insurance contribution, the income limit for Class 1 contributions is a *weekly* exemption. Thus, someone earning £89.10 in some weeks and £88.50 in others pays contributions in weeks where earnings were £89.10, even if her average for the year was under £89. These contributions are not refundable, in sharp contrast with the operation of income tax in similar circumstances. Uneasy relationships like this have generated pressure for an integrated system of income tax and national-insurance contributions (see Hills 2003, and the discussion in Chapter 11, Section 3.2).

Employers' contributions are analogous, except that the contribution rate is 12.8 per cent and there is no upper limit. There is a reduced rate for contracted-out employees.

Both employee and employer Class 1 contributions are collected alongside income tax. They pay for national-insurance benefits and also contribute to the cost of the National Health Service.

THE SELF-EMPLOYED pay both Class 2 and Class 4 contributions. The Class 2 contribution is flat rate (£2 per week in 2003/4). Class 4 contributions are a percentage of profits collected by the Inland Revenue as part of the individual's income-tax assessment. In 2003/4, the class 4 contribution was 8 per cent of profits between £4,615 (the income-tax threshold for a single person) and £30,940, and 1 per cent of profits above that. These contributions do not entitle a self-employed person to all the benefits available to an employee. There is no support while unemployed and no earnings-related retirement pension. Someone who is both employed and self-employed is potentially liable to pay Class 1, Class 2, and Class 4 contributions, subject to an annual ceiling on total contributions.

THE NON-EMPLOYED, broadly, are not current members of the labour force—for example, students or married women who are not employed or self-employed. To maintain an un-broken contributions record, people in that situation can pay a voluntary flat-rate Class 3 contribution (£6.95 per week in 2003/4). The payment of Class 3 contributions gives no right to immediate benefit, but may protect future entitlement. As discussed further in Chapter 9, Section 1, a woman (or in certain circumstances a man) staying at home to look after young children or a disabled person can avoid breaks in her contributions record without paying Class 3 contributions because she receives home responsibilities protection—that is, receives a credit for her contribution.

2.2. The National Insurance Fund

National-insurance benefits are paid from the National Insurance Fund, and all other central government benefits from the Consolidated Fund. The distinction is important for operational purposes and for understanding the structure of government accounts but has less economic significance.

REVENUE. On the revenue side, the relation between the two funds is straightforward. The income of the National Insurance Fund derives mainly from the contributions of insured persons. Virtually all other central government revenues go into the Consolidated Fund.

In 2003/4 total gross national-insurance contributions were £74.5 billion, the great bulk from Class 1 contributions. For the most part, these contributions paid for benefits in 2003/4—i.e. the system was organized on a Pay-As-You-Go basis. Whether the Fund should be organized on actuarial lines (i.e. have a reserve sufficient to pay all expected future liabilities) is a central topic in Chapter 9.

Two general points should be noted. First, as Table 7.1 shows, national-insurance contributions were over 20 per cent of central government revenue from all other sources; only income tax produced significantly more revenue. In effect there is a third estate alongside the Inland Revenue and Customs and Excise. Secondly, the budgetary procedures for this revenue differ from those for public spending generally; for example, the accounts of the National Insurance Fund are kept separate from the general accounts.

EXPENDITURE. On the expenditure side, matters are less tidy. In principle, benefits from the National Insurance Fund (e.g. for unemployment) are paid only to individuals with an appropriate contributions record, while similar benefits paid from the Consolidated Fund are awarded on the basis of other criteria, such as low income or number of children (e.g. child benefit). As the foot of Table 7.3 shows, spending on contributory benefits in 2003/4 was £56 billion, just below half of total benefit spending of £115 billion (to which should be added some £12 billion in tax credits). Spending on non-contributory benefits is of two sorts: benefits awarded without a contributions record or income test (£23 billion in 2003/4) and those awarded on the basis of an income test (£35 billion in 2003/4).

In practice, however, many people receive benefits from both sources, so that it is more informative to discuss them together. Table 7.3 divides benefits into three groups:

- those intended to offer insurance against events that might happen or might not, notably unemployment, ill health, and widowhood (these benefits—which in principle could be addressed through private insurance—are discussed in Chapter 8);

- those intended primarily to provide consumption smoothing—that is, redistribution to oneself over the life cycle, notably retirement pensions (these benefits—which in principle could be addressed through saving—are discussed in Chapter 9);

- those relieving poverty, including income-tested poverty relief, employment subsidies, and family support (these benefits are discussed in Chapter 10).

The largest of the three (£48 billion in 2003/4) is consumption smoothing, mainly through the state old-age pension (the figure excludes income-tested benefits for pensioners, notably the pension credit, which are included in the anti-poverty benefits). The major insurance-type benefits (£24 billion in 2003/4) concern ill health. A clear conclusion is the importance of consumption smoothing and insurance, which together make up nearly two-thirds of spending on cash benefits.

Benefits intended to relieve poverty can be divided into three groups. First is a series of general income-tested benefits, notably income support (an income-tested benefit of last resort for people below pensionable age) and the pension credit, the parallel benefit for people above pensionable age. Secondly, and as large as those two benefits, is a series of income-tested benefits to assist people with their housing costs. Thirdly, there are benefits (mostly not income tested) to assist families with children (£10 billion in 2003/4), of which the largest is child benefit, a tax-free cash payment in respect of each child, payable weekly to (usually) the mother.

Table 7.3. Cash benefits, UK, 2003/4 (est.) (£m.)

Insurance against specific contingencies

Unemployment

Jobseeker's allowance—contribution based	504	
Jobseeker's allowance—income based	2,261	
Job grant	25	
		2,790

Ill-health

Statutory sick pay	32	
Incapacity benefit	6,876	
Attendance allowance	3,341	
Invalid care allowance	1,040	
Severe disablement allowance	945	
Disability living allowance	7,433	
Industrial disablement and death benefits	674	
		20,341

Widowhood

Widows'/bereavement benefits	1,070	
		1,070

Total insurance	24,201

Consumption smoothing

Benefits for elderly people

State retirement pension—basic	39,591	
State retirement pension—earnings related	6,718	
Winter fuel payments	1,718	
Over-75 TV licence	375	

Total consumption smoothing	48,402

Poverty relief

General income tested

Income support	9,882	
Pension credit[a]	5,141	
Social fund	377	
		15,400

Housing benefits

Housing Benefit Rent Allowance and rent rebate[b]	12,620	
Council Tax Benefit[b]	3,291	
		15,911

Benefits for families with children

Child benefit	9,102	
Guardian's allowance/child's special allowance	2	
Maternity benefits	1,047	
		10,151

Total poverty relief	41,462
Other	587
TOTAL	114,652

of which	
Contributory	55,960
Non-contributory, not income tested	22,981
Non-contributory, income tested	35,290

[a] The pension credit replaces Income Support for people aged 60 and over.
[b] Housing Benefit and Council Tax benefit figures are total amounts, including payments by the central Department and spending by local authorities.
Source: UK DWP (2002a): table 7.

3. Benefits in kind

This section surveys very briefly the finances of the National Health Service and of the state educational system (for details, see Glennerster et al. 2000; Glennerster 2003*a*: chs. 4–6). As we shall see in Chapter 12, the original intention of the National Health Service that all health care should be free has largely been realized. Medical attention is generally free, with the exception of certain items (e.g. prescription drugs) for which charges apply to some people. Of total spending on the National Health Service in the early 2000s, about 95 per cent came from general taxation and from national-insurance contributions, with about 2.5 per cent from charges. Table 7.1 shows that total spending on health care in 2003/4 was £75 billion, with an additional £13 billion for social care (for further detail see Table 12.1). The National Health Service, clearly, is not a contributory scheme, and any assessment of its finances must discuss the tax system as a whole (see Section 4).

Education is discussed in Chapters 13 and 14. Historically, school education was both produced and financed locally. Table 7.1 shows that spending on education and related activities was £59 billion (for further detail see Table 13.1). Though most education spending is at the local level, the extent of central government grants to local authorities means that it is largely financed from the Consolidated Fund. I shall abstract from most of the central versus local debates and discuss school education for the most part as a non-contributory scheme financed from general taxation, and differing from the National Health Service only to the extent that there is a larger role for local government. Higher education raises very different issues, taken up in Chapter 14.

Table 7.1 shows that net spending on housing in England in 2003/4 was £6 billion, with substantial involvement by both central and local government. This figure under-states public spending on housing. It omits tax relief for owner-occupiers, which, like all tax allowances, is an invisible item in government accounts. More importantly, it omits the large amount of income-tested benefit spending designed to assist people to meet their housing costs, shown in Table 7.3. Benefits for housing are discussed in Chapter 10 in the context of poverty relief.[7]

4. Assessing the welfare state

4.1. Incidence considerations

Assessing the efficiency and redistributive impacts of the welfare state is a vast undertaking that raises both methodological and measurement problems (see Atkinson and Stiglitz 1980: lecture 9). This section limits itself to outlining some of the issues of principle,

---

[7] As explained in Chapter 1, Section 2.1, housing (like food) is an area where the major *economic* problem is one not of market allocation but of income distribution. Poor people live in bad housing not because they do not have the information to make better decisions but because they cannot afford anything better. For the purposes of this book, housing is therefore discussed in the context of poverty relief.

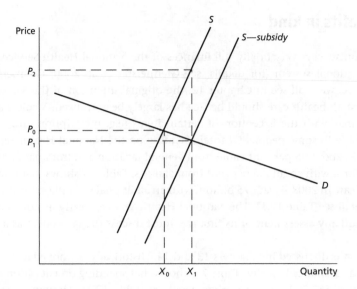

Fig. 7.1. Partial equilibrium incidence of a subsidy

leaving more detailed discussion to later chapters. Two aspects assume special relevance: the notion of tax incidence; and the importance of considering benefits and taxes together.

THE SIMPLE TAX INCIDENCE ARGUMENT is illustrated in Figure 7.1, which analyses the partial equilibrium incidence of a housing subsidy. Suppose the housing market is in equilibrium at price P_0 and quantity X_0. A specific rent subsidy shifts the supply curve vertically downwards to S—*subsidy*; this reduces the price paid by the tenant from P_0 to P_1 (i.e. only a small reduction), and increases the price received by the landlord substantially from P_0 to P_2.

The result is that, if landlords are rich and tenants poor (not that this is necessarily the case), then a seemingly redistributive housing subsidy might of itself be regressive. Similarly, suppose that labour is supplied inelastically to the market (empirically plausible for primary workers).[8] A reduction in income tax or national-insurance contributions can be analysed as a labour subsidy, and Figure 7.1 shows how the subsidy reduces unit wage costs to the employer from P_0 to P_1 (since P_1 is on the demand curve for labour), and increases the wage received by the employee from P_0 to P_2 (since P_2 is on the labour-supply curve). In this case the tax reduction benefits mainly the employee. But the result is reversed where labour supply is elastic.

THE GENERAL EQUILIBRIUM INCIDENCE ARGUMENT. However, to be sure of the efficiency of any policy or of its redistributive effects, it is necessary also to see how the *general* equilibrium of production, consumption, and distribution is affected. There has been some work

---

[8] The primary labour force consists of 'breadwinners'—i.e. people who would normally be in the labour force full-time. It consists traditionally of men aged 18 to 65 and unmarried women aged 18 to 60. The secondary labour force consists of people who are not *necessarily* full-time members of the labour force—e.g. people under 18, people past retiring age, and married women.

on applied general-equilibrium analysis (see the Further Reading), though no detailed analysis of the impact of the welfare state.

The discussion of incidence concentrates on the effect, *ceteris paribus*, of changes in taxation or expenditure on the relative position of different income groups. The crucial words are *ceteris paribus* and the *relative* position of individuals or groups. The *ceteris paribus* condition is important because we are trying to separate the distributional effect of a given change in tax (or expenditure) from any other change in the system. This makes it necessary in principle to introduce a countervailing tax that (*a*) is distributionally neutral and (*b*) keeps the budget balance unchanged. It should be clear that this procedure is fraught with difficulty.

Assuming that this can be done by one means or another, the effect of a tax change on the relative position of different income groups will depend on several sets of factors. Suppose individual A sells factor *m*, which is used to make good *x*, and B sells factor *n*, which is used to make good *y*; and suppose that a tax change raises the relative price of *x*. Individual A is then better off:

1. the greater the increase in his pre-tax income (i.e. the greater the rise in the relative price of *m*);
2. the smaller the taxes he pays;
3. the greater the extent to which he consumes (relatively cheaper) *y* rather than *x*.

The first two items together determine A's net disposable income, and are often jointly referred to as the 'sources' side; the third item concerns the 'uses' side. The three factors show the effect on relative incomes of a tax change considered in isolation. To complete the distributional picture, it is crucial to add that A will be advantaged relative to B also:

4. the greater the benefit derived by A (relative to that received by B) from goods/services provided by government out of the taxes paid by A and B.

It should be clear that discussion of distributional effects that limits itself to tax changes on their own (i.e. 2 above) looks at only part of the picture, and one that may be completely altered by other changes, particularly under 3 and 4.

4.2. Redistribution: Preliminary discussion

THE MEANING OF PROGRESSIVITY is illustrated by an individual's average tax rate—that is, his tax bill as a proportion of his total income. A tax is progressive if the average rate is higher for someone with a higher income. Suppose that an individual can earn £5,000 tax free per year, and pays tax at a marginal rate of 25 per cent on anything above this. Someone earning £5,000 pays no tax; someone earning £10,000 pays £1,250 (12.5 per cent of his income); and someone with £15,000 pays £2,500 in tax (16.7 per cent of his income). Thus the tax (which is a stylized version of the UK system) is progressive, even though most people face the same marginal rate of 25 per cent.[9]

---

[9] Whether the degree of progression is the *right* one is an entirely different question.

In assessing the progressivity of a tax it is necessary, in addition to its formal structure, to know the number of people affected: a tax of 25 per cent on income up to £50,000 and 80 per cent thereafter may sound highly progressive, but if nobody has income over £50,000 the tax in practice is proportional. It is also necessary to know the extent to which the formal tax rates apply in practice: a tax is less progressive than it appears if the highest rates are never applied—that is, if tax avoidance or evasion[10] are proportionately more frequent at higher incomes. These considerations apply equally to benefits, whose distributional effects have become more complicated because they have increasingly been subject to tax while contributions to private pensions attract tax relief.

CONSIDERING TAXES AND BENEFITS TOGETHER. The discussion in Section 4.1 has two implications. First, in assessing the finance of the welfare state it may be necessary to consider simultaneously a variety of taxes contributing to the Consolidated Fund, the National Insurance Fund, and local revenues. Suppose a government tries to help the poor by increasing the employer national-insurance contribution relative to the employee contribution. The discussion underlying Figure 7.1 suggests that it is of no analytical consequence whether a tax is imposed on the buyer or the seller. In the case of national insurance, it is therefore (except in the very short term) the combined employer and employee contribution that matters; any attempt to increase one and reduce the other is little more than window dressing.

Secondly, it is frequently the *overall* system that matters—that is, taxation and expenditure should be considered together. At its simplest, a scheme that uses a proportional tax to subsidize mink coats will usually be regressive; the same tax used to finance poverty relief is progressive.

The logic is simple. Consider a commodity (e.g. health care) that is publicly supplied without charge, and financed by a specific contribution. This arrangement is redistributive from rich to poor *if (rich) individual A pays more in contributions than (poor) B, if each consumes the same quantity; it is also progressive if A consumes twice as much as B, but pays more than twice as much in contributions.*

In practice matters are more complicated because it is hard to identify precisely which contributions/taxes have paid for the commodity—that is, which tax(es) would be reduced or abolished if it were no longer publicly supplied. It might be argued that health care is redistributive so long as A (who consumes twice as much as B) pays more than twice as much in taxes. But this implicitly assumes that health care is financed by a proportionate share of all taxes. The definition in the previous paragraph must therefore be qualified: health care is financed progressively if A consumes twice as much as B, but pays more than twice as much in whatever taxes are used to finance it.

REDISTRIBUTIVE IMPLICATIONS. These factors must be borne in mind in considering the extent to which the welfare state is financed progressively. This is done for unemployment and sick pay in Chapter 8, Section 3.2, for pensions in Chapter 9, Section 5.2, and for the major non-contributory benefits in Chapter 10, Section 3.5. These benefits all redistribute from rich to poor to a greater or lesser extent. Nevertheless, as discussed

---

[10] Tax avoidance is legal (e.g. reducing one's tax liability via a mortgage); tax evasion is illegal (e.g. concealing part of one's income).

in Chapter 1, Section 3, and Chapter 6, Sections 2.3 and 4.3, poverty and inequality both increased over the 1980s.

The redistributive effects of the National Health Service and school education are discussed in Chapter 12, Section 4.3, and Chapter 13, Section 4.3, and of higher education in Chapter 14, section 4.3. It was traditionally thought that these systems redistributed from rich to poor, but Le Grand (1982) argued the contrary. The core of his argument is that, though these benefits are financed progressively, in that the rich pay more towards them in taxes and contributions than the poor, they are used even more progressively, so that the overall result can be regressive. For example, if the rich pay twice as much in taxes as the poor to finance education, but use it proportionately ten times as much, then it is not the rich who subsidize the poor, but the other way round. We return to these arguments in Chapters 12–14.

Thus there is a limited presumption that at least the cash side of the welfare state is progressive. But any such view is rendered somewhat tentative by incidence considerations; by conceptual difficulties (e.g. the validity of the Gini coefficient); and by measurement and data problems.

■ QUESTIONS FOR FURTHER DISCUSSION

1. Would it increase the redistributive power of the welfare state if a larger fraction of social-security contributions was imposed on the employer and a smaller fraction on the worker?

2. What are the likely redistributive effects if higher education is paid from general taxation?

■ FURTHER READING

Glennerster (2003a) covers the ground of this chapter in greater detail. For a historical perspective, see Peacock and Wiseman (1967).

For data on taxation and public spending, the annual *Financial Statement and Budget Report* can be downloaded from http://www.hm-treasury.gov.uk, as can *Public Expenditure: Statistical Analyses* (UK Treasury 2003b). For general data, see *The UK National Accounts* (the 'Blue Book'), which can be downloaded from http://www.statistics.gov.uk. More detailed spending proposals are set out each year in a series of departmental reports that can be downloaded from http://www.dwp.gov.uk for cash benefits, http://www.dh.gov.uk for spending on the NHS and personal social services, and http://www.dfes.gov.uk for education spending.

On the planning and control of public expenditure, see Thain and Wright (1995) for detailed discussion up to the early 1990s; Glennerster (2003a: ch. 9) gives an overview and is more up to date.

The institutions of national-insurance contributions (and other state benefits) are described in Child Poverty Action Group (2003) (the 2003 version of an annual publication), or on the Department for Work and Pensions web site (http://www.dwp.gov.uk). On the finances of cash benefits, the National Health Service, personal social services, and education, see Glennerster et al. 2000, and Glennerster 2003a.

The theory of tax incidence is set out in Stiglitz (2000: ch. 18) and, more formally, in Atkinson and Stiglitz (1980; lectures 6, 7). The pioneering work on applied general equilibrium analysis is Harberger (1962); for later developments, see Ballard et al. (1985) and Piggott and Whalley (1985, 1986).

8 Insurance: Unemployment, sickness, and disability

The plan covers all citizens without upper income limit, but has regard to their different ways of life; it is a plan all-embracing in scope of persons and of needs.

(Beveridge Report, 1942)

1. Introduction and institutions

1.1. The issues

AIMS AND METHODS. Historically the main aim of cash benefits was *poverty relief* (objective 4 in Chapter 1, Section 2.2), in particular the prevention of *absolute* poverty. Motives were controversial, ranging from altruism to capitalist oppression (Chapter 2, Section 7.1, Chapter 3, Section 5.3, and Chapter 4, Section 4.1), but with widespread agreement about the aim itself. Over the twentieth century other aims became important. Policy has aimed at alleviating *relative* poverty. *Insurance* (objective 5) is concerned with protection in the face of stochastic contingencies such as unemployment, ill health, or widowhood. *Consumption smoothing* (objective 6) relates to life-cycle effects such as retirement or the presence of dependent children. The objective of *inequality reduction* is more controversial, particularly the aim of redistribution from rich to poor. Other aims discussed in Chapter 1, Section 2.2, concern *efficiency* and *ease of administration*. These aims all recur in the following chapters.

More specifically, unemployment benefit, sickness benefit, and widows' benefits contribute to the insurance objective, the major subject of this chapter. If the benefit formula is weighted towards the lower paid, they also contribute to poverty relief and to vertical redistribution. One of the major purposes of explicit social-insurance contributions is to give recipients an entitlement to benefit, thereby fostering social solidarity. If properly constructed, the benefits minimize adverse labour-supply effects, thereby contributing to the incentives objective. In addition, in that unemployment is uninsurable in private markets (a major argument in this chapter), state-organized unemployment compensation can contribute to the micro-efficiency objective.

The methods available for income protection vary enormously, but schemes can usefully be classified into three types—private, public, and mixed. Pure private arrangements include the voluntary purchase of actuarial insurance and voluntary charity. Mixed schemes involve public participation in private arrangements through regulation (e.g. minimum standards for private insurance) and/or through finance. The latter frequently takes the form of tax expenditures (Chapter 7, Section 1.1)—for example, tax relief for private pension contributions. Public schemes embrace the forms of institution discussed in Chapter 1, Section 2.1 *Social insurance* is awarded on the basis of a contributions record and the occurrence of a specified contingency, such as unemployment or being above a specified age. *Social assistance* is financed from taxation and awarded on the basis of a means test. *'Universal' benefits* are awarded on the basis of a specified contingency (e.g. having dependent children), without either a contribution or an income test.

Which method is preferred depends on the relative weights given to different aims, which in turn depends on political perspective. Libertarians make a sharp distinction between two forms of income transfer.

- Under actuarial insurance an individual provides for his *own* benefits through his previous contributions, and can therefore legitimately choose any desired level of benefit.

- Under a non-contributory scheme, his benefits are paid by *others*. In this case the aim of cash transfers should be to prevent *absolute* poverty—that is, benefits should be at subsistence.

To a libertarian the preferred methods for achieving these aims are voluntary private insurance and private charity, respectively.

Socialists, in contrast, see income transfers as contributing to their egalitarian aims, and therefore favour publicly organized transfers to prevent *relative* poverty and to reduce inequality. Liberals take an intermediate line. We saw in Chapter 6, Section 2.1, that poverty cannot be defined analytically, so its definition is partly ideological. The alleviation of poverty, however defined, can be through insurance (private or public, voluntary or compulsory); through cash transfers out of tax revenues; via private charity; or through whatever mix of these approaches best meets stated aims. The pros and cons of these methods are the subject of Part 2 of the book. This chapter is about benefits whose primary purpose is insurance. Chapter 9 considers consumption smoothing, notably old age pensions. Chapter 10 is about benefits aimed primarily at poverty relief. Chapter 11 discusses reform strategies.

QUESTIONS about national insurance are of two sorts. The first (Section 2) is whether it should be national (i.e. publicly provided). This in turn raises questions about the circumstances in which people insure voluntarily, and those where it might be appropriate for the state to make insurance compulsory and/or to provide insurance itself. The second issue (Section 3) is the effectiveness of the existing system, including its impact on work effort and saving. Where necessary, different benefits are discussed separately. The major conclusions about cash benefits are set out at the end of Chapter 11.

NON-ECONOMIC ARGUMENTS. Three types of argument are commonly used to justify publicly provided cash transfers. First, 'the state has a duty to protect its less fortunate members', or 'everyone has a right to protection from catastrophic income loss'. Both value judgements are widely accepted. Both, however, beg the crucial question of *how* individuals are best helped. It is precisely this issue that is the main subject of this chapter and the next. The second type of argument is that 'without national insurance the poor could not afford adequate cover'. The weakness of this position was discussed in Chapter 4, Section 7.2. If there are no technical problems with private insurance, the market can supply it efficiently. In such cases, distributive aims are generally best achieved through income transfers.

A third argument is that 'it is immoral for insurance companies to profit from people's misfortunes'. This is tenable as a value judgement. But it has been argued (Chapter 4, Section 7.2) that the question of public-versus-private production and allocation is less a moral issue than a technical one. Hence insurance against income loss should be publicly provided if that is more efficient and/or just; but, where private insurance is more efficient, equity aims can generally be achieved through income transfers. We do not, after all, say that food should be publicly provided because it is immoral for food manufacturers to exploit the fact that without it people would starve.

1.2. Institutions

National insurance refers to benefits payable to people with the necessary contributions record; in economic terms it is an insurance scheme against income loss due to events such as unemployment, ill health, or old age. The development of the Beveridge system after 1948 was discussed in Chapter 2, Section 6.1, and contribution arrangements in Chapter 7, Section 2.1. This section briefly summarizes benefit institutions in 2004 (for detailed discussion, see the Further Reading). Table 8.1 shows the level of the major benefits.

UNEMPLOYMENT. *Jobseeker's allowance* is paid at a flat rate to people who are capable of work, available for work, and actively seeking work. Benefit is paid on the basis of *either* a contributions record *or* a means test, cutting across the traditional divide between contributory and non-contributory benefits. The contributory benefit is payable for a maximum of six months.

HEALTH-RELATED ABSENCE FROM WORK. Sickness benefit, introduced in the first wave of post-war institutions, has been replaced by a range of benefits.

Statutory sick pay is administered by employers. Benefit, which depends on a contributions record and is taxable, is paid to eligible people at a weekly flat rate. A medical certificate is required only where sickness lasts more than seven days. Someone who is still unwell after twenty-eight weeks is eligible for incapacity benefit, discussed shortly.

Statutory maternity pay is directly analogous. Benefit, which is taxable, is paid by employers on the basis of a contributions test for up to eighteen weeks, for the first six weeks at 90 per cent of the person's average weekly earnings, and thereafter at a flat rate.

Both statutory sickness payments and statutory maternity payments are made by employers, who deduct outgoings from their monthly national-insurance contribution receipts. The advantage is the administrative ease of subjecting benefit to tax and national-insurance contributions. Both benefits, however, continue to be paid from the National Insurance Fund. Thus both are publicly funded, with administration hived off to employers.

Table 8.1. Main national-insurance benefit rates, 2003/4

Type of benefit	Weekly benefit
Jobseeker's allowance (contributions based)	
Person age 16–17	£32.50[a]
Person aged 18–24	£42.70[a]
Person aged 25 or over	£53.95[a]
Statutory sick pay	
Standard rate	£63.25[a]
Maternity benefits	
Statutory maternity pay	
Higher rate	90% of earnings
Lower rate	£75.00[a]
Incapacity benefit (under state pension age)	
Short term, lower rate	£53.50[a]
Short term, higher rate	£63.25[a]
Long term, basic rate	£70.95[a]
Disability benefits	
Disability living allowance	
Care component	£14.00–£56.25
Mobility component	£14.90–£39.30
Industrial injuries benefit	
Disablement pension (aged over 18, 100% rate)	£114.80[a]
Retirement pension	
Basic state retirement pension	
Single person	£75.50[a]
Married couple	£120.70[a]
State earnings-related pension	earnings-related
Bereavement	
Bereavement allowance (standard rate)	£75.50[a]
Widowed parent's allowance	£75.50[a]
Miscellaneous benefits	
Guardian's allowance (in addition to child benefit)	£9.65–£11.35

Note: Updated rates of benefit can be found at http://www.dwp.gov.uk.
[a] Benefit subject to income tax.

Incapacity benefit has three components. Short-term incapacity benefit is paid at the lower rate for up to twenty-eight weeks to people (e.g. self-employed or unemployed) who cannot claim statutory sick pay, and at the higher rate thereafter. A person who is still ill after a year receives long-term incapacity benefit. Eligibility for the first twenty-eight weeks is assessed on the basis of an 'own-occupation' test—that is, whether the person is incapable of carrying out his normal job. After twenty-eight weeks, a less stringent test—whether the person is capable of carrying out other, less demanding, work—is normally applied.

Severe disablement allowance is a tax-free benefit for someone who has not been able to work for at least twenty-eight consecutive weeks because of ill health, whose contributions record does not entitle him to incapacity benefit.

COPING WITH DISABILITY. Several benefits assist with the extra costs of living independently, and for that reason are often paid irrespective of a person's income or contributions record.

Disability living allowance is a tax-free benefit, normally payable without a contributions test or an income test. The benefit has two components: the care component, payable at one of three weekly rates, is awarded to people who are physically or mentally disabled to the point where they need help caring for themselves; the mobility component assists people who are unable or virtually unable to walk. The benefit is normally awarded only to people under 65. Eligible individuals can receive either or both components.

Attendance allowance is the analogue to disability living allowance for people whose need for help with personal care because of illness or disability starts when they are 65 or over. The benefit is tax free and awarded without a contributions test.

Help for people in work. The Working Tax Credit (see Chapter 10, Section 1) contains an additional element for someone whose disability (physical or mental) puts him at a disadvantage in finding a job or restricts his earning potential.

Industrial injuries disablement benefit. Someone who is disabled because of an accident at work or industrial disease is eligible for industrial injuries disablement benefit, which is tax free, and payable for the entire duration, temporary or permanent, of any loss of faculty, whether or not the person is unable to work. Benefit is payable when statutory sick pay/sickness benefit ceases, or from three days after the accident if there is no incapacity for work. Various additional payments can be made where injury is exceptionally severe.

BEREAVEMENT. *Bereavement allowance*, subject to contribution conditions, is paid for one year to a surviving spouse aged between 45 and pensionable age, the size of the payment rising with the age of the recipient. *Widowed parent's allowance*, subject to contribution conditions, is payable to a widow or widower with at least one child. The benefit comprises a basic allowance with increases for each dependent child.

CARING FOR OTHERS. A range of benefits is available at least partially to compensate people who care for others.

Invalid care allowance is a taxable benefit for someone of working age who is caring for a severely disabled person (i.e. someone who is receiving one of the major health-related benefits).

Guardian's allowance is paid for each child in addition to child benefit. The benefit is paid where the parents of a child are dead, to anyone who looks after a child as part of his or her family.

Increases for dependants. The level of many of these benefits may be increased if the beneficiary has dependants (adult or child) whom he or she supports. In the latter case, child benefit is normally payable in addition.

Most benefits are uprated annually according to a statutory formula. Total spending in 2003/4 was £115 billion (Table 7.3).

2. Theoretical arguments for state intervention

2.1. Efficiency 1: Regulation

Are efficiency and social justice assisted by state involvement in insurance markets in the ways just described? In particular, would individuals in a private market buy the *socially efficient* quantity of insurance against income loss? This breaks down into three separate questions: (*a*) why do people insure at all; (*b*) why does the state make membership compulsory; (*c*) why does the state provide such insurance itself?

The first question was answered in Chapter 5—a rational risk-averse individual will insure voluntarily so long as the value of certainty exceeds the net cost of insurance. Why, secondly, is membership of national insurance compulsory? The standard argument for voluntarism is that it is efficient for an individual to make her own decision so long as she bears fully the costs of so doing. If I do not insure my Picasso, society regards this as my prerogative. Similarly, it might be argued that I should be free not to insure against income loss because of unemployment or ill health. If I then lose my job and starve that is my fault.

The flaw in the voluntarism argument in this case is that it overlooks the external costs that non-insurance can impose on others. Suppose someone chooses not to insure, and then loses his job. If society bails him out by paying a non-contributory benefit, the external cost falls upon the taxpayer. Alternatively, if he is given no help, he may starve, which imposes costs on others in a variety of ways. First, non-insurance may bring about not only his own starvation, but also that of his dependants. There are also broader costs, including any resulting increase in crime, and the financial costs of disposing of his body, or the health hazards if it were left where it fell. Additionally, though more arguably, it is possible to specify a psychic externality, where people do not like the idea of a society that allows people to starve. If so, the individual's death from starvation imposes external costs by reducing the utility of others directly.[1]

Where an activity causes an external cost, one form of intervention is a Pigovian tax.[2] Here, however, the aim is not marginally to influence consumption through marginal price changes, but to prevent non-insurance. Making insurance compulsory (i.e. regulation) is likely to be a more effective way of achieving this.

In sum, the major efficiency argument for compulsory membership is that uninsured losses due to unemployment, illness, or industrial injury may impose costs on others, including dependants such as spouses and children. There is an analogy with automobile insurance, which is also compulsory in most countries. But, quite correctly on efficiency grounds, compulsion is limited to insurance to cover the damage I might inflict on *others*. I can choose whether to take out insurance to cover damage to my *own* car or person.

---

[1] This psychic cost would not arise if members of society had different utility functions—another manifestation of the impossibility of a Paretian liberal (see Chapter 3, Section 3.1).

[2] See, in ascending order of completeness, the Glossary, the Appendix to Chapter 4, para. 15, and/or Chapter 4, Section 3.2.

2.2. Efficiency 2: Public provision

To continue the analogy, the state makes car insurance compulsory, but does not supply insurance itself. Why, then, does it provide national insurance? This question brings us back to the discussion in Chapter 5, Section 4.1, of the circumstances in which private insurance markets are efficient. The end of this section considers the demand conditions. However, it is useful to look first at the supply conditions: the relevant probability must be independent across individuals, less than one, known or estimable, known equally to all parties (i.e. no adverse selection), and exogenous (i.e. no moral hazard). Efficiency arguments about the appropriateness of public provision hinge on whether these five assumptions hold for the risks covered by national insurance.

UNEMPLOYMENT INSURANCE. We need to consider separately each of the assumptions discussed in Chapter 5, Section 3.

1. Whether individual probabilities of becoming or remaining unemployed are independent is controversial. Simple Keynesian theory suggests that unemployment reduces demand and contributes to further unemployment, thus making unemployment a common risk. Those who believe in a natural rate of unemployment deny this conclusion except in the short run. Individual probabilities may be partly correlated, though this problem alone is unlikely to make private insurance impossible.

2. The overall probability of being unemployed is less than one, though for some sectors of the labour force, such as unskilled young people, it may be too high for private insurance to be viable. Individuals returning to the labour force after a long break in employment and unemployed school-leavers cause additional problems.

3. The average probability of being unemployed is well known—it is simply the aggregate unemployment rate. There is also considerable knowledge of the probability of unemployment for subgroups of the labour force.

4. Adverse selection: a private insurance company could ask about an applicant's previous employment record. This is not a complete solution, however: the process is costly; verification is not always possible; and not everyone has a past employment record.

5. Much the greatest problem with private unemployment insurance is moral hazard. The insured individual may be able to influence, first, the probability of *entering* unemployment by bringing about his own redundancy ('I'll work for you this week for nothing if you then make me redundant'). Secondly, and of greater importance, he can influence the probability of *leaving* unemployment—that is, the duration of unemployment.

A key question is how costly (financial and psychic) it is for an individual to remain unemployed. Since psychic costs are unobservable, it is not possible to distinguish two cases.

- The psychic cost to the individual is high (case 1 in Chapter 5, Section 3.2), and continuing unemployment is caused by a lack of jobs.

- The cost is low (case 3), and the individual remains unemployed in part by choice.

The first is an insurable risk; the second is not—the insurer is imperfectly informed and, as discussed shortly, the problem is worse for unemployment than for most other risks.

As we shall see (Section 3.1), the relationship between the level of benefits and the level and duration of unemployment is hotly disputed. It should be noted, however, that to say that individuals with insurance devote more time to job search is not *necessarily* to imply inefficiency. In principle, the efficient duration of unemployment for the ith individual, x_i, is that period that he would rationally choose if he had to finance his unemployment from accumulated savings or by borrowing in a perfect capital market. Inefficiency arises when an individual chooses to be unemployed for longer than x_i because insurance has reduced the marginal cost to him of so doing. It was for this reason that Beveridge insisted on full employment, because 'the only satisfactory test of unemployment is an offer of work' (Beveridge Report 1942: 163).

We saw in Chapter 5, Section 3.1, that an actuarial premium is calculated as

$$\pi_i = (1 + \alpha)p_i L, \tag{8.1}$$

where p_i is the probability of the ith individual becoming or remaining unemployed, L is the unemployment benefit, and α the loading to cover the insurance company's administrative costs and normal profit. Moral hazard of the sort described above means that p_i can be manipulated by the insured individual in ways the insurer cannot monitor, making it impossible for the insurance company to calculate a premium.

The theory is borne out by empirical evidence. There are virtually no private policies I can buy to top up the (low, flat-rate) UK state unemployment benefit, and such policies as do exist (discussed next) all incorporate highly restrictive conditions. In contrast, policies offering sick pay appear regularly in my junk mail.

Further support for the impossibility of *general* private unemployment insurance arises from an attempt by Beenstock and Brasse (1986) to show the opposite. They discuss mortgage protection policies, which make mortgage repayments during unemployment. Such policies have three salient characteristics. They are open, by and large, only to the best risks: owner-occupiers tend to be in more secure jobs, and so have a lower-than-average probability of *entering* unemployment; they are also more mobile (since owner-occupiers are generally less affected than renters by housing market rigidities), increasing the probability of *leaving* unemployment. Secondly, such policies can typically be started only at the time the mortgage is taken out, on the grounds that few people will seek to buy a house if they know their job is at risk; this reduces adverse selection. Thirdly, owner-occupiers tend to have higher-than-average earnings, and so face lower replacement rates, thus minimizing moral hazard. Mortgage protection policies are therefore limited to the best risks, impose restrictions that minimize adverse selection, and sidestep the worst problems of moral hazard.

Other policies offer unemployment insurance that is not tied to a mortgage, but they are generally expensive (i.e. with premiums several multiples of the overall unemployment rate) and hedged about by restrictions (e.g. no benefit is paid for the first 120 days of unemployment). All such policies are genuinely private insurance, but they offer no basis whatever on which to generalize. A careful study by Burchardt and Hills (1997: ch. 4) reaches the same conclusion; for fuller discussion, see Barr (2001a: ch. 3).

Thus unemployment is not a risk that accords well with the model of actuarial insurance. First, as discussed in Chapter 5, Section 4.2 (see also Atkinson 1995*a*: ch. 11), the risk itself is a social construct arising out of the nature of employment in industrial labour markets. Secondly, the probability is to some extent endogenous to the individual. Thus it is not surprising that earlier schemes under the 1911 National Insurance Act and during the 1920s ran into trouble (Chapter 2, Sections 2.2 and 3.2). The theoretical conclusion, supported by empirical evidence, is twofold.

- If income support is to exist for the unemployed, it will have to be publicly provided. This outcome can be supported on *efficiency* grounds because of information problems in insurance markets, of which problems no mention is made in Hayek's attack (1960: ch. 19) on publicly provided benefits. The libertarian predilection for private markets and voluntarism in this instance is untenable.

- The resulting institutions do not look actuarial. The argument in Chapter 5, Section 4.2, suggests that no other result is possible.

Unemployment insurance protects people against income loss by paying benefit to people who are unemployed—that is, by subsidizing unemployment. An alternative approach—known variously as activation policies, welfare to work, and making work pay—subsidizes employment, notably through working tax credits. This latter approach, an important topic in Chapter 10, has increasingly influenced policy in the UK, the wider EU, and the USA since the mid-1990s.

SICK-PAY INSURANCE. If we ask the same questions about sick-pay insurance,[3] the individual probabilities of absence from work because of ill health are unrelated, except during a major epidemic (i.e. the likelihood of my missing work for health reasons is independent of your state of health). Except for the chronically ill, the probability of absence is less than one, and can be estimated. There is no major problem of adverse selection, since a private insurance company can ask about an applicant's previous health and record of absence. Nor is there a serious problem of moral hazard. The probability of missing work is broadly exogenous, since making oneself genuinely ill is costly, and pretended illness can, at least up to a point, be policed by requiring claimants to provide a doctor's certificate.

Thus there is no substantial technical difficulty with private sick-pay insurance, and such institutions exist in many countries. The only efficiency justification for public provision is through a two-step argument.

1. There are economies of scale from running unemployment and sick-pay insurance jointly, since it is administratively cheaper to collect both contributions together.

2. Unemployment benefits must be publicly provided for technical reasons.

Given 2, it follows from 1 that administrative savings arise from running a public sick-pay scheme alongside unemployment insurance. This argument, though valid, is not overriding.

---

[3] Discussion here is concerned with income replacement during health-related absence from work, not with insurance against the cost of medical treatment, which is discussed in Chapter 12.

THE SMALLER NATIONAL-INSURANCE BENEFITS. Voluntary maternity insurance may face problems of adverse selection (i.e. only women intending to become pregnant would insure), making private supply impossible. However, as we saw in Chapter 5, Section 4.1, compulsion can sidestep the problem. Thus, if maternity insurance is compulsory, it would not necessarily have to be publicly provided.

Similar arguments apply to the guardian's allowance, which is payable when one or both parents are dead, and also to increases for dependants more generally. What we are talking about here is a form of life insurance, with which the private market is well able to cope. If private insurance is feasible for the individual, it is also feasible for her dependants (e.g. we saw in Chapter 5, Section 2.3, how an annuity can cover a spouse).

In the case of industrial injury insurance, again, there is no strong efficiency argument for public provision. The probability of injury is independent across individuals, less than one, and can be estimated. Nor do serious problems arise with adverse selection or moral hazard (for instance, it would not generally pay an individual deliberately to injure himself). It is true that some occupations are riskier than others, but this simply means that private insurance would require higher premiums for riskier occupations.

In all these cases, there is an overwhelming case for compulsion but not for public provision. Counter-arguments to the latter position are that there might be administrative economies if all social benefits were organized together; and there might be administrative difficulties in enforcing compulsion if supply were private. The issue of public-versus private pensions is deferred to Chapter 9, Section 3.1.

DEMAND-SIDE CONDITIONS. Alongside these supply-side considerations, it is necessary also to consider the demand side. Here, the central question is whether purchasers of insurance against income loss due to unemployment or ill health are well informed. With short-term policies (i.e. this year's premium pays for this year's potential benefit), individuals can acquire information about different policies, as currently with car insurance. There is a case for regulating standards, but not for public provision. As discussed in Chapter 5, Section 4.1, the situation may be different for complex long-run policies—for example, long-term care in old age (discussed shortly) or pensions. Where information problems are serious, the benefits from competition are diminished and may largely disappear.

Two other arguments have been put forward to explain or justify public provision of national insurance. Marxists argue (Chapter 3, Section 5.3) that such institutions are a form of social control, whose main aim is to prevent social unrest. This argument may *explain* the existence of national insurance, but it does not necessarily *justify* it. In particular, it does not establish why we have publicly organized social insurance rather than, say, non-contributory benefits. It also used to be argued, along Keynesian lines, that national insurance generally, and unemployment benefit in particular, is a built-in stabilizer. But asserting that this might be a consequence (albeit a beneficial one), again, does not necessarily *justify* national insurance.

2.3. A view to the future: Long-term-care insurance

Long-term-care in old age is expensive. Many people never need it, but some people do. On the face of it, therefore, the existence of long-term-care insurance would be welfare enhancing. Specifically, suppose that one in six people will need long-term care, and that the average duration of such care is two years. Thus a representative person will require care for four months (i.e. one-third of a year). If high-quality care costs £30,000 per year, I could buy actuarial cover for a premium of £10,000. Like all competitive insurance, the premium is based on the *average* experience. In contrast, if there were no insurance, I would have to save enough to cover the *maximum* duration of long-term care. I might need care at age 80 and live to 100. Twenty years of premiums would require savings of more than £500,000.

Is private insurance (*a*) feasible and (*b*) efficient? On the demand side, policies, being long term, are inevitably complex (Burchardt and Hills 1997: ch. 6), calling into question the quality of consumer information. On the supply side, insurers face at least two of the problems discussed in Chapter 5, Section 3.1. First, they may not know the relevant probability. It is known today, but may change over the course of a long-run contract: it might decline through medical advances that help me to care for myself; equally, medical progress, by extending my life, might increase the likelihood that I will require care. Thus not even the direction of change is known. Over a long time horizon, we are therefore talking about uncertainty, not risk. Secondly, probabilities may not be independent: a medical advance that does not prevent or cure disability but that prolongs life once a person has become disabled affects the probability of *all* policy-holders.

Thus there are good reasons for arguing that private long-term-care insurance policies, though they exist, are unlikely to be efficient.

If there is too little information . . . to ascertain whether [long-term-care] insurance products . . . represent value for money, can consumers make an informed choice about purchase? If insurers likewise suffer from a lack of reliable data . . . premiums may turn out to be higher than they need to be; but if not, insurers may be unable to meet their commitments. Given this uncertainty, it must be questioned whether private insurance is a suitable way to meet the security needs of a large part of the elderly population.   (Burchardt and Hills 1997: 44–5)

Not least for those reasons, since 2003 such policies have been subject to regulation by the UK Financial Services Authority.

There are strong arguments suggesting that long-term care is a suitable case for social insurance. First, the scope for differences in individual choice is limited. Secondly, these are not risks that fit the actuarial mechanism very well. With social insurance, in contrast, the contract need not be fully specified, making it easier to adapt to changing social and medical circumstances (see also the discussion in Chapter 5, Section 4.1). Thirdly, the costs of long-term care are much lower than for pensions because on average people require care for a much shorter period than they require a pension. For precisely such reasons, the costs of long-term care in Germany are covered by a specific element of the social insurance contribution (see Schneider 1999).[4] The UK Royal Commission on Long Term Care (1999) advocated tax funding, though its recommendations were only partially implemented. This remains an unresolved area. For fuller discussion, see the Further Reading.

---

[4] Germany has taken the integration of the finance of long-term care into social insurance one step further: 'the Constitutional Court ruled that at the end of 2004, childless workers will have to pay a higher premium into the country's compulsory nursing insurance scheme than will workers with children. The reasoning . . . is that childless workers . . . do not bear the main costs of raising the next generation of contributors to the pay-as-you-go insurance, and they reap the benefits from the insurance premiums paid by the younger generation' (Neil Gilbert 2002: 181).

2.4. Social justice

What are the equity arguments for publicly provided insurance? Horizontal equity is concerned with such goals as minimum standards for certain commodities and/or equal access to them. It was argued in Chapter 4, Section 4.3, that these occur automatically where the assumptions of perfect information and equal power hold. Thus the demand-side conditions, just discussed in the context of efficiency, are also relevant here. Where consumers are well informed there is no case for intervention on horizontal equity grounds; where they are badly informed, the case for publicly organized insurance can be argued on both efficiency and equity grounds.

Similar arguments apply to the equal-power assumption. Where insurance is competitive, what matters is not whether individuals have more or less power, but whether they can afford an actuarial premium. Automobile insurance premiums are generally related to age and previous driving record, but there is no evidence of a systematic relationship between premiums and social class. Similarly, there is no reason to expect substantial discrimination with unemployment and sick-pay insurance. This argument is less strong, however, with complex, long-term policies, for which it can be argued that more articulate people will be better placed to ask assertive questions about the degree of cover offered.

Vertical equity concerns redistribution from rich to poor. The standard argument, that 'the state must provide insurance, because otherwise the poor would not be able to afford adequate cover', is false (Section 1.1). A somewhat more subtle variant is that actuarial insurance cannot redistribute from rich to poor, only from 'lucky' to 'unlucky', and therefore should be publicly provided to redistribute income. Again, the key argument in Chapter 4, Section 7.2, suggests that, without efficiency reasons for provision, distributive goals should be pursued through income transfers except, possibly, where there are consumption externalities (Chapter 4, Section 4.2). In the presence of consumption externalities, the rich may want the poor to consume insurance, and so impose it as a merit good; and the poor may feel less stigmatized by receiving 'insurance benefit' than 'welfare'. Both reasons offer an explanation (though not necessarily a justification) of public provision for reasons of vertical equity.

Finally, it can be argued (Chapter 4, Section 7.2, and Chapter 5, Section 4.1) that, if there are *efficiency* grounds for making membership of national insurance compulsory, it is not inappropriate to finance the scheme so as to redistribute from rich to poor. We return to this issue in the next section.

3. Assessment of insurance benefits

3.1. Efficiency and incentives

Arguments of principle

This part of the chapter briefly assesses the UK system in the light of earlier theoretical argument (for fuller discussion of the UK and other countries, see the Further Reading). The major issues are empirical, but we start with a number of issues of principle: should national insurance be national (i.e. publicly provided); does the state provide the optimal quantity of insurance; and are the resulting institutions insurance?

SHOULD IT BE NATIONAL? The efficiency arguments rest on externalities, justifying compulsion, and technical (mainly information) failures on the supply side of the insurance market and, for longer-term policies, also on the demand side, justifying provision of the major benefits, though with a somewhat weaker argument for sick pay than for the other schemes. If we ignore consumption externalities, the main equity arguments are (a) that the poor may feel less stigmatized by insurance, and (b) that, if insurance is publicly provided for efficiency reasons, it can then be used as a redistributive device. These arguments are compelling. Some areas could, indeed, be returned to the private sector—for example, short-term sick pay. However, unemployment is an uninsurable risk and, as argued in Chapter 9, so is unanticipated inflation, with major efficiency implications for public involvement in pensions. Since spending on elderly people and unemployed people makes up over half of all income transfers, if we ask 'Should national insurance be national?' the short answer is yes.

DOES THE STATE PROVIDE THE OPTIMUM QUANTITY OF INSURANCE? Where insurance is compulsory and publicly provided, inefficiency arises if the state, through misperception of individual preferences, constructs a larger or smaller than optimal scheme. In a first-best world, the ith individual (assumed rational and risk averse) will choose to insure against a loss L_i for which she pays the actuarial premium shown in equation (8.1). All N individuals make this utility-maximizing decision, resulting in a vector of optimal insurance purchases

$$(L_1, L_2, \ldots, L_N). \tag{8.2}$$

The L_i vary across individuals depending *inter alia* on their risk aversion.

Will national insurance offer these optimal quantities? The answer must be no, because the insurance offered is a sort of average that does not cater for differences in tastes. However, national insurance is less inefficient than the free market outcome, not least because risks like unemployment are uninsurable; and individuals can buy additional insurance against risks such as sickness and disability.

A separate issue is whether there are missing benefits, long-term-care insurance being a case in point.

IS IT INSURANCE? On the face of it, national insurance does not look much like insurance.

1. Contributions are not related to individual risk. In the scheme envisaged by Beveridge, contributions were geared to the *average* risk, as shown in equation (5.16), and adverse selection avoided by making membership compulsory. This principle was violated because retirement pensions from 1946 onwards were not actuarial (see Chapter 9); because from 1975 contributions by the employed (Class 1) and self-employed (Class 4) were related not to average risk but to the contributor's income; and because of the existence of credits for the unemployed, and for people at home looking after young children or a disabled person.

2. Entitlement to benefit does not depend only on the occurrence of the insured event. Benefits (but not contributions) are higher where the contributor has dependants; contributions and benefits taken together are redistributive from rich to poor; and

until 1989 pensions in the first five years after normal retirement age were subject to an earnings test (i.e. pension was withdrawn for individuals who continued working). In other countries, additional restrictions may be imposed—for example, 'workfare' requires recipients of unemployment and related benefits to undertake work or training.

3. The scheme is not financed on actuarial lines. As discussed in Chapter 9, state pensions, unlike most private schemes, generally make no provision for future liabilities.

4. The contract is not fully specified, in that the risks covered can change over time. Some people view this as a disadvantage, since the state can renege on past promises. On the other hand, it is an advantage because (as discussed in Chapter 5, Section 4.2) it enables the state to respond to unforeseen risks. Social insurance, unlike private insurance, thus offers protection not only against risk but also against uncertainty.

The conclusion is that national insurance is insurance in the sense that it offers protection against risk, but not insurance where premiums bear an actuarial relationship to individual risk. In the sense discussed in Chapter 5, Section 4.2, the mechanism is social insurance rather than actuarial insurance. For the reasons given in Section 2.2, no other result is possible.

It is important to be clear that social insurance does not *have* to be redistributive from rich to poor. Its precise form will depend on the objectives of policy. It is perfectly possible to have social-insurance arrangements that closely mimic actuarial arrangements (e.g. the original Beveridge scheme, or a scheme in which both contributions and benefits are strictly proportional to individual earnings). Over the years there has been much confusion about the purposes of social insurance. There are good reasons for thinking of it both as a technical instrument for dealing with market failure *and* as a redistributive device. But the two cases are argued on very different grounds and should be carefully distinguished.

Incentive issues

In discussing the incentive effects of social insurance two questions dominate: is the system itself a contributory cause of unemployment; and does it reduce the rate of saving and capital accumulation (the latter issue being particularly relevant in the case of pensions)?

ARE UNEMPLOYMENT BENEFITS A CONTRIBUTORY CAUSE OF UNEMPLOYMENT? The discussion of moral hazard in Section 2.2 has already hinted at this issue. With a high replacement rate (i.e. the ratio of income when unemployed to post-tax-and-transfer income in work), the low paid may be little worse off (and in the short run perhaps better off) out of work. In 2000/1 nearly 7 per cent of the workforce faced replacement rates of 70 per cent and over (UK DSS 2001: 13), creating an 'unemployment trap' whereby an unemployed person had little financial incentive to seek work (this should be contrasted with the 'poverty trap' (Chapter 10, Section 3.4), under which an individual doing at least some work is given no incentive to work longer hours).

The logic of the disincentive argument is appealingly straightforward. Simple theory suggests that higher replacement rates tend to reduce work effort that is financially motivated, an argument that informed policy throughout the 1980s and later. 'When increases in benefits narrow the gap between in-work and out-of-work incomes, work becomes less attractive; the effect is to encourage dependency' (UK DSS 1997: 52).

The quantitative literature is large, complex and controversial. There are major statistical problems, not least because individual labour supply is frequently a function of household joint decisions. There are also major measurement problems; for example, the interaction of the tax and benefit systems makes it difficult to estimate benefits accurately. Attempts to estimate the individual's potential entitlement face the problem that the sample may not contain sufficient information. On the other hand, using actual benefit receipts causes statistical difficulties where unobserved individual characteristics influence *both* the level of benefit *and* the probability of accepting a particular job offer; for example, if I am lazy (unobserved), I may have a poor employment record and consequently receive less benefit *and* be less keen to accept a new job.

One strand of research (Atkinson and Micklewright 1991; Layard et al. 1991; Atkinson 1995a: ch. 10) emphasizes cross-country data, making it possible to include institutional differences as explanations of why unemployment was more persistent over the 1980s in most European countries than in the USA and Japan. Particular emphasis is placed on three aspects of the labour market. First are aspects of the benefit structure additional to the replacement rate, such as the maximum duration of benefit, qualification conditions for benefit, the proportion of the unemployed receiving benefit, and the stringency with which the 'actively-seeking-work' condition is enforced. Secondly, there are active labour-market policies, such as placement and counselling services, training, and job creation.[5] Thirdly there is the structure of the labour market, including the power of trade unions and the extent of centralized wage bargaining. The conclusion is that, though the replacement rate has an effect, labour supply is influenced more by other aspects of the benefit structure, in particular the maximum duration for which benefit can be received. In short, the hypothesis that unemployment benefits exert a substantial upward effect on the level of unemployment receives only limited empirical support.

Policy, however, continues to be based on the assumption that unemployment benefits have significant incentive effects. Atkinson and Micklewright (1989) list thirty-eight changes during the 1980s to UK benefits for the unemployed, mostly making benefits less generous. As Atkinson (1995a: 179–80) later summarized the 1980s:

Insurance benefits [have] been eroded by . . . the tightening of the contribution conditions [and] the extension of the disqualification period . . . their value has been reduced by the taxation of benefits: and the abandonment of statutory indexation has made the position of recipients insecure. These measures add up to a substantial reduction in the amount and extent of National Insurance benefit paid to the unemployed.

To argue that the simple relationship between the level of benefit and unemployment duration is not strong does not, however, mean that incentives are unimportant (see the Further Reading). Since the late 1990s, governments in the UK, the wider EU, and north America have increasingly looked at benefit structures more holistically to encourage labour-force participation, notably through working tax credits. The strategy exemplified by the Atkinson quote above is based on the stick of reduced benefits; working tax credits are based on the carrot of tying an increasing range of benefits to work so as to make work pay. The latter set of policies is discussed in Chapter 10, section 3.

---

[5] For an assessment, see Robinson (2000).

DISABILITY BENEFITS AND LABOUR SUPPLY. Spending on health-related cash benefits, as Table 7.3 shows, is substantial and has risen significantly over the years. To the extent that this is a manifestation of more generous benefits, it can be argued that disability benefits reduce labour supply. It is, however, possible to argue the reverse: recipients of disability benefit rose as unemployment increased; taken literally, this means that disability benefit is not a *cause* of unemployment, but a *consequence*. Both theories are almost certainly too simple (see Disney and Webb 1991); though data are improving (see Barmby et al. 2002), the study of causation remains work in progress.

OTHER INCENTIVE EFFECTS. Pensions and labour supply may also be related if pensions induce early retirement. It is also argued that publicly provided pensions financed out of tax revenues may reduce savings, capital accumulation, and economic growth. Both sets of issues are discussed in Chapter 9, Section 5 (see also the Further Reading to Chapter 9).

3.2. Equity issues

HORIZONTAL EQUITY. It can be argued that national insurance gives everyone equal access to income support. One of the major themes of the Beveridge Report was that national insurance should be comprehensive, unified, and compulsory. This aim has largely been achieved in that there is no evidence of discrimination in the payment of benefits, nor of substantial maladministration.

However, not all groups receive equal coverage, despite Beveridge's intention to the contrary. Fifty years ago most single-parent families resulted from widowhood, which therefore received extensive coverage, especially where there were young children. It is argued that this group, which today comprises only a small fraction of lone-parent families, is treated generously relative to families separated by other causes, such as divorce. The difficulty (and the prominence of the latter group among the poor) arises largely because benefits are conditioned on cause (e.g. widowhood) rather than outcome (i.e. being a lone parent).

There is also criticism that the relative treatment of men and women is inequitable. During the 1980s some benefits of particular relevance to women (e.g. the universal maternity grant) were withdrawn, others (child benefit, one-parent benefit, free school meals, and the state earnings-related pension) became less generous, and there were continuing complaints that childcare costs could not be offset against earnings for income support. Reforms after 1997 brought some improvement, a trend strengthened by reform in 2003 that extended tax credits to support children and to assist with the costs of childcare. Improvement, though welcome, has not resolved all problems (see Bennett 2002).

VERTICAL EQUITY. How redistributive is national insurance? The major difficulties include conceptual problems (Chapter 7, Section 4) and many of the measurement problems discussed in Chapter 6. A definitive answer requires general equilibrium analysis of the joint incidence of contributions and benefits. No such work exists, so we must be content with more rough-and-ready answers. National-insurance contributions for most people rise disproportionately with income for all except the highest earners (Table 7.2). The state pension is redistributive from rich to poor (Chapter 9, Section 5.2). Unemployment compensation is also redistributive, since people with lower incomes pay smaller contributions, generally for fewer weeks, and receive benefit more frequently than some-one with a higher income. The various incapacity benefits are redistributive to the extent that claims are more common among the lower paid. The combined effect of all cash benefits in 2002/3 was to reduce the Gini coefficient by about 14 per cent (Lakin 2003: table 27). The same body of analysis (ibid.: table 4) found that before all taxes and benefits the average income of the richest 20 per cent of households was eighteen times as large as that of the poorest 20 per cent; the effect of all taxes and benefits (including benefits in kind) was to reduce the ratio to about four to one.

Another aspect is whether benefits are pitched at the right level. This raises two further questions. First, and largely an efficiency matter, is whether the level of benefit is that which would have been chosen voluntarily by a hypothetically well-informed, rational individual. This is the issue, discussed earlier, of whether national insurance provides the optimal quantity of insurance. Secondly, are the insurance benefits high enough to keep people out of poverty? If we use the level of income support as the yardstick of poverty, it can be argued that the main national-insurance benefits, which are generally below the income-support level, are too low. We return to the subject in Chapter 10, Section 3.

■ **QUESTIONS FOR FURTHER DISCUSSION**

1. 'If people want to insure against income loss due to unemployment, ill health, or old age, they should buy private insurance.' What are the counter-arguments? In particular, why is national insurance (a) compulsory and (b) publicly organised?

2. Is unemployment insurance insurance?

3. A significant number of people require long-term care in old age. Should insurance against the costs of such care be mandatory? If so, could such insurance be left to private institutions?

■ **FURTHER READING**

For compendious description of institutions (including legal sources), see Child Poverty Action Group (2003) (the 2003 version of an annual publication). For assessment, recent developments, and statistical data, see Glennerster (2003a: ch. 7), the Department for Work and Pensions, *Departmental Report* (UK DWP 2003a) (the 2003 version of an annual publication), and the Department for Work and Pensions web site (http://www.dwp.gov.uk). On institutions in the EU, see the various country reports and overview documents on http://europa.eu.int/comm/employment_social/soc-prot/index_en.htm

For institutions worldwide, see US Social Security Administration (2002, 2003), downloadable from http://www.ssa.gov/policy/pubs/index.html. See also the various government portals in the list of useful web sites at the start of the book.

On the theory of insurance, see the Further Reading at the end of Chapter 5. The application to social insurance is discussed by Stiglitz (2000: ch. 14) and Rosen (2002: ch. 9).

The effectiveness of unemployment benefit and sick pay in offering insurance is discussed by Di Tella and MacCulloch (2002) and Gertler and Gruber (2002), the latter a study in a developing country (Indonesia) but with findings that apply more broadly.

The incentive effects of unemployment benefits are discussed by Meyer (2002), Fredriksson and Holmlund (2003), and Røed and Zhang (2003). For discussion of the broader determinants of unemployment, including labour-market institutions, see Blanchard and Wolfers (2000) and Blanchard and Portugal (2001). On the incentive effects of sickness benefits, see Barmby et al. (2002), and of pensions the Further Reading to Chapter 9.

Long-term care is discussed by Burchardt and Hills (1997), UK Royal Commission on Long Term Care (1999), and Barr (2001*a*: ch. 5). For assessment of the situation in the UK, see Glennerster (2000: 218–20) and Brooks et al. (2002: chs. 5, 7) and for projections of the demand for long-term care, Wittenberg et al. (2002). On Germany (which has incorporated the finance of long-term care into its system of social insurance), see Schneider (1999), and on the USA, the relevant chapters in Fuchs (1996).

On policy in the UK, see the symposium on welfare reform in *Fiscal Studies*, 23/4 (Dec. 2002), Brewer et al. 2002 (an overview), Hills 2002 (an analysis of public attitudes), and Bennett 2002 (on gender dimensions)). See also Glennerster (2000: ch. 10) and Nickell and Quintini (2002). Baldwin and Falkingham (1994) discuss the ways in which the original Beveridge model no longer conforms with social conditions, and Hills (2003) discusses the contributory principle. Burchardt and Hills (1997) analyse private mortgage protection insurance and insurance covering long-term care. On distributional impacts of national insurance, see Evans (1998) and the Further Reading at the end of Chapter 6, and, for discussion of gender aspects, Bennett (2002).

On policy in the EU and USA, see the Further Reading at the end of Chapter 10.

9 | Consumption smoothing: Old-age pensions

'You are old, Father William,' the young man said,
'And your pension has almost run out;
And yet you insist that funding is safe
It's no wonder you're all up the spout.'
'In my youth', Father William replied to his son,
'They told me my savings would grow;
But, now that I'm perfectly sure I have none,
I'd prefer you to Pay as I Go.'

(With apologies to Lewis Carroll)

1. Introduction and institutions

The previous chapter discussed benefits whose major purpose is to offer insurance. This chapter discusses old-age pensions, one of whose central roles is consumption smoothing, as analysed in the simple Fisher model in Chapter 4, Section 3.2.[1] Pensions also contribute to some of the other objectives in Chapter 1, Section 2.2. They can assist vertical redistribution. Like other contributory benefits, they can strengthen social solidarity. The relative terms on which men and women receive pensions (e.g. whether there is a common retirement age) raise important issues of horizontal equity.

Questions broadly parallel those of Chapter 8. Section 2 discusses different methods of organizing pensions, and their pros and cons. The efficiency and equity arguments for state intervention, and the effects of different types of intervention, are analysed in Sections 3 and 4. The state old-age pension and related benefits are assessed in Section 5.

THE STATE SCHEME. The 1975 Social Security Pensions Act (UK DHSS 1974) was one of the most important pieces of social-security legislation since the National Insurance Act 1946 (Chapter 2, Section 5), and, as subsequently amended, is the basis of the arrangements described here.

The contributions side was discussed in Chapter 7, Section 2.1. To qualify for a full pension, an individual must generally have contributed for at least forty-four years (men) or forty years (women). Where this requirement is not met, pension is awarded on a sliding scale. *Home-responsibilities protection* ensures that years spent by a parent at home

---

[1] Another element of consumption smoothing, student loans, is discussed in Chapter 14.

looking after children or a disabled dependant will not result in loss of pension. Thus a woman who drops out of the labour force for fifteen years to look after children has to work for only twenty-five years (i.e. 40–15) to qualify for a full pension.

On the benefits side, the major provisions of the 1975 Act may be summarized as follows, noting subsequent amendments, and in particular a number of important changes (motivated by cost containment) for people retiring after 2000.

1. The weekly pension comprises the flat-rate *basic component* and the *earnings-related* component, also referred to as the state earnings-related pension scheme (SERPS).

2. The basic component for a single person is about one-fifth of national average earnings.

3. For people retiring after 2010, the earnings-related component for someone with a full contributions record is calculated as 20 pence of pension per pound of pensionable earnings between the lower and upper earnings limits. The pension was formerly based on the individual's best twenty years, but for people retiring since 2000 is based on the person's entire contribution record.

4. The same pension formula applies to men and women. Pensionable age is 65 for men and 60 for women. An increase in women's pensionable age will be phased in from 2010, leading to a common pensionable age of 65 by 2020.[2]

5. A man receives an increase in his pension if he is married unless his wife has a pension in her own right, in which case she receives the full pension to which she is entitled on the basis of her earnings. Where a couple has two contribution records, the surviving spouse inherits half of his or her partner's earnings-related pension.

6. The basic pension is uprated in line with price increases. The earnings-related component is protected in two ways. First, the earnings on which the pension is calculated are revalued each year in line with the general movement of earnings, so that the earnings-related pension, when first awarded, reflects a person's *real* earnings record. Secondly, the earnings-related component, once in payment, is uprated each year in line with price increases.

7. The pensions of people who work beyond pensionable age are increased by 7.5 per cent (in real terms) for each year by which pension is deferred.

8. Membership of the flat-rate scheme is compulsory. It is possible to contract out of the earnings-related component by belonging to a private scheme—either an occupational pension or a personal pension. Since 1995 (another important change), approved occupational and personal pensions must offer *limited price indexation*—that is, must index pensions for annual rates of inflation up to 5 per cent. The central topic of pensions in the face of inflation emerges repeatedly in subsequent discussion.

[2] Under the reforms, the key date is 6 April 1950. For women born before that, pensionable age will continue to be 60. Pensionable age for a woman born on 6 May 1950 (i.e. one month after the key date) would be 60 years and one month, for a woman born of 6 June 1950, 60 years and two months, and so on. Thus for women born on or after 6 April 1955 pensionable age will be 65.

Many people receiving a national-insurance pension are also eligible for additional income-tested assistance, such as the pension credit and housing benefit (Chapter 10).

PRIVATE PENSION SCHEMES vary widely but are broadly of two sorts: *occupational schemes*, generally organized by employers, and *personal pensions*. Private pensions in industrialized countries share key features. Almost all are *funded*.[3] They are *supplemental*, in that they replace only part of the state pension. They are *constrained* in two ways: individual choice, particularly under occupational schemes, is generally limited; and pension companies are regulated to protect consumers. Virtually all private pension schemes are *subsidized* on a substantial scale through tax expenditures. Finally, though an increasing number of schemes offer *limited indexation*, virtually none offers complete protection against inflation.

The coverage of private pensions has grown substantially over the years. By 1991, half of all UK employees, including a growing number of women, belonged to an occupational scheme. Employers can choose whether or not to offer occupational pensions in place of the state earnings-related scheme; and, where an occupational scheme exists, employees can choose whether to join or, instead, to have their own personal pension, either run by a financial institution or, even more individually, self-managed.

2. Methods of organizing pensions

THE ECONOMICS OF PENSIONS can be confusing, because writers easily become bemused by their *financial* aspects (i.e. analysis of insurance companies' portfolios of financial assets). I shall try to simplify matters by concentrating on the essential *economic* issues (i.e. the production and consumption of goods and services).

From an individual viewpoint, the economic function of pensions is consumption smoothing. By contributing to a pension scheme, an individual consumes today less than she produces, so as to continue to consume when she has retired and is no longer producing. In principle, an individual can transfer consumption over time in two ways, and in *only* two ways: she can store current production; or she can acquire a claim to future production.

One way to ensure future consumption is to set aside part of current production for future use—for example, by digging a hole in one's back garden and adding to its contents each year tins of baked beans, shoelaces, and soap powder. Though this is the only way Robinson Crusoe could guarantee future consumption, the method has major inefficiencies. Storing current production is costly in terms of the potential return to savings forgone, and also because storage costs for many commodities are high. A second problem is uncertainty—for example, about what quantities to store, what new goods might become available, and how one's tastes might change. Thirdly, some services can be transferred over time by storing the physical wealth that generates them (e.g. it is possible to store housing services by being an owner-occupier); but it is not possible, even in principle, to store services deriving from human capital, medical services being a particularly important

---

[3] i.e. pay benefits out of a previously accumulated fund, as explained in detail in Section 2.

example. Organizing pensions by storing current production on a large scale is therefore a non-starter.

The alternative is for individuals to exchange current production for a claim on future output. There are two ways in which I might do this: by saving part of my wages each week I could build up a pile of *money* that I would exchange for goods produced by younger people after my retirement; or I could obtain a *promise* that I would be given goods produced by others after my retirement. The promise could be from my son ('Don't worry, dad, I'll look after you when you're old'), or from government. The two most common ways of organizing pensions broadly parallel these two sorts of claim on future production. So-called *funded* schemes follow the first; *Pay-As-You-Go* (PAYG) or unfunded schemes the second.[4]

FUNDED AND PAY-AS-YOU-GO SCHEMES. In a funded scheme, contributions are invested in financial assets, the return on which is credited to its members. When an individual retires, the pension fund will be holding all his past contributions, together with the interest and dividends earned on them. This usually amounts to a large lump sum that is converted into an annuity (Chapter 5, Section 2.3)—that is, a pension of £X per year. Funding, therefore, is simply a method of accumulating money, which is exchanged for goods at some later date. Most occupational schemes are of this type.

Funded schemes take many forms, of which two in particular should be distinguished. Under a *defined-contribution* scheme, the contribution rate is fixed, so that a person's pension is determined *only* by the size of the lump sum accumulated during working life. As discussed in Chapter 5, Section 2.3, insurance protects the individual against the risks associated with longevity, but leaves her facing those associated with varying real rates of return to pension assets, including:

- the risk that her pension portfolio will do better or worse, depending on (*a*) overall economic risk and (*b*) the potential for managerial slack; and

- the risk that unanticipated inflation after retirement will exceed whatever indexation provisions the pension offers.

Under a *defined-benefit* scheme, usually run at a firm or industry level, the firm promises to pay an annuity at retirement. In so-called final-salary schemes, the annuity depends on the employee's wage in her final year (or final few years) of work and upon length of service (a typical formula is one-eightieth of final salary per year of service, up to a maximum of forty years). In another form of defined benefit, the relevant wage is not final salary but an average over a longer period. Whatever the wage reference period, the annuity is, in effect, wage indexed until retirement. The employee contribution is generally a fraction of her salary. Thus, the employer's contribution becomes the endogenous variable. In a defined-benefit scheme, it is the firm or industry that bears the risk in the face of unanticipated changes in the real rate of return to pension assets.[5]

---

[4] There are other ways of organizing pensions. The so-called *book* method makes advance provision for pensions on the company's balance sheet in the same way as provision is made for other deferred liabilities (e.g. future tax payments). Money is not transferred out of the company (as with funded schemes) but is retained for use by the company. At the same time a reserve is set up in the balance sheet to reflect the estimated liability. In *cash* terms there is little difference between book reserving and Pay-As-You-Go.

[5] For comparison of defined-benefit and defined-contribution schemes, see Bodie et al. (1988).

Occupational schemes can be either defined benefit or defined contribution; individual pensions are all defined contribution. Funded schemes of both sorts have two major implications: in principle they always have sufficient reserves to pay all outstanding financial liabilities (since an individual's entitlement is simply his past contributions plus the interest earned on them); and a representative individual, or a generation as a whole, gets out of a funded scheme no more than he has put in—that is, with funding, a generation is constrained by its own past savings. Other implications emerge throughout the chapter.

Pay-As-You-Go (PAYG) schemes are usually run by the state. They are contractarian in nature, based on the fact that the state need not accumulate funds in anticipation of future pension claims, but can tax the working population to pay the pensions of the retired generation. Almost all state pension schemes are PAYG.

From an economic viewpoint, PAYG can be looked at in several ways. As an individual contributor, my claim to a pension is based on a promise from the state that, if I pay contributions now, I will be given a pension in the future. The terms of the promise are fairly precise; they are set out in each country's social-security legislation. From an aggregate viewpoint, the state is simply raising taxes from one group of individuals and transferring the revenues thereby derived to another. State-run PAYG schemes, from this perspective, appear little different from explicit income transfers.

The major implication of the PAYG system is that it relaxes the constraint that the benefits received by any generation must be matched by its own contributions. Samuelson (1958) showed that, with a PAYG scheme, it is possible in principle for *every* generation to receive more in pensions than it paid in contributions, provided that real income rises steadily; this is likely when there is technological progress and/or steady population growth.

PRELIMINARY COMPARISON. PAYG schemes have important advantages. First, they minimize impediments to labour mobility, since pension entitlement depends on earnings and years of service but not on how many jobs a person has had. Secondly, full pension rights can be built up quickly, since pensions are paid not by one's own previous contributions, but by those of the current workforce. Thirdly, PAYG schemes are generally able to protect pensions in payment against inflation and, fourthly, they can generally increase the real value of pensions in line with economic growth.

Table 9.1 illustrates the latter two points. In period 1 the total income of the workforce is £1,000, so that a contribution rate of 10 per cent yields £100. Suppose by period 2 prices and earnings have risen by 100 per cent (column 2). A contribution of 10 per cent now yields £200, which has a purchasing power of £100 at the old price level, and so maintains the real value of pensions in the face of inflation. Alternatively, suppose (column 3) that economic growth raises earnings to £2,000, while prices stay at their original level. In this case the 10 per cent contribution rate has a *real* yield of £200, and so it is possible to double the real value of pensions.

Against these undoubted advantages must be offset the problem that PAYG is sensitive to any change in the age structure of the population that reduces the workforce relative to the number of dependants. The key variable is the so-called age dependency ratio,

$$\frac{P}{W}, \tag{9.1}$$

Table 9.1. Financing a Pay-As-You-Go pension scheme in the presence of inflation and growth

Income, contributions, and real pensions	Period 1 (1)	Period 2 (inflation) (2)	Period 2 (growth) (3)
1. Total income of workforce	£1,000	£2,000	£2,000
2. Price index	100	200	100
3. Pension contribution rate	10%	10%	10%
4. Available for pensions	£100	£200	£200
5. Real value of pensions ($=$[row (4)/row (2)] $\times$ 100)	£100	£100	£200

where P is the number of pensioners and W the number of workers. Influences like increased longevity raise the number of pensioners, and longer education reduces the size of the workforce. Lowering the retirement age simultaneously reduces the workforce and increases the number of pensioners. Finally, as we shall see, any large 'bulge' in the birth rate can cause serious difficulties.

Another claimed disadvantage of PAYG finance is that it makes pensioners dependent on the future workforce. This is true. But, as we shall see in Section 3.2, the same is true of funded schemes. In both cases pensioners are dependent on future generations, since both schemes build pensions round claims on future production rather than by storing current production.

The disadvantages of funded schemes tend to mirror the advantages of PAYG. The formula of defined-benefit occupational schemes tends to favour long-serving workers. This is a deliberate feature of such schemes (see Hannah 1986) to encourage loyalty and help the management of internal labour markets, but it has the effect of impeding labour mobility. Secondly, it takes a long time to build up full pension rights, because it takes an individual many years to build up a lump sum sufficiently large to generate an annuity that will support him fully in retirement. Thirdly—and fundamental to any discussion of funded schemes—there is the issue of inflation, discussed shortly.

Against these disadvantages, it is often claimed that funding has the major advantage of being insensitive to changes in the dependency ratio. The argument is that a funded scheme always has sufficient resources to pay the pensions of its members, since the present value of a representative pension stream exactly equals past contributions plus interest. It is true that a funded scheme will have sufficient resources to pay all *money* claims against it; but it does *not* follow that funding, on that account, offers pensioners better protection against demographic change. This controversial topic is addressed in detail in Sections 3.2 and 5.1.

PENSIONS AND INFLATION. Inflation is particularly relevant to defined-contribution schemes. It is important to distinguish (*a*) pensions in build-up, when contributions are still being paid, and (*b*) pensions in payment. Defined-contribution schemes can generally cope with inflation during the build-up of pension rights, and with a given rate of *anticipated* inflation once the pension is in payment. But they do not cope well with unanticipated post-retirement inflation. The reason is straightforward. A pensioner under a funded scheme builds up over his working life a lump sum, which he exchanges upon retirement for an annuity. The present value of an actuarial annuity equals the lump sum. From equation (5.11) the annuity thus depends on the lump sum, and on the *real* rate of interest facing the insurance company (i.e. the excess of the nominal interest rate over the rate of inflation). Two cases need discussion.

- *Certainty*: if inflation is 5 per cent each year with certainty, it is an easy matter to offer an annuity that rises by 5 per cent each year. Inflation is no problem.

- *Uncertainty*: as discussed in Section 3.1, inflation is a common shock and thus an uninsurable risk. A possible way out where inflation is purely domestic is to hedge through an internationally diversified portfolio of pension assets. Another escape route, from the insurer's perspective, is to offer limited indexation. If the limit is 5 per cent, then, so far as the insurer is concerned, the situation is similar to the certainty case above—the risk of inflation beyond 5 per cent is transferred to the pensioner.

The conclusion is that, once pensions are in payment, private, defined-contribution schemes can cope with limited inflation (i.e. can offer indexation up to some pre-specified level). But they face major problems with inflation beyond that level. The point is much more than academic. The price index in the UK in January 1974 was 100; in September 1978, in the wake of the first oil shock, it was 200. With 5 per cent indexation, pensions would have increased from 100 to about 133, rather than to 200. Pensions in payment would have lost one-third of their value. Two points are noteworthy: the loss is permanent—in contrast with pensions during build up, there is no opportunity to make up any of the lost ground; and, with rising life expectancy, people are retired today for many more years than previously.

The relative ability of PAYG and funding to cope with inflation is due less to the method of finance *per se* than to the fact that in many instances only the state can guarantee indexed amounts. Funded schemes can cope with inflation if their assets are indexed by the state—for example, where the state sells indexed gilts or where it underwrites directly the indexation component once funded pensions are in payment. However, the part of the return that compensates for inflation is paid out of current tax revenues—that is, on a PAYG basis. More generally, any receipts of funded schemes deriving from current tax revenues, whether the return to indexed government bonds[6] or the tax advantages they currently enjoy, constitute a PAYG element in such schemes.

3. Efficiency arguments for state intervention

Section 3.1 discusses efficiency aspects of public-versus-private provision, and Section 3.2 looks at the PAYG-versus-funding controversy. Social justice is discussed in Section 4.

---

[6] See the Glossary.

3.1. Public-versus-private provision

Efficient consumption smoothing requires that individuals buy the *socially* efficient *real* level of pension. The three major policy issues are why people would voluntarily contribute to a pension scheme, why the state makes membership compulsory, and why it provides retirement pensions itself.

In a world of certainty, including certainty about one's life expectancy, consumption smoothing takes place through saving. In practice, however, people do not know how long they will live and so a mixture of saving and insurance (i.e. the purchase of an annuity) is generally more efficient. Thus a rational, risk-averse individual will join a pension scheme so long as its net cost does not exceed the value of the certainty he thereby derives (Chapter 5, Section 2.1). Membership is compulsory because of the external costs that arise if an individual does not buy pension rights (Chapter 8, Section 2.1). The issue of public provision is more complicated. The private market provides pensions efficiently only if the standard assumptions of perfect information, perfect competition, and no market failures hold. Potential problems on the demand side were discussed in Chapter 5, Section 4.1. A central issue is whether buyers of a technically complex financial instrument are well informed. On the supply side, it is necessary to consider separately the five technical conditions (Chapter 5, Section 3) that must hold if the private market is to supply insurance efficiently.

The probability of living to a given age for pensioner A is independent of that for pensioner B, and is known and less than one. Data on mortality rates are generally reliable in all industrialized countries. Nor is there any problem of adverse selection—by and large people do not know when they are going to die. Moral hazard is not a problem either; suicide is costly to the individual, and works in the insurance company's favour.

The initial conclusion, therefore, is that there is no technical problem with private pension provision. This, however, overlooks inflation. Consumption smoothing, as its name implies, relates to a future consumption bundle—that is, to the *real* value of a person's pension. This can occur without intervention only if the private market can supply insurance against unanticipated inflation. Such insurance is not possible for two reasons.

- The probability distribution of different future levels of inflation is unknown.[7]
- Inflation is a common shock. The probability of pensioner A experiencing a given rate of inflation is *not* independent of that for pensioner B—the rate of inflation facing one pensioner will (by and large) face them all.

Inflation is therefore an uninsurable risk. Thus pensioners cannot insure each other. To what extent might they be able to find protection through some other mechanism—for example, by buying assets whose value keeps pace with inflation? That would be possible without intervention if real rates of return were independent of inflation. As an empirical matter, this is not the case. The dependence is partly the result of distortions elsewhere (e.g. non-indexed tax systems), which could in principle be corrected. However, where an inflationary shock represents other adverse movements in the economy, no private

---

[7] Inflation is not a problem for car repairs, for example, because automobile insurance, unlike pensions, is financed by *current* premiums.

agency can offer a complete hedge against inflation. Bodie's survey (1990: 36) points out that 'virtually no private pension plans in the US offer automatic inflation protection after retirement'.

The conclusion is that private pensions can offer limited indexation, as discussed in Section 2, but protection beyond that must ultimately come from government. Thus there is an efficiency argument, at a minimum, for state intervention to assist private schemes with the costs of unanticipated inflation once pensions are in payment. The state is able to offer such a guarantee because it can use current tax revenues on a PAYG basis. This will introduce a PAYG element into even the purest funded scheme. It should be clear that an indemnity against inflation, if publicly provided, is not true insurance (because it cannot be), but a form of tax/transfer. Since efficient consumption smoothing requires individuals to make decisions about the real value of the pension they purchase, and since the appropriate guarantees against inflation can be given only by the state on a PAYG basis, there is a cast-iron efficiency argument for at least some public involvement with pensions. Whether this should stop at the provision of inflation indemnities for private schemes, or whether the state should step in to provide pensions itself on either a PAYG or a mixed funded/PAYG basis, is an open issue upon which most of the rest of the chapter has a bearing.

3.2. Funding versus Pay-As-You-Go: Theoretical arguments

Having established the case for at least some public involvement, the next question is whether any state scheme should be funded or PAYG and, in particular, the relative merits of the two methods in the face of demographic change.

THE DEMOGRAPHIC PROBLEM is analysed by Barr (1979, 2002a), on which this section draws.[8] The root of the problem (Figure 9.1) is the peak in the birth rate in the 1940s, followed by the larger bulge in the 1960s in which more than ten million babies were born. These cohorts of 'bulge' babies will retire between 2010 and 2030, and will have to be supported in old age by the smaller succeeding generations. Specifically, in 1991 about 16 per cent of the population was 65 or over; the projected figure for 2041 is 24 per cent. The problem is not unique to the UK. A startlingly similar pattern exists in the USA, in most of the EU countries, and also in Australia, New Zealand, and Japan.[9]

How relevant is funding to the problem? The widely held (but false) view that funded schemes are inherently 'safer' than PAYG is an example of the fallacy of composition.[10] For *individuals*, the economic function of a pension scheme is to transfer consumption over time. But (ruling out the case where current output is stored in holes in people's

---

[8] The analysis is similar in spirit to Samuelson (1958).

[9] This is a remarkable fact. Why should countries as different as Denmark (Protestant and highly industrialized) and Italy (Catholic and with some less industrialized parts) have a similar pattern of birth rates? Australia, which escaped much of the recession of the 1970s, nevertheless had a declining birth rate. And Japan faces the same problem despite large differences in religion, social organization, and patterns of industry. No one has yet given a satisfactory explanation.

[10] It is a fallacy of composition to assume that because something is true for an individual it will *necessarily* be true on aggregate. For instance, if I stand on my seat in the theatre I will get a better view, but if everybody does so nobody will get a better view.

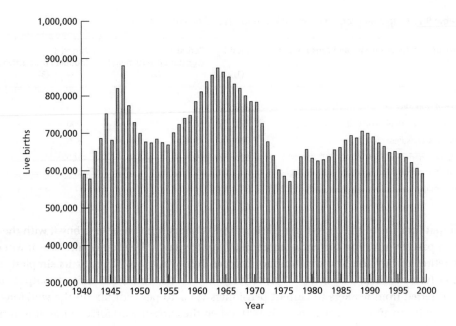

Fig. 9.1. Live births per 1,000 population, 1938–2001

Source: UK Government Actuary's Department.

gardens) this is not possible for society as a whole; the consumption of pensioners as a group is produced by the next generation of workers. From an *aggregate* viewpoint, the economic function of pension schemes is to divide total output between workers and pensioners—that is, to reduce the consumption of workers so that sufficient output remains for pensioners. Once this point is understood, it becomes clear why PAYG and funded schemes, which are both financial mechanisms for dividing output between workers and pensioners, should not fare very differently in the face of demographic change.

THE SIMPLE MODEL highlights the argument under strong assumptions, which are subsequently relaxed. These simplify the analysis without substantially altering the conclusion. They are:

1. Output per head remains constant over time, and is the same whether pensions are funded or PAYG.

2. The number of workers remains constant.

3. Wages are fixed in real terms, pensions in nominal terms.

4. There is no trade with other countries.

The simplest case is illustrated by the first column of Table 9.2. There are 10 workers who produce an output of 1,000. Assume that there are no taxes, so that workers receive the whole of their output; and assume that each unit costs £1. Now suppose that workers use 900 units of output for current consumption, and set the remaining 100 units aside for their retirement. Pension provision can take two forms. Workers can sell 100 units of

Table 9.2. Output and consumption with workforces of different sizes

Size of workforce, output, and consumption	Period 1 (1)	Period 2 (constant productivity) (2)	Period 3 (doubled productivity) (3)
Size of workforce	10	5	5
Total output = total income of workforce	1,000	500	1,000
Workers' consumption	900	450	900
Workers' non-consumption	100	50	100

Note: Output is measured in physical units.

output for £100 to the current generation of pensioners, who are able to buy it with their own past savings. The current generation of workers saves the money, and uses it when it retires to buy the non-consumption of the then workforce. This, at its simplest, is how funded schemes operate.[11] Alternatively, in a PAYG world, 100 units of output are transferred from workers to current pensioners via a 10 per cent tax on the workforce, so that it can afford to consume only 900. When the current workforce retires, it in turn receives 100 units of output.

Under the stated assumptions both schemes can continue indefinitely and both lead to the same three conclusions.

- Pensioners can consume only what workers produce but do not consume.
- Pensioners always depend on succeeding generations to provide the labour to produce the goods which they consume.
- Under the stated assumptions PAYG and funding lead to identical results.

THE EFFECTS OF A DECLINE IN THE WORKFORCE. The previous assumptions stand, except that the labour force halves, as shown in the second column of Table 9.2. With output per worker unchanged (by assumption) output halves to 500, and workers' consumption to 450, leaving 50 units for pensions. Under PAYG, the 10 per cent tax mentioned above leads to exactly this result. With a funded scheme matters are more complicated. The current pensioner generation is the previous workforce of 10 in column 1, which has accumulated sufficient funds to buy an output of 100 at the initial price of £1 per unit. If the saving behaviour of workers does not change, total spending will be £450 by workers on current consumption, plus £100 by pensioners from accumulated funds. The total of £550 is greater than the value at current prices of output of 500: though pensioners get their £100 in *money* safely transferred to their retirement, they will not necessarily receive 100 units of *consumption*.

In economic terms, if there is a large accumulation of pension funds when the workforce is declining, the high level of spending by pensioners out of their accumulated

[11] In practice things can be more complicated: contributions can come from employers and the government as well as from workers; and contributions may not be entirely at the expense of workers' consumption. These factors complicate the analysis but do not change the logic of the underlying argument.

savings will reduce the rate of saving in the economy. Pensioner consumption is greater than saving by workers (i.e. the excess of workers' production over their consumption at current prices); and at full employment this causes demand inflation, which erodes the purchasing power of pensioners' accumulated funds, and hence their consumption. The precise mechanism of this inflationary process is spelled out in Barr (1979), which shows that, if the labour force halves, then, under the stated assumptions, output will halve, the price level will double, and pensioner consumption will halve. In the extreme, it does me no good to accumulate a huge fund if on the day I retire the last worker flies to Australia—I will have plenty of ten pound notes, but no mechanism for transforming them into consumption.[12]

RELAXING THE ASSUMPTIONS. Suppose first that workers' wages are not necessarily indexed, nor pensions necessarily fixed in money terms. If the labour force halves (the other assumptions remaining in force), output will halve (column 2 of Table 9.2). This output can be divided between workers and pensioners in different ways; but their joint demand is constrained by total supply. The relative shares of the two groups will depend on such factors as their political and bargaining strengths—that is, whether pensioners are more powerful lobbying for current tax revenues (PAYG) or as the owners of capital. There is no difference of principle between the two methods, only a practical issue.

Suppose, next, that productivity doubles, but is unaffected by the method of pension finance. If the other assumptions still hold, a smaller workforce of 5 can now produce the same output as previously produced by 10 (column 3). Workers can consume 900, leaving 100 for pensioners. The system is in equilibrium, in this case because supply has adjusted. In a world of funding, the growth in output makes possible sufficient extra saving by the smaller workforce to match dissaving by the larger group of pensioners. Under PAYG, a tax at an unchanged rate of 10 per cent enables government to transfer to pensioners the 100 units of output promised to them.

Relaxing the demographic assumptions is straightforward. Suppose that the decline in the working-age population is entirely offset by increases in the labour-force participation of women, and in the retirement age. In this case, column 1 of Table 9.2 applies in period 2, notwithstanding demographic change. The problem is entirely resolved, again on the supply side, for both types of pension scheme, for the same reason as in the previous paragraph. A similar conclusion arises from any combination of increased productivity and labour-force participation that prevents output from falling.

Finally, it is possible to maintain the consumption of both workers and pensioners with goods produced abroad, provided the country has sufficient overseas assets to do so—for example, by owning factories in countries with a younger population. This approach, which is compatible with either PAYG or funding, increases the workforce by importing labour—analytically the same solution as in the previous paragraph.

Two conclusions emerge.

- If changes in productivity and labour-force participation are independent of the method of finance, then relaxing the assumptions does not change the previous results. In particular, it remains the case that funding and PAYG are not substantially different

---

[12] Australian producers would be unlikely to accept pounds in exchange for Australian goods in this situation.

in their ability to cope with demographic change. This should not be surprising. The task of both schemes is to reduce workers' consumption; PAYG does this by taxing workers, funding by allowing or forcing them to save. The only difference is that PAYG makes explicit the notion that pensions involve current resources.

- The crucial variable is *output*. A decline in the labour force causes problems only if it causes a fall in output; the problem is solved to the extent that this can be prevented.

The choice between PAYG and funding in the face of demographic change is therefore relevant only to the extent that funding (as is sometimes argued) systematically *causes* output to be higher. This is a matter of considerable controversy both theoretically and empirically, and is a central topic in Section 5.1.

OTHER ASPECTS. This section digresses briefly to a number of other issues about PAYG and funding, mainly to make clear that they have little or nothing to do with the central issue of paying for pensions. The main arguments are that funded schemes are safer, give more freedom, and impose greater financial discipline.

The question of safety, as we have seen, turns on whether pensioners as a group are better able to fight for their share of national output as recipients of current tax revenues or as the owners of capital. The PAYG mechanism makes clear both the quarrel over output shares and the dependence of pensioners on younger workers. Funding hides both issues, but does not remove them. It is, indeed, possible for the state to break promises under a PAYG scheme. But funded schemes are also vulnerable and also political (consider the political sensitivity of tax advantages for pension funds).[13] As a practical matter, the purchasing power of the flat-rate component of the national-insurance retirement pension in 2002/3 was 2.6 times its value in 1948. Funded benefits have frequently failed to keep up with inflation.

A related argument asserts that taxes in a PAYG world curtail individual liberty. The issue of freedom, however, is raised less by the way pensions are organized than by compulsion. A compulsory funded employer scheme gives no more freedom than PAYG; and a compulsory personal pension offers only constrained choice.

A final argument is that funding imposes greater financial discipline. With PAYG, the state makes promises now, but may not have to pay anything till later. The immediate revenue charge is negligible relative to the potential future liability, leading, it is argued, to irresponsible promises (an example of government failure discussed in Chapter 4, Section 5). With funding, promises of higher future benefits must be matched by increased contributions immediately, thereby, it is argued, guarding against government failure. Though factually true, this argument points both ways. The ability of social insurance (of which PAYG is an example) to respond to changing social and economic circumstances can equally be regarded as one of its advantages. Of course, PAYG can be abused, but—as with automobiles and pain-killing drugs—that is not a watertight argument for abolition.

---

[13] While on the subject, it should not be imagined that storing current output at the bottom of one's garden gives complete protection against *all* contingencies. The state can always expropriate such output either explicitly, or by a tax on individual wealth, or, more subtly, by engineering inflation and imposing a non-indexed capital-gains tax on an accruals basis. In similar vein, funded schemes run a potential risk of state direction of their investment portfolios, a besetting problem in Latin America (see Mesa-Lago 1990). For specific discussion of the safety of different pension regimes, see Diamond (1996).

4. Social justice

4.1. Public-versus-private provision

This section closely parallels Chapter 8, Section 2.4, and considers the equity arguments for public organization of pensions. Horizontal equity concerns goals like a guaranteed minimum standard of some commodities, or equal access to them. These occur without intervention (Chapter 4, Section 4.3) where individuals have perfect information and equal power, a line of argument that lends little support to public provision of pensions. If individuals did not have perfect information, they would generally be able to buy it. At most there is a case for regulation of minimum standards. The fact that individuals do not have equal power lends further support to minimum standards, but, again, there is no argument for public provision.

I have already discussed in Chapter 8, Section 2.4, and elsewhere the weakness of the vertical-equity argument that the state should provide pensions because otherwise the poor could not afford them. The earlier conclusions apply equally here—that public provision solely to foster redistribution is justified only by a consumption externality, where the rich confer pensions on the poor as a merit good.

Consumption externalities apart, equity reasons for public provision must appeal to efficiency arguments. In the case of pensions, these arise out of the inability of private institutions to guarantee protection against inflation, giving an efficiency justification for public involvement at least in underwriting the indexation component of pensions, and possibly (depending on the outcome of the funding-versus-PAYG debate) of some or all of the pension. As discussed in Chapter 4, Section 7.2, once a commodity is publicly provided on *efficiency* grounds, it is not inappropriate to finance it redistributively. In addition, the fact that membership is compulsory, by imposing a pooling solution, avoids the worst problems of adverse selection (Chapter 5, Section 4.1); in consequence, premiums based on income rather than individual risk need cause no major inefficiency. These efficiency arguments for compulsion and public provision, taken together, suggest that using publicly organized pensions for distributional purposes does not necessarily cause substantial efficiency losses.

4.2. The redistributive effects of pensions

A pension scheme, depending on its precise construction, can redistribute from young to old, from rich to poor, and from men to women. It will also redistribute over the life cycle. It is necessary to consider PAYG and funded schemes, and in each case to ask three questions: is such redistribution possible; is it inevitable; and to what extent does it occur in practice?

REDISTRIBUTION FROM YOUNG TO OLD. PAYG enables a generation as a whole to receive more than the sum of its past contributions. Thus redistribution from the workforce to the retired generation is *possible*. But it is not *inevitable*, since a PAYG scheme could be organized to pay actuarial benefits. *In practice*, as we shall see in Section 5.2, there has been substantial redistribution from young to old in many countries over the post-war period.

With funded schemes it is necessary to consider separately the cases of stable and unstable price levels. In a world with no inflation, the funded benefits of any generation are constrained by its past contributions, rendering redistribution from young to old impossible. The effect of unanticipated inflation is to bring about unintended redistribution from old to young, and vice versa for unanticipated price deflation.

REDISTRIBUTION FROM RICH TO POOR can, and usually does, occur with PAYG pensions. In many schemes there is *formula redistribution*, in that individual B with half the income of individual A generally pays half the contribution, but receives a pension that is more than half of A's. The UK system was described in Section 1. In the USA, though the formula has changed over time, it has always been explicitly redistributive. The same is true in the systems of most industrialized countries.

The effect of formula redistribution is partially offset by *differential mortality*, to the extent that the rich live longer than the poor. But redistribution is not inevitable—it is possible to organize a PAYG scheme in which pensions are proportional to contributions, as with 'notional defined-contribution' schemes in several countries, including Sweden.[14]

It might be possible to devise a (compulsory) funded scheme that redistributes from rich to poor. But, where membership is voluntary, the present value of the annuity received by a representative individual must equal the lump sum accumulated over his working years. This implies, *ceteris paribus*, that pensions must be proportional to contributions, thus ruling out systematic redistribution.

REDISTRIBUTION FROM MEN TO WOMEN. The following is broadly the case in the UK.[15]

- The normal retiring age for men is 65, at which age a man has a life expectancy of 80.5. The average man is thus retired for 15.5 years.

- The normal retiring age for women is 60, at which age women have a life expectancy of 83, so that the average woman is retired for 23 years.

- It is therefore $\frac{23}{15.5}$, or roughly 1.5 times, as expensive to provide a given weekly pension for a woman as for a man.

- If men and women pay equal contributions and receive equal weekly benefits, there is redistribution from men to women. Since women live longer than men, abolishing the differential retirement age would reduce the subsidy but would not eliminate it.

Redistribution from men to women occurs for these reasons in both funded and PAYG schemes. The phenomenon is widespread, but is particularly strong in the UK, which was an outlier in international terms in having a lower retiring age for women (a subject to

[14] Sweden introduced a 'notional defined-contribution' scheme in 1998 (Sweden: Federation of Social Insurance Offices, 1998). The scheme is financed through social-insurance contributions, but the pension a person receives bears a strict actuarial relationship to her notional lifetime pension accumulation (the amount being adjusted for the cohort's life expectancy). In addition, there is a safety net pension for people with low lifetime earnings and credits for periods spent caring for children.

[15] Interim figures from the Government Actuary's Department, based on data for 1999–2001.

which we return in Section 5.2).[16] Two issues arise: is such redistribution inevitable; and is it desirable? On the first point, one could devise a scheme (PAYG or funded) in which women receive benefits related to their longevity. A woman could receive a lower monthly pension than a man with an identical contributions record—that is, a definition of equity as a pension stream of equal present value. Alternatively, women could pay a higher contribution and receive the same monthly pension as men—that is, equity consists of women receiving a pension stream with a higher present value, matched by a larger contributions stream. Thus there are two definitions of equity: equal present value, or equal monthly value. Either is defensible, but they are different, hence the equity problem.

Redistribution from men to women in pensions, though not inevitable, is almost universal, partly from a belief that any differential is a form of discrimination. A decision by the US Supreme Court (1978) declared differential pensions unconstitutional even if calculated actuarially (i.e. on the basis of equation (5.11)).[17] Nor is such redistribution undesirable. Analytically, it occurs because women pay the same premiums as men despite being (from the insurer's viewpoint) worse risks because they live longer. As we saw in Chapter 5, Section 4.1, efficiency generally requires that premiums should be proportional to risk; where insurance is compulsory, however, low-risk individuals are not able to opt out, and charging the same premium for all categories of risk does not cause adverse selection. It is possible that secondary inefficiency might arise—for example, the possible distortion of labour-supply decisions that non-actuarial contributions might cause. To the extent that this is not a substantial problem, the decision whether all classes of risk should pay the same premium can be made mainly on equity grounds.

REDISTRIBUTION OVER THE LIFE CYCLE. Where none of the earlier types of redistribution occurs, redistribution over the life cycle (i.e. consumption smoothing) is the only redistributive effect of pensions. In comparison with PAYG, funded schemes generally have less redistribution from young to old and less from rich to poor. Thus a larger fraction of funded pensions will relate to redistribution over time than to redistribution between people.

5. Assessment of old-age pensions

5.1. Efficiency and incentives

Background questions

This section asks whether the national-insurance pension is efficient and equitable, starting with the *a priori* questions of Chapter 8, Section 3.1: should pensions be national (i.e. publicly provided), are they optimal in quantity and type, and are they actuarial?

---

[16] The Old Age Pensions Act 1908 established a common retirement age of 70, which was reduced to 65 under the Old Age and Widows and Orphans Contributory Pensions Act 1925. Women's retirement age was reduced to 60 in 1940, partly because of a campaign by women's organizations (for details of the events leading to the change in 1940, see Thane 1982: 245). Women's retirement age will over time be raised to 65; see note 2.

[17] Though tenable on equity grounds, the decision was based on a failure to understand the nature of insurance.

SHOULD PENSIONS BE NATIONAL? The efficiency arguments for state involvement rest on externalities, justifying compulsion, and technical failures in the insurance market, justifying public provision at a minimum of some sort of indemnity against inflation. It is agreed (*a*) that it should be compulsory for people to belong to a pension scheme, at least up to some minimum level, and (*b*) that efficiency is enhanced where people are able to reallocate consumption over their lifetime. Decisions about consumption smoothing are therefore efficient if inflation can be ignored; but only the state can guarantee full indexation. Thus there is a role for public provision at least of indexed assets for use by private, funded schemes. The efficiency argument for public provision of the whole pension is less clear-cut.

DOES THE STATE PROVIDE THE OPTIMAL QUANTITY AND TYPE OF PENSION? Only tentative answers are possible. Does the state provide the optimal level of pensions? Martin Evans (1998: table 7.7) shows that about one-third of increased state pension spending between 1973 and 1994 related to rising numbers of pensioners; the remaining two-thirds related to rising real pensions. For this and other reasons, the fraction of pensioners requiring additional means-tested assistance fell over the period from 22 per cent to 14 per cent. For the most part, this outcome resulted from deliberate government policy. The state has also acted to protect private pensions against inflation—for example, by issuing indexed bonds.

It can be argued that the increasing role of the state in indexing public and private pensions has contributed to the relative certainty with which individuals can plan for the future, and has therefore increased efficiency, albeit imperfectly because the state scheme makes no allowance for different degrees of risk aversion between individuals.

A second set of questions concerns the efficiency of private institutions. Though private pensions in the UK are well established and, for the most part, work well, they have had problems, largely connected with imperfect consumer information. Occupational pensions faced the so-called Maxwell scandal, in which the assets of an occupational scheme were illegally siphoned off for other purposes. Proposals to tighten regulations (UK Pension Law Review Committee 1993) led eventually to private pensions being regulated by the Financial Services Authority. With personal pensions the problem was different. 'What is clear . . . is that there is considerable inefficiency within the personal pensions market because of the high management costs and poor advice offered to savers. Individual purchasers have little chance of gaining full information about the wide array of highly complex long-term financial instruments on offer' (Johnson and Rake 1997: 44).

What this suggests is *not* that the state necessarily does a better job than the private sector but—as argued in Chapter 4, Section 7.1—that the choice of instruments is complex. In the case of pensions, the best way forward is to retain private institutions, with state intervention through stronger regulation and, possibly, an element of subsidy.

ARE PENSIONS ACTUARIAL? Chapter 8, Section 3.1, pointed out that national-insurance contributions are not geared to risk, that the scheme is not funded, and that rights to benefit are not determined solely by the occurrence of the insured event. In addition, as we shall see in Section 5.2, the scheme redistributes to the poor, and offers credits for people at home looking after young children, and for the unemployed. These arrangements are a considerable departure from the Beveridge scheme, whose lump-sum contributions and benefits ruled out redistribution from rich to poor (assuming, for example, equal life expectancy); and, since the original proposals were for a funded scheme, they would also have ruled out redistribution from young to old.

For these reasons, some writers have questioned whether the basic pension should continue to be contributory. The counter-argument is that pensions are social insurance, as defined in Chapter 5, Section 4.2: they are insurance in the sense of offering protection against longevity and inflation risks, but not in the sense of being an actuarial mechanism. As discussed in Chapter 8, Section 3.1, social insurance, though it *enables* redistribution from rich to poor, does not *require* it. The extent to which social insurance is redistributive therefore depends on the relative weights attached to the different objectives in Chapter 1, Section 2.2.

Incentive issues

The incentive effects of pensions are the subject of considerable debate. This section makes no attempt to survey the large literature (see the Further Reading) but seeks only to sketch out why the issue is controversial. Two issues predominate: does PAYG restrict saving and output growth; and do pensions reduce labour supply?

PENSIONS, SAVING, AND ECONOMIC GROWTH. It is often regarded as self-evident that saving, and hence economic growth, will be higher with funding than under PAYG. But this assertion faces at least three major qualifications.

1. *Increases in saving, if any, occur only during the build-up of the fund.* It should be clear from column 1 of Table 9.2 that in the long run workers save 100 and pensioners dissave 100, so that net saving is zero.

2. *Does funding increase saving even during the build-up phase?* Opinion is divided. The issue can be posed simply. Suppose that my mandatory pension contribution of 100 is moved from a PAYG scheme to a funded scheme. Two illustrative outcomes are interesting.

- My voluntary savings behaviour (e.g. for retirement or bequests to my children) does not change. Thus my saving increases by 100.

- I reduce my voluntary saving by 100; thus there is no increase in my saving.

The issue, therefore, is the extent to which any increases in mandatory saving are offset by reductions in voluntary saving.

The issue is ancient. In the context of the 1908 Old Age Pensions Act (Chapter 2, Section 2.2), Sydney and Beatrice Webb (1909: 334) reported that 'some of our witnesses . . . have taken the view . . . that such non-contributory pensions would be likely to discourage thrift and saving'. Current debate was reopened by Feldstein (1974). His empirical work concluded that the US PAYG social-security (i.e. pension) scheme reduced personal saving by about 50 per cent, thereby reducing the capital stock by 38 per cent below what it would have been in the absence of the social-security system. That work was hotly disputed (e.g. Leimer and Lesnoy 1982). Gale (1998) argues that the savings offset is larger than previously supposed because of econometric biases in earlier work. The debate continues.

A second central question in considering the effect of funding on savings is what happens to the pensions of the older generation. If they are reduced, consumption falls, and hence, *ceteris paribus*, savings will indeed rise. But, if pensions are not reduced, they have to be paid from taxes or government borrowing. Extra taxation exerts downward pressure on saving; extra borrowing at least partially offsets additional private capital formation. These macroeconomic effects could swamp moves from PAYG to funding. It is therefore not surprising that an IMF study (Mackenzie et al. 1997: 1) concluded: 'Studies of the U.S. economy, on which most research has been done, provide some moderately strong evidence that the introduction and development of the public pension plan have depressed private sector saving, although the extent of this impact has proved hard to estimate. Studies of other countries as a group have tended to be inconclusive . . .'.

3. *Do increased savings lead to increased output?* The third qualification is that an increase in saving does not *necessarily* raise output. There are not one, but three links in the argument that future output will be higher with funding than with PAYG:

- funding leads to a higher rate of saving in the build-up period than PAYG;
- this higher saving is translated into more and better investment; and
- this investment leads to an increase in output.

None of the three links *necessarily* holds. The evidence on the first, as just discussed, is mixed. On the second, increased saving does not necessarily lead to new investment; pension savings could instead be used to buy old masters. So far as the third link is concerned, the objective is to channel resources into their most productive investment use. But it cannot just be *assumed* that pension managers make more efficient choices than other agents. More generally, the declining growth performance of the Communist countries over the 1970s and 1980s, despite very high rates of investment, makes it clear that the volume of investment is not the sole determinant of growth—its quality is also of central importance.

As with the second link, there is also an important macroeconomic argument. The claim that higher savings contributes to growth is of dubious relevance in a small open economy, since investors can borrow internationally. Thus higher saving by people in countries such as Poland, New Zealand, South Africa, or Chile might well translate into higher income for them in the future, but will have little effect on the level of investment in those countries. The argument is less true in the USA, whose international borrowing, because of its size, will drive up world interest rates. Thus the USA (from which most of the literature emanates) is a special case.

All three links have to hold before it can be asserted that funding will lead to greater increases in output than PAYG. At best the assertion is not proven.

PENSIONS AND LABOUR SUPPLY. The question here is whether pensions (either PAYG or funded) reduce labour supply. The problems are similar to those affecting empirical analysis of the labour-supply effects of unemployment benefits (Chapter 8, Section 3.1). On the contributions side, the theoretical analysis of taxation on work effort is generally accepted (see Atkinson and Stiglitz 1980: 23–61). The effect of national-insurance contributions is to drive a wedge between gross and net money wages. If workers discount future benefits entirely, contributions have the same effect as an income tax; at the other extreme, where future benefits bear an actuarial relationship to contributions, and are perceived to do so, national-insurance contributions are not a tax but simply the price of insurance, which, like any other price, has little if any distortionary effect on labour supply.

The impact of future benefits, on the other hand, is harder to analyse. They are payable only in certain contingencies, can be changed by legislation, and will depend on marital status; and it is not possible to borrow against future benefits, which must therefore be weighted by the probability that each benefit will be received at some given future date. The weighted benefits must then be discounted to present value using the market rate of interest or, for people who cannot borrow as much as they wish, at a personal rate of time preference. Similar problems arise in valuing pension rights considered as part of personal wealth.

As a result, modelling the effect of pensions on labour supply is complex, with studies (see the Further Reading) reaching very different conclusions. That said, recent evidence paints a clear picture that badly designed schemes affect retirement decisions. Two potential distortions have to be considered: (*a*) retirement decisions and (*b*) labour-market responses earlier in life.

So far as the retirement decision is concerned, what matters is that pensions should be related *at the margin* to individual contributions, and that contributors and beneficiaries should perceive this to be so. The argument is important. It is possible to have a pension formula that is redistributive in the sense that worker A, with twice the earnings of worker B over his working life, gets a pension that is higher than B's, but less than twice as high. However, if either A or B retires early, his pension should be actuarially reduced relative to the pension he would have received at age 65.

In contrast, earlier labour-market behaviour depends not only on the marginal relationship between contributions and benefits, but on the effect of an increase in earnings on the total pensions package. In this case, labour-market distortions are minimized where contributions bear a fully actuarial relationship to benefits. This is the case with private defined-contribution schemes. It is also the case with state schemes which pay benefits strictly proportional to a person's contributions record—for example, the notional defined-contribution scheme in Sweden and other countries noted earlier (see note 14).

There is growing evidence that badly designed schemes, whether private or public, cause labour-market distortions. Gruber and Wise (1998, 1999; see also Gruber and Wise 2002), reporting on a study of eleven industrial countries, find a strong relationship between the design of public pensions and early retirement. In particular, they examine the fact that most countries increase pensions for people who delay retirement by less than the actuarial amount, thereby creating an incentive for people to leave the labour force at the age at which their pension wealth is maximized. Gruber and Wise call this 'the tax force to retire', and find a strong association between that variable and the labour-force departure of older men.

Such distortions also exist in private schemes. Employer schemes can encourage labour immobility—indeed, vesting rules (which specify the length of service before a worker gains title to any pension benefits) may be deliberately designed to discourage workers from leaving (Hannah 1986; Campbell 1999). Publicly organized defined-benefit schemes, being universal, do not impede labour mobility, since members can change jobs without changing to a new pension scheme.

Two conclusions are noteworthy. First, questions about labour supply, though highly significant, are logically separate from the PAYG-versus-funding controversy: what matters is pension design, not whether a scheme is private or public. Secondly, labour supply should not be considered in isolation: what matters is not labour supply but economic welfare. A defined-benefit scheme might reduce labour supply at the margin; but if the utility loss from lower output is more than offset by the utility gain from greater security, defined-benefit arrangements may be welfare improving even if they do reduce labour supply.

Dealing with future problems

Britain's demographic problems are less acute than elsewhere in Europe. In addition, since the mid-1980s the state pension has been tied to changes in prices rather than earnings, the resulting savings being sufficient to keep contributions fairly constant despite population ageing. In many ways, therefore, Britain's pensions 'crisis' is not a crisis at all, but a matter that has largely been resolved (Hills with Gardiner 1997). This section therefore concentrates more on the logic of dealing with demographic problems than with the specifics of any particular country.

POLICIES IN THE FACE OF THE DEMOGRAPHIC PROBLEM. We saw earlier that the Eurotoddlers of the 1950s and 1960s will cause a sharp rise in the dependency rate when they retire in the years after 2010. Any solution to the declining population of working age must reduce the demand for goods and services and/or increase their supply. This implies one or more of three outcomes. Demand can be reduced (a) by increasing contributions, thereby reducing the average consumption of workers, and/or (b) by reducing benefits, thereby reducing the average consumption of pensioners. The UK has adopted (b) by deciding to increase pensions in line with prices rather than earnings.

Alternatively, on the supply side, workers and pensioners can have the consumption they currently expect, so long as (c) output rises sufficiently to maintain average consumption per head (hence the emphasis in Section 3.2 on the central importance of output). In theory, raising output involves either or both of two strategies. *Increased output per worker* can arise from increases in the quantity and quality of capital, and from increases in the quality of labour. *Increased numbers of workers* can arise from increased labour-force participation by those of working age; from an increase in the retirement age; and/or by importing labour.

In practice, supply-side policies in the face of a declining workforce should therefore include some or all of the following:

1. introducing policies to increase the capital stock and its quality, e.g. robots (which have the added advantage of not requiring pensions);
2. increasing investment in labour through education and training;
3. increasing labour-force participation by reducing unemployment and by encouraging more women to join the labour force (e.g. by improving child-care facilities);
4. raising the average retirement age;
5. importing labour directly, through immigration;
6. importing labour indirectly by exporting capital to countries with a young labour force.

Policy 4 has major advantages to which we return shortly.

TO WHAT EXTENT IS FUNDING A SOLUTION? Funding is clearly irrelevant to policies 2–5, which can all be pursued by *direct* methods. If funding makes any difference via policy 1, it can be so only if it (*a*) leads successively to an increase in saving, in investment, and in output (i.e. policy 1), *and* (*b*) does so more effectively than any other method of garnering resources and channelling them into productive investment. The stringency of these conditions should be clear from earlier discussion. The evidence on (*a*), both theoretically and empirically, is mixed, inconclusive, and controversial, and that on (*b*) is unlikely to be less so.

The effect of policy (6) requires discussion. Pensioners can consume goods made abroad so long as they can organize a claim on those goods. If British workers use some of their savings to buy Australian factories, they can in retirement sell their share of the factory's output for Australian money to buy Australian goods, which they then import to the UK. Though useful, this policy is not foolproof. It breaks down if Australian workers all retire; thus the age structure of the population in the destination country is important. Secondly, if large numbers of British pensioners exchange Australian dollars for other currencies, the Australian exchange rate might fall, reducing the real value of the pension. Thus the ideal country in which to invest has a young population *and* products one wants to buy. Accumulating assets in countries with younger populations is thus one way to maintain claims on future output. Overseas investment by pension funds is one way to implement this policy. But there are other ways: I could, for example, hold part of my saving in Australian equities or mutual funds. Funding *per se* is not paramount—what is paramount is saving.

The funding-versus-PAYG controversy can therefore be argued rather to miss the point by concentrating on a method of increasing output that is both indirect (namely, the three steps in (*a*)) and debatable. Since the issue is one of economic growth, it seems easier and more reliable to adopt direct methods of effecting policies 1–6.

This is *not* an argument against funding; but it *is* an argument against reliance on funding *alone* to address demographic problems. The analysis suggests three conclusions.

- In the face of demographic problems the key variable is output.
- Policy should consider the entire menu of policies that promote output growth directly.
- From a macroeconomic perspective the choice between PAYG and funding is secondary. Neither method (indeed, no method) can insure against common shocks. The future is full of uncertainties (about rates of inflation, output growth, birth rates, and the like), which affect pension schemes just as they affect most other institutions.

In short, the argument that funding insulates pensioners from demographic change should not be overstated. From an economic point of view demographic change is not a strong argument for a shift towards funding.

THE REAL SOLUTION: RAISING THE AGE OF RETIREMENT. Reforms in the UK since the mid-1980s have exerted downward pressure on state-pension spending by indexing pensions only to price changes, and by increasing the emphasis on private pensions. The first is a response to the demographic and global pressures discussed in Chapter 1, Section 3. The second results from fiscal incentives and is also to some extent the expression of people's choices. By the mid-1990s, six million people were contributing to the state earnings-related pension, while fifteen million had contracted out, and were contributing to occupational or personal pensions. To some extent, therefore, people were voting with their feet.

Though the decline in the state pension halted in the years after 2000, a series of reforms and proposals for reform have continued a movement towards private arrangements, though the resulting institutions are subject to criticism and continuing discussion. A Green Paper (UK DSS 1998) foreshadowed the introduction of a state second pension (essentially a top-up to the basic rate pension for low earners) and of stakeholder pensions (simple individual funded accounts with low administrative costs aimed at low earners). However, the arrangements had significant problems, not least their complexity.[18] A further Green Paper (UK DWP 2002d) did not really address these problems: pensioner poverty continued, and the system remained complex, leading to calls for a higher basic state pension paid by raising the retirement age.[19]

All the advanced industrial countries, and many other countries, face a similar collision of demographics and fiscal pressures. A series of proposals in the USA has analysed the role of funding (Feldstein 1996; Diamond 1998; National Academy of Social Insurance 1998; Cogan and Mitchell 2003). In Europe, proposals for pension reform in the early 2000s created political turbulence but relatively little action.

Virtually none of the proposals got fully to grips with the real solution—raising pensionable age. The logic is straightforward. People today live much longer than 100 years ago. That is a wonderful outcome that we should all applaud. To talk about the 'problem' of ageing is grotesquely to miss the point. The problem is not that people are living longer but that they are retiring too early.

In considering the forces that drive pension spending, three issues cumulate.

(a) People are living longer and thus receive a pension for longer; at a given real pension that increases the total cost of providing for each pensioner.

(b) People are joining the workforce later because of increased education and training; thus there are fewer people producing the goods that pensioners consume.

(c) The high birth rates of the late 1940s and the 1960s were followed by lower birth rates; thus the population is ageing, raising the age-dependency ratio.

It should be noted that (a) and (b) would make it harder to finance pensions even in the absence of (c); the main effect of population ageing is to make the problem worse.

What can be done to accommodate these pressures? As discussed earlier in this section, there are four and only four ways in which pension finance can be improved.

1. *Increasing output* is possible by raising labour productivity and/or by increasing the number of workers: output growth sufficient to meet the growing demands of pensioners, if that is possible, is a complete solution. With a steady rise in life expectancy, however, that is unlikely.

---

[18] For critiques, see Agulnik (1999), Disney et al. (1999), Falkingham and Rake (1999), Agulnik and Barr (2000), and Rake et al. (2000).

[19] For the state of play in 2003, see Glennerster (2003a: 214–17); for overall assessment, see Emmerson and Wakefield (2003); on pensioner poverty, see Hancock (1998) and Goodman et al. (2003); for a critique and reform proposals, see Brooks et al. (2002: chs. 4, 6).

2. *Reducing the living standards of workers* by increasing pension contributions: this solution is problematic, first, because increased contributions, especially in a PAYG scheme, can create labour-supply disincentives, emigration being the extreme example, thus hindering growth. Reducing workers' living standards is also likely to be politically unpopular.

3. *Reducing the living standards of pensioners* faces analogous problems—the policy can create pensioner poverty (as in the UK) and will be politically unpopular.

4. *Raising the age of retirement* (more accurately, raising pensionable age): later retirement increases the number of workers and *simultaneously* reduces the number of pensioners—it is not double counting to include both effects, hence raising the retirement age is a powerful policy instrument.

It is also a good one. When pensions were first introduced they incorporated a retirement age that was very old relative to life expectancy (65 in the 1898 New Zealand pension, 70 in the 1906 Lloyd George legislation in the UK). Since then life expectancy has increased in the advanced countries on a linear trend, with no evidence that the curve is flattening. It is rational to embrace this extra life expectancy with open arms, but irrational to keep the retirement age fixed at 65 forever. By the time that people live to be 110 (not that implausible), they will work for 45 years (20–65) and then be retired for another 45.

As well as being good macroeconomic policy, raising pensionable age is also good social policy. First, a significant number of people would actively prefer to work longer.[20] Secondly, the policy contains pension spending not by reducing living standards in old age, but by reducing the duration of retirement. Even those who look forward to retirement would generally prefer the latter option. Thirdly, since adjustment to longer life expectancy could come either from lower consumption or from longer working life, it seems strange to adopt a corner solution by ignoring the latter option.

These arguments notwithstanding, the average retirement age in many countries has continued to fall, creating a problem that policy-makers have yet to face but which they will have no choice but to face.

What, then, should policy be? The most efficient and equitable policy is to raise the average retirement age to accommodate aggregate resource pressures, but to offer choice over retirement, in the face of efficient incentives, to accommodate individual preferences. Specifically, any well-designed pension scheme should have four elements:

- an initial retirement age that makes it fiscally possible to provide a genuinely adequate state pension;
- a subsequent retirement age that increases in line with rising life expectancy in a way that is rational and transparent, so that people know long in advance broadly when they will be able to retire;
- a flexible labour market that allows people to move from full-time work towards full retirement along a phased path of their choosing;
- public understanding of the simple economics of pensions.

---

[20] The US Age Discrimination in Retirement Act 1978, which enables (but does not compel) broad classes of people to defer retirement until they are 70, was not a top-down measure motivated by budgetary control, but a legislative response to grass-roots activism by people who resented compulsory retirement.

5.2. Equity issues

The discussion in Chapter 8, Section 3.2, of equity aspects of national insurance applies equally to pensions. This section concentrates on a number of other issues.

REDISTRIBUTION OVER THE LIFE CYCLE. Hills (with Gardiner 1997) looks at the combined effects of taxation and benefits. He finds that of every £1,000 of cash benefits (mostly pensions) paid to a representative person, nearly three-quarters is self-financed. To a significant extent, therefore, the welfare state acts as a 'piggy bank'. The point is broadly echoed in Table 7.3, where spending on benefits aimed at insurance and consumption smoothing was £72 billion, some 63 per cent of total benefit spending.

REDISTRIBUTION FROM RICH TO POOR. The system of benefits (Section 1) and contributions (Chapter 7, Section 2.1) together imply considerable formula redistribution (see Section 4.2). At its simplest, from Table 7.2, someone with weekly earnings of £120 pays a contribution of about £3.40 per week, and someone earning £500 pays about £45. If each received only the basic pension, the 'poor' person would receive thirteen times as much pension per pound of contribution. Because of the earnings-related component, the effect is not as strong as the example suggests; but, *ceteris paribus*, there is still redistribution from rich to poor. In 2002/3, the effect of taxes and benefits was to reduce the Gini coefficient for retired households from 66 for original income to 33 for post-tax income (Lakin 2003: table 11).

Other factors, however, work in the opposite direction. There is differential mortality, since the better off have a greater life expectancy (and hence collect their pensions longer) and tend to stay in education longer (and hence start to pay contributions later). Secondly, it is disproportionately the better off who contract out of the state scheme, and this, too, reduces its redistributive impact.

The overall redistributive effect is therefore complex and results are far from definitive. An implication of the life-cycle results just discussed is that about one-quarter of cash benefits are not self-financed. Hills (with Gardiner 1997: fig. 12) shows that the 'lifetime poor' are net gainers and the 'lifetime rich' net losers. Alongside redistribution over the life cycle, therefore, the system also redistributes from rich to poor.

REDISTRIBUTION FROM YOUNG TO OLD. The real purchasing power of the UK basic state pension increased by 260 per cent between 1948 and 2002, far beyond pensioners' actuarial entitlement. In the USA many retirees receive a social-security pension at least twice their actuarial entitlement. Whether this is more equitable than a funded scheme with no such redistributive possibilities is a matter of judgement.

REDISTRIBUTION FROM MEN TO WOMEN can occur in both funded and PAYG schemes as a consequence of differential life expectancy (Section 4.2). This type of redistribution is particularly strong in the UK, which is unusual in having a lower retirement age for women. To the extent that this redistribution is caused by the differential retirement age, it is inequitable. First is the anomaly whereby a woman who retires at 65 will receive a higher pension than a 65-year-old man with an identical contributions record, because she has worked beyond her normal retirement age.[21] Secondly, there is the discrimination against women who would prefer to work longer. Thirdly, the earlier retirement age gives a woman fewer years to make up any deficiency in her contributions record. For these, as well as for fiscal reasons, women's retirement age will be increased to 65.

Removing this indefensible anomaly reduces the transfer from men to women but does not eliminate it. What, if anything, could or should be done about it? One answer is to recognize the fact but, having recognized it, to leave it at that. As discussed in Section 4.1, this is defensible, not least because compulsory membership means that the subsidy will not cause inefficiency in insurance markets through adverse selection.[22]

OTHER ASPECTS. Redistribution also takes place between households of different sizes. From Table 8.1, the basic pension for a married couple is 60 per cent higher than for a single person making the same contribution; in the USA the situation is broadly comparable.

Finally, note should be taken of the important relation between accrued pension rights —particularly to the state pension—and the distribution of personal wealth. Because pension rights are distributed more equally than most other forms of non-human wealth, the overall wealth distribution is more equal when they are included. The size of the effect, however, is controversial, depending on (a) precisely which types of pension wealth are included (e.g. how should national-insurance pension rights be treated?), and (b) the valuation placed on entitlements to a future income stream. The latter problem is particularly intractable (see Banks and Tanner 1996; Hamnett and Seavers 1996).

5.3. Conclusion

Empirical investigation suggests that funding is likely to make little difference, if any, to growth rates. The funding solution is indirect in its mechanism, controversial in its outcome, and likely in any case to have only a second-order effect. It would, therefore, be highly dangerous to imagine that simply by embracing funding the demographic problem would be solved. In addition, efficiency arguments of principle point strongly towards a public role at least in underwriting indexation. The efficiency case for continued public, PAYG involvement is therefore strong. Such an argument accepts that it is appropriate for people to use the state as a collective institution for consumption smoothing and insurance where it is able to perform these functions more cheaply and efficiently than any private alternative. This does not mean that PAYG schemes have never made profligate promises. But the efficiency case for state involvement is, at its very least, a counterblast to the government failure arguments in Chapter 4, Section 5.

Aaron (1982) contrasts the absence of conclusive evidence that PAYG schemes have deleterious efficiency effects, with the strong evidence that their equity impact is beneficial, in that they have greatly improved the economic status of the elderly. He argues that decisions about the future of state pensions should therefore be made mainly on equity grounds.

---

[21] The real pension is increased by 7.5% for each year of work beyond normal retiring age (section 1); thus a woman retiring at 65 receives a pension 37.5% higher than that of an identical 65-year-old man.

[22] Voluntary personal pensions do not offer unisex benefits. Reform would require EU-wide action.

■ QUESTIONS FOR FURTHER DISCUSSION

1. Pensions are said to be in crisis. What is the source of that crisis?

2. Is funding a solution to the problems of pension finance?

3. What solutions are there other than funding to the problems of pension finance?

■ FURTHER READING

For compendious description of institutions (including legal sources), see Child Poverty Action Group (2003) (the 2003 version of an annual publication) or UK DWP (2002e) (a detailed guide for pensions advisers), or other items on the Department of Work and Pensions web site (http://www.dwp.gov.uk). On institutions in the EU including discussion of pension regimes in different countries, see the various reports and overview documents on http://europa.eu.int/comm/ employment_social/soc-prot/index_en.htm, and for survey of pensions in twelve countries, Pensions Policy Institute (2003). For institutions worldwide, see US Social Security Administration (2002, 2003), downloadable from http://www.ssa.gov/policy/pubs/index.html. See also the various government portals in the list of useful web sites at the start of the book. For a survey of private pension arrangements, see International Social Security Association/International Network of Pension Regulators and Supervisors (2003).

On the analytics of pensions, see, in ascending order of technical difficulty, Thompson (1998), Barr (2002a), Rosen (2002: ch. 9), Diamond (2002), and Diamond (2003), the last of which analyses social security as a particular example of optimal taxation theory. The classic articles are by Samuelson (1958) and Aaron (1966).

See Poterba et al. (1996), Mackenzie et al. (1997), and Gale (1998) for the effects of pensions on saving, and, for labour-supply effects, see Gruber and Wise (1998, 1999, 2002), Blundell et al. (2002) and Disney and Smith (2002).

The distributional effects of the UK state pension are discussed by Hills with Gardiner (1997) and Martin Evans (1998). On pensioner poverty, see Hancock (1998) and Goodman et al. (2003) and, on gender aspects, Falkingham and Rake (1999) and Bennett (2002).

There is a huge literature on pension reform. On the UK, see Agulnik (1999), Agulnik and Barr (2000), Brooks et al. (2002), and Glennerster (2003a: ch. 7). On the USA, see Feldstein (1996), Arnold et al. (1998), National Academy of Social Insurance (1998), and Lee and Skinner (1999). For pension reform in Europe, see Forni and Giordano (2001) (Italy), Angel (2002) (Spain), Ploug (2003) (Denmark), Cornelisse and Goudswaard (2002) (on convergence within the EU), and Andrietti (2001) (on the portability of supplementary pension rights within the EU). On pension reform in Central and Eastern Europe, see the symposium in the *International Social Security Review*, 54/2–3 (April–September 2001), Augusztinovics et al. (2002), and Schmähl and Horstmann (2002). On Australia, see Whiteford and Angenent (2001), and on South-East Asia, Asher (1998).

There is also a huge debate. For contrasting overviews, see Arnold et al. (1998), Disney (2000), Barr (2002a), Lindbeck and Persson (2003) and Diamond (2004). Cogan and Mitchell (2003) discuss perspectives of US pension reform in the early 2000s; for a specific US proposal, see Diamond and Orszag (2004). A major international debate about pension reform grew out of World Bank (1994), which strongly favoured a move to funded pensions in developing as well as developed economies; for a more recent World Bank view, see Holzmann (2000). For counterviews, see Gillion (2000), and also Hemming (1999), which (emanating from the IMF) argues that the gains from funding are relatively minor. Queisser (2000) and Scherman (2000) probe for the existence of an emerging consensus. On the political economy of pension reform, see Müller (2001) on Central and Eastern Europe, Mesa-Lago and Müller (2002) on Latin America, and Müller (2003) for a comparison.

10 Poverty relief

Poverty is a great enemy to human happiness; it certainly destroys liberty, and it makes some virtues impracticable, and others extremely difficult.

(Samuel Johnson, 1709–94)

Social security has increasingly become a reactive ambulance, picking up the casualties of social, economic and ideological change. It would be perverse to blame motorway accidents on ambulances, even though they appear every time there is one.

(Martin Evans, 1998)

1. Introduction and institutions

This chapter discusses the third main function of cash benefits—poverty relief. The benefits are many and various, those listed in Table 7.3 being only the most important. They differ widely: some are administered centrally, some locally; some are mandatory, others discretionary; some take the form of cash grants for specific purposes (scholarships), others reduce the price of specific goods (rent subsidies, free pharmaceutical drugs). In addition, poverty is often multidimensional (Sen 1999; Burchardt et al. 2002b). This chapter, however, concentrates on income poverty and the effect of cash benefits in relieving it. For present purposes, such benefits can usefully be divided into three sorts:

- benefits awarded on the basis of an income- or wealth test—that is, only where income or wealth falls below a prescribed limit, the main examples discussed here being income support (i.e. 'welfare') and housing benefit;

- benefits based on an income test and additional criteria—for example, the requirement to be in paid employment, the main example being the working tax credit;

- so-called universal benefits, awarded without a contributions test or an income test, on the basis of other criteria, the example discussed in this chapter being child benefit.

These benefits reflect the various the aims set out in Chapter 1, Section 2.2. Their major objective is poverty relief. They also contribute to vertical redistribution. Child benefit also provides consumption smoothing in the face of life-cycle effects. Since transfers are financed out of progressive taxation, they also contribute to vertical redistribution; and benefits awarded without an income test can foster social solidarity.

This chapter starts by briefly describing the most important of these benefits in the UK (see also the Further Reading). Section 2 considers the arguments for state intervention and Section 3 assesses the various benefits, including a brief survey of empirical evidence.

INCOME SUPPORT is the final safety net for people under 60 for whom family income from all other sources falls below a specified minimum, and also acts as a 'passport' to other benefits such as housing benefit. Expenditure is large (just below £10 billion in 2003/4 (Table 7.3)). The numbers involved are also large: in 2003/4 there were 2.1 million recipients. Anyone aged 16 or over who is not working for more than sixteen hours per week may be eligible, whether or not he has a national-insurance record or is receiving national-insurance benefit. Benefit is normally conditional on registering for work, with exceptions such as people with major health problems and single parents of children under 16. People aged 60 and above are eligible for poverty relief through a different benefit, the pension credit, discussed shortly.

Benefits are of two sorts: income support itself, which offers a weekly benefit, and the social fund, from which single payments are made. The determination of income support rests on two considerations:

- requirements—that is, how much benefit is awarded to a family with no other income, determined by reference to family size and such factors as disability;
- resources—that is, how much income the family has. In principle all income is included, in particular child benefit and the major national-insurance benefits. For income-support purposes the relevant magnitude is 'net' earnings after tax and national-insurance contributions, and after allowing for limited work expenses, including fares. Some income is disregarded, normally only a small amount except, for example, where a person is receiving certain types of disability benefit.

A family's benefit is calculated as the difference between its requirements and its resources. If requirements are estimated at £150 and resources at £70 per week, benefit will normally be £80. At the margin an extra pound of earnings therefore costs £1 of benefit, in economic terms a 100 per cent implicit tax rate. Thus the implicit tax on disregarded income is 0 per cent; on most other income, including most national-insurance benefits, it is 100 per cent. Income support can therefore be thought of as 'topping up' family income from whatever source to bring it up to a basic minimum.

PENSION CREDIT is the parallel benefit for people aged 60 and over. It guarantees that a person's income will reach at least a minimum level (just over £100 per week for a single person in 2003/4). The income test excludes a range of other benefits such as Attendance Allowance and Disability Living Allowance (discussed in Chapter 8) and Housing Benefit and related benefits, discussed shortly. Importantly, it also has a significantly higher disregard for personal wealth than income support, the intention being explicitly to avoid penalizing elderly people with small savings. Expenditure is large, reaching £5.1 billion in 2003/4, when about two million households received the benefit.

HOUSING BENEFIT is administered by local authorities and provides means-tested assistance with rent and Council Tax (i.e. local taxation). Total spending in 2003/4 was £12.6 billion (Table 7.3). For individuals in receipt of income support, housing benefit is normally equal to the full amount of rent. Otherwise, benefit depends on the claimant's gross income (including that of his or her spouse), household size, and the amount of rent. As with income support, some income is disregarded. Where family income, after disregards, exceeds a specified limit, benefit is lost at a rate of 65 pence per pound of income above the limit.

WORKING TAX CREDIT, as the name implies, is aimed at the working poor, with the twin objectives of relieving poverty and increasing labour-force participation, broadly analogous to the Earned Income Tax Credit in the USA. The mechanism for doing so is to offer income-tested poverty relief, but to make the benefit conditional on the recipient working at least X hours per week. The benefit is administered by the tax authorities and delivered as a net addition to a person's pay packet (hence the name 'tax credit').

Benefit is available to anybody aged 25 or over who works sixteen hours a week or more. There is a basic element and a range of additional elements for single parents and couples, for people who work for thirty hours a week or more, and for people with a severe disability; there is also an element to contribute towards the costs of child care. A person earning below a threshold level of income (£5,060 per year in 2003/4) receives the full benefit. For earnings above that, benefit is withdrawn at a rate of 37 pence per pound of earnings. Benefit is normally awarded on an annual basis; thus an increase in earnings, unless large, will not lead to a reduction in benefit until a person is reassessed.

CHILD TAX CREDIT. Families with children are eligible also for Child Tax Credit, which parallels working tax credit but—importantly—is not conditional on being in work, thus spanning the in and out of work divide. The benefit, which is paid by the income-tax authorities directly to the person mainly responsible for the children, offers one-source support for families, also providing the family element of income support and the non-contributory unemployment benefit. The child tax credit is paid in addition to child benefit (below): it contains a basic element paid to all eligible families plus a child element for each child in the family. Where a family is entitled to working tax credit, it receives child tax credit in addition. A family with earnings below the threshold in the previous paragraph receives in full all the elements of working tax credit and child tax credit to which it is entitled; above that, 37 pence of benefit is withdrawn for each pound of earnings.

CHILD BENEFIT is a flat-rate, tax-free weekly payment (£16.05 for the first child and £10.75 for each subsequent child in 2003/4) paid—normally to the mother—without an income test.[1] The benefit cost £9 billion in 2003/4 (Table 7.3) and was awarded to over seven million families with over twelve million children.

2. Theoretical arguments for state intervention

2.1. Arguments for intervention

EFFICIENCY AND SOCIAL JUSTICE. The benefits listed above, and others, cover three broad categories of people. First are those whose national insurance (despite compulsory membership) leaves them in poverty. Such people are eligible also for income support, child

---

[1] A child for these purposes is under 16, or under 19 if in full-time education.

tax credit, and child benefit. Secondly, there are those without national-insurance cover because they have exhausted their entitlement or because they never had any (e.g. a school leaver, or a recently divorced woman with no recent contributions). Finally, there are those whose reason for poverty is not covered by national insurance—for example, the parent of a large family in low-paid work, who has to rely on working tax credit, child tax credit, and child benefit.

None of these categories can readily be dealt with by private insurance; and none except the first can be helped by raising national-insurance benefits or by extending their coverage. Much poverty is associated with children and/or high housing costs, neither of which is an insurable risk. Two conclusions emerge: private insurance is not possible in most of these cases; nor is extending national insurance a complete answer.

The state could, of course, do nothing, and let people face the risk of starvation, but, even ignoring equity arguments, this has a range of *efficiency* costs, including social unrest/crime among those facing starvation; the death by starvation of dependants including children (the future labour force); and the fact that malnutrition causes poor health, thereby raising health-care costs and lowering the capacity of adults to work and of children to absorb education. These costs (cf. the nineteenth-century national-efficiency arguments in Chapter 2, Section 2.1) give efficiency grounds for publicly provided income support.

From the viewpoint of social justice, libertarians incline towards private charity where poverty is caused by a non-insurable risk. However, various difficulties (Chapter 4, Section 4.1), including the free-rider problem, suggest that voluntary giving will be inefficiently low even by libertarian standards. Thus writers such as Friedman and Hayek do not oppose subsistence payments out of public funds, though they favour every inducement to encourage people to work. Socialists, in contrast, argue for generous benefits paid on the basis of need, to advance their egalitarian objectives.

Thus there are solid arguments in terms of efficiency and social justice for public provision of subsistence benefits on a non-insurance basis. Whether benefits should be above subsistence and, if so by how much, has no definitive answer (Chapter 6, Section 2).

CRITERIA FOR ASSESSING REDISTRIBUTIVE SCHEMES. How effective are benefits in relieving poverty? This question is tackled for national-insurance benefits, health care, and education in terms of their efficiency and equity. But for poverty relief the argument is illuminated by three somewhat different criteria that cut across the efficiency/equity distinction.

The level of benefits. Does the scheme give recipients a socially acceptable standard of living—that is, does it relieve poverty? This involves, first, *money benefits*: does the scheme pay enough to allow people to buy an adequate consumption bundle? Secondly, the issue of *stigma*: for any given level of money support a person's living standard (in utility terms) is reduced to the extent that he feels stigmatized by receiving benefit.

Targeting. In Weisbrod's terminology (1969), targeting has two aspects.

- Vertical efficiency is concerned with avoiding leakages—that is, benefits should go *only* to those who need them. This reduces the cost of the scheme, but may involve high implicit tax rates and the poverty trap (Section 3.4).

- Horizontal efficiency is concerned with avoiding gaps—that is, benefits should go to *all* the poor. Failure can arise either because *eligibility rules* prevent some needy groups from applying, or because *take-up* is less than 100 per cent.

The cost criterion embraces the benefits themselves and administrative costs.

These three criteria interact in important ways that emerge in subsequent discussion. Cost constrains the freedom to have high benefits. There is an important interaction between cost and the level of benefit: as we shall see, increasing, say, income support by *x* per cent is likely to increase cost by much more than *x* per cent. A further interaction is between cost and targeting: again it transpires that reducing the rate at which benefits are withdrawn as family income rises disproportionately affects costs.

2.2. The simple analytics of targeting

There are three basic approaches to targeting: via an *income test*, where the amount of benefit is directly related to individual or family income; or via *indicators* of poverty, where benefits are based on easily observable characteristics that are highly correlated with poverty—for example, ill health, old age, or the presence of children in the family. A third possibility is *self-targeting*. There are also examples that are a mix of the pure cases.

TARGETING VIA AN INCOME TEST. The idea is simple: poor people are identified by the fact that they have low incomes. The major advantage of this approach is that, at its best, it can target benefits very tightly.

Income testing, however, has important costs. First, it can create major disincentives to work effort and saving. The central economic issue (discussed in detail in Chapter 11, Section 2.2) concerns the shape of the income distribution—that is, how many poor people there are relative to the number of potential taxpayers. If there are many people in poverty and a small tax base, the tax rates necessary to finance poverty relief will be high, creating labour-supply disincentives for taxpayers. There will also be disincentives for recipients: if benefits are to be kept in the hands of the poor (which is necessary to meet fiscal constraints), they must be clawed back rapidly as the income of recipients rises. At its extreme, as discussed in Section 3.1, benefit is withdrawn pound for pound with recipients' marginal earnings. This implicit tax rate creates an obvious labour-supply disincentive.

A second problem is that assessing income can be intrusive and hence stigmatizing, particularly if the income unit is the family or extended family rather than the individual, so that the determination of eligibility requires all family members to reveal their income. Thirdly, measuring income is administratively demanding.

INDICATOR TARGETING uses indicators of poverty that can be measured more easily than income (the classic article is by Akerlof 1978). The idea is best illustrated by example. Assume:

- only redheads are poor;
- all redheads are poor;
- there is no hair-dyeing technology.

In these circumstances it is theoretically possible completely to eliminate poverty, as defined by the poverty line, by paying a redhead benefit; additionally, because benefits go *only* to the poor, expenditure is minimized; and because identification is easy, administrative demands are small.

These results follow, first, because having red hair is a necessary condition for poverty (the first assumption); thus targeting is horizontally efficient; were this not the case, a redhead benefit would leave gaps by failing to cover poor people who did not have red hair. It is also a sufficient condition (the second assumption); targeting is therefore vertically efficient; were this not the case, benefits would 'leak out' to redheads who were not poor. Thus having red hair is perfectly correlated with poverty. Furthermore, having red hair is wholly exogenous to the individual (the third assumption), thus minimizing deleterious incentives. Thus the ideal indicators are:

- highly correlated with poverty, to ensure accurate targeting;
- beyond the control of the individual, to minimize disincentives; and
- easy to observe, to assist administration.

Indicator targeting can have significant advantages over income testing. Disincentives for recipients are weaker (since only the income effect works against labour supply). Where the indicator is easily observable (e.g. the number of children in a family), it is less demanding administratively. Thirdly, as discussed shortly, it is possible, with care, to use an indicator which facilitates self-targeting.

There are disadvantages, however. Gaps in coverage arise because some individuals with incomes below the poverty line may not have the relevant characteristics (i.e. the indicators are not completely horizontally efficient). And there may be leakages because some people may possess the necessary characteristics but not be poor (i.e. the indicators are not completely vertically efficient).

SELF-TARGETING. In some circumstances, it is possible to improve targeting by creating an incentive structure under which the choices of claimants act as a signalling device. Two approaches are usefully distinguished.

Price subsidies. This approach subsidizes a carefully chosen bundle of goods consumed disproportionately by the poor. If, for example, only poor people eat black bread, it is possible to offer it at subsidized prices. Other examples include services that have a higher-quality higher-priced substitute, such as public transport. Though analytically valid, the number of commodities that (*a*) have a negative income elasticity of demand, *and* (*b*) form a significant fraction of the consumption of the poor, is very limited.

Conditional benefits. This approach conditions benefit on specific actions by the recipient. The simplest example is 'workfare', where an unemployed person is awarded benefit only so long as she undertakes some form of work or training. This has the advantage that it benefits *all* who come forward and *only* those who come forward; and the only people who claim are those who genuinely cannot find higher paying work. Workfare has these beneficial incentive effects because it imposes costs on recipients in one of two ways: it makes it difficult or impossible for a person to receive benefit while continuing to work unofficially—that is, it 'taxes away' the person's earnings from other work; and, where people are using benefit, in effect, to subsidize their leisure, it 'taxes away' their leisure. In both cases, workfare reduces the individual's replacement rate—in the first case by the reduction or elimination of unofficial earnings, in the second by the forgone leisure—and thus increases the incentive to find work. In principle, the only people who claim benefit are those for whom unemployment benefit plus workfare is genuinely the least-bad option.

There are two potential disadvantages. First, targeting may be imperfect: there are gaps (for instance, because some genuinely poor people are physically unable to work), and leakages (for instance, because public-works employment may crowd out some other wage work). Secondly, not everyone agrees that this approach contributes to social justice: is workfare an example of less eligibility (Chapter 2, Section 1.1) or of the dignity of labour?

MIXED METHODS OF TARGETING. One example is the working tax credit, which is a mixture of income testing and self-targeting. Similarly, child tax credit is a mixture of indicator targeting (i.e. the presence of one or more children in the family) and income testing. Other examples are discussed in Chapter 11, Section 4.

3. Assessment of poverty relief

3.1. Income-tested benefits

Income support

LEVEL. Does income support—the benefit of last resort—offer benefits high enough to relieve poverty? With an absolute definition of poverty (Chapter 6, Section 2.1) the answer is generally yes: nobody starves; and the level of income support in 2003/4 was over twice the real value of its 1948 predecessor. Concerns remain, however—about hypothermia among the elderly, about rising numbers of people sleeping on the streets, and about rising numbers of people suffering multiple deprivation. The problem was serious enough for the government to introduce a Social Exclusion Unit in the late 1990s, chaired by the Prime Minister, to coordinate policy across departments.

The social fund, which makes single payments to cover specific emergencies, has been criticized (see Howard 2003): it works within a fixed budget; most of the payments are loans; and most awards involve local discretion. Though the last aspect is, up to a point, inevitable in a scheme designed to meet exceptional needs, the former two are not. As a result, it is argued, the social fund fails in a significant number of cases to meet the poverty-relief objective, in that take-up is well below 100 per cent.

A separate but equally important issue is whether benefits are high enough not just to *relieve* immediate poverty but to *prevent* it in the longer term (cf. preventive medicine).[2] Again, there is a question mark. Spending cuts in the mid-1990s affected relief to people caring for Alzheimer sufferers. Such benefits, by keeping families together, have obvious social benefits; they are also much cheaper than paying for residential care. Benefits for lone parents are similarly cost effective if, by keeping families together, they keep young people out of (very costly) jail.

TARGETING is concerned with both horizontal and vertical efficiency.

---

[2] In many ways this is the poverty-relief analogue of dynamic efficiency.

Horizontal efficiency. The eligibility rules for income support are broad, reflecting its status as a benefit of last resort. The USA has no comparable scheme for non-aged adults without children. Income support from that point of view does well.

However, a sizeable proportion of eligible recipients do not receive benefit—that is, take-up is incomplete. On the supply side, some eligible applicants might not be awarded benefit: an official may impose a harsh interpretation on regulations or be unaware of certain entitlements. Such difficulties cannot entirely be avoided, but there is little evidence of systematic discrimination in the enforcement of rules (e.g. by race) in the award of benefit.

Take-up can be incomplete also for demand-side reasons, in that an unknown number of eligible people do not apply for benefit. Three sets of theories seek to explain why: ignorance, inconvenience, and stigma. It is not surprising that many people are ignorant of their entitlement under the benefit system, notwithstanding considerable efforts to make information more available and easier to understand.

Inconvenience is concerned with the cost to the applicant of making a claim, including the time spent filling in forms, and the need to answer potentially embarrassing questions about income and family circumstances. Some writers (Nichols and Zeckhauser 1982; Blackorby and Donaldson 1988) argue that such costs may be deliberate, to avoid the worst problems of adverse selection and moral hazard. The underlying argument is that the imposition of costs on claimants assists the operation of self-targeting.

Stigma in its pure form arises if individuals feel that, if they receive certain benefits, they will be labelled as belonging to a socially rejected group. Hence there is a psychological cost to claiming benefit additional to the convenience costs just discussed.

Vertical efficiency aims to withhold benefit from those who do not need it. Viewed narrowly, income support scores well. Once a family has used up its small disregard (Section 1), it normally loses £1 of benefit for every pound of additional net earnings, which, in effect, imposes a 100 per cent implicit tax rate on earnings. This targets benefits very tightly.

Figure 10.1 shows the combination of leisure and income for someone on income support with an initial endowment at b of 24 hours of leisure. The line ab shows her earning opportunities. Suppose a scheme is now introduced under which income is not allowed to fall below Oc. This is shown by the line cde. Someone choosing 24 hours of leisure receives an income of $Oc = be$. If she works, the first £5 (say) of net earnings is disregarded, and spendable income rises above the income-support level, shown by the line eg. But, once her disregards are exhausted, she loses benefit pound for pound with earnings, and so her spendable income is fixed, shown by the dotted line fg. This is equivalent to an implicit marginal tax of 100 per cent, since all extra earnings are 'taxed away' by the loss of benefit: it is impossible for recipients to raise their net disposable income; it also removes any financial incentive to work. Where people work only to earn money, the budget constraint collapses to the two segments af and ge; nobody will choose a point on the segment fg (since at point g the individual has the same income as at f, but more leisure). If a person receives £120 in income support, which is lost pound for pound with earnings above £5, then fg covers earnings from £5 to at least £125. This strong potential labour supply disincentive is the price of targeting benefit tightly on those in need—in short, vertical efficiency through means testing is inherently in conflict with labour-supply incentives.

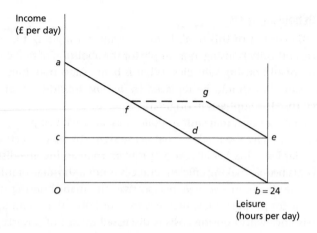

Fig. 10.1. Stylized representation of the budget constraint under income support

COST. Expenditure has risen sharply over the years largely—though by no means wholly —because of rising unemployment and other reasons for non-participation. When national insurance was introduced in 1948 it was thought that eventually everyone would be self-supporting through work or insurance, and that national assistance (as it was then called) would dwindle. But over time the number of recipients grew, as did the complications.

Administrative costs have also risen. In 2003/4 administrative spending by the Department for Work and Pensions was £5.8 billion (UK DWP 2003*a*: table 5), to which must be added the costs of collecting national-insurance contributions and paying out working tax credit and child tax credit, which are administered by the Inland Revenue.

THE SCOPE FOR IMPROVEMENT is reduced by interactions between the three criteria. First, could benefits be increased? Suppose a family of given size receives £100 per week, which is reduced pound for pound with earnings (disregards are ignored for simplicity). Doubling benefit from £100 to £200 would roughly double the cost of benefits to existing recipients (i.e. by assumption those earning less than £100 per week); but, in addition, more people (by assumption those earning between £100 and £200) would become eligible. Another possible improvement would be to reduce the rate at which benefits are withdrawn as earnings rise. This would increase the transfer receipts of families with other income; and it might reduce stigma, in as much as means testing (the main cause of stigma) could be reduced. Unfortunately, the room for manœuvre in this direction is also limited. In the example just discussed, with a 100 per cent implicit tax rate only those earning below £100 are eligible; with a 50 per cent rate anyone earning below £200 is eligible. Halving the tax rate, like doubling the benefit level, raises costs both by increasing benefits to existing recipients *and* by increasing the number of potential beneficiaries. The increase in costs associated with either change is accentuated by the shape of the income distribution, which in almost all countries is skewed towards lower incomes. The number of people with incomes between 1 and 1.5 times the income-support level is large, correspondingly reducing the scope for increasing benefits.

Assistance with housing costs

In the first (1987) edition of this book I wrote: 'I am not arguing for the abolition of subsidies to local authority housing, nor simply for the abolition of rent control, nor even for the abolition of all housing subsidies. What is being suggested, quite simply, is that over time *price* subsidies should be replaced by *income* subsidies in all sectors of the housing market' (p. 410, emphasis in original).

Over the intervening years, that shift in policy has largely taken place, so that housing is now largely allocated by the market. That is the right strategic direction, since inadequate housing is far less a market-allocation problem than an income-distribution problem; what prevents people making efficient choices is not a shortage of information but a shortage of income. From an *economic* perspective, the main housing problem is how to make it possible for people on low incomes to afford decent accommodation and, for that reason, assistance with housing costs is discussed as part of poverty relief. Other—substantial—problems with housing raise issues about which economics does not have a lot to say.

A range of income-tested benefits helps with rental costs and council tax (i.e. local property taxation). Recipients of income support and income-based jobseeker's allowance are automatically entitled to the full rate of housing benefit and council tax benefit. As family earnings rise, income support is lost pound for pound with earnings, as discussed above. When entitlement to income support is exhausted, most families still have some entitlement to housing benefit, at which stage they face a 67 per cent withdrawal rate. Housing benefit and council tax benefit thus raise very similar issues to income support: benefit is tightly targeted to contain costs, but at the expense of serious labour-supply disincentives.

3.2. Working tax credits

One of the main causes of low income is the lack of a job. Chapter 8 discussed one approach, unemployment insurance, which addresses the risk by subsidizing unemployment. An alternative approach, subsidizing employment, has been tried in several countries since the mid-1990s (see the Further Reading). Some of the motivation for the policy direction has been important changes in the market for low-skilled workers, in particular a reduction in (*a*) the relative earnings of people with low skills, and (*b*) their labour-force participation rates.

Schemes such as the Working Tax Credit in the UK, the Earned Income Tax Credit in the USA, and similar schemes in other countries have twin objectives: to increase the income of poor people, both now and in the future; and to increase labour-force participation. The mechanism for doing so is to offer income-tested poverty relief, but conditional on the recipient working at least X hours per week. The benefit (henceforth, generically, working tax credits) is thus targeted using all three of the targeting methods discussed in Section 2.2. The amount of benefit a person receives depends on an income test, on indicator targeting (e.g. the requirement in some schemes that there are children in the family), and on self-targeting (i.e. the work-contingent eligibility rule). The logic is that, by tieing benefit to work, people have an incentive to find (or to keep) work so as to qualify (see Besley and Coate 1992; Blundell 2000).

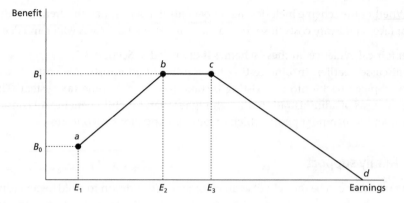

Fig. 10.2. Stylized operation of a working-tax-credit scheme

In Figure 10.2 a person must work for at least (say) 10 hours per week before he is entitled to an initial level of benefit, B_0. Thereafter, for every pound he earns, he receives an additional x pence; thus take-home pay rises faster than wages, shown by the line segment $a–b$. At some point, he reaches the maximum benefit offered by the scheme, B_1. In many schemes he is allowed to keep that maximum over a range of earnings, usually fairly short, $E_3–E_2$. As earnings continue to rise, however, it becomes necessary to claw back the credit, shown by the line segment $c–d$, to ensure that benefit does not leak out to non-poor people.

A number of variables are central to the design of such schemes.

- The size of the maximum benefit, B_1. With a larger benefit, poverty relief is stronger, and so is the incentive to join the workforce; however, the fiscal costs will be higher—not only the cost of benefit for people with earnings below E_2, but also because the taper beyond point c takes place at higher levels of earnings; hence more people qualify for at least some benefit.

- The minimum number of hours worked to qualify (implied by a). Again, there is a balance: if a is small, the incentive to participate is stronger, but hours worked might well be lower.

- The rate at which benefit is clawed back (shown by the slope of $c–d$). The rate of clawback raises the standard targeting dilemma of costs versus disincentives: a steeper slope (i.e. a faster rate of clawback) makes a corner solution at c more likely (i.e. reduces labour supply) but reduces fiscal costs.

- The speed with which benefits respond to changes in income. In the working tax credit, importantly, benefit is awarded on an annual basis. As discussed in Section 3.4, such fixed-period awards can soften the trade-off between costs and incentive effects.

- Whether entitlement is assessed on the basis of individual earnings or family earnings. As discussed in Section 3.5, if the relevant basis is family earnings, the benefit is better targeted but at the expense of a stronger effect on the incentives facing *all* family members, since over the range $c–d$ they all face both an income and a substitution effect against increasing hours worked.

- Whether the scheme includes higher benefits if a person has children, or is disabled, or faces child-care costs. If so, the capacity to relieve poverty is wider and deeper.

The empirical evidence on these schemes is discussed in Section 3.5.

As discussed earlier, income testing has significant administrative costs. Tax credits, however, piggy back onto an existing income test—the income tax system. Thus the marginal costs of administration, though higher than for child benefit, are considerably lower than for income support, which requires a stand-alone income test.[3]

3.3. Family support

CHILD TAX CREDIT can be thought of as an income-tested addition to child benefit (discussed below); saying the same thing in a different way, all families get some support to reflect the costs of bringing up children, but poor families receive additional, income-tested support.

The analysis of tax credits for families with children directly parallels previous discussion. Higher benefits improve poverty relief and incentives to participate, but tend to reduce work effort by those already in the labour force (discussed in Section 3.5); and higher benefits increase costs both through higher payments to low earners along a–b in Figure 10.2, and by increasing the total number of beneficiaries, by enlarging the range of earnings over which the segment c–d operates.

Tax credits to cover the costs of child care have a particular importance. Because they offset (wholly or in part) one of the major costs of moving into work, they unambiguously improve both poverty relief and participation.

CHILD BENEFIT. It has been argued that child benefit, because it is not income tested, is poorly targeted. This argument ignores the idea of indicator targeting.

Having children is highly correlated with poverty and is thus a good indicator. This is no accident. Parents are typically in the younger segments of the population, and thus at a relatively low part of their lifetime earnings trajectory; and the arrival of children frequently reduces second-earner income. For both reasons, family income tends to be low precisely at the time when the demands on that income are high. For life-cycle reasons, families with children *systematically* have low income relative to needs, an argument borne out by the empirical evidence in Section 3.5. It is, of course, possible to point to specific high-income families with children; that merely makes the point that child benefit is not *perfectly* targeted. Pointing to exceptions is analogous to arguing that heavy smokers who live into their nineties disprove the ill-health effects of smoking.

This line of argument shows that child benefit, in addition to offering poverty relief, also allows life-cycle redistribution. A similar result could in theory be attained by borrowing, but capital-market imperfections largely rule out that option in policy terms.

Child benefit (like the child tax credit) also assists targeting within the family. If paid to the mother, the benefit helps to empower women. Secondly, the empirical evidence on intra-family distribution (Pahl 1989; Kempson et al. 1994; Goode et al. 1998) suggests that paying family support to the mother improves the targeting of benefits on children.

---

[3] Even so, administration is not entirely straightforward, for example because the credits are based on household income while income tax is based on individual income.

In addition, since targeting involves no income test, the labour-supply disincentive of the benefit is reduced.[4] The incentive, particularly for secondary earners, to work at least part-time is considerably enhanced, since (in contrast with child tax credit awarded on the basis of a family income test) extra earnings by the secondary worker do not increase the tax liability of other family members.

The administration of an income test is costly, not least because information needs to be updated regularly. Child benefit is administratively cheap because it generally has a single, once-and-for-all information requirement—a birth certificate. Thereafter benefit can be paid automatically for sixteen years.

3.4. The poverty and unemployment traps

As discussed above, income support has a 100 per cent rate of benefit withdrawal. As a result, an increase in earnings, being wholly offset by a decline in benefits, has no effect on a family's living standards and, as a result, constitutes a major labour-supply disincentive. The same problem arises for people who do not receive income support, but a variety of other benefits. Thus someone earning an extra pound could face income tax, national-insurance contributions, a loss of working tax credit/child tax credit and a loss of housing benefit, the cumulative total facing the person with a very high implicit tax rate.

In the discussion of the measurement of poverty (Chapter 6, Section 2.3), the three important questions concerned how many people were poor (the 'headcount'), by how much they fell below the poverty line (the 'poverty gap'), and for how long they remained there. In the case of the poverty trap, analogously, we need to ask how high are implicit tax rates; how many people do they affect; and for how long do they apply or not apply?

THE INTENSITY OF THE POVERTY TRAP. Many individuals/families continue to face high marginal rates. The resulting ill effects are twofold. First, low-income families cannot raise their net income. The effect is striking. Official figures in the mid-1990s (UK DSS 1995: table 1.8) showed that, if the pre-tax wages of a family rose from £50 to £200 per week, weekly spendable income increased by less than £10. The second ill effect is that high tax rates bring about a strong substitution effect against work effort, and so are potentially a major labour-supply disincentive.

A complete analysis, however, must take account of the complexity of the benefit formulas. The more benefits are introduced, the greater the variation in implicit tax rates and the greater the complexities when different benefits interact. The structure of implicit tax rates facing any particular family will depend both on its size and composition, and on the precise mix of benefits it receives.

HOW MANY PEOPLE FACE THE POVERTY TRAP? It is not enough to analyse the case of a 'typical' family. To assess the impact of the poverty trap we also need to know how many families face such rates—that is, how many families of different sizes and types there are at each income level; which benefits they actually receive (the take-up question); and which margin we are discussing, that for the primary or a secondary earner.

---

[4] There is a disincentive arising via the income effect but, unlike income-testing, none via the substitution effect.

MITIGATING FACTORS: THE IMPORTANCE OF FIXED-PERIOD AWARDS. As well as asking how high are implicit tax rates and how many people face them, we need also to ask for how long people face or do not face these rates. Here, fortunately, there are mitigating factors, the most important of which are the existence of fixed period awards.

As mentioned earlier, working tax credit and child tax credit are awarded for a year, during which the authorities need not normally be informed of any increases in family income. Awarding benefit for a year has the obvious administrative convenience of not having to reassess a family each time its income changes, but also has a substantial and beneficial behavioural effect. Any increase in earnings that occurs during an award period does not result in any immediate loss of benefit, and so the marginal tax rate is zero, at least in the short run. And, even if an increase in earnings is permanent, so that benefits at some future date are assessed on the basis of a higher income, any loss of benefit that occurs not at the time of the increase in earnings, but only later, is likely at least partly to be discounted, and hence to be less of a disincentive.

Conventional presentation of the poverty trap shows that a family earning an extra pound could lose up to (say) 80 pence in benefit. Where benefits are awarded for a fixed period, this figure must be reinterpreted. It is certainly the case that family A receives 80 pence less than family B if its earnings are £1 higher. Thus the high implicit tax rates apply cross-sectionally. But our interest is the effect on family A's benefits of an increase in its earnings. This is a time-series question, and has a different answer.

Fixed-period awards thus have important policy implications. They enable the poor to raise their net income more easily, since benefit need not be lost at the time earnings rise. To that extent, the tendency for families to be trapped in poverty is less acute than the traditional view suggests. Secondly, labour-supply incentives may be improved. Temporary changes in earnings (e.g. overtime at Christmas) will not affect benefits; and even where increases are expected to persist, the tax rate relevant to labour-supply decisions is that *perceived* by recipients, which will depend on their rate of time preference. This is almost certainly high, both because their income is low and because any increase in earnings may only be temporary. A poor worker is unlikely to reject an opportunity to increase his earnings because it might cost him benefit six months later.

In addition to their beneficial impact on (*a*) family poverty and (*b*) labour supply, fixed-period awards have two further advantages. If taxes are fully discounted, the withdrawal of benefit as income rises is analytically equivalent to a lump-sum tax collected at some time in the future, with all the welfare properties of lump-sum taxation. Furthermore, fixed-period awards ameliorate the dilemma faced by public policy between the desire to preserve incentives by keeping tax rates low, and the need to reduce costs by targeting benefits tightly on those in need (hence withdrawing benefits rapidly as income rises). Fixed-period awards cushion the impact of high rates of withdrawal, while avoiding the high expenditure that would be involved in substantially reducing them.

3.5. Empirical issues and evidence

Two issues predominate: the effectiveness of poverty relief and the resulting incentive effects.

How effective is poverty relief?

Poverty relief is assessed in terms of the level of benefits, their horizontal efficiency (i.e. are there significant gaps), and their vertical efficiency (how large are leakages to the non-poor).

THE LEVEL OF BENEFITS. The key question—are benefits high enough to relieve poverty—has no definitive answer, not least because there is no definitive poverty line (see Chapter 6, Section 2). Thus different people give different answers.

British governments from the mid-1980s gave poverty alleviation a low weight, so that Martin Evans (1998: 299) took the view that 'it is possible to argue that "poverty" as a state concept of commitment disappeared'. In sharp contrast, the UK government in 1997 for the first time explicitly acknowledged the existence of poverty and introduced official targets for the eradication (note—eradication, not alleviation) of child poverty within twenty years.

However poverty is defined, it rose significantly in Britain (as in many other countries) over the 1980s and 1990s. In 2001/2, official figures showed that 13.3 million people, just over 23 per cent of the population, lived in households with below half the average income after housing costs (UK DWP 2003b: table 3.4). In 1979 only 9 per cent of the population were poor. Child poverty was high, around 20 per cent of children living in households receiving income support (the comparable figure in 1979 was just over 7 per cent). Not everyone who is poor, however, remains poor: in any four-year period between 1991 and 2000, about one-third of individuals experienced some poverty, but only about 1 in 10 was below 60 per cent of median household income for three or more years, and only 1 in 20 for all four years (UK DWP 2003b: 7; for more detailed studies of poverty dynamics, see the Further Reading). Official figures (UK Treasury 2002c: table 3.2) projected that tax and benefit reforms lifted 2.2 million children out of poverty (relative to a poverty line of 50 per cent of median income) between 1997/8 and 2003/4.

The average poverty rate across the EU was 15 per cent in 1999, but with considerable variation across countries, ranging from 9 per cent in Sweden to 21 per cent in Greece and Portugal.[5] In the absence of social transfers, the overall poverty rate would have been 40 per cent. Across the EU as a whole, the risk of persistent poverty (i.e. poor in 1999 and in at least two of the previous three years) was 9 per cent.

Poverty relief in the USA differs in two strategic ways: the level of benefit can be inadequate because there is no automatic relation between the official US poverty line (which is federal) and benefit levels (which are set by states); and coverage is incomplete because there is no equivalent to income support, for which *anyone* is in principle eligible. The main post-war social-assistance benefit, Aid to Families with Dependent Children (AFDC), became more generous over the 1960s, but after the first oil shock was increasingly restricted. AFDC was replaced in 1996 by a new benefit, Temporary Assistance for Needy Families. Under the new benefit, states have more discretion over benefit design;

---

[5] Dennis and Guio (2003: statistical appendix). The figures refer to the percentage of the population living in households with equivalized disposable income below 60 per cent of the median equivalized income of the country they live in. The 15 per cent figure for the EU as a whole is a population-weighted average of the national figures.

the federal contribution is a block grant rather than a matching grant; and the federal contribution is fixed in nominal terms so its real value will decline over time (for fuller discussion, see Blank 2002 and the Further Reading). Such policy directions will do nothing to reverse the rising US poverty headcounts discussed in Chapter 6, Section 2.3.

TARGETING 1: HORIZONTAL EFFICIENCY. Do benefits go to those who need them (i.e. are they horizontally efficient)? This boils down mainly to take-up, of which there are two main measures: the *caseload* take-up rate refers to the proportion of eligible *claimants* who receive benefit; the *expenditure* measure relates to the fraction of total expenditure (assuming hypothetical full take-up) that is actually claimed. Take-up is far from easy to measure (see Atkinson 1989: ch. 11). It has risen over the years, in part as a result of deliberate action. In 1994/5 around £9 out of every £10 of available benefit was being claimed, and about four out of every five eligible people were claiming. Take-up was lower for the other main means-tested benefits.

A separate aspect of horizontal efficiency is the gender implications of targeting. The feminization of poverty was noted in Chapter 6, Section 2.3; see also Bennett (2002).

If we draw the threads together, cash benefits may fail to relieve poverty for three sets of reasons: (*a*) the absolute level of benefits may be too low; (*b*) coverage may be inadequate for certain groups, in the sense that they are poor but not eligible for benefit; and (*c*) take-up may be incomplete either (on the demand side) because of ignorance about entitlement, or stigma, or (on the supply side) out of maladministration and/or discrimination.

TARGETING 2: VERTICAL EFFICIENCY. The extent to which benefits are restricted to the poor has two aspects: to what extent does income testing restrict benefits to the poor; and how well targeted are categorical benefits awarded on the basis of non-income criteria?

Income-testing. For three main reasons—rising unemployment, joblessness connected with lone parenthood and disability, and changes in social-security policy—there was a dramatic rise in the number of people dependent on means-tested benefits, from 8 per cent of the population in the mid-1970s to almost 21 per cent twenty years later (Martin Evans 1998: table 7.22). As mentioned earlier, in 2001/2 around 20 per cent of children lived in households on income support.

There are two key questions about income testing: the issue of implicit tax rates, and the extent to which benefits go to lower income groups. On the former, there has been significant progress. Before 1998, 740,000 people faced marginal deduction rates of over 70 per cent; after the introduction of the working tax credit and child tax credit in 2003, the figure was 260,000. There was a price, however—the number facing marginal deduction rates of over 60 per cent increased from 760,000 in 1998 to nearly 1.5 million in 2003, largely because working tax credit extended benefits to low-income workers who had previously not been eligible for benefit.[6]

To what extent do benefits go to poorer families? In 2001/2, households (adjusted for household size) in the bottom income quintile received £5,530 in cash benefits, just over half of their total income from all sources; in the second quintile, the comparable figure

---

[6] These figures ignore the fact that working tax credit and child tax credit are normally awarded for a year, and are unaffected by changes in earnings of less than £2,500 per year. The effect of this fixed-period award, as discussed in Section 3.4, is to ameliorate the effect of marginal deduction rates.

was £5,650, about 40 per cent of income. Benefits fell sharply for better-off households: the top income quintile received cash benefits of £1,150, or 2.6 per cent of total household income after all taxes and transfers (Lakin 2003: table 4).

The interpretation of these figures highlights the dilemma discussed earlier—tightly targeted benefits score well in terms of containing costs, but only by trapping people in poverty and giving them little incentive to increasing their earnings.

Indicator targeting. A second aspect of vertical efficiency is the extent to which benefits can be targeted through non-income criteria. The *a priori* arguments why child benefit is likely to be well targeted, set out in Section 3.3, are borne out in practice: 'Children are disproportionately present in low-income households, 21 per cent of children . . . were living in households with below 60 per cent of median income (before deduction of living costs) in Great Britain in 2000/01' (UK Office for National Statistics 2003).

Finally, in assessing the effectiveness of income transfers in relieving poverty, we should remind ourselves of major and unavoidable methodological questions. First, there are the many problems in defining the poverty line, the unit of receipt, and the distribution of income within that unit (Chapter 6, Section 2.1). Secondly, there is the value placed by recipients on the transfers: the value of cash benefits may be reduced by stigma, and that placed on in-kind transfers may be less than their market price (though see Chapter 4, Section 4.2). Thirdly, and possibly of greatest intractability, there is the incidence of the transfers (Chapter 7, Section 4.1). Calculations assume (because no other procedure is practicable) that a family's pre-transfer income is that which it would have been in the absence of any system of income support. This is, to say the least, a strong assumption. Similarly, it is assumed that benefits paid to those in work, including family credit and child benefit, have no effect on wage rates.

Incentive effects

When we turn to the incentive effects of cash transfers, the waters are, if anything, even murkier. The incentive effects of unemployment benefit (Chapter 8, Section 3.1) and pensions (Chapter 9, Section 5.1) are closely linked with the present discussion, which is consequently brief.

In assessing the incentive effects of benefits, two issues are relevant: does the benefit increase the number of hours worked by people who are in the labour force; and does the benefit encourage non-participants to join the labour force.

The disincentive effects—on both participation and hours worked—of high marginal deduction rates were discussed earlier (see the Further Reading). More interesting are the incentive effects of working tax credits in the UK, the earned income tax credit in the USA, and similar schemes in other countries, which are designed deliberately to avoid the worst incentive problems by subsidizing employment rather than unemployment.

There is a large and growing literature on the topic (for surveys, see Blundell 2000, Ellwood 2000, Walker and Wiseman 2003, and the Further Reading). Evidence from schemes in the USA and UK conforms with what theory predicts.

- The schemes are associated with an increase in participation of single people. This is partly because of the direct incentive effects of the wage subsidy, and also because some schemes contribute to child-care costs and thus address the fixed costs of work.

- The effect on the hours worked of a single person, given that he or she has entered work, is less clear-cut. Someone along the segment $a–b$ in Figure 10.2 faces incentives to work longer hours, but someone working along the segment $c–d$ may be induced to work fewer hours; and there is evidence from some schemes of a move towards part-time work.

- Schemes that determine eligibility in terms of family income create incentives for reduced work effort by the secondary earner. If the effect of a wife working extra hours is to move her husband from the segment $a–b$ to the segment $c–d$ in Figure 10.2, she is less likely to work the extra hours.

- At least some of the schemes show a 'spike' in hours of work around the minimum necessary to qualify.

- The more generous the segment $a–b$, the stronger the inducement to participate but, equally, the more stringent the necessary clawback in $c–d$, creating incentives to restrict hours of work to the line segment $b–c$. Thus benefit design faces a trade-off between encouraging individuals to enter the labour force, and creating incentives for those already in the labour force to move from full-time to part-time work.

Blundell's conclusion (2000: 42) from reforms in a number of countries is that,

careful design . . . can significantly increase family incomes while providing reasonable incentives for parents to work. It also appears that any offsetting negative effect on hours worked by those already in employment is not strong enough to counter this overall positive increase in labour supplied. However, since these programmes are generally based on family income, there is evidence of a negative offsetting effect on the labour supply of married women in households with young children.

Other approaches to poverty relief also seek to target benefits in ways that rely less on income testing. Regulation involves policing individual behaviour—for example, by enforcing job search or by pursuing child support from absent fathers more vigorously. As examples of the latter, in Australia, child support is enforced through the income tax system; the UK Child Support Agency has a similar function. Alternatively, indicator targeting seeks to minimize distortions by paying more generous benefits to groups (e.g. pensioners) with less elastic labour supplies, a case in point being the more generous wealth test in the UK pension credit (Section 1).

3.6. Conclusion

The UK's income distribution, like that in almost all industrialized countries, is heavily skewed towards lower incomes. We want to support the poor (the level criterion), but the income distribution makes it inevitable that benefits must be withdrawn fairly rapidly if limited resources (the cost criterion) are to be targeted on the most needy. This focus can be achieved in various ways: benefit can be withdrawn as family income rises, either immediately (income support) or eventually (working tax credit); or it can be removed when an individual's status changes (e.g. the loss of unemployment benefit upon resumption of work, or loss of child benefit when a child reaches the age of 16). Whatever the method, a poverty trap in one form or another is largely inevitable, an observation that brings us naturally to Chapter 11.

■ QUESTIONS FOR FURTHER DISCUSSION

1. 'Targeting is a matter of some subtlety and has a number of different dimensions' (Atkinson 1995*b*). Which are the major forms of targeting? What are the advantages and disadvantages of each?

2. 'Unless a benefit is awarded on the basis of an income test it will be poorly targeted.' Discuss.

■ FURTHER READING

For compendious description of institutions (including legal sources), see Child Poverty Action Group (2003) (the 2003 version of an annual publication) or the Department of Work and Pensions web site (http://www.dwp.gov.uk). On social protection in the EU, see the various country reports and overview documents on http://europa.eu.int/comm/employment_social/ soc-prot/index_en.htm. For institutions worldwide, see US Social Security Administration (2002, 2003), downloadable from http://www.ssa.gov/policy/pubs/index.html. On family support in a range of countries, see Bradshaw and Finch (2002), and, for the evolution of such policies in the UK since 1975, Adam et al. (2002). See also the various government portals in the list of useful web sites at the start of the book.

The analytics of targeting are discussed by Weisbrod (1969), Akerlof (1978), Besley and Kanbur (1993), Atkinson (1995*a*: ch. 12; 1995*b*), and Sen (1995*b*). For empirical discussion, see Grosh (1994) and Ravallion and Datt (1995).

For assessment of poverty relief in the UK, see Evans (1998) for assessment of the late 1980s and 1990s and, for the period since then, Sutherland et al. (2003), and on child poverty, Sutherland and Piachaud (2001) and Brewer et al. (2003). On poverty dynamics, see Gardiner and Hills (1999), Hobcraft (2002), and Burgess and Propper (2002) (which also includes some discussion of developments in the OECD).

On poverty in Europe, see Atkinson (1998), Gordon and Townsend (2000), Dennis and Guio (2003), and, on child poverty and child benefits, Immervoll et al. (2000).

The methodology of poverty measurement in the USA is discussed by Glennerster (2002*a*). For general discussion of poverty relief, see Jorgenson (1998), Levy (1998), Triest (1998), and Blank (2000), and on child poverty in Britain and the USA, Dickens and Ellwood (2003). For assessment of welfare reform in the USA, see Blank (2002, 2003) (the latter also discusses lessons for Europe), Blank and Ellwood (2002) and Grogger (2002).

Poverty in OECD countries is discussed by Jäntti and Danziger (2000), Vleminckx and Smeeding (2000), and Burtless and Smeeding (2001).

The analytics of activation policies such as working tax credits are set out by Besley and Coate (1992) and Blundell (2000). For the institutions of working tax credit in the UK, see UK Treasury (2002*c*) and, for assessment, Brewer (2003) and Walker and Wiseman (2003). On policies in the EU, see Lødemel and Trickey (2001) and Dauderstädt and Witte (2002). Analogous policies in the USA are discussed by Ellwood (2000) and Haveman and Wolfe (2000); see also Solow (1998). On Australia and New Zealand, see Mitchell (2002). For comparison between the UK and USA, see Brewer (2001), and, for an international survey, Martin Evans (2001).

11 Strategies for reform

If a free society cannot help the many who are poor, it cannot save the few who are rich.

(John F. Kennedy, 1961)

1. Approaches to income support

The last three chapters discussed the cash side of the welfare state in some detail. This chapter considers more generally the pros and cons of different forms of income support. It is a discussion not of specific proposals, but of different strategies. The starting point is how most usefully to identify the poor. Chapter 10, Section 2.2, distinguished two approaches.

- Benefits can be conditioned on *income* (i.e. means-tested), the archetypal example being the sort of negative income tax discussed in Section 2 below.

- Alternatively, benefits can be conditioned on the *characteristics* of recipients, using indicators such as being unemployed, sick, or retired. This strategy—sometimes called the 'Back-to-Beveridge' approach—is discussed in Section 3.

Section 4 considers mixed strategies. Section 5 summarizes the major conclusions to emerge from Chapters 8 to 11.

The distinction between categorical and non-categorical schemes is important. The former stress the *causes* of poverty, and institute programmes for specific groups. Historically, it was thought that most people would be self-supporting through work, through insurance against income loss due to unemployment or sickness, or through saving and other forms of consumption smoothing; and that the few who fell outside these groups could be categorized into the disabled, the blind, etc. Underlying this approach is the distinction between the 'deserving' poor (e.g. widows with young children) and the 'undeserving'. Such thinking lay behind the Poor Law, and permeated much of the 1930s New Deal legislation in the USA. The Beveridge Report (1942: 124–5), though liberal in its attitude, distinguished eight 'reasonable' causes of poverty.

Non-categorical schemes, in contrast, regard recipients as a spectrum that includes the self-supporting, the very poor, and large numbers in between. Such schemes concentrate on *outcome* rather than cause, and classification is made only in terms of need. The approach is attractive because there are few gaps through which 'difficult' cases can fall, but has the disadvantage of requiring a means test in one form or another.

The bottom line is that the ultimate constraint on poverty relief is the shape of the income distribution, which in virtually all countries is skewed towards people with low incomes. As a result, there are no easy solutions to poverty. This is not an argument against increased redistribution, but a warning that it will not be brought about without an awareness of the difficulties involved.

2. Income-testing: The negative income-tax approach

Negative income taxation is the archetype of cash support conditioned on an income test. This section sets out the analytics of such schemes. Section 2.2 discusses large-scale negative income taxation, and Section 2.3 how a small-scale scheme could be part of a package of wider reform.

2.1. The idea

The basic idea is outlined in terms of a simple income-tax system shown in Figure 11.1a by the line OBA: a person's income is tax free up to £B; thereafter it is taxed at t per cent. Suppose that $B = £4,000$ and $t = 25$ per cent. The simplest negative income tax is shown by the line G_0BA: if an individual's income is above £4,000, he pays tax of 25 per cent of the excess over £4,000; if it is below £4,000, he *receives* 25 per cent of the shortfall below £4,000. Someone with an income of £4,500 pays 25 per cent of £500—i.e. £125; someone with an income of £3,500 receives £125. More generally, it is possible to have a different tax rate above and below the break-even income (shown by the line G_1BA), and a higher break-even point for larger families.

Formally, the simplest negative income tax relates the individual's tax bill, T (positive or negative), to his income, Y, as

$$T = t(Y - B), \qquad (11.1)$$

where t is the tax rate applied above and below the break-even income, B, as shown by the line G_0BA. It is often more useful to think of the system in a different way: an individual with zero income receives 25 per cent of the amount by which his income falls below £4,000, i.e. £1,000; from equation (11.1) it is entirely equivalent to give *everyone* a transfer of £1,000, and to tax *all* other income at 25 per cent. Thus

$$T = tY - G \qquad (11.2)$$

where $G = tB$ is a lump-sum transfer to the individual, who then pays tax at a rate, t, on all his other income, Y. Similarly, an individual could be given a larger transfer, say G_1 in Figure 11.1a, and taxed at 50 per cent on the first £B of his income and 25 per cent thereafter. A scheme that gives everyone a lump sum and taxes all other income goes under the generic name of a *guaranteed-income scheme*. Equations (11.1) and (11.2) show that guaranteed-income schemes and negative income taxes are analytically equivalent. Such arrangements have been given various names: minimum-income guarantee, reverse income tax, basic-income guarantee, and social-dividend schemes. Though their

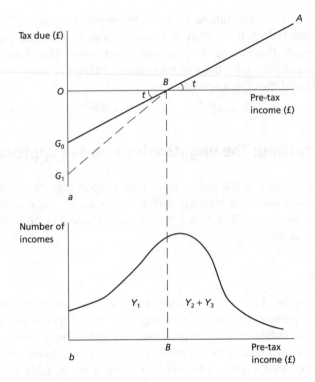

Fig. 11.1. The cost of negative income tax

administration is different, all are completely identified by two features: the size of the transfer, G, to an individual with no income, and the tax structure applied to any other income.

2.2. An assessment of large-scale negative income-tax schemes

Negative income-tax schemes have attracted widespread support (see the Further Reading): from libertarians because cash transfers are compatible with market allocation, and so can loosen what they see as the stranglehold of in-kind transfers under the welfare state, and from socialists because the scheme guarantees everyone at least a minimum income as a right of citizenship and without a means test. Additionally, it is claimed that negative income tax will boost take-up, reduce stigma, and, by bringing all individuals under a single umbrella, enable government to be better informed about the economic condition of the population. Possibly the most important claims are that negative income tax can solve the poverty trap and increase the redistributive power of the welfare state.

Why then, despite widespread support, has no country adopted a large-scale scheme? The short answer, given the shape of the income distribution, is its cost. This implies a large increase in tax rates, which aggravates the poverty trap and/or creates labour-supply disincentives.

Issues of cost

A useful starting point is the distinction between a small-scale scheme, which offers a low guaranteed income like G_0 in Figure 11.1a, and a large-scale scheme giving a higher transfer like G_1. Under the first, the cost is not large, and no high tax rates are necessary; but the guaranteed income is low, so no substantial help is given to the poor, and the need for additional benefits remains. If negative income tax is the sole anti-poverty device, it is necessary to have a high guaranteed income like G_1. This raises problems of cost, as illustrated in Figure 11.1. The intercept, G_0, and slope, t, of negative income tax completely characterize the position of an individual or family. But the aggregate cost of the scheme and its redistributive strength depend *both* on the tax/benefit function *and* on the size distribution of income. The society shown in Figure 11.1b contains many poor people with income less than B, and relatively few rich people; consequently, the cost of the scheme shown in Figure 11.1a will be higher, because of the larger number of net beneficiaries relative to net contributors, than in a richer country (i.e. one in which the left-hand tail, Y_1, is smaller).

THE LOGIC OF THE COST ISSUE is straightforward. Atkinson (1983: 275) illustrates the point: if the guaranteed income for an average family is x per cent of average income, and if income tax currently raises y per cent of average income for purposes other than income support, then the average income tax rate must be $x + y$. With plausible values for x and y (Atkinson suggests 35 per cent and 15 per cent), the *average* rate of *income* tax (i.e. ignoring all indirect taxes, etc.) is at least 50 per cent.

Why are large-scale schemes so costly? The intuitive answer is that 'ordinary' income tax needs to finance benefits *only* (or largely) for poor people, whereas negative income tax pays benefit to *everyone*. The resulting increase in taxation can be viewed in two ways: either because higher gross benefit payments require higher taxation; or because higher taxes are necessary to claw back benefits paid to rich people.

It is necessary, however, to dig deeper. Consider the society shown in Table 11.1 with five poor individuals (assumed to have no income) and ten rich people (whose income is £10,000 per year) as shown in rows 1 and 2. The tax base (i.e. pre-transfer personal income) is £100,000 (line 3), and the tax threshold £4,000 under income tax and £0 under negative income tax (row 4). The poverty line, by assumption, is £4,000 per year (row 5). Under 'ordinary' income tax (columns 1 and 2), £4,000 is transferred to each of the five poor individuals in the form of 'welfare' benefits; rich individuals receive no transfer (row 6a). The total cost of the scheme is £20,000 (row 7), requiring a tax rate on income above the threshold of $33\frac{1}{3}$ per cent (rows 8 and 9); post-transfer incomes of poor and rich are £4,000 and £8,000, respectively (row 10). Under an otherwise identical negative income tax (columns 3 and 4), both poor *and* rich receive a transfer of £4,000 (row 6b). The cost of the scheme is £60,000, requiring a tax rate on all income of 60 per cent (rows 7–9). Post-transfer incomes of rich and poor are identical to the income tax case: poor individuals have £4,000; rich individuals each receive £4,000 but have to pay £6,000 in tax, leaving a net income of £8,000. The introduction of a negative income tax with a uniform tax rate has had no effect on post-transfer incomes but, by tripling the cost of income support, has tripled the average tax rate (row 11) to ensure that rich individuals still pay £2,000 net tax despite receiving an initial transfer of £4,000.

Table 11.1. Hypothetical effect of negative income tax on tax rates

Basic economic data	'Ordinary' income tax and benefits		Negative income tax	
	Poor individual (1)	Rich individual (2)	Poor individual (3)	Rich individual (4)
Assumptions				
1. Number of individuals	5	10	5	10
2. Pre-transfer income of each individual (per year)	£0	£10,000	£0	£10,000
3. Tax base (= total pre-transfer personal income)	10 × £10,000 = £100,000	10 × £10,000 = £100,000	10 × £10,000 = £100,000	10 × £10,000 = £100,000
4. Tax threshold	£4,000	£4,000	£0	£0
5. Poverty line (per year)	£4,000	£4,000	£4,000	£4,000
6a. Cash transfer to each *poor* individual under income tax	£4,000	£0		
6b. Guaranteed income to *all* individuals under negative income tax			£4,000	£4,000
Implications				
7. Total cost of income support (row (1) × row (6))	5 × £4,000 = £20,000	5 × £4,000 = £20,000	15 × £4,000 = £60,000	15 × £4,000 = £60,000
8. Total taxable income (from rows (3) and (4))	10 × (£10,000 − £4,000) = £60,000	10 × (£10,000 − £4,000) = £60,000	10 × £10,000 = £100,000	10 × £10,000 = £100,000
9. Tax rate on taxable income (from rows (7) and (8))	£20,000/£60,000 = 33$^{1}/_{3}$%	£20,000/£60,000 = 33$^{1}/_{3}$%	£60,000/£100,000 = 60%	£60,000/£100,000 = 60%
10. Post-transfer income	£4,000	£4,000 + (1 − $^{1}/_{3}$)£6,000 = £8,000	£4,000	£4,000 + (1 − 0.6)£10,000 = £8,000
11. Average tax rate on personal income (from rows (7) and (3))	£20,000/£100,000 = 20%	£20,000/£100,000 = 20%	£60,000/£100,000 = 60%	£60,000/£100,000 = 60%

Note: it is assumed that
1. taxation is levied only to finance cash transfers;
2. there are no transactions costs.

However, Table 11.1 to some extent hides the fact that negative income tax may not increase taxation *per se* so much as *replace implicit by explicit taxation*.[1] There are two cases. In the first, both the level of benefits and their coverage remain unchanged under negative income tax, as in Table 11.1. Identical recipients receive identical benefits; total net expenditure is unchanged; no increase in net revenue is necessary; and nobody's post-transfer income has changed. Negative income tax has produced an exact mimic of the previous system by a different administrative mechanism: nothing has been done to relieve poverty; and the poverty trap and labour-supply disincentives are unchanged. The only difference is that in Table 11.1 someone whose income rises from £0 to £10,000 under income tax will (*a*) lose £4,000 via implicit taxation, and (*b*) pay an additional £2,000 in explicit income tax; under negative income tax he pays £6,000 in explicit tax. The only effect of negative income tax in this case is to make *all* withdrawal of benefit part of *explicit* taxation. From one perspective this is a difference more of form than of substance; from another it forecloses the possibility of minimizing incentive effects through devices like fixed-period awards (Chapter 10, Section 3.4), or—as discussed in Section 3— the conditioning of benefits not on income but on factors like family size, age, and health and employment status.

A second, and very different, case arises where net benefits and/or coverage are increased by negative income tax. This raises the net income of at least some poor people; but net expenditure rises, necessitating an increase in taxes over and above the replacement of implicit by explicit taxation.

The logic of what is happening is seen most easily in terms of two hypothetical states of the world, in which benefits are paid *only* to the poor (state A) or to *everyone* (state B). Then:

1. *Total tax revenue*: gross expenditure, and hence on a revenue-neutral basis also gross tax revenues, must be higher in state B than in state A.

2. *Average tax rate* (ATR): if tax revenues are greater in state B then ATR must be higher.

3. *Marginal tax rates* (MTR): if ATR is higher, then MTR must be higher for at least some groups. There are two polar cases: *either* the increase in MTR is concentrated wholly on the poor, in which case (*a*) the poverty trap is institutionalized, and (*b*) there is a potential labour-supply problem for the poor; *or* the increase in MTR is concentrated wholly on the rich, in which case (*a*) the poverty trap is in principle 'solved', but (*b*) there is a potential labour-supply problem for the rich.

Thus negative income tax inevitably increases explicit tax rates.

FORMAL ANALYSIS (Non-technical readers can proceed directly to 'Major implications', below). The cost of any scheme is the tax/benefit function in Figure 11.1*a* weighted by the income distribution in Figure 11.1*b*. Thus:

$$C = AG - \int_{0}^{\infty} t(Y)D(Y)\, dY \tag{11.3}$$

---

[1] See the Glossary.

where:

G = the guaranteed income per individual/family,

A = the total number of individuals/families,

Y = personal income,

$t(Y)$ is the tax function (given in Figure 11.1a by the tax parameter, t), and

$D(Y)$ is the distribution of pre-tax income (given in Figure 11.1b).

Any issue of cost boils down to an empirical question about the elements of equation (11.3). For a given population, A, guaranteed income, G, and tax function, $t(Y)$, the cost of the scheme and its redistributive strength depend on the size distribution of pre-tax personal income $D(Y)$, and in particular on the relative size of the left-hand tail of Figure 11.1b.

Within this framework it is possible (see Barr 1975) to estimate the cost of different tax regimes—'ordinary' income tax and two variants of negative income tax. Each of the systems comprises two elements—gross expenditure and gross revenue. For income tax, gross expenditure consists of total spending on cash benefits, S, and all remaining expenditure, R, out of income-tax revenue. R, in other words, is the required surplus of income tax over expenditure on cash benefits. Under a large-scale negative income tax, S is omitted (since all existing cash benefits are, by assumption, abolished), and gross expenditure consists of R and the cost of the guaranteed income payments, AG in equation (11.3). On the revenue side, total personal income, Y, is split into three components: Y_1 is the income of 'poor' individuals/families with pre-transfer income below the tax threshold (i.e. the left-hand tail of Figure 11.1b); Y_2 is income below the tax threshold of families whose total income exceeds the tax threshold (equivalent to the personal allowances under income tax); and Y_3 is income above the tax threshold. Formally,

$$Y_1 = \int_0^B D(Y)\,dY$$

$$Y_2 + Y_3 = \int_B^\infty D(Y)\,dY \tag{11.4}$$

where B is the income-tax threshold. Attention is focused on a very simple form of the tax function, $t(Y)$, in equation (11.3), with tax rates t_1 and t_2 applying, respectively, to income above and below the tax threshold.

Income tax is shown by the line *OBA* in Figure 11.2. Gross expenditure consists of cash benefits, S, plus the required surplus, R. On the revenue side, income below the tax threshold, $Y_1 + Y_2$, is not taxed (i.e. $t_1 = 0$); income above the threshold, Y_3, is taxed at the basic rate of income tax (including national-insurance contributions), $\bar{t}$. Thus a simplified version of income tax is

$$C_1 = S + R - \bar{t}Y_3 \tag{11.5}$$

where, by definition, $C_1 = 0$.

Dual-rate negative income tax consists on the expenditure side of the gross cost of the guaranteed income, AG (replacing existing cash benefits, S), and the required surplus, R.

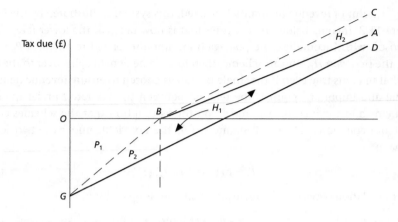

Fig. 11.2. The redistributive effects of negative income tax

On the revenue side, taxes are levied at rates t_1 and t_2 on the relevant parts of the tax base, as shown by the line GBC in Figure 11.2. Dual-rate negative income tax is constructed so as to keep benefits in the hands of the poor by ensuring that all benefits are taxed away by the time the tax threshold, B, is reached. A benefit of £80 and a threshold of £100 implies that $t_1 = 80/100 = 0.8$, i.e. the restriction

$$t_1 = \frac{G}{B}$$

(11.6)

and the cost of the system is

$$C_2 = AG + R - \frac{G}{B}(Y_1 + Y_2) - t_2 Y_3.$$

(11.7)

Compared with income tax, the poor gain an amount related to the area P_1 in Figure 11.2.[2] Since all benefits are taxed away by the time the tax threshold is reached, the rich are invariant between the two systems if the tax rate on income above the threshold remains unchanged. But, as drawn, the dual-rate scheme imposes a higher rate than income tax above the tax threshold (i.e. BC has a steeper slope than BA), so the rich lose an amount related to the area H_2. Benefits remain in the hands of the poor.

Single-rate negative income tax is a special case where the same tax rate is levied on all income. Thus $t_1 = t_2$, and from equation (11.7)

$$C_3 = AG + R - t_2 Y$$

(11.8)

where by definition (from Figure 11.1*b* and equation (11.4))

$$Y = \int_0^\infty D(Y)\, dY = Y_1 + Y_2 + Y_3.$$

(11.9)

[2] Understood as weighted by the appropriate section of the income distribution.

If the constraint of revenue neutrality is relaxed, this system is illustrated by the line GD in Figure 11.2. Income below the tax threshold is now taxed at the lower rate, t_2, so in comparison with income tax the poor gain an amount related to the area $P_1 + P_2$. As drawn, the rich gain H_1.[3] In this scheme, therefore, some benefit spills over to the rich, a result that remains true even if the single tax rate is chosen to ensure revenue neutrality.

A final and important point is the relation between the tax rate t under the single-rate scheme and the dual rates t_1 and t_2, on the assumption that the schemes cost the same. From equations (11.7), (11.8), and (11.9) the tax yields under the two schemes are equal if

$$tY = t_1(Y_1 + Y_2) + t_2Y_3. \tag{11.10}$$

Hence the relation between the single and dual rates is given by

$$t = \theta t_1 + (1 - \theta)t_2 \tag{11.11}$$

where

$$\theta = \frac{Y_1 + Y_2}{Y}. \tag{11.12}$$

Two important implications follow from equation (11.11). First, t can be thought of as the marginal rate applied to all income, *or* as a weighted average of the dual rates, *or*, more generally, as the average of any set of marginal rates with the same tax yield. Secondly, if t_1 is higher than t_2 (which is likely if the poverty trap is a problem), then t is higher the larger is θ: put another way, t is higher the smaller is Y_3 as a proportion of total income— that is, the lighter the upper tail of the income distribution.

MAJOR IMPLICATIONS. The foregoing apparatus demonstrates earlier results more precisely. Equation (11.6) shows that under the dual-rate scheme (which keeps all benefits in the hands of the poor) the tax rate, t_1, on low income rises in parallel with the level of benefits. Thus negative income tax recreates the poverty trap in another form. The first conclusion, therefore, is that, *in a scheme that keeps all benefits in the hands of the poor, the more successfully poverty is alleviated, the more serious is the problem of the poverty trap.* The situation is no different from that under the present benefit system.

The solution to the poverty trap is to withdraw benefits more slowly, in which case the break-even income rises above the tax threshold. This is the case under the single-rate scheme, which lowers the marginal tax rate on the poor. But, from equation (11.7), if the poor pay lower taxes on Y_1, then the rich pay lower taxes on Y_2. It follows, on an equi-cost basis, that more revenue will have to be collected from Y_3. Thus, for a given guaranteed income, *the poverty trap can be alleviated only by increased taxation of the rich.* This, as we shall see, can cause labour-supply problems.

The last result, emphasized by equation (11.11), is that the average tax rate t will be higher the smaller is Y_3 as a proportion of the tax base. This gives rise to a fundamental (but often overlooked) conclusion—that for a given level of benefit *it is the shape of the*

---

[3] Again weighted by the appropriate section of the income distribution.

income distribution that 'creates' the poverty trap—changing the system of cash transfers will not solve the problem so long as benefits are conditioned on income.

Negative income tax thus increases tax rates at some or all levels of income: it institutionalizes the poverty trap and/or leads to higher tax rates on incomes above the poverty line. Given the shape of the income distribution in virtually all countries, the level of benefit and its cost can be reconciled only by the imposition of punitive taxation. This raises two consequential problems: the redistributive power of negative income tax, as we shall see shortly, is not high despite the presence of high tax rates; and there is potentially a serious labour-supply problem.

Redistributive effects

Negative income taxation has implications for both horizontal and vertical redistribution. A large-scale scheme paying benefits equal to the poverty line may improve horizontal efficiency in two ways: it can increase take-up; and it can reduce stigma, because there is no longer a benefit system for the poor and a tax system for the non-poor, but one system that covers everyone.

On vertical efficiency, negative income tax scores less well. At first glance it might appear that, by benefiting the poor at the expense of the non-poor, it is strongly redistributive. This is not necessarily so. The cost of negative income tax, as we have seen, depends on the size distribution of income. So too does the redistributive strength of any particular scheme, simply because a 1 per cent increase in the average tax rate raises more revenue for redistribution to the poor the greater the proportion of taxpayers who are non-poor.

Since virtually all countries have an income distribution heavily skewed towards lower incomes, negative income tax will not be a strong re-distributor for two reasons. First, as benefits are increased, the average tax rate has to be raised to finance them. Secondly, there are many people with low incomes and relatively few with high incomes; the tax increase necessary to finance a high guaranteed income therefore falls substantially on those with low and average incomes, thus clawing back a substantial proportion of the benefit to the poor. In consequence, the redistributive effects, though not trivial, are muted.

CONCLUSION 1. Given (*a*) the shape of the income distribution, and (*b*) current benefit levels, two results follow.

- A universal negative income tax will be very costly; this will necessitate high tax rates which are likely to cause labour-supply problems.
- Negative income taxation will not be a strong redistributor.

2.3. The role of a small-scale negative income tax

Given this conclusion, there are three potential ways forward: a small-scale negative income tax in combination with other forms of income support; the 'Back-to-Beveridge' approach discussed in the next section; and schemes that combine the two approaches (Section 4).

A small-scale scheme will not solve poverty, and therefore contributes to poverty relief only if it makes other schemes more effective. As an example, consider a scheme that pays child benefit for each child, as currently, and pays each adult a negative income tax guarantee equal to the 'cashed-out' value of the income-tax personal allowance.[4]

We saw in Chapter 6, Section 2.3, that one of the major difficulties in identifying and counting the poor arises because the tax authorities know little about them. A key feature of a universal negative income-tax scheme is not that it would help the poor directly (because the guaranteed income would be small), but that for the first time the great bulk of the population would be brought under the tax authority's umbrella. This would make it possible to search out the poor, thereby increasing the take-up of other benefits. The strategy is to use a universal negative income tax not to *solve* poverty, but to enhance the effectiveness of benefits aimed specifically at poverty relief.

A scheme of this sort, as well as improving take-up, alleviates the poverty trap in two ways. First, the guaranteed income being universal, all other cash benefits become devices only for 'topping up' income, rather than mechanisms for total income support. This has the important advantage that the tax implicit in benefit withdrawal applies over a shorter range of income. Suppose a family receives £100 in income support; under the present system (ignoring disregards) it faces a 100 per cent implicit tax on the first £100 of its net earnings. But, if its weekly guaranteed income was £60, it would receive only £40 in income support, and so face a 100 per cent tax rate on only the first £40 of net earnings. Secondly, fixed-period awards (Chapter 10, Section 3.4) would further reduce the poverty trap. A family receiving a guaranteed income of £60, if awarded housing benefit of £40 per week for six months, would receive £100 per week *irrespective of changes in income*. Thus, by the back door, it is possible to pay a larger guaranteed income to families with low incomes. For a detailed proposal of a scheme of this type, see Parker (1989).

CONCLUSION 2. The only feasible role for a pure negative income-tax scheme is not as a major redistributor of income, but as a *search device* to discover low-income families, in order to increase take-up rates. For this purpose, the guaranteed income need be no higher than the cashed-out value of current income-tax allowances; thus costs are not excessive, minimizing problems with the poverty trap.

3. Indicator-targeting: The 'Back-to-Beveridge' approach

3.1. The idea

Negative income taxation seeks to raise low incomes by paying benefits conditioned on income. The so-called Back-to-Beveridge strategy makes benefits conditional on other characteristics—for example, being unemployed, ill, retired, or having children. In its pure form, the approach is based wholly on indicator targeting, with no means testing at all.

As discussed in Chapter 10, Section 2.2, the ideal indicators are (*a*) highly correlated with poverty, to ensure accurate targeting, (*b*) exogenous to the individual, to minimize distortionary incentives, and (*c*) easy to observe, to assist administration.

---

[4] If the tax threshold is £4,000 per year and the tax rate 25%, the cashed-out value of the personal allowance is £1,000.

What does the approach imply in practice? Empirically, the major correlates of poverty are unemployment; ill health; large families; single-parent families; old age; and high housing costs; in developing economies, geographical location (i.e. place of residence) or being landless may also be highly correlated with poverty (see Lipton and Ravallion 1995). Benefits paid to people in these categories embrace a majority of the poor. How exogenous are these characteristics?

- The endogeneity of the level and duration of unemployment is controversial (Chapter 8, Section 3.1).

- With ill health, the problem is less acute because genuine ill health is costly to the individual, and because policing is possible through certification procedures.

- The incidence of large families is exogenous with respect to benefits unless family size is influenced by the existence of family benefits; similarly, the occurrence of single-parent families is exogenous unless the decision by parents to separate is substantially influenced by the benefit system. A crucial issue in this context is whether having children/separating is more strongly endogenous than labour supply.

- Reaching retirement age is entirely beyond the individual's control. Individuals may choose voluntarily to defer retirement, but this works in the 'right' direction by increasing labour supply.

- Housing costs are far from exogenous under any system that, like housing benefit, bases assistance on *actual* costs. Matters could be improved if assistance were related to a regional index of *average* housing costs.

Particularly where administrative capacity is limited, good indicators are pregnancy, infancy, and school attendance by young children. Such characteristics are not *necessarily* associated with poverty, but the correlation is generally high; there are no major problems of endogeneity (the existence of benefits for very young children is not usually a *primary* motive for pregnancy); and the characteristics are easily observed. In such cases, direct in-kind transfers are both well targeted and non-transferable. Pregnant women and infants benefit from nutritional programmes such as free orange juice at maternity clinics and medical check-ups; schoolchildren can be given free milk, meals, and health checks. Such programmes are aimed at a precise, and largely captive group, and they are not readily tradeable. More generally, targeted family support, particularly for nutritional and medical purposes, can be a useful instrument (for further discussion, see Grosh 1994). Another possible indicator is visible old age. Such benefits would empower the elderly (disproportionately women), thereby, through grandmother's discretion, offering family support.

Some comments on indicator targeting are necessary. First, the strategy offers the possibility of sidestepping the poverty trap by concentrating the entire loss of benefit on a change of category (e.g. accepting a job, or regaining health). Exogeneity in this context is clearly crucial.

Secondly, some individuals with incomes below the poverty line will fall outside the characteristics just described (i.e. the characteristics are not completely horizontally efficient). For this group at least, a residual income-tested scheme is necessary. There are also people within the six categories (hence qualifying for benefit) whose pre-transfer

income is above the poverty line (i.e. the categories are not completely vertically efficient). For this reason there is a case for making all benefits taxable in the same way as
earned income.

Finally, it should be noted that the indicator approach can, at least in part, be organized
through the institutions of social insurance (as currently for unemployment, ill health,
and old age), but does not have to be (e.g. child benefit). The issue of whether some forms
of income support are organized through social insurance therefore remains open (for
discussion, see Hills 2003).

3.2. An example

The following example is based on a proposal by James Meade (1978), who advocated a
system that (*a*) paid all national-insurance benefits at or above the poverty line defined by
income support; (*b*) paid child benefit at the income-support level; (*c*) paid additional
benefits to one-parent families, people with disabilities, etc.; and (*d*) phased out many
means-tested benefits. In addition, (*e*) the income-tax threshold should be raised to the
poverty line.

Proposals of this sort can alleviate the poverty trap in two ways. First, the major benefits
are at or above the poverty line, thus reducing the number of people receiving income
support and facing its 100 per cent implicit tax. Secondly, these benefits are not affected
by changes in income, but only by a change in the recipient's category—for example, the
loss of unemployment benefit upon resumption of work. This does not remove the poverty
trap so much as sidestep it by concentrating the entire tax effect on the change in status.

The resulting advantages are twofold. Families are not trapped in poverty (an equity
gain). Secondly, the arrangements will have beneficial incentive effects (an efficiency
gain), since the criteria on which benefits are awarded are largely exogenous to recipients.

4. Mixed strategies

Sections 2 and 3 discussed the two strategies for the most part in isolation. As a guide to
practical policy, however, neither on its own will succeed. Benefits conditioned on income
generally run into problems of high tax rates, with consequent problems of disincentives
and administrative cost; and pure categorical schemes face intractable problems of gaps
in coverage, benefits 'leaking' to the non-poor, and problems with defining and administering borderline cases. Targeting, as Atkinson (1995*b*) points out, is a matter of some
subtlety and has a number of different dimensions.[5] The most promising way forward is
through a mix of the two strategic approaches.

The main purpose of this chapter has been to set out the logic of different strategies for
reform, so no attempt is made here to go beyond a brief listing of some proposed reforms.

[5] For references on the analytics of targeting, see the Further Reading to Chapter 10.

BASIC INCOME PROPOSALS. The Basic Income Scheme (Parker 1989) has several variants. The most promising pays a guaranteed income roughly equal to the cashed-out value of income-tax allowances, superimposed on which are social-insurance benefits. Some versions have the desirable characteristic that benefit is invariant to age (if below pensionable age), sex, marital status, and employment status, thus minimizing distortionary incentives. The scheme can be regarded as a universal negative income tax whose intercept varies with the characteristics of recipients, and thus as a blend of the two approaches.

THE PARTICIPATION INCOME SCHEME. Atkinson (1995a: 300) argues that 'it is a mistake to see basic income as an *alternative* to social insurance . . . It is more productive to see [it] as complementary . . . I would see [the] partnership between social insurance and basic income not just as a transitional compromise, but as an alternative conception of basic income' (emphasis in original).

What Atkinson calls the Participation Income Scheme is, in essence, a negative income-tax scheme—but one in which benefit is conditioned on some form of participation. Participation is interpreted broadly. A person is eligible if he or she is working (employed or self-employed), retired, unable to work because of ill health, unemployed and available for work, engaged in education or training, caring for young, old, or disabled dependants, or undertaking approved types of voluntary work.

On the benefits side, the scheme pays a participation income to everyone aged 18 or over who participates in one or more of these ways; and it pays a basic income to all children in place of child benefit. People would also continue to be eligible for social insurance benefits. On the taxation side, all income, including all social insurance benefits, is taxed, the only exception being a disregard on the first £10 of weekly earnings (early 1990s prices). Thus the participation income and social insurance complement and reinforce each other—an explicit mix of the negative income-tax approach and the indicator-targeting approach, with the advantages of both, but few of the disadvantages.

WORKING TAX CREDIT SCHEMES. These schemes, discussed in Chapter 10 (see the Further Reading to Chapter 10), include the UK working tax credit and child tax credit, and the US earned income tax credit. Such schemes (generically referred to as working tax credits) are a mixture of income testing, indicator targeting (extra credits for children, for lone parents, and for disability), and self-targeting (because of the work requirement). Thus tax credits can be regarded as a negative income tax scheme, but one that applies only to lower earners. Middle- and high-earners face ordinary income-tax; lower earners face a negative income-tax threshold (G_0 in Figure 11.1(a), but with a higher tax rate (i.e. the taper) on low earnings. Moffitt (2003) analyses working tax credits in this way. After many years of debate between income testing and categorical benefits, it may be that there is finally some convergence on mixed modes of targeting.

5. Conclusion: Cash benefits

The discussion in Part 2 is shaped by four fundamental sets of constraints.

- Technical problems—largely information problems—that can make voluntary, private arrangements for insurance and consumption smoothing inefficient or impossible: the central argument is that the choice between private and public solutions is more technical than ideological.

- The age distribution—that is, the rising fraction of elderly people, which shapes options for pension reform: a major conclusion is that demographic change is a problem, not a crisis.

- The income distribution—that is, the fact that the income distribution is skewed towards lower incomes, which constrains a country's ability to relieve poverty: one result is that a poverty trap in one form or another is inescapable.

- The fact that factor supply is endogenous—that is, people in a free society have choice about how many hours to work and in which country to live: thus incentives matter.

The chapters in Part 2 discuss two sorts of mechanism. *Self-help* is necessary for people who are self-supporting on a lifetime basis but need a system of insurance (Chapter 8) and consumption smoothing (Chapter 9) to iron out discontinuities. *Poverty relief* (Chapter 10) is necessary for those who are unable to support themselves over their lifetime as a whole. Thus the welfare state has both a 'piggy-bank' function and a 'Robin Hood' function.

The menu of methods of self-help includes private insurance, voluntary saving, and state activity, the latter in the form of social insurance or through transfers out of current tax revenues. Poverty relief can be achieved by private charity, or through publicly organized transfers out of tax revenues (note that actuarial insurance cannot systematically redistribute from rich to poor). The respective merits of these methods can be summarized as follows.

ACTUARIAL VERSUS SOCIAL INSURANCE. The private market cannot always supply the efficient quantity and type of insurance against all causes of income loss.

1. Because non-insurance may cause an externality, there is an efficiency argument for making some forms of insurance compulsory (Chapter 8, Section 2.1).

2. Private insurance in several important areas will be inefficient or non-existent: unemployment is not well covered by actuarial insurance, mainly because of moral hazard (Chapter 8, Section 2.2); and, in the context of pensions, inflation is an uninsurable risk (Chapter 9, Section 3.1). These technical problems give an efficiency justification for public provision of unemployment compensation and, at a minimum, underwriting on a PAYG basis the indexation component of pension schemes. The efficiency arguments for public provision of sickness benefits and the smaller national-insurance benefits are weaker.

Social insurance was discussed in Chapter 5, Section 4.2. It can deal with risks that market failures prevent actuarial insurance from covering. It can also adapt to changing social and economic circumstances. These can occur because some risks (unemployment, retirement) are in important respects social constructs, the nature of which has changed over time; they can also arise because technical advances such as genetic testing can create new uninsurable conditions (see Barr 2001*a*: ch. 5).

THE INSURANCE PRINCIPLE—is it possible, necessary, or desirable? It is *possible* for the state to create institutions similar to private, actuarial insurance—for example, the original Beveridge concept of flat-rate contributions based on average risk, giving entitlement to flat-rate benefits, or notional defined-contribution schemes (see the Glossary) in countries like Sweden. For non-insurable risks (unemployment, inflation), these merely mimic private institutions but are not true insurance. It does not follow that actuarial institutions (i.e. with risk-related premiums) are *necessary*. If membership is compulsory, it is possible, without the likelihood of substantial inefficiency, to impose a pooling solution in which premiums are not based on individual risk (Chapter 5, Section 3.2, and Chapter 8, Section 3.1).

It is an open question whether adherence to the contributory principle in a state scheme is *desirable* (Chapter 8, Section 3.1; see also Hills 2003). Social assistance has the advantage of flexibility, since entitlement to benefit does not depend on a contributions record; the corresponding disadvantages are that benefits conditioned on income may be stigmatizing, and can cause a poverty trap (Chapter 10, Section 3). Contributory schemes, while less flexible, may have advantages because they sidestep the poverty trap (Chapter 11, Section 3); because individuals might perceive contributions differently from taxes, with correspondingly different labour-supply effects; and because recipients might feel less stigmatized by benefits conditioned on previous contributions rather than an income test.

PENSION FINANCE. No definitive answer is possible.

1. Moving national insurance pensions onto a funded basis will not by itself address the problems caused by demographic change (Chapter 9, Section 5.1). The important policies are those that increase national output directly: through investment in new technology and improvements in the quality of labour (both of which increase productivity per worker); and through increased labour-force participation, including lower unemployment, increased participation by women, and—a central part of the solution—later retirement.

2. Theoretical and empirical analysis of the effects of pension schemes on saving and labour supply have produced conflicting results (Chapter 9, Section 5.1).

3. The choice between PAYG and funding depends largely on views about income redistribution and policy flexibility (Chapter 9, Sections 3.2 and 5.3).

POVERTY RELIEF. In part because of the free-rider problem, redistribution through private charity is likely to be suboptimal even from a libertarian perspective and *a fortiori* from a Rawlsian or socialist viewpoint (Chapter 4, Section 4.1). Thus at least some publicly organized redistribution through the tax system can be justified under any theory of society, though with considerable disagreement about how much (Chapter 4, Sections 2.2 and 4.4). Any such redistribution will be constrained by the size distribution of income (Chapter 11, Section 2.2). As a result:

1. Income-tested poverty relief is withdrawn rapidly as the income of recipients rises, thereby containing costs and targeting benefits on the poorest families. The price of these advantages is the poverty trap, which makes it difficult for families to increase their standard of living, and therefore creates a labour-supply disincentive (Chapter 10, Section 3.1).

2. Awarding benefit for a fixed period can mitigate the worst disincentive effects; so can working tax credits that make benefit conditional on work (Chapter 10, Section 3.4).

REFORM

1. Benefits conditioned on income (whether means-tested explicitly or in the form of a large-scale negative income tax) suffer from the necessity of high tax rates to finance them. This causes a poverty trap with major efficiency and equity costs.

2. For this reason large-scale negative income-tax schemes cannot solve poverty on their own. Their cost is a consequence not of the negative income-tax mechanism *per se* but of (*a*) the existing size distribution of income, (*b*) the poverty line chosen, and (*c*) the empirical fact that labour supply is endogenous (Chapter 11, Section 2.2).

3. Benefits conditioned on indicators other than income can circumvent some of these difficulties, particularly if the criteria are exogenous to the recipient and highly correlated with poverty. Such indicator targeting offers some hope of improvement (Chapter 10, Section 2.2, and Chapter 11, Section 3). The most hopeful route for reform is a careful blend of the two approaches (Chapter 11, Section 4).

What are the implications of these largely technical arguments? The preferred libertarian methods of voluntary insurance and voluntary charity rather fall by the wayside. Private insurance will frequently be inefficient, sometimes because, with complex, long-term contracts, consumers might be badly informed, but more often because of technical problems on the supply side. Libertarians might therefore concede an element of compulsion in view of the externality caused by non-insurance (Chapter 8, Section 2.1), and allow in addition a limited role for non-actuarial, tax-financed transfers to raise to subsistence those incomes that remain low despite private charity. This will be especially relevant to non-insurable risks. Libertarians criticize national insurance as exceeding the scope necessary to achieve this limited purpose, thereby curtailing the freedom of taxpayers to make their own decisions.

Socialists favour public organization of cash transfers, financed by progressive taxation; benefits should be awarded on the basis of need, and should be above subsistence so as to reduce inequality. Whether insurable risks are dealt with out of tax revenues or by social insurance is an area of debate. However, many socialists abhor means testing, partly because of the poverty trap and partly as a legacy of the Poor Law. In the absence of a universal guaranteed income, this brings us back to insurance, at which point there is some convergence between socialist and liberal views.

■ QUESTIONS FOR FURTHER DISCUSSION

1. Evaluate the case for introducing a 'basic income' scheme.

2. Explain how the 'Back to Beveridge' approach works, using indicators of poverty rather than an income test.

■ FURTHER READING

There is a huge literature on negative income tax: see Christopher et al. (1970) (tending to the libertarian), Meade (1972) (a cogent liberal appeal), and Parker (1989). In the US context, see Tobin et al. (1967), Christopher Green (1967), Tobin (1968), and Aaron (1973). On the costs of negative income tax, see Barr (1975) and Atkinson (1989: ch. 16).

One of the best accounts of the US negative income-tax experiments, including details of the experimental design and an analysis of the labour-supply responses, can be found in the contributions to Pechman and Timpane (1975); for an account of the experiments in rural areas, see Palmer and Pechman (1978). The official findings from the New Jersey experiment on labour supply are presented in Watts and Rees (1977). For a survey of the large literature on the incentive effects of the experiments, see Burtless (1986).

On the case for 'Back to Beveridge', see Meade (1978: ch. 13), and, for discussion of the contributory principle, Hills (2003).

For mixed schemes, see Parker (1989), Atkinson (1995a: ch. 15), Brittan (1995: ch. 13), Field (1996), Moffitt (2003), and the references to working tax credit schemes in the Further Reading at the end of Chapter 10.

PART 3

Benefits in Kind

Three intellectual threads run through this book: information problems, issues of social justice, and problems of definition and measurement. The discussion of cash benefits was concerned mainly with the first two; in the case of benefits in kind the third assumes special importance. Many of the arguments about health care and education turn crucially on the first and the third, particularly the measurement of private and social costs and benefits. In part because of these problems, the issues raised by benefits in kind are particularly complex. It is therefore unfortunate that health care and education are bedevilled by emotional polemics, most of which confuse aims and methods. The main purpose of these chapters is not to give the 'right' answer, but firmly to establish the right battleground.

Chapters 12–14 look at health care, school education, and higher education. The theoretical analysis in Chapter 12—which is largely, though not wholly, about insurance—points to strong efficiency arguments for state involvement in the finance of health care, though with no similarly strong conclusion about its production. Chapters 13 and 14—which are largely, though far from wholly, about consumption/investment smoothing—are in important respects mirror images of each other. Chapter 13 points to efficiency arguments for substantial state involvement with both the finance and production of school education. Chapter 14, using the identical body of theory, reaches a very different conclusion—that the state should fund part of the costs of higher education, but that market forces, with some regulation, are both more efficient and more equitable on the production side. These very different conclusions are rooted in the economics of information—that is, they are much more technical than ideological.

Each chapter has a common outline. After a brief introduction (Section 1), the aims of policy are discussed in Section 2 and the theoretical arguments about state intervention in Section 3. Policy analysis concentrates on assessment of the current UK system (Section 4) and reform strategies in the UK and elsewhere (Section 5). The conclusions are set out in Section 6. Many of the theoretical arguments are similar, so theoretical sections are written to bring out the parallels and contrasts rather than to be repetitive.

12 Health and health care

Risk varies inversely with knowledge.

(Irving Fisher, 1930)

That any sane nation, having observed that you could provide for the supply of bread by giving bakers a pecuniary interest in baking for you, should go on to give a surgeon a pecuniary interest in cutting off your leg, is enough to make one despair of political humanity.

(George Bernard Shaw, 1911)

1. Introduction

Given the size of the topics, the next three chapters are inevitably eclectic. The main questions asked are: how efficient/just is a competitive market for health care, school education, or higher education likely to be; to what extent would public production and allocation be more efficient/just; and would any mixed system perform better than either of the pure cases? Several important issues receive little mention, including the detailed finances of health care and education (see Glennerster 2003*a* and the Further Reading).

NON-ECONOMIC ARGUMENTS. It is useful to remind ourselves of earlier discussion of bad economic arguments. They are generally of two sorts: either they fail to understand the nature and limitations of market allocation; or they confuse aims and methods. Libertarians argue that health care is an 'ordinary' commodity that should be distributed in accordance with income, tastes, and relative prices; if we do not like the distribution of health care, we should change the distribution of income. As argued below, this is a mistake of the first kind.

Arguments that confuse aims and methods were discussed in Chapter 4, Section 7.2. The view that 'health care and education are basic rights and therefore should be provided by the state' is illogical because the words 'and therefore' simply do not follow from the initial premiss. If health care, etc., are basic rights, then so is food, which is provided well enough by the private sector. For the same reason, the argument that 'health care, etc. should be publicly provided because otherwise the poor could not afford them' does not stand up. Poverty may justify cash transfers but is not, without considerable qualification, a justification for public provision.

The same arguments can be viewed from the political perspectives discussed in Chapter 3. Many socialists believe that health care and education should be provided collectively. This view is tenable as a value judgement, but the consequent policies will be unsuccessful unless they go with rather than against the grain of economic theory. Libertarians argue that virtually all goods, including health care and education, should be supplied privately, because collective provision is both inefficient and a violation of individual liberty. This view, again, is workable only if it accords with economic theory. Markets can fail entirely (unemployment insurance) or be inefficient (many forms of health-care insurance)— devout hopes are not enough. Liberals reject both lines of argument because each makes the *method* of provision (market or state) a primary *aim*. As argued in Chapter 4, Section 7.2, a better approach is to choose aims on the basis of personal values and ideology, and then to select on technical grounds whichever method best achieves them.

INSTITUTIONS are described in Section 4.1. During the early part of the chapter virtually no institutional knowledge is necessary. As a good approximation, the National Health Service (NHS) is financed out of central government revenues, and health care (with minor exceptions) provided publicly and without charge, both for treatment by a general practitioner (i.e. family doctor) and for hospital in- and out-patient treatment. Most hospital doctors and nurses in the NHS are paid a salary. Family doctors are paid in a complex way reflecting *inter alia* the numbers and ages of their patients. Throughout the NHS there is relatively little fee-for-service. Alongside the NHS is a small private sector.

2. Aims

2.1. Concepts

Social welfare is maximized by the joint pursuit of efficiency[1] and social justice (or equity). This section outlines the meaning of these ideas as they apply to the health sector and then turns to the more difficult problem of measuring them.

The starting point is the obvious, but often overlooked, distinction between health and health care. The primary objective of health policy, it can be argued, is to improve people's health. Health, however, derives from many sources, including (*a*) overall living standards, (*b*) individual choice—for example, about diet (plenty of fruit and vegetables) and lifestyle (exercise, avoiding smoking, etc.), (*c*) the general external environment (e.g. pollution), (*d*) the individual environment, such as the type of job (or *having* a job), (*e*) the quality and availability of health care, and (*f*) a person's inheritance (e.g. physical and emotional strength). Medical treatment is thus only part of the story. Health policy should look at all of (*a*)–(*e*), not just at health care narrowly defined; policy, for example, should include action on food quality and public education about the health benefits of diet and lifestyle decisions as well as the resourcing and management of the NHS.

Efficiency is as important here as elsewhere. If we spent nothing on health, some people would die unnecessarily of trivial complaints; if we spent the whole of GDP on health care, there would be no food and we would all die of starvation. The optimal

---

[1] The concept of efficiency is defined in Chapter 4, Section 2.1.

quantity lies somewhere between—in principle where the value gained from the last health intervention is equal to the marginal value that would be derived from the alternative uses to which the resources involved could be put. This is the quantity X^* in Figure 4.1.

Allocative efficiency (sometimes referred to in discussions of health and education as *external efficiency*) is concerned with producing the quantity, quality, and mix of health interventions (including preventive care and health education) that bring about the greatest improvement in health.[2] External efficiency relates both to the overall size of the health sector as a proportion of gross domestic product (the macro-efficiency aim in Chapter 1, Section 2.2) and to the way resources are divided between alternative uses within the health sector (the micro-efficiency aim). Separately, productive efficiency (Chapter 4, Section 2.1) (sometimes referred to as *internal efficiency*) is concerned, for example, with running medical institutions as efficiently as possible.

Equity is more elusive.[3] Le Grand (1982: 14–15) distinguishes four definitions of equity in consumption: equality of public expenditure; equality of use—that is, individuals with the same need should consume the same quantity; equality of cost—that is, *ceteris paribus*, individuals should face the same 'price' for the service (including such factors as forgone earnings, time, etc.); and equality of outcome. Two definitions are of particular interest. Equality of utilization implies that everyone in a given condition should receive the same quantity; the problem is that people differ in the extent to which they choose to consume health care or education. Equality of outcome implies an unequal allocation such that everyone enjoys an equal state of health or level of educational attainment. Whether or not such an aim is thought desirable, it is not fully feasible.

To avoid some of these difficulties equity will be defined as a form of *equality of opportunity*, as described in Chapter 6, Section 3.1 (especially equation (6.18)). This does not mean that individuals can necessarily obtain as much health care as they want (since health-care resources are scarce, no system can satisfy everyone's wants). But it does mean that any individual should receive as much health care as anyone else in the same medical condition, regardless of any factors that are thought to be irrelevant—for example, income. The same argument applies to education.

Problems remain, however. Le Grand (1996) assesses health systems in terms of their efficiency, equity, and administrative feasibility and concludes that no rationing device can simultaneously satisfy all three. Hence evaluation of any system will depend on the relative weights accorded each of the criteria.

Once we have decided the efficient level of health activities and their equitable distribution, the remaining question is who should pay for them—that is, to what extent is it appropriate to finance health care progressively? This is the issue of vertical equity discussed in Chapter 4, Section 4.1. It was argued in Chapter 4, Section 7.2, that if, for example, health care is allocated efficiently by the market, then equity aims are generally best achieved through cash transfers. But, where health care is publicly produced and

---

[2] It can be argued that by emphasizing the *greatest* improvement in health the policy-maker's choice is given precedence over the individual's and, in that sense, the objective is extra-welfarist. For discussion, see Hurley (2000, especially Section 2, which discusses a range of definitions of efficiency).

[3] See Chapter 4, Section 4, and Chapter 6, Section 3.1. See also Le Grand (1996) and Wagstaff et al. (1999).

allocated for *efficiency* reasons, it may be appropriate to finance it out of progressive taxation; if so, it is possible, though not inevitable (Section 4.3), that in-kind transfers will redistribute from rich to poor.

2.2. Measuring costs and benefits

The concept of efficiency is well understood. But attempts to make it operational by measuring costs and benefits must of necessity be rough and ready because of serious measurement problems, particularly in quantifying benefits. The total cost of the NHS and its component parts is readily available (See Table 12.1). The costs of different types of treatment are harder to establish, *inter alia* because of the familiar problem of apportioning overheads and the need to distinguish short- and long-run marginal costs, but these problems are not insurmountable.

MEASURING BENEFITS faces three major problems.

Health is hard to measure. Health care is only an *input*; the outcome is improved health. Expenditure on health care can be estimated, but health itself is hard to measure except in terms of broad indicators such as infant mortality, life expectancy, and estimates of the burden of disease.

Causality is complex. To what extent is any improvement in health *caused* by medical care? A patient's complete recovery could be due entirely to the treatment she has received; or it could be due, wholly or in part, to her natural powers of recovery. The influence of intangible factors (the 'will to live') is crucial, but impossible to measure. Similarly, improvements in health outcomes (e.g. life expectancy) may be due to improved diet, reduced smoking, cleaner air, and the like. If such factors are ignored, we will tend to overestimate the benefits of health care.

Improved health is hard to value. The difficulties are illustrated by the extensive literature on valuing human life (see the Further Reading). Such attempts are sometimes regarded as immoral. But all sorts of policies affect the risks faced by individuals, and hence the number of deaths. Many accident victims would be saved if they could receive medical attention rapidly; nevertheless, we do not have casualty departments on every street corner. Thus we are not prepared to spend infinite sums of money to save one life. The question therefore arises of how much we should be prepared to spend to reduce the risk of death by 1 per cent or, more generally, to reduce the extent or duration of ill health.

The measurement problems are obvious once we realize that the benefits of improved health are twofold. There are *output benefits*—that is, the increased output/income of the individual whose affliction is reduced or removed. This is hard enough to measure. In addition, there are intractable problems in measuring the *utility benefits* arising from any reduction in the physical and emotional suffering of the patient and his or her family.

ASSESSING EFFICIENCY is therefore problematical. There are three approaches: cost-benefit analysis, cost-effectiveness analysis, and cost-utility analysis. Cost-benefit studies are limited by the difficulties of measuring health benefits. Cost-effectiveness analysis considers a specific medical condition, and examines the costs of alternative forms of treatment. Thus it avoids the need to measure benefits; major difficulties remain, however, because evidence on the effectiveness of most medical treatment is limited.

Cost-utility analysis looks not at the *health* benefits of treatment but at the *utility* benefits, based round the idea of a Quality Adjusted Life Year (QALY). A QALY starts from the premiss that the outcome of medical care should be measured in terms not only of the quantity of extra life it produces, but also of its quality. Though measuring quality inevitably involves subjective judgement (e.g. of how much a restriction in mobility reduces the quality of life), QALYs have the merit of incorporating subjective values explicitly and systematically. QALYs look at the extra years (adjusted for quality) result-ing from treatment, and divide them by its cost. Some forms of treatment represent an inefficient use of resources—for example, the treatment is unpleasant, it does not extend life by much, and the time remaining is full of pain and discomfort. Other types of treat-ment, in contrast, are underused. One example is a hip replacement: it is a one-off proce-dure that (relative to many medical interventions) is not expensive; and, though it does not prolong life, it considerably improves its quality. For further discussion, see Williams (1985) (the classic article) and Wagstaff (1991), and, for discussion of an alternative measure, Healthy Year Equivalents, Bleichrodt (1995) and Culyer and Wagstaff (1995).

The conclusion to which this leads is simple but depressing. The efficiency aim for health is clear enough in principle (and the same will turn out to be true for education), but measurement problems make definitive empirical answers unlikely, if not impossible. The definition of equity is more elusive but, as we shall see in Section 4.3, empirical work has made some headway.

3. Methods

3.1. Theoretical arguments for intervention 1: Efficiency

This section looks at how the aims discussed in Section 2 might be achieved, in particular *why* the state intervenes (Sections 3.1 and 3.2) and *how* in theory it might intervene so as jointly to maximize efficiency and equity (Section 3.3).

Private markets allocate efficiently only if the *standard assumptions* hold—that is, per-fect information, perfect competition, and no market failures such as external effects (Chapter 4, Section 3.2, and the Appendix to Chapter 4, paras. 5–17). The underlying question is why health care is 'different' from equally vital commodities like food.

Information problems

Does medical care conform with the standard assumptions? First, are individuals perfectly informed about the nature of the product (i.e. is their indifference map well defined)? The answer, clearly, is no. Many people are unknowingly ill, particularly the elderly, and people with ailments that have no obvious symptoms. In addition, individuals are often ignorant about which types of treatment are available, and about the outcome of different treatments, which is often probabilistic. Furthermore, what little the patient knows is generally learnt from the provider of medical services; and many types of treatment (e.g. setting a broken leg) are not repeated, so that much of what a patient learns is of little future use.

There are other areas (hi-fi, used cars) where the consumer has to rely on the supplier for information. But in these cases it is usually possible to buy information (e.g. consumer magazines, or a report by the Automobile Association), and legislation offers increasing consumer protection.[4] With medical care:

- much (though not all) the information is technically complex, so that a person would not necessarily understand the information even were it available;
- mistaken choice is costlier and less reversible than with most other commodities;
- an individual generally does not have time to shop around if his condition is acute (contrast the situation with a car repair);
- consumers frequently lack the information to weigh one doctor's advice against another's;
- emotions can be strong—for example, ignorance may in part be a consequence of fear, superstition, etc.

To a considerable extent, therefore, consumers are poorly informed about the quantity of treatment they need and about the quality of the care they receive; and, even if information were available, health care is inherently a technical subject, so that there is a limit to what consumers could understand without themselves becoming doctors. Thus there is not only an information problem, but also (as discussed in Chapter 4, Section 3.2; see also New 1999) an information-processing problem. The availability of large amounts of information online does nothing to address the latter. Matters are made worse by the existence of groups who could not use information even if they had it, such as victims of road accidents.

Ignorance is not necessarily evidence of inefficiency. Information may be costly, and its acquisition therefore inefficient if the resulting gain is small. Some degree of ignorance may be optimal, though less than would prevail under a private health-care market.

If consumers are to make rational choices, they need to have the necessary information, and also the power to enforce their decisions. Efficiency therefore requires equal power, in the sense that there should be no constraint on the ability of individuals to consume health care (or education) apart from differences in their money income—that is, people may have different incomes, but there should be no discrimination. This assumption was presented in Chapter 4, Section 3.2, as a precondition of perfect competition, but the issue is closely related to perfect information and so fits naturally into the discussion at this point. In the context of health care and education, power consists largely of knowledge about their uses and benefits, knowledge about one's rights in respect of the NHS and the educational system, and the ability and confidence to be articulate. It is implausible to imagine that this is the state of affairs for all consumers, though in the final analysis the issue is empirical.

Because of imperfect information and unequal power, consumers will choose inefficiently, though with room for debate about the extent of the problem (this is one of the key issues in any discussion of health care). It is also not clear whether the result will be under- or over-consumption. If the 'true' marginal private valuation in Figure 12.1 is

---

[4] It has been suggested that a consumer magazine about medicine might be called *Which Doctor?*

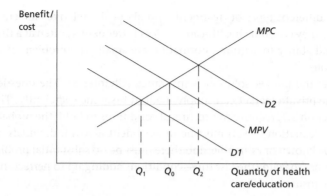

Fig. 12.1. The effects of consumer ignorance on individual demand for health care/education

shown by the curve *MPV*, consumer ignorance can result in demand curves *D1* (under-consumption) or *D2* (over-consumption). In addition, where knowledge and power are systematically related to socio-economic status, there is also inequity (Section 3.3).

What solutions exist? Providing information on a scale sufficient for rational individual choice may be too costly, in which case decisions about treatment must be delegated to the doctor, who acts as an agent for the patient. Minimal intervention takes the form of regulation—for example, only individuals with approved qualifications are allowed to practise medicine. But, where the information problem is serious, the performance of the market may be so inefficient that more extensive state involvement—either through substantial regulation of private production or through public production and allocation—might be a better solution. We return to this issue in Section 4.2.

A separate question is whether consumers are adequately informed about prices (formally, whether their budget constraint is well defined). Here, again, it can be argued that most consumers are ignorant of what a particular form of treatment 'should' cost; and, because much medical care is not repeated, information often has no future use. Nor would it help if consumers were well informed about prices. Rational choice requires simultaneous knowledge both of prices and of the nature of the product (i.e. of both budget constraint *and* indifference map); knowledge of prices without adequate information about different types of treatment will not ensure efficiency.

The result is inefficiency of the type discussed above, and summarized in Figure 12.1. If the *only* problem were inadequate information about prices, the appropriate intervention would be regulation, either in the form of a published price list or through price controls. But where information about the nature of the product is imperfect, ignorance about prices adds further weight to the argument for more substantial state involvement.

Insurance problems

The third information assumption—knowledge about the future—fails with health care, as stressed in Arrow's classic article (1963). Patients do not know when, or how much, health care they will demand; they lack information about the probabilities of different outcomes for different types of treatment, and about the relative efficiency of different providers; and they consume health-care services infrequently, often at a time when their judgement and ability to acquire information are small. The problem of uncertainty is therefore serious.

In principle, the market solution is insurance (Chapter 5). The question, therefore, is whether the private market can supply medical insurance efficiently. This, we saw in Chapter 5, Section 3.1, requires five technical conditions to hold: the probability of needing treatment (equation (5.12)) must be independent across individuals, and less than one; it must be known or estimable; and there must be no substantial problem of adverse selection or moral hazard (the last three conditions adding up to perfect information on the part of the insurer).[5]

Looking at the first condition, the probability of requiring treatment is independent across individuals except during major epidemics.

Secondly, the probability of requiring treatment of a particular type is less than one for ailments like appendicitis or a broken leg. But the condition fails for chronic medical problems (e.g. diabetes) arising before a policy is taken out. Also—a major future problem—it will fail as developments in genetic testing, by improving knowledge of future health problems, create more and more uninsurable conditions (Barr 2001a: ch. 5; see also UK DoH 2003a).[6] The libertarian solution is insurance starting before birth. More realistically, regulation is needed.

Thirdly, the probabilities relevant to medical insurance are generally estimable. However, problems arise with policies whose benefits are a long time in the future, clouding knowledge of the relevant risks—for example, long-term incapacity to work (Burchardt and Hills 1997: ch. 5) and long-term care insurance, discussed in Chapter 8, Section 2.3.

Finally, problems arise of both adverse selection and moral hazard (Chapter 5, Section 3.2).

ADVERSE SELECTION occurs where an individual can conceal from the insurer that he is a bad risk, in which case equilibrium can be inefficient, unstable, or non-existent. Akerlof (1970: 492–3) asks why Americans over 65 cannot easily buy medical insurance, and concludes 'that as the price [of insurance] rises the people who insure themselves will be those who are increasingly certain that they will need the insurance; for error in medical check-ups, doctors' sympathy with older patients, and so on make it much easier for the applicant to assess the risks involved than the insurance company'. Similarly, if employees know better than their employers that they are likely to have high medical bills, employers providing good medical benefits will disproportionately attract employees with health problems, thus discouraging the provision of fringe benefits.

Notwithstanding debate about the magnitude of the problem (see Pauly 1986), there is evidence about the instability of pooling equilibria (see Chapter 5, Section 3.2) in the face of competitive pressures: Blue Cross/Blue Shield, the main US non-profit insurer, originally practised community rating (charging everyone in a locality the same premium), but was forced by competitive pressures from commercial insurers to adopt experience rating (related to the risk of individual subscribers).

---

[5] The classic article is Arrow (1963); see also Pauly (1974, 1986) and, for a summary, Culyer (1993).
[6] A related (but different) point is that treatment of long-term illness is generally expensive, so that competitive pressures act to reduce premiums at the expense of long-term coverage.

MORAL HAZARD can arise in two generic ways: patients may be able to influence either the probability of requiring medical treatment, or its cost. Taking the probability issue first, individuals with full insurance might take fewer health precautions; this is the problem (case 2 in Chapter 5, Section 3.2) addressed by Pauly (1974, 1986). Secondly, both the decision to consult one's family doctor and pregnancy can be matters of *choice* that lead to the consumption of medical services. Elective medical care of this sort (case 3 in Chapter 5, Section 3.2) is not well covered by voluntary policies: some risks are uninsurable in private markets, at least for voluntary individual policies.

Moral hazard arises also through the *third-party payment* problem (case 4 in Chapter 5, Section 3.2). The problem arises because (*a*) the insurance company is largely divorced from the decisions of doctor and patient, and (*b*) the doctor is paid a fee for service. At its simplest, if medical insurance covers all costs, health care is 'free' to the patient, and the supplier is not constrained by the patient's ability to pay. Patient and doctor both face zero *private* costs, even though the *social* costs of health care are positive and frequently large, and both have an incentive to consume all health care that yields *any* private benefit. The result is over-consumption—i.e. Q_1, greater than the efficient outcome, Q^*, in Figure 12.2.

Matters, however, can be more complex. The doctor is an agent for *two* principals—the patient and the insurance company. As a result, 'the relation between health care and health outcomes is so loose that performance guarantees cannot be given to either principal; this is a kind of information asymmetry that faces both ways and that is perhaps even shared by the agent him- or herself' (Blomqvist 1991).

An additional problem—transactions costs—requires separate discussion. We saw earlier (equation (5.17)) that insurance, even if efficient on the supply side, can be provided at a price that the individual is prepared to pay only if his degree of risk aversion is sufficient to cover the insurer's administrative costs and normal profit. If transactions costs are too high, some risk-averse individuals will choose not to insure. This is not *per se* inefficient if high transactions costs are unavoidable. But it is inefficient if an alternative system could avoid them—for example, private medical insurance in the USA has high accounting costs; these are avoided by the NHS, which rarely has to send patients a bill.

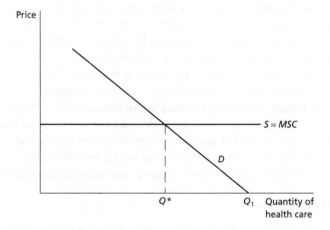

Fig. 12.2. A simple market for health care

The theory thus predicts that conventional medical insurance will face two sets of problems.

- *Gaps in coverage* arise for risks such as chronic and congenital illness, the medical needs of the elderly, and primary health care.
- *Inefficiency* occurs in various forms, particularly over-prescription of medical care as a result of third-party incentives.

The first set of difficulties, plus the problem that arises if transactions costs are high, all lead to *under-consumption*. Third-party payments cause *over-consumption*.

SOLUTIONS. There are two lines of attack on these problems: market solutions and the adoption of different forms of intervention. As discussed in Chapter 5, Section 3.2, insurers have adopted various devices to contain costs. They can limit cover: premiums can rise disproportionately with the degree of cover sought; and there can be less-than-full cover through deductibles (where the insured person pays the first X of any claim) and coinsurance (where the insured person pays x per cent of any claim). Such devices reduce the demand for treatment. None is a complete solution: deductibles, except for small claims, do nothing to face individuals with the *marginal* cost of treatment; and, with a coinsurance rate of, say, 20 per cent, the patient's private marginal cost is only 20 per cent of marginal social cost. Alternatively, insurers can seek to influence the supply side by restricting treatment to certain providers, who then face competitive pressures to retain approved status.

However, there is no complete solution to moral hazard for two reasons. As discussed in Chapter 5, Section 3.2, the root problem is the imperfect information of insurers about the behaviour of the insured (hence the description of moral hazard as 'hidden action'). In addition, as discussed in Section 2.2, 'health' is hard both to define and to measure, making it difficult to specify contractually what treatment is covered for different medical conditions.

Intervention can reduce inefficiency in a number of ways. Insurance could be compulsory to prevent the externalities caused by non-insurance (Chapter 8, Section 2.1), with cover starting before birth to cope with the congenitally and chronically ill. As discussed in Chapter 5, Section 3.2, a partial solution to adverse selection is to make membership (e.g. of an employer scheme) compulsory to prevent low risks opting out. Alternatively, regulation could prevent insurance companies from withholding cover from high-risk individuals, simultaneously regulating the conditions under which they could increase premiums. Compulsory membership of national, provincial, or work-related systems of social insurance in various industrialized countries has a similar effect. Moral hazard would have to be left to dubiously effective devices like coinsurance, or to different types of insurance, like health maintenance organizations (discussed in Section 5).

Most industrial countries (the USA is an outlier) do not use actuarial insurance as the primary vehicle for finance. Two models predominate. Social insurance (as defined in Chapter 5, Section 4.2) abandons the model of actuarial insurance because it does not fit health care very well. Alternatively, medical care can be financed through the tax system.

The remaining assumptions

COMPETITION. The assumption of equal power was discussed earlier. The next step is to consider the applicability of perfect competition—that is, whether the markets for inputs such as skilled manpower and drugs are competitive. Doctors, it is argued, do not act like the profit-maximizing monopolists of elementary textbooks. Two sets of issues are relevant: doctors' motivation and the economic environment in which they operate.

Doctors may be motivated more by professional reputation than by money: that reputation may depend more on assessment by professional peers than on evaluation by the consumer; and peer approval is more easily achieved by developing more advanced techniques (e.g. heart transplants). Thus, there can be a bias towards certain glamorous types of treatment. Alternatively, a doctor's motivation may be individually determined. Le Grand distinguishes two sets of motives: a 'knight' is motivated by public service—for example, the benefit of the patient; a 'knave' pursues his or her self-interest—for example, maximizing charges and minimizing hours of work (see Le Grand 2003; ch. 7 discusses health care explicitly).

Doctors' behaviour is determined jointly by their motives and their economic environment. As discussed above, doctors may not face the costs of their decisions, but are reimbursed by insurers. There is no budget constraint facing doctors individually; and on aggregate they are constrained only by the willingness of consumers or employers to pay insurance premiums. These arguments point towards oversupply of health care generally. In addition, the *composition* of that supply may be distorted in favour of glamorous areas.

What solutions exist for non-competitive behaviour? At a minimum, regulation is required on standards (e.g. doctors must have approved qualifications), plus perhaps some regulation of prices and possibly also monitoring of doctors' activities. Another potential solution is the libertarian approach (see the Further Reading) of removing entry barriers to medical practice, thereby enhancing competitiveness on the supply side and largely removing the need for state intervention of the type just described. This solution may be more apparent than real. The advantages of competition are that it increases consumer choice and minimizes costs. As we saw in Chapter 4, Section 3.2, however, an increase in the range of choice improves efficiency only where consumers are sufficiently well informed to make choices, which is frequently not the case with health care; and, if competitive forces push down prices, consumers, for the same reason, are unable to assess whether quality has declined, and if so whether they want the lower-quality product at the lower price. The counter-argument to the proponents of unrestricted market systems for health care is that *the advantages of competition are contingent on perfect information.*

The conclusion is that supply-side deviations from competitive behaviour may cause inefficiency; but removing restrictions to competition is unlikely *on its own* to improve economic welfare.

EXTERNALITIES AND INCREASING RETURNS TO SCALE. The literature on health care distinguishes two sorts of externality: 'caring' externalities, such that my utility is reduced if you receive less health care than I think you should (these are a matter more of the *distribution* of health care than the efficiency of its production (see Section 3.2)); and technological externalities.[7] The latter arise mainly via communicable diseases (e.g. if I am vaccinated against polio I benefit, and also confer a benefit on you because you cannot now catch

---

[7] On the definition and effects of externalities, and possible remedies, see Chapter 4, Section 3.2, and/or the Appendix to Chapter 4, para. 15.

polio from me). In the context of today's medical technology, these externalities, though real, are only a small fraction of the total value of health care. It is a standard proposition that technological external benefits, if uncorrected, cause under-consumption by creating a divergence between private and social benefits. The problem can be solved in a variety of ways, the most relevant here being regulation (e.g. making vaccination compulsory) or a Pigovian subsidy. Externalities are not *per se* a justification for public production and allocation.

It is sometimes argued that health care is subject to increasing returns to scale (Chapter 4, Section 3.2, and Figure 4.4). In that case, health care would be a natural monopoly that, if uncorrected, would lead to under-consumption. However, the range of output over which health care exhibits increasing returns to scale is small, so the problem is unlikely to arise except, possibly, in sparsely populated areas.

For all these reasons, according to Blaug (1997: 4): 'the thrust of [Arrow's (1963)] essay was to show that health care markets *invariably* fail and that the best we can do is to minimise the consequences of market failure . . . what we can never do is entirely to eradicate the inherent inefficiencies of resource allocation in health' (emphasis added).

3.2. Theoretical arguments for intervention 2: Equity

HORIZONTAL EQUITY was discussed in Chapter 4, Section 4.3, in terms of perfect information (necessary for rational decisions) and equal power (necessary to enforce those decisions). Both may be lacking for consumers of health care (and school education). Equity issues arise most acutely where these problems affect the lower socio-economic groups most strongly (a likely occurrence if information is costly to acquire). Thus lower-income individuals may have less information relevant to choices about health; in addition, they may be less able to make use of any information they acquire. In such cases intervention in the following forms may improve equity as well as efficiency.

Regulation would be concerned with the professional qualifications of doctors and nurses, with drugs, and with medical facilities in both public and private sectors.

Where imperfect information causes under-consumption, a subsidy might be applied either to prices (e.g. free medical prescriptions) or to incomes. In most circumstances price subsidies are cheaper (Lindsay 1969): if the price of health care is subsidized, consumption will increase via both income *and* substitution effects; with an income subsidy only the income effect operates, so a larger subsidy is generally needed to bring about a given increase in consumption.

Where problems of inadequate information and inequality of power are serious, efficiency and equity may jointly be maximized by public allocation and/or production. In broad terms this depends on two factors: whether the private or public sector is more efficient at producing health care; and whether monitoring of standards is more effective in one sector or the other. This issue is discussed in Section 3.3.

VERTICAL EQUITY concerns the extent to which health care does or should redistribute from rich to poor. We saw in Chapter 7, Section 4, that (subject to various caveats) publicly provided health care is redistributive if (rich) individual R pays more tax contributions to its cost than (poor) P where each consumes the same quantity, and also if R consumes twice as much as P but pays more than twice as much in contributions. Why might this be thought desirable—why, in other words, might people care about the distribution of health care? A formal explanation is given by the voting model discussed in Chapter 4, Section 4.2. Suppose R's utility rises both with his own consumption and with P's. In particular, suppose that R's utility rises with 'good' consumption by P (e.g. health care or education) but falls with P's 'bad' consumption (e.g. beer and karaoke). This is a consumption externality of the type described by equation (4.17). It might, therefore, be rational for R to offer P a transfer of health-care costing, say, £300, but a cash transfer of only £100 (since P might spend the latter on 'bad' consumption). Given these offers, P might prefer the in-kind transfer to the lower cash amount (see Figure 4.6). If the difference between the two offers is sufficiently large, both rich *and* poor might vote for compulsory in-kind transfers of health care.

It is worth delving more deeply into the nature of the consumption externality. 'Good' consumption by the poor can raise the utility of the rich for two entirely different reasons. The rich might vote for transfers of health care for reasons of efficiency/self-interest. They might believe that a healthier workforce fosters economic growth; or that increased health care for the poor raises their productivity and/or reduces the cost of caring for them; or that such transfers prevent social unrest. This is the 'national-efficiency' argument (Chapter 2, Section 2.1) that gives rise to the Marxist interpretation of the welfare state (Chapter 3, Section 5.3). A completely different explanation is that some rich individuals care about the distribution of health care for reasons of altruism.

Thus, alongside efficiency arguments for public production and allocation, there may be powerful equity motives making it politically easier to make transfers in kind. The rich may favour them for selfish or altruistic reasons; and the poor may prefer them, either because the in-kind transfer is more generous than the cash offer, and/or because they feel less stigmatized by receiving benefits in kind than through means-tested cash transfers.

The voting model explains why *some* transfers of health care take place. But is the amount *optimal*? This was discussed in Chapter 4, Section 4.4. Libertarians support in-kind transfers as voluntary action by the rich, but not as coercion by the poor through the ballot box (Chapter 4, Section 4.1), and argue that redistribution under the existing system is greater than optimal. Socialists support in-kind transfers for their own sake, because they increase equality, and argue that redistribution of health care is almost certainly suboptimal.

THE ROLE OF GIVING. Previous discussion suggested two reasons for intervention to enhance equity: inadequacies of information or power may justify intervention to improve horizontal equity; and consumption externalities can explain in-kind transfers. The role of giving raises a third set of arguments. The analysis so far has treated health care as a commodity to which the standard economic arguments apply. But most societies, for generally accepted ethical reasons, decree that certain commodities that in principle are readily marketable should be excluded from the usual economic calculus. Thus, there is a free market for the purchase and sale of cattle but, in most countries, no similar market for babies, for wives, or for slaves. Titmuss (1970) argues that, for ethical and philosophical reasons, there should similarly be no market for blood, which should be donated to recipients. This, he argues, is a morally superior method of distribution.

Two questions arise: how valid are Titmuss's views about blood; and do the arguments generalize to other commodities? Whether blood should be given rather than allocated by the market is ultimately one of social values, so that no answer is unambiguously right or wrong. But Titmuss's views are rightly respected on moral grounds, and also because certain characteristics of blood make its allocation as a gift both feasible and (arguably) also efficient. The reasons for the latter view are threefold: the opportunity cost of the act of giving blood (e.g. the time and discomfort) is small; and that of losing a pint of blood effectively zero; furthermore, blood donation can create an altruistic externality, in as much as donors often experience a utility gain, not from the act of giving but from the thought of the benefit the blood will confer on others. These considerations together suggest that the marginal social cost of blood is likely to be low, and may be zero. In this case giving might be both morally superior *and* efficient.

This makes blood a special case, so that it is dangerous indiscriminately to generalize the notion of giving into areas like health care and education. The main reason is that the marginal social cost of health care is positive and often large. It is, therefore, an economic commodity. If a doctor spends more time with one patient, she will have less time to spend with others; and resources devoted to health care are at the expense of other uses (contrast the case of blood, the giving of which has virtually no opportunity cost to the donor, and which (*pace* Dracula) has no non-medical uses).[8] Thus, voluntary giving of health care and education, even if regarded as morally superior, will generally run into major allocative problems that do not arise with blood.

3.3. Types of intervention

Sections 3.1 and 3.2 discussed *why* the state might intervene. The next question is *how* best it might do so. Since the aim is jointly to maximize efficiency and equity, they are discussed together. Three types of regime are considered: market production and allocation (with or without income transfers); public production and allocation; and intermediate strategies. The analysis of market production is closely linked to privatization discussed in Chapter 4, Section 6, which should be read alongside this section (see especially Table 4.1, which is referred to extensively).

In bygone times, medical technology was cheap, so health care could be treated as a basic right like voting privileges; costly advances are making this approach unsustainable. Advances in medical technology, by increasing the range of feasible medical interventions, contribute to rising medical spending. Thus macro-efficiency (i.e. expenditure on health care as a proportion of national income) has become increasingly important in all industrial economies (Section 4.1). It is therefore more than usually important to be dispassionate in considering methods of allocation.

PURE MARKET PROVISION. Some writers (see the Further Reading) argue that health care is similar to food. On the demand side, consumers have preferences that they should be allowed to translate into their utility-maximizing consumption pattern. Supply will

---

[8] Though resources used in *processing* and *storing* blood do have alternative uses and hence a positive opportunity cost.

adjust to these preferences more efficiently if it is competitive. Government intervention destroys the fit between demand and supply, and the destruction is greatest if intervention takes the form of public production. Writers of this ilk favour privatization to the greatest extent possible—that is, ideally row 1 in Table 4.1, or for low-income families row 2.

We saw in Section 3.1 that health care comes nowhere near conforming with the standard assumptions, so that unrestricted market allocation is not a theoretically promising approach. But analysis of the pure market case is important to understanding the problems raised by health care. To focus the argument, discussion concentrates on two simple cases, initially assuming away non-competitive supply-side behaviour, and concentrating on problems of imperfect information on the demand side of the product market and the supply side of the insurance market.

Case 1. Assume initially that there is no insurance, so that consumption is constrained by price. In the presence of consumer ignorance (and to some extent also because of unequal power), the demand curve is not properly defined, but 'wobbly', as shown in Figure 12.1, so that the market-clearing quantity can be above or below the optimum. Uncorrected externalities lead to under-consumption, and non-competitive supply-side behaviour to under- or over-consumption, depending on doctors' motivation and the incentives they face. The result is inefficiency in the total volume of resources (i.e. macro-inefficiency), possibly substantial, though with no clear presumption of its direction, and also micro-inefficiency (i.e. the allocation of resources to different types of health care). There is also considerable inequity; the distribution of health care is determined by inequalities in the income distribution; and these inequalities are heightened if knowledge and power are correlated with income, and also by the absence of insurance and perfect capital markets. The overall result is likely to be *under-consumption* of health care.

Case 2. Assume that the insurer pays all bills in full. Consumption is no longer constrained by price, and is therefore determined mainly by the supplier; as a result, the indeterminacy of the patient's demand curve is less important. On the supply side, the doctor has no incentive to ration demand to the efficient quantity Q^* in Figure 12.2. Both patient and doctor can behave as though the cost of health care were zero, leading to *over-consumption* Q_1.[9] There is also inequity, since some individuals are unable to buy insurance (the old, the chronically ill, etc.), and others cannot afford insurance premiums that over-consumption has raised to an inefficiently high level.

These arguments do not necessarily apply to inputs, many of which can be privately produced—for example, food products (the NHS does not grow its own vegetables), drugs, beds, towels, X-ray machines, and so on. Some inputs of services might also be privately produced (e.g. food or laundry), provided that the costs of quality control are not excessive.

MIXED PUBLIC/PRIVATE INVOLVEMENT. To what extent might health care be based on mixed public/private involvement so as to avoid the worst problems of pure private provision? The desirability of such a package depends on two factors: would it be more efficient and

---

[9] There might be some pressures to economy—for example, from employers who pay for medical insurance for their employees.

equitable than other methods; and might it be politically more acceptable than NHS-type arrangements (as might be the case, for instance, in the USA)?

Production. The supply of medical treatment in a private market is crucially influenced by fee for service and third-party payments. Thus, as we saw above, the market output, Q_1 in Figure 12.2, exceeds the efficient output, Q^*. Third-party payments create a divergence between private and social costs and benefits, and hence cause a particular kind of externality. These, we know, can be dealt with in a number of ways, of which two are of special relevance. First, output could be restricted to Q^* by *regulation*; this would involve policing doctors' decisions, either by administrative means or through the imposition of a budget constraint (e.g. row 3(*b*) in Table 4.1).

Alternatively, it is possible to *internalize the externality* by merging the activities of doctor and insurance company, thereby forcing doctors to face the social marginal cost of the treatment they prescribe. The outstanding example of this approach is the notion of a *health maintenance organization* of the type now widespread in the USA (see the fuller discussion in Section 5.1). The essence of a health maintenance organization in this context is that *doctors* provide the insurance. As a result, the externality is internalized and there is no longer an incentive to over-prescribe. It might be possible by one of these methods to constrain private production to its efficient level.

Finance could be organized in one of two generic ways. One possibility is private finance plus residual state finance. 'Easy' cases (i.e. the insurable conditions of non-poor individuals) are financed by private insurance, subject to regulation in two ways: there would be minimum standards of coverage; and insurance would be compulsory because of the externality caused by non-insurance (see Chapter 8, Section 2.1). Two difficulties arise: non-insurable risks and the poor. The former, as we saw in Section 3.1, include congenital and chronic health problems, the medical needs of the elderly, visits to family doctors, and pregnancy. The state could deal with these cases either by subsidizing private insurance or by paying for treatment, through a residual public insurance scheme or out of tax revenues. The poor could be assisted similarly. This approach raises serious problems: there is the difficulty of defining borderlines, both as between the types of health-care problem that qualify for state assistance, and over the income level below which the poor are subsidized; policing would be necessary to prevent oversupply; and the familiar poverty trap (Chapter 10, Section 3) could arise for the poor.

A second possibility is state finance. Here the state pays medical bills through social insurance or from tax revenues. An analytically equivalent arrangement is compulsory membership of regulated, private, non-profit insurance institutions acting, in effect, as agents of the state. The advantages of this arrangement are twofold: the scheme's compulsory nature makes it possible with no efficiency loss to gear premiums to ability to pay rather than to risk (Chapter 5, Section 4.1); and its universal coverage (with respect to individuals and to type of illness) avoids problems with borderlines. Such social-insurance institutions, precisely because they are not strictly actuarial (i.e. because premiums are not risk-rated on an individual basis), can avoid the gaps of private schemes (cf. Chapter 8, Section 2.2, for the case of unemployment benefits).

These considerations suggest two coherent mixed strategies. Suppose that health care is *produced* by health maintenance organizations of some kind; that membership is compulsory for all individuals; and that insurance premiums are *financed* by individuals (in the case of the poor out of transfer incomes). This arrangement has the flavour of row 3(*a*) in Table 4.1. Alternatively, suppose health care is produced privately, but not by health maintenance organizations; payment is made by the state (directly, through social insurance, or through regulated medical insurance); and total output or expenditure is controlled by the state either directly or via a global budget constraint. This mechanism (broadly that of Canada) follows the general thrust of row 3(*b*) for health care *per se* and of row 6 for health-care insurance.

PUBLIC PRODUCTION, ALLOCATION, AND FINANCE. The elements of row 8 in Table 4.1 require separate justification. Consumer sovereignty is appropriate where information is sufficient for rational choice, a process that may be assisted by regulation of quality. In the case of health care, the patient's information is often so imperfect that the individual consumption decision is best made on his behalf by an agent (column 3). The argument for publicly financed health care (column 4) rests on the problems just discussed of private insurance—namely, the imperfect information of insurance companies (which contributes to the third-party-payment problem), and the fact that not all medical conditions are insurable. The third-party-payment problem can also justify public production as a method of controlling the resulting large and inefficient increases in the output of health care. More formally, the imperfect information of consumers justifies control of *quality*, and that of insurers control of *quantity* (column 2). Both forms of policing might be more effective if production itself were public (column 1).

The argument for public production and allocation thus turns in a crucial though complex way on the issue of information. To justify this arrangement, however, it is necessary to show not only that the conditions for market efficiency fail, but also that public production and allocation are less inefficient than other arrangements. The first point is relatively easy to establish, the second less so.

Because of information problems the NHS strategy can be regarded as feasible—an institution motivated largely by equity works because it goes with the grain of *efficiency* considerations. The strategy has four cornerstones. Dealing with demand-side problems:

- treatment is decided by doctors, thus addressing problems of consumer ignorance;
- health care is (mostly) tax financed and (mostly) free at the point of use.

These features avoid gaps in insurance by abandoning the insurance principle even as a fiction; and medical care is made available without stigma. On the supply side:

- there is little fee for service, reducing third-party-payment incentives to oversupply;
- health care is explicitly rationed, in part by administrative means, and partly by the existence of a budget constraint for the NHS as a whole. The idea, at least in principle, is to restrict consumption to the quantity Q^* in Figure 12.2.

Furthermore, once it is established that public production and allocation are justifiable on efficiency grounds, it is legitimate to finance health care so as to further distributional aims (Chapter 4, Section 7.2). In theory, therefore, the strategy is feasible in both efficiency and equity terms. We turn now to assessment of the practice.

4. Assessment of the UK system of health care

4.1. Institutions

This part of the chapter starts with an overview of the institutions of the National Health Service (NHS) and of private health care, and then attempts to assess the extent to which the NHS meets the aims of efficiency (Section 4.2) and social justice (Section 4.3).

The operation of the national health service

THUMBNAIL HISTORY. Since its inception, the NHS has been almost entirely publicly funded. On the delivery side, it is possible to see four phases.[10]

* Prior to 1991, the regime was essentially one of central planning.
* The period 1991–7 saw experiments with quasi-markets, discussed below, which introduced some competition between public providers.
* From 1997, there was a partial move away from market forces.
* From 2003 onwards, there was a partial reintroduction of competition.

Discussion is organized round the four areas in Table 4.1: the production of health care; the individual consumption decision (i.e. the system from the viewpoint of the consumer); finance; and the aggregate production decision (i.e. budget setting).

PRODUCTION OF HEALTH CARE UNDER THE NHS has a dual structure of primary health care, and hospitals and community health services.

Primary health care. The main element is the system of general practitioners (i.e. family doctors). Every individual is registered with a general practitioner (GP), who deals with straightforward complaints and chronic conditions, and refers patients to hospital and specialist services. In the latter case, the GP acts both as guide (to steer patients to the appropriate specialist) and as gatekeeper (to prevent trivial complaints being taken to a specialist). GPs also have a role in preventive medicine, including immunization, family planning, and cervical screening. Innovations introduced after 2000 include access to primary care through NHS Direct (a telephone system) and NHS Walk-in Centres.

Other major types of primary medical care are dentistry, pharmaceutical services, and ophthalmic services. Dentists are paid on a fee-for-service basis on an agreed scale, net of consumer charges (also on an agreed scale). Pharmacists dispense drugs, etc., for which they are reimbursed on the basis of costs plus a profit margin, but net of the consumer charges discussed below.

Hospitals and community health services. In the late-1990s, the hospital sector in England directly employed over 780,000 people, including 60,000 medical personnel and about 340,000 nursing staff (UK DoH 2002*b*: table D1). Hospital doctors are paid a salary rather than a fee for service, though, as discussed below, they may combine salaried work for the NHS with private practice.

---

[10] The health services in England, Wales, Scotland, and Northern Ireland are run separately and have differences. What follows is generic where possible; otherwise it describes the system in England.

Until 2004, most hospitals were overseen by governing bodies (Trusts) ultimately appointed by the Secretary of State, and were subject to considerable central control and target setting. Under legislation in 2003, Foundation Trusts, with a majority of local representation, were gradually to replace them. Foundation Trusts are able to borrow for capital purposes and to negotiate local wage rates. They finance their current expenditure from contracts with Primary Care Trusts (discussed below), which are responsible for ensuring their local populations have access to the full range of specialist care (see Glennerster 2003a: ch. 4). There are also a small number of private hospitals, about 4 per cent of beds, used by private fee-paying patients; and NHS hospitals can also take a small number of private fee-payers.

Community health services, also generally provided by trust-type organizations, have two functions: preventive health services, including health education, health visiting, screening and vaccination programmes, and maternity and child-welfare clinics; and cooperation with personal social-services departments, so that wherever possible health and social care can be dealt with together. Like hospitals, they, too, reach service agreements with Primary Care Trusts and are funded by them, increasingly in collaboration with local social-services departments.

THE INDIVIDUAL CONSUMPTION DECISION. Apart from the charges described below, health care under the NHS is free. The main source of health care for most people is their GP. Individuals are free to register with any NHS GP in their area who is prepared to add them to his list of patients. Anyone who wishes, for whatever reason, to change to another GP may do so. No charge is made for consultations or for home visits. The GP prescribes treatment or, in more complex or serious cases, refers the patient to an NHS hospital.

Where a GP prescribes drugs, the patient pays a fixed charge per item—for example, per bottle of tablets. Broad classes of people are exempt, notably children, expectant mothers, older people, and people with low incomes. As a result, about 85 per cent of prescriptions are free—disproportionately for people who make the greatest use of drugs. As in other countries, the UK's drug bill has increased sharply in recent years.

A patient is usually referred to hospital by his GP, but in emergencies this procedure is bypassed. Treatment is free, including tests, consultations with doctors, nursing, drugs, and intensive care, whatever the complaint and however long the hospital stay. All the facilities of the NHS are available to anyone living in the UK, apart from temporary residents. Historically, GPs were limited as to which hospitals they could refer patients. Under new plans, by 2005 patients will be able to choose their hospital, and the hospital will be paid for the treatment given.

FINANCE. Expenditure on the NHS (around 7 per cent of GDP in 2003/4) has been low by international standards. Expenditure has risen since the mid-1970s for several reasons. There was a 'bulge' in the birth rate in 1948 and another in the mid-1960s (Figure 9.1). The number of old people has increased, intensifying the demand on facilities.[11] Costly new techniques have led to increased expectations. The relative price effect has raised

---

[11] Health spending per person by age is U-shaped, being very high at birth and in old age, and low in between (see UK DoH 2002c: figure 6.3).

Table 12.1. Health, UK, 2003/4 (est.) (£m.)

National Health Service		
NHS hospitals, community health, NHS Trusts	66,826	
NHS family health services	7,589	
Other	1,629	
		76,044
Charges and capital receipts		−3,924
Other		2,729
Total health		74,849
Personal social services[a]		12,526
TOTAL HEALTH AND PERSONAL SOCIAL SERVICES		87,375

[a] England.
Sources: UK Treasury (2002a: tables 7.1, 7.2, A3); UK DoH (2002c: annex A4).

the cost of health care by more than the average increase in prices.[12] Separately, a political decision was taken in 2002 to increase spending on the NHS towards a target of 9.4 per cent of GDP in 2007/8, bringing the UK more into line with spending levels in the rest of Western Europe.

The funding of the NHS is discussed in detail by Glennerster (2003a: ch. 4). Of the total cost of the NHS shown in Table 12.1, about 74 per cent came from general taxation, about 20 per cent from national-insurance contributions and about 2.5 per cent from charges.

Primary Care Trusts, introduced in 1997, are allocated funds by the national government on a population basis, weighted to take account both of differential demand and of unmet need, estimated in terms of readily measurable characteristics of the relevant population such as age, sex, socio-economic indicators, and health status. The budgets are used to purchase hospital care, community and domiciliary services like home nursing, and the drugs prescribed by GPs. Primary Care Trusts are thus a form of health maintenance organization (discussed in Section 5), but determined on the basis of residence rather than individual choice.

General practitioners' remuneration has been complex ever since they were persuaded to join the new NHS in 1948 as private individuals. Historically, the NHS contracted with individual GPs, who were paid a given sum for each patient for whom they agreed to take full responsibility. In addition, they were paid for a range of costs of maintaining their practice, with additional funding if they provided extra services. Under a new contractual relationship introduced in 2003, the NHS contracts not with individuals GPs, but with 'practices', usually a group of GPs plus supporting primary care staff. Each practice must provide a standard range of services and can be paid extra for providing

---

[12] The relative price effect (also referred to as 'excess medical inflation') measures the extent to which the price of services like health care tends to rise faster than prices generally. There are two reasons: first, throughout the economy the price of labour tends to rise faster than the general price level (i.e. real earnings rise); and, secondly, health care has a higher than average direct labour content, about three-quarters of NHS current spending being on directly employed staff. The same, broadly, is true of education. See Baumol (1996).

more specialist services previously supplied by hospital outpatient departments or community agencies.

Hospitals, until 1991, were generally both financed and managed by Health Authorities, institutional budgets being incrementally negotiated each year. Reforms in 1991 sought to improve efficiency by separating the finance of health care from its provision. The intention was that Health Districts should buy health care from the most efficient providers, public or private, inside or outside their District, to which GPs could then refer their patients (some larger general practices could act like Health Districts in this respect). Since 1997, hospitals have been financed mainly by the Primary Care Trusts just discussed.

Consultants. NHS hospitals have specialist consultants who are contracted to work for the NHS, but can choose whether to do so full-time or part-time. In changes introduced in 2003, each consultant's contract is directly with a hospital Trust, in contrast with previous arrangements where the contract was with a much higher-level unit of administration: the idea behind the change is to facilitate loyalty to the Trust. The same reforms also introduced stronger financial incentives to work full-time for a Trust rather than partly in private practice.

THE AGGREGATE PRODUCTION DECISION—that is, setting budget limits. The annual budget for the NHS is determined in the same way as the budget for defence or any other government service, as the result of negotiation between the Treasury and spending departments, as modified by subsequent discussion in Cabinet. The figure that emerges is a global budget for the NHS as a whole, which is divided between England, Scotland, Wales, and Northern Ireland. Within England, resources are allocated by the Secretary of State to each District on the basis of a complex formula related to population and estimates of medical need. The process is therefore largely one of 'top-down' allocation, constrained by expenditure in previous years. Primary Care Trusts and Districts are cash limited (i.e. they have to operate within a fixed annual budget).

Private health care

Alongside the NHS is a system of private health care. An individual can consult a GP privately, in which case he pays the GP's fees and the full cost of any drugs; he can be referred to a consultant either through the NHS or privately; and the consultant can refer him to hospital either through the NHS or privately. Though the private sector has grown somewhat over the years, it remains small. In 2000, 11.5 per cent of the population had some private medical insurance, up from 4 per cent twenty-five years earlier (Mossialos and Thomson 2002). Benefits are only a small fraction of NHS spending. Private medical care is used mainly for the convenience of a private room or (more contentiously) by those facing a long wait for treatment under the NHS, and only for a narrow range of less complex treatment.

Most private health care is financed by voluntary insurance, which historically has been cheap in the UK for four reasons: most patients use an NHS GP even if they see a specialist privately; the NHS provides a back-up if patients present complications beyond the capacity of a private hospital; people with private insurance are usually young and employed (their health-care insurance is often a fringe benefit) and hence low risk; finally, health care is cheaper in the UK than, for example, the USA, not least because UK doctors and nurses are paid less.

The relationship between private health care and the NHS has been a source of continuing controversy. NHS hospitals have specialist consultants who are contracted to work for the NHS, but can choose whether to do so full-time or part-time. The existence of 'pay beds' within the NHS has aroused the greatest controversy. It is argued that people with money can jump the queue without necessarily paying the full economic cost of treatment, and many regard this as inequitable. Others argue that private patients bring extra income to some consultants, and that to ban private practice by NHS employees would result in large and costly pay demands, and possibly the loss of highly skilled specialists. The issue remains highly contentious.

International comparisons

Before turning to an assessment of the NHS, it is helpful to have some perspective on the organization and problems of systems elsewhere (see the Further Reading). In the broadest of terms, all industrialized countries adopt one of the three models.

- *The quasi-actuarial approach* is characterized by employer-based or individual insurance, and by private ownership of medical factors of production. The closest approximation (and the only major example among OECD economies) is the USA.
- *Earnings-related social-insurance contributions* are characterized by compulsory coverage financed by earnings-related employee contributions and/or an employer payroll tax, possibly supplemented by tax funding. Such funding regimes are compatible with a larger (Canada) or smaller (Germany) role for the private sector.
- *'Universal' medical care* is characterized by tax funding and public ownership and/or control of the factors of production (e.g. Sweden, the UK).

PROBLEMS. Inspection of the international scene suggests considerable similarity in two strategic areas: the pervasiveness of regulation in *all* health-care systems and problems of cost containment (on the latter, see Mossialos and Le Grand 1999). Since fee for service paid by a third party is the most common way of paying doctors, it is not surprising, despite the variety of their institutions, that most countries have at one time or another experienced a dramatic escalation in health expenditures because of the third-party-payment problem (Section 3.1). The UK is one of the few countries to have escaped these pressures, largely because of parliamentary control of public expenditure.

The situation in the USA is a textbook example. Prior to the 1960s the system was broadly one of private production financed by private medical insurance. But problems arose, and as a response Medicare (for the old) and Medicaid (for the poor) were introduced in the mid-1960s. The modification they introduced was simple: the poor and old continued to receive private treatment, but their medical bills were now paid out of federal/state funds. The effect of these unlimited third-party payments was entirely predictable: public spending on health care rose sharply to the point where health spending became the second largest item in the federal budget, slightly smaller than income support, but larger than defence and debt interest (the classic article is Robert G. Evans 1974; see also Fuchs 2000, Charles Jones 2002). Not least for this reason, as Table 12.2 shows, US medical spending is by a long way the highest of any country, at 13.9 per cent of GDP in 2001; the comparable figures for Canada are 9.7 per cent and the UK just over

Table 12.2. Health spending per head and as per cent of GDP, various countries, 2001

Country	Health spending per head, US$ PPP	Health spending, per cent of GDP
Australia	2,350[a]	8.9[a]
Austria	2,191	7.7
Belgium	2,490	9.0
Canada	2,792	9.7
Czech Republic	1,105	7.3
Denmark	2,503	8.6
Finland	1,841	7.0
France	2,561	9.5
Germany	2,808	10.7
Greece	1,511	9.4
Hungary	911	6.8
Iceland	2,643	9.2
Ireland	1,935	6.5
Italy	2,212	8.4
Japan	1,984[a]	7.6[a]
Korea	893[a]	5.9[a]
Luxembourg	2,719[a]	5.6[a]
Mexico	586	6.6
Netherlands	2,626	8.9
New Zealand	1,710	8.1
Norway	3,012	8.3
Poland	629	6.3
Portugal	1,614	9.2
Slovak Republic	682	5.7
Spain	1,600	7.5
Sweden	2,270	8.7
Switzerland	3,160[a]	10.9
United Kingdom	1,992	7.6
United States	4,887	13.9
OECD average		8.4

[a] 2000.
Source: OECD (2003a).

7 per cent. The differences in real spending per head of population are even larger, at $4,887 in the USA, $2,792 in Canada, and $1,992 in the UK. France, which came out top of the World Health Organization rankings in 2002 (World Health Organization 2001: annex table 1) had spending figures very close to those in Canada.

There are two possible arguments against the assertion that high medical spending in the USA is, at least in part, an inefficient response to inadequately policed third-party incentives. Americans might have a greater taste for health care than the British (i.e. demand is higher in the USA); or Americans might suffer more health problems (i.e. need is greater). If the former, we would expect high-spending countries to enjoy better health; if the latter, that they suffer more illness. Neither phenomenon is the case. Notwithstanding the spending figures just discussed, infant mortality and life expectancy in the USA are no better than in the UK. The US story is taken up in Section 5.1.

SOLUTIONS. Two broad classes of solution—regulation, and the use of incentives—have been adopted to try to contain costs (for fuller discussion, see Barr 2001*a*: ch. 4).

Regulation is pervasive and inescapable. The logic is simple: expenditure = price × quantity. Successful cost containment must (*a*) control total spending directly, or (*b*) control price and quantity, or (*c*) use price control to reinforce an overall spending constraint. Control of medical fees (i.e. price control) with open-ended budgets only partially contains costs because of the incentive for doctors to increase output to compensate for lost income. This is exactly what happened with Medicare in the USA (Robert G. Evans 1974; Robert G. Evans et al. 1989). Canada, in contrast, managed to avoid the worst of the Medicare cost explosion because it adopted both price control *and* a global budget ceiling. European countries, too, have developed systems that combine price and expenditure control (Mossialos and Le Grand 1999).

Whatever the system, successful methods of restricting supply to around its efficient level all include the imposition of budget limits either on public expenditure (the UK, Sweden) or on insurance disbursements (Canada). This is an important conclusion because the demand for health care will increase in the future not only with advances in medical technology but also because of population ageing in many countries.

Incentives to economy take various forms. The third-party-payment problem arises because health-care providers are reimbursed retrospectively on what is, in effect, a cost-plus basis. The idea of *prospective payment* is becoming increasingly widespread. In one form, each hospital receives a fixed annual global budget that it can spend as it wishes. Other mechanisms, including diagnosis-related groups and health maintenance organizations, are discussed in Section 5.1.

Other forms of incentive have also been tried, including cost sharing (where the patient pays part of the cost of treatment), privatization, and (particularly in the USA) attempts to increase competition between providers.

4.2. Assessment 1: Efficiency

As discussed in Section 2.1, efficiency can be defined in principle but is hard to measure, mainly because of difficulties in measuring (*a*) the benefits of health care as opposed to other activities (the *macro*-efficiency issue), and (*b*) the relative benefits in different areas of health care (*micro*-efficiency). Quantitative work on both is scant, so that relatively little is known about the health gains deriving from different types of intervention. Thus discussion is largely based on *a priori* argument.

Assessment of the efficiency, or otherwise, of the NHS is organized under four broad heads: advantages in principle; advantages in practice; criticisms with little validity; and criticisms that are valid. The NHS has at least four efficiency advantages in principle.

1. *Supply-side incentives* to economize arise, first, from the way remuneration is organized. Doctors are not generally paid a fee for service. Thus there is no financial incentive to oversupply. There is no argument of principle against paying doctors a high salary—the crucial point is that it is not related to medical activity. GPs are paid mainly on the basis of capitation, to contain costs, with some fee for service to encourage particular preventive activities. A pure capitation system gives GPs an incentive to increase the size of their lists, but to decrease the time spent with any one patient. To that extent there is an incentive for GPs either to *undersupply* or to pass patients to the hospital sector. The argument should not be overstated, however. First it assumes that doctors are 'knaves' (Le Grand 2003). Secondly, even for knavish doctors the fee-for-service element encourages preventive activity. Thirdly, a patient who feels she is receiving inadequate attention can transfer to another doctor, thereby reducing the original GP's income.[13]

A second form of constraint is the NHS budget (a macro-efficiency point), coupled with the control exercised by the NHS over doctors' behaviour and the traditions of the medical profession in the UK. The overall result is that there is no financial incentive to supply excessive medical care, Q_1 in Figure 12.2, rather than the socially optimal quantity, Q^*. This is true both for health care as a whole and for different types of treatment, though with a question mark over the possibility of undersupply by GPs.

2. *The individual-consumption decision.* The decision about treatment is generally made by doctors. This ameliorates the information problem. In addition, a patient may place more trust on a decision based on clinical judgement unclouded by financial motives.

3. *Finance* for the most part is from general taxation, avoiding problems in insurance markets (Chapter 5, Section 3 and Section 3.1). To the extent that taxes are based on ability to pay there are also equity advantages, discussed below.

4. *Treatment* is mostly free at the point of use. This encourages early diagnosis, reduces the externality problem, and has equity advantages.

The system has advantages also in practical terms.

5. *Macro-efficiency.* As Table 12.2 shows, the NHS is cheap by international standards, though health outcomes are not out of line with those elsewhere. Klein's argument (1984: 15) that 'the NHS seems to be a remarkably successful instrument for making the rationing of scarce resources socially and politically acceptable' remains broadly true, though political pressures led to the significant increases in funding discussed in point 9, below.

6. *Micro-efficiency.* We shall see shortly that the NHS is not above criticism for the way it allocates resources to different areas of health care. But it also has advantages. Its unified structure enables action to be taken on overall medical priorities (see points 10 and 11 below); and the absence, for the most part, of fee for service reduces adverse incentives.

Two criticisms sometimes made of the NHS do not hold water.

7. *The NHS is a monopoly.* The first argument is that consumers have no choice. This is not the case. They are free to choose (and change) their GP, to ask for a second opinion, or to opt for private medical care. A different argument is that the NHS spends too much

---

[13] The capitation element of GPs' pay under the NHS thus approximates to a voucher system.

on bureaucracy. In fact, NHS administrative spending is low by international standards. In the USA, in contrast, Himmelstein and Woolhandler (1997) estimate that administrative costs averaged 26 per cent of total hospital costs.[14] Davis and Cooper (2003) found that the combined administrative spending of public and private programmes in 2002 was $111 billion (broadly equivalent to the entire NHS budget), with a projected figure for 2012 of $222 billion. A third argument is that the NHS is too centralized. Centralization, however, can have advantages: it makes it possible to establish priorities; and the NHS can use its powers as a monopsony to negotiate lower prices for drugs. In addition, reforms since the early 1990s have given hospital Trusts considerable autonomy.

8. *Work effort.* Doctors, it is argued, work less hard if they are not paid a fee for service and/or the best and most innovative individuals will be lost to the profession (this is the issue of *dynamic* efficiency). There are two lines of attack on this position. It assumes uncritically that labour supply is motivated solely by financial gain, but loses plausibility if one allows for non-money wages and a tradition of service. Many professionals—academics, lawyers, and accountants—are paid salaries, yet it is not argued that they should be paid a fee for service. In Le Grand's terms (2003), doctors can be knights as well as knaves. A second counter-argument is that, even if work effort/innovation is substantially motivated by high pay, it might well suffice to base remuneration on high salaries rather than fee for service.

To rebut these arguments is not to say that no criticism is possible.

9. *Macro-inefficiency.* Some commentators argue that too few resources are devoted to the NHS, aggravating waiting lists for non-urgent (and some urgent) treatment. Pro-market writers argue that the NHS *causes* too few resources to be devoted to medical care; but international comparison suggests that private systems can lead to excessive production that regulation has only partly curtailed. There are at least two reasons why there is no definitive answer to the funding question: first, the health benefits of different medical interventions are hard, if not impossible, to measure; secondly, 'the optimal level of health funding is a normative question dictated partly by the aggregate tastes and preferences of society' (McGuire 1994: 147). For these and other reasons, there is little *scientific* support for the idea of a major funding crisis in the NHS (see McGuire 1994; Dixon 1997; A. H. Harrison et al. 1997*a*, *b*). There is considerably more *political* support for additional funding. Not least for these reasons, in 2002 the government announced a substantial increase in spending on the NHS, aiming to reach 9.4 per cent of GDP by 2007/8.

10. *Micro-inefficiency in the geographical allocation of resources.* The initial location of facilities was largely a matter of historical accident and over time matched the location and age structure of the population less well. The Resource Allocation Working Party (UK DHSS 1976) made specific proposals for geographical reallocation on the basis of the size and demographic structure of the population in an area, health indicators such as local mortality and fertility, and gaps in existing provision. As a result, resources were shifted away from London and the south-east of England. A range of policies over the

---

[14] The overall figure broke down into 34% of the costs of private, for-profit hospitals, 24.5% for private, non-profit hospitals, and 23% for public hospitals.

years continued to improve the match of resources with need, so that by 2000/1 only three health authorities in England were more than 4 per cent away from the amount specified by the formula. Subsequent policy established a more ambitious aim. Instead of seeking to equalize access to health care, policy aimed at reducing health inequalities by targeting additional resources on areas with poorer health outcomes (see Glennerster 2003a: 64, and, for a historical overview, Glennerster et al. 2000).

11. *Micro-inefficiency in the allocation of resources to different types of health care*. Reforms after 2002 (see Section 5.3) were introduced to address a series of problems. Incentives could be perverse—for example, a consultant who treats more patients gets extra work but no extra resources. Secondly, over-centralization, particularly through national pay agreements, led to staffing problems in high-wage parts of the country like London. Thirdly, there was a lack of accountability: no one knew what anything cost or whether they were keeping within their budget. Fourthly, the system was inflexible—for example, it was difficult to close an unwanted hospital.

In addition to action to increase efficiency within the NHS, there is also scope for better coordination between NHS activities and related activities paid from the social-security budget and local-authority budgets. Care for the frail elderly, for example, gives respite to their carers and thus helps to keep older people out of hospital or long-term residential care; similarly, care packages for elderly people waiting to leave hospital can reduce hospital stays, with benefits for both the person concerned and the NHS budget.

Greater efficiency requires two sorts of information:

- technical information, in particular on the costs and health benefits of different types of treatment;
- social and political information to generate a set of weights to be applied to relevant non-medical criteria (e.g. whether the patient has dependants).

Information on the first is woeful. The problem is largely intractable because of the major problems (particularly of measuring health and of attributing causality) discussed in Section 2.2; thus progress is likely to be slow and incomplete. That said, a legitimate criticism of the NHS is that it gathers *too little* information.

12. *Productive inefficiency* (i.e. internal inefficiency) is also a problem, which the 2002 reforms (Section 5.3) sought to address.

4.3. Assessment 2: Equity

As we saw in Chapter 4, Sections 2.2 and 4.3, equity cannot be defined unambiguously, but depends on political values; in addition (Chapter 6, Section 3.1), the definition of equality is fraught with ambiguities. For present purposes horizontal equity is defined in terms of equality of opportunity in respect of health care, as set out in Section 2.1. Thus individuals A and B with identical medical conditions should receive equal treatment unless other relevant differences exist (e.g. one of them has young or old dependants); irrelevant considerations (e.g. that A is rich and B poor) should make no difference. How closely does the NHS approximate this ideal?

13. *The unimportance of income.* The quantity of health care an individual receives is largely (though as we shall see not wholly) unconstrained by her income. No one is denied health care because of poverty; and no one goes in fear of financial ruin as a result of expensive medical treatment.

14. *The system accords with British notions of social justice* and, notwithstanding increasing pressures from the late 1990s, remains popular politically. A leaked report of a proposal in the late 1980s under Margaret Thatcher's government to introduce significant privatization caused such a political backlash that reforms in 1991 preserved the basic principles of publicly funded and publicly produced health care.

15. *The system allows action on the distribution of health care by region*, which, as a result of the policy discussed in point 10, is considerably more equal than previously.

16. *The distribution of health* is controversial. Black's conclusion (1980) that disparities in health across UK socio-economic groups had widened over the lifetime of the NHS were disputed by Le Grand (1987*a*, 1989). The essence of Le Grand's argument was that the composition of socio-economic groups had changed, so that the lowest group in the 1980s was more disadvantaged relative to the median than the lowest group forty years earlier. Le Grand therefore measured inequality in health outcomes not through data on socio-economic *groups* but by measuring the Gini coefficient (see Chapter 6, Section 4) for *individual* data on age-at-death. Le Grand (1987*a*: table 1) concluded that the most equal countries included the UK, the Netherlands, and Sweden; the least equal countries included the USA (measuring mortality inequality in terms of the Gini coefficient, the only country consistently less equal than the USA was Romania).

Recent findings point to a striking relationship between health and socio-economic variables (for a cogent survey, see Robert G. Evans 1996). Wilkinson (1996) finds that among developed countries it is not the richest societies that have the best health but the most equal. Smaller income differences raise average life expectancy. Morris et al. (1994) find a significant link between loss of employment and mortality. Studies of British civil servants (Marmot et al. 1991; North et al. 1993) find that people with less control over their work suffer poorer health outcomes. Not least because of such findings, the Labour government in the years after 1997 placed renewed emphasis on the links between poverty, inequality, and ill health.

17. *The distribution of health care.* Three issues arise: the empirical facts; the explanation of those facts; and implications for policy. Le Grand (1982: ch. 3) argues that the NHS does not achieve equality of use. 'The evidence suggests that the top socio-economic group receives 40 per cent more NHS expenditure per person reporting illness than the bottom one' (Le Grand 1982: 46).

This result can be explained (see Figure 12.3) in terms of two sets of factors. The benefits of health care perceived by poorer people (MPV_P) may be lower than those of the rich (MPV_R) (e.g. if the poor have worse information); or the poor might rationally place a lower value on health (e.g. smoking might be one of the few pleasures of someone whose life is otherwise miserable); or the actual benefits to poorer people might be lower if doctors treat them less effectively than middle-class patients. Probably of greater importance, the poor face higher costs of health care. Since treatment is free, the main cost is time. Travel time is generally higher for poorer people, who more often have to rely on public

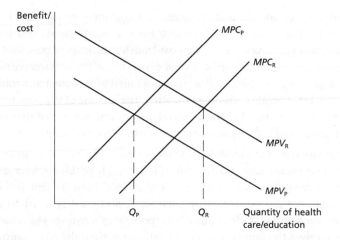

Fig. 12.3. Differences in the costs and benefits of health care/education by socio-economic group

transport; and the cost of time is generally higher for the poor, who often lose pay if they spend a morning in a hospital outpatient clinic, a cost not faced by people on salaries. These factors taken together can explain why in practice Q_R in Figure 12.3 is 40 per cent higher than Q_P.

These results were controversial. Powell (1995) disputes Le Grand's premiss, that equality is *the* objective. Consider the ratio B_R/B_P, where B_R is the benefit going to the rich and B_P that going to the poor. The objectives of the welfare state include:

- *insurance and consumption-smoothing*: for these purposes, $B_R/B_P > 1$ may well be right; for the purposes of consumption smoothing, for example, pensions should rise with income;

- *poverty relief*: for this purpose B_R/B_P should be less than one; the tighter the targeting the greater the extent to which B_R/B_P should tend to zero;

- *social cohesion*, which implies that B_R/B_P should tend to one.

Thus whether $B_R/B_P > 1$ is a problem depends in part on the objective. Inequality in the distribution of welfare state benefits is not *necessarily* a sign of failure.

Secondly, various writers, using more disaggregated data, dispute Le Grand's empirical results. They find that people with lower incomes receive more health care but have poorer health, and conclude that the NHS delivers broadly equal care for equal need (Propper 2001).

What implications can be drawn from these results? Even if it does not fully achieve the objective of equal treatment for equal need, the NHS can still be an equalizing force. First, the NHS cannot be regarded as a failure unless an alternative system of health care is more equalizing. International comparison offers no strong evidence for such a proposition.

Secondly, whether or not the NHS is an equalizing force depends not only on the distribution of benefits but also on whether expenditure is discussed not in isolation but, more properly, in conjunction with the taxation which finances it (Chapter 7, Section 4.2). The argument is important, and worth spelling out. Suppose that the pre-transfer incomes of poor and rich are 20 and 80; that all income is taxed away by the state to provide free goods and services; and that the rich receive twice as many goods and services as the (equally numerous) poor. As a result, the post-transfer incomes of poor and rich are $33\frac{1}{3}$ and $66\frac{2}{3}$, respectively. From the perspective of expenditure, the rich receive twice as much as the poor, suggesting that public allocation has failed as an equalizing force. But when expenditure and taxation are considered together, the income of the poor has been raised both absolutely from 20 to $33\frac{1}{3}$, and relatively, from one-quarter of that of the rich to one-half. On either count, the system taken as a whole is equalizing.

18. *Redistributive effects of the NHS.* To what extent is the NHS thus financed progressively? In practice, measurement raises almost insuperable problems, *inter alia* because of the difficulty of measuring the incidence of taxes and benefits, but the *logic* is clear (Chapter 7, Section 4.2, as qualified by Chapter 7, Section 4.1). If (rich) individual R contributes on average, say, twice as much as (poor) P in whatever tax is used to pay for the NHS, but receives the same quantity of health care, then the NHS redistributes from rich to poor (i.e. is progressive). But if R contributes twice as much but consumes four times as much as P then the NHS is regressive.

Empirically, the NHS is financed progressively. Propper (1995: 202) concludes that 'the gainers are those in the lowest six decile groups and women, the losers are those in the top four decile groups and men'.

Additionally, even if the redistributive effect is weak, the NHS is still an equalizing force if it reduces inequality more than any alternative system. International studies (Wagstaff et al. 1999; Gerdttham and Jönsson 2000) find that the NHS scores well in this respect. A plausible conclusion is not that the NHS has failed, but that it may not be as strong an equalizing force as some of its supporters hoped. This suggests that egalitarian aims are likely to be served better by keeping and improving the NHS than by replacing it.

5. Reform

This section discusses three strategic reform directions: addressing the problems of mainly private systems; systems with privately produced but publicly funded health care; and reforms within the NHS, including discussion of quasi-markets.

5.1. Mainly private approaches

RADICAL PRIVATIZATION. The failure of virtually all the standard assumptions[15] (Section 3.1) suggests that an unrestricted private market (i.e. rows 1 or 2 in Table 4.1) is likely to be highly inefficient for technical reasons (Section 3.1), and also inconsistent with widely held notions of social justice (Section 3.2). That view, as we saw in Section 4.1, is confirmed by empirical observation. Countries that have adopted careless *ad hoc*

---

[15] i.e. the assumptions necessary for the market to allocate efficiently—see Chapter 4, Section 3.2, or the Appendix to Chapter 4, paras. 6–17.

modifications to private health-care systems have typically experienced sharp and unexpected cost increases.

Any rapid expansion of private medical care in the UK also raises political economy issues. If private treatment is only a marginal activity, it can be a useful device for enhancing consumer choice and alleviating excess demand. But if the private sector grows beyond a certain (unknown) size, it is possible that 'the most demanding consumers of health care [would] exit from the public sector so diminishing the political voice for more spending in the public sector' (Klein 1984: 23–4). Such an outcome would have two effects. It would shift medical resources from the poor to the rich; whether this is desirable depends on one's definition of social justice. In addition, if the private health-care sector becomes large, it is likely to run into the cost-containment problems faced by other countries (Section 4.1).

If radical privatization is not the answer, what package of reform might be feasible? The main conclusion of the theoretical discussion in Section 3 is that it is not possible to make health care efficient and equitable by *ad hoc* tinkering. What is needed is a *strategy*. Since virtually all health care is financed by third parties (i.e. insurers or the taxpayer), the marginal cost to the consumer is zero, and he will generally demand an inefficiently high quantity, Q_1 in Figure 12.2. The heart of the issue, therefore, is rationing treatment to Q^*. In principle this can be done in two ways: (*a*) by making medical providers face the marginal social cost of health care; or (*b*) by imposing a budget constraint on total expenditure.

MANAGED CARE IN THE USA. This is the case of private production and private insurance subject to extensive management and regulation. The approach is also applied in the public sector.

The discussion at the end of Section 4.1 pointed to two complementary approaches to containing costs: regulation and the use of incentives. Managed care has both ingredients.[16]

- Regulation takes the form of *intensive management* of medical provision. Since the mid-1980s, the USA has increasingly moved from a system in which doctors had free rein to a management-controlled model.

- Incentives are based round *prospective payment*. If expenses are reimbursed *ex post*, medical providers face no incentive to economize; if, in contrast, they are paid *ex ante* (e.g. a prepayment of $X for a hip replacement), they face strong incentives to use resources carefully. The following institutions translate the idea into practice.

Health maintenance organizations (HMOs). Under this approach, individuals pay a lump-sum annual contribution to a 'firm' of doctors (the HMO), which promises to provide the contributor with a comprehensive range of medical services. The doctors provide primary care themselves and buy in hospital care as necessary. The HMO's income, which consists of the contributions of its members, is used to pay for health care, including the salaries of the doctors. Any surplus (like that of any firm) can be distributed to the doctors as

---

[16] For fuller discussion, see Marmor and Hacker (1999) and Glied (2000). Note that, Medicaid apart, regulation is private, rather than imposed by government.

higher pay, or to members as lower contributions, or ploughed back into the HMO to improve its service.

An important theoretical advantage of HMOs is that the doctor provides both health care *and* medical insurance. The HMO is thus analytically equivalent to merging the activities of doctor and insurance company. As discussed in Section 3.3, this internalizes the externality caused by third-party payments, giving doctors an incentive to economize —for example, providing preventive care or early treatment to nip an incipient problem in the bud.

Though evidence suggests that HMOs do exert some downward pressure on medical costs, it is well not to be too optimistic. First, HMOs may ameliorate one strategic insurance problem—exploding costs—but they do nothing to deal with the other—uninsurable risks.[17] Anecdotal evidence suggests that, as with any prepayment system, attempts are made in the USA to restrict membership to the best risks, an effect that is becoming stronger as the US population ages.[18] Secondly, HMOs do not *necessarily* provide the efficient quantity Q^* in Figure 12.2. Theory suggests that they will provide less than Q_1; but it does not follow that they provide Q^*.

Diagnosis-related groups (DRGs) are another form of prospective payment. Hospital in-patient cases are classified into different types, and hospitals paid a fixed price per case, depending primarily on its DRG. Once more, the idea is no panacea. Like any classification system, costs vary *within* each category, giving hospitals an incentive to select cheaper cases of each type. Pressures therefore grew for more refined DRGs. That, however, gave incentives to 'DRG creep', where hospitals classify as 'severe' as many cases as possible.

Preferred provider organizations (PPOs). Increasingly insurers in the USA and elsewhere give patients an incentive to choose from a limited range of providers, inviting institutions to tender competitively to become such a preferred provider. The idea is to exert downward pressure on price.

Over the years, the USA has moved increasingly towards prospective payment methods, up to a point moderating the increase in spending (though doing little to address gaps in coverage). HMOs are now the main form of health finance. Medical providers have responded by more intensive management. The duration of hospital stays has fallen by about 50 per cent, partly because of medical advances, but largely because of financial incentives and consequent managerial pressures. Notwithstanding these changes, the USA continues to face problems both with containing costs and with gaps in coverage (see Anderson et al. 2003; Davis and Cooper 2003; Glied 2003; Hoffman and Wang 2003).

THE STANFORD PLAN. Can these problems be solved within a mainly private system? The scheme, described below, offered by Stanford University and subsequently by Harvard and elsewhere, shows what is possible, but also the scale of intervention necessary.

---

[17] Given the problems of actuarial insurance discussed in Section 3.1, it is not surprising that in 2001 about 41 million people, about one in six non-elderly Americans, had inadequate or no medical insurance (Hoffman and Wang 2003: 3).

[18] It is said that some HMOs have offices on the third floor of buildings with no elevator; if you are fit enough to get to the office, you are fit enough to join the HMO.

(*a*) The university contracts with a small number of insurers, mainly HMOs.

(*b*) As a condition of joining Stanford's 'club', each insurer offers a policy with three elements: an agreed core package of health care; a structure of premiums that may differ with family size, etc., but must be unrelated to a person's medical risk; and agreement to accept all applicants.

(*c*) The university operates a redistributive pooling arrangement such that schemes with a worse-than-average risk group receive transfers.

(*d*) Employees can choose which scheme to join.

(*e*) The university contributes a fixed sum to each person's package, broadly equal to the cost of the cheapest of the approved policies.

Under (*a*) and (*b*), the university acts as agent for badly informed consumers, ensuring that insurance contains no hidden snags. Element (*b*) rules out cream skimming and ensures that nobody is excluded from cover, and (*b*) and (*e*) together ensure that everyone can afford cover. Element (*c*) protects insurers from adverse selection. Element (*e*) assists cost containment, since the individual faces the full marginal cost of joining a more expensive scheme. This is efficient.

Such an arrangement is thus a genuine strategy.[19] The interesting question is what sort of strategy. From a US perspective, this is a private scheme hedged by sufficient regulation and transfers to deal with market failures. But the scheme can equally be described as decentralized social insurance, its key features being central regulation, universal coverage, premiums unrelated to individual risk, and the existence of transfers to schemes with a disproportionate number of high risks.

The latter perspective points to a powerful conclusion: *that any strategy for addressing the problems of actuarial medical insurance leads inescapably to institutions with the major characteristics of social insurance*. Thus it should not be surprising that the USA is alone among industrial countries in using competitive private insurance as the major instrument for financing medical care. Elsewhere, two models predominate. Social insurance (Chapter 5, Section 4.2) abandons the model of actuarial insurance because it does not fit health care very well. Alternatively, medical care can be financed via the tax system.

5.2. Systems with public funding and private production

This package of private production, public funding, and extensive regulation embraces more public involvement than the previous one. *Production* of health care is private, fee for service. There is *regulation* of the quality of treatment and, crucially, also its quantity. The latter, as discussed in Section 4.1, could be achieved, as in Canada, through a combination of price control and global spending limits. *Finance* is public (private, non-profit institutions (as in Germany), acting in effect as agents of the state, could achieve the same result). Finance could be arranged in one of two ways. With compulsory insurance, premiums could be income related with no efficiency loss (Chapter 5, Section 4.1).

---

[19] This should not be surprising, since Alain Enthoven, a Stanford faculty member and one of America's leading health economists, chaired the committee that designed the scheme.

Alternatively, the state could drop the idea of actuarial insurance because it does not fit health care very well, and finance the scheme from general taxation. The general thrust of these arrangements follows row 3(*b*) of Table 4.1 for health care, and row 6 for health insurance. This is broadly the Canadian system.

The approach has two advantages. The problems of private insurance are largely avoided; and the incentive to oversupply, resulting from fee-for-service and third-party payments, is moderated by controlling total expenditure. The strategy rests crucially on effective imposition of a budget constraint, which in turn depends on political will and administrative capacity. Such arrangements can undoubtedly be successful, as, for example, the Canadian system (Robert G. Evans et al. 1989; Blendon et al. 1995).

5.3. NHS reforms

The NHS strategy (approximately row 8 in Table 4.1) has powerful advantages. But it also has problems, so that some reforms are desirable.

In macro-efficiency terms, a central question is whether the NHS is underfunded, as manifested, for example, by waiting lists and old hospital buildings. There is no scientific support for this view (point 9). To the extent that there *is* a problem, the solution is to devote more resources to the NHS. There are also problems of micro-efficiency, not least for lack of technical information on the costs and benefits of treatment, and of clearly stated priorities about different types of treatment and different classes of recipient. The solution is to gather more information of the type discussed in point 11. It is in this context that proposals for *internal (or quasi-) markets*, discussed shortly, offer prospects of improvement.

As for equity issues, the distribution of medical care by social class is one of the more intractable of the problems discussed. One approach is to reduce the cost of treatment for less-well-off groups—for example by compensating outpatients for transport costs and forgone earnings (as is done already with jurors). This process would be assisted by more general equalizing measures—for example, further income redistribution and better education. These measures may appear rather pale. It may be that we simply have to accept that inequality in health care, like inequality generally, cannot easily be reduced beyond a certain point. This does not mean that we should not try—merely that we should not expect easy answers. At a minimum we should not forget that the distribution of health care under the NHS, unequal though it might be, is more equal than that in many (if not most) other countries. The balance between realism and complacency is never easy.

Finally, there is growing evidence that a powerful factor in improving health (as opposed to health care) is rising income and greater equality. In that respect progress in health depends on events well outside the health sector.

THE 1990S: INTRODUCING QUASI-MARKETS. In a rare case of professional unanimity, the great weight of advice to a parliamentary inquiry (UK House of Commons Social Services Committee 1988; see also Barr et al. 1989), was to retain tax funding and introduce some competition on the supply side. Reforms in the early 1990s attempted to do just that. They left much unchanged: the NHS continued to provide comprehensive medical care; access remained universal; medical care continued to be funded mainly out of general taxation and was free at the point of use.

Changes in 1991 allowed larger GP practices to become fundholders, with freedom to buy certain types of care on behalf of their patients—in essence a small HMO. Such a move increased the power of GPs relative to consultants and hospitals, increasing pressure on hospitals to be efficient. Secondly, purchasers (Districts and GPs) were separated from providers (hospitals)—that is, demand and supply were separated. Districts changed from *providers* to *purchasers*, again increasing competitive pressures on hospitals. Thirdly, well-managed hospitals could become self-governing Trusts.

These changes introduced an internal market, or quasi-market, into the NHS. The traditional welfare-state model was based on public funding and public production, usually by a monopoly state supplier. Quasi-markets retain public funding but decentralize demand and supply. The trends reflect a growing convergence among OECD countries: continued reliance on public funding, political control of total health spending, and the use of managed markets or quasi-markets to foster efficiency on the supply side. Similar trends are also occurring in education (Chapter 13, Section 5), and in other areas.

More specifically (see the Further Reading), quasi-markets are markets in the sense that they introduce market forces. But they differ from the market for, say, food.

- On the supply side, they introduce competition (e.g. between hospitals or schools), but the suppliers are not necessarily private, nor necessarily profit maximizing.

- On the demand side, consumers do not spend cash; their purchasing power is expressed as an earmarked budget (e.g. capitation payments to GPs or to primary schools). This is, in effect, a form of voucher.

- Consumers may make their own choice (e.g. of school), or choice may be made on their behalf by an agent (a GP or District Health Authority).

The case for competition is that it improves internal (but not necessarily external) efficiency. Though simple in principle, the approach raises a series of strategic questions.

Incentives for quality. At the heart of quasi-markets is an inherent tension. Either medical providers face the costs of their decisions, or they do not. If they do not, they face no incentives to productive efficiency. But if providers do face the costs of their decisions, downward cost pressures may affect quality, which imperfectly informed consumers may be unable to judge (another example of asymmetric information). Alternatively, GPs (like HMOs) will face incentives to weed out costly patients (another example of cream skimming). Thus quality control and monitoring of medical outcomes become critical.

Can quality be monitored cost effectively? Thus the question is whether the purchaser (District or GP) can ensure quality by specifying contracts sufficiently tightly and by monitoring providers. This is difficult, not least (as discussed in Section 2.2) because of the problems of measuring health outcomes, making it hard to decide which supplier offers the most efficient and effective treatment.

How useful is competition? There are two questions: how much competition results from the reforms; and is such competition desirable? On the first, competition can be exaggerated. The existence of waiting lists points to at least some excess demand, reducing competitive pressures; and competition is limited outside metropolitan areas. Secondly, the benefits of competition are contingent on perfect information (Section 3.1). Patients are certainly not well informed; and the difficulties of measuring quality mean that Districts and GPs, acting as agents, will not necessarily be perfectly informed either.

Assessing these reforms faces at least three sets of difficulties. The problems in evaluating the health gains from different interventions have already been discussed. Secondly, the reforms were introduced with a significant increase in funding, making it difficult to disentangle the effects of increased resources from those of the reforms themselves. Thirdly there is the problem of self-selection: Bartlett and Le Grand (1994) argue that the first wave of hospital Trusts was the most entrepreneurial and hence not typical.

Writers like Glennerster (1994) conclude that decisions are best located at the lowest level (i.e. GPs), where information about consumers is richest. From this perspective, the movement towards GP fundholding was a move in the right direction. There is some support that this was so (Le Grand et al. 1998; Le Grand 1999). GP fundholding encouraged more flexible methods, reduced referrals to hospital and encouraged quicker discharge, and reduced the rate of growth of spending on pharmaceuticals. There is less evidence on the impact of fundholding on patient satisfaction or health outcomes.

Attempts to give hospitals greater freedom met with more mixed evaluation. Le Grand (1999) concluded that the introduction of hospital Trusts had made little difference, though later work by the same author (2002a) offers a more optimistic assessment.

REFORMS SINCE 1997 appeared to move from competition towards central planning, but a second wave began to reverse that policy (for fuller discussion, see Glennerster 2003a: ch. 4; Le Grand 2002b).

GP fundholding was replaced by Primary Care Trusts. At core, these are larger versions of GP fundholding, covering populations of 100,000 or more. This brings economies of scale but also means that decisions are no longer taken at the level with greatest information about patients. Separately, government downplayed the role of competition.

In the hospital sector, similarly, the government in the late 1990s to some extent moved away from competition, introducing a series of bureaucratic measures, including quantitative targets for waiting lists and similar variables (UK DoH 2000). Two sets of problems resulted. The targets were based on what was measurable (waiting lists, average length of hospital stay, bed utilization rates) rather than on what mattered (patient satisfaction and improved health outcomes produced in cost-effective ways). As a result, medical priorities were distorted—waiting-list targets created incentives to give priority to non-urgent treatment of people who had been on the waiting list for a long time over clinically more urgent treatment of people newly on the waiting list. Separately, there was evidence that hospital productivity was declining.

In part to address these problems, an inquiry was set up (UK Treasury 2002d (the Wanless Report)). The report highlighted the importance of 'a more productive and flexible workforce, more effective use of technology, policies to promote better disease prevention and putting in place improved incentives to ensure more efficient use of resources' (UK Treasury 2002a: para 7.2; see also UK DoH 2002a). The emphasis on incentives led to two strategic changes in direction. First, the balance between targets and incentives changed, with a return of the internal market, with money following the patient for certain types of treatment.

Resources and responsibility for delivery will progressively be devolved to local organisations, with the greatest freedoms and flexibilities going to the highest performing organisations. By 2004 local primary care trusts will hold 75 per cent of NHS resources . . . to commission care from a range of providers to provide patients with high quality care in both community and hospital settings. (UK Treasury 2002a: para. 7.9)

Targets were retained but broadened: some (maximum waiting times, improved appointment systems) related to process, but others (reducing health inequalities, reducing mortality from cancer and heart disease) concerned health outcomes and their distribution, and thus started to focus on what really matters.

The second strategic change, as discussed in Section 4.2, was the decision substantially to increase the resources going to the NHS, from 7 per cent of GDP in 2003/4 to 9.4 per cent by 2007/8.

THE FUTURE. Discussion earlier in this section pointed to the conflicting incentives between cutting costs and maintaining quality (see also Propper 2001). Public bodies such as the National Institute for Clinical Excellence (NICE) and the Commission for Health Care Audit and Inspection (CHAI) thus have a central role in monitoring quality both of process and—particularly—of outcomes.

A more radical approach (King's Fund 2002) argues that even the more decentralized form of planning in the proposals just described is not enough. What is needed is a body outside the immediate control of central government, whose sole remit is the quality of health care and health outcomes (to some extent analogous with operational independence of the central bank in some countries). Providers of primary care and hospital services should be turned into competitive not-for-profit entities facing active competition, including the possibility of bankruptcy. Such organizations are not out of line with those found in many countries (see European Observatory on Health Care Systems 2002 and the Further Reading). Glennerster (2003a: 77) argues that the reforms outlined above can be regarded as early steps along this route.

6. Conclusion

Health derives from many sources, including income, diet, and lifestyle and—it is increasingly clear—broader socio-economic factors (Section 4.3, point 16). Improved health, therefore, depends in part on developments well outside the health sector.

But health care is also important. Yet no system of health care can be perfect—the real issue is to choose the least inefficient and inequitable form of organization. Radical privatization (as defined in Chapter 4, Section 6) is no way of doing so. This conclusion rests not on personal values but on the *technical* nature of health care, and particularly, though not exclusively, on information problems.

Health care conforms only minimally with the assumptions necessary for market efficiency. The imperfect information and unequal power of consumers, externalities, and technical difficulties with private medical insurance cause serious problems on the demand side of a hypothetical private market; non-competitive behaviour by doctors can cause problems with supply, and third-party payments cause inefficiency via both demand and supply (Section 3.1). *A priori* there is an overwhelming presumption that an unrestricted private market will be highly inefficient, and also inconsistent with widely held notions of social justice. This view is confirmed by empirical observation (Section 4.1). Countries with little public involvement in health care, or that adopted careless *ad hoc* modifications to private systems, typically experienced sharp, unplanned increases in expenditure. Efficiency requires, at a minimum, considerable regulation and state financial involvement (Section 3.3).

Because of information problems, the NHS strategy has major advantages—an institution motivated largely by equity is successful because it goes with the grain of efficiency arguments. On the demand side, decisions about treatment are made by doctors, alleviating the worst effects of consumer ignorance; the problems of private insurance are resolved by abandoning insurance even as a fiction; and treatment is largely free at the point of use, which reduces the externality problem and goes a long way towards eliminating the influence of income on consumption. On the supply side, doctors are not as a rule paid a fee for service, thus removing incentives to oversupply. Health care is rationed partly by administrative means and partly by the NHS budget. Furthermore, if public production and allocation can be defended on efficiency grounds, it is legitimate to finance health care redistributively for reasons of social justice (Chapter 4, Section 7.2). In theory, therefore, the strategy is feasible in both efficiency and equity terms.

The practice (Section 4) is far from perfect: waiting lists for non-urgent (and even some urgent) conditions continued well after 2000; there is room for improvement in both external and internal efficiency; and the distribution of health by social class remains an issue. However, a good deal can be said on the plus side.

- The NHS is cheap by international standards, yet health standards are not out of line with those in other countries.
- Doctors have no financial incentive to over-prescribe and (partly because of this) patients generally trust their doctor.
- Treatment is free whatever the extent and duration of illness; no one is denied access because of low income; and no one goes in fear of financial ruin.

The NHS thus has much to commend it; and many of its remaining problems could largely be resolved by giving it some more resources and by gathering more and better information.

Its advantages notwithstanding, the NHS is not the only system that makes sense. The strategy has, however, served the UK well, is widely popular, and can be drastically changed only at considerable risk of throwing out the baby with the bathwater. Institutions in other countries show that the adoption of a different system is likely to raise problems very similar to those of the NHS, and additional and more intense problems as well. My preferred reform for the UK, therefore, is to keep the NHS; the principle should be retained, and the system improved within the existing strategy along the lines suggested in Section 5.3.

However, the political economy and the structure of the medical profession in many other countries make it unlikely that they would readily adopt a system of public production. This is especially true of the USA, where the mixed public/private arrangements described in Section 5.1 might be a more satisfactory solution. The Canadian model of publicly funded, privately produced health care has much to offer; and a system based on regulated health maintenance organizations buttressed by income transfers may offer an alternative.

The crucial point is that any system of health care must constitute a genuine *strategy*—*ad hoc* tinkering is a guaranteed road to disaster. Both theory and international experience point to two effective strategies:

- mainly public funding (taxation or social insurance) plus public production; or
- mainly public funding plus private production *plus* regulation to contain costs.

At a strategic level the problems a country faces are largely predictable consequences of its chosen health strategy. Consider four broad objectives of a health-care system: (*a*) equitable access, (*b*) cost containment, (*c*) no waiting lists, and (*d*) consumer choice. A country like the USA, with largely private funding, faces the problems discussed in Section 3.1, so that its major problems are (*a*) and (*b*). In countries like Canada, with public funding of private production, the pressure point is (*b*). Countries like the UK, with mainly public funding of mainly public production, score well on (*a*) and (*b*), but tend to face problems on (*c*) or (*d*). There is no perfect solution. The trick is to learn from theory and experience to choose the least bad second-best option. For an ambitious attempt to rank health-care systems worldwide, see World Health Organization (2001: annex table 1).

■ QUESTIONS FOR FURTHER DISCUSSION

1. People buy food of their choice at market prices on the basis of what they can afford. Why should the same mechanism not be used for health care?

2. 'The UK national health service is a genuine strategy for addressing pervasive technical problems in the markets for medical care and medical insurance.' Explain why this is so.

3. The USA relies heavily on private insurance to finance health care. Explain why the resulting problems are entirely predictable. What types of reform might improve matters?

4. [More difficult] 'No health-care system is perfect. The problems of the health system in each country are predictable outcomes of its chosen health-care strategy.' Discuss with examples from at least two countries.

■ FURTHER READING

On the institutions of health care, recent developments, and statistical data in the UK, see Glennerster (2003*a*: ch. 4), the Department of Health *Departmental Report* (UK DoH 2003*b*) (the 2003 version of an annual publication) and the Department of Health web site http://www.dh.gov.uk. For a survey of systems in a range of countries (Australia, Denmark, France, Germany, the Netherlands, New Zealand, Sweden, and the UK), see the European Observatory on Health Care Systems (2002), the European Observatory web site: http://www.who.dk/observatory, and the various government portals in the list of useful web sites at the start of the book. On institutions in the EU, see the various country studies and overview reports on http://europa.eu.int/comm/employment_social/soc-prot/healthcare/healthcare_en.htm.

For general discussion of the economics of health, see Rosen (2002: ch. 10) and Stiglitz (2000: ch. 12). On the nature of health care, including problems with insurance, see Arrow (1963) (the classic article) and Culyer (1993). Problems with medical insurance are discussed by Pauly (1974, 1986), Culyer (1993), and Cutler and Zeckhauser (2000); Barr (2001*a*: ch. 5) discusses the implications of genetic testing for insurance. On equity in health care, see Wagstaff et al. (1999), Gerdttham and Jönsson (2000), and Propper (2001), and on the impossibility of rationing health care in a way that is simultaneously efficient, equitable, and administratively feasible, Le Grand (1996).

The case for market provision of health care is set out *inter alia* by Friedman and Friedman (1980: ch. 4). For UK discussion, see Propper and Green (2001). On the role of giving, the classic work is Titmuss (1970).

On the socio-economic determinants of health, see Robert G. Evans et al. (1994), Wilkinson (1996), Benzeval et al. (2000), and, for a cogent survey, Robert G. Evans (1996). For attempts to quantify the benefits of health care, such as QALYs and similar measures, see Williams (1985), Wagstaff (1991), Bleichrodt (1995), and Culyer and Wagstaff (1995). On why health matters, see Shapiro (1993), a riveting but sobering account of the Russian mortality crisis.

For recent proposals to reform the NHS, see UK DoH (2000, 2002*a*) and UK Treasury (2002*d*). For assessment of the NHS from the mid-1970s to the mid-1990s, see Le Grand and Vizard (1998). On quasi-markets, see the symposium in the *Economic Journal* (September 1991) (Glennerster 1991; Le Grand 1991*b*; Maynard 1991), for an assessment of the strategy, Bartlett et al. (1998), and, for evaluation of the NHS internal market, Le Grand et al. 1998. For reviews of the NHS, see Propper (2001) and King's Fund (2002), and, for assessment, Glennerster (2003*a*: ch. 4) and Le Grand (1999, 2002*a,b*).

On developments in Europe, see Mossialos and Le Grand (1999) on cost containment, Saltman (2003) on increasingly flexible boundaries between public and private systems, and Mossialos and Thomson (2002) on voluntary health insurance.

On the USA, see Anderson et al. (2003), Davis and Cooper (2003), and Glied (2003). Reinhardt (2000) offers a US perspective on lessons from other countries. On the reform of Medicare, see Fuchs (2000) and McClellan (2000), and, on the determinants of health, James P. Smith (1999).

13 | School education

Man is the most versatile of all forms of capital.

(Irving Fisher 1930)

1. Introduction

This chapter, about school education, and the next, about higher education, are matching twins so far as the underlying economic theory is concerned but—using the same theory—reach sharply different conclusions about the role of the state.

This chapter discusses the aims of education (Section 2), theoretical arguments about state intervention in pursuit of efficiency and equity (Section 3), assessment of UK school education (Section 4), possible reforms (Section 5), and major conclusions (Section 6).

During the early part of the chapter little knowledge is needed of the institutions described in Section 4.1. Education is compulsory to age 16. Primary (age 5 to 11) and secondary education (age 11 to 18) are publicly funded and publicly produced.[1] There is also a small private sector.

2. Aims

2.1. Concepts

Social welfare is maximized through the pursuit of economic efficiency[2] and social justice (or equity). This section discusses how these concepts apply to education.

The primary objective of education policy is to improve educational outcomes. As discussed in Chapter 12, Section 2.1, good health derives from many sources, of which health care is only one. Good educational outcomes, analogously, derive from many sources, of which formal education is only one: parenting is key; there is increasing evidence of the link between childhood poverty and poor educational outcomes (see Section 4.2, point 4); and natural ability is also part of the story.

---

[1] Chapter 4, Section 6, discusses in detail the distinction between public and private production and finance.
[2] The concept of economic efficiency is defined in Chapter 4, Section 2.1.

What, however, do we mean by 'good educational outcomes'? The main purpose of education is to transmit knowledge and skills *and*, as important, attitudes and values. Education is not only technical but also cultural: it is essential if a country is 'to be a successful nation in a competitive world, and to maintain a cohesive society and rich culture' (UK NCIHE 1997*b*: 7). Part of the objective is to produce agreement about values. As examples, consider the following statements: students should never disagree with their teachers; women should sit in class and just listen; answers get higher marks if they conform with the teacher's ideology. In the West there is strong disagreement with the values contained in such statements, the prevailing value being that what matters is the analytical *content* of the argument, not the gender or status of the *person* making it. Instilling such values is part of the purpose of education. Another part of the objective is to allow diversity. Families will have different views about subject matter, the role of discipline, and the place of religion. We saw in Chapter 6 that it is not possible to quantify a value-free definition of poverty or inequality. Analogously, the education package, and hence the meaning of a 'good' education, is multidimensional, will depend on the economic, political, and social structure of the country concerned,[3] and will vary far more than the definition of good health.

Achieving this primary objective involves a number of subsidiary ones. Efficiency is important. If we spent nothing on education, children would all be illiterate; if we spent the whole of national income on education, there would be no food or health care. The optimal quantity clearly lies somewhere between—in principle where the value gained from the last unit of education is equal to the marginal value that would be derived from the alternative use to which the resources involved could be put. This is the quantity X^* in Figure 4.1.

Allocative efficiency (sometimes referred to in discussion of education as *external efficiency*) is concerned with producing the types of educational activities that equip individuals—economically, socially, politically, and culturally—for the societies in which they live. External efficiency applies to the totality of resources devoted to education (the macro-efficiency aim in Chapter 1, Section 2.2), and also to the division of resources between different types and levels of education (the micro-efficiency aim), so as to produce the optimal quantity, quality, and mix. Separately, productive efficiency (Chapter 4, Section 2.1), sometimes referred to as *internal* efficiency, is concerned with running schools and other institutions as efficiently as possible.

Equity is more elusive (see the discussion in Chapter 12, Section 2.1). To sidestep some of these difficulties equity will be defined as a form of *equality of opportunity* (Chapter 6, Section 3.1, especially equation (6.18)). This does not mean that individuals can necessarily obtain as much education as they want. However, it implies that, if individuals A and B have similar tastes and ability, they should receive the same education, irrespective of factors that are regarded as irrelevant—for example, income. This definition of equity at least has the merit that it apportions scarcity in a just way.

Once we have decided the efficient level of production of different types of education and their equitable distribution, the remaining question is how to finance education.

---

[3] See Barr (2001*a*: ch. 15) for discussion of how education in Communist countries was well suited to the needs of central planning and totalitarian government.

This is an issue of vertical equity discussed in Chapter 4, Section 4.1. It was argued in Chapter 4, Section 7.2, that, if education is allocated efficiently by the market, then equity aims are generally best achieved through income transfers. But where education is publicly produced and allocated for *efficiency* reasons, it may be appropriate to finance it out of progressive taxation; if so, it is possible, though not inevitable (Section 4.3), that in-kind transfers will redistribute from rich to poor.

2.2. Measuring costs and benefits

Measuring costs, as with health care (Chapter 12, Section 2.2), presents no insurmountable problems. We know the direct costs of the state educational system and its components (Table 13.1). The problem of apportioning overheads is broadly the same as for health care. For people past school-leaving age it is also necessary to include an estimate of forgone earnings.

Measuring benefits faces a series of major problems, with distinct echoes of the discussion of defining and measuring poverty (Chapter 6, Section 2). In both cases, there is no wholly satisfactory solution.

- *Output cannot be measured.* Since there is no single definition of a 'good' education, there is no unambiguous measure of output. We can measure test scores, but (*a*) such measures are imperfect even in their own terms, and (*b*) educational outputs are much broader than such technical benefits. Education has *consumption benefits*—that is, the enjoyment of the educational process itself; *investment benefits*, including higher pay, job satisfaction and the enjoyment of leisure; and various *external benefits*, including shared values. Most of these are unmeasurable, but that does not make them unreal.

- *Connecting inputs and outputs* (the education production function) *is problematical.* It is possible to measure the quantity of some inputs (teachers' and pupils' time, buildings, equipment). But it is not possible to measure their quality. Nor is it possible to measure other inputs, such as natural ability and the quantity of quality of parenting. Secondly, as just discussed, output can be measured only in terms of test scores. Thirdly, the production function is hard to estimate. Studies typically assume (because no other assumption is available) that schools have a single, narrow objective—maximizing pupils' test scores.[4]

- *Causality cannot be established.* Even if these measurement problems were solved, a further problem remains. As discussed shortly, the screening hypothesis questions the causal link between post-primary education and increased individual productivity. Is an individual productive because she is naturally able, or because she has been well educated?

THE HUMAN CAPITAL MODEL attempts to explain the demand for education in terms of its production and utility benefits. It is argued, in the case of the former, that an individual

---

[4] See Todd and Wolpin (2003) for discussion of estimating education production functions. Akerlof and Kranton (2002) set out a theoretical approach which integrates the sociological and the economic approach to analyzing education.

who acquires more education becomes more productive. This approach sees education as a type of investment, analogous to improving machinery. From the individual viewpoint, this investment is profitable to the extent that it increases future income by more than its initial costs, including forgone earnings. Empirically there is a strong correlation between an individual's education and his lifetime earnings. The overall pattern summarized by Blaug (1970: 27) still applies—that is, that 'within a few years after leaving school . . . better educated people earn more than less educated people; their advantage continues to widen with age and . . . the favourable differential persists until retirement'.

Utility benefits arise because education might have consumption benefits in the present as well as investment benefits in the future. The individual return to education also includes non-money rewards such as job satisfaction and the enjoyment of leisure.

To clarify the *individual* return to education, it is helpful to set out his individual investment decision. The initial assumptions of the simplest human capital model are:

1. Education raises the individual's marginal product in the future and therefore his future money income.

2. This increase in money income is the *only* benefit from education—i.e. we rule out consumption benefits and future non-money returns.

If B_t is the benefit to the individual from an extra year's education, and r is his personal rate of time preference, the *gross present value*[5] (GPV) of an additional year of education is

$$\text{GPV} = \frac{B_1}{1+r} + \frac{B_2}{(1+r)^2} + \ldots + \frac{B_N}{(1+r)^N}. \tag{13.1}$$

The *net present value* (NPV) is

$$\text{NPV} = \sum_{t=0}^{N} \frac{B_t}{(1+r)^t} - C_0, \tag{13.2}$$

where C_0 is the cost of an additional year of education (including forgone earnings). The individual will continue to acquire education so long as GPV > C_0—i.e. up to the point where NPV = 0. This is the level of education Q_0 in Figure 13.1, where the marginal private value (MPV) of education is the marginal gross present value from equation (13.1), and the marginal private cost (MPC) is the cost of education to the individual.

Relaxing the second assumption does not change the flavour of the results. Consumption benefits reduce C_0 and non-money returns increase B_t in equation (13.2), thus increasing the quantity of education an individual will choose to acquire.

THE SCREENING HYPOTHESIS. It might seem, therefore, that by measuring the money income benefits (though not the utility benefits) to the individual we can establish a lower bound on the production benefits of education. This is valid if we are prepared to assume that education is *causally* related to increases in individual productivity. This is the strong first assumption made above. In contrast, the screening hypothesis argues that education is *associated* with increased productivity but does not *cause* it.[6]

---

[5] For further discussion of cost–benefit analysis, see Stiglitz (2000: ch. 11).

[6] The large literature on this and other aspects of the economics of education is surveyed by Blaug (1976, 1985) and Glennerster (1993). For fuller discussion of screening, see Riley (2001).

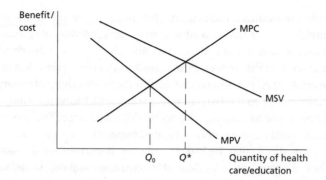

Fig. 13.1. A simple human capital model of the individual decision to invest in health care/education

The screening hypothesis argues, first, that education beyond a basic level does not increase individual productivity and, secondly, that firms seek high-ability workers but are unable, prior to employing them, to distinguish them from those with low ability. The problem is analytically similar to adverse selection in insurance markets (Chapter 5, Section 3.2), or more generally to 'lemons' (Akerlof 1970), in the sense that one side of the market has better information than the other. Individuals therefore have an incentive to make themselves distinctive by some sort of signal. According to the screening hypothesis, post-primary education fills exactly this function: it gives a signal to prospective employers, which it is in the *individuals'* (though not necessarily society's) interests to acquire. Just as an individual's good health may be due more to a naturally strong constitution than to medical care, so, according to this view, is productivity the result of natural ability rather than post-primary education.

There are various counter-arguments. Where education includes professional training (e.g. medicine), there is a direct contribution to productivity. The strong form of the hypothesis also assumes that there is only one type of job. In practice, skills and job characteristics are heterogeneous, so that it is necessary to match workers and jobs, giving education an additional social return as a matching device. Whether there is *some* validity in the hypothesis is an empirical matter. The verdict is undecided and likely to remain so, since individual productivity is determined in part by unmeasurable influences such as natural ability and family background.

The conclusion from the individual viewpoint is that it is possible to measure the money income benefits (but not the utility benefits) *associated* with different levels of education, but the *causal* relationship is less clear. The screening hypothesis leaves the *individual* decision to invest unaffected, and so leads to the same result as the human capital model. But, to the extent that it is true, screening has profound implications for the *socially* optimal level of investment in education, to which we turn next.

EXTERNAL BENEFITS. Setting the screening hypothesis to one side for the moment, education may create benefits to society over and above those to the individual in a number of ways.[7] There is at least one strong external benefit. Education, to the extent that it raises

---

[7] The theory of externalities is discussed in Chapter 4, Section 3.2, and the Appendix to Chapter 4, para. 15.

an individual's future earnings, increases her future tax payments; in the absence of any subsidy, an individual's investment in education confers a 'dividend' on future taxpayers.[8]

Does education create external benefits over and above this tax dividend? It is part of the conventional wisdom that it does. *Production benefits* arise if education not only makes someone more productive, but also contributes to the productivity of others (your ability to use email increases my productivity as well as your own). Individuals may become more adaptable and better able to keep up with technological change. The economic spin-offs of higher education and a more mobile educated population are relevant in this context. It is not surprising that much high-tech industry is concentrated round clusters of universities—for example, Cambridge (Massachusetts) and Cambridge (England). Education lies at the heart of theories of endogenous growth (Romer 1993). Measuring these benefits is difficult, not least because it is hard to separate the effects of education from other determinants of productivity, such as natural ability and the quantity and quality of capital.

Education can also create *cultural benefits* external to the recipient in at least two ways. A common experience (music, art, literature) may foster communication generally, both at the time and in the future. In addition, there may be neighbourhood effects; the mechanics of taking children to school, parent–teacher associations, and the like, bring people into contact and may foster shared attitudes locally. More fundamentally, one of the purposes of education is to inculcate core values that underpin social cohesion. Separate but related, education may also create *civic benefits*: Dee (2003) reports a strong relationship between educational attainment and civic engagement in such forms as voter participation and support for free speech.

Thus the externality argument is strong in presumptive terms, but, once more, measurement problems make definitive answer impossible. Estimates of private rates of return are suspect because, of necessity, they omit all non-money returns. Estimates of the social rate of return are doubly suspect: they omit non-money returns and can take account of screening only very approximately. Because of the 'tax-dividend' point, there is an unarguable external benefit, but it is not possible to show how much.

If education (*a*) increases individual productivity and (*b*) creates external production benefits, the amount of education chosen by an individual in a market system, Q_0 in Figure 13.1, will generally be less than the optimal amount, Q^*, an issue discussed in more detail in Section 3.1. However, if the claims of the screening hypothesis are valid, then education leads to (but does not *cause*) an increase in individual income, but does not raise output. In this case individuals may acquire *more* education than is socially efficient.

RATE-OF-RETURN STUDIES, despite these difficulties, attempt to measure the benefits of education. The rate of return, r_0, is that rate of interest that equates the present value of the stream of future benefits in equation (13.2) to the initial cost of acquiring an additional unit of education—that is, r_0 is the rate of interest that reduces the *net* present value of additional education to zero. It is vital to distinguish the private rate of return (which determines individual decisions) from the social rate (which is the relevant variable for public policy).

---

[8] This line of argument can be used to justify a subsidy for any type of investment that raises future income. That is precisely what usually happens through the tax system in the case of business investment.

Two conclusions tend to emerge from empirical studies.[9] The rate of return is highest for primary education, and then declines; and the private rate of return exceeds the social rate at all levels of education (mainly because in all countries education subsidies reduce costs to the individual but not to society). These results must be heavily qualified. First, they are based on *money* returns. No account is taken of the consumption value of education, nor of its future non-money returns. Where these factors are present, empirical estimates *understate* both private and social benefits to an unknown extent. Secondly, such estimates can measure only the *association* between education and earnings. But, to the extent that the screening hypothesis is true, the causal link is weakened, in which case the measured social (though not the private) benefits of post-primary education will be *overstated* by an unknown amount.

THE RELATIONSHIP BETWEEN EDUCATION AND ECONOMIC GROWTH. For these and other reasons, quantification remains a major challenge. Output growth depends on the increase in the quantity and quality of the capital stock, on the increase in quantity and quality of the labour force, and on a variety of non-economic factors. Education affects only one of these, the quality of the labour force. The problem is to separate the quantitative effect of this variable given the influence of all the others. Early work established the unsurprising conclusion that no country has experienced a substantial degree of economic development without first achieving a level of basic literacy in a substantial proportion of its population.

More recent work has started to establish more firmly the link between human capital formation and output growth. Wolf's analysis (2002) rightly cautions against complacently taking it for granted that increased education spending necessarily translates into faster growth, the most blatant example being the latter days of Communism. Clearly the quality and relevance of education are central: the level of spending is relevant, but so is the responsiveness of the system to the needs of students and employers. An OECD study uses panel data for the advanced industrial countries to assess the influence on growth rates of a series of variables, and concludes: 'The improvement in human capital has been one of the key factors behind the growth process of the past decades in all OECD countries . . .' (Bassanini and Scarpetta 2001: 39; see also OECD 2003*b*). At a minimum, such findings suggest that under-investing is a risky strategy.

3. Methods

3.1. Theoretical arguments for intervention 1: Efficiency

The arguments about the conformity of primary and secondary education with the standard assumptions in many ways parallel those for health care (see the discussion in Chapter 12, Section 3.1), so discussion is brief.

---

[9] For an international study, see Psacharopoulos (1994) and OECD (2003*b*). On the UK, see Blundell et al. (1999).

PERFECT INFORMATION. Do consumers of school education have perfect information about the nature of the product (i.e. are indifference maps well defined); about prices (i.e. do they know their budget constraint); and about the future? Knowledge of the nature of the product is certainly not perfect. Children (the immediate consumers) are not well informed. In a market system decisions are therefore left to parents, at least for early education. But parental preferences can cause inefficiency in two ways: they might themselves have imperfect information; or they might not consider the child's best interests but those of the family as a whole, themselves included. The issue is further complicated by the particular difficulty in defining 'the product'.

Such complexities can make rational decisions difficult. In addition, consumers of education are likely to differ in the extent of their confidence and articulateness (the issue of unequal power). The result of these factors is inefficiency, though both its extent and its direction (see Figure 12.1) are open to debate. But it is likely that imperfect information leads to under-consumption, particularly by the lowest socio-economic groups (see Section 3.2).

Solutions can take several forms. In contrast with health care, the market itself might supply information—for example, advisory centres, or a 'Good Schools Guide' that includes relevant performance indicators. But it can be argued that, where children or their families have imperfect information and/or where families cannot be relied on to act in their best interests, there is an efficiency argument for intervention, particularly in the form of regulation. This would embrace mandatory school attendance (discussed below), and the establishment of minimum standards and inspection to ensure conformity with those standards. Only if the information problem is regarded as major is there an argument on this account for public production and allocation.

A second issue is the extent to which consumers or their families are well informed about prices. If education were privately produced, this information would be provided by the market. But, as with health care, it should be remembered that improved knowledge of prices increases efficiency only where consumers are well informed also in other respects. If intervention on efficiency grounds were thought necessary, it would take the form of publishing a list of school fees, or regulating them.

The problem of information about the future is minor. Parents know that their children will need education at least until minimum school-leaving age. In a market system they would make financial provision for their children's education out of current income, out of savings, or, if they were uncertain of their future income or lifespan, by taking out an endowment policy, the proceeds of which could be used to pay school fees in the future. Uncertainty (as opposed to poverty) raises no substantial problems in this context.

PERFECT COMPETITION. The proposition that the advantages of a competitive market for health care are contingent on perfect information (Chapter 12, Section 3.1) applies equally here. But the information problem is perhaps less severe for education, so this section is concerned not with the desirability of competition but with its feasibility. Two issues arise: the supply of education; and the supply through the private market of finance for education. There is no reason why schools in cities should not act competitively (a topic to which we return in Section 5.2). But a rural school may have a local monopoly and, if run to maximize profits, would under-provide. The standard solution is price regulation (Chapter 4, Section 3.2).

Education finance raises different issues, which recur in the discussion of higher education in Chapter 14. From an efficiency viewpoint we do not normally worry if an individual cannot afford more than x units of a good. If someone cannot afford smoked salmon and therefore buys none, there are no efficiency implications. But if an individual cannot afford an adequate diet and becomes malnourished, there are efficiency losses as well as equity costs. Similar losses arise if an individual cannot afford to buy the socially efficient amount of education—for example, basic literacy, numeracy, and computer skills. With perfect capital markets, children could finance their own education by borrowing against their future earnings, as illustrated by the Fisher model (see Figure 4.5 and the surrounding discussion). But, as discussed in more detail in Chapter 14, Section 3.1, capital markets are not perfect, not least because students seeking to borrow cannot offer physical or financial collateral. In a pure market system this would lead to under-consumption, giving an efficiency (as well as a possible equity) justification for intervention. This could take several forms: the state could act as guarantor for loans made by private institutions to children for educational purposes; it could provide loan finance itself; or it might choose to subsidize education.

MARKET FAILURES. Education is not a public good;[10] nor does it generally face increasing returns to scale. But we saw in Section 2.2 that education creates important external benefits concerning productivity, shared values, and civic participation. These benefits are hard to quantify, but cannot on that account be ignored. Intervention can involve regulation in the form of compulsory attendance at school until age 16 to prevent under-consumption (see the analogous argument for compulsory membership of an unemployment insurance scheme in Chapter 8, Section 2.1); and an appropriate Pigovian subsidy could in principle achieve a similar effect.

3.2. Theoretical arguments for intervention 2: Equity

HORIZONTAL EQUITY relates to perfect information (to assist rational choice) and equal power (to enforce that choice). Both may be lacking for consumers of education. A major equity issue arises where these problems are greater for individuals in lower socio-economic groups (which is likely if information is costly to acquire). Thus parents with little education may have less information than better-educated parents over school choice; in addition, they may be less able to make use of any information they do acquire. In such cases intervention may improve equity as well as efficiency.

Regulation would be concerned with the professional qualifications of teachers, minimum physical facilities, school attendance, and, possibly, curricula. Where imperfect information causes under-consumption, a subsidy might be applied either to prices or to incomes. Income subsidies usually take the form of cash transfers, but education vouchers (Section 5.1) can be thought of as a form of tied transfer.

Where inadequate information and inequality of power are serious problems, efficiency and equity may both be increased by public allocation and/or production, depending on whether (*a*) the private or public sector is more efficient at producing education and (*b*)

---

[10] See the definition of public goods in the Appendix to Chapter 4, paras. 13, 14.

regulation of standards is more effective in one sector or the other. The issue is discussed in Section 3.3.

VERTICAL EQUITY concerns the extent to which education does or should redistribute from rich to poor. As discussed in Chapter 7, Section 4, publicly provided education, subject to caveats, is redistributive if (rich) individual R pays more taxes to pay for education than (poor) P where each consumes the same quantity, and also if R consumes twice as much as P but pays more than twice as much in contributions. The voting model in Chapter 4, Section 4.2, offers an explanation of why this might happen. If R's utility rises with P's 'good' consumption (education for P's children) but falls with P's 'bad' consumption, we have a consumption externality of the sort described by equation (4.17). In those circumstances, it might be rational for R to offer an in-kind transfer of education worth £1,000, but to make a cash offer of only £200 (since P might spend the latter on 'bad' consumption). If the difference between the two offers is large enough, P might prefer the in-kind offer to the lower cash amount (see Figure 4.6).

Analogous to the arguments about health care, the rich may have an interest in the education of the poor for two reasons. They might support transfers of school education for reasons of efficiency/self-interest: a well-educated workforce might foster economic growth, and/or might reduce social unrest. This is the 'national-efficiency' argument (Chapter 2, Section 2.1), which gave rise to the Marxist interpretation of the welfare state (Chapter 3, Section 5.3). Alternatively, rich individuals might care about the distribution of education for altruistic/equity reasons.

Thus efficiency arguments for public production and allocation may be reinforced by equity motives that make it politically easier to make transfers in kind. The rich may favour them for selfish or altruistic reasons; and, if the offer is sufficiently generous, the poor might also prefer in-kind transfers.

The voting model offers an explanation of why *some* transfer of education takes place. But is the amount transferred *optimal*? As discussed in Chapter 4, Section 4.4, libertarians support in-kind transfers only as voluntary action by the rich, but not as a result of government failure in the face of coercive electoral behaviour by the poor (Chapter 4, Section 5). They therefore argue that redistribution under the current system is greater than optimal. Many socialists support in-kind transfers for their own sake (particularly in the case of education) because they increase equality, and argue that redistribution is almost certainly suboptimal.

3.3. Types of intervention

Sections 3.1 and 3.2 discussed *why* the state might intervene. The next issue is *how* best it might do so. The theoretical arguments raised by school education largely parallel those for health care. The main differences are that the problem of information (though not of equal power) may be less acute; that problems with private insurance are not relevant; and that the issues of imperfect capital markets and of external effects are more important.

PURE MARKET PROVISION (i.e. rows 1 or 2 of Table 4.1). Critics of public provision (Friedman and Friedman 1980: ch. 6) wish to see education produced, allocated, and financed privately. But they recognize some of the problems described earlier, so their policy proposals (Section 5.1) are of private production, with mixed public/private finance and some regulation.

The argument against market production and allocation of pre-university education is the failure of many of the assumptions necessary for market efficiency. Regulation can be justified by imperfect information and unequal power, and the presence of externalities and local monopolies. Subsidies can be justified by externalities, and subsidies or the provision of loan guarantees (or of loans themselves) by capital market imperfections. The issue of public production rests largely on the extent of information problems. It should be clear that a pure market system is likely to be highly inefficient, and also inequitable to the extent that knowledge, power, and access to capital markets are correlated with socio-economic status. Unrestricted market provision of pre-university education is theoretically implausible and, in practice, does not exist in any country.

MIXED PUBLIC/PRIVATE INVOLVEMENT (e.g. row 4(*a*) in Table 4.1). The issue is whether it is possible to devise an efficient and equitable package whereby the state regulates education and subsidizes it wholly or in part, but where production takes place in the private sector. This is the way universities operate in many countries, and proposals to extend these arrangements to schools ('voucher' schemes) are discussed in Section 5.1.

Several ingredients are necessary for this approach to be efficient and equitable. The state would have to regulate education in one or more of the following areas: mandatory school attendance to some minimum age; course content; minimum qualifications for teachers; certification of schools (i.e. would an individual need permission to start a school?); inspection to ensure an adequate quality of service; and fee levels (i.e. should schools be allowed to charge what they liked?). Though the principle of regulation is accepted, commentators disagree about how far it should go.

Subsidies to education can be justified in both efficiency and equity terms. In a libertarian world, individuals pay for the private benefits they receive from education, but are subsidized to the extent that external benefits are thereby conferred upon others. This degree of subsidy might, however, be insufficient. Individuals from lower socio-economic groups might face imperfect capital markets; in addition they (and their families) might have poorer information about the benefits of education and/or be reluctant to incur large debts. Any resulting tendency to under-consumption suggests a larger subsidy than the externality argument implies, and maybe a 100 per cent subsidy, at least for school education. Additionally, if the subsidy is only partial, it may be necessary on both efficiency and equity grounds for the state to provide loan capital.

Private production is likely to be efficient only if quality is adequately monitored. Libertarians dispute this view, arguing that dissatisfied parents can move their child to another school, and that, if a school has a bad reputation, it will go out of business. This argument has two weaknesses. Parents may not have enough information to realize that their child is being badly educated or may not have the confidence to do anything about it. Secondly, education is not a repeatable experiment. It is true that a restaurant that provides bad service will go out of business; its former clients suffer nothing worse than a bad meal, and can spend the rest of their lives going to better restaurants. Education, in contrast, is largely a once-and-for-all experience; a child who has had a bad year in school may never recover. In addition, there are emotional costs (changing friends, etc.) in changing school. A more apt analogy is a restaurant whose food is so bad that it might cause permanent ill health.

Finally, private-consumption decisions are likely to be efficient and equitable only if families have sufficient information, and if they use it in the child's best interests. The issue of whether the state or the family is better qualified to make educational decisions in the name of an individual child is controversial to say the least. Some parents are capable of more informed decisions than the state; others make poorer decisions. If the quality of parental choice is systematically related to socio-economic status and the effect is strong, then private allocation can be argued to be less equitable than state allocation, irrespective of the balance of argument about efficiency. It is not surprising that the advocates of parental choice almost invariably belong to the better-off socio-economic groups.

PUBLIC PRODUCTION, ALLOCATION, AND FINANCE (i.e. row 8 in Table 4.1). Is public funding, together with public production and allocation, less inefficient and inequitable than the sort of arrangements just described? The allocation issue should be argued on the basis of perceptions about imperfect information and social cohesion, and that of public production on whether it is, or is not, likely to be more efficient than the private market. These issues, we have seen, turn crucially on the answers to two questions.

- Do parents on average make better or worse decisions than the state about their children's education?
- If the quality of parental choice varies systematically with socio-economic status, how do we weight the claims of middle-class children and their parents to be allowed unrestricted choice, relative to those of children in lower socio-economic groups, whose interests might be served better by the state?

The answer to the first question is empirical. The answer to the second depends on political stance. Libertarians argue that state allocation interferes with parental freedom and therefore reject it. To socialists the aim of equality is paramount; the claim of children from poorer families therefore takes priority, and state allocation is preferred. Liberals try to recognize the claims of both groups. This involves a system either of public allocation, which takes account of stated parental preferences, or of parental choice subject to careful scrutiny.

The *a priori* arguments about the provision of school education are more finely balanced than those about health care.[11] But it is fair to say that the failures of the assumptions necessary for market efficiency are sufficiently strong to make public production, allocation, and finance of school education a tenable strategy. To the extent that this is the case on efficiency grounds, it is appropriate to finance education redistributively for reasons of social justice (Chapter 4, Section 7.2).

Finally, since education is not a homogeneous whole, it is necessary to ask whether the same answers apply to all types of education. Should there be one set of answers for compulsory education and another for education beyond the minimum school-leaving

---

[11] It is therefore curious that the educational systems of different countries vary much *less* than their systems of health care. In particular, it is surprising from an *economic* point of view that school education in the USA is publicly produced, allocated, and financed (i.e. row 8 in Table 4.1).

age; should some types of education be free and others not; are market solutions more applicable to higher education than to school education; should higher education be financed in part by loans and, if so, on what terms should the loan be made or repaid? These and other questions are taken up in Chapter 14.

4. Assessment of UK school education

4.1. Institutions

This section describes the school system (public and private) under the four heads of Table 4.1—that is, production, the individual-consumption decision, finance, and the aggregate production decision. Sections 4.2 and 4.3 assess the efficiency and equity of the system.

The operation of school education

The ultimate responsibility for education in England rests with the Secretary of State for Education, who is responsible for the Education Department and is accountable to Parliament.[12] Under the Department are over 100 Local Education Authorities (LEAs), each providing pre-school, primary, and secondary education. The state sector includes a significant number of religious denominational schools, particularly at the primary level, which retain the right to determine the content of religious education; the current expenditure and most capital spending of such schools is met by the state. There is also a small school private sector. Universities, discussed in Chapter 14, are not part of the legal framework established by the 1944 Education Act, nor are they the responsibility of LEAs.

Schools are inspected by an independent central body, the Office for Standards in Education, whose reports on individual schools are publicly available. State schools must keep to a national curriculum, and must test pupils at 7, 11, and 14. There is a nationally regulated school leaving examination (the General Certificate of Secondary Education (GCSE)) and a university entrance level exam (Advanced Level). Each school's results in the various tests and examinations are published. Thus parents have access to significant information on the quality of each school.

PRODUCTION. Education for the under-5s has been given increasing priority; by 2002 all 4-year-olds had access to pre-school education, with the intention that that entitlement should be extended rapidly to all 3-year-olds. All children receive compulsory primary education from age 5 to 11, usually at schools funded by LEAs. Secondary education is provided by LEAs for children aged 11 to 19 years. It is free, and compulsory till age 16. Most teachers are employed by the LEA and paid on an agreed national scale. Total public spending on school education in 2002/3 (Table 13.1) was £30 billion.

---

[12] Education is administered separately in Wales, Scotland, and Northern Ireland. Scottish educational institutions differ significantly from those in the rest of the UK, the difference being larger than for cash benefits and health care. Discussion is limited, for the most part, to the system in England.

Table 13.1. Education, England, 2002/3, estimated outturn (£m.)

Schools		
Under fives	3,173	
Primary	9,273	
Secondary	11,948	
Other	3,440	
Capital spending	2,196	
		30,031
Further education		
Further education and adult learning	5,141	
Student support	280	
		5,422
Higher education		
Spending on teaching and research	5,392	
Student support	1,065	
		6,457
Administration		1,479
		43,388

Notes:
The data in this table do not match those in Fig. 1.1. The data here are for England in 2002/3, the aggregate figure in Fig. 1.1 is that for the UK in 2003/4.
Figures are inflated to 2002/3 prices.   *Source*: UK DfES (2003a: table 3.3).

The third arm of the statutory system is further education, which covers the vocational, cultural, social, and recreational needs of everyone over school-leaving age who is not in full-time secondary or higher (i.e. university) education. The system provides education relevant to people's working lives, and is often dovetailed with the practical training provided by industry. A second function is to provide for people's leisure. This involves a huge variety of courses, for most of which charges are levied.

THE INDIVIDUAL-CONSUMPTION DECISION. A child normally attends a local primary school, and then proceeds to a local comprehensive school. Children normally take the General Certificate of Secondary Education (GCSE) in up to ten subjects, both arts and sciences, at about the age of 16. At that stage some children leave school; in 2000/1 89 per cent of pupils passed five or more GCSE subjects, and only 5 per cent left school with none. Advanced Level (A level) is taken at about the age of 18, usually in three or four subjects. The number of students staying on till 18 increased sharply over the 1990s. Universities do not normally admit students unless they have two or three A levels or the equivalent.

Issues of individual choice arise in at least three ways. First, there is the decision to continue education beyond the minimum leaving age. This is the individual investment decision discussed in Section 2.2, to which we return later. Second is the extent to which parents can choose which school their child attends. The 1944 Education Act allowed parents considerable discretion, but the exercise of that choice often conflicted with attempts by the LEA to balance numbers and quality of intake across schools within their jurisdiction and to set boundaries for each school's catchment area. Legislation in the 1980s increased the right of parents to choose any state school, limited only by the maximum size of school (set by the Secretary of State) and priorities given to those living nearest the school.

A third aspect of individual choice is the extent to which parents and their children have (or should have) any influence over the LEA and the teaching profession in the running of schools. After many years of debate, legislation in 1986 extended parental representation on schools' governing bodies. As mentioned earlier, the 1988 Education Reform Act introduced a national curriculum, which applies to all state schools. The Act also specifies 'attainment targets' at ages of 7, 11, 14, and 16. The national curriculum specifies programmes of study to achieve these targets, and also establishes a system of assessment.

FINANCE. Public spending on education roughly doubled in real terms between 1960 and 1976, when it peaked at nearly 7 per cent of gross national product. The increase was partly the result of higher birth rates in the late 1940s and mid-1960s; partly because expectations about educational standards rose; and partly because of the relative price effect.[13] Thereafter, spending declined to 4.7 per cent at the end of the 1980s—a cut unparalleled even under the Great Depression of the 1930s (Chapter 2, Section 3) (see Glennerster 1998). Spending rose somewhat over the 1990s. In 2000, public and private spending on education (Table 13.2) was somewhat below the OECD average of 5.3 per cent. Austria, France, and the Nordic countries stand out as high spenders. UK spending subsequently rose towards the OECD average, as real funding per pupil aged 4–19 in England increased by over one-quarter between 1997/98 and 2003/4, most of the increase taking place after 2000.

Spending on schools in England absorbed about two-thirds of the education budget in 2003/4 (Table 13.1).[14] Since few charges are levied, basic education is financed mainly by the state out of taxation. Since the mid-1990s, about three-quarters of education spending came from central government. There are also limited sources of non-governmental finance: schools can raise funds through their own efforts to pay for 'extras'; and the voluntary sector contributes to the cost of some schools (see Glennerster 2003a: ch. 6).

THE AGGREGATE PRODUCTION DECISION (i.e. setting budget limits). In the past most decisions about educational expenditure were a more or less complex mix of decisions at central and local levels. Since 1991, however, the bulk of education finance, and hence the aggregate production decision, has been a central government responsibility (Glennerster 2003a: ch. 6).

Private schools

Alongside the state sector, a small number of private schools (often confusingly called 'public' schools) provide education, for about 6 per cent of all pupils, a percentage that has remained static since the mid-1980s (Glennerster 2002b: annex table 1). The existence of a private sector is controversial. Private schools over the years have come under heavy attack. It is argued that they cream off scarce resources of academically gifted children and teachers, and of finance, making it difficult for state schools to maintain high

---

[13] See Chapter 12, note 12.

[14] Table 13.1 is for England not the UK, both because education is largely funded by local authorities and because it is more devolved to the different countries of the UK than the National Health Service.

Table 13.2. Education spending as percentage of GDP, OECD, 2000

	Primary and secondary education			Tertiary education			Total
	Public	Private	Total	Public	Private	Total	
Australia	3.7	0.7	4.4	0.8	0.7	1.6	6.0
Austria	3.7	0.2	3.9	1.2	negligible	1.2	5.1
Belgium	3.4	0.2	3.6	1.2	0.1	1.3	4.9
Canada	3.3	0.3	3.6	1.6	1.0	2.6	6.2
Czech Republic	2.8	0.3	3.1	0.8	0.1	0.9	4.0
Denmark	4.1	0.1	4.2	1.5	negligible	1.6	5.8
Finland	3.5	negligible	3.5	1.7	negligible	1.7	5.2
France	4.0	0.2	4.3	1.0	0.1	1.1	5.4
Germany	2.9	0.7	3.6	1.0	0.1	1.0	4.6
Greece	2.7	0.2	3.0	0.9	negligible	0.9	3.9
Hungary	2.8	0.2	3.0	0.9	0.3	1.1	4.1
Iceland	4.6	0.2	4.9	0.8	negligible	0.9	5.8
Ireland	2.9	0.1	3.0	1.2	0.3	1.5	4.5
Italy	3.2	0.1	3.3	0.7	0.1	0.9	4.2
Japan	2.7	0.2	2.9	0.5	0.6	1.1	4.0
Korea	3.3	0.7	4.0	0.6	1.9	2.6	6.6
Mexico	3.3	0.5	3.8	0.8	0.2	1.1	4.9
Netherlands	3.0	0.1	3.1	1.0	0.2	1.2	4.3
New Zealand	4.6	n.a.	4.6	0.9	n.a.	0.9	5.5
Norway	3.6	negligible	3.7	1.2	negligible	1.3	5.0
Poland	3.7	n.a.	3.7	0.8	n.a.	0.8	4.5
Portugal	4.1	negligible	4.1	1.0	0.1	1.1	5.2
Slovak Republic	2.7	0.1	2.8	0.7	0.1	0.8	3.6
Spain	3.1	0.2	3.3	0.9	0.3	1.2	4.5
Sweden	4.4	negligible	4.4	1.5	0.2	1.7	6.1
Switzerland	3.8	0.4	4.3	1.2	n.a.	1.2	5.5
Turkey	2.4	n.a.	2.4	1.0	negligible	1.0	3.4
United Kingdom	3.4	0.4	3.8	0.7	0.3	1.0	4.8
United States	3.5	0.4	3.9	0.9	1.8	2.7	6.6
OECD average	3.3	0.4	3.6	0.9	0.9	1.7	5.3

Notes: The data in this table, being based on different definitions, are not comparable with those in table 13.1. Numbers do not always add, due to rounding.
n.a. = not available.   *Source*: OECD (2003c: table B2.1b).

standards; and, through their hold on recruitment to key positions, that they perpetuate and accentuate economic and social divisions. The counter-arguments centre on their high quality, the beneficial effects of competition, and the freedom of parents to choose their favoured education.

The finance of private schools is complex. The bulk of their income comes from fees, though some have income from private endowments and appeals to former pupils. They also benefit from tax expenditures. Their charitable status gives them exemption from paying Value Added Tax on fees and from income tax, corporation tax, and local council tax.

In short, the production and finance of school education in the state sector are both public (approximating row 8 of Table 4.1). Private schools approximate to row 1, with elements of row 2.

4.2. Assessment 1: Efficiency

The measurement problems discussed in Section 2.2 create enormous difficulties for the assessment of external efficiency. Much of the argument is, therefore, of necessity *a priori*. Efficiency advantages and disadvantages are more finely balanced than with health care—one person's 'sign of a civilized society' is another's 'society is going to the dogs'. Discussion of efficiency therefore concentrates on four areas, with no attempt at division into advantages and disadvantages.

1. *The individual consumption decision* is substantially influenced by the state and the teaching profession both centrally and locally. Children must attend school until they are 16; the LEA can influence (or in some cases control) the choice of school; and state schools are bound by the national curriculum. These constraints mitigate to some extent the problem of imperfect information, but at the expense of consumer sovereignty.

During the 1990s and thereafter, there was a major effort to improve parental choice. The introduction of the national curriculum made it possible to introduce national Standard Achievement Tests at age 7, 11, and 14. The results of these tests, and the reports of the Office for Standards in Education on each school, were published. Taken together, these changes substantially increased the quantity and quality of information available to parents, and made access to such information easy. The second element in the strategy was to strengthen the power of parents to choose their child's school, not least by giving the Secretary of State the power to determine the size of each school (and hence the ability at least at the margin to expand numbers at schools for which demand was high).

2. *Primary and secondary education is free*, or nearly so. Such subsidies avoid the externality problem and have equity advantages. However, according to the screening hypothesis (Section 2.2), they may be inefficient beyond primary education.

3. *Macro-efficiency*. What is the efficient volume of resources to devote to school education? Though the question is central, the conceptual and measurement problems discussed in Section 2.2 make definitive quantification impossible. Educational achievement depends not only on schooling, but also on the quantity and quality of parenting, family income, family size, and the influence of television and neighbourhood. Thus it should not be surprising that the link between educational resources and pupil achievement is complex and, more generally, that the focus on inputs rather than outcomes may be mistaken (for a survey, see Hanushek 2003a). Such findings suggest that attempts to equalize the distribution of educational inputs may do little to reduce inequality.

Though quantitative analysis is fraught with difficulty, there are good qualitative arguments for increasing investment in education. The nature of technological change is a key driver. First, though it can reduce the need for skills—for example, computers have become more user-friendly—technological advance mostly increases the demand for skilled workers and reduces the demand for unskilled workers. Secondly, change is increasingly rapid, so that knowledge has a shorter half-life: thus skills need to be up-dated, and need to be flexible enough to adapt to changing technology. Put another way, investment in broad, flexible skills offers a hedge against technological dynamism. Specific skills may become redundant, but education and training should give people general skills, saving the resources that would otherwise have to be devoted to retraining labour whose skills had become outdated or, at worst, to supporting workers socially excluded as a result of technological advance.

These changes explain the movement into the 'information age', meaning a need for education and training that is (*a*) larger than previously, (*b*) more diverse, and (*c*) repeated, in the sense that people will require periodic retraining. They also explain the close links between low educational achievement and social exclusion (Sparkes and Glennerster 2002).

Demographic change creates a second argument for increased investment in education and training. The rising proportion of older people in many countries presages high spending on pensions and other age-related activities such as medical and long-term care. As discussed in Chapter 9, Section 3.2, the solution is to increase output sufficiently to meet the combined expectations of workers and pensioners. If the problem is that workers are becoming relatively more scarce, the efficient response is to increase labour productivity. Demographic change is thus an argument for additional spending on investment both in technology and in human capital.

Notwithstanding the impossibility of quantifying the efficient level of spending on education, training, and retraining, the qualitative arguments that education contributes to personal and national goals are strong.

4. *Micro-efficiency*. Having asked (but failed wholly to answer) the question 'are we spending the right amount on education?', we need next to ask the other half of the external-efficiency question: 'are we doing the right things with educational resources?' First, are schools efficient? Gundlach et al. (2001) argue that school productivity declined in OECD countries. Glennerster (2002*b*) offers a counterblast so far as the UK is concerned. He points to a series of reforms in 1988 (see Section 5.2), notably the introduction of (*a*) national standards and a national curriculum and (*b*) a quasi-market (see point 1 above), together with (*c*) devolution of management to schools. The resulting competition, alongside a series of more specific reforms in the late 1990s and early 2000s, Glennerster argues, contributed significantly to improved educational outcomes, most strikingly in primary schools. The topic is taken up in Section 5.2.

School productivity, however, is only part of the story. Just as good health is due at least as much to factors outside the health sector, such as diet and lifestyle choices, as to clinical interventions, so there is growing evidence that the sources of educational outcomes are much wider than the schooling a person receives. Feinstein (1998, 2003) analyses data from the UK 1970 Birth Cohort Survey, a particularly rich dataset that includes test scores at ages 22 months, 42 months, 5 years, and 10 years. His findings are dramatic. First, early child development matters: there is a statistically significant relationship between test scores at 22 and 42 months and later achievement. As an example, over half of the children whose test scores at 42 months are in the top quartile went on to get A-level qualifications or higher; for children in the bottom quartile of test scores, the comparable figure was 17 per cent (Feinstein 2003: table 3).

A second conclusion is that socio-economic status has a major influence. At 22 months there was a 13 per cent difference in the average scores of children in the top and bottom socio-economic groups; by age 10 that had widened to 28 per cent (ibid., figure 1). Even more dramatically (ibid., figure 2), consider two children: A is from a poor background but in the top quartile of test scores at 22 months; B is from a well-off background but is in the bottom quartile. By age 6, B has started to overtake A. Social background has overcome the effects of early poor development.

A number of implications follow. First, schooling from age 5 is not enough to overcome polarization; intervention is needed much earlier. Government policy—for example, the Sure-Start programme—is beginning to address the gap (see Section 5.2). Secondly, the quality of parenting, a topic that is starting to receive the attention in research it deserves, is crucial. 'The production of human capital depends as much on the investment of parental time and skill in children as it does on formal schooling' (Glennerster 2003a: 103; see also Sparkes and Glennerster 2002). Thus the efficient division of resources devoted to educational achievement should not focus on the formal school system alone, but also on broader determinants of achievement.

4.3. Assessment 2: Equity

As discussed in Chapter 4, Sections 2.2 and 4.3, equity is hard to define and depends on political perspective. Following Section 2.1, horizontal equity is taken to imply that children A and B should have an equal *opportunity* (as defined in Chapter 6, Section 3.1) to acquire an education of equal quality and duration, irrespective of whether, for example, A comes from a middle-class family and B from a lower socio-economic group. Equality of opportunity, as discussed in Chapter 6, Section 3, does not necessarily imply equality of outcome for at least three reasons: A may be luckier than B; they may have different tastes where (and the proviso is crucial) both are well informed; and A may be more 'able' than B, where such differences are not related to educational and other circumstances earlier in their lives.

5. *The role of income.* The intention of the 1944 Education Act and subsequent policies was that access to education should not be constrained by family income. This aim has not been fully achieved for either schools or higher education. Though no fees are charged, school attendance still involves parental expenditure—for example, on uniforms or sports gear; and schools are allowed to charge for individual music tuition and for some outside-hours activities. In addition, too many children leave school at 16 not because they want to or because they do not have the ability to proceed further, but because their family needs their earnings. School education after age 16 (for which financial support, though improving, remains limited), like health care under the NHS, is not 'free', but imposes a

cost in forgone earnings that bears disproportionately on the lower socio-economic groups. This disproportion has major implications (discussed in Chapter 14) for university attendance.

6. *Reducing inequality of achievement*. Compared with countries like France and Germany, England historically has a bad record in terms of people leaving school with no qualifications, and also in terms of intermediate technical skills. However, the level of academic achievement, once the preserve of the better-off, has increased and the variance in achievement within the UK declined. Between 1970/1 and 1993/4, the fraction of children leaving school without any qualification fell from 44 per cent to 6 per cent, and the numbers gaining one or more passes at A level doubled (Glennerster 1998: table 3.5). And, as measured by the ability to achieve at least some passes at GCSE, the class gradient at 16 had largely been levelled (ibid., table 3.11). In the years since 1995, both trends strengthened. Glennerster (2002b: table 5) shows sharp improvements between 1995 and 2001 in test results at ages 7, 11, and 14. He also found (ibid., table 6) that the poorest-performing schools and—separately—the schools with the largest number of pupils from poor backgrounds improved more than average schools—that is, inequality of outcomes reduced.

Equality increased in other ways. Girls' achievements improved unambiguously. In 1980/1 boys did better at A level; by the mid-1990s the situation had reversed; and by the mid-1990s women slightly outnumbered men at university (Glennerster 1998: table 3.7). The achievements of ethnic minority children also improved. The general pattern was a tendency to do less well in primary school, but to catch up later, in some instances surpassing the performance of white pupils (Glennerster 1998).

As earlier discussion of Feinstein's results (point 4) makes clear, however, the pattern of declining inequality does not mean that all is well. Middle-class parents can better exercise choice within the state sector, both directly and by moving to areas with good schools, and some increase their choice further by sending their children to private schools. At this point the conflict between equity and individual freedom is at its sharpest.

Similar incentives arise on the supply side. The move towards quasi-markets (Section 5.2) increases competitive pressures on schools. Chapter 12 discussed the problems that arise when private medical insurers attempt to screen out all but the best risks. Glennerster (1991) argues that schools face similar incentive to cream skimming. We know that (*a*) performance is determined largely by socio-economic background, and (*b*) schools in greater demand can attract more pupils and hence more funds. A school achieves (*b*) by maximizing the examination results of its pupils; it does that at minimum cost by selecting students from higher socio-economic backgrounds. Just as medical insurers seek healthy clients, schools seek potentially high-achieving pupils. Evidence suggests that worries about cream skimming are real (see West and Pennell 2002).

A countervailing incentive is to target more resources on pupils from poorer backgrounds (analogous to paying doctors a higher capitation allowance for chronically ill or elderly patients). Glennerster (2002b: 130) concludes:

The government has not done enough to compensate schools for the extra demands that poorer-performing or difficult pupils put on the school. Ideally, a school should be indifferent between accepting a child with lower potential or greater problems compared with another pupil. If it were to receive sufficient additional rewards for taking difficult pupils, that indifference could be achieved. We have to find a more rigorous and evidence-based allocation to schools in deprived areas.

How much should we worry if education is distributed unequally? Differential access *could* in principle be caused entirely by exogenous differences in tastes and abilities, in which case no issue of inequality arises.[15] A person would be brave (or foolish) to argue that this is the whole explanation but, to the extent that it is part of the story, a simple observation of outcomes tends to overstate inequality. Secondly, if this inequality is genuine, should we be concerned about it? Is education the engine of economic prosperity or the plaything of the rich? If the former, it is appropriate to be concerned about its distribution on efficiency as well as equity grounds. If the latter (i.e. if the screening hypothesis holds), post-compulsory education may have no *social* benefits, thereby diminishing the importance of the efficiency question. But, since education confers *private* benefits, its distribution, if inequitable, remains a proper concern. Thirdly, it is necessary to remind ourselves that a different system of education would not *necessarily* be more egalitarian. As with the NHS, it is not enough to argue that the present system is imperfect; it is also necessary to suggest an alternative that will do better. If none can be found, egalitarian goals must be pursued by other means.

These caveats notwithstanding, the distribution of education is clearly influenced by inequalities in society. Individuals from less fortunate backgrounds have less information about the value of education, and less know-how to make the best use of 'the system'. They have lower incomes, and are therefore less able to afford the earnings forgone by continuing education. Nor should it be forgotten that education is an investment that, like all investments, takes time to pay off; but the pursuit of long-run goals requires *hope*; and hope, too, is distributed unequally by social class. The expectations of children are formed largely on the experience of their parents, whose lives may give little encouragement to long-run optimism. For all these reasons, children from low-income families tend to receive education of a lower quality, and to avail themselves of a smaller quantity. There is inequality in education, and the inequality is much greater than in health care.

7. Redistributive effects of school education. We have seen (Chapter 7, Section 4.2, as qualified by Chapter 7, Section 4.1) that education is financed progressively if (rich) individual R consumes (say) twice as much education as (poor) individual P, so long as R pays more than twice as much as P in the taxes that pay for education. For the system as a whole, historical evidence shows education spending on a child of a family in socio-economic group 1 (henceforth for short a 'rich' child) was about 50 per cent higher than for a 'poor' child (Le Grand 1982: table 4.1). If so, the system is financed progressively if on average the tax contribution towards education of an individual in the highest socio-economic group exceeds that of someone in the lowest by more than 50 per cent. As with the NHS (see the discussion in Chapter 12, Section 4.3), this is likely if we are prepared to assume that education is financed out of taxation generally—that, if all public expenditure on education were withdrawn, there would be, for example, a reduction in income tax, or an equi-proportionate reduction in all taxes, rather than a reduction of a regressive tax.

[15] Murphy (1981: 182) sums up the issue neatly: 'though no necessary relationship exists between class *disparity* in education and class *inequality* in education, educational commentators have conventionally taken the existence of one to indicate the existence of the other' (emphasis added).

In contrast with the NHS, however, matters cannot be left there. The different parts of the educational system must be discussed separately. The conclusion of Chapter 14 is that the redistributive effects of publicly funded higher education are regressive.

5. Reform

Section 5.1 looks at private approaches to reform, in particular proposals for voucher schemes. Section 5.2 assesses a series of reforms to the school system in England.

5.1. Mainly private approaches

RADICAL PRIVATIZATION. Section 3.1 discusses the failure of many of the standard assumptions.[16] *A priori* we would therefore expect an unrestricted private market for school education (i.e. row 1 or 2 in Table 4.1) to be inefficient for technical reasons (Section 3.1), and also inconsistent with widely held views of social justice (Section 3.2). Complete privatization offers no solution, so it is not surprising that no advanced country has a system of school education remotely approximating a pure private market. It is more useful to ask whether any mixed public/private package offers hope of improvement.

VOUCHER SCHEMES FOR SCHOOL EDUCATION. The idea is that parents receive an education voucher for each child—that is, a tied grant to be 'spent' by parents at a school of their choice. There are many variants, of which two best illustrate the mechanism.

The Friedman proposal (1962) has three defining characteristics.

- The value of the voucher is the average cost of a place in a state school, or a proportion of that cost.
- 'Topping up' is allowed (i.e. if the voucher does not fully cover fees, parents can top it up out of their own pockets).
- Parents and schools are unconstrained: parents can spend the voucher at any school, public or private, and schools have complete freedom in their choice of pupils and organization of waiting lists.

The Jencks scheme (1970) is very different.

- The basic voucher covers the full average cost of state education.
- Topping up is not allowed, but low-income parents receive a larger voucher, thus giving extra resources to schools with larger numbers of disadvantaged children.
- Schools where demand exceeds supply are constrained in that they must allocate at least half of their places by ballot.

---

[16] i.e. the assumptions necessary for the market to allocate efficiently—see Chapter 4, Section 3.2, or the Appendix to Chapter 4, paras. 6–17.

Thus the Jencks scheme has more of an equalizing effect on expenditure. Both Friedman and Jencks are concerned with consumer sovereignty and efficiency, but Jencks's scheme places more emphasis on distributional goals.

The essence of the voucher idea is that education is at least in part produced in the private sector, with intervention to increase efficiency and equity by subsidy (i.e. the voucher) and regulation (e.g. compulsory school attendance, minimum standards, and, in some schemes, restrictions on topping up and the allocation of places). The Friedman scheme is therefore a mixture of rows 1 and 2 of Table 4.1 (because parents can choose their child's school, and are free to top up the voucher) and row 4(a) (since education up to a certain age is compulsory). The Jencks scheme is a combination of row 2 and line 4(b), the latter because the 'no-topping-up' rule imposes a constraint on total output.

Voucher schemes, it is argued, increase efficiency, enhance consumer sovereignty, and reduce the risk of political indoctrination. Parents choose their child's school; and education is privately produced and competitive, so that schools are responsive to parental demand. Proponents also claim as an advantage that voucher schemes avoid the situation where parents who send their children to private schools receive no tax relief in respect of costs from which they thereby relieve the state system.

To opponents of voucher schemes, their efficiency advantages are debatable and their equity effects almost certainly deleterious. The efficiency issue, as we saw in Section 3.1, hinges on whether parents are sufficiently well informed to make the right choices for their children and to police the standards of their child's school. To the extent that middle-class parents are better able to exercise choice, competitive pressures are mainly to their advantage. Secondly, as discussed in point 6 above, schools face incentives to screen out low-achieving applicants, improving the quality of a school's intake being the cheapest and easiest way to improve its outcomes.

Voucher schemes also have major distributional effects, though less so in the case of a Jencks type of scheme than under the Friedman proposals. Extending vouchers to private schools would increase subsidies to people already choosing private education, mainly the better off; spending the money on improving the state system would do more to equalize educational outcomes. Allowing parents to top up vouchers would accentuate disparities in the distribution of education, both quantity and quality. Vouchers might well have advantages for middle-class families, but only at the expense of less well-informed choices by lower socio-economic groups. The equity issue therefore turns on the relative weight given to the claims of the two groups. Finally, voucher schemes are criticized because privately produced education is likely to reduce social cohesion.[17]

My own conclusion is that voucher schemes that offer public funding of mainly privately produced education offer questionable efficiency gains, and increase inequality both in access and outcomes. As discussed in point 6 above, however, increased competition between schools in the state sector (an implicit voucher scheme) offers potential gains in both efficiency and equity. This is the direction that UK reform has taken.

---

[17] As a graphic illustration of differences of opinion about what constitutes a good education, note the chasm between 'reduce social cohesion' here and 'reduce the risk of political indoctrination' above.

5.2. Reforms in the UK

The strategy of public production, regulation, and finance (row 8 in Table 4.1), at least for school education, is common to all industrialized countries. Though the strategy is not seriously questioned, worries about efficiency and equity generate continuing reform.

Quasi-markets and the 1988 education reform act

The basic idea of quasi-markets is to retain public funding but to increase efficiency and responsiveness by introducing market forces *within* the state system. The 1988 Education Reform Act includes provisions specifically designed to do this, reinforced by a 1992 Act that requires schools to publish the examination performance of their pupils, leading to the publication of league tables. It is useful to draw out the different strands of quasi-markets as they apply to education.

Competition. The argument for competition is that it improves efficiency. As with health care (Chapter 12, Section 5.3), optimism should not be uncritical. Problems include imperfect consumer information on the demand side and local monopoly on the supply side. In addition, as discussed in Section 4.3, point 6, competition gives schools incentives to recruit students from better-off backgrounds to maximize school performance, hence (given league tables) maximizing the demand for places. Competition thus creates two contradictory pressures: towards the efficient use of resources and towards 'cream-skimming'.

Local management of schools allows individual schools to manage their current (but not capital) resources. The argument for decentralized management is that it improves efficiency and allows schools to respond to competitive pressures. Local managers have better information than managers at the Local Education Authority or the central Education Department. In addition, if management is central, information flows become distorted by local managers so as to maximize their freedom. Empirical evidence from the USA (Chubb and Moe 1990) supports the view that decentralized school systems produce better results, measured in terms of educational outcomes.

Open enrolment and formula funding. Under open enrolment parents, within limits, can choose to which school to send their child. Formula funding introduced a capitation element into school finance, such that any pupil signing on at a state school triggers a payment by the LEA to the school; thus schools that attract more pupils receive more resources. This implicit voucher arrangement means that school finance is determined in part by parental choice rather than by bureaucratic decision.

The national curriculum can be viewed in very different ways. In its favour, it can be regarded as regulating education markets, analogous to managed health care. Secondly, and complementarily, it can be argued to increase equality of opportunity by spreading best practice. The assessment targets are outcome measures against which school performance can be measured and, where necessary, remedial action can be taken.

A very different view, thirdly, is that the national curriculum exemplifies a centralizing tendency and interferes with the individual/family consumption decision. Schools wishing to experiment, which was possible under the old system subject to *local* agreement, now require *central* agreement from the Secretary of State. Only parents who can afford private education have genuine freedom (private schools are not bound by the national curriculum). The national curriculum, according to this view, reduces efficiency, equity, and individual freedom.

A fourth view, drawing on the experience of other countries, is that the national curriculum politicizes education achievement, since politicians will not like to see large numbers of pupils failing the tests.

Reforms since 1997

In schools (in contrast with health care and higher education) the government elected in 1997 continued the competitive reforms of its predecessors. It also introduced further changes.

- Given the very early roots of disadvantage (point 4 above), policies targeted early childhood. Sure-Start provided child care and training for mothers on low incomes. A National Child Care Strategy included increased availability of affordable child care. Nursery school places for 3-year-olds were increased, covering 88 per cent of children by 2003. The right to enter pre-school was given to 4-year-olds.

- There was increased emphasis on basic skills. The literacy hour, introduced in 1998, spent an hour each day exclusively on developing and improving reading and writing skills. A parallel numeracy hour was introduced in 1999.

- Education Maintenance Allowances, after a pilot scheme, went nationwide in 2004 for pupils from poor families from the age of 16, to encourage them to stay at school. The scheme includes a £30 weekly allowance plus periodic bonuses where recipients keep to the terms of a learning agreement with their school or college.

- There was action on literacy and numeracy also for young adults, a problem identified in UK DfES (1999).

- Increasingly after 2000, there was a sharp increase in funding per pupil.

Glennerster (2001b) reports three sets of outcomes. First, test scores improved, most strikingly in primary schools. In 1995, 45 per cent of pupils reached the mathematics targets for 11-year-olds; by 2001 the figure was 70 per cent. For the same two years, the percentage of pupils reaching the reading targets rose from 49 per cent to 81 per cent (ibid., table 5). Secondly, in contrast with outcomes earlier in the 1990s, this achievement was not concentrated at the top end: the schools that had performed least well in 1995 improved more than the average or the best schools (ibid., table 6). Thirdly, the same, broadly, is true of schools with the most students from poor backgrounds (ibid., table 7). Thus average attainment increased and inequality of outcome declined.

Three sets of questions arise. First, can we take the numbers at face value? Are the improvements genuine, or have pupils and teachers simply got better at taking tests? The counter-argument is that the improvement has been steady and sustained. Secondly, if the improvement is real, can it be attributed to increased competition? Logic suggests that the combination of (*a*) targets, (*b*) published exams results, and (*c*) a system of finance in which a school's income depends on its ability to attract pupils should create powerful incentives to improve outcomes, as attested by the huge amount of attention schools pay to their performance in league tables.

Third, are the equity gains as large as they might be, or are they significantly reduced by competitive pressures to selectivity? Some writers (West and Pennell 2002, 2003; West and Hind 2003) argue that these pressures have significantly reduced access to the best schools for disadvantaged pupils. More optimistically, Glennerster, based on his own findings and those of Bradley et al. (1999) and Bradley and Taylor (2000), concludes that:

> The results are clear. Those schools that faced most competition from nearby schools improved their performance most. The greater the competition the more the improvement, and the longer this persisted, the more they improved.
>
> The evidence suggests . . . that the quasi-market has . . . increased efficiency. It may have done so at the cost of encouraging selectivity, although the evidence is weaker. It is possible to counter this disadvantage by increasing schools' financial and other incentives to accept more difficult or slower learners. (Glennerster 2003a: 122–3).

The conclusion—an important one—is that competition within the state sector opens up the possibility of improving outcomes *and* of reducing disparities in achievement. The story is ongoing, however, not least because the improvements have been sharpest in primary schools, with fewer gains in secondary education.

6. Conclusion

Educational outcomes derive from many sources, including family income, parenting, and natural ability (Section 4.2), and thus depend not only on classroom activity but on much broader factors. Conceptual and measurement problems make the area highly controversial, and controversy is compounded by differences over the meaning of a 'good' education, which includes not only technical matters but also attitudes and values (Section 2.1).

So far as school education is concerned, many of the assumptions necessary for market efficiency fail, the main problems being imperfect information, imperfect capital markets, and external effects. From an equity viewpoint, the most important problem is that knowledge about the operation and value of education is likely to be correlated with socio-economic status. Substantial public involvement is therefore essential (Section 3.3), although, because the information problem is less acute than with health care, the theoretical arguments about public production (as opposed to regulation and finance) are rather more finely balanced. It is, therefore, not surprising that no advanced country has a system of school education that even remotely approximates a pure private market. State-school systems universally are publicly regulated and financed; they are also all publicly produced. To the extent that this strategy is valid on efficiency grounds, it is legitimate for education to be financed in accordance with distributional goals (Chapter 4, Section 7.2).

The practice of education in the UK is far from unblemished. Measurement problems (Section 2.2) make the assessment of efficiency problematic, though—at least as measured by test scores—outcomes have improved and disparities in achievement declined. Access in terms of gender, ethnicity, and social class has also improved. However, substantial differences remain: the better off receive higher-quality school education and make more intensive use of the system, and the latter difference cannot be explained entirely by differences in tastes and ability.

However, those who argue for a more private school system have to demonstrate not that the current system is imperfect (which is not in dispute), but that a more market-oriented solution would do better. So far as school education is concerned, opponents of the broad thrust of existing arrangements have yet to prove their case. The advocates of a mixed public/private system of school education offer only limited evidence in support of their views. The efficiency effects of vouchers for a mainly private school system are unclear *a priori* and not proven empirically. In equity terms they are likely to increase inequalities in the distribution of education, and in particular to benefit the middle class at the expense of lower socio-economic groups (Section 4.3).

The significant improvements in the performance of the school system suggest a policy of seeking improvement within the existing strategy. But it should be clear from earlier discussion that the determinants of educational outcomes are much broader than school activities, family and other influences in early childhood being particularly important. To the extent that inequalities in education are the result of broader inequalities, progress in the former will depend in part on improvements in the latter. Thus education policy needs to be explicitly rooted in broader social policies.

■ QUESTIONS FOR FURTHER DISCUSSION

1. What problems arise in attempting to assess the social benefits of increased investment in education?

2. Assess the case for introducing market forces into school education, for example through a system of vouchers. Would you give the same answer for university education?

■ FURTHER READING

On the institutions of school education, recent developments and statistical data in the UK, see Glennerster (2003a: ch. 4), the Department for Education and Skills *Departmental Report* (UK DfES 2003a) (the 2003 version of an annual publication), and the Education Department web site, http://www/dfES.gov.uk, and, for statistical information, UK DfES (2003b). OECD (2003c) contains compendious statistical information on education systems throughout the advanced industrial countries. See also the various government portals in the list of useful web sites at the start of the book.

The case for market provision of education is set out by Friedman and Friedman (1980: ch. 6); for a critique, see Bosanquet (1983: chs. 11, 12).

For an introduction to the underlying theory, see Stiglitz (2000: ch. 16), and for general texts on the economics of education, Blaug (1970), Johnes (1993) (a UK text), Cohn and Geske (1990) (a US text), and, for collections of major articles, Hanushek (2003b) and Johnes and Johnes (2004). On the vast literature on the theory of human capital and its applications, see Blaug (1970: ch. 1); the classic work is Becker (1975). The screening literature is assessed by Riley (2001). See also the Further Reading on the theoretical literature on information problems at the end of Chapter 5.

For the relationship (or lack of it) between educational inputs, educational attainment, and the distribution of income, see Krueger and Whitmore (2001), Hanushek (2003a), and Krueger (2003).

On measuring the returns to education, see Psacharopoulos (1994), Blundell et al. (1999), Dee (2003), and OECD (2003b). McMahon (2002) discusses returns in developing countries.

For discussion of the relation between education and growth, see Hanushek and Kimko (2000), Bassanini and Scarpetta (2001), Krueger and Lindahl (2001), Gylfason and Zoega (2003), and OECD (2003b). For a more sceptical view, see Wolf (2002).

On competition and voucher schemes, see Epple and Romano (1998), Hoxby (2000), Ladd (2002), and Neal (2002). Angrist et al. (2002) offer a case study based on evidence from Columbia.

As general reinforcement of the material in this chapter, see Glennerster (1998; 2003a: ch. 6). The first assesses the UK educational experience from the mid-1970s to the mid-1990s, the second, the finance of education and more recent developments. For assessments of reform since 1997, see Glennerster (2002b, 2003a) (more optimistic) and West and Pennell (2002, 2003) (who accept the gains in achievement but are less optimistic about access). On education and social exclusion, see Sparkes and Glennerster (2002), and, on the early roots of poor educational performance, Feinstein (1998, 2003). UK DfES (2002) is a White Paper on schools setting out the government's agenda for subsequent years.

For a survey that analyses OECD countries and also some developing countries, see Hanushek (2002), and, for US discussion, Lazear (2002) and the articles about competition listed above.

14 | Higher education

All that is spent during many years in opening the means of higher education to the masses would be well paid for if it called out one more Newton or Darwin, Shakespeare or Beethoven.

(Alfred Marshall, 1842–1924)

1. Introduction

The previous chapter set out the strong case for public funding and public production of school education.[1] This chapter, its twin, applies the same theory to university education and reaches very different conclusions: that funding should be shared between the taxpayer and the recipient, and that production should be substantially through market forces. A core message in Chapter 12 is the ill effects if policy treats health care as though it were food, uncritically adopting market forces where the standard assumptions do not apply.[2] Analogously, this chapter shows the ill effects of treating a food-type good as though it were health care. The resulting problems are predictable: underfunded universities, inadequate student support, and a poor record on access.

The chapter discusses the aims of higher education (Section 2), theoretical arguments about state intervention in pursuit of efficiency and equity (Section 3), assessment of higher education in the UK (Section 4), reform directions (Section 5), and conclusions (Section 6). There is much that the chapter leaves out. The theoretical discussion in Sections 2 and 3 is broadly applicable to all post-compulsory education and training, including further education and vocational training. Because of constraints both of space and expertise, however, the latter part of the chapter concentrates on higher education.

2. Aims

Chapter 13, Section 2.1, discussed the aims of education in general terms and should be reread at this stage. A key point is that educational outcomes comprise *both* knowledge and skills *and* attitudes and values. Higher education therefore contributes both to national

---

[1] Chapter 4, Section 6, discusses in detail the distinction between public and private production and finance.
[2] i.e. the assumptions necessary for the market to allocate efficiently—see Chapter 4, Section 3.2, or the Appendix to Chapter 4, paras. 6–17.

economic performance and to the promotion of core values, and thus has a significant cultural dimension that will vary across people within a country and across countries.

In parallel with the discussion of school education, achieving the primary objective—better educational outcomes—rests on secondary objectives: using resources efficiently and distributing them equitably.

EFFICIENCY. Allocative (or external) efficiency applies to the totality of resources devoted to tertiary education (the macro-efficiency aim in Chapter 1, Section 2.2), and also to the division of resources between the different parts of tertiary education and, within higher education, their division between subjects and universities, and between spending on universities and on student support (the micro-efficiency aim). Separately, productive efficiency (Chapter 4, Section 2.1), sometimes referred to as *internal* efficiency, is concerned with such factors as the quality of university management. The acute problems involved in measuring these variables, discussed in Chapter 13, Section 2.2, apply equally here.

The specific efficiency aims of higher education include the efficient *size* of the sector, the efficient *quality*, and the efficient *subject mix* to maximize student satisfaction, meet the needs of employers, and maximize national economic performance.

EQUITY, as discussed in Chapter 13, Section 2.1, is harder to define. I shall adopt the same definition as for school education in defining equity as a form of equality of opportunity (Chapter 6, Section 3.1, especially equation (6.18)). Thus *access* to higher education, the key equity aim, should be based on a person's ability and tastes, but not on family income or socio-economic status, nor on gender or ethnicity. Improved access contributes to equity. It also contributes to efficiency, in that it minimizes the waste of talent.

FREEDOM, an objective that economists do not discuss very much, is important in this context. *Intellectual freedom and diversity* are important both for their own sake, as a core value, and because a thriving, diverse system of higher education contributes to democratic pluralism. Separately, the *pursuit of knowledge for its own sake* is an objective, partly for intrinsic reasons and also, more practically, because it is often unclear in advance whether a particular line of research might have practical benefits, the study of binary numbers in nineteenth-century mathematics being a case in point.

3. Methods

3.1. Theoretical arguments for intervention 1: Efficiency

The analysis of health care in Chapter 12, Section 3.1, discussed separately the market for health care and the market for medical insurance. Analogously, discussion here focuses separately on (*a*) the market for higher education and (*b*) the finance of higher education.

Higher education
PERFECT INFORMATION. As discussed in Chapter 4, Section 3.2, consumer sovereignty is more useful (*a*) the better is consumer information, (*b*) the more cheaply and effectively

it can be improved, (c) the easier it is for consumers to understand available information, (d) the lower are the costs of choosing badly, and (e) the more diverse are consumer tastes. There are good reasons for optimism in applying these criteria to higher education. First, information is available, and more can be made available. There are already good university guides, and universities publish detailed information on the Internet. Secondly, students can, for the most part, understand and evaluate that information. The process is easier because going to university can be anticipated (contrast finding a doctor to deal with injury after a road accident), so that the student has time to acquire the information and advice he needs. Thirdly, though the costs of mistaken choice can be large, it is not clear that a central planner would do better; moreover, the move towards modular degrees, allowing students to change subjects and, increasingly, institutions, reduces those costs. It should be noted, fourthly, that students make choices already.

Finally (item (e) above), consumer tastes are diverse, degrees are becoming more diverse, and change is increasingly rapid. For all these reasons, students are more capable than central planners of making choices that conform with their own needs and those of the economy. In contrast, attempts at manpower planning are even more likely than hitherto to be wrong because of the increasing complexity of post-industrial society. Consumer sovereignty can thus be regarded as more useful for higher education than for schools.

On the demand side, therefore, it can be argued that students are well-informed consumers. Though that proposition is robust for most students, there is an important exception: students from poorer backgrounds might not be well informed. It has been argued that relatively poor people will borrow to buy a house, so why not to buy a degree? Apart from the tax advantages, when someone buys a house (a) he knows what he is buying, since he has lived in a house all his life, (b) the house is unlikely to fall down, and (c) over most periods the value of the house is likely to go up. When people borrow for a degree (a) they may be imperfectly informed about the nature of the product if from a family with no graduates, (b) there is a high risk (or at least a perceived high risk, which again is higher for people with no previous university experience in their family) of failing the degree, and (c) though the *average* private return to a degree is positive (Blundell et al. 2000; OECD 2003b), there is considerable variance around it. For all three reasons, borrowing to buy a degree is more risky than borrowing to buy a house, and the risks are likely to be greater for people from poorer backgrounds and for women. These issues have major implications, discussed below, for the design both of student loans and of redistributive policies.

On the supply side, central planning, whether or not it was ever desirable, is no longer feasible. Forty years ago, with an elite system (only 5–6 per cent of young people went to university), it was possible, as a polite myth, to assume that all universities were equally good ('parity of esteem') and hence could be funded broadly equally. Responding to technological change, however, advanced countries increasingly have mass higher education, meaning more universities, more students, and greater diversity of subject matter. Thus the myth of parity of esteem and approximate parity of funding is no longer sustainable. In principle, differential funding allocations could be made by an omniscient central planner, but the problem is too complex for that to be the sole mechanism: mass higher education requires a funding regime in which institutions can charge differential prices to reflect their different costs and missions.

Perfect information about prices can be addressed by requiring universities to publish charges on their web site. Perfect information about the future is not an issue in the sense that higher education raises no insurance problems.

PERFECT COMPETITION AND MARKET FAILURES. In most countries there are a fairly large number of universities and similar institutions, and students, unlike schoolchildren, are old enough to study away from home. Thus it is reasonable to regard higher education as competitive, an argument reinforced by international competition and distance learning.

Higher education is not a public good, nor are there increasing returns to scale. As discussed in Chapter 13, Section 2.2, however, there are strong arguments that higher education creates benefits to society above those to the individual—benefits in terms of growth, the transmission of values, and the promotion of social cohesion.[3] Note that the latter two externalities arise whether or not the screening hypothesis holds (see Chapter 13, Section 2.2). Those arguments suggest a continuing taxpayer subsidy for higher education. Equally, however, there is overwhelming evidence that students receive a significant private benefit from their degrees. Thus it is efficient and equitable that the costs of higher education should be shared between the taxpayer and the direct recipient.

It can therefore be argued that higher education conforms reasonably well with the standard assumptions. The strategy that follows is to use market forces (with regulation where relevant) to allocate resources, with taxpayer subsidies in respect of external benefits and redistributive activity to promote access. The role of the state in assisting efficiency and equity is taken up in Section 3.3.

Financing higher education

Parallel to the question of how resources are best allocated within higher education is the question of how the finance of higher education should be organized.

WHY STUDENT LOANS? There is a head-on collision worldwide between two competing imperatives:

- the need for mass investment in human capital (Chapter 13, Section 4.2, point 3); and
- fiscal constraints in the face of demographic pressures and international competition (Chapter 15, Section 2.2).

Funding higher education entirely through the tax system is a blind alley. As discussed in Section 3.3, it is not only unaffordable in fiscal terms, but also inefficient, given the private benefits to recipients, and regressive, since higher education is consumed mainly by people from better-off backgrounds, who therefore benefit most from tax funding.

Thus public funding must be supplemented on a significant scale by private funding, for which there are six potential sources:

1. family resources;
2. a student's earnings while a student;

---

[3] See the definition of externalities, public goods and increasing returns to scale in the Appendix to Chapter 4, paras. 13, 14.

3. a student's future earnings—that is, loans;

4. employers;

5. entrepreneurial activities by universities; and/or

6. gifts—for example, from charitable foundations or bequests in people's wills.

If we look at these in turn, family resources are not bad in themselves, but do nothing to promote access. Student earnings are generally small. The USA, with flexible labour markets and a tradition of combining study with work, is an outlier. In addition, earning activities compete with study time and leisure. These are not arguments against this approach, but caution against excessive reliance.

Employer contributions, contrary to popular belief, are likely to be small. This is systematic and predictable. When jobs were for life, it was rational for an employer to invest in the skills of his workers, since he would reap the benefits of that investment. Today, in contrast, labour is mobile. Thus it remains in the interests of employers *as a whole* to want training to take place, but in the interests of each *individual* employer to leave it to other employers to pay for training, and then to poach the resulting trained people. In short, there is an externality, leading to under-investment in training by employers.

Entrepreneurial activities by universities, as a practical matter, yield little net revenue. They need very different skills from those of running the academic side of the institution. At worst, they risk diverting scarce institutional capacity to lower-priority activities. Even at the most prestigious US universities, income from such things as intellectual property rights is only a small fraction of university income.

Gifts, analogous with student earning opportunities, are a useful potential source of funds, but are rarely more than a marginal contribution, except in the USA, which has a culture of giving and highly developed institutions to encourage it. In addition, while gifts may be important to some top universities, they are much less relevant to the generality of universities, and of virtually no relevance to other tertiary institutions.

Having ruled out (*a*), (*b*), (*d*), (*e*), and (*f*) as *major* sources of private funds, we are left with loans as the only approach with the potential to yield resources on a large scale and in an equitable way. The design of loans, however, is critical.

WHAT TYPE OF LOAN: THE ARGUMENT FOR INCOME-CONTINGENT REPAYMENTS Loans can be organized in different ways.

- *Mortgage-type loans*—for example, home loans or bank overdrafts—have fixed repayments of £X per week.

- With *income-contingent loans*, in contrast, repayments take the form of x per cent of the borrower's subsequent earnings until the loan plus interest has been repaid. Thus the duration of repayment is variable.

- With a *graduate tax*, repayments continue for life, or until retirement. High-earning graduates may therefore repay more than they have borrowed.

Because of major capital-market imperfections, mortgage-type loans create problems on both sides of the market.

On the demand side, they are risky from the student's viewpoint and so are likely to deter applicants, particularly from poorer backgrounds. This is inefficient, because it wastes talent, and is inequitable. As discussed earlier, borrowing to pay for an education qualification is more risky than borrowing to buy a house. This is for several reasons.

- Though the average real return is positive, the variance of outcomes is generally larger for educational qualifications.
- There is no security for the loan. If someone takes out a loan to buy a house and subsequently earns less than anticipated, he can sell the house and use the proceeds to repay the loan. This is not an option with a qualification.
- Both risks apply to all students, but particularly to those from poorer backgrounds who tend to be (a) less well informed and (b) less able to absorb financial risk.

On the supply side, long-term loans are risky also to the lender: there is no collateral; and students are better informed than lenders about whether they aspire to careers in financial markets or the arts (another example of asymmetric information).

Friedman (1962) is clear about these capital-market imperfections. He points out that

the device adopted to meet the corresponding problem for other risky investments is equity investment plus limited liability on the part of shareholders. The counterpart for education would be to 'buy' a share in an individual's earning prospects; to advance him the funds needed to finance his training on condition that he agree to pay the lender a specified fraction of his future earnings. (p. 103)

On that basis he advocates loans from government, in return for which

the individual . . . would agree to pay to the government in each future year a specified percentage of his earnings in excess of a specified sum for each $1,000 that he received . . . The payment could easily be combined with payment of income tax and so involve a minimum of additional administrative expense. (p. 105)

Thus Friedman, starting from the benefit principle (he who benefits should pay), ends up advocating a graduate tax (as defined above). A different approach starts from a predisposition towards free, tax-financed education, abandoning that model only because of its regressiveness in the case of higher education. Glennerster et al. (1968: 26) point out that

in the United Kingdom, higher education is now financed as a social service. Nearly all the costs are borne out of general taxation . . . But it differs radically from other social services. It is reserved for a small and highly selected group . . . It is exceptionally expensive . . . [And] education confers benefits which reveal themselves in the form of higher earnings. A graduate tax would enable the community to recover the value of the resources devoted to higher education from those who have themselves derived such substantial benefit from it.

Thus the benefit principle and the ability-to-pay approach, despite their very different starting points, lead to an identical policy prescription—income-contingent repayments. This is an important conclusion. Someone with low earnings makes low repayments, and someone with low lifetime earnings does not fully repay his or her loan. Thus income-contingent loans have in-built insurance against inability to repay, addressing the demand-side capital market imperfection—the uncertainty to the individual about the return to a degree.

There is one further point. Consumption smoothing, and the role of the welfare state in assisting it, is a central theme of this book.[4] Pensions redistribute from a person's younger to her older self; student loans, analogously, redistribute from middle years to earlier years. Income-contingent loans are thus also consistent with the idea of social insurance.[5]

3.2. Theoretical arguments for intervention 2: Equity

Suppose that every student has an income-contingent loan large enough to cover realistic living costs and all tuition charges. Thus higher education is free at the point of use, and the borrower repays only if his or her subsequent earnings warrant. It might therefore be argued that going to university is a low-risk choice, and hence a large enough income-continent loan is all that is needed to ensure equal access.

To illustrate why that argument does not stand up, it is necessary to explore more deeply the roots of exclusion. Someone might be (a) badly informed about the benefits of a degree (shortage of information), (b) come from a low-income background (shortage of money), and/or (c) attend a low-quality school (a shortage of education). Thus a person might not apply to university for a variety of reasons.

- She has not thought of it, or wrongly thinks she is not suited for it (root (a)).

- She has left school at 16, either for lack of aspiration (root (a)), or because her family needs her earnings (root (b)), or because her school has not inspired her to stay on (root (c)).

- She is debt averse. At one level this could be regarded as irrational, in that loans have income-contingent repayments. If, however, she is badly informed and, as a result, underestimates the benefits of a degree and overestimates the costs (root (a)), the decision could be entirely rational given what she knows. In addition, if she is from a low-income family (root (b)), the capacity to absorb financial risk is lower; again, unwillingness to borrow, even on the most advantageous terms, could be rational.

Thus the state has a significant role in three strategic ways to promote access:

- *improving information*, particularly for schoolchildren to raise their aspirations (i.e. tackling root (a)), to encourage them to stay on in school and, having done so, to apply to university;

- *providing money* in at least two ways. First, to address root (b), the state should provide financial assistance to encourage pupils to stay at school after age 16, an example being education maintenance allowances, discussed in Chapter 13, Section 5.2. Secondly, the state should pay grants (i.e. scholarships) to university (and other tertiary) students from poor backgrounds, thus addressing debt aversion;

- *improving the quality of school education*, which is necessary to address root (c).

---

[4] See the Fisher model in Figure 4.5 and surrounding discussion.

[5] For that reason my original (1989: ch. 5) proposal was for income-contingent repayments added to national-insurance contributions rather than to income tax.

3.3. Types of intervention

Sections 3.1 and 3.2 discussed *why* the state might intervene. The next issue is *how* best it might do so.

SCHOOLS AND UNIVERSITIES: TWO VERY DIFFERENT STRATEGIES. Earlier chapters contrasted food and health care. With food, people are generally able to make well-informed choices, supporting a strategy that pursues efficiency through market allocation and distributional objectives through income transfers—for example, paying pensions to the elderly, who then buy food in the same shops as the rest of us, and at the same prices. With health care, in contrast, there are major information problems in the market for medical care and, separately, in the market for medical insurance, suggesting a much greater role for the state.

In considering whether higher education (or tertiary education more generally) is more like food or more like health care, there are three important gradients.

- *Age*. As students get older, they become better informed. It is clearly right that someone makes educational choices on behalf of a small child. A university student, in contrast, is better informed about her needs than anyone else. At some stage in between the balance tips, arguably at the age at which education stops being compulsory.

- *Diversity*. There are strong arguments for considerable homogeneity in what schools offer, in terms both of technical matters (a common package of basic knowledge and skills) and of attitudes and values, to strengthen social cohesion. The higher up the education scale one goes, the weaker the claims for uniformity and the greater the desirability of diversity, particularly of subject matter.

- *Socio-economic status*. Compulsory education, by definition, is attended by children from all socio-economic groups. However, for the reasons discussed in Section 3.2— notably the socio-economic gradient in access to high-quality schooling and to information about the benefits of a degree—it is mainly people from better-off backgrounds who stay at school beyond minimum leaving age and go on to university. This issue arises in all countries; it is acute in the UK.

The first two gradients point in the same direction. Younger children have limited capacity to make choices, and there is a strong case for uniformity of educational experience, pointing to a centrally planned package, with space for local, cultural, and religious diversity. School education thus has more in common with health care than with food.

In contrast, the capacity of young adults to make choices is generally good and the case for diversity strong. Post-compulsory education is more like food than health care. It is thus consistent to question competitive private provision of school education, as in Chapter 13, but to support market mechanisms in combination with income transfers and other government intervention for tertiary education.

In short, theory suggests that higher education is more like food than like health care, suggesting that market forces are useful. The third gradient does not invalidate this conclusion, which holds for the generality of students, but gives a cogent justification for the access measures in Section 3.2, which are a central plank in the reform strategy in Section 5.1.

The rest of this section draws out four lessons from economic theory: (*a*) the days of central planning are gone; (*b*) the costs of higher education should be shared between the taxpayer and the recipient; (*c*) well-designed student loans have essential characteristics; and (*d*) government has an important continuing role.

WHO SHOULD MAKE THE DECISIONS? A major conclusion from Section 3.1 and the preceding discussion is that the days of central planning of higher education have gone. Consumer sovereignty is useful, since students are generally well informed and could (and should) be given more and better information. Secondly, producer sovereignty is essential, given the size and diversity of higher education and the speed with which content is changing. Thus decisions should be taken not through central planning but as a result of choices by all the major stakeholders—students, universities, employers and government.

WHO SHOULD PAY? A second major conclusion is that the costs of higher education should be shared between the taxpayer and the recipient. Given the external benefits higher education creates, it is efficient that taxpayer subsidies should be a permanent part of the landscape.

Why not finance higher education from taxation, as with school education? Earlier discussion suggests three reasons why tax funding beyond that commensurate with external benefits or aimed at improving access is the wrong way forward in terms of the objectives in Section 2.

Tax funding is unaffordable—that is, violates the objective of macro-efficiency. This is the conflict discussed in Section 3.1 between (*a*) the imperative for a large, high-quality tertiary sector in the interests of national economic performance and (*b*) fiscal constraints arising from population ageing and international competitive pressures.

Tax funding is also inefficient, given the private benefits to recipients, violating the micro-efficiency objective.

Thirdly, tax funding is regressive—that is, violates the equity objective. To the extent that higher education is disproportionately consumed by people from better-off backgrounds, it is they who benefit most from tax funding. To many, as a value judgement, this is wrong. Even worse, excessive reliance on tax funding diverts to students from better-off backgrounds the resources that should be used to finance the wide-ranging activities needed to improve access, discussed in Section 3.2.

The fact that tax funding, beyond a certain point, is regressive is no accident. Some people argue that higher education should be treated as a tax-funded social good that a civilized country should offer. This is a beguiling vision, which was possible when higher education was a consumption good for a small number of people. But those times have gone. There are three steps in the argument.

- Technological advance means that mass higher education is essential for national economic performance.

- We live in a free society, so that people can choose how hard to work and can emigrate. Both facts impose limits on taxation, and those limits are reinforced by international capital mobility.

- Mass higher education, which is expensive, plus limited taxation lead to rationing of places and funding. In any rationing system, middle-class families are likely to do better (see the discussion on the roots of exclusion in Section 3.2), leading to disproportionate middle-class use. Thus—systematically and predictably—excessive reliance on tax funding is regressive.

HOW SHOULD LOANS BE ORGANIZED? Well-designed student loans have three essential features.

Income-contingent repayments. As discussed in Section 3.1, income-contingent repayments promote efficiency by protecting borrowers against risks that would otherwise lead to inefficiently low levels of investment in higher education, and equity, since their inbuilt insurance against inability to repay assists access.

Large enough to cover all fees and realistic living costs. Large enough loans resolve student poverty and promote access by making higher education free at the point of use. Student loans are a device to assist consumption smoothing. If students face an intertemporal budget constraint that incorporates an efficient interest rate (discussed shortly), there is no good reason for restricting loans—for example, via an income test. This is an argument not for unlimited loans, but for loans large enough to cover realistic costs.

An unsubsidized interest rate. In broad terms, the interest rate on student loans should be related to the government's cost of borrowing. Blanket interest subsidies cause four major problems.[6]

- They violate the macro-efficiency objective. They are very expensive in fiscal terms, with potentially deleterious effects on the quality of higher education, since student support, being politically salient, crowds out the funding of universities.

- They are inefficient in microeconomic terms. A subsidized interest rate distorts choices between present and future consumption: because of the fiscal cost of interest subsidies, loans tend to be too small, reducing their effectiveness in providing consumption smoothing.

- They are inequitable because they impede access. Loans are expensive, therefore rationed, and therefore too small. The result impedes access because students from poor backgrounds may not have access to family support, putting them at risk from expensive credit-card debt.

- They are inequitable, in addition, because they are deeply regressive, the main beneficiaries being successful professionals in mid-career. To illustrate the point, ask who benefits from interest subsidies. They do not help students (graduates make repayments, not students). They help low-earning graduates only slightly, since unpaid debt is eventually forgiven. They do not help high-earning graduates early in their careers—with income-contingent loans, monthly repayments depend only on earnings; thus interest rates *have no effect on monthly repayments*, but only on the

---

[6] A separate issue is that Islamic law does not allow interest payments. But it is possible to buy a house in ways compatible with Islamic law by making monthly rental payments for an agreed duration, after which ownership of the house is transferred to the occupant, a method facilitated by recent UK reforms of the stamp duty payable on the transfer of ownership. Formulating student loans as a capped graduate tax offers an analogous way forward.

duration of the loan. Thus the major beneficiaries are successful professionals in mid-career, whose loan repayments are switched off earlier because of the subsidy than would otherwise be the case.

WHAT ROLE FOR GOVERNMENT? The argument for market forces does not mean that government has no role. Government continues to have important tasks.

Funding. This includes taxpayer subsidies justified by external benefits and also (though not discussed in this chapter) research funding.

Promoting access. Action to promote access includes the type and range of measures discussed in Section 3.2.

Ensuring quality assurance in the interests of consumer protection. This could be by a central inspectorate, analogous to the Office for Standards in Education for schools. A more light-handed approach stresses incentives more than regulation. A minimalist model would require universities to publish accurate performance data on their web sites—for example, the destination of its recent graduates—giving prospective students the information they need to vote with their feet.

Setting incentives. Government will have views about the shape of higher education. It might, for example, wish to encourage subjects less able to flourish in a more market-oriented system, such as music, drama, or some languages. For different reasons, it might wish to encourage teacher training. In either case, it could bring this about by targeting resources on such activities.

Government will also have views about the degree of competition it wishes to see. In a simple-minded vouchers model, institutions compete for students; those that attract large numbers flourish and expand, those that fail to attract students go to the wall. Universities, however, are not the conventional firms of economic theory (Winston 1999): they do not make a homogeneous product; they do not maximize profit; and the 'product' is not well defined. Thus red-in-tooth-and-claw competition is not the best environment for higher education. It is a mistake, however, to think that this is the only approach to competition. At the other extreme, government, as in the UK in the early 2000s, could decide how many students studied which subjects at which university, and issue vouchers accordingly. Such a regime simply mimics central planning. Thus a market-oriented model should be thought of as a continuum, from 0 per cent constrained (law of the jungle) to 100 per cent constrained (pure central planning) or anywhere in between. The degree of competition is a policy variable, and different answers are possible for different subjects. Thus government continues to have an important role, but as setter of incentives, not as central planner.

Organizing student loans. Capital market imperfections explain why the private sector provides large-scale home loans but no analogue to finance investment in human capital. Government action is therefore needed at a minimum to ensure the administrative infrastructure is in place and to provide targeted subsidies for people with low lifetime earnings who, with income-contingent repayments, will not repay their loans in full. Mostly, government will also have to provide the loan capital.

4. Assessment of UK higher education[7]

4.1. Institutions

THUMBNAIL HISTORY. The funding of higher education can be divided into four phases.

- Until 1990, tuition fees were paid from taxation and living expenses by a mixture of tax-funded grant and, for better-off families, a parental contribution.
- Between 1990 and 1998, tax funding of tuition fees continued, but a student loan covered part of living costs, alongside a smaller system of grants and parental contributions.
- In 1998, a fixed charge for tuition fees was introduced, from which poor people were exempt; the grant was abolished, and living costs financed by a mixture of loan and parental contributions. Thus there were tuition fees but no market forces.
- Under reforms announced in 2003, grants were due to return in 2005; and from 2006, universities were to be allowed some variation in the fees they charge, thus introducing market forces.

The following discussion describes the higher education system under the four heads of Table 4.1: production, the individual-consumption decision, finance, and the aggregate production decision. Sections 4.2 and 4.3 assess the organization of the system and outcomes.

PRODUCTION. Higher education comprises what used to be two sets of institutions: polytechnics and universities. Polytechnics, formerly under the control of Local Education Authorities, became independent under the 1988 Education Reform Act. Universities have always been independent, self-governing bodies. The formal distinction between universities and polytechnics disappeared in 1992.

THE INDIVIDUAL-CONSUMPTION DECISION. UK students choose to which universities they apply, and universities choose which students to accept. Places are offered mainly on the basis of academic qualifications, usually A levels. Students do not have a right to a place; they are carefully selected, and the drop-out rate is low by international standards. The tuition fees of UK full-time undergraduates at a UK university were paid from public funds until 1998, after which a tuition charge was levied except for students from poor backgrounds.

Until 1998, British undergraduate students in full-time higher education were also eligible for a maintenance grant to cover living costs. The grant varied according to where the student studied and whether or not he continued to live in the parental home, and was means-tested on family income. Students from the best-off families received no grant. Where students received less than the full amount, parents were expected to make up the difference.

---

[7] The discussion in Sections 4 and 5 will at times have a more campaigning note than parallel discussion in previous chapters, since I have been a participant in the UK debate since the first (1987) edition of this book.

In its early days the system worked well. Over the years, however, a combination of rising student numbers and fiscal constraints put the system under pressure. Partly for that reason, grants were supplemented by student loans from 1990. Higher education is thus subsidized for UK students, particularly undergraduates. Overseas students are not generally eligible for public funding. They pay full tuition fees and must finance their own living costs.

FINANCE. The 1960s were a golden age for UK higher education (the same was true in the USA). The Anderson Report (UK Department of Education 1960) advocated generous maintenance grants; and the Robbins Report (UK Committee on Higher Education 1963)—a major milestone in British higher education—recommended sharp expansion of student numbers. Higher education in the 1960s was generously funded from taxation, with few questions asked. The good times drew to a close in the mid-1970s. Tax funding declined, and universities were given increasing 'guidance' about how money should be spent.

Reforms after 1988. The Education Reform Act 1988 greatly extended central planning of higher education. From 1992, universities in England were funded by the Higher Education Funding Council for England (HEFCE), with separate bodies for the other parts of the UK. Universities 'bid' to teach N students at a price of £X each. As a result, they received public funds from three main sources: income from HEFCE; students' tuition fees (paid by government); and research funds, channelled largely through the Research Councils. Universities also increasingly earned money in the private sector: from the fees of privately funded UK students and of overseas students; from privately funded research activity; from a variety of commercial activities; and (in some cases) from their own endowments. From 1991, research funding became more selective, based on a four-yearly Research Assessment Exercise.

Reform in 1998. A Committee of Inquiry (UK NCIHE 1997*a,b* (The Dearing Committee)) reported in 1997, and government responded with a series of reforms that took effect in 1998. For present purposes, the key features of the reform were:

- The mortgage-type student loan introduced in 1990 was replaced by a loan with income-contingent repayments.

- The maintenance grant (to cover part of living costs) was abolished and replaced by an income-contingent loan.

- A tuition fee of £1,000 per year was introduced; the fee was the same on all courses at all universities. There was no loan to cover the tuition fee.

- Both loan and fee were income tested. A student from a poor background paid no fee and was entitled to the maximum loan; a student from a well-off background paid the full fee and received a loan that was generally at least 75 per cent of the full loan.

This system is assessed in Sections 4.2 and 4.3.

THE AGGREGATE-PRODUCTION DECISION. In the 1960s and early 1970s, somewhat to over-simplify, higher-education institutions decided how many students to admit and the state made available sufficient funds to make this possible. There was a major expansion of the university sector in the aftermath of the 1963 Robbins Report. After 1975, these policies were to some extent reversed, or at any rate halted. In 1990, only 14 per cent of the relevant age group started full-time degree courses. As well as restricting the *size* of the higher-education sector, there was also growing government influence on its *composition*. What used to be virtually untied transfers to higher education became increasingly like tied grants.

A dramatic expansion in student numbers between 1990 and 1995 requires explanation. In 1990, the then Secretary of State for Education established a target of a 30 per cent participation rate by the turn of the century. From 1991, teaching and research were funded separately; thus expansion, being based only on teaching costs, became cheaper. Each university was given a contract to teach N students, funded at the full estimate of teaching costs. However, universities were allowed to attract students in excess of N. For such students, they were paid a lower sum. Since this was the only way cash-strapped universities could get any more money, they expanded rapidly—so rapidly that in 1996 government reimposed limits on student numbers.

Thus participation rose sharply (the good news), so that the UK moved from an elite system of higher education in 1960 to a mass system by 1995. However (the bad news), funding failed to keep pace; over the twenty years from 1980 real funding per student in higher education almost halved. In 2000, UK spending on tertiary education was 1 per cent of GDP, significantly below the OECD average of 1.7 per cent and a long way below the US figure of 2.7 per cent (Table 13.2).

In short, the production of higher education is private, and finance for UK students largely public (row 2), but with increasing elements of row 4(*b*), given the growing control over the disposition of public funds.

4.2. Assessment 1: The organization of higher education

This section assesses the system of higher-education finance introduced in England in 1998.[8] Section 5 assesses reform foreshadowed for 2006. It is helpful first to assess the way higher education is organized (i.e. the process) before assessing the outcomes.

1. *Income-contingent loans.* There is one piece of unambiguously good news. Income-contingent loans, with repayments collected alongside income tax, were introduced for UK students starting their degrees in or after 1998.

Unfortunately, even in 2003 the wider public remained largely unaware that repayments were income contingent, and hence a payroll deduction like income tax, but paid only by graduates and switched off once the loan was repaid. Such ignorance impeded access. The fault was largely the government's, who did little to explain the system, in particular that student loans were not like mortgage-type debt.

The bad news is that income contingency is all the good news. Higher education in the years after 2000 faced a series of problems that were both predictable and predicted

---

[8] For a fuller discussion, see Barr and Crawford (1998*b*) and Barr (2002*b*). The arrangements in Scotland and Wales are somewhat different—see the Further Reading.

(Barr and Crawford 1998*b*; Barr 2002*b*): continuing interest subsidies, inadequate funding of universities, deficient design of student loans, a highly complex system of student support, continued central planning, and a woeful record on widening access. The root problems were two fundamental distortions: interest subsidies and continued central planning.

2. *Interest subsidies*. In the UK, graduates pay an interest rate on their loans equal to the rate of inflation rather than the government's cost of borrowing. The resulting problems graphically illustrate the analytical arguments in Section 3.3. The focus of attack is *blanket* interest subsidies; a strong case can be made for *targeted* subsidies—for example, for people who are unemployed, to make sure that their debt does not spiral upwards.

The motivation for interest subsidies is to promote access. There is universal agreement about the objective, but interest subsidies actively impede its achievement.

Problem 1. Loans were too small—in particular there was no loan to cover fees. Interest subsidies are expensive: about one-third of money lent to students never came back because of the cost of the subsidy. As a direct consequence, the Treasury rationed loans: the full loan did not cover realistic living costs; loans were means-tested, so that not all students were eligible for a full loan; and there was no loan to cover fees. As a result:

- The system was inefficient, because loans could not provide all the consumption smoothing that students would have liked.

- It was inequitable, because it caused student poverty, and even more inequitable because the problem was worse for students from poorer families.

- It impeded access, because worries about student poverty and/or credit-card debt deterred an unknown number of people from applying to university.

Problem 2. Interest subsidies are regressive. As discussed in Section 3.3, the major beneficiaries of interest subsidies are successful professionals in mid-career, whose loan repayments are 'switched off' earlier because of the interest subsidy than they would be otherwise. Thus the effect of interest subsidies is to transfer money from the pockets of students (because loans are too small) to the pockets of people in mid career and (because inadequate loans force students to used credit-card debt) to the pockets of credit-card companies. This is not what policy-makers intended.

Problem 3. The system of student support was complex. Someone from a poor background paid no tuition fee and was entitled to a full loan. The assessment of a student's financial position was based on parental (or spouse) income. Parental income had two effects: as income rose, the tuition fee rose; once the fee reached its maximum (£1,125 in 2003/4), the effect of additional parental income was to reduce the size of the loan to which the student was entitled. All students, however rich their parents, were entitled to a loan equal to about 75 per cent of the maximum loan *except* that scholarship and similar income, if high enough, could reduce loan entitlement below that 75 per cent minimum. Alongside these arrangements were a series of other schemes to assist students from poor backgrounds that—notwithstanding attempts at simplification in 2002— remained complex.

To a considerable extent, this complexity resulted from (*a*) the income test and (*b*) the need to supplement loans that are too small—both further consequences of interest subsidies. Students, prospective students, and their parents could not understand the system; it was a nightmare to administer; and complexity, *per se*, impeded access.

3. *Continued central planning*. This chapter and the previous one argue for central planning of school education but against central planning of higher education. Yet higher education continued to be centrally planned, first, through controls on price and quantity. For UK and EU undergraduates, the price (i.e. the tuition fee) was the same at all universities and for all courses, and was set by law. The central planner also established the number of students at each university and on each degree, though latterly such controls were slightly relaxed.

A second strategic element in central planning was a bureaucratic approach to quality control. It is right that universities are accountable publicly and transparently for the public funds they receive, but the procedure was heavily bureaucratic. The process of assuring teaching quality in the late 1990s and early 2000s provoked particular hostility because of its intrusive nature and considerable additional workload.[9] Teaching quality assurance was only the tip of the bureaucratic iceberg.

The resulting ill effects are discussed below. However, one in particular should be discussed immediately—the control of fees as another price distortion alongside the interest subsidy. An efficiency problem, discussed in points 4 and 5 below, is that universities were underfunded; thus central planning impeded quality. Price control also impeded access because the fees of home students were controlled, but universities could charge whatever they wanted to non-EU students. The problem was predicted.

A further impediment to access is the incentive to discriminate against British students. A flat fee will continue the erosion of quality at the best universities, which face the biggest shortfalls in funding. British students could suffer in one of two ways. The quality of the best institutions might fall; though British students could still get places, the quality of the degree would be less. Alternatively, the best institutions will largely stop teaching British undergraduates (for whom they receive on average £4,000 per year) and will use the fees from foreign undergraduates (around £8,000 per year) to preserve their excellence. The government is considering trying to prevent British universities from charging additional fees to UK/EU students. Again, this is done for equity reasons; again, it ends up harming the very people it is aimed at helping.   (Barr and Crawford 1998*b*: 80)

In addition, most people would regard it as unfair if a student at Banbury University (a small, mythical local university) has to pay the same tuition fee as one at nearby Oxford.

Points 2 and 3 suggest that higher education in England and Wales (and to a lesser extent in Scotland) faced two fundamental problems: universities were underfunded, and students were poor. In addition (point 6 below), the proportion of students from the lowest two socio-economic backgrounds had not changed significantly in forty years.

4.3. Assessment 2: Outcomes

How do points 1–3 map onto the objectives in Section 2?

---

[9] A prized possession is the picture I took of the fourteen filing cabinets of material for the 3½-day visit to assess LSE's teaching of politics in October 2000.

4. *Macro-efficiency*. UK higher education has a record of high quality, at its best world class, and is a major export industry. But by 2003, if not earlier, there was universal agreement that the system was underfunded and that quality had been eroded.

In the late 1980s I argued (Barr 1989: ch. 1) that the UK higher-education sector was too small, with 14 per cent of the age group going to university. By the early 2000s, participation had risen to over 40 per cent. The problem was then different—that of quality—given real cuts in funding per student. As an illustration, each university teacher on average had responsibility for 40 per cent more students in 1996 than in 1989 (UK Committee of Vice-Chancellors and Principals 1996: 4). One of the roots of the funding problem was interest subsidies: since student support is politically salient, interest subsidies at the margin crowded out resources. A second root was continued central planning, in particular the control of tuition fees. As a result, universities were neither (*a*) adequately funded out of taxation nor (*b*) given the freedom to charge for their core activities. Either (*a*) or (*b*) is a potentially coherent approach; to have neither is by definition incoherent. Though quantification is impossible, there was a powerful efficiency case for more resources for higher education, a case all the stronger because of international competition.

5. *Micro-efficiency*. The loan system created a series of inefficiencies. Loans were too small and hence inefficiently constrained choices over consumption smoothing. The interest subsidy created incentives to borrow as much as possible, if only to make a profit by putting the money into a bank account paying a higher rate of interest. Third, the complexity of student support (another indirect consequence of interest subsidies) was inefficient because it left people imperfectly informed and because of its excessive absorption of administrative resources.

Central planning created additional inefficiencies. With a large, growing, and increasingly diverse sector, the ability of a central planner to make decisions about the efficient number of students at different institutions and in different subjects was increasingly deficient. This is not a criticism of the Higher Education Funding Council for England but of its inappropriate remit.

Central setting of prices (i.e. tuition fees) created further inefficiencies and inequities. The logic of economic theory is particularly ruthless in this context. Price ceilings erode incentives to investment and quality improvement (whose costs cannot be covered by price increases); price floors erode incentives to increased efficiency (whose benefits cannot be appropriated through lower prices). Flat fees, being both a floor and a ceiling, are thus particularly inimical to efficiency.

Finally, central planning was costly in terms of time and paperwork.

6. *Access*. As with school education, access improved somewhat, to an extent that is greater than is apparent from the raw statistics. The point is identical to that for health care (Chapter 12, Section 4.3, point 16): 'the unskilled manual group may form a low percentage of students but there are far fewer people in that position to start with' (Glennerster 1998: 59). For that reason, disparities should be measured not by data on groups but by data on individuals. Hellevick and Ringen (1995), comparing the cohort born in the 1960s with that of the 1930s, found that inequality in educational achievement halved, as measured by the Gini coefficient applied to individual data. Glennerster (1998: table 3.11) reaches a similar conclusion: in 1974 children with professional

and managerial parents were over-represented among degree-holders by a factor of 2.7 relative to their overall numbers in the population; by 1990, the disproportion had fallen to 1.4.

That said, England still had a poor record both absolutely and in comparison with other countries. In 2002, 81 per cent of children from professional backgrounds went into higher education; the comparable figure for children from unskilled backgrounds was 15 per cent (UK Education and Skills Select Committee 2002: 19).

What can be said about causes? A central point is that the real barriers to access arose earlier in the system. The roots of exclusion were discussed in Section 3.2: a lack of information, lack of money, and/or lack of high-quality schooling. All three elements are critical determinants of whether or not a person leaves school at 16. Of people with A levels good enough to go to university in the early 2000s, 90 per cent did so, with virtually no socio-economic gradient. Hence £1 million spent raising GCSE scores and encouraging people to continue to A level does more for access than increased subsidies of higher education for people who would have gone to university anyway. Some of the policies designed to increase staying-on rates are discussed in Section 5.

A second set of causes lay within higher education itself. The problems of student support discussed earlier impeded access—notably the fact that loans were too small and that fees had to be paid upfront because there was no loan entitlement to cover them. In addition, excessive tuition fee subsidies (a consequence of flat fees) disproportionately benefited middle-class students, crowding out resources for targeted transfers to promote access.

7. *Equity 1: general.* Equity issues arise in ways other than unequal access. The introduction of loans with income-contingent repayments in 1998 was an unambiguous improvement in equity as well as efficiency terms.

As discussed earlier, however, major inequities arose from the interest subsidy: loans were too small, creating poverty and impeding access, and the subsidies were deeply regressive (point 2, above).

Flat fees, as well as being inefficient, are also inequitable: as discussed earlier (point 3), it can be argued to be unfair to charge the same tuition fee at a small local university as at a world-class one; in addition, there is the potential discrimination against home students.

8. *Equity 2: what is wrong with tax funding?* The introduction of fees in 1998 was attacked by some who thought it wrong to charge *any* fee and by others (Barr and Crawford 1998*b*) because the proposal did not go far enough—the flat-rate nature of the fee, in essence, enshrining continued central planning. The way to show why variable fees improve not only efficiency but also equity is to consider the inequity of tax funding.

Given the external benefits of higher education, it is efficient that tax funding of part of its costs should be a permanent part of the landscape. Tax funding beyond that faces three inescapable problems.

Problem 1. It does not work. As discussed in point 6, access remains highly unequal.

Problem 2. It will not happen. Given increasingly acute fiscal constraints, higher education will always lose out to the National Health Service, nursery education, and schools.

Problem 3. It should not happen. As discussed in Section 3.3, excessive reliance on tax funding is both inefficient and deeply regressive. If the money comes from general taxation, the taxes of the hospital porter pay for the degree of the old Etonian. If it is unfair for graduates to pay more of the cost, as the proponents of tax funding argue, it is even more unfair to ask non-graduate taxpayers to do so.

The counter-argument is to make direct tax more progressive. Suppose the government raised £5 billion that way. The question that advocates of tax funding must then answer is: why should that money be spent on students from better-off backgrounds who will generally go on to become the richest, rather than on nursery education (see the discussion in Chapter 14, Section 4.2, point 4), vocational education, action to improve the staying-on rate post-16, and more generous grants?

9. *Redistributive effects of higher-education finance.* We have seen (Chapter 7, Section 4.2, as qualified by Chapter 7, Section 4.1) that education is financed progressively even if (rich) individual R consumes (say) twice as much education as (poor) individual P, so long as R (or her parents) pays more than twice as much as B in the taxes that pay for education. The previous chapter concluded that school education, for the most part, was financed redistributively. However, it is necessary to discuss separately the different parts of the education system. It is possible to argue that post-compulsory secondary education might still be progressive; but the finance of further education is at best proportional, and that of universities almost certainly regressive. A similar conclusion was reached, for similar reasons, by Hansen and Weisbrod (1969, 1978) for the heavily subsidized system of public higher education in California.

The regressivity of university finance is compounded by noting that education has major intergenerational aspects. The children of poor parents tend to have lower-quality education, and less of it. Thus the taxes of poor families contribute to consumption by the rich of a university education which helps to keep them rich.

The assessment of the system of higher education in the UK[10] is an illustration in practice of the theoretical discussion in Chapter 4, Section 7.2—namely that, where the conditions necessary for the market to operate efficiently hold, the use of price subsidies in pursuit of equity objectives frequently ends up not only creating inefficiency, but also harming the very people the subsidies were intended to help.

- The interest subsidy on student loans harms access because loans are too small and because their cost crowds out the income transfers that would do much more to promote access. More generally, the interest subsidy is such a major distortion that it also impedes the objectives of quality and expansion.

- Flat tuition fees cause inefficiency (point 5), harm access (point 6), and are inequitable in other ways (point 7).

The UK government after 1997 was genuinely committed to access, but the policies they put in place did little to improve matters. What should they have done?

---

[10] Though much of the specific discussion in Section 4 is about England, the general point applies to the UK as a whole.

5. Reform

5.1. A strategy for reform

A reform strategy—broadly applicable to all industrialized countries—has three elements.

DEFERRED VARIABLE FEES. Universities should be free to vary their tuition fees, bringing in additional resources to improve quality. Students should be helped to pay the charges as described below. Of central importance, charges should be deferred: thus graduates make repayments, not students.

Thinking on fees can be muddled. Many people (including me) agree that higher education is a right for those with the wish and the aptitude, but it does not follow that it must be free (food, equally, is a right, yet nobody demonstrates outside shops or restaurants). Another confusion is between social elitism, which is abhorrent, and intellectual elitism, which is both necessary and desirable. There is nothing inequitable about intellectually elite institutions. The access imperative is a system in which the brightest students can study at the most intellectually demanding institutions irrespective of their socio-economic background.

ADEQUATE AND UNIVERSAL INCOME-CONTINGENT LOANS. The second element in the strategy is student loans large enough to cover fees and realistic living costs and available to all students. This package eliminates upfront fees, making higher education free at the point of use. It ends student poverty. It is simple to understand. And it is vastly simpler to administer than a system that relies heavily on income testing.

ACTIVE MEASURES TO PROMOTE ACCESS. As discussed in Section 3.2, there are three causes of exclusion: information poverty, financial poverty, and poor access to good schools. Any strategy to promote access must address all three.

- *Financial resources*. Financial support post-16 is essential to encourage young people to stay in school. Once at university, grants are vital; so are extra resources to provide intellectual support for students whose road to higher education has been difficult, to assist the transition. Further measures are needed to help people with low earnings after university.

- *Information*. Action to inform schoolchildren and raise their aspirations is equally critical. The saddest impediment to access is someone who has never even thought of going to university. Action needs to start young (see Chapter 13, Section 4.2, point 4).

- *Improved school quality*. The problems of access to higher education cannot be solved entirely within the higher-education sector. More resources are needed earlier in the system to improve the quality of the lower tail of school education.

5.2. Proposed reforms: The 2003 White Paper

CONTENT. A wide-ranging White Paper was published in 2003. Discussion here is limited to the funding proposals, under the same three heads as the reform strategy, above.

Fees raise three separate questions: should fees be the same at all universities or different; should students pay fees upfront or deferred; and should universities receive fees upfront or deferred? The White Paper answered all three questions correctly. From 2006 fees will no longer be fixed, but variable between 0 and £3,000 per year. However, there will no longer be an upfront charge, since fees will be fully covered by a loan. Universities, however, receive the fee income upfront.

Student support continues broadly the same as the 1998 regime assessed in Section 4. The maximum maintenance loan was increased, but entitlement continues to be income tested. Loans attract a zero real rate of interest—that is, interest subsidies continue.

Access. The White Paper aimed to promote access directly in several ways. It brought back a grant of at least £1,000 per year, subsequently increased to £2,700 per year.

Seen through the eyes of lurid press coverage, the proposals were horrible—high fees, large debts. That view is thoroughly misleading. The strategy has two elements: it (*a*) redistributes from better off to worse off, and (*b*) ends communism—that is, brings in genuine competition.

STRATEGY ELEMENT 1: REDISTRIBUTION FROM BETTER OFF TO WORSE OFF. The underlying principle is that those who can afford to pay more do so, releasing resources to improve quality and promote access, where 'can afford' refers to their income as a graduate, not to their family circumstances as a student. This approach is entirely consistent with the first and third legs of the strategy above.

At its core, this part of the strategy comprises two complementary sets of actions (see Figure 14.1):

- a price increase, raising the average tuition fee from p_0 to p_1. This leads to a movement *along* the demand curve from *a* to *b*. Taken alone, this action obviously reduces demand and harms access. However, the fees are deferred for everyone; in addition, there are:
- targeted transfers to groups for whom access is fragile. This moves their demand curve *outward*, increasing their demand to *c*.

Thus the strategy is deeply progressive. It shifts resources from today's best off (who lose some of their fee subsidies) to today's worst off (who receive a grant) and tomorrow's worst off (who, with income-contingent repayments, do not repay their loan in full).

Earlier arguments lend strong support to the strategy, which can be seen in a very different perspective from the high-fees, high-debt portrayal.

- The proposals can be thought of as the restoration of universal grants: higher education is largely free at the point of use, paid in part by a temporary addition to the income tax of graduates.
- A graduate tax and income-contingent loan repayments are both payments levied on top of income tax. From the viewpoint of the graduate, the only difference is that with a graduate tax the duration of payment is fixed and with an income-contingent loan variable. Thus loans can be thought of as a capped graduate tax, which is switched off once the graduate has paid a set contribution towards the cost of her degree.[11]

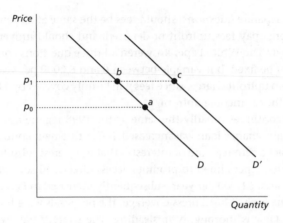

Fig. 14.1. The twofold strategy to promote access

- Another perspective, discussed in Section 3.1, is to think of student loans as social insurance—a case of consumption smoothing that is the mirror image of pensions.

Core argument 1: deferred variable fees are fair.

- They resolve the serious inequities of tax funding, a graduate tax, or flat fees.
- Those who can afford to pay a larger contribution after graduation do so.
- The system protects access in two ways: students face no upfront charges; and graduates repay only if their earnings warrant.
- As illustrated in Figure 14.1, the system actively promotes access because it frees resources to increase the staying-on rate post-16 and to restore grants, thereby focusing resources on those who need help most, rather than spending wastefully and regressively on blanket subsidies.

STRATEGY ELEMENT 2: THE END OF COMMUNISM. As well as being fair, variable fees shift the balance of power from the central planner and producers to students and employers by (*a*) giving universities an independent source of income and (*b*) strengthening competition.

Core argument 2: variable fees make funding open ended. If fees are set by government, rising fee income can be offset by falling taxpayer contributions. Thus government controls the total volume of resources going into higher education—funding is closed ended. Australia is a graphic example: government introduced centrally set fees in 1989 to address a funding crisis; by 2000, the system was back in crisis. Equally, the introduction of fees in the UK did not net any extra money.[12] A graduate tax has the same problem: government controls the volume of resources going into higher education, and universities compete in a zero-sum game. With variable fees, in contrast, if tax funding falls, each

[11] For clear exposition, see Alasdair Smith, 'A fair and flexible tax on graduates', *Financial Times*, 6 December 2002.
[12] This was also predicted—see Barr and Crawford (1998*b*: 78).

university has a policy response under its own control, and thus has an independent source of income. The central planner no longer controls the funding envelope of the state-owned enterprise.

Core argument 3: variable fees introduce competition. As the whole of this book makes clear, my support for competition is not ideological. Competition does not always improve outcomes, most particularly where there are information problems. This chapter has argued that—in sharp contrast with schools—competition in higher education is useful. Variable fees expose universities to more competition, empowering the choices of students, and indirectly also employers. The change in the balance of power is fundamental to creating a diversified system of higher education suitable to a technological age. This is not an argument for law-of-the-jungle competition. As discussed in Section 3.3, government has an important continuing role, but as regulator and setter of incentives, not as central planner.

The potential benefits from competition are large, but so are the resulting changes, creating political opposition. The supply-side response is predictable. The White Paper strategy has profound implications for the management of universities. The elite universities—like Poland and Hungary in 1990 at the time Communism was overthrown—welcomed the new freedoms, but some institutions were unenthusiastic, seeing the new arrangements as more a threat than an opportunity. The demand-side response was also understandable. Students, like the Poles in 1990, saw prices rising, but not yet the resulting benefits of reform. Once the changes are in place, students should greatly prefer the new system, which transforms their power by giving universities strong incentives to give them such things as accelerated courses and part-time options.

BRIEF ASSESSMENT. In conclusion, did the reform proposals get it right? In large measure, as indicated above, the answer is yes. However, there are doubts about three issues. First, fees were capped at £3,000; will this turn out to be too low? If all or most universities charge the full amount, the system reverts to one with flat fees, restoring central planning by the back door. Second, the reforms did not grasp the nettle of interest subsidies for student loans, the wide and deep pernicious effects of which are discussed in Sections 3.3 and 4.2, point 2. Finally, will there be sufficient political support to see through a set of highly controversial proposals?

In early 2004, the crystal ball remained murky. For contemporary assessment, see Barr (2003, forthcoming) and UK Education and Skills Select Committee (2003).

5.3. An emerging international consensus?

In the second half of the 1980s writers in different countries were converging on similar conclusions about the design of loan systems—particularly the centrality of income-contingent repayments—through similar reasoning in the face of similar problems (see Barr 1991). In the late 1990s, a consensus grew about broader aspects of higher-education finance, not least because of the contradictory imperative (*a*) towards higher participation in higher education and (*b*) fiscal constraints connected with population ageing and international competition.

- *Element 1.* There should be a continuing taxpayer subsidy to universities.

- *Element 2.* There should also be mechanisms for targeting taxpayer subsidies at *particular* students to promote access. However, the *generality* of students should contribute, because of the private benefits they receive.

- *Element 3.* Fees should vary across universities, reflecting diversity of activity and cost. Within a regulatory framework, each university should determine its own fee level and structure.

- *Element 4.* Students should be able to pay fees and living costs through a system of loans—that is, there should be no upfront fees. Those loans should have income-contingent repayments (the 1980s consensus).

6. Conclusion

Reform of higher-education finance, including a well-designed loan scheme, would open up capital markets to allow investment in human capital and make it possible to restore erosions in quality (both micro-efficiency gains). Loans can also improve equity by reducing the regressivity of higher-education finance and by freeing resources to promote access. Loans, however, are far from a complete answer. The regressivity of university finance has two roots: the extent of tax finance; and the fact that too few children from poorer backgrounds go to university. Loans address the first root but do little to eradicate the second. Increasing university attendance by working-class children requires not only expansion of higher education, but also, and importantly, action to improve equity within the school system.

■ QUESTIONS FOR FURTHER DISCUSSION

1. What are the economic arguments for greater reliance on student loans to finance higher education. How should such loans be organized?

2. 'University education is a basic right. It should therefore be free.' Discuss

3. Why is it argued that market forces in higher education are not only useful, but essential? What implications does the theory have for the determination of tuition fees?

■ FURTHER READING

On funding universities in England, see Higher Education Funding Council for England (2002). On Scotland, see Scotland Higher Education Review Board (2003), on Wales, Stroud (2001) and Wales Education and Lifelong Learning Committee (2002), and, for an overview of the UK scene, Glennerster (2003*a*: ch. 6). See also the various government portals in the list of useful web sites at the start of the book. OECD (2003*c*) contains compendious statistical information on education systems throughout the advanced industrial countries.

The nature of higher education is discussed by Winston (1999). On income-contingent repayments, see Friedman (1962: ch. 6), Glennerster et al. (1968, reprinted as Glennerster 2003*b*), and, for an overview, Barr (2001*a*: ch. 12). Palacios (2003) proposes a method that would allow private contracts with income-contingent repayments.

For methodological discussion and estimates of rates of return to higher education in the UK, see Blundell et al. (2000), and, for an explanation of the importance of tertiary education in explaining widening disparities in earnings, Acemoglu (1999). See also the Further Reading at the end of Chapter 13.

For a critique of the UK system in the 1990s, see Barr and Crawford (1998*a*). The post-1998 arrangements are assessed by Barr and Crawford (1998*b*), Barr (2002*b*), Greenaway and Haynes (2003), and UK National Audit Office (2002*a*,*b*). For a generally supportive critique of the 2003 reform proposals, see Barr (2003, forthcoming).

For discussion of other countries, see Barr (2001*a*: ch. 13) (which discusses the USA, UK, the Netherlands, Sweden, Australia and New Zealand) and Productivity Commission (2002) (a study of Australia, Canada, Hong Kong, Ireland, the Netherlands, New Zealand, Singapore, Sweden, the UK, and the USA). See also Johnstone (2000), Kane (2001), and the International Comparative Higher Education Finance and Accessibility Project web site (http://www.gse.buffalo.edu/org/IntHigherEdFinance). On the USA, see Ehrenberg (2002), Carnevale and Rose (2003), and the articles in Yaeger et al. (2001). Useful US web sites include the Office of Postsecondary Education, US Department of Education (http://www.ed.gov/offices/OPE), the Association for the Study of Higher Education (http://www.ashe.missouri.edu), the National Center for Public Policy and Higher Education (http://www.highereducation.org/index.shtml), the National Center for Education Statistics (http://nces.ed.gov), the Advisory Committee on Student Financial Aid (http://www.ed.gov/offices/AC/ACSFA), and the College Board (http://www.collegeboard.com/highered).

Chapman and Ryan (2003) discuss the impact of income-contingent repayments in Australia. For discussion of New Zealand, see LaRocque (2003).

PART FOUR

Epilogue

15 | Conclusion

A democratic capitalist society will keep searching for better ways of drawing the boundary lines between the domain of rights and the domain of dollars. And it can make progress. To be sure, it will never solve the problem, for the conflict between equality and economic efficiency is inescapable. In that sense, capitalism and democracy are really a most improbable mixture. Maybe that is why they need each other—to put some rationality into equality and some humanity into efficiency.

(Arthur M. Okun, 1975)

1. Arguments for a welfare state

1.1. Theory

The welfare state is the outcome of diverse forces over nearly four centuries of developing social policy. Two aspects, in particular, stand out from the historical discussion in Chapter 2: debates about ideology (which are taken up in Chapter 3), and the welfare state's functional purposes, notably economic efficiency (Chapters 4 and 5). Ideological aims vary widely. To libertarians (Chapter 3, Section 2) the primary goal is individual freedom, which is best achieved by unrestricted private markets. Empirical libertarians such as Hayek and Friedman therefore espouse minimal intervention and oppose all but the most austere welfare systems, whose purpose is limited to poverty relief. Marxists (Chapter 3, Section 4.2) regard the market system by its very nature as incompatible with their primary aim of meeting need. They therefore reject it, and give the state a primary role in production and allocation. Marxists have mixed feelings about the welfare state (Chapter 3, Section 5.3). In part it accords with their aim of meeting need and is therefore to be applauded; yet it serves also to support a capitalist system that they regard as inherently unjust.

Liberals take a more eclectic view. The utilitarian aim (Chapter 3, Section 3.1) is the maximization of total welfare, leaving open the question of whether it is to be achieved by private markets, by public production and allocation, or by a mix of the two. Rawls (Chapter 3, Section 3.2) argues that goods, liberty, and opportunity should be distributed equally unless any other arrangement is to the advantage of the least well off. Again, the issue of how this is best achieved is left open. For the purposes of this book, the single feature that above all distinguishes liberal theories is the treatment of private property as an issue that is contingent, not dogmatic—that is, the treatment of private property is not an end in itself but a means towards the achievement of stated aims.

Society has functional as well as ideological goals, notably the achievement of economic efficiency, as defined in Chapter 4, Section 2.1. Where there is a trade-off between efficiency and social justice, their relative weights will vary between libertarians, liberals, and Marxists. But an increase in efficiency that does not impair social justice is an unambiguous gain under *any* of these theories of society (Chapter 4, Section 2.2).

Efficiency can be achieved by market allocation, notably in a competitive environment with no market failures and, importantly, with no significant information failures (Chapter 4, Section 3.2). Similar conditions are necessary if insurance is to be efficient: at least some individuals must be risk averse (Chapter 5, Section 2.1), and there must be no technical problems with privately supplied insurance (Chapter 5, Section 3). These conditions, referred to collectively as the *standard assumptions*, must all hold if the market is to be relied on to allocate efficiently.

The distinction between *aims* and *methods* (i.e. between the *what* and the *how*) is crucial. The functional and ideological aims of policy can be encapsulated in large measure in the twin goals of economic efficiency and social justice. Once the aims have been chosen, the next step is to select methods to achieve them, including (Chapter 4, Section 3.1) no state intervention at all; intervention in the form of cash transfers; or interference with the market mechanism through regulation, through financial involvement, and/or through public production. The approach can be summarized in two statements: (*a*) the proper place of ideology is in the choice of aims, particularly the definition of social justice and its trade-off with economic efficiency; (*b*) once these aims have been agreed, the choice of method should be treated as a *technical* issue.

Whether a good is better produced publicly or privately should be decided on the basis of which method more closely achieves specified aims; and a major purpose has been to give a rationale in any situation for choosing the method(s) most likely to do so. This was given in the form of two propositions (Chapter 4, Section 7.2).

- If the standard assumptions hold, market allocation will be efficient; in this case social justice should generally be pursued via income transfers (e.g. so that poor people can buy food at market prices).
- Suppose the standard assumptions fail in a way that justifies public production and allocation on *efficiency* grounds; social justice may then appropriately be pursued through transfers in kind (e.g. free medical care under the National Health Service).

Whether a particular commodity should be publicly or privately produced is thus contingent on its technical characteristics—that is, a liberal approach in the sense described above (for libertarian and Marxist counter-arguments, see Chapter 4, Section 7.3). The welfare state should not be judged in dogmatic terms, but should be supported only if it contributes more than alternative arrangements to the achievement of agreed policy objectives.

1.2. Policy

Chapter 1 started with two questions: what theoretical arguments justify the existence of the various parts of the welfare state; and, given these arguments of principle, how well do the British and other systems perform? The answers are summarized in Chapter 4, Section 7, for the underlying theory, Chapter 11, Section 5, for cash benefits, and the concluding sections of Chapters 12, 13, and 14 for health care, school education, and higher education, respectively, so only the most important conclusions are set out here.

The aims of cash benefits (Chapter 1, Section 2.2) include insurance, consumption smoothing, and poverty relief; more controversially, they also include reducing inequality. Their achievement requires mechanisms to foster self-help and vertical redistribution.

INSURANCE AND CONSUMPTION SMOOTHING are necessary for an individual who is self-supporting over his lifetime, but needs a mechanism to allow him to redistribute from himself at one time (e.g. when working) to himself at another (e.g. when unemployed or retired). In principle, one part of the answer is voluntary private insurance. That, however, is not a tenable strategy (Chapter 8). On the demand side, non-insurance imposes external costs on various groups including taxpayers, giving an efficiency reason for making insurance compulsory (Chapter 8, Section 2.1). On the supply side, the private market is unable for technical reasons to provide the efficient quantity and type of insurance against all causes of income loss; in particular, unemployment and inflation are not insurable risks. Another part of the answer is consumption smoothing (see Figure 4.5 and surrounding discussion) through voluntary private savings plus the eventual purchase of an annuity. As discussed in Chapter 9, Section 3.2, this approach faces a number of technical problems, including the difficulty of insuring against inflation.

Several important results follow. There are strong efficiency grounds for a major public role in offering mechanisms for insurance and consumption smoothing, including public provision of unemployment compensation (Chapter 8, Section 2.2) and, at a minimum, underwriting the indexation component of retirement pensions (Chapter 9, Section 3.1). For these benefits at least, public involvement, whatever the form it takes, will not (because it cannot) be actuarially related to individual risks. For the major risks covered by the state scheme, adherence to strict actuarial principles is neither possible (except as a mimic of private institutions) nor necessary, and only arguably desirable. Various reforms of the insurance system are possible, but a substantial return to voluntary private insurance and pure, private, funded pensions is not one of them (Chapters 8, Section 3.1, and Chapter 9, Section 5.1). Social policy requires that individuals are protected against income loss; but strict adherence to market supply enables them to acquire protection only where risks can be covered by actuarial mechanisms. This puts the cart before the horse by making *social* policy subservient to *technical* considerations. A bridge is needed between the two sets of issues.

POVERTY RELIEF is relevant to those who cannot support themselves over their lifetime. In principle it can be organized through private charity or by the state. Partly because of the free-rider problem, voluntary redistribution is likely to be suboptimal even by libertarian standards, and even further below the Rawlsian or socialist optimum (Chapter 4, Section 4.1). Redistribution through the tax system may therefore be justified in both efficiency and equity terms (Chapter 10, Section 2) under any theory of society, though with considerable disagreement as to how much redistribution is desirable (Chapter 4, Section 4.4) or feasible (Chapter 11). The overall success of cash benefits in practice is also controversial (Chapter 8, Section 3, Chapter 9, Section 5, and Chapter 10, Section 3). The

UK has a wide-ranging system of insurance benefits; these are buttressed by assistance benefits organized on a national basis, for which *everyone* is potentially eligible. Many other countries have less comprehensive systems (Chapter 2, Section 6). Nevertheless, poverty remains (Chapter 10, Section 3.5). Indeed, poverty in the UK and the USA increased over the 1980s and 1990s.

Reform can follow one of two strategies. Benefits can be conditioned on income by an explicit means test or through a negative income tax (Chapter 11, Section 2), though this approach can easily aggravate the poverty trap.[1] Alternatively, it may be possible to sidestep the worst of the poverty trap by adopting the 'Back to Beveridge' approach (Chapter 11, Section 3), under which benefits are conditioned on carefully chosen characteristics of recipients, such as being unemployed or retired, or having children. The most hopeful reform strategy is through a judicious combination of the two approaches (Chapter 11, Section 4).

BENEFITS IN KIND. The theoretical discussion of public involvement in health care, school education, and higher education is set out in the early parts of Chapters 12, 13, and 14, respectively. The issues are complex, not least because of intractable measurement problems (Chapter 12, Section 2.2, and Chapter 13, Section 2.2). There are strong *a priori* arguments suggesting that unrestricted private markets for health care and school education (Chapter 12, Section 3, and Chapter 13, Section 3) will be inefficient, and also inequitable to the extent that information, power, and access to capital markets are correlated with socio-economic status. The precise form of public involvement has two aspects. The *allocation* issue rests crucially on whether individuals or 'experts' (doctors, teachers, etc.) are better informed and/or better able to act in the interests of consumers. The question of *production* depends largely on whether quality/quantity can be monitored more effectively with production in the public or private sector. The theoretical arguments for public production and allocation of health care and school education (Chapter 12, Section 3.3, and Chapter 13, Section 3.3), though not irrefutable, are strong, largely because of information problems.

The National Health Service is not without problems, but has powerful advantages (Chapter 12, Section 4). In comparison with other countries, the system is cheap, yet health outcomes in the UK are close to the average for advanced countries. Theoretical argument and international comparison both suggest that radical 'privatization' (whatever its advocates mean by the term) will not solve old problems, and is likely to create new and larger ones. The evidence for the UK, overwhelmingly, is that the National Health Service should be retained, and improvement sought within the existing strategy by increasing its resources, gathering and using more and better information, and continuing experiments with quasi-markets. Though the case for public funding is robust, that does not mean that public production is the only possible model. Other countries with different political traditions and different medical structures have adopted other sensible *strategies* of mixed public/private provision—for example, private production and public funding subject to a budget constraint, as in Canada (Chapter 12, Section 5).

---

[1] See the Glossary.

School education also has problems (Chapter 13, Section 4), not least that middle-class children continue to receive a disproportionate share of resources. However, the introduction of competition into state education was associated with improved outcomes —especially in primary education—in the late 1990s and early 2000s, in terms both of test scores and a relative improvement in low-performing schools. Though problems remain, they are not *necessarily* an indictment of state education. Opponents have to show not that the state sector is imperfect (which is not in dispute), but that a private system would do better. Vouchers for private education (Chapter 13, Section 5.1) offer no such prospect. Their efficiency effects are unclear *a priori* and unproven empirically; in equity terms they are likely to benefit middle-class children more than other groups.

The problems of higher education (Chapter 14, Section 4) are greater. This is an area of the welfare state that works badly, not through choosing controversial aims (Chapter 14, Section 2), but by adopting methods that will not achieve them. The theoretical arguments (Chapter 14, Section 3) point to a strategy of allocation through market forces, supported by a well-designed loan scheme, appropriate regulation, and the pursuit of equity objectives via income transfers. That line of argument does not, however, deny a substantial role for government (Section 3.3). The historical strategy, however, has been of public funding plus central planning. Though tenable when the system was small, with today's mass higher education (which is essential for national competitiveness) the system faces entirely predictable problems: universities are underfunded, harming quality; student support is inadequate, harming access; and, because higher education continues to be a mainly a middle-class activity, the finance of the system is regressive. The reforms discussed in Chapter 14, Section 5, therefore adopt a strategy with three elements: universities charge variable tuition fees; all fees and realistic living costs are covered by an income-contingent loan entitlement, addressing the financing needs of the generality of students; and a range of policies actively promote access, both through money measures such as grants, and through action to improve the information of children from poorer backgrounds. The strategy is deeply progressive. It shifts resources from today's best off (who lose some of their fee subsidies) to today's worst off (who receive a grant) and tomorrow's worst off (who, with income-contingent repayments, do not repay their loan in full).

One of the most important points I have tried to convey is that the approach to higher education (and to the other areas) is advocated *not* for ideological reasons but because of its substantial advantages in terms of efficiency and social justice. Higher education and health care are equally important from the viewpoint of social policy, but there are substantial differences in their *technical* natures. As a result, they require different solutions.

1.3. Why have a welfare state?

This book has asserted the powerful arguments in favour of the welfare state: it addresses major issues of market failure; it achieves equity objectives that many people support; and it contributes to important broader objectives such as social cohesion. Virtually all parts of the welfare state address all three aspects. School education from a functional perspective is a form of investment in the next generation of workers and citizens, and, provided 'free', it acts also to help the poor and enhance social cohesion; analogous arguments apply to health care. Publicly provided income transfers, similarly, have an efficiency role where the private market is unable to supply insurance (e.g. against unemployment) even to individuals able to support themselves on a lifetime basis.

Several important conclusions emerge. First, to the extent that the welfare state has a substantial functional aspect, opposition by writers such as Hayek and Friedman is misplaced. The single theoretical issue that, more than any other, divides their arguments from those in this book is their failure to take account of the major implications of information problems, which affect consumers of increasingly complex products, and also arise in important ways in insurance markets. Information problems of this sort greatly strengthen the efficiency case for the welfare state. The debate with libertarians (Chapter 4, Section 7.3), surprisingly, turns out to be at least as much technical as ideological. As a result, it is less public involvement *per se* that should be controversial than its precise form and the choice of its distributional objectives.

This theoretical conclusion has historical support. A British study concluded that 'the welfare state, and indeed welfare itself, is very robust. Over the thirteen years from 1974 to 1987, welfare policy successfully weathered an economic hurricane in the mid-1970s and an ideological blizzard in the 1980s. The resources going to public welfare were maintained; [and] welfare indicators continued to show a steady improvement' (Le Grand 1990: 350). In the USA, 'the Reagan era ended with the welfare state substantially intact, though somewhat frayed around the edges. It is now tilted more toward its middle-class beneficiaries than it was a decade ago, but the broad contours remain essentially as they have evolved since the 1930s, when the welfare state began' (Peterson 1991: 133). 'Popular perceptions notwithstanding, the degree of welfare state roll-back, let alone significant change, has so far been modest' (Esping-Andersen 1996a: 10).

Once the welfare state's efficiency role is understood, these findings should not be surprising. The argument is not diminished by the fact that it can explain only part of the variation across countries.[2] The major efficiency role of social institutions makes them relevant to the population at large, not just to the poor. The welfare state is much more than a safety net; it is justified not simply by any redistributive aims one may (or may not) have, but because it does things that private markets for technical reasons either would not do at all, or would do inefficiently. We need a welfare state of some sort for efficiency reasons, and would continue to do so even if all distributional problems had been solved.

That said, the welfare state is not—even in principle—a complete solution. It may make unemployment more bearable, but it does little to reduce the number of people out of work; nor does it improve working conditions for those in employment; and many people— for example, women, ethnic minorities—are underprivileged for reasons not directly connected with poverty. There is room for debate about the nature of these problems and about appropriate ameliorative action, but little disagreement that each is a legitimate concern of public policy. Their omission is not because they are unimportant but because (with the exception of unemployment) economics has little to say about them.

---

[2] See Alesina et al. (2001) on why the USA does not have a European-style welfare state.

2. A changing world: Debates

Notwithstanding strong arguments supporting the general idea of the welfare state, there is major and continuing debate round two broad sets of questions.

- Is the welfare state desirable, particularly in terms of its effects on incentives and on economic growth?
- Even if desirable, is a welfare state any longer feasible, given the challenges discussed in Chapter 1, Section 3, of demographic and social change, and global and political pressures?

2.1. Is the welfare state desirable?

MISTAKEN OBJECTIVES? Libertarians, espousing freedom and choice, criticize the welfare state's emphasis on equality and security. Since these are matters of fundamental value judgements, the opposite view is equally plausible. Libertarians also argue that the welfare state is a threat to individual freedom. The validity of this view depends on two factors: the weight given to freedom compared with other objectives; and how freedom is defined (to a Libertarian, freedom means absence of coercion, to a socialist it includes an element of security (Chapter 3, Section 4.2)).

AN INHERENTLY MISTAKEN ENTERPRISE? Libertarians attack the welfare state on theoretical grounds, arguing that it is not possible to have a large purposeful collective enterprise. In many ways this is an appeal to the coordination/information-processing problems that beset central planning. The welfare state, however, is not a monolith, but comprises many smaller components. Secondly, many of these components are publicly *financed* but privately and *competitively* produced—welfare does not have to be state welfare. Thirdly, where market failures are severe, state action, albeit imperfect, may produce the least-bad outcomes.

Libertarians also attack the practice as inefficient and ineffective in terms of the services it provides. As already indicated, imperfect state action may be the least-bad way. Furthermore, a major thrust of modern policy is to introduce competition on the supply side, as exemplified by the discussion of quasi-markets in Chapter 12, Section 5.2, and Chapter 13, Section 5.1, precisely to improve internal incentives to efficiency.

DAMAGING TO ECONOMIC GROWTH? The argument is that the welfare state harms growth because the level of welfare-state spending is too high or (separately) because its rate of growth is too rapid. In consequence, high or rising levels of taxation drag down economic growth.

Does the welfare state reduce growth? It is not controversial to argue that beyond a certain point taxation harms growth. What *is* controversial is (*a*) where that point is, and (*b*) the precise mechanism by which welfare-state spending might reduce growth. The issue remains disputed, as Atkinson's survey (1995*a*: ch. 6) makes clear.

- As Figure 1.2 shows, welfare-state spending varies widely around the OECD average, with no evidence that growth has been slower in high-spending countries or higher in low-spending countries.

- If the charge is that the *level* of welfare-state spending is too high, then, as Atkinson (1995*a*: 123) points out, 'the Welfare State is no more than a co-defendant with other elements of the state budget'.

- Causation can be problematic. Do countries with higher spending reduce their growth rate, or do countries with lower growth and more poverty need to spend a larger fraction of GDP alleviating poverty?

- Looking at aggregates can obscure other influences on growth, notably the detailed structure—and hence the incentive effects—of benefits. Benefits awarded without an income test, for example, may cost more but have less powerful adverse incentives.

For these and other reasons, Solow, in an assessment of cross-country comparative analysis (1994: 51, quoted by Atkinson 1995*a*: 124), concluded: 'I do not find this a confidence-inspiring project. It seems altogether too vulnerable to bias from omitted variables, to reverse causation, and above all to the recurrent suspicion that the experiences of very different national economies cannot be explained as if they represented different "points" on some well-defined surface.'

Are assessments of the welfare state well specified? Economists of all people should need no reminder of the flaws in an argument that considers costs but ignores benefits. Atkinson (1999*a*: 8) addresses the argument that the welfare state is unsustainable and should therefore be rolled back, and criticizes it as being too simple.

The emphasis by economists on the negative economic effects of the welfare state can be attributed to the theoretical framework adopted . . . which remains rooted in a model of perfectly competitive and perfectly clearing markets. *[This] theoretical framework incorporates none of the contingencies for which the welfare state exists* . . . The whole purpose of welfare state provision is missing from the theoretical model.   (emphasis added)

Atkinson's point is that a model based on perfect information and market clearing systematically rules out the market failures that it is one of the fundamental tasks of the welfare state to address. The choice of such a model means that analysis inescapably focuses only on costs, and implicitly rules out some of the welfare state's main benefits, including insurance and consumption smoothing. The richer theoretical treatment of this book incorporates market failure and government failure, leading to a more complex range of outcomes than the simple unsustainability argument allows. This does not argue that fiscal constraints should be ignored, merely that fiscal constraints, market failure, and government failure are each important.

Is reduced growth necessarily a problem? Even if the welfare state does reduce growth, that is not the end of the argument. The issue for policy-makers is to balance costs and benefits. Suppose that, in state-of-the-world A ('pure capitalism'), there is little security but rapid growth. If the electorate is prepared to trade slightly lower growth for greater security—in some ways analogous to an insurance premium—mechanisms to increase security are welfare enhancing. At its broadest, this is a stylized representation of the development of the welfare state in advanced countries in response to rising real incomes and electoral pressures over the twentieth century. In state of-the-world B ('communism'), in contrast, there is considerable material security, but growth rates are low. People are therefore willing (as in the former Communist countries) to adopt market mechanisms, offering the potential for higher living standards but at a cost of reduced security. In short, too little security reduces well-being; so does too much.

DAMAGING INCENTIVE EFFECTS? Writers like Murray (1984: ch. 12) argue that social benefits, far from being the cure to social ills, are part of their *cause*. According to this argument, which echoes nineteenth-century British debates about poverty relief (Chapter 2, Section 1.1), social assistance is too generous, thereby creating a 'culture of poverty'. The counter-view (e.g. Levy 1998) is that labour-market behaviour, crime, and single parenthood are far too complex to be explained only—or even mainly—by the incentives offered by social benefits.

A more sophisticated argument (Dufwenberg and Lundholm 2001; Lindbeck et al. 2003) is that over an extended period the existence of social benefits changes social norms. To paraphrase the argument, a typical person in (say) the 1930s felt stigmatized by receiving benefits; in the early post-war period, partly because of deliberate policy, stigma (Chapter 10, Section 3.1) was felt less acutely; by the 1980s benefits were regarded as an entitlement—not something to be avoided if at all possible but, along with wages and the tax system, part of a person's budget constraint. In economic terms, in the 1930s a pound of income transfers was worth less in utility terms than a pound of earnings; by the 1980s, according to this line of argument, the difference was much smaller, with predictable effects on behaviour.

2.2. Is the welfare state sustainable?

Even if we conclude that these problems are minor or surmountable, and hence that the welfare state is desirable, it is still necessary to discuss whether it is any longer feasible.

COMPATIBLE WITH A GLOBAL ECONOMY? As discussed in Chapter 1, Section 3, the core of the globalization argument is that, because of technological change, much economic activity has become 'dematerialized'—that is, takes the form of computer-transmitted information. As a result, national boundaries become porous, making competition global and reducing the freedom of any country to conduct an independent economic policy. The argument is important. Many activities are genuinely becoming more global, but the implications for the welfare state are not necessarily apocalyptic.

The world is not wholly global. Though global competition is powerful, it is not all-powerful. Not all goods are tradeable. Nor are all factors mobile: labour mobility is reduced both by choice (people prefer to stay with their language, culture, and family) and because of constraints such as immigration controls.

Western countries can adapt. It is vital to keep two issues logically separate.

- What should be the *scale* of the state's activities—that is, the level of public spending on income transfers, health care, education, and the like?
- What is the appropriate *structure* of activity—that is, the public/private mix?

The first is largely a matter of budgetary balance—a macroeconomic issue. The second is microeconomic. It is concerned with which activities are most efficiently privately funded and/or privately produced and which are not. The distinction is important: a budgetary crisis is *not* a ground for privatization.

Globalization means that countries—for instance, in South-East Asia—with low social spending, can exert competitive pressures on OECD countries. That, however, is not an argument for dismantling the welfare state, still less for radical structural change such as privatization. Rather, it is an argument for some reduction in the scale of some welfare-state activities. For this reason as well as for demographic ones, governments in virtually all the OECD countries have tried to restrain welfare-state spending.

The newly industrialized countries may also adapt. A third reason why globalization is not the death knell for the welfare state is that, in all the industrialized countries, social spending has been a superior good: as incomes have risen, electorates have voted to increase the share of such spending in GDP. In some countries the process has perhaps gone too far,[3] but that does not mean that the premiss is flawed. Unless the countries of East Asia are very different, rising incomes and the weakening of extended family ties will lead to demands for rising social expenditure.

A plausible outcome of global competition, therefore, is some convergence between the OECD and Asian countries. Competition will continue to exert downwards pressure on wage costs and on the generosity of social benefits in the OECD; and over time rising incomes will lead to increased social spending in the newly industrializing countries.

DEMOGRAPHICALLY SUSTAINABLE? Rising life expectancy and falling birth rates in many countries result in an ageing population. The facts are not in dispute. As discussed in Chapter 9, Section 5.1, however, a whole range of policies can address the problem: increasing the quantity and quality of capital; increasing labour-force participation; more generous immigration policies; and—most powerful of all—raising the age of retirement.

A CRISIS OF THE WELFARE STATE? Esping-Andersen (1996a) argues that political and other institutions are enormously important for managing potential conflict between efficiency and distributional objectives. He goes on to argue that during the 1950s and 1960s, and in some countries longer, it was possible to pursue distributional objectives with little efficiency cost because there was a consensus of accepting wage restraint in return for full employment (see also Atkinson and Mogensen 1993). That consensus, it can be argued, was what underpinned the early success of Keynesian policies, providing a positive-sum solution to the trade-off between growth and equity. According to this view, institutions have become more fragmented. Because of changes in social norms and a weakening of some institutions, the trade-off between growth and equity had by the 1990s become less favourable than formerly. What has emerged is a zero-sum trade-off.[4]

Though the issue is of critical importance, it does not counsel despair. It is unarguable that parts of the system require change—generous tax-funded pensions are more feasible the fewer the number of pensioners (Chapter 9); similarly, free, tax-funded

---

[3] Government failure is discussed in Chapter 4, Section 5.

[4] For theoretical discussion of how social customs can influence economic outcomes, see Akerlof (1980).

university education is possible with an elite system but not with the mass system required by modern technology (Chapter 14). In these areas, as elsewhere, the welfare state is adapting.

- There is particular emphasis in many countries on improving the incentive structure of the benefit system.
- The generosity of some benefits is being reduced, for both economic and, in some countries, political reasons.
- Other reforms, such as raising the age of retirement, are part of the menu of options.

The welfare state will continue to adapt. Some of those adaptations can be foreseen.

- Demographic and global change will continue to create pressure to contain total spending. In consequence, pensions and health care will continue to face resource constraints, creating upward pressure on the age of retirement.
- Not least because of labour-market trends, inequality will be a continuing problem. A consequence will be pressures more carefully to distinguish the insurance and consumption-smoothing functions of cash benefits from their poverty relief function. This may lead to social insurance becoming more actuarial; more generally, pensions will, up to a point, become more individualized. Such moves, if well designed, could (*a*) facilitate labour-market flexibility and (*b*) enable women, in the face of more fluid family structures, to have their own pension entitlement.
- There will be mounting pressure for new insurance instruments (public, private, or mixed) to cover contingencies such as requiring long-term care in old age.
- New lending instruments will emerge. Income-contingent loans will increasingly pay for part of the costs of post-compulsory education and training. In the face of labour-market developments, especially reduced job security and the increasing prevalence of part-time work, there will also be pressure for more flexible lending for house purchase.

POLITICALLY SUSTAINABLE? The survival of the welfare state depends on political as well as economic sustainability. Libertarians argue that the state takes on tasks (e.g. the abolition of poverty) that are impossible, that failure undermines the state, and, to that extent, that the welfare state contains the seeds of its own political demise. The exact opposite can be asserted. It is the welfare state that has made capitalism, with all its attendant benefits of economic growth, politically feasible, as the quote by Arthur Okun at the head of the chapter suggests. Failure to address poverty can be destabilizing and hence politically damaging—a key problem in many of the reforming former Communist countries.

Libertarians also argue that the welfare state leads to the formation of powerful interest groups. This is true. It is also true that capitalist lobbies create powerful interest groups, such as employers' organizations, Chambers of Commerce, and the like. These, it can be argued, are all desirable activities within democratic pluralist societies.

In the face of all these controversies, it is not surprising that there is a flourishing political debate about whether the UK or other countries can afford a welfare state. The easy complacency of earlier years about the continued growth of social spending has been replaced by discussion of whether or not there is a crisis in welfare. The argument in this book is that the discussion should not be about *whether* there should be a welfare state, but about its precise form and its distributional objectives. Glennerster reaches a similar conclusion. He points out two crucial facts. First, the level of taxation and social spending, though high in all the Western industrial economies, varies widely and is not correlated in any obvious way with economic performance. These facts contradict the simple view that the present scale of the welfare state or something rather larger or smaller is incompatible with a substantial capitalist sector. Secondly, fifty years ago, 'in a ravaged economy, when real incomes were less than half what they are today, people voted for what came to be called the welfare state, and paid the price, and voted to continue affording it' (Glennerster 1997: 298).

Thus the future of the welfare state depends not only on economic feasibility, but also very much on what people, through the political process, decide that they want.

COULD WE MANAGE WITHOUT A WELFARE STATE? A defence against these various accusations, however robust, understates the strong positive case for the welfare state.

- The core argument of this book is that the welfare state exists not just to provide poverty relief (its 'Robin Hood' function) but also to offer insurance and consumption smoothing (the 'Piggy Bank' function) in areas that private institutions are able to cover incompletely, if at all. It also has an important role in fostering social cohesion.

- Looking to the future, the insurance element will become increasingly important. Risk and uncertainly are likely to intensify. This is the core argument in OECD (2003*d*), which concentrates on five sets of uncertainties: natural disasters, technological accidents, infectious diseases, food safety, and terrorism. Actuarial insurance is not able to address problems of this type or on this scale.

- There is increasing evidence that the roots of exclusion lie in early childhood, stressing the need for policy to support and enhance families (Esping-Andersen 1999; Esping-Andersen et al. 2002; Neil Gilbert 2002; Hills et al. 2002). Such policies— a confluence of economics and social policy—involve cash benefits, health care, and education, as well as broader policies to improve parenting. They also involve significant redistribution, major efforts to improve information, and considerable coordination of different types of activity. Again, such activities require state action.

None of the ideas in this book is intended to be a detailed blueprint, but more to illustrate an approach that has been, throughout, to entertain moderately egalitarian aims while avoiding dogmatism about methods. The result shows how, with care, it is possible to create institutions both within the welfare state and more broadly that contribute to a society characterized simultaneously by economic efficiency and social justice.

■ **QUESTIONS FOR FURTHER DISCUSSION**

1. 'Globalization is the death knell for the welfare state.' Discuss.

■ FURTHER READING

The classic defence of the mixed economy is by Okun (1975), and the classic attack on the welfare state by Murray (1984).

For broadly supportive assessments of the welfare state, see Atkinson (1999*a,b*; 2003), Esping-Andersen (1999); Esping-Andersen et al. 2002; Neil Gilbert (2002). For worries about incentive effects, see Lindbeck et al. (2003).

Atkinson (2003) discusses the implications of globalization for the welfare state. On the implications of European integration, see Sinn (1998). Alesina et al. (2001) discuss the reasons why the USA does not have a European-type welfare state.

For a broader discussion of emerging risks and policies to address them, see OECD (2003*d*).

REFERENCES

Aaron, Henry J. (1966), 'The Social Insurance Paradox', *Canadian Journal of Economics and Political Science*, 33/3 (Aug.), 371–4; repr. in Barr (2001*b*: ii. 79–82).

—— (1973), *Why is Welfare so Hard to Reform?* (Washington: Brookings Institution).

—— (1982), *Economic Effects of Social Security* (Washington: Brookings Institution).

Abel Smith, Brian (1964), *The Hospitals, 1800–1948* (London: Heinemann).

—— and Townsend, Peter (1965), *The Poor and the Poorest* (London: Bell & Sons).

Acemoglu, Daron (1999), 'Changes in Unemployment and Wage Inequality: An Alternative Theory and Some Evidence', *American Economic Review*, 89/5 (Dec.), 1259–78.

Adam, Stuart, Brewer, Mike, and Reed, Howard (2002), *The Benefits of Parenting: Government Financial Support for Families with Children since 1975*, Commentary 91 (London: Institute for Fiscal Studies).

Aghion, Philippe, Caroli, Eve, and García-Penalosa, Cecilia (1999), 'Inequality and Economic Growth: The Perspective of the New Growth Theories', *Journal of Economic Literature*, 37/4 (Dec.), 1615–60.

Agulnik, Phil (1999), 'The Proposed State Second Pension', *Fiscal Studies*, 20/4: 409–21.

—— and Barr, Nicholas (2000), 'The Public/Private Mix in UK Pension Policy', *World Economics*, 1/1 (Jan.–Mar.), 69–80.

Akerlof, George A. (1970), 'The Market for "Lemons": Qualitative Uncertainty and the Market Mechanism', *Quarterly Journal of Economic*, 84 (Aug.) 488–500; repr. in Barr (2001*b*: i. 308–20).

—— (1978), 'The Economics of "Tagging" as Applied to the Optimal Income Tax, Welfare Programs and Manpower Planning', *American Economic Review*, 68: 8–19; repr. in Barr (2001*b*: ii. 298–309).

—— (2002), 'Behavioral Macroeconomics and Macroeonomic Behavior', *American Economic Review*, 92/3 (June), 411–33.

—— and Kranton, Rachel E. (2002), 'Identity and Schooling: Some Lessons for the Economics of Education', *Journal of Economic Literature*, 40 (Dec.), 1167–1201.

Alesina, Alberto, Glaeser, Edward, and Sacerdote, Bruce (2001), *Why Doesn't the US Have a European-Style Welfare State*, Harvard Institute of Economic Research, Discussion Paper No. 1933, http://post.economics. harvard.edu/hier/2001papers/2001list.html.

Altmeyer, A. J. (1966), *The Formative Years of Social Security* (Madison: University of Wisconsin Press).

Anderson, Gerard, Reinhardt, Uwe, Hussey, Peter, and Petrosyan, Varduhi (2003), 'It's the Prices, Stupid: Why the United States Is So Different from Other Countries', *Health Affairs* (May/June), 89–105.

Andreoni, J. (1989), 'Giving with Impure Altruism: Applications to Charity and Ricardian Equivalence', *Journal of Political Economy*, 97: 1447–58.

—— (1990), 'Impure Altruism and Donations to Public Goods: A Theory of Warm-Glow Giving', *Economic Journal*, 100: 464–77; repr. in Barr (2001*b*: ii. 613–26).

—— and Payne, A. Abigail (2003), 'Do Government Grants to Private Charities Crowd out Giving or Fund-Raising', *American Economic Review*, 93/3 (June), 792–812.

Andrietti, Vincenzo (2001), 'Portability of Supplementary Pension Rights in the European Union', *International Social Security Review*, 54/1 (Jan.–Mar.), 59–83.

Angel, Francisco Blanco (2002), 'The Spanish Public Retirement Pension System: Principal Challenges and Recent Developments', *International Social Security Review*, 55/3 (July–Sept.), 57–72.

Angrist, Joshua, Bettinger, Eric, Bloom, Erik, King, Elizabeth, and Kremer, Michael (2002), 'Vouchers for Private Schooling in Columbia: Evidence from a Randomized Natural Experiment', *American Economic Review*, 92/5: 1535–58.

Apps, Patricia F. (1981), *A Theory of Inequality and Taxation* (Cambridge: Cambridge University Press).

—— and Rees, Ray (1996), 'Labour Supply, Household Production and Intra-Family Welfare Distribution', *Journal of Public Economics*, 60: 199–219; repr. in Barr (2001*b*: i. 665–85).

Arnold, Douglas, Graetz, Michael, and Munnell, Alicia (1998) (eds.), *Framing the Social Security Debate: Values, Politics, and Economics* (Washington: Brookings Institution).

Arrow, Kenneth F. (1963), 'Uncertainty and the Welfare Economics of Medical Care', *American Economic Review*, 53: 941–73; repr. in Cooper and Culyer (1973: 13–48), Diamond and Rothschild (1978: 348–75), and Barr (2001*b*: i. 275–307).

—— (1973), 'Some Ordinalist–Utilitarian Notes on Rawls's Theory of Justice', *Journal of Philosophy*, 70 (May), 245–63.

Asher, Mukul G. (1998), 'The Future of Retirement Protection in Southeast Asia', *International Social Security Review*, 51/1 (Jan.–Mar.), 3–30.

Atkinson, Anthony B. (1970), 'On the Measurement of Inequality', *Journal of Economic Theory*, 2. 244–63; repr. (including a non-mathematical summary) in Atkinson (1980: 23–43) and Barr (2001*b*: i. 592–612).

—— (1980) (ed.), *Wealth, Income and Inequality* (2nd edn., Oxford: Oxford University Press).

—— (1983), *The Economics of Inequality* (2nd edn., Oxford: Oxford University Press).

—— (1989), *Poverty and Social Security* (Brighton: Harvester Press).

—— (1995*a*), *Incomes and the Welfare State: Essays on Britain and Europe* (Cambridge: Cambridge University Press).

—— (1995*b*), 'On Targeting Social Security', in van de Walle and Nead (1995), 25–68.

—— (1996), 'Seeking to Explain the Distribution of Income', in Hills (1996*b*), 19–48.

—— (1998), *Poverty in Europe* (Oxford: Basil Blackwell).

—— (1999*a*), *The Economic Consequences of Rolling Back the Welfare State* (London and Cambridge, Mass.: MIT Press).

—— (1999*b*), 'The Economics of the Welfare State: An Incomplete Debate', in Marco Buti, Daniele Franco, and Lucio R. Pench (eds.), *The Welfare State in Europe: Challenges and Reforms* (Cheltenham and Northampton, Mass.: Edward Elgar), 57–70.

—— (2000), *Poverty in Europe* (Oxford: Basil Blackwell).

—— (2003), *Income Inequality in OECD Countries: Data and Explanations*, CESIfo Working Paper No. 881 (Munich: CESifo), downloadable from http://www.cesifo.de.

—— and Bourguignon, François (2000) (eds.), *Handbook of Income Distribution* (Amsterdam: Elsevier).

—— and Brandolini, Andrea (2001), 'Promise and Pitfalls in the Use of "Secondary" Data-Sets: Income Inequality in OECD Countries as a Case Study', *Journal of Economic Theory*, 39/3 (Sept.), 771–99.

—— and Micklewright, John (1989), 'Turning the Screw: Benefits for the Unemployed 1979–1988' in Andrew Dilnot and Ian Walker (eds.), *The Economics of Social Security* (Oxford: Oxford University Press), 17–51.

—— —— (1991), 'Unemployment Compensation and Labour Market Transitions: A Critical Review', *Journal of Economic Literature*, 29/4 (Dec.), 1679–727.

—— —— (1992), *Economic Transformation in Eastern Europe and the Distribution of Income* (Cambridge: Cambridge University Press).

—— and Mogensen, Gunnar V. (1993), *Welfare and Work Incentives: A North European Perspective* (Oxford: Oxford University Press).

—— and Stiglitz, Joseph E. (1980), *Lectures on Public Economics* (London and New York: McGraw-Hill).

—— Maynard, Alan K., and Trinder, Chris (1983), *Parents and Children* (London: Heinemann).

—— Rainwater, Lee, and Smeeding, Timothy M. (1995), 'Income Distribution in European Countries', in Atkinson (1995a), 41–63; repr. in Barr (2001b: ii. 502–26).

—— Cantillon, Bea, Marlier, Eric, and Nolan, Brian (2002), *Social Indicators: The EU and Social Inclusion* (New York and Oxford: Oxford University Press).

Augusztinovics, Mária, with Gál, Róbert, Matits, Ágnes, Máté, Levente, Simonovits, András, and Stahl, János (2002), 'The Hungarian Pension System before and after the 1998 Reform', in Elaine Fultz (ed.), *Pension Reform in Central and Eastern Europe, Volume 1: Restructuring with Privatization: Case Studies of Hungary and Poland* (Geneva: ILO), 25–93.

Baldwin, Sally, and Falkingham, Jane (1994), *Social Security and Social Change* (Hemel Hempstead: Harvester Wheatsheaf).

Ballard, Charles L., Shoven, John B., and Whalley, John (1985), 'General Equilibrium Computations of the Marginal Welfare Costs of Taxes in the United States', *American Economic Review*, 75/1: 128–38.

Banks, J., and Tanner S. (1996), 'Savings and Wealth in the UK: Evidence from Micro-Data', *Fiscal Studies*, 17/2 (May), 37–64.

Barmby, Tim A., Ercolani, Marco G., and Treble, John G. (2002), 'Sickness Absence: An International Comparison', *Economic Journal*, 112/480 (June), F315–31.

Barr, Nicholas A. (1975), 'Negative Income Taxation and the Redistribution of Income', *Oxford Bulletin of Economic and Statistics*, 37/1 (Feb.), 29–48, as revised in 38/2 (May 1976), 147.

—— (1979), 'Myths My Grandpa Taught Me', *Three Banks Review*, 124 (Dec.), 27–55; repr. in Barr (2001b: ii. 83–111).

—— (1981), 'Empirical Definitions of the Poverty Line', *Policy and Politics*, 9/1: 1–21.

—— (1987), *The Economics of the Welfare State* (1st edn.; London: Weidenfeld & Nicolson, and Stanford, Calif.: Stanford University Press).

—— (1989), *Student Loans: The Next Steps* (Aberdeen University Press for the David Hume Institute, Edinburgh, and the Suntory-Toyota International Centre for Economics and Related Disciplines, London School of Economics).

—— (1991), 'Income-Contingent Student Loans: An Idea Whose Time has Come', in G. K. Shaw (ed.), *Economics, Culture and Education: Essays in Honour of Mark Blaug* (Aldershot: Edward Elgar), 155–70; repr. in Barr (2001b: iii. 583–600).

—— (1992), 'Economic Theory and the Welfare State: A Survey and Interpretation', *Journal of Economic Literature*, 30/2: 741–803; repr. in Barr (2001b: i. 24–86).

—— (1994a), 'The Role of Government in a Market Economy', in Barr (1994c), 29–50.

—— (1994b), 'Income Transfers: Social Insurance', in Barr (1994c), 192–225.

—— (1994c) (ed.), *Labor Markets and Social Policy in Central and Eastern Europe: The Transition and Beyond* (New York and Oxford: Oxford University Press for the World Bank) (also available in Hungarian, Romanian, and Russian).

—— (1999), 'Comments on "Economic Policy and Equity: An Overview" by Amartya Sen', in Vito Tanzi, Ke-young Chu, and Sanjeev Gupta (eds.), *Economic Policy and Equity* (Washington: International Monetary Fund), 44–8.

—— (2001a), *The Welfare State as Piggy Bank: Information, Risk, Uncertainty and the Role of the State* (Oxford and New York: Oxford University Press).

—— (2001b) (ed.), *Economic Theory and the Welfare State, i. Theory, ii. Income Transfers, and iii. Benefits in Kind*, Edward Elgar Library in Critical Writings in Economics (Cheltenham and Northampton, Mass.: Edward Elgar).

—— (2002a), 'Reforming Pensions: Myths, Truths and Policy Choices', *International Social Security Review*, 55/2 (Apr.–June), 3–36 (also in French, German, and Spanish).

—— (2002b), 'Funding Higher Education: Policies for Access and Quality', House of Commons, Education and Skills Committee, *Post-16 Student Support*, Sixth Report of Session 2001–2002, HC445, London: TSO, Ev 19–35.

—— (2003), 'Financing Higher Education: Lessons from the UK Debate', *Political Quarterly*, 74/3 (June), 371–81.

—— (forthcoming), 'Higher education funding', *Oxford Review of Economic Policy*, 20/2.

—— and Crawford, Iain (1998*a*), 'Funding Higher Education in an Age of Expansion: Submission to the National Committee of Inquiry into Higher Education', *Education Economics*, 6/1: 45–70.

—— —— (1998*b*), 'The Dearing Report and the Government's Response: A Critique', *Political Quarterly*, 69/1 (Jan.–Mar.), 72–84.

—— and Hall, Robert E. (1981), 'The Probability of Dependence on Public Assistance', *Economica*, 48/190 (May), 109–23.

—— and Whynes, David (1993) (eds.), *Issues in the Economics of the Welfare State* (London: Macmillan).

—— Glennerster, Howard, and Le Grand, Julian (1989), 'Working for Patients? The Right Approach?', in *Resourcing the National Health Service: The Government's White Paper: Working for Patients* (House of Commons Social Services Committee, Session 1988–9, HC 214-I; London: HMSO), 17–22; repr. in Social Policy and Administration, 23/2 (Aug.), 117–27.

Barry, Brian (1973), *The Liberal Theory of Social Justice* (Oxford: Oxford University Press).

Bartlett, Will, and Le Grand, Julian (1994), 'The Performance of Trusts', in Ray Robinson and Julian Le Grand (eds.), *Evaluating the NHS Reforms* (London: King's Fund Institute), 54–73.

—— Roberts, Jennifer, and Le Grand, Julian (1998) (eds.), *A Revolution in Social Policy: Lessons from Developments of Quasi-Markets in the 1990s* (Bristol: Policy Press).

Bassanini, Andrea, and Scarpetta, Stefano (2001), 'The Driving Forces of Economic Growth: Panel Data Evidence for the OECD Countries', *OECD Economic Studies*, No. 33, 2001/II, 10–56.

Baumol, William (1996), 'Children of the Performing Arts, the Economics Dilemma: The Climbing Costs of Health Care and Education', *Journal of Cultural Economics*, 20/3: 183–206.

—— and Blinder, Alan (2000), *Economics: Principles and Policy* (Fort Worth: Dryden Press).

Becker, Gary (1975), *Human Capital* (2nd edn., Cambridge, Mass.: National Bureau of Economic Research).

—— (1983), 'A Theory of Competition among Pressure Groups for Political Influence', *Quarterly Journal of Economics*, 98 (Aug.), 371–400.

—— (1985), 'Public Policies, Pressure Groups, and Dead Weight Costs', *Journal of Public Economics*, 28 (Dec.), 329–47.

Beenstock, Michael, and Brasse, Valerie (1986), *Insurance for Unemployment* (London: Allen & Unwin).

Begg, David, Fischer, Stanley, and Dornbusch, Rudiger (2003), *Economics* (7th edn., Maidenhead: McGraw Hill).

Bennett, Fran (2002), 'Gender Implications of Current Social Security Reforms', *Fiscal Studies*, 23/4 (Dec.), 559–84.

Bentham, Jeremy (1789), *An Introduction to the Principles of Morals and Legislation* (London: Payne).

Benzeval, Michaela, Taylor, Jayne, and Judge, Ken (2000), 'Evidence on the Relationship between Low Income and Poor Health: Is the Government Doing Enough?', *Fiscal Studies*, 21/3 (Sept.), 375–99.

Besley, Timothy, and Coate, Stephen (1992), 'Workfare versus Welfare: Incentive Arguments for Work Requirements in Poverty Alleviation Programs', *American Economic Review*, 82/1: 249–61.

—— and Kanbur, Ravi (1993), 'Principles of Targeting', in Michael Lipton and Jacques van der Gaag (eds.), *Including the Poor* (Washington: World Bank), 67–90; repr. in Barr (2001*b*: ii. 310–34).

Beveridge, William (1944), *Full Employment in a Free Society* (London: Allen & Unwin).

Beveridge Report (1942), *Social Insurance and Allied Services*, Cmd 6404 (London: HMSO).

Black, Douglas (1980), *Inequalities in Health* (the Black Report), Report of a Research

Working Group chaired by Douglas Black (Department of Health and Social Security, London), published in Peter Townsend and N. Davidson, *Inequalities in Health* (London: Penguin, 1982).

Blackorby, Charles, and Donaldson, David (1988), 'Cash versus Kind, Self-Selection, and Efficient Transfers', *American Economic Review*, 78: 691–700.

Blanchard, Olivier, and Portugal, Pedro (2001), 'What Hides behind an Unemployment Rate: Comparing Portugese and US Labor Markets', *American Economic Review*, 91/1 (Mar.), 187–207.

—— and Wolfers, Justin (2000), 'The Role of Shocks and Institutions in the Rise of European Unemployment: The Aggregate Evidence', *Economic Journal*, 110/462 (Mar.), C1–C33.

Blank, Rebecca (1994) (ed.), *Social Protection versus Economic Flexibility* (Chicago: University of Chicago Press).

—— (1997), *It Takes a Nation: A New Agenda for Fighting Poverty* (Princeton: Princeton University Press).

—— (2000), 'Fighting Poverty: Lessons from Recent US History', *Journal of Economic Perspectives*, 14/2 (Spring), 3–19.

—— (2002), 'Evaluating Welfare Reform in the United States', *Journal of Economic Literature*, 40/4: 1105–66.

—— (2003), 'Lessons from US Welfare Reform', *CESifo Economic Studies*, 49/1: 49–74.

—— and Ellwood, David T. (2002), 'The Clinton Legacy for America's Poor', in J. A. Frankel and P. R. Orszag (eds.), *American Economic Policy in the 1990s* (Cambridge, Mass.: MIT Press).

Blaug, Mark (1970), *An Introduction to the Economics of Education* (London: Penguin).

—— (1976), 'The Empirical Status of Human Capital Theory: A Slightly Jaundiced Survey', *Journal of Economic Literature* (Sept.), 827–56; repr. in Blaug (1987), 100–28, and Barr (2001*b*: iii. 313–41).

—— (1985), 'Where Are We Now in the Economics of Education?', *Economics of Education Review*, 4/1: 17–28; repr. in Blaug (1987), 129–40 and Barr (2001*b*: iii. 342–53).

—— (1987), *The Economics of Education and the Education of an Economist* (Aldershot: Edward Elgar).

—— (1997), 'Where Are We Now in British Health Economics?', Presentation to the Twenty-Fifth Anniversary of the UK Health Economists' Study Group (Centre for Health Economics, York: University of York).

Bleichrodt, H. (1995), 'QALYs and HYEs: Under What Conditions Are They Equivalent?', *Journal of Health Economics*, 14/1 (May), 17–37.

Blendon, R. J., Benson, J., Donelan, K., Leitman, R., Taylor, H., Koeck, C., and Gitterman, D. (1995), 'What Has the Best Health Care System? A Second Look', *Health Affairs*, 14/4: 220–30.

Blomqvist, A. (1991), 'The Doctor as Double-Agent: Information Asymmetry, Health Insurance and Medical Care', *Journal of Health Economics*, 10/4 (Nov.), 411–32.

Blundell, Richard (2000), 'Work Incentives and 'In-Work' Benefit Reforms: A Review', *Oxford Review of Economic Policy*, 16/1: 27–44.

Blundell, Richard, Dearden, Lorraine, Meghir, Costas, and Sianesi, Barbara (1999), 'Human Capital Investment: The Returns from Education and Training to the Individual, the Firm and the Economy', *Fiscal Studies*, 20/1 (Mar.), 1–23.

—— —— Goodman, Alissa, and Reed, Howard (2000), 'The Returns to Higher Education in Britain: Evidence from a British Cohort', *Economic Journal*, 110/461 (Feb.), F82–F99.

—— Meghir, Costas, and Smith, Sarah (2002), 'Pension Incentives and the Pattern of Early Retirement', *Economic Journal*, 112 (Mar.), C153–C170.

Boardman, Anthony, and Vining, Aidan (1989), 'Ownership and Performance in Competitive Environments: A Comparison of the Performance of Private, Mixed and State-Owned Enterprises', *Journal of Law and Economics*, 32 (Apr.), 1–33.

Bodie, Zvi (1990), 'Pensions as Retirement Income Insurance', *Journal of Economic Literature*, 28 (Mar.), 28–49.

—— Marcus, Alan J., and Merton, Robert C. (1988), 'Defined Benefit versus Defined Contribution Plans: What Are the Real Tradeoffs?', in Zvi Bodie, John B. Shoven, and David Wise (eds.), *Pensions in the US Economy* (Chicago: Chicago University Press), 139–60; repr. in Barr (2001*b*: ii. 167–88).

Booth, Charles (1902), *Life and Labour of the People of London*, 17 vols. (London: Macmillan).

Bosanquet, Nicholas (1983), *After the New Right* (London: Heinemann).

Bowley, Marion (1937), *Nassau Senior and Classical Economics* (London: Allen & Unwin).

Bradley, S., and Taylor, J. (2000), *The Effect of the Quasi-Market on the Efficiency-Equity Trade-Off in the Secondary School Sector*, Centre for Research in the Economics of Education, Discussion Paper EC9/00 (Lancaster: University of Lancaster).

—— Johnes, G., and Millington, J. (1999), *School Choice, Competition and the Efficiency of Secondary Schools in England*, Centre for Research in the Economics of Education, Discussion Paper EC3/99 (Lancaster: University of Lancaster).

Bradshaw, J., and Finch, N. (2002), *A Comparison of Child Benefit Packages in 22 Countries*, Department for Work and Pensions Research Report No. 174 (Leeds: Corporate Publishing Services), downloadable from http://www.dwp.gov.uk/asd/asd5/index.html.

Brainerd, Elizabeth (1998), 'Winners and Losers in Russia's Economic Transition', *American Economic Review* 88/5 (Dec.), 1094–116.

Brewer, Mike (2001), 'Comparing In-Work Benefits and the Reward for Work for Families with Children in the US and the UK', *Fiscal Studies*, 22/1 (Mar.), 41–77.

—— (2003), *The New Tax Credits*, Briefing Note No. 35 (London: Institute for Fiscal Studies).

—— Clark, Tom, and Goodman, Alissa (2003), 'What Really Happened to Child Poverty in the UK under Labour's First Term?',

Economic Journal, 113/488 (June), F240–F257.

—— —— and Wakefield, Matthew (2002), 'Social Security in the UK under New Labour: What did the Third Way Mean for Welfare Reform?', *Fiscal Studies*, 23/4 (Dec.), 505–37.

Brittan, Samuel (1995), *Capitalism with a Human Face* (Aldershot and Brookfield, Vt.: Edward Elgar).

Brooks, Richard, Regan, Sue, and Robinson, Peter (2002), *A New Contract for Retirement* (London: Institute for Public Policy Research).

Bruce, Maurice (1972), *The Coming of the Welfare State* (4th edn., London: Batsford).

Buchanan, James M., and Tullock, Gordon (1962), *The Calculus of Consent* (Ann Arbor, Mich.: University of Michigan Press).

Buhmann, Brigitte, Rainwater, Lee, Schmaus, Guenther, and Smeeding, Timothy (1988), 'Equivalence Scales, Well-Being, Inequality, and Poverty: Sensitivity Estimates across Ten Countries, Using the Luxembourg Income Study (LIS) Database', *Review of Income and Wealth*, 34/2: 115–42.

Burchardt, Tania, and Hills, John (1997), *Private Welfare Insurance and Social Security: Pushing the Boundaries* (York: Joseph Rowntree Foundation).

—— Le Grand, Julian, and Piachaud, David (2002*a*), 'Introduction', in Hills et al. (2002), ch. 1, 1–12.

—— —— —— (2002*b*), 'Degrees of Exclusion: Developing a Dynamic, Multidimensional Measure', in Hills et al. (2002), ch. 3, 30–43.

Burgess, Simon, and Propper, Carol (2002), 'The Dynamics of Poverty in Britain', in Hills et al. (2002), ch. 4, 44–61.

Burtless, Gary (1986), 'The Work Response to a Guaranteed Income: A Survey of Experimental Evidence', in Alicia H. Munnell (ed.), *Lessons from the Income Maintenance Experiments* (Federal Reserve Bank of Boston), 22–52.

—— (1987), 'The Adequacy and Counter-Cyclical Effectiveness of the Unemployment System', Testimony to the Committee on

Unemployment and Means, US House of Representatives, 15 Dec. 1987.

—— (1996), 'Trends in the Level and Distribution of US Living Standards: 1973–1993', *Eastern Economic Journal*, 22/3 (Summer), 271–90.

—— and Smeeding, Timothy M. (2001), 'US Poverty in a Cross-national Context', in Sheldon, H. Danziger and Robert H. Haveman (eds.), *Understanding Poverty* (New York: Russell Sage Foundation), 162–91.

Campbell, Nigel (1999), *The Decline of Employment among Older People in Britain*, Centre for the Analysis of Social Exclusion, Case Paper No. 19 (London: London School of Economics).

Carnevale, Anthony P., and Rose, Stephen J. (2003), *Socioeconomic Status, Race/Ethnicity, and Selective College Admissions* (New York: Century Foundation), downloadable from www.equaleducation.org.

Castles, Frances (1996), 'Needs-Based Strategies of Social Protection in Australia and New Zealand', in Esping-Andersen (1996*b*), 88–115.

Chadwick, Edwin (1842), *Inquiry into the Sanitary Condition of the Laboring Population of Great Britain* (London: HMSO).

Champernowne, David G., and Cowell, Frank A. (1998), *Economic Inequality and Income Distribution* (Cambridge and New York: Cambridge University Press).

Chapman, Bruce, and Ryan, Chris (2003), *The Access Implications of Income-Contingent Charges for Higher Education: Lessons from Australia*, Discussion Paper No. 463 (Apr.), (Centre for Economic Policy Research, Canberra: Australian National University).

Chaudhuri, Shubham, and Ravallion, Martin (1994), 'How Well Do Static Indicators Identify the Chronically Poor?', *Journal of Public Economics*, 53: 367–94; repr. in Barr (2001*b*: ii. 407–34).

Child Poverty Action Group (2003), *Welfare Benefits and Tax Credits Handbook 2003/4* (5th edn., London: Child Poverty Action Group).

Christopher, A., et al. (1970), *Policy for Poverty*, Research Monograph 20 (London: Institute of Economic Affairs).

Chubb, J. W., and Moe, T. M. (1990), *Politics, Markets and America's Schools* (Washington: Brookings Institution).

Coase, Ronald H. (1960), 'The Problem of Social Cost', *Journal of Law and Economics*, 3 (Oct.), 1–44.

Cogan, John F., and Mitchell, Olivia S. (2003), 'Perspectives from the President's Commission on Social Security Reform', *Journal of Economics Perspectives*, 17/2 (Spring), 149–72.

Cohn, E., and Geske, T. G. (1990), *The Economics of Education* (3rd edn., Oxford: Pergamum Press).

Collard, David (1983), 'Economics of Philanthropy: A Comment', *Economic Journal*, 93/371 (Sept.), 637–8.

Cooper, Michael H., and Culyer, Anthony J. (1973) (eds.), *Health Economics* (London: Penguin).

Cornelisse, Peter A., and Goudswaard, Kees, P. (2002), 'On the Convergence of Social Protection Systems in the European Union', *International Social Security Review*, 55/3 (July–Sept.), 3–17.

Coulter, Fiona, Cowell, Frank, and Jenkins, Stephen (1992), 'Equivalence Scale Relativities and the Extent of Inequality and Poverty', *Economic Journal*, 102/414 (Sept.), 1067–82.

Cowell, Frank A. (1995), *Measuring Inequality* (2nd edn., Hemel Hempstead: Prentice Hall/Harvester Wheatsheaf).

—— (2000), 'Measurement of Inequality', in A. B. Atkinson and F. Bourguignon (eds.), *Handbook of Income Distribution* (Amsterdam: Elsevier).

—— (2003) (ed.), *The Economics of Poverty and Inequality Vols I and II*, Edward Elgar Library in Critical Writings in Economics (Cheltenham and Northampton, Mass.: Edward Elgar).

Crosland, Anthony (1956), *The Future of Socialism* (London: Cape).

Cullis, John, and Jones, Philip (1998), *Public Finance and Public Choice* (2nd edn., Oxford: Oxford University Press).

Culyer, Anthony J. (1993), 'Health Care Insurance and Provision', in Barr and Whynes (1993), 153–75.

—— and Wagstaff, Adam (1995), 'QALYs versus HYEs: A Reply to Gafni, Birch, and Mehrez', *Journal of Health Economics*, 14/1 (May), 39–45.

—— —— (1996) (eds.), *Reforming Health Care Systems: Experiments with the NHS: Proceedings of Section F (Economics) of the British Association for the Advancement of Science, Loughborough 1994* (Cheltenham and Brookfield, Mass.: Edward Elgar).

Cutler, David M., and Zeckhauser, Richard J. (2000), 'The Anatomy of Health Insurance', in Anthony J. Culyer and Joseph P. Newhouse (eds.), *Handbook of Health Economics, Volume 1A* (Amsterdam: North Holland), ch. 11, 563–643.

Dalton, H. (1920), 'The Measurement of the Inequality of Income', *Economic Journal*, 30: 348–61.

Daniel, Caroline (1997), 'Socialists and Equality', in Franklin (1997), 11–27.

Daniels, N. (1975) (ed.), *Reading Rawls* (Oxford: Basil Blackwell).

Danziger, Sheldon, and Gottschalk, Peter (1995), *America Unequal* (New York: Russell Sage Foundation; Cambridge, Mass., and London: Harvard University Press).

Dauderstädt, Michael, and Witte, Lothar (2002) (eds.), *Work and Welfare in the Enlarging Europe* (Bonn: Friedrich Ebert Stiftung).

Dasgupta, Partha (1993), *An Inquiry into Well-Being and Destitution* (Oxford: Oxford University Press).

Davis, Karen, and Cooper, Barbara S. (2003), 'American Health Care: Why So Costly?', Invited Testimony, Senate Appropriations Committee, Subcommittee on Labor, Health and Human Services, Education and Related Agencies, Hearing on Health Care Access and Affordability: Cost Containment Strategies, downloadable from http://www.cmwf.org/programs/quality/davis_senatecommitteetestimony_654.pdf.

Davis, O. E., and Whinston, A. (1965), 'Welfare Economics and the Theory of Second Best', *Review of Economic Studies*, 32/89 (Jan.), 1–14.

Dee, Thomas S. (2003), *Are There Civic Returns to Education?* Working Paper No. W9588 (Cambridge, Mass.: NBER).

Dennis, Ian, and Guio, Anne-Catherine (2003), 'Poverty and Social Exclusion in the EU after Laiken-part 1', *Statistics in Focus, Population and Social Conditions*, Theme 3–8/2003, Luxembourg: Eurostat, downloadable from http://europa.eu.int/comm/eurostat/.

Derthick, Martha (1979), *Policymaking for Social Security* (Washington: Brookings Institution).

Desai, Meghnad (1979), *Marxian Economics* (Oxford: Basil Blackwell).

Di Tella, Rafael, and MacCulloch, Robert (2002), 'Informal Family Insurance and the Design of the Welfare State', *Economic Journal*, 112/481 (July), 481–503.

Diamond, Peter A. (1996), 'Insulation of Pensions from Political Risk', in Salvador Valdes-Prieto (ed.), *The Economics of Pensions: Principles, Policies and International Experience* (Cambridge: Cambridge University Press), 33–57.

—— (1998), 'The Economics of Social Security Reform', in Douglas Arnold, Michael Graetz, and Alicia Munnell (eds.), *Framing the Social Security Debate: Values, Politics, and Economics* (Washington: Brookings Institution), 38–64; repr. in Barr (2001*b*: ii. 189–217).

—— (2002), *Social Security Reform*, The Lindahl Lectures (Oxford and New York: Oxford University Press).

—— (2003), *Taxation, Incomplete Markets and Social Security* (Cambridge, Mass.: MIT Press).

—— (2004), 'Social Security', *American Economic Review*, 94/2 (May), 94/1 (March), 1–24.

—— and Orszag, Peter R. (2004), *Saving Social Security: A Balanced Approach* (Washington: Brookings Institution).

—— and Rothschild, Michael (1978) (eds.), *Uncertainty in Economics: Readings and Exercises* (New York: Academic Press).

Dickens, Richard, and Ellwood, David T. (2003), 'Child Poverty in Britain and the United States', *Economic Journal*, 113/488 (June), F219–F239.

Disney, Richard (2000), 'Crises in Public Pension Programmes in OECD Countries: What Are the Reform Options?' *Economic Journal*, 110/461 (Feb.), F1–F23.

—— and Smith, Sarah (2002), 'The Labour Supply Effect of the Abolition of the Earnings Rule for Older Workers in the United Kingdom', *Economic Journal*, 112 (Mar.), C126–C152.

—— and Webb, Steven (1991), 'Why Are There So Many Long-Term Sick in Britain?', *Economic Journal*, 101: 252–62.

Disney, Richard, Emmerson, Carl, and Tanner, Sarah (1999), *Partnership in Pensions: An Assessment*, Commentary No. 78 (London: Institute for Fiscal Studies).

Dixon, Jennifer (1997), 'The British NHS—A Funding Crisis?', *Eurohealth*, 3/1 (Spring), 36–7.

Douglas, P. H. (1925), *Wages and the Family* (Chicago: University of Chicago Press).

—— (1939), *Social Security in the United States: An Analysis of the Federal Social Security Act* (New York: McGraw-Hill).

Downs, Anthony (1957), *An Economic Theory of Democracy* (New York: Harper & Row).

Dufwenberg, Martin, and Lundholm, Michael (2001), 'Social Norms and Moral Hazard', *Economic Journal*, 111/473 (July), 506–25.

Dunleavy, Patrick (1985), 'Bureaucrats, Budgets and the Growth of the State: Reconstructing an Instrumental Model', *British Journal of Political Science*, 15: 299–328; repr. in Barr (2001*b*: i. 433–62).

Ehrenberg, Ronald G. (2002), *Tuition Rising: Why College Costs So Much* (Cambridge, Mass.: Harvard University Press).

Ellwood, David T. (2000), 'Anti-Poverty Policy for Families in the Next Century: From Welfare to Work—and Worries', *Journal of Economic Perspectives*, 14/1 (Winter), 187–98.

Emmerson, Carl, and Wakefield, Matthew (2003), *Achieving Simplicity, Security and Choice in Retirement? An Assessment of the Government's Proposed Pensions Reforms*, Briefing Note No. 36 (April) (London: Institute for Fiscal Studies), downloadable from http://www.ifs.org.uk/pensions/bn36.pdf.

Epple, Dennis, and Romano, Richard E. (1998), 'Competiton between Private and Public Schools, Vouchers, and Peer-Group Effects', *American Economic Review*, 88/1 (Mar.), 33–62; repr. in Barr (2001*b*: iii. 402–31).

Esping-Anderson, Gøsta (1990), *The Three Worlds of Welfare Capitalism* (Cambridge: Polity Press).

—— (1996*a*), 'After the Golden Age? Welfare State Dilemmas in a Global Economy', in Esping-Andersen (1996*b*), 1–31.

—— (1996*b*) (ed.), *Welfare States in Transition: National Adaptations in Global Economies* (London: Sage).

—— (1999), *Social Foundations of Post-Industrial Economies* (Oxford and New York: Oxford University Press).

—— with Gallie, Duncan, Hemerijck, Anton, and Myles, John (2002), *Why We Need a New Welfare State* (Oxford and New York: Oxford University Press).

Estrin, Saul (1994), 'The Inheritance', in Barr (1994*c*), 53–76.

—— (2002), 'Competition and Corporate Governance in Transition', *Journal of Economic Perspectives*, 16/1 (Mar.), 101–24.

European Observatory on Health Care Systems (2002), *Health Care Systems in Eight Countries: Trends and Challenges*, European Observatory on Health Care Systems, London: London School of Economics, downloadable from www.hm-treasury.gov.uk.

Eurostat (2001), *European Social Statistics: Income, Poverty and Social Exclusion* (Luxembourg: European Statistical Office).

Evans, Martin (1998), 'Social Security: Dismantling the Pyramids?', in Glennerster and Hills (1998), 258–307.

—— (2001), *Welfare to Work and the Organisation of Opportunity: Lessons from Abroad*, Centre for the Analysis of Social Exclusion, CASE Report No. 15 (London: London School of Economics).

Evans, Robert, G. (1974), 'Supplier-Induced Demand: Some Empirical Evidence and Implications', in M. Perlman (ed.), *The Economics of Health and Medical Care* (London: Macmillan), 162–73; repr. in Barr (2001*b*: iii. 147–58).

—— (1996), 'Health, Hierarchy and Hominids—Biological Correlates of the Sociological Gradient in Health', in Culyer and Wagstaff (1996), 35–64; repr. in Barr (2001*b*: iii. 5–34).

—— Lomas, Jonathan, Barer, Morris, L., et al. (1989), 'Controlling Health Expenditures: The Canadian Reality', *New England Journal of Medicine*, 320/9: 571–7.

—— Barer, Morris L., and Marmor, Theodore R. (1994) (eds.), *Why Are Some People Healthy and Others Not? The Determinants of Health of Populations* (New York: Aldine).

Falkingham, Jane, and Rake, Katherine (1999), 'Partnership in Pensions: Delivering a Secure Retirement for Women', in *Partnership in Pensions? Responses to the Pensions Green Paper*, Centre for the Analysis of Social Exclusion, CASEpaper 24 (London: London School of Economics).

Feinstein, C. H. (1972). *Statistical Tables of National Income, Expenditure and Output of the UK, 1855–1965* (Cambridge: Cambridge University Press).

Feinstein, Leon (1998), *Pre-School Educational Inequality? British Children in the 1970 Cohort*, Discussion Paper 404 (London: London School of Economics, Centre for Economic Performance), downloadable from http://cep.lse.ac.uk.

—— (2003), 'Inequality in the Early Cognitive Development of British Children in the 1970 Cohort', *Economica*, 70/277: 73–98.

Feldstein, Martin S. (1974), 'Social Security, Induced Retirement and Aggregate Capital Accumulation', *Journal of Political Economy*, 82: 905–26.

—— (1996), 'The Missing Piece in Policy Analysis: Social Security Reform', *American Economic Review*, 86/2 (May), 1–14; repr. in Barr (2001*b*: ii. 247–60).

Field, Frank (1996), *Stakeholder Welfare* (London: Institute for Economic Affairs).

Finer, S. E. (1952), *The Life and Times of Sir Edwin Chadwick* (London: Methuen).

Fischer, Claude, S., Hout, Michael, Jankowski, Martin, Lucas, Samuel R., Swidler, Ann, and Voss, Kim (1996), *Inequality by Design: Cracking the Bell Curve Myth* (Princeton: Princeton University Press).

Fisher, Irving (1930), *The Theory of Interest* (New York: Macmillan).

Forni, Lorenzo, and Giordano, Raffaela (2001), 'Funding a PAYG Pension System: The Case of Italy', *Fiscal Studies*, 22/4 (Dec.), 487–526.

Foster, James E. (1984), 'On Economic Poverty: A Survey of Aggregate Measures', *Advances in Econometrics*, 3: 215–51.

Franklin, Jane (1997) (ed.), *Equality* (London: Institute for Public Policy Research).

Fraser, Derek (1984), *The Evolution of the British Welfare State* (2nd edn., London: Macmillan).

Fredriksson, Peter, and Holmlund, Bertil (2003), *Improving Incentives in Unemployment Insurance: A Review of Recent research*, CESifo Working Paper No. 922 (Munich: CESifo), downloadable from http://www.cesifo.de.

Freeden, M. (1978), *The New Liberalism: An Ideology of Social Reform* (Oxford: Oxford University Press).

Friedman, Milton (1962), *Capitalism and Freedom* (Chicago: University of Chicago Press).

—— and Friedman, Rose (1980), *Free to Choose* (London: Penguin).

Fuchs, Victor R. (1996) (ed.), *Individual and Social Responsibility: Child Care, Education, Medical Care, and Long-Term Care in America*, National Bureau of Economic Research Conference Report Series (Chicago and London: University of Chicago Press).

—— (2000), 'Medicare Reform: The Larger Picture', *Journal of Economic Perspectives*, 14/2 (Spring), 57–70.

Galal, Ahmed, et al. (1994), *Welfare Consequences of Selling Public Enterprises: An Empirical Analysis* (New York: Oxford University Press).

Gale, William (1998), 'The Effects of Pensions on Wealth: A Re-Evaluation of Theory and

Evidence', *Journal of Political Economy*, 106/1: 706–23.

Gardiner, Karen, and Hills, John (1999), 'Policy Implications of New Data on Income Mobility', *Economic Journal*, 109/453 (Feb.), F91–F111.

Gauldie, E. (1974), *Cruel Habitations: A History of Working-Class Housing, 1780–1918* (London: George Allen & Unwin).

George, Victor, and Wilding, Paul (1994), *Welfare and Ideology* (Hemel Hempstead: Harvester Wheatsheaf).

Gerdttham, Ulf-G., and Jönsson, Bengt (2000), 'Cross-Country Studies of Health Care Expenditure', in Anthony J. Culyer and Joseph P. Newhouse (eds.), *The Handbook of Health Economics, Volume 1A* (Amsterdam: North-Holland), ch. 1, 11–53.

Gertler, Paul, and Gruber, Jonathan (2002), 'Insuring Consumption against Illness', *American Economic Review*, 92/2 (Mar.), 51–70.

Gilbert, Bentley B. (1973), *The Evolution of National Insurance in Great Britain* (London: Michael Joseph).

Gilbert, Neil (2002), *Transformation of the Welfare State: The Silent Surrender of Public Responsibility* (New York and Oxford: Oxford University Press).

Gillion, Colin (2000), 'The Development and Reform of Social Security Pensions: The Approach of the International Labour Office', *International Social Security Review*, 53/1 (Jan.–Mar.), 35–63.

Gini, C. (1921), 'Measurement of Inequality of Incomes', *Economic Journal*, 31: 124–6.

Gilmour, Ian (1992), *Dancing with Dogma* (Hemel Hempstead: Simon & Schuster).

Ginsburg, N. (1979), *Class, Capital and Social Policy* (London: Macmillan).

Gintis, H., and Bowles, S. (1982), 'The Welfare State and Long-Term Economic Growth: Marxian, Neoclassical and Keynesian Approaches', *American Economic Review, Papers and Proceedings*, 72/1: 341–5.

Glennerster, Howard (1991), 'Quasi-Markets for Education?', *Economic Journal*, 101/408 (Sept.), 1268–76; repr. in Barr (2001*b*: iii. 393–401).

—— (1993), 'The Economics of Education: Changing Fortunes', in Barr and Whynes (1993), 176–99.

—— (1994), *Implementing GP Fundholding* (Milton Keynes: Open University Press).

—— (1997), *Paying for Welfare: Towards 2000* (3rd edn., Hemel Hempstead: Prentice Hall/Harvester Wheatsheaf).

—— (1998), 'Education: Reaping the Harvest?', in Glennerster and Hills (1998), 27–74.

—— (2000), *British Social Policy since 1945* (Oxford and Malden, Mass.: Blackwell Publishers).

—— (2002*a*), 'US Poverty Studies and Poverty Measurement: The Past Twenty-Five Years', *Social Service Review* (Mar.), 83–107.

—— (2002*b*), 'United Kingdom Education 1997–2001', *Oxford Review of Economic Policy*, 18/2: 120–36.

—— (2003*a*), *Understanding the Finance of Welfare: What Welfare Costs and How to Pay for it* (Bristol: Policy Press).

—— (2003*b*), 'A Graduate Tax Revisited', *Higher Education Review*, 35/2 (Spring), 25–40.

—— and Hills, John (1998) (eds.), *The State of Welfare II: The Economics of Social Spending* (2nd edn., Oxford: Oxford University Press).

—— Merrett, Stephen, and Wilson, Gail (1968), 'A Graduate Tax', *Higher Education Review*, 1/1: 26–38, reprinted in Barr (2001*b*: iii. 570–82), and as Glennerster (2003*b*).

—— Hills, John, and Travers, Tony (2000), *Paying for Health, Education and Housing* (Oxford: Oxford University Press).

Glied, Sherry (2000), 'Managed Care', in Anthony J. Culyer and Joseph P. Newhouse (eds.), *Handbook of Health Economics, Volume 1A* (Amsterdam: North Holland), ch. 13, 707–753.

—— (2003), 'Health Care Costs: On the Rise Again', *Journal of Economic Perspectives*, 17/2 (Spring), 125–48.

Goode, Jackie, Callender, Claire, and Lister, Ruth (1998), *Purse or Wallet: Gender Inequalities and Income Distribution within Families on Benefits* (Bristol: Policy Press).

Goodman, Alissa, Johnson, Paul, and Webb, Steven (1997), *Inequality in the UK* (Oxford: Oxford University Press).

—— Myck, Michal, and Shephard, Andrew (2003), *Sharing in the Nation's Prosperity? Pensioner Poverty in Britain*, Commentary 93 (London: Institute for Fiscal Studies), dowloadable from http://www.ifs.org.uk.

Gordon, David M. (1969), 'Income and Welfare in New York City', *Public Interest*, 16 (Summer), 64–88.

—— and Townsend, Peter (2000) (eds.), *Breadline Europe: The Measurement of Poverty* (Bristol: Policy Press).

Gorovitz, S. (1975), 'John Rawls: A Theory of Justice', in A. de Crespigny and K. R. Minogue (eds.), *Contemporary Political Philosophers* (London: Methuen), 272–89; repr. in Barr (2001*b*: i. 122–39).

Gottschalk, Peter (1997), 'Inequality, Income Growth and Mobility: The Basic Facts', *Journal of Economic Perspectives*, 11/2 (Spring) 21–40; repr. in Barr (2001*b*: ii. 435–54).

—— and Smeeding, Timothy M. (1997), 'Cross-National Comparisons of Earnings and Income Inequality', *Journal of Economic Literature*, 35/2 (June), 633–87; repr. in Barr (2001*b*: ii. 527–81).

—— —— (2000), 'Empirical Evidence on Income Inequality in Industrial Countries', in A. B. Atkinson and F. Bourguignon (eds.), *Handbook of Income Distribution* (Amsterdam: Elsevier), 261–308.

Gough, I. (1979), *The Political Economy of the Welfare State* (London: Macmillan).

Green, Christopher (1967), *Negative Taxes and the Poverty Problem* (Washington: Brookings Institution).

Greenaway, David, and Haynes, Michelle (2003), 'Funding Higher Education in the UK: The Role of Fees and Loans', *Economic Journal*, 113/485 (Feb.), F150–F166.

Grogger, Jeffrey (2002), 'The Behavioral Effects of Welfare Time Limits', *American Economic Review*, 92/2 (May), 385–9.

Gronbjerg, K., Street, D., and Suttles, G. D. (1978), *Poverty and Social Change* (Chicago: University of Chicago Press).

Grosh, Margaret (1994), *Administering Targeted Social Programs in Latin America: From Platitudes to Practice* (Washington: World Bank).

Gruber, Jonathan, and Wise, David A. (1998), 'Social Security and Retirement: An International Comparison', *American Economic Review*, 88/2 (May), 158–63; repr. in Barr (2001*b*: ii. 161–6).

—— —— (1999), *Social Security and Retirement around the World* (Chicago: University of Chicago Press).

—— —— (2002), *Social Security Programs and Retirement around the World: Micro Estimation*, Working Paper No. W9407 (Cambridge, Mass.: NBER).

Gundlach, Erich, Wossman, Ludger, and Gmelin, Jens (2001), 'The Decline of Schooling Productivity in OECD Countries', *Economic Journal*, 11/471 (May), C135–C147.

Gylfason, Thorvaldur, and Zoega, Gylfi (2003), *Education, Social Equality and Economic Growth*, CESifo Working Paper No. 876 (Munich: CESifo), downloadable from http://www.cesifo.de.

Hamnett, Chris, and Seavers, Jenny (1996), 'Home-Ownership, Housing Wealth and Wealth Distribution in Britain', in Hills (1996*b*), 348–73.

Hancock, Ruth (1998), 'Can Housing Wealth Alleviate Poverty among Britain's Older Population?', *Fiscal Studies*, 19/3 (Aug.), 249–72.

Hannah, Leslie (1986), *Inventing Retirement* (Cambridge: Cambridge University Press).

Hansen, W. Lee, and Weisbrod, Burton A. (1969), 'The Distribution of Costs and Direct Benefits of Public Higher Education: The Case of California', *Journal of Human Resources*, 4/2 (Spring), 176–91; repr. in Barr (2001*b*: iii. 531–46).

—— —— (1978), 'The Distribution of Subsidies to Students in California Public Higher Education: Reply', *Journal of Human Resources*, 13/1 (Winter), 137–9.

Hanushek, Eric A. (2002) (ed.), 'Publicly Provided Education', in Alan J. Auerbach and Martin Feldstein (eds.), *Handbook of*

Public Economics. Volume 4 (Elsevier Science), 2045–141.

—— (2003*a*), 'The Failure of Input-Based Schooling Policies', *Economic Journal*, 113/485: F64–98.

—— (2003*b*) (ed.), *The Economics of Schooling and School Quality, Vols. I and II*, Edward Elgar Library in Critical Writings in Economics (Cheltenham and Northampton, Mass.: Edward Elgar).

—— and Kimko, Dennis D. (2000), 'Schooling, Labor-Force Quality, and the Growth of Nations', *American Economic Review*, 90/5 (Dec.), 1184–208.

Harberger, Arnold C. (1962), 'The Incidence of the Corporation Income Tax', *Journal of Political Economy*, 70/3 (June), 215–40.

Harris, Jose F. (1972), *Unemployment and Politics, 1886–1914* (Oxford: Oxford University Press).

—— (1997), *William Beveridge: A Biography* (rev. edn., Oxford: Oxford University Press).

Harrison, A. H., Dixon, J., New, B., and Judge, K. (1997*a*), 'Is the NHS Sustainable?', *British Medical Journal*, 314: 296–8.

—— —— —— —— (1997*b*), 'Can the NHS Cope in the Future?', *British Medical Journal*, 314: 139–42.

Harrison, J. (1978), *Marxist Economics for Socialists* (London: Pluto).

Hattersley, Roy (1987), *Choose Freedom: The Future for Democratic Socialism* (London: Michael Joseph).

Haveman, Robert, and Wolfe, Barbara (2000), 'Welfare to Work in the US: A Model for Other Developed Nations?', *International Tax and Public Finance*, 7/1: 95–114.

Hay, J. R. (1975), *The Origins of the Liberal Welfare Reforms 1906–1914* (London: Macmillan).

Hayek, Friedrich A. (1944), *The Road to Serfdom* (London: Routledge; Chicago: Chicago University Press).

—— (1945), 'The Use of Knowledge in Society', *American Economic Review*, 35: 519–30.

—— (1960), *The Constitution of Liberty* (London: Routledge & Kegan Paul; Chicago: Chicago University Press).

—— (1976), *Law, Legislation and Liberty*, ii. *The Mirage of Social Justice* (London: Routledge & Kegan Paul).

Hellevick, O., and Ringen, S. (1995), 'Class Inequality and Egalitarian Reform' (Oxford: Department of Applied Social Studies).

Hemming, Richard (1999), 'Should Public Pensions be Funded?', *International Social Security Review*, 52/2 (Apr.–June), 3–29.

Hicks, John R. (1946), *Value and Capital* (2nd edn., Oxford: Oxford University Press).

Higgins, Joan (1981), *States of Welfare: Comparative Analysis in Social Policy* (Oxford: Basil Blackwell and Martin Robertson).

Higher Education Funding Council for England (2002), *Funding Higher Education in England: How the HEFCE Allocates its Funds*, Report 02/18, Higher Education Funding Council for England, downloadable from www.hefce.ac.uk.

Hills, John (1996*a*), 'Introduction: After the Turning Point', in Hills (1996*b*), 1–16.

—— (1996*b*) (ed.), *New Inequalities: The Changing Distribution of Income and Wealth in the United Kingdom* (Cambridge: Cambridge University Press).

—— (1998), 'Housing: A Decent Home within the Reach of Every Family?', in Glennerster and Hills (1998), 122–88.

—— (2002), 'Following or Leading Public Opinion? Social Security and Public Policy Attitudes since 1997', *Fiscal Studies*, 23/4 (Dec.), 539–58.

—— (2003), *Inclusion or Insurance: National Insurance and the Future of the Contributory Principle*, Centre for the Analysis of Social Exclusion, CASE paper 68 (London: London School of Economics).

—— with Gardiner, Karen (1997), *The Future of Welfare: A Guide to the Debate* (rev. edn., York: Joseph Rowntree Foundation).

—— Le Grand, Julian, and Piachaud, David (2002) (eds.), *Understanding Social Exclusion* (Oxford: Oxford University Press).

Himmelstein, David, U., and Woolhandler, Steffie (1997), 'The Costs of Care and Administration at for Profit and Other Hospitals in the US Health Care System',

New England Journal of Medicine, 336/11: 769–74.

Hirschleifer, J., and Riley, John G. (1992), *The Analytics of Uncertainty and Information*, Cambridge Surveys of Economic Literature (Cambridge and New York: Cambridge University Press).

Hobcraft, John (2002), 'Social Exclusion and the Generations', in Hills, Le Grand, and Piachaud (2002), 62–83.

Hobsbawn, E. J. (1964), *Labouring Men* (London: Weidenfeld & Nicolson).

Hobson, J. A. (1908), *The Problem of the Unemployed* (4th edn., London: Methuen).

—— (1909), *The Crisis of Liberalism: New Issues of Democracy* (London: King & Son).

Hochman, Harold, and Rodgers, James (1969), 'Pareto Optimal Distribution', *American Economic Review*, 59/4: 542–57.

Hoffman, Catherine, and Wang, Marie (2003), *Health Insurance Coverage in America: 2001 Data Update*, Kaiser Commission on Medicaid and the Uninsured, downloadable from http://www.kff.org/content/2003/4070/4070.pdf.

Holzmann, Robert (2000), 'The World Bank Approach to Pension Reform', *International Social Security Review*, 53/1 (Jan.–Mar.), 11–34.

Hoxby, Caroline M. (2000), 'Does Competition among Public Schools Benefit Students and Taxpayers?', *American Economic Review*, 90/5 (Dec.), 1209–38.

Howard, Marilyn (2003), *Lump Sums: Roles for the Social Fund in Ending Child Poverty* (London: Child Poverty Action Group).

Hume, David (1770), 'Enquiry Concerning the Principles of Morals', in *Essays and Treatises on Several Subjects* (London: Cadell).

Hurley, Jeremiah (2000), 'An Overview of the Normative Economics of the Health Sector', in Anthony J. Culyer and Joseph P. Newhouse (eds.), *Handbook of Health Economics, Volume 1A* (Amsterdam: North Holland), ch. 2, 55–118.

Immervoll, Herwig, Sutherland, Holly, and de Vos, Klaas (2000), *Child Poverty and Child Benefits in the European Union*, Working Paper No. EM1/00 (Cambridge: EUROMOD).

Inman, Robert P. (1987), 'Markets, Governments and the "New" Political Economy', in Alan J. Auerbach and Martin S. Feldstein (eds.), *Handbook of Public Economics*, ii (Amsterdam: North Holland), 647–777.

International Social Security Association/International Network of Pension Regulators and Supervisors (2003), *Complementary and Private Pensions throughout the World 2003* (Geneva: International Social Security Association/International Network of Pension Regulators and Supervisors).

Jäntti, Markus, and Danziger, Sheldon (2000), 'Income Poverty in Advanced Countries', in A. B. Atkinson and F. Bourguignon (eds.), *Handbook of Income Distribution* (Amsterdam: Elsevier).

Jarvis, Sarah, and Jenkins, Stephen P. (1997), 'Low Income Dynamics in 1990s Britain', *Fiscal Studies*, 18/2: 123–42.

—— (1998), 'How Much Income Mobility is there in Britain', *Economic Journal*, 108/447 (Mar.), 428–43.

Jencks, Christopher (1970), *Education Vouchers: A Report on the Financing of Elementary Education by Grants to Parents* (Cambridge, Mass.: Cambridge Center for the Study of Public Policy).

Johnes, Geraint (1993), *The Economics of Education* (London: Macmillan).

Johnes, Geraint, and Johnes, Jill (2004), *The International Handbook on the Economics of Education* (Cheltenham and Northampton, Mass.: Edward Elgar).

Johnson, Paul, and Rake, Katherine (1997), 'The Case of Britain', in *Pension Systems and Reforms—Britain, Hungary, Italy, Poland, Sweden: Final Report* (Budapest: European Commission's PHARE ACE Programme, Research Project P95-2139-R), 25–50.

Johnstone, D. Bruce (2000), 'Student Loans in International Perspective: Promises and Failures, Myths and Partial Truths', downloadable from http://www.gse.buffalo.edu/org/IntHigherEdFinance/publications.html.

Jones, Andrew M., and Posnett, John W. (1993), 'The Economics of Charity', in Barr and Whynes (1993), 130–52.

Jones, Charles I. (2002), *Why have Health Expenditures as a Share of GDP Risen so Much?* Working Paper W9325 (Cambridge, Mass.: NBER).

Jorgenson, Dale W. (1998), 'Did We Lose the War on Poverty', *Journal of Economic Perspectives*, 12/1 (Winter), 79–96.

Kaim-Caudle, P. (1973), *Comparative Social Policy and Social Security: A Ten-Country Study* (Oxford: Martin Robertson).

Kaldor, Nicholas (1955), *An Expenditure Tax* (London: Allen & Unwin).

Kane, Thomas J. (2001), 'Assessing the US Financial Aid System: What We Know, What We Need to Know', in *Ford Policy Forum 2001* (Cambridge Mass.: Forum for the Future of Higher Education, Massachusetts Institute of Technology), 25–34.

Karoly, Lynn A., and Burtless, Gary (1995), 'Demographic Change, Rising Earnings Inequality and the Distribution of Personal Well Being, 1959–89', *Demography*, 32/3: 379–405.

Katznelson, Ira (1978), 'Considerations on Social Democracy in the United States', *Comparative Politics*, 11: 77–99.

Kay, John A. (2003), *The Truth about Markets: Their Genius, their Limits, their Follies* (London: Allen Lane).

Kempson, Elaine, Bryson, Alex, and Rowlingson, Karen (1994), *Hard Times: How Poor Families Make Ends Meet* (Bristol: Policy Press).

King, Mervyn A. (1983), 'An Index of Inequality: With Applications to Horizontal Equity and Social Mobility', *Econometrica*, 51: 99–115.

King's Fund (2002), *The Future of the NHS: A Framework for Debate* (London: King's Fund).

Klein, Rudolf (1984), 'Privatisation and the Welfare State', *Lloyds Bank Review*, 151 (Jan.), 12–29.

Krueger, Alan B. (2003), 'Economic Considerations and Class Size', *Economic Journal*, 113/485: F34–63.

—— and Lindahl, Mikael (2001), 'Education for Growth: Why and for Whom?', *Journal of Economic Literature*, 39/4 (Dec.), 1101–36.

—— and Whitmore, Diane M. (2001), 'The Effect of Attending a Small Class in the Early Grades on College-Test Taking and Middle School Test Results: Evidence from Project Star', *Economic Journal*, 111/468 (Jan.), 1–28.

Ladd, Helen F. (2002), 'School Vouchers: A Critical View', *Journal of Economic Perspectives*, 16/4 (Fall), 3–24.

Lakin, Caroline (2003), 'The Effects of Taxes and Benefits on Household Income, 2001–02', *Economic Trends* (May), downloadable from http://www.statistics.gov.uk.

LaRocque, Norman (2003), *Who should Pay: Tuition Fees and Tertiary Education Financing in New Zealand* (Wellington: Education Forum), downloadable from www.educationforum.org.nz.

Laski, Harold (1967), *A Grammar of Politics* (5th edn., London: Allen & Unwin).

Layard, Richard, Nickell, Stephen, and Jackman, Richard (1991), *Unemployment* (Oxford: Oxford University Press).

Lazear, Edward (2002) (ed.), *Education in the Twenty-first Century* (Stanford, Calif.: Hoover Institution Press).

Le Grand, Julian (1982), *The Strategy of Equality* (London: George Allen & Unwin).

—— (1984), 'Equity as an Economic Objective', *Journal of Applied Philosophy*, 1/1: 39–51; repr. in Barr (2001*b*: i. 156–68).

—— (1987*a*), 'Inequalities in Health: Some International Comparisons', *European Economic Review*, 31: 182–91; repr. in Barr (2001*b*: iii. 74–83).

—— (1987*b*), 'The Middle-Class Use of the British Social Services', in Robert Goodin and Julian Le Grand (eds.), *Not Only the Poor: The Middle Classes and the Welfare State* (London: Allen & Unwin), 91–107.

—— (1989), 'An International Comparison of Distribution of Ages-at-Death', in J. Fox (ed.), *Health Inequalities in European Countries* (London: Gower), 75–91.

—— (1990), 'The State of Welfare', in Hills (1990), 338–62.

—— (1991*a*), *Equity and Choice: An Essay in Applied Philosophy* (London and New York: Harper Collins).

—— (1991*b*), 'Quasi-Markets and Social Policy', *Economic Journal*, 101/408 (Sept.), 1256–67.

—— (1996), 'Equity, Efficiency and Rationing of Health Care', in Culyer and Wagstaff (1996), 150–63; repr. in Barr (2001*b*: iii. 133–46).

—— (1999), 'Competition, Cooperation, or Control? Tales from the British National Health Service', *Health Affairs*, 18/3: 27–39.

—— (2002*a*), 'Further Tales from the British National Health Service', *Health Affairs*, 21/3: 116–28.

—— (2002*b*), 'The Labour Government and the National Health Service', *Oxford Review of Economic Policy*, 18/2: 137–53.

—— (2003), *Motivation, Agency and Public Policy: Of Knights and Knaves, Pawns and Queens* (Oxford and New York: Oxford University Press).

—— and Robinson, Ray (1984) (eds.), *Privatisation and the Welfare State* (London: George Allen & Unwin).

—— and Vizard, Polly (1998), 'The National Health Service: Crisis, Change or Continuity?', in Glennerster and Hills (1998), 75–121.

—— Propper, Carol, and Robinson, Ray (1992), *The Economics of Social Problems* (3rd edn., London: Macmillan).

—— Mays, Nicholas, and Mulligan, Jo-Ann (1998), *Learning from the NHS Internal Market—A Review of the Evidence* (London: The King's Fund).

Lee, Ronald, and Skinner, Jonathan (1999), 'Will Aging Baby Boomers Bust the Federal Budget', *Journal of Economic Perspectives*, 13/1 (Winter), 117–40.

Leimer, Dean R., and Lesnoy, Selig D. (1982), 'Social Security and Private Saving: New Time-Series Evidence', *Journal of Political Economy*, 90: 606–42.

Letwin, William (1983) (ed.), *Against Equality* (London: Macmillan).

Levy, Frank (1998), *Dollars and Dreams: The Changing American Income Distribution* (2nd edn., New York: Russell Sage Foundation).

Lindbeck, Assar (1997), 'The Swedish Experiment', *Journal of Economic Literature*, 35 (Sept.), 1273–319.

—— and Persson, Mats (2003), 'The Gains from Pension Reform', *Journal of Economic Literature*, 41/1 (Mar.), 74–112.

—— Nyberg, Sten, and Weibull, Jorgen (1999), 'Social Norms and Economic Incentives in the Welfare State', *Quarterly Journal of Economics*, 114/1: 1–35.

—— —— —— (2003), 'Social Norms and Welfare State Dynamics', *Journal of the European Economic Association*, 1 (Apr.–May), 533–42.

Lindsay, Cotton M. (1969), 'Medical Care and the Economics of Sharing', *Economica*, 36: 351–62; repr. in Cooper and Culyer (1973), 75–89.

Lipsey, Richard G., and Lancaster, Kelvin (1956), 'The General Theory of Second Best', *Review of Economic Studies*, 24/63 (Jan.), 11–32.

Lipton, Michael, and Ravallion, Martin (1995), 'Poverty and Policy', in J. Behrman and T. N. Srinavasan (eds.), *Handbook of Development Economics*, iii. (Amsterdam: North Holland).

Lødemel, Ivar, and Trickey, Heather (2001) (eds.), *An Offer you Can't Refuse: Workfare in International Perspective* (Bristol: Policy Press).

Lorenz, M. O. (1905), 'Methods for Measuring Concentration of Wealth', *Journal of the American Statistical Association*, 9: 209–19.

Lucas, Robert E. (1987), *Models of Business Cycles* (Oxford: Basil Blackwell).

Lundberg, Mattias, and Squire, Lyn (2003), 'The Simultanous Evolution of Growth and Inequality', *Economic Journal*, 113/487 (Apr.), 326–44.

Luxembourg Income Study (2000), *LIS Quick Reference Guide* (Syracuse, NY: Center for Policy Research, Luxembourg Income Study, The Maxwell School), downloadable from http://www.lis.ceps.lu/lisquick.htm.

McClellan, Mark (2000), 'Medicare Reform: Fundamental Problems, Incremental Steps', *Journal of Economic Perspectives*, 14/2 (Spring), 21–44.

McCreadie, C. (1976), 'Rawlsian Justice and the Financing of the National Health

Service', *Journal of Social Policy*, 5/2 (Apr.), 113–30.

McDonagh, O. (1960), 'The Nineteenth Century Revolution in Government: A Reappraisal Reappraised', *Historical Journal*, 2.

McGuire, Alistair (1994), 'Is There Adequate Funding of Health Care?', in Culyer and Wagstaff (1996), 134–49.

Mackenzie, G. A., Gerson, Philip, and Cuevas, Alfredo (1997), *Pension Regimes and Saving*, Occasional Paper 153 (Washington: International Monetary Fund).

McMahon, Walter W. (2002), *Education and Development: Measuring the Social Benefits* (New York and Oxford: Oxford University Press).

Mandel, E. (1976), 'Introduction' to Karl Marx, *Capital*, i (London: Penguin).

Marmor, Theodore R., and Hacker, J. S. (1999), 'Managed Care in the 21st Century: A Critical Commentary', *Michigan Law Review*, 32/4 (Summer), 661–84.

Marmot, M. G., Davey Smith, G., Stanseld, S., Patel, C., North, F., Head, J., White, I., Brunner, E., and Feeney, A. (1991), 'Health Inequalities among British Civil Servants: The Whitehall II Study', *The Lancet*, 8 June, 337, 1387–93.

Marsh, D. (1980), *The Welfare State* (2nd edn., London: Longman).

Marshall, Thomas H. (1975), *Social Policy in the Twentieth Century* (4th edn., London: Hutchinson).

Maynard, Alan (1991), 'Developing the Health Care Market', *Economic Journal*, 101/408 (Sept.), 1277–86.

Meade, James E. (1952), 'External Economies and Diseconomies in a Competitive Situation', *Economic Journal*, 62: 54–67.

—— (1972), 'Poverty in the Welfare State', *Oxford Economic Papers*, 24: 289–326.

—— (1978), *The Structure and Reform of Direct Taxation* (London: Institute for Fiscal Studies and George Allen & Unwin).

Megginson, William, Nash, Robert C., and van Randenborgh, Matthias (1994), 'The Financial and Operating Performance of Newly Privatized Firms: An International Empirical Analysis,' *Journal of Finance*, 49/2: 403–52.

—— and Netter, Jeffry M. (2001), 'From State to Market: A Survey of Empirical Studies on Privatization', *Journal of Economic Literature*, 39/2 (June), 321–89.

Menscher, S. (1967), *Poor Law to Poverty Program* (Pittsburgh: University of Pittsburgh Press).

Merrett, Stephen (1979), *State Housing in Britain* (London: Routledge & Kegan Paul).

Mesa-Lego, Carmelo (1990), *Economic and Financial Aspects of Social Security in Latin America and the Caribbean: Tendencies, Problems and Alternatives for the Year 2000*, World Bank, Latin American and the Caribbean Region, Technical Department, Human Resources Division, Report No. IDP-095 (Washington: World Bank).

Mesa-Lago, Carmelo, and Müller, Katharina (2002), 'The Politics of Pension Reform in Latin America', *Journal of Latin American Studies*, 34: 687–715.

Meyer, Bruce D. (2002), 'Unemployment and Workers' Compensation Programmes: Rationale, Design, Labour Supply and Income Support', *Fiscal Studies*, 23/1 (Mar.), 1–49.

Milanovic, Branko (1998), *Income, Inequality and Poverty during the Transition from Planned to Market Economy* (Washington: World Bank), downloadable from http://www.worldbank.org/research/inequality/inequalityandtransition.htm.

—— (1999), 'Explaining the Increase in Inequality during Transition', *Economics of Transition*, 7/2: 299–341.

—— (2002), 'True World Income Distribution, 1988 and 1993: First Calculation Based on Household Surveys Alone', *Economic Journal*, 112/477 (Jan.), 1–92.

—— and Yitzhaki, Shlomo (2002), 'Decomposing World Income Distribution: Does the World Have a Middle Class?', *Review of Income and Wealth*, 48/2: 155–78.

Miliband, Ralph (1969), *The State in a Capitalist Society* (London: Weidenfeld & Nicolson).

Mill, John Stuart (1863), *Utilitarianism* (London: Parker, Son & Bourn).

Miller, David (1976), *Social Justice* (Oxford: Oxford University).

Mishra, Ramesh (1981), *Society and Social Policy* (London: Macmillan).

Mitchell, Deborah (2002), 'Participation and Opportunity: Redefining Social Security in Australia and New Zealand', *International Social Security Review*, 2002/4: 127–41.

Moffitt, Robert A. (2003), 'The Negative Income Tax and the Evolution of US Welfare Policy', *Journal of Economic Perspectives*, 17/3 (Summer), 119–40.

Morris, J. K., Cook, D. G., and Shaper, A. G. (1994), 'Loss of Employment and Mortality', *British Medical Journal*, 308 (6937), 30 April, 1135–9.

Mossialos, Elias, and Le Grand, Julian (1999) (eds.), *Health Care and Cost Containment in the European Union* (Aldershot: Ashgate).

—— and Thomson, Sarah (2002), 'Voluntary Health Insurance in the European Union', *International Journal of Health Services*, 32/1: 19–88.

Mueller, Dennis C. (2003), *Public Choice III* (Cambridge: Cambridge University Press).

Murphy, J. (1981), 'Class Inequality in Education: Two Justifications, One Evaluation but No Hard Evidence', *British Journal of Sociology*, 32/2 (June), 182–201.

Murray, Charles (1984), *Losing Ground: American Social Policy, 1950–1980* (New York: Basic Books).

Müller, Katharina (2001), 'The Political Economy of Pension Reform in Eastern Europe', *International Social Security Review*, 54/2–3 (Apr.–Sept.), 57–79.

—— *Privatising Old-Age Security: Latin American and Eastern Europe Compared* (Cheltenham and Northampton, Mass.: Edward Elgar).

Myers, R. J. (1965), *Social Insurance and Allied Government Programs* (New York: Irwin).

National Academy of Social Insurance (1998), *Evaluating Issues in Privatizing Social Security*, Report of the Panel on Privatization of Social Security (Washington: National Academy of Social Insurance), downloadable from http://www.nasi.org.

Neal, Derek (2002), 'How Vouchers could Change the Market for Education', *Journal of Economic Perspectives*, 16/4 (Fall), 25–44.

New, Bill (1999), 'Paternalism and Public Policy', *Economics and Philosophy*, 15: 63–83.

Newfield, Jack (1978), *Robert F. Kennedy: A Memoir* (New York: Berkley Publishing Corporation).

Nichols, Albert L., and Zeckhauser, Richard J. (1982), 'Targeting Transfers through Restrictions on Recipients', *American Economic Review, Papers and Proceedings*, 72: 372–7; repr. in Barr (2001*b*: ii. 366–71).

Nickell, Stephen, and Quintini, Glenda (2002), 'The Recent Performance of the UK Labour Market', *Oxford Review of Economic Policy*, 18/2: 202–20.

Nisbet, R. (1974), 'The Pursuit of Equality', *Public Interest*, 35 (Spring), 103–20; repr. in Letwin (1983: 124–47).

Niskanen, William A. (1971), *Bureaucracy and Representative Government* (Chicago: Aldine Atherton).

North, F., Syme, S. L., Feeney, A., et al. (1993), 'Explaining Sociological Differences in Sickness Absence: The Whitehall II Study', *British Medical Journal*, 306, 6 Feb., p. 363.

Nozick, Robert (1974), *Anarchy, State and Utopia* (Oxford: Basil Blackwell).

OECD (2000), *Purchasing Power Parities for OECD Countries, 1970–1999* (Paris: OECD), downloadable from http://www.oecd.org.

—— (2002), *Society at a Glance: OECD Social Indicators 2002* (Paris: OECD).

—— (2003*a*), *OECD Health Data 2003: A Comparative Analysis of 30 Countries* (Paris: OECD).

—— (2003*b*), *Financing Education: Investments and Returns: Analysis of the World Education Indicators 2002 Edition* (Paris: OECD).

—— (2003*c*), *Education at a Glance: OECD Indicators 2003* (Paris: OECD).

—— (2003*d*), *Emerging Risks in the 21st Century: An Agenda for Action* (Paris: OECD).

Okin, S. M. (1989), *Justice, Gender and the Family* (New York: Basic Books).

Okun, Arthur M. (1975), *Equality and Efficiency: The Big Tradeoff* (Washington: Brookings Institution).

Oppenheim, Carey, and Harker, Lisa (1996), *Poverty: The Facts* (3rd edn., London: Child Poverty Action Group).

Palacios, Miguel (2003), *Financing Human Capital: A Capital Markets Approach to Student Funding* (Cambridge: Cambridge University Press).

Palmer, J. L., and Pechman, J. A. (1978) (eds.), *Welfare in Rural Areas: The North Carolina–Iowa Income Maintenance Experiment* (Washington: Brookings Institution).

Pahl, Jan (1989), *Money and Marriage* (Basingstoke: Macmillan).

Parker, Hermione (1989), *Instead of the Dole: An Enquiry into Integration of the Tax and Benefit System* (London: Routledge).

Pauly, Mark V. (1974), 'Overinsurance and Public Provision of Insurance: The Roles of Moral Hazard and Adverse Selection', *Quarterly Journal of Economics*, 88: 44–62; repr. in Barr (2001*b*: i. 321–39).

—— (1986), 'Taxation, Health Insurance and Market Failure in the Medical Economy', *Journal of Economic Literature*, 24 (June), 629–75.

Peacock, Alan T., and Wiseman, Jack (1967), *The Growth of Public Expenditure in the United Kingdom* (rev. edn., London: George Allen & Unwin).

Pechman, Joseph A., and Timpane, P. Michael (1975) (eds.), *Work Incentives and Income Guarantees: The New Jersey Negative Income Tax Experiment* (Washington: Brookings Institution).

—— Aaron, Henry J., and Taussig, Michael K. (1968), *Social Security: Perspectives for Reform* (Washington: Brookings Institution).

Pelling, Henry (1979), *Popular Politics and Society in Late Victorian Britain* (2nd edn., London: Macmillan).

Pen, Jan (1971), 'A Parade of Dwarfs (and a Few Giants)', extract from *Income Distribution* (London: Penguin); repr. in Atkinson (1980: 47–55) and Barr (2001*b*: i. 557–68).

Pensions Policy Institute (2003), *State Pension Models—A Primer* (London: Pensions Policy Institute), downloadable from http://www.pensionspolicyinstitute.org.uk.

Peterson, Wallace C. (1991), *Transfer Spending, Taxes and the American Welfare State* (Boston, Mass.: Kluwer).

Phillips, Anne (1997), 'What has Socialism to do with Sexual Equality?', in Franklin (1997), 101–21.

Piachaud, David (1987), 'Problems in the Definition and Measurement of Poverty', *Journal of Social Policy*, 16/2: 147–64.

—— (1993), 'The Definition and Measurement of Poverty and Inequality', in Barr and Whynes (1993), 105–29.

—— and Sutherland, Holly (2002), 'Child Poverty', in Hills, Le Grand, and Piachaud (2002), 141–54.

Piggott, John, and Whalley, John (1985), *UK Tax Policy and Applied General Equilibrium Analysis* (Cambridge: Cambridge University Press).

—— —— (1986) (eds.), *New Developments in Applied General Equilibrium Analysis* (Cambridge: Cambridge University Press).

Piketty, Thomas, and Saez, Emmanuel (2003), 'Income Inequality in the United States, 1913–1998', *Quarterly Journal of Economics*, 118/1: 1–39.

Ploug, Neils (2003), 'The Recalibration of the Danish Old-Age Pension System', *International Social Security Review*, 56 (Apr.–June), 65–80.

Poterba, James M., Venti, Steven, F., and Wise, David A. (1996), 'How Retirement Saving Programs Increase Saving', *Journal of Economic Perspectives*, 19 (Fall), 91–112.

Powell, M. (1995), 'The Strategy of Equality Revisited', *Journal of Social Policy*, 24/2: 163–91.

Prest, Alan R., and Barr, Nicholas (1985), *Public Finance in Theory and Practice* (7th edn., London: Weidenfeld & Nicolson).

Productivity Commission (2002), *University Resourcing: Australia in an International Context* (Melbourne: Productivity Commission), downloadable from http://www.pc.gov.au/research/studies/highered/finalreport/index.html.

Propper, Carol (1995), 'For Richer, for Poorer, in Sickness and in Health: The Lifetime Distribution of NHS Health Care', in Jane Falkingham and John Hills (eds.), *The Dynamic of Welfare: The Welfare State and the Life Cycle* (Hemel Hempstead: Prentice-Hall/Harvester Wheatsheaf, 1995), 184–203.

—— (2001), 'Expenditure on Healthcare in the UK: A Review of the Issues', *Fiscal Studies*, 22/2: 151–83.

—— and Green, K. (2001), 'A Larger Role for the Private Sector in Financing UK Health Care: The Arguments and the Evidence', *Journal of Social Policy*, 30/4: 685–704.

Psacharopoulos, George (1994), 'Returns to Investment in Education: A Global Update', *World Development*, 22: 1325–44.

Quah, Danny (1996), *The Invisible Hand and the Weightless Economy*, Occasional Paper No. 12 (London: London School of Economics, Centre for Economic Performance, May).

—— (2003), *Digital Goods and the New Economy*, Discussion Paper No. 563; (London: London School of Economics, Centre for Economic Performance, March).

Queisser, Monika (2000), 'Pension Reform and International Organizations: From Conflict to Convergence', *International Social Security Review*, 53/2 (Apr.–June), 31–45.

Radford, R. A. (1945), 'The Economic Organisation of a POW Camp', *Economica*, NS 12/48 (Nov.), 189–201.

Rake, Katherine, Falkingham, Jane, and Evans, Martin (2000), 'British Pension Policy in the Twenty-First Century: A Partnership in Pensions or a Marriage to the Means-Test?', *Social Policy and Administration*, 34/3: 296–317.

Ravallion, Martin (1996), 'Issues in Measuring and Modeling Poverty', *Economic Journal*, 106 (Sept.), 1328–44; repr. in Barr (2001*b*: ii. 391–406).

—— and Datt, Gaurav (1995), 'Is Targeting through a Work Requirement Effective?', in van de Walle and Nead (1995), 413–44.

—— van de Walle, Dominique, and Gautam, Madhur (1995), 'Testing a Social Safety Net', *Journal of Public Economics*, 57/2 (June), 175–99.

Rawls, John (1972), *A Theory of Justice* (Oxford: Oxford University Press).

Rees, Ray (1989), 'Uncertainty, Information and Insurance' in John Hey (ed.), *Current Issues in Microeconomics* (London: Macmillan, 1989), 47–78.

Reinhardt, Uwe, E. (2000), 'Health Care for the Aging Baby Boom: Lessons from Abroad', *Journal of Economic Perspectives*, 14/2 (Spring), 71–83.

Ricardo, David (1817), *On the Principles of Political Economy and Taxation* (London: Murray).

Riley, John G. (2001), 'Silver Signals: Twenty-Five Years of Screening and Signalling', *Journal of Economic Literature*, 39/2 (June), 432–78.

Rimlinger, G. (1971), *Welfare Policy and Industrialisation in Europe, America and Russia* (New York: Wiley).

Robbins, Lionel C. (1977), *Political Economy Past and Present: A Review of Leading Theories of Economic Policy* (London: Macmillan).

—— (1978), *The Theory of Economic Policy in English Classical Political Economy* (2nd edn., London: Macmillan).

Robinson, Peter (2000), 'Active Labour-Market Policies: A Case of Evidence-Based Policy-Making', *Oxford Review of Economic Policy*, 16/1: 13–26.

Robson, William A. (1976), *Welfare State and Welfare Society* (London: George Allen & Unwin).

Røed, Knut, and Zhang, Tao (2003), 'Does Unemployment Compensation Affect Unemployment Duration?', *Economic Journal*, 113/484 (Jan.), 190–206.

Romer, Paul (1993), 'Ideal Gaps and Object Gaps in Economic Development', *Journal of Monetary Economics*, 32: 338–69.

Rose, M. E. (1972), *The Relief of Poverty 1834–1914* (London: Macmillan).

Rosen, Harvey S. (2002), *Public Finance* (6th edn., London and New York: McGraw-Hill Irwin).

Rothschild, Michael, and Stiglitz, Joseph E. (1976), 'Equilibrium in Competitive Insurance Markets: An Essay on the Economics of Imperfect Information', *Quarterly Journal of Economics*, 90: 629–49; repr. in Barr (2001*b*: i. 340–60).

Rowntree, B. Seebohm (1901), *Poverty: A Study of Town Life* (London: Longman).

—— (1941), *Poverty and Progress: A Second Social Survey of York* (London: Longman).

—— and Lavers, G. R. (1951), *Poverty and the Welfare State* (London: Longman).

Sainsbury, Diane (1994) (ed.), *Gendering Welfare States* (London: Sage).

Salanié, Bernard (2000), *Microeconomics of Market Failures* (London and Cambridge, Mass.: MIT Press).

Saltman, Richard B. (2003), 'Melting Public–Private Boundaries in European Health Systems', *European Journal of Public Health*, 13/1 (Mar.), 24–9.

Samuelson, Paul A. (1954), 'The Pure Theory of Public Expenditures', *Review of Economics and Statistics*, 36/4 (Nov.), 387–9.

—— (1958), 'An Exact Consumption-Loan Model of Interest with or without the Social Contrivance of Money', *Journal of Political Economy*, 66/6 (Dec.), 467–82; repr. in Barr (2001*b*: ii. 63–78).

Scherman, K. G. (2000), 'A New Social Security Reform Consensus? The ISSA's Stockholm Initiative', *International Social Security Review*, 53/1 (Jan.–Mar.), 65–82.

Schmähl, Winfried, and Horstmann, Sabine (2002) (eds.), *Transformation of Pension Systems in Central and Eastern Europe* (Cheltenham and Northampton, Mass.: Edward Elgar).

Schneider, Ulrike (1999), 'Germany's Social Long-Term Care Insurance: Design, Implementation and Evaluation', *International Social Security Review*, 52/2 (Apr.–June), 31–74.

Schottland, C. I. (1963), *The Social Security Program in the United States* (New York: Appleton-Century-Crofts).

Scotland Higher Education Review Board (2003), *A Framework for Higher Education in Scotland: Higher Education Review: Phase 2* (Edinburgh: The Stationery Office), downloadable from http://www.scotland.gov.uk.

Sen, Amartya K. (1970), 'The Impossibility of a Paretian Liberal', *Journal of Political Economy*, 78/1 (Jan.–Feb.), 152–7; repr. in Barr (2001*b*: i. 96–101).

—— (1973), *On Economic Inequality* (Oxford: Oxford University Press).

—— (1982), *Choice, Welfare and Measurement* (Oxford: Oxford University Press).

—— (1985), *Commodities and Capabilities* (Amsterdam: North Holland).

—— (1987), *The Standard of Living* (Cambridge: Cambridge University Press).

—— (1992), *Inequality Reexamined* (Oxford: Oxford University Press).

—— (1995*a*), *Mortality as an Indicator of Economic Success and Failure*, Innocenti Lectures (Florence: UNICEF).

—— (1995*b*), 'The Political Economy of Targeting', in van de Walle and Nead (1995), 11–24.

—— (1999), 'Economic Policy and Equity: An Overview', in Vito Tanzi, Ke-young Chu, and Sanjeev Gupta (eds.), *Economic Policy and Equity* (Washington: International Monetary Fund), 28–43.

—— and Williams, Bernard (1982) (eds.), *Utilitarianism and Beyond* (Cambridge: Cambridge University Press).

Shapiro, Judith (1993), 'The Russian Mortality Crisis and its Causes', in Anders Aslund (ed.), *Russian Economic Reform at Risk* (London and New York: Pinter); repr. in Barr (2001*b*: iii. 44–73).

Shorrocks, A. F. (1983), 'Ranking Income Distributions', *Economica*, 50/197 (Feb.), 3–17.

Simons, Herbert (1938), *Personal Income Taxation* (Chicago: University of Chicago Press).

Sinn, Hanns-Werner (1998), 'European Integration and the Future of the Welfare State', *Swedish Economic Policy Review*, 5/1: 113–32, and comment by Henry Ohlsson, 133–6.

Smith, Adam (1776), *An Inquiry into the Nature and Causes of the Wealth of Nations* (repr. Oxford: Oxford University Press, 1976).

Smith, James P. (1999), 'Healthy Bodies and Thick Wallets: The Dual Relation Between Health and Economic Status', *Journal of Economic Perspectives*, 13/2 (Spring), 145–66.

Smith, Stephen (1992), 'Taxation and the Environment: A Survey', *Fiscal Studies*, 13/4 (Nov.), 21–57.

Solow, Robert M. (1994), 'Perspectives on Growth Theory', *Journal of Economic Perspectives*, 8: 45–54.

—— (1998), *Work and Welfare* (Princeton, NJ: Princeton University Press).

Sparkes, Jo, and Glennerster, Howard (2002), 'Preventing Social Exclusion: Education's Contribution', in Hills, Le Grand, and Piachaud (2002), 178–201.

Spence, Michael A. (1973), 'Job Market Signalling', *Quarterly Journal of Economics*, 87/3 (Aug.), 355–74.

—— (2002), 'Signaling in Retrospect and the Informational Structure of Markets', *American Economic Review*, 92/3 (June), 434–59.

Spencer, Herbert (1884), *The Man versus the State* (New York: Appleton).

Stern, Nicholas (2002), *A Strategy for Development* (Washington: World Bank).

Stevens, R. B. (1970) (ed.), *Statutory History of the United States: Income Security* (New York: McGraw-Hill).

Stiglitz, Joseph E. (1983), 'Risk, Incentives and Insurance: The Pure Theory of Moral Hazard', *Geneva Papers on Risk and Insurance*, 8/26: 4–33; repr. in Barr (2001b: i. 361–90).

—— (1989), 'The Economic Role of the State', in Arnold Heertje (ed.), *The Economic Role of the State* (Oxford: Basil Blackwell).

—— (1993), *Information and Economic Analysis* (Oxford: Oxford University Press).

—— (2000), *The Economics of the Public Sector* (3rd edn., New York and London: Norton).

—— (2002), 'Information and the Change in the Paradigm in Economics', *American Economic Review*, 92/3 (June), 460–501.

—— and Walsh, Carl E. (2002), *Economics* (3rd edn., New York: Norton).

Stroud D. (2001), 'Further and Higher Education Participation and Student Support Arrangements, with Special Reference to Wales: A Description and Evaluation' (Cardiff: Independent Investigation Group on Student Hardship and Funding in Wales), downloadable from http://www.wales.gov.uk/investinginlearners.

Sugden, Robert (1982), 'On the Economics of Philanthropy', *Economic Journal*, 92/366 (June), 341–50; repr. in Barr (2001b: ii. 603–12).

—— (1983a), 'On the Economics of Philanthropy: Reply', *Economic Journal*, 93/371 (Sept.), 639.

—— (1983b), *Who Care? An Economic and Ethnical Analysis of Private Charity and the Welfare State*, Occasional Paper 67 (London: Institute of Economic Affairs).

—— (1984), 'Reciprocity: The Supply of Public Goods through Voluntary Contributions', *Economic Journal*, 94/376 (Dec.), 772–87.

Sutherland, Holly (1997), 'Women, Men and the Redistribution of Income', *Fiscal Studies*, 18/1: 1–22.

—— and Piachaud, David (2001), 'Reducing Child Poverty in Britain: An Assessment of Government Policy 1997–2001', *Economic Journal*, 111/469 (Feb.), F85–F101.

—— Sefton, Tom, and Piachaud, David (2003), *Poverty in Britain: The Impact of Government Policy since 1997* (York: Joseph Rowntree Foundation).

Sweden: Federation of Social Insurance Offices (1998), '*Sweden*', *The Future of Social Security* (Stockholm: Federation of Social Insurance Offices), 192–203; for updates see also http://www.pension.gov.se.

Sweezy, Paul (1942), *The Theory of Capitalist Developement* (London: Dennis Dobson).

Tawney, R. H. (1953), *The Attack and Other Papers* (London: Allen & Unwin).

—— (1964), *Equality* (4th edn., London: George Allen & Unwin).

Taylor, Alan J. (1972), *Laissez-faire and State Intervention in Nineteenth-Century Britain* (London: Macmillian).

Thain, C., and Wright, M. (1995) *The Treasury and Whitehall: The Planning and Control of Public Expenditure, 1976–1993* (Oxford: Oxford University Press).

Thane, Pat (1982), *The Foundations of the Welfare State* (London: Longman).

Theil, Henri (1967), *Economic and Information Theory* (Amsterdam: North Holland).

Thompson, Lawrence (1998), *Older and Wiser: The Economics of Public Pensions* (Washington: Urban Institute).

Thurow, Lester C. (1971), 'The Income Distribution as a Pure Public Good', *Quarterly Journal of Economics* (May), 327–36.

Tiebout, Charles (1956), 'A Pure Theory of Local Expenditure', *Journal of Political Economy* (Oct.), 416–24.

Timmins, Nicholas (1996), *The Five Giants: A Biography of the Welfare State* (London: Fontana).

Titmuss, Richard M. (1958), *Essays on 'The Welfare State'* (London: Allen & Unwin; 3rd edn., 1976).

—— (1968), *Commitment to Welfare* (London: Allen & Unwin; 2nd edn., 1976).

—— (1970), *The Gift Relationship* (London: Penguin).

Tobin, James (1968), 'Raising the Incomes of the Poor', in K. Gordon (ed.), *Agenda for the Nation* (Washington: Brookings Institution).

—— Pechman, J., and Mieszkowski, P. (1967), 'Is a Negative Income Tax Practical?', *Yale Law Journal*, 77: 1–27.

Todd, Petra, E., and Wolpin, Kenneth I. (2003), 'On the Specification and Estimation of the Production Function for Cognitive Achievement', *Economic Journal*, 113/485: F3–33.

Triest, Robert K. (1998), 'Has Poverty Gotten Worse?', *Journal of Economic Perspectives*, 12/1 (Winter), 97–114.

Tullock, Gordon (1970), *Private Wants, Public Means* (New York: Basic Books).

—— (1971), 'The Charity of the Uncharitable', *Western Economic Journal*, 9: 379–92; repr. in Letwin (1983: 328–44).

—— (1976), *The Vote Motive*, Hobart Paperback No. 9 (London: Institute of Economic Affairs).

UK Board of Education (1943), *Educational Reconstruction*, Cmd 6458 (London: HMSO).

UK Committee of Vice-Chancellors and Principals (1996), *Our Universities, our Future: Part 4: The Case for a New Funding System—Special Report*, The CVCP's evidence to the National Committee of Inquiry into Higher Education (London: Committee of Vice-Chancellors and Principals).

UK Committee on Higher Education (1963), *Higher Education* (The Robbins Report), Cmnd 2154 (London: HMSO).

UK Department of Education (1960), *Grants for Students* (The Anderson Report), Report of the Committee Appointed by the Minister of Education and the Secretary of State for Scotland, Cmnd 1051 (London: HMSO).

UK Department of Labour (1944), *Employment Policy*, Cmd 6527 (London: HMSO).

UK DfES (1999): UK Department for Education and Skills, *Improving Literacy and Numeracy* (the Moser Report) (London: TSO).

—— (2002): UK Department for Education and Skills, *Schools: Achieving Success* (London: TSO), downloadable from http://www.dfes.gov.uk.

—— (2003*a*): UK Department for Education and Skills, *Departmental Report 2003*, Cm 5902 (London: TSO), downloadable from http://www.dfes.gov.uk.

—— (2003*b*): UK Department for Education and Skills, *Statistics of Education: Education and Training Expenditure since 1993–4*, Issue No. 04/03 (London: TSO), downloadable from http://www.dfes.gov.uk.

UK DHSS (1974): UK Department of Health and Social Security, *Better Pensions Fully Protected against Inflation*, Cmnd 5713 (London: HMSO).

—— (1976), *Sharing Resources for Health in England: Report of the Joint Resource Allocation Working Party* (London: HMSO).

—— (1985*a*), *Reform of Social Security*, Cmnd 9517 (London: HMSO).

—— (1985*b*), *Reform of Social Security: Background Papers*, Cmnd 9519 (London: HMSO).

—— (1985*c*), *Reform of Social Security: Programme for Action*, Cmnd 9691 (London: HMSO).

UK DoH (1944): UK Department of Health, *A National Health Service*, Cmd 6502 (London: HMSO).

—— (2000): UK Department of Health, *The NHS Plan: A Plan for Investment, a Plan for Reform*, Cm 4818-I (London: TSO), downloadable from http://www.dh.gov.uk.

—— (2002*a*): UK Department of Health, *Delivering the NHS Plan*, Cm 5503 (London: TSO), downloadable from http://www.dh.gov.uk.

—— (2002*b*): UK Department of Health, *Health and Personal Social Services Statistics, England* (London: TSO), downloadable from http://www.dh.gov.uk

—— (2002*c*): UK Department of Health, *Department of Health Expenditure Plans 2002–03 to 2003–04, Departmental Report*, Cm 5403 (London: TSO), downloadable from http://www.dh.gov.uk

—— (2003*a*), UK Department of Health, *Our Inheritance, our Future: Realising the Potential of Genetics in the NHS*, Cm 5791-II (London: TSO), downloadable from http://www.dh.gov.uk.

—— (2003*b*), UK Department of Health, *Departmental Report 2003*, Cm 5904 (London: TSO), downloadable from http://www.dh.gov.uk.

UK DSS (1995), *Tax Benefit Model Tables* (Department of Social Security, Analytical Services Division; London: HMSO).

—— (1997), *The Government's Expenditure Plans 1997–98 to 1999–2000: Social Security Departmental Report*, Cm 3613 (London: HMSO).

—— (1998), *A New Contract for Welfare: Partnership in Pensions*, Cm 4179 (London: TSO).

—— (2001), *The Government's Expenditure Plans 2001–02 to 2003–04: Social Security Departmental Report*, Cm 5115 (London: TSO).

UK DWP (2002*a*): UK Department of Work and Pensions, *Departmental Report: The Government's Expenditure Plans 2002–03 to 2003–04*, Cm 5424 (London: TSO), downloadable from http://www.dwp.gov.uk.

—— (2002*b*): UK Department of Work and Pensions, *Households below Average Income (HBAI) 1994/95–2001/02* (London: TSO), downloadable from http://www.dwp.gov.uk.

—— (2002*c*): UK Department of Work and Pensions, *Work and Pension Statistics 2002* (London: TSO), downloadable from http://www.dwp.gov.uk.

—— (2002*d*): UK Department of Work and Pensions, *Simplicity, Security and Choice: Working and Saving for Retirement*, Cm 5677 (London: TSO), downloadable from http://www/dwp.gov.uk.

—— (2002*e*): UK Department for Work and Pensions, *A Guide to State Pensions* (London: TSO), downloadable from http://www.dwp.gov.uk.

—— (2003*a*): UK Department for Work and Pensions, *Departmental Report 2003*, Cm 5921 (London: TSO), downloadable from http://www.dwp.gov.uk.

—— (2003*b*): UK Department of Work and Pensions, *Households below Average Income 1994/95–2001/02* (London: TSO).

UK Education and Skills Select Committee (2002), *Post-16 Student Support*, Sixth Report of Session 2001–2002, HC445 (London: TSO), Ev 19–35, downloadable from http://www.parliament.uk/ parliamentary_committees/education_ and_skills_committee.cfm.

—— (2003), *The Future of Higher Education, Fifth Report of Session 2002–03, Volume II, Oral and Written Evidence*, HC 425-II (London: TSO), Ev 292–309, downloadable from http://www.parliament.uk/ parliamentary_committees/education_ and_skills_committee.cfm

UK Government (1944), *Social Insurance*, Pt. I, Cmd 6550, and Pt. II (Workmen's Compensation), Cmd 6551 (London: HMSO).

UK House of Commons Social Services Committee (1988), *Fifth Report: The Future of the National Health Service*, Session 1987–88, HC 613 (London: HMSO).

UK National Audit Office (2002*a*), *Improving Student Achievement in English Higher Education*, Report by the Comptroller and Auditor General, HC486, Session 2001–2002 (London: TSO).

—— (2002*b*), *Widening Participation in Higher Education in England*, Report by the Comptroller and Auditor General, HC485, Session 2001–2002 (London: TSO).

UK NCIHE (1997*a*): UK National Committee of Inquiry into Higher Education (the Dearing Committee), *Higher Education in the Learning Society: Summary Report* (London: HMSO).

—— (1997*b*), *Higher Education in the Learning Society: Report of the National Committee* (London: HMSO).

UK Office for National Statistics (2003), *Social Trends*, 33 (London: TSO).

UK Pension Law Review Committee (1993), Pension Law Reform, Report of the Pension Law Review Committee, Vol. I *Report*, and Vol. II *Research* (London: HMSO).

UK Royal Commission on the Distribution of Income and Wealth (1979), *Report No. 7: Fourth Report on the Standing Reference*, Cmnd 7595 (London: HMSO).

UK Royal Commission on Long Term Care (1999), *With Respect to Old Age: A Report by the Royal Commission on Long Term Care*, Cm 4192-I (London: TSO).

UK Select Committee on Tax Credit (1973), *Report and Proceedings*, Session 1972–73, HC 341-I, 341-II, 341-III (London: HMSO).

UK Treasury (2002*a*), *Opportunity and Security for All: Investing in an Enterprising, Fairer Britain. New Public Spending Plans 2003–2006*, Cm 5570 (London: TSO), downloadable from http://www/hm-treasury.gov.uk

—— (2002*b*), *Budget Report 2002: The Strength to Make Long-Term Decisions: Investing in an Enterprising, Fairer Britain* (London: TSO), downloadable from http://www/hm-treasury.gov.uk.

—— (2002*c*), *The Child and Working Tax Credits: The Modernisation of Britain's Tax and Benefit Systems*, Number Ten (London: HM Treasury).

—— (2002*d*), *Securing our Future Health: Taking a Long-Term View, Final Report* (the Wanless Report) (London: HM Treasury), downloadable from www.hm-treasury.gov.uk

—— (2003*a*), *Budget Report 2003: Building a Britain of Economic Strength and Social Justice* (London: TSO), downloadable from http://www/hm-treasury.gov.uk.

—— (2003*b*), *Public Expenditure: Statistical Analyses 2003*, Cm 5901 (London: TSO), downloadable from http://www/hm-treasury.gov.uk.

UNICEF (2000), 'A League Table of Child Poverty in Rich Nations', Innocenti Report Card 1 (Florence: UNICEF Innocenti Research Centre, June), downloadable from http://www.unicef-icdc.org.

US Advisory Council on Social Security (1938), *Final Report*, S. Doc. 4, 76 Cong. 1 sess. (1939).

US Federal Emergency Relief Administration (1942), *Final Statistical Report of the Federal Emergency Relief Administration* (Washington: US Government Printing Office).

US National Resources and Planning Board (1942), *Long Range Work and Relief Policies: Report of the Committee on Long Range Work and Relief to the National Resources Planning Board* (Washington: US Government Printing Office).

US Panel on Poverty and Public Assistance (1995), *Measuring Poverty: A New Approach* (Washington: National Academy Press).

US President's Commission on Income Maintenance Programs (1969), *Poverty amid Plenty: The American Paradox*, Report of the President's Commission on Income Maintenance Programs (Washington: US Government Printing Office).

US Social Security Administration (2002), *Social Security Programs throughout the World 2002–2003: Europe 2002, Asia and the Pacific 2002* (Washington: US Social Security Administration), downloadable from http://www.ssa.gov/policy/pubs/index.html.

—— (2003), *Social Security Programs throughout the World 2002–2003: Africa 2003, Americas 2003* (Washington: US Social Security Administration), downloadable from http://www.ssa.gov/policy/pubs/index.html.

US Supreme Court (1978), *City of Los Angeles, Department of Water and Power* et al. v. *Manhart* et al., Case No. 76–1810.

van de Walle, Dominique, and Nead, Kimberly (1995) (eds.), *Public Spending and the Poor: Theory and Evidence* (Washington and London: Johns Hopkins University Press).

Varian, Hal R. (2002), *Intermediate Microeconomics: A Modern Approach* (6th edn., New York: Norton).

Vickers, J., and Yarrow, G. (1988), *Privatization: An Economic Analysis* (London and Cambridge: Mass.: MIT Press).

Vleminckx, Koen, and Smeeding, Timothy (2000) (eds.), *Child Well-Being, Child Poverty and Child Policy in Modern Nations: What do we Know?* (Bristol: Policy Press).

Wagstaff, Adam (1991), 'QALYS and the Equity-Efficiency Tradeoff', *Journal of Health Economics*, 10: 21–43.

—— van Doorslaer, Eddy, et al. (1999), 'Equity in the Finance of Health Care: Some Further International Comparisons', *Journal of Health Economics*, 11: 389–411.

Wales Education and Lifelong Learning Committee (2002), *Policy Review of Higher Education*, National Assembly for Wales, downloadable from http://www.wales.gov.uk.

Walker, Robert, and Wiseman, Michael (2003), 'Making Welfare Work: UK Activation Policies under New Labour', *International Social Security Review*, 56/1 (Jan.–Mar.), 3–29.

Watts, Harold W., and Rees, Albert (1977) (eds.), *The New Jersey Income Maintenance Experiment*, ii, *Labor Supply Responses* (New York and London: Academic Press).

Weale, Albert (1978), *Equality and Social Policy* (London: Routledge & Kegan Paul).

Weaver, Caroline L. (1982), *The Crisis in Social Security: Economic and Political Origins* (Durham, NC: Duke University Press).

Webb, M. (1984), 'Privatisation of the Electricity and Gas Industries', in D. Steel, and D. Heald (eds.), *Privatizing Public Enterprises* (London: Royal Institute of Public Administration, 1984), 87–100.

Webb, Sidney, and Webb, Beatrice (1909), *The Break Up of the Poor Law*, Minority Report of the Poor Law Commission, Part I (London: Longman).

Weisbrod, Burton A. (1969), 'Collective Action and the Distribution of Income: A Conceptual Approach', in Joint Economic Committee, *The Analysis and Evaluation of Public Expenditures* (Washington: US Government Printing Office); repr. in Barr (2001*b*: ii. 277–97).

West, Anne, and Hind, Audrey (2003), *Secondary School Admissions in England: Exploring the Extent of Overt and Covert Selection* (London: Research and Information on State Education Trust), downloadable from http://www.risetrust.org.uk/admissions.html.

—— and Pennell, Hazel (2002), 'How New is New Labour? The Quasi-Market and English Schools 1997 to 2001', *British Journal of Educational Studies*, 50/2: 206–24.

—— —— (2003), *Underachievement in Schools* (London: Routledge Falmer).

West, Edwin G. (1970), *Education and the State* (2nd edn., London: Institute of Economic Affairs).

Whiteford, Peter, and Angenent, Gregory (2001), *The Australian System of Social Protection: An Overview*, 2nd edn, Occasional Paper No. 6 (Canberra: Department of Family and Community Services).

Wilensky, Harold L., and Lebeaux, Charles N. (1965), *Industrial Society and Social Welfare* (New York: Free Press; London: Collier-Macmillan).

Wiles, Peter J. D. (1974), *Distribution of Income: East and West* (Amsterdam: North Holland).

Wilkinson, Richard (1996), *Unhealthy Societies: The Afflictions of Inequality* (London: Routledge).

Williams, Alan (1985), 'Economics of Coronary Artery Bypass Grafting', *British*

Medical Journal, 3 Aug., 326–9; repr. in Barr (2001*b*: iii. 201–4).

Winston, Gordon C. (1999), 'Subsidies, Hierarchy and Peers: The Awkward Economics of Higher Education', *Journal of Economic Perspectives*, 13/1 (Winter), 13–36.

Witte, E. E. (1962), *The Development of the Social Security Act* (Madison: University of Wisconsin Press).

Wittenberg, Raphael, Hancock, Ruth, Comas-Herrera, Adelina, and Pickard, Linda (2002), 'Demand for Long-Term Care in the UK: Projections of Long-Term Care Finance for Older People to 2051', in Richard Brooks, Sue Regan, and Peter Robinson (eds.), *A New Contract for Retirement: Modelling Policy Options to 2050* (London: Institute for Public Policy Research).

Wolf, Alison (2002), *Does Education Matter: Myths about Education and Economic Growth* (London: Penguin Books).

Wolff, Edward N. (1998), 'Recent Trends in the Size Distribution of Household Wealth', *Journal of Economic Perspectives*, 12/3 (Summer), 131–50.

World Bank (1994), *Averting the Old Age Crisis* (New York: Oxford University Press).

—— (1996), *World Development Report 1996: From Plan to Market* (New York and Oxford: Oxford University Press).

—— (2000), *Making Transition Work for Everyone: Poverty and Inequality in Europe and Central Asia* (Washington: World Bank).

—— (2002), *Transition: The First Ten Years* (Washington: World Bank).

World Health Organization (2001), *World Health Report 2000* (Geneva: World Health Organization).

Yaeger, John, et al. (2001) (eds.), *Finance in Higher Education*, ASHE Reader Series (Boston: Pearson Custom Publishing).

Zaidi, Asghar, and Burchardt, Tania (2003), *Comparing Incomes when Needs Differ: Equivalisation for the Extra Costs of Disability in the UK*, Centre for the Analysis of Social Exclusion, CASE Paper No. 64 (London: London School of Economics).

GLOSSARY

absolute poverty poverty line defined in terms of a subsistence standard of living; as opposed to **relative poverty**

activation policies see **working tax credit**

actuarial insurance An actuarial contribution is based on two factors: (*a*) the size of the benefit to be paid if the insured event (e.g. becoming ill) occurs; and (*b*) the probability of the event occurring. The probability needs to take into account mortality, morbidity, inflation, and all other relevant factors. This is the way in which private insurance works

administrative efficiency see **productive efficiency**

adverse selection situation in which an individual who is a poor risk can conceal the fact from the insurance company

AFDC Aid to Families with Dependent Children

Aid to Families with Dependent Children formerly the main US **income-tested benefit** for families with no (or virtually no) other income

allocative efficiency the allocation of scarce resources in such a way that no reallocation can make any individual better off without making at least one other individual worse off; also referred to as efficiency, **external efficiency**, Pareto efficiency, or Pareto optimality

annuity the payment of an income of £*x* per year for life; often given to an individual in exchange for a single, lump-sum payment at the time he retires; see Chapter 5, Section 2.3

block grants a block grant (for example, from central government to a lower level of government) is a fixed transfer, irrespective of the level of spending of the lower level of government, in contrast with a **matching grant**

cardinal utility If utility is *cardinally* measurable, we can make statements like 'A gets twice as much utility from his first ice cream as from his second' or 'B gets the same utility as A from an ice cream'. When utility is measurable only *ordinally*, we can say only that A gets *more* utility from his first ice cream than from his second, but not how much more; and it is not possible to make interpersonal comparisons between A's and B's utility. See also **utility**.

cash benefits income support in the form of cash, in contrast with benefits in kind like free health care; cash benefits generally include **social insurance** and **social assistance**

child benefit UK system of weekly, tax-free cash payment of £*x* for each child in the family, generally payable to the mother

collectivist view that gives priority to the achievement of equality or meeting need; can take various forms, including **democratic socialist** or **Marxist**

comprehensive school UK secondary school for pupils of all abilities, generally covering the age range 11–18

consumption smoothing allows a person to maximize his lifetime utility by redistributing over the life cycle, from his younger to his older self—for example, by saving—or from his older to his young self, by borrowing

contributory benefit benefit payable only to individuals who (*a*) have a **National Insurance** contribution record, and (*b*) are unemployed, retired, or suffering from ill health, etc.; see also **social insurance** and **non-contributory benefit**

Council Tax the system of property tax in England

cream skimming attempt by the supplier of services to select the least costly clients; frequently used in connection with medical insurers who face incentives to try to screen out all but the best risks

cross section series of observations on different entities during a single period of time—for example, the Family Expenditure Survey gathers data on the expenditure patterns of a large number of families in a given week; as opposed to **time series**

defined-contribution pensions in a defined contribution scheme, a person's pension is an annuity whose size, given life expectancy, etc., is determined only by the size of his lifetime pension accumulation; thus the individual faces the risk that his pension portfolio might perform badly; contrasts with **defined-benefit pensions**

defined-benefit pensions under a defined benefit scheme, often run at firm or industry level, a person's pension is based on his wage and upon length of service; thus his annuity is, in effect, wage indexed until retirement, and the risk of varying rates of return to pension assets falls on the employer; contrasts with **defined-contribution pensions**

democratic socialist view that **collectivist** goals can be achieved within a mixed economy; see also **libertarian**, **liberal**, **Marxist**

disregard amount of earnings or other income that is disregarded (i.e. ignored) in calculating the benefit to which an individual or family is entitled

earned income tax credit see **working tax credit**

earnings-related benefits in contrast with **flat-rate benefits**, are paid as a percentage of previous earnings; thus, individuals with higher previous earnings receive higher benefits

economic efficiency see **allocative efficiency**

efficiency see **allocative efficiency**

engineering efficiency see **productive efficiency**

equity a goal relating to the way in which resources should be distributed or shared between individuals, hence synonymous with **social justice**; see also **horizontal equity** and **vertical equity**; equity *may* imply equality, but does not have to—see also **libertarian**, **liberal**, **collectivist**

external efficiency synonymous with **allocative efficiency**; often used in the context of health care and education. It means, for example, the allocation of resources so as to maximize the health gain from a given budget or the production of the mix of educational activities that equip individuals—economically, socially, and politically—for the societies in which they live

Family Credit UK system of supplementing the incomes of low-income working families; introduced in 1988 to replace Family Income Supplement

Family Income Supplement see **Family Credit**

FIS Family Income Supplement

flat-rate benefits, in contrast with **earnings-related benefits**, are paid at a fixed monthly rate (though they may be higher for larger families) and are not related to previous income; thus, for a given family type, all recipients receive the same benefits

funded pensions are paid from an accumulated fund built up over a period of years out of contributions of its members; contrasts with **Pay-As-You-Go** schemes

general practitioner family doctor

Gini coefficient a measure of the overall inequality in society; it takes on values between zero (when income is distributed equally) and one (when one individual has all the income)

GP general practitioner

Green Paper consultative document issued by UK central government, inviting discussion and comment; as distinct from a **White Paper**

Health Maintenance Organization a 'firm' of doctors, which charges individuals/families an annual premium, in return for which it provides the individual/family with a comprehensive range of medical services; see Chapter 12, Section 5

Higher Education Funding Council for England (HEFCE) a body that finances universities and colleges on the basis of contracts; replaces the former **Polytechnics and Colleges Funding Council** and **Universities Funding Council**

HMO Health Maintenance Organization

HMSO Her Majesty's Stationery Office

horizontal efficiency is concerned with ensuring that benefits should go to *all* the poor. Failure can arise either because eligibility rules prevent some needy groups from applying, or because **take-up** is less than 100 per cent. Thus horizontal efficiency is concerned with avoiding gaps, as opposed to **vertical efficiency**, which is concerned with avoiding leakages

horizontal equity distribution in accordance with equal treatment of equals—for example, the relative tax treatment of families of different sizes at a given level of income; see also **equity** and **vertical equity**

housing benefit UK system of assistance with rent and local taxation for low-income householders

implicit tax rate a tax that arises when a family in receipt of an **income-tested benefit** earns extra income, and as a consequence loses benefit; if benefit is lost pound for pound with earnings, the implicit tax rate is 100 per cent; see Chapter 10, Section 3

income-contingent repayments with a conventional loan, repayments are £*x* per month for a fixed period; with income-contingent repayments, in contrast, repayments are calculated as *x* per cent of the borrower's monthly earnings; thus the duration of the loan is variable

income-related benefit see **income-tested benefit**

Income Support UK system of **means-tested**, **non-contributory** benefits, for which individuals/families are eligible if their income from all other sources is less than the poverty standard; replaced **Supplementary Benefit** in 1988

Income-Tested Benefit benefit awarded to individuals/families with low incomes, and withdrawn as income rises; as distinct from benefits awarded on the basis of other criteria—for example, having a contributions record; also referred to as income-related benefit; see also **contributory benefit** and **means-tested benefit**

indexed government bonds an ordinary 10-year bond sold in 2000 for £100 would pay, say, £10 interest per year and repay the £100 loan in 2010. A similar indexed bond makes a lower interest payment, but repays in 2010 not £100, but the initial sum indexed for changes in the price level. If prices double over the period, the bond-holder receives £200 plus interest (also indexed) in 2010

insurance used with two different meanings: as a device that offers individuals *protection against risk*, or as an *actuarial mechanism* normally organized in the private sector; on the latter, see also **actuarial insurance**

internal efficiency see **productive efficiency**

laissez-faire used in this book in its most frequent sense as 'a belief in the efficacy of a free market economy' (Taylor 1972: 11); see also **libertarian**

LEA see **Local Education Authority**

less eligibility condition that the standard of living of those in receipt of **Poor Law** benefits should be lower than that of the poorest worker

liberal view of property rights and income distribution as contingent matters rather than as items of dogma. Note the confusing ambiguity in the use of the word. In the nineteenth century it was used as a label for classical Liberal thinkers such as Bentham and Nassau Senior; and today a writer like Friedman, in calling himself a liberal, is using the term in the same way. Throughout the book such writers are referred to as **libertarians**

libertarian view that gives priority to individual liberty, usually associated with a belief in the free market and *laissez-faire*; see also **liberal** and **collectivist**

Local Education Authority the body that organizes most forms of education at a local level, including building schools and employing teachers

Local Rates former UK system of local taxation, based on the annual rental value of property

macro-efficiency concerns the proportion of national resources devoted to a particular activity such as health care or education; as opposed to **micro-efficiency**

market failure impediment to the efficient working of the market, in particular externalities, public goods, or increasing returns to scale (see Appendix to Chapter 4, paras. 12–16); see **standard assumptions**

Marxist view that **collectivist** goals are incompatible with capitalism, and can be achieved only under state ownership of major productive resources; see also **libertarian**, **liberal**, and **democratic socialist**

matching grant a grant from (say) central government in the form of a fixed percentage of spending by (say) local government on a particular activity, in contrast with a **block grant**

means test see **means-tested benefits**

means-tested benefits benefits paid to individuals whose income and wealth from all other sources are below a given amount; the term thus embraces both income testing and wealth testing

micro-efficiency concerns the division of total medical resources between the different parts of the health-care system, or that of educational resources between different areas of education, etc.; as opposed to **macro-efficiency**

moral hazard situation in which an insured person can affect the insurance company's liability without its knowledge

National Health Service UK system under which medical care is (*a*) provided by the state, (*b*) financed mainly out of general tax revenues, and (*c*) supplied to patients mostly without charge

National Insurance UK system of **social insurance** in respect (e.g.) of unemployment, ill health, and retirement; see also **contributory benefit**

negative income tax a system in which income support and income taxation are integrated by using the tax system, both to pay benefits to those with low incomes and to levy taxes on those with higher incomes

NHS the UK **National Health Service**

NIT **negative income tax**

non-contributory benefit benefit awarded without the need for a contributions record, and financed out of general tax revenues (in contrast with a **contributory benefit**); may be **income-tested**, or awarded on the basis of non-income criteria—for example, **child benefit**

notional defined-contribution pensions pensions financed through social insurance contributions, where a person's pension bears a strict actuarial relationship to his lifetime pension contributions; pensions may be adjusted for the cohort's life expectancy, and may offer credits for periods spent caring for children

OECD Organisation for Economic Cooperation and Development: an organization of the world's advanced industrial countries

ordinal utility see **cardinal utility**

original position hypothetical situation (used by the philosopher John Rawls) in which rational negotiators behind the **veil of ignorance** negotiate a just constitution for a country in which they will all have to live

outdoor relief benefits paid under the **Poor Law** to individuals, principally the elderly, who were not required to live in the **workhouse**

Pareto efficiency see **allocative efficiency**

Pareto optimality see **allocative efficiency**

Pay-As-You-Go pensions paid (usually by the state) out of current tax revenues, rather than out of an accumulated fund; contrasts with **funded** schemes

PAYG **Pay-As-You-Go**

Pigovian subsidy/tax where an activity creates an external benefit, an unrestricted private market will supply an inefficiently small quantity. One way of restoring supply to its efficient level is to pay a so-called Pigovian subsidy. Analogously, a Pigovian tax discourages excessive supply in the present of an external cost. See Chapter 4, Section 3.2, and/or the Appendix to Chapter 4, para. 15

Poor Law UK system for the relief of destitution, from late sixteenth century; it was phased out over the first half of the twentieth century

poverty trap situation in which individuals/families earning an extra £1 lose £1 or more in income-tested benefits, and hence make themselves absolutely worse off. Such people have no financial incentive to work longer hours. As distinct from the **unemployment trap**; see also **implicit tax rate**

productive efficiency the allocation of resources so as to produce the maximum output from given inputs; also referred to as administrative efficiency, engineering efficiency, or internal efficiency; a component of **allocative efficiency**

progressive taxation tax system in which tax paid as a proportion of income is higher for individuals with higher incomes; see also **proportional taxation** and **regressive taxation**

proportional taxation tax system in which tax paid is the same proportion of income at all income levels; see also **progressive taxation** and **regressive taxation**

quasi-markets are used to improve the efficiency of public providers by introducing market forces. But they differ from the market for, say, food: on the supply side, they introduce competition (e.g. between hospitals or schools), but the suppliers are not necessarily private, nor necessarily profit maximizing. On the demand side, consumers do not spend cash; their purchasing power is expressed as an earmarked budget. Consumers may make their own choice (of school), or choice may be made on their behalf by an agent (much medical care)

rates see **Local Rates**

regressive taxation tax system in which tax paid as a proportion of income is lower for individuals with higher incomes; see also **progressive taxation** and **proportional taxation**

relative poverty poverty line defined relative to the average standard of living—for example, as a proportion of average income; as opposed to **absolute poverty**

replacement rate ratio of income when unemployed or retired to income (post-tax and transfers) when in work

revenue neutral a policy change is revenue neutral if any resulting increase in expenditure is accompanied by a matching increase in taxation

risk with risk, the probability of an event (e.g. breaking a leg or becoming unemployed) is known; with uncertainty, in contrast, the relevant probability is not known—for example, the probability distribution of future rates of inflation

SERPS UK State Earnings-Related Pension Scheme

social assistance state benefits paid out of general tax revenues without contribution condition, but usually subject to a **means test**; see also **income-tested benefit**

social dividend scheme form of **negative income tax**

social insurance form of organization, originally modelled on private insurance, under which individuals receive state benefits in respect of (e.g.) unemployment or retirement, often without any test of means or need, on the basis of previous (usually compulsory) contributions; see also **contributory benefit** and **National Insurance**

social justice a goal relating to the way in which resources should be distributed or shared between individuals; see also **equity, horizontal equity,** and **vertical equity**; for different definitions of social justice, see **libertarian, liberal, collectivist**

social security all publicly provided cash benefits. Note that this standard British usage differs from the narrower American definition of social security as retirement benefits, and the broader EEC definition, which includes health services; throughout the book the term is used with its British meaning

standard assumptions the assumptions under which the market will, in theory, allocate resources efficiently—namely, perfect information, perfect competition, and no **market failures** (see Chapter 4, Section 3.2, or the Appendix to Chapter 4, paras. 5–17)

stigma loss of **utility** because income is received in the form of (usually) **income-tested** benefits, rather than from some more congenial source (e.g. earnings or insurance benefits)

supplementary benefit former UK system of **means-tested**, **non-contributory** benefits, for which individuals/families were eligible if their income from all other sources was less than the poverty standard; replaced the earlier system of National Assistance in 1966; replaced in 1988 by **Income Support**

take-up the number of people receiving a particular benefit as a proportion of those potentially eligible

tax expenditures public expenditure implicit in the granting of tax relief to certain activities—for example, approved private pension contributions or mortgage interest payments, as opposed to explicit expenditure; see Chapter 7, Section 1.1

third-party payment problem situation in which the insurance company pays the whole of an individual's (e.g.) medical bill; as a result neither patient nor doctor has an incentive to economize; technically, a form of **moral hazard**

time series series of observations on a single entity (or aggregate) over several periods—for example, data on the level of unemployment benefits, the number of people out of work, etc. in a country each year from 1960–1980; as opposed to **cross section**

uncertainty see **risk**

unemployment trap situation in which an individual/family is better off (or little worse off) when unemployed than when in work, and hence has little financial incentive to seek work. This situation arises particularly for those with low earnings and/or with large families. As distinct from the **poverty trap**, under which an individual doing at least some work is given no financial incentive to work longer hours

unfunded see **Pay-As-You-Go**

Universities Funding Council (UFC) body that financed universities in Britain on the basis of contracts from 1990 to 1993, after which it was replaced by the **Higher Education Funding Council**

uprating increase in the value of almost all cash benefits, usually at annual intervals, and usually in line with changes in the price level

utility individual well-being or satisfaction; see also **cardinal utility**

veil of ignorance hypothetical situation in which rational individuals in the **original position** have to negotiate a just constitution for a country in which they will all have to live, but *without knowing who they will be* (i.e. whether they will be born as one of the most or the least fortunate)

vertical efficiency concerned with ensuring that benefits go *only* to people who need them. This reduces the cost of benefits, but may involve high **implicit tax rates** and the **poverty trap** (see Chapter 10:3.2). Thus vertical efficiency is concerned with avoiding leakages, as opposed to **horizontal efficiency**, which is concerned with avoiding gaps in coverage

vertical equity the extent of redistribution of income, consumption, or wealth from rich to poor; see also **equity** and **horizontal equity**

welfare US usage for **income-tested benefits**; see also **social assistance**

White Paper firm statement of government intent; as distinct from a **Green Paper**

workhouse institution giving work and rudimentary accommodation to the destitute, under the **Poor Law**

workhouse test condition that recipients of benefits under the **Poor Law** must live in the **workhouse**

working tax credit a benefit that offers income-tested poverty relief, conditional on the recipient working at least X hours per week

■ AUTHOR INDEX

■ SUBJECT INDEX